Awakening

*Entering the Ascension Timeline
of the Golden Age*

Book One

ALSO BY LORI TOYE

AWAKENING

—— *Entering the* ——

ASCENSION TIMELINE

of the Golden Age

The ASCENDED MASTERS
received through

LORI ADAILE TOYE

I AM AMERICA PUBLISHING & DISTRIBUTING
P.O. Box 2511, Payson, Arizona, 85547, USA.
www.iamamerica.com

I AM America Maps and Books have been marketed since 1989 by I AM America Seventh Ray Publishing and Distributing, through workshops, conferences, and numerous bookstores in the United States and internationally. If you are interested in obtaining information on available releases please write or call:

I AM America, P.O. Box 2511, Payson, Arizona, 85547, USA. (928) 978-6435, or visit:
www.iamamerica.com
www.loritoye.com

Graphic Design and Typography by Lori Toye
Host and Questions by Lenard Toye

Love, in service, breathes the breath for all!

Print On Demand Version

10 9 8 7 6 5 4 3 2 1

❧

*"Humanity is on the brink of great evolution
and Spiritual Awakening."*

- Saint Germain

Lord Sananda
World Teacher
Hierarch of Shalahah

Saint Germain
Lord of the Golden Cities
Sponsor, I AM America Map
Hierarch of Wahanee

El Morya
Sponsor, Map of Exchanges
Hierarch of Gobean

Kuthumi
Sponsor, Map of Exchanges
Hierarch of Malton
and Gandawan

Lord Macaw (Meru)
Sponsor, Map of the Ancients
Hierarch of Gobi

Mother Mary
Manu of the New Children
Hierarch of Marnero, Swaddling Cloth

Kuan Yin
Sponsor, Greening Map
Hierarch of Jehoa

The Master Teachers of Awakening

(Top, left) Lord Sananda is also known as the *Lord of the Transition* and as *World Teacher* oversees all aspects of the Earth Changes Maps and their Prophecies. He is also known as one of *Four Pillars*, four Master Teachers who oversee the *I AM America Teachings*. (Top, middle) Saint Germain is the *Lord of the Golden Cities*, a sponsor for the *I AM America Map* (United States, Canada, Greenland), and is a Four Pillars Master Teacher. (Top, right) El Morya is the sponsor of the *Map of Exchanges* (Europe) and is a Four Pillars Master Teacher. (Middle row, left) Kuthumi is the sponsor for the *Map of Exchanges* (Africa, Middle East), and is a Four Pillars Master Teacher. (Middle, right) Lord Macaw is the sponsor of the *Map of the Ancients*. (Bottom, left) Mother Mary is the Manu for the New Children and oversees the *Swaddling Cloth* (Brazil). She is also a sponsor of the *I AM America Map*, (Central and South America). (Bottom, right) Kuan Yin is the sponsor for the entire *Greening Map* (Asia and the Far East: India, Australia, China, Russia, Siberia, and Japan).

CONTENTS

SECTION ONE

Points of Perception

Earth Healing   55

Love's Service   59

Changing of the Guard   66

The Fourth Dimension   75

The Work of a Master   81

No Need for Change?   87

Weaving the New Web   95

Golden City Classes   102

Closing the Circle　　　118

Fountain of Life   124

The First Golden City   129

The Ever Present Perfection   133

SECTION TWO

Light of Awakening

Light a Candle — 155

Emanation — 158

Behind the Interplay   171

A New Day   176

A Quickening   186

Golden City Rays   196

Blue Illumination   204

The Light of a Thousand Suns 209

Divine Destiny

Template of Light   219

Conscious Creation   228

Divine Destiny   233

Map of the Ancients   239

The Time of Testing   249

Memory Is Freedom   259

Growth of the Soul   267

The New Children   275

APPENDICES

Author's Introduction

Spiritual Awakening is a profound evolutionary process that almost every conscious, aware human inevitably encounters. You can't, however, predict exactly when it will occur. It can shake one from a deep, lethargic sleep with a startling, bright light. For some it is a calmer process, like floating down a peaceful, lazy river with undercurrents of dark, baptismal waters. The process can certainly be gauged by its effect, but the experience is rarely calculated or predictive. A small dose of transformational experience is enlightening, but as change increases, the consequent loss of what you used to be can be inordinately painful. As your transformation progresses, you will encounter a necessary, life-giving development with both noticeable and subtle layers that define for you what is happening. Most importantly, know that Spiritual Awakening is transformational, and rest assured that once a glint of its transmuting light lessens the length of your shadow, life's trajectory is forever changed.

Beginnings are sometimes difficult to identify and often after a profound Spiritual Awakening, one begins to remember other moments and pronounced *a-has* that led or played an important role in getting you to where you are. I have no doubt that when Saint Germain appeared at the foot of my bed in 1983, the electrical energies initiated my system into a rapid Fourth-Dimensional Awakening. Yet, before that, I had several experiences also worth noting that I'd like to share.

My early twenties were not easy. In fact, if I were to measure my life by the early years of that decade it is no less than a miracle that my life was ever touched by a Spiritual Master, and an even greater wonder that I could ever assist the Masters—even in a small way. After attending a few years of college and marrying my high-school sweetheart, I left the inland prairies of Idaho and lived near the Strait of Juan de Fuca, on the Olympic Peninsula in Washington State. I worked at a local newspaper as a bookkeeper, and my office was located in the upper floor of a central building in downtown Sequim, Washington. Just down the stairs and around the corner my best girlfriend, Margie, also worked as a bookkeeper for a local drugstore. We met for lunch almost every Wednesday where we'd plot our next Friday night escape from our weeklong drudgery of number crunching and counting money. These were the days of disco, and in our small region there was only one club for young adults that offered live music along with the pulsing beat of Boz Skaggs, Donna Summer, Pablo Cruise, and of course the Bee Gees. Friday Night was definitely our girls' night out.

Since Margie was single and my husband literally hated to dance, more often than not, the two of us would meet up with more friends, and afterwards go out for coffee and breakfast in the early morning. The Sun was just beginning to backlight the eastern horizon with hues of pink and blue as we drove home and turned off the main highway onto a gravel road, a short-cut through the forest to my apartment. Morning light began to stream through the tall fir trees, and each Ray seemed inordinately alive and filled with a conscious light force that I had never sensed or noticed before. I commented several times to Margie about this, and she slowed down to enjoy what seemed to be a magical journey through a gateway of heavenly light. Suddenly a voice spoke within me, "Come to me!" and I immediately noticed a distinct beam of light, focused on the side of the road. Its golden force diffused into small particles, and I could literally see thousands of small rainbows of light swirling and churning within the cascading beam. Margie also noticed the majestic beam, and as we approached it she pulled over to the side of the road. We both sat for a minute staring at the mesmerizing light. As the light grew in size and intensity, it seemed magnetic, drawing both of us to its indescribable awe and profound beauty. Before either of us could exchange another word I impulsively opened the car door and dashed across the gravel road about twenty feet to stand directly in its glowing center, now a radiating floodlight of energy.

The light enfolded me and within seconds my body disappeared, each cell absorbed into its beauty. I could barely recognize the form of my body and it seemed with each inhale, my breath infused even more light into my being. I could not tell where I began or ended, I was literally ONE with the light. Years later I read a Summit Lighthouse decree from Master Kuthumi that accurately portrayed my experience. Here is an excerpt:

"I AM light, glowing light,
Radiating light, intensified light.
God consumes my darkness,
Transmuting it into Light.
This day I AM a focus of the Central Sun.
Flowing through me is a crystal river,
A living fountain of light . . ."

I basked in the morning light for what seemed an eternity, my consciousness no longer my personal possession. I had transformed, literally, into a "living fountain of light."

My friend never let me live down that transcendental encounter, and would later jokingly refer to it as my "Jesus moment." Funny though, I never felt the presence of Jesus . . . the incident seemed more universal and complete than conventional, profane religion. Noticeably, within a few months I had yet another unusual Awakening experience.

My husband and I often struggled as newlyweds. It seemed like what pleased me, did not please him. And we were both young, in fact, too immature for the commitment we had made to one another. Often, we would disagree over small things that led to intense quarrels. Plus, since we had recently moved we were also adapting to new jobs, friends, and an altogether new environment. Personally, I loved my new life but at times felt uncertain and grew weary of our relationship's state of constant emotional turmoil. At times I questioned if we should even remain married. After another long day of work, followed by yet another senseless argument, I decided to sleep on our hide-a-bed couch. I was both physically and mentally exhausted.

I closed my eyes and crossed into a space of soothing, yet almost hypnotic sleep. My mind was drifting and my breath was measured—slow and rhythmic. It seemed like I had entered a trance-like state that was other-worldly, and rapidly disconnecting from the heaviness of this world. Every muscle in my body was relaxed, almost like I was drugged. Floating in space, I noticed a face in the distance . . . familiar in some way, but one I couldn't recognize. The being of light is swiftly moving toward me, and suddenly a face hovers directly over mine. Our eyes meet and the light being is a young man, with light blond hair and distinctive greenish gold eyes. His face is chiseled and his look, though not stern, is somewhat serious, yet I feel a depth of compassion and empathy. His eyes convey an intense focus and it seems as if his energy enters my consciousness, my being, literally touching the vital essence of my soul. And everywhere there is light—golden effulgent light, similar to my experience in the forest. Eventually his face fades, and I awake, but his haunting image is indelibly etched into my memory.

Nearly fifteen years later, while visiting a metaphysical bookstore in Sedona, Arizona, I immediately recognize the ethereal face that had visited me years ago. The image was Master Hilarion, an Ascended Master whose service to humanity is focused upon the Green Ray of healing, service to humanity, truth, and science. It is alleged that Master Hilarion applies the flame of living truth to assist his students and chelas, but I am of the opinion that his personal visit was to trigger a Spiritual Awakening within me and instigate what I now know to be an Overlighting process. This spiritual method is essential for a new student—an aspirant—and the Master Teacher initiates a critical shakti—a dynamic energy that imbues certain qualities to initiate specific activities. In addition, the Spiritual Master follows and monitors the student through a critical phase of spiritual development and assists the student through upcoming difficulties.

Vedic knowledge clearly identifies three types of shakti activated by the Green Ray. The first is *Visasleshana*, a paralyzing, hypnotic gaze that assists one to discover and explore the depth of the soul through intuition and concentration. The second is *Arohana*, which empowers one with the courage and the ability to win battles through the masterful use of resources. The final and third shakti is *Kshiradyapani*, a vibrant healing energy that provides nourishment and Divine Protection. Undeniably, in a future timeline I would need to tap into each of these qualities to progress my spiritual mission with I AM America.

My introduction to the Ascended Masters and their teachings was nothing short of memorable. Although these experiences were profound, I had yet to meet a Spiritual Teacher who could guide and direct my development and growth. Several months after Master Hilarion's visitation my employer surprisingly moved me from the front desk and bookkeeper position into an advertising sales position. One day at work, I received a life-changing call to pick up an ad from a local health food store.

When I walked in the door and up to the counter of the small store to introduce myself, the owner stood up, pointed her finger at me, and stated, "You have work to do for Master Saint Germain!" Intrigued, I asked, "Who is Saint Germain?" The owner motioned for me to follow her through rows of neatly tiered vitamins to her office. On the wall hung a picture with the words *Comte de Saint Germain* carefully scripted in gold letters on the painting.

As I viewed the antique portrait of the eighteenth-century Frenchman, I had absolutely no idea who he was or why I felt so drawn to his aristocratic features and the details of his story. I was twenty-two years old, and the owner of his framed picture further explained that he was her spiritual teacher, and also an Ascended Master. I had never heard the term

"Ascended Master," nor did I understand how Saint Germain, who had obviously lived over two hundred years ago, could be a contemporary. After all, it was 1978.

The owner of that store, Florence, became a good friend and my first mentor of the Ascended Master tradition. Through her guidance and knowledge I entered a profound stage of Spiritual Awakening and enlightenment while learning about karma, reincarnation, the evolution and immortality of the soul, and the great mission of the Ascended Masters, also known as the Great White Brotherhood.

For many years Florence had been a member of a mystery school based out of Seattle, the *Aquarian Foundation*, founded by the medium Keith Milton Rhinehart. Reverend Rhinehart, (1936-1999), was a scientifically tested and researched medium expert in telekinesis, levitation, trumpet direct voice, apportation, and full and partial materialization of Ascended Masters through the mediumistic use of ectoplasm. Keith grew up in Colorado, and his mother's spiritualist teacher predicted that he would become a world famous medium. After falling asleep during a church service, dozens of roses appeared out of thin air and dropped from the teenager's aura. Reverend Rhinehart would often state that these demonstrations of the Ascended Masters were, "not for the sake of phenomena alone, but rather to establish clearly the Divine Source." During many of Reverend Rhinehart's sessions the Ascended Masters would appear in ectoplasm bodies to share spiritual teachings and to perform many of the miracles shared in the Bible, such as healing the sick and alchemically changing water into wine.

Reverend Rhinehart was not a Master, but was considered an adept, and throughout many decades brought forth teachings from Saint Germain, Master Morya, Sanat Kumara, and Kuthumi — many of the well-known Master Teachers of Theosophy and the I AM Movement. This is the venerated *lineage of gurus* written about in many of the I AM America Teachings. The lineage of gurus carries a specific energy similar to a shakti that is transmitted from this ancestry of esoteric knowledge through their spiritual teachings, whether channeled, trance-received, or by automatic writing. A trained disciple can quickly detect its presence. Several years after I had begun my career as a clairaudient trance channel I was contacted by yet another student of Keith Rhinehart.

Susan Liberty Hall had traveled with Reverend Rhinehart throughout the late sixties and early seventies, and had journeyed with him throughout the United States, Mexico, and South America. During this time she was not only a member of his church and organization, but worked as his secretary-assistant and had personally witnessed hundreds of live teachings and messages from the Ascended Masters in numerous sessions. When she contacted me in the early nineties, she immediately knew that the I AM America Teachings were indeed authentic. "I instantly recognized our beloved Master Saint Germain," she often reiterated. Susan wrote of her knowledge of the Ascended Masters in her foreword for *Building the Seamless Garment*, "The moment I heard the words I *AM America* I knew she was in service to Saint Germain, his teachings based on the I AM Presence, and the importance of the I AM Race, freedom, and democracy." Both Florence and Susan shared a vital tenet of Ascended Master Teaching — *the Golden Rule*. To paraphrase this significant passage from the Bible found in both Luke 6:31 and Matthew 7:12, "Do unto others as you would have them do unto you." Most importantly, Susan often added that for Christians who wished to evolve their devotion, faith, and practice, "Ascended Master Teaching is the *next* step."

Once encountered, Spiritual Awakening is an ongoing process and recurs with incremental steps. Our Awakening Process can transpire at many different levels and can encompass the Mental Body through exposure to new theories, facts, truths, and evidence. We can expand our Emotional Body through the practice of empathy, forgiveness, and compassion. Our intellect develops Divine Wisdom through applying purposeful listening and the memorization of sacred texts and passages. And above all, our innate spiritual divinity becomes activated and further honed through the continuous engagement of spiritual practices that include meditation, contemplation, prayer, decree, and positive visualization. This is the stable foundation which supports the cultivation of the HU-man super-senses.

Since the information presented in this book was first published over a dozen years ago, and received another dozen years before then, some may consider this information dated. I assure you, it is not. In fact, when reading this material to write new sub-titles I was continuously amazed and sometimes a bit surprised at the contemporary nature of the messages and teachings. For instance, Saint Germain coins an interesting phrase to describe the Earth's future collective consciousness as, "When insanity becomes sane," and prophesies stolen elections and alien governments who control populations through genetic interference. I remember at the time these prophecies seemed a bit edgy, but the fact is that years ago I did not wholly understand. Since then I have grown and (thankfully) awakened at new levels.

Moving through these teachings you will find the underpinnings of many important principles that are developed and expanded upon in future teachings. Saint Germain aptly explains multi-dimensional experience which is a primer to the HU-man Co-creation of simultaneous realities and multiple timelines. These are the metaphysical laws that help move conventional consciousness out of propaganda and possible theory, and drive human experience into the New Times — the Golden Age.

The second section of this book is primarily devoted to the knowledge of the Seven Rays of Light and Sound and their continuous interaction with the human aura through spiritual development. In my earlier years of study I could not find consistent information regarding the Ray Forces. It seemed that each Spiritual Teacher and school of Ascended Master teaching interpreted the Seven Rays differently. However, there were also essential elements of confluence; for instance the Yellow Ray was almost always associated with wisdom, the Pink Ray with love, and the Blue Ray with power and the application of personal will. I yearned to find a simple, yet consistent system that could seamlessly teach this important knowledge without confusion.

In 1996 I experienced an enlightening Spiritual Awakening that introduced me to ancient Vedic Astrology — *Jyotish*, which in Sanskrit means *Science of Light*. During a family vacation, I stepped into a bookstore. I immediately walked toward the metaphysical section where I noticed the title *Ancient Hindu Astrology for the Modern Western Astrologer* by James Braha. The book magnetized into my hands. For weeks, I pored over its pages that fully explained the vast and intricate systems of the wisdom of the Seven Rays. Here, at last, was the practical knowledge I sought that described and interpreted the Rays as both a tangible and an accessible energy.

Jyotish (pronounced Joe-teesh) is the ancient astrology of India, and likely originates from a time of greater light on Earth—the epoch of *Dvapara-Yuga* over six-thousand years ago. Legend states that the wise Rishi Teachers of India knew our Earth would soon enter a time of psychic corruption and darkness, Kali-Yuga. Jyotish, the personal exacting science of the Rays, was humanely bestowed so one could ably contact and achieve *moksha*—the natural and innate ability to liberate and inevitably free our human consciousness (aka the Ascension Process) in a prophesied time of spiritual shadows.

The foundation of Jyotish is based on the traditional Hindu Vedas—ancient spiritual scriptures—as one of the six disciplines (Vedanga) necessary to understand the Vedas. An experienced Jyotishi (astrologer) can accurately interpret the language of the stars and affirm with stunning accuracy personal predictions or forecast worldwide events; yet, most importantly, the practice of Jyotish opens subtle doors beyond this world and reveals the creation beyond our Earthly awareness, or better yet, the creation *behind* this creation. My Jyotish counselor explained how Jyotish ideally opens our instinctive psychic abilities, while simultaneously grounding each vision in its spiritual law that was observed thousands of years ago.

I took a full year's sabbatical from my work at I AM America to study Jyotish and discovered the complex and compelling parallels to the Seven Rays and Ascended Master Teaching. During this period my dreamtime became unusually vivid. I found myself entering celestial classrooms where many of the intricate topics of Jyotish were addressed. Often I would wake in the morning with a particular assignment from the heavenly instructor, such as: "Today, you will study Shad-Bala." Or, "Re-read and memorize the properties of the grahas (planets)." This process of conscious and dream-state education continued for approximately one year, and for months afterwards I still had numerous questions. Many of these inquiries were telepathically relayed to the Master Teachers and addressed in our channeled sessions. Several of these lessons are contained in the *Light of Awakening* section.

The third and final section of this book, *Divine Destiny*, evolves a more complex understanding of the Rays and their relationship to the Golden Cities. To clearly appreciate and comprehend this knowledge you must engage another vital principle of Awakening; that is, you must *empty your Cup*. I suggest that you discard, at least while in the process of absorbing this information, preconceived ideas and notions that may hinder your growth. We are now living in a time of unparalleled evolution through the metaphysical appearance of the Gold Ray that is dispersed and regulated to Earth through activated Golden Cities and our solar system's movement through an energized Photon Belt. This planetary anomaly is creating a worldwide Awakening of humanity through a unification of science, philosophy, religion, and spirituality. Many of the principles that you held to be bedrock truths are contrarily different from the unique esoteric histories and narratives found in *Divine Destiny*. For instance, the Ascended Masters claim that within our Earth is yet another Sun—smaller than our solar Sun—known as *Earth's Inner Sun*. Our entire solar system rotates around yet another larger Sun, the Galactic Center. This spiritual principle was not a mystery to the ancient people of both India and Mesoamerica; however, it is a well known fact in the Ascended Master tradition that this Great Central Sun emits a unique and life-evolving energy that calibrates spiritual growth and development; this includes the expanse of our intelligence and the span of our lifetime.

As the teachings evolve in this first book of the *Ascension Timeline Series, Awakening*, it becomes apparent that in order to enter the New Times and embrace the Golden Age that we must first overcome the old patterns and consciousness that have held us prisoners to suppression, false beliefs, and the oppressive manipulation by others for economic gain and exploitive control. Saint Germain reiterates, "The light that emanates from the Great Central Sun is the light that shall free you all. It is the light of Awakening!"

Divine Destiny also features spiritual insight and esoteric histories from the Ascended Master Lord Macaw (Meru), a Spiritual Teacher whose soul's biography dates back to both Mu and Lemuria. His instruction presents the age-old maxim that in order to move forward, we must embrace the past. This teaching is both literal and metaphoric.

He literally presents a new map, brought forward from the Akashic Records of Earth's prehistoric history—the *Map of the Ancients*. Its landforms depict Earth in a much earlier time and present controversial knowledge from the lost ages of Mu, Lemuria, and Atlantis. Lord Macaw claims that this map was not imparted to teach geology, or for that matter, Prophecy. Instead, its spiritual significance is the map's provenance of ancient civilizations, and how each culture was formed through the focus of the magnificent Seven Rays of Light and Sound.

The Map of the Ancients was presented, drawn, explained, and then re-drawn as Lord Macaw patiently corrected our discrepancies. When we finished we could vaguely recognize the continents of Earth. However, with later research—contained in the appendices of this book—the information parallels the many myths and scientific theories of epochs past.

The metaphoric understanding of our own past is also presented for personal examination. Saint Germain explains, "The karmas, the actions that have been taken in the past, seem to follow us and become part of our present." The perceptive re-telling of past events—personal or worldwide—is also a profound element within the Co-creation process. The Ascended Masters refer to this as "the *Re-membering* of *His-story*." This process incites the healing of old wounds, the psychological "baggage" we are inclined to carry for far too long. More importantly, this practice re-calibrates our consciousness to carefully see, hear, and perceive our pasts. This careful refinement is the flame that ignites our inner-light, and this source of truth enlightens our present and leads our journey toward the mysterious unknown and onward to transcendence.

I'd like to close with some insights shared by Saint Germain and Lord Sananda throughout the I AM America Teachings regarding the Awakening Process:

"The degree of Awakening is measured through choice."
-*Saint Germain*

"Carry the Great Awakening in your activity!
As you spread this message of change, remind all you meet of all cultures,
that the prophecy of change is an Awakening to Liberty and Grace!"
-*Lord Sananda*

"To be Awakened is to know what one wants to create."
-*Saint Germain*

"In the Awakening Process, one is always at odds with the ego."
-*Saint Germain*

"Is there not that moment of Awakening of seeing this nonsense
with great humor, tears, and laughter?"
-*Saint Germain*

"Move in small, incremental steps, and you will not miss one bit along the way.
It is important to understand each stage of consciousness
as you move along in your Awakening."
-*Saint Germain*

"The Awakening of divinity within comes through openness and receptivity,
the trust and acceptance that the Master is truly within."
-*Saint Germain*

"The minutes and seconds click and the Awakening is at hand.
The time has come for man to receive the gift."
-*Lord Sananda*

SECTION ONE

Points of Perception

Based on the Prophecies and Spiritual Teachings of

Saint Germain

CHAPTER ONE

Earth Healing

cs

Saint Germain in Bend, Oregon.

Greetings in that Mighty Christ Light, I AM Saint Germain. I stream forth on the Mighty Ray of Mercy and Forgiveness. As usual, Dear hearts, chelas, and students, I must ask permission to come forth.

Response: "Please come forth, Dear one."

PROPHECIES OF PEACE

The work upon the Earth Plane and Planet is one where we shall say, tarry not. For this Time of Transition[1] that comes is indeed, as we have said, a time when that Lady shall open her legs and you would perceive, in essence, a birth scream or a howl. But yet, we see this as that Time of Awakening, a Time of Transition, and a time for the opening of the Prophecies of Peace and Grace. May peace stream forth into your hearts, Dear ones, and be forever your infinite and eternal decree. Peace and grace, that which is, shall we say, that Law of the Best and Highest Good, that which streams forth from that Ray of Divine Will and that Ray of Divine Love.

We ask for you, Dear ones, dear Brothers and Sisters, chelas and students. Those who are gathered here for the ushering in of that Mighty Law of Grace. To hold within their hearts, that Mighty Light of God that never fails. We ask for you at all times to see yourself as that transmitter, that generator, that mighty servant of light, who allows these energies to come and bring forth an enactment of the Divine Will upon the Earth Plane and Planet.

Dear hearts, the Time of Peace now comes to the planet. And, you as forerunners, as lovers of this peace, we ask you to play them as a grand symphony, one string harmonizing one with the next. Or have we not taught that the first law that streams forth, is the Law of Harmony? And now, we as members and as servants of lovers of peace and grace, ask that each of you consider that not only is this a Time of Change and Earth Change for that matter, but also a time which will be a Time of Peace and Prophecies of Peace.

The Spiritual Hierarchy of this Lodge has, for some time, decided that Earth Changes Prophecy will no longer be given for a short time. However, we will now allocate this time to bring forth what are known as those Prophecies of Peace.

HARMONY AND AGREEMENT

For Dear ones, as you have known, your attention is where energy flows! Have you not noticed this in all Co-creation and manifestation? And, have you not noticed this in the work-about world in which you live?

Each and every one of you asks daily, "How is it that I can apply these teachings and utilize them for my life? How can I serve this Spiritual Awakening? How can I best serve my Brothers and Sisters?" I say to you, each and every one of you, that it is as simple as living in that Law of Harmony.[2]

But first, that Law of Harmony is built upon agreement. That is, again, that harmonious response to thought — for it is the

---

1. This twelve-year era of spiritual change marks a turning point in the momentum of the Earth's energy. It begins with the implementation of a benevolent plan: one that activates the Law of Love while encouraging Divine Awareness among humanity. Beginning in 1988 and ending in 2000, (however some I AM America prophecies suggest a longer duration) the beloved Ascended Masters, Archangels, and Elohim flood the Earth with light (the Rays) to restore mankind's spiritual growth and acuity. Many people know and understand this period as the Spiritual Awakening. During this short but intense interval of Transformation, the proliferation of alternative self-help and healing groups spawns a renewed zeal for other forms of faith. And as the spirituality of the global community gels, the human consciousness — like a river changing course — flows from secular concerns to spiritual viewpoints. The Time of Transition, as a result, fosters an understanding and an experience of Unity among spiritual thoughts, customs, and cultures. And though this Divine Age ended nearly a decade ago, humanity can still tap into the readily available spiritual infusion of energy to initiate the dawning of human consciousness for the New Dimensions.

2. The First Jurisdiction. The Twelve Jurisdictions are an integral part of the Prophecies of Peace and are specific teachings of spiritual practices. When applied, these spiritual laws move consciousness beyond fear-based thinking and into Co-creative-based experience. Harmony is based on the spiritual teachings of cooperation, agreement, and balance. "All energy, in order to be sustained for creation, must be maintained in balance — balance is the continuous cycle of harmony."

thought that is the premise of all Creation. And we would ask that each and every one of you consider to align your thoughts to that plan of the best and the highest good. Allow a frequency and a vibration to come forth that serves that mighty plan of the Divine Will!

THE CHANGE WITHIN

In the days to come, yes, there will be the shaking and the rattling of the Earth forces. Not only shall we see eruptions in that Cascade Range, but also into the Sierra Madres, and in a counter-clockwise positing of that Pacific Rim. These were all the prophecies that we have dispensed in the I AM America material and we will continue to give brief updates on.

However Dear chelas and students, we ask for you to place your attention not only on the element of change, but to look deep within the heart of your own being and recognize the change that is happening within your heart. Are we not now in the middle of a spiritual transition? Are we not now in the middle of a Spiritual Awakening? I ask you Dear stalwart students of the Mighty Flame of Truth, to come forward in that breath of the Mighty ONE; come forward in that breath of that Mighty ONE Peace.

The Time of Transition is a time when we are transiting not only from the Third Dimension, but onward into the Fourth and the Fifth Dimension. For it is, shall we say, in the harmony of the spheres, where peace is gained; and the bitter cup is taken from your lips. You have sought the sensation of this elusive reality and have found so contained within that duad, that form of clay, your body; and now we move into that Time of ONE, that Time of Monad, that Time of ALL Interconnectiveness of All Life!

Your emotions, your feelings, even your thoughts, Dear ones, run rampant at this time. And we would ask that you discipline them through enacting that first Mighty Law of Harmony. Call forth harmony in all your agreements; call forth harmony in all your transactions. Remember, you are a Oneship as beloved Kuan Yin has stated, "Each and every one of you shares this life." This ONE life that is contained upon the planet is ONE that is contained in your own being. You have studied the energetics of change and also the energetics related to not only the

human or electromagnetic field, but also study Dear chelas and students, that electromagnetic force that is of the planet itself.

THE VORTICES SERVE HUMANITY

Understand that each of the fifty-one Vortices, which have been brought forth in service to the awakening of humanity, are also those mighty focuses of energy contained upon the planet — and for her transit into what we would call, a quantum leap in Collective Consciousness.

The positing of your location at this moment is the location of one of those older Vortices of the planet. And yes, while you carry forward a readjustment and re-alignment of, that electromagnetic body, the impulse body, a natural feeling body of the planet, you are also assisting in anchoring in the energies which align to the Golden City Vortex known as Klehma.[3] And we would ask that in your heart and in your thought today, that you hold forth that thought of Continuity, Cooperation, and Balance.[4]

---

3. See Appendix A1: *The Golden City Vortex, Golden City Structure*, and *Ray Force Entering a Golden City*.

4. The existence of Vortices is the foundation of the I AM America Prophecies — that's why the understanding of this concept is paramount to grasping the teaching of the Ascended Masters. The Vortex is a polarized motion body, meaning it creates its own electromagnetic field. It's characterized by a concentration of energy and, in some cases, psychic gravity. Rock formations act as energizing points for the Earth's electromagnetic energies.

Vortices often form at the intersection lei lines (the Earth's energy meridians), also known as "power spots." Think of it as the geographic equivalent of the longitudinal and the latitudinal coordinates that circle the globe. The convergence of meridian lines can warp time and energy, and align molecular structure with phenomenal accuracy. Vortices and lei lines also embrace animate characteristics: the yin and yang; female and male.

Although all Vortices embody electromagnetic properties, they fall into two general categories: electric and magnetic. Electrical Vortices, the yin or the feminine, tend to open the central nervous system and stimulate neural passages. Magnetic Vortices, however, identify with spiritual or ethereal energies, and the yang or the masculine essence. These Vortices encourage deep meditation and physical rejuvenation. A person's psychic awareness — along with his or her telepathy and the frequency of lucid dreaming — may intensify in these areas.

Many Vortices are highly sacred places where dimensions interplay like cracks between worlds. For instance, the geomancy — or divination of earth material — of the Sedona Vortices is well documented. These formations serve as hallowed highways, ferrying spiritual energies to the material realm. Here, the healing of physical, emotional, and spiritual maladies is optimal.

COOPERATION

As members of this Lodge, Dear hearts, remember at all times we hold within our hearts, first, that Mighty Law of Cooperation. And we would ask each and every one of you to become not only a symbol of this cooperation, but also to carry it forward in your daily demonstration. Choose and you shall act; act and you shall choose.

As we have stated before, Dear ones, "as above so below." We ask for this Divine Will to stream forth in you — this day. And with these Prophecies of Peace, carry them forward not only in your heart, but also in that active hand.

POLARIZATION AND BALANCE

In the times to come, after that time where that polarization of energy is balanced, we shall see not only changes in government, but also within the social structures, these, first starting with the family unit. The Time of Equity now comes to the planet, and that Inner Marriage or marriage of the Kundulini energies will now be woven, not only as male and female, but the activation of the Christ.

DIVINE CONCEPTION

In the family units, even conception as you have understood it, will come forward in a different manner. You have worries of the clay vessel and the carrying forth of energies in the human duad. We ask for you to consider forms of sponsorship of energy that are carried forward in consciousness and in thought.

Beloved Mother Mary brought forward, that first idea of divine conception. Held first immaculately in her inner eye, in her inner vision. We ask you now, Dear students, to hold that forward, to hold that perfect thought.

CREATIVE THOUGHT AND THE POWER OF CHOICE

To assist the accelerations of energies upon the Earth Plane and Planet, we will encounter what is known as holo-leaping or the movement between the Third and Fourth Dimensions.

How do we do this, Dear ones? Through what are known as our energy fields. How do we direct our energy fields? Through creative thought.

Many lifestreams from other planets now seek entry into the Earth Plane and Planet. However, at this time, we are seeing the ending (lifting) of the Mighty Law of Cause and Effect. This, you have known through many lifestreams, and through some, shall I say, even limited teachings as karma. But we ask you to consider this as dharma. For is it not joyful now to be ending this portion of the path, Dear hearts, this portion of the journey?

Now we have climbed to this new positing. And we look over the valley and we say, "It is good." Is it good for you, Dear ones? Is this, in that Law of the Best and the Highest Good? These are the choices that lay in front of you in this Time of Transition.

SEVENTH MANU

During these times that await us, as I have stated, many lifestreams are preparing themselves now to come upon the planet known as the Seventh Manu.[5] I have spoken of them in previous discourse. Not only do they await entry through your

---

5. The word Manu comes from the Hindu word "to think," an apt root for this highly evolved society of young souls prophesied to incarnate on the Earth during the New Times. But the idea of Manu is expansive; its significance reaches far beyond the context of the I AM America Prophecies.

Manu refers to a root race or a group of souls inhabiting a vast time period (era or epoch) on Earth. The concept of Manu is found among Native American tribes, too. The Hopis describe this term as "worlds" e.g. fourth world, fifth world. Manu is also a mythical, cosmic being who oversees the souls during their incarnation processes throughout the duration of that specific time period. Some consider Manu a type of spiritual office, not unlike a "World Teacher." For example, one evolved cosmic being will serve as Manu for one world cycle, and when it ends, it moves on in the evolutionary process. A different entity serves as Manu for the next group. Each group of souls has a different energy and purpose. Seventh Manu children will possess advanced capabilities — astute intellect, vast spiritual knowledge, and keen psychic abilities. Forerunners of the Seventh Manu will pave the way for this metaphysically venerated population. Carrying less karmic burden than those of the past, these forbearers of ever-increasing enlightenment promote a sense of higher consciousness. As dharma flourishes, the Seventh Manu, sponsored by the Beloved Mother Mary, proliferates.

The majority of this Seventh-Manu generation will settle in an area of Brazil known as the *Swaddling Cloth*. (You can view the geo-physical perimeters of the Swaddling Cloth on the I AM America Freedom Star World Map.) Others will be born in the Golden City Vortices.

conscious thought, but also through those Mighty Vortices on the planet.

They come to bring their service, Dear ones, and to bring their service not only to humanity, but to those other kingdoms of creation: Devas, Elementals, and Elohim. They come, in essence, to raise the vibrational frequencies of the planet, for these are the Times of Peace that await us!

THE MIGHTY SPARK

Will a time come when humanity will again live in harmony with its environment? This I say — so! (yes) In this illusion, there is always an element of chaos! You are blessed, Dear ones, as Co-creators, inheritors that possess, that mighty spark, the Monad, the ONE.

As all life contains within it that One Mighty Breath, we ask for you to consider, Dear chelas, stalwart students of truth, that it is held within the frequency and the Vibration of your thought, the development of your consciousness.

GATHER IN GROUPS

These small exercises, the gathering of a group to hold collective thought, to hold Collective Consciousness, are those first steps that allow that involution of consciousness to become an evolution of humanity.

CONSCIOUSNESS OF SOURCE

And then those higher frequencies are allowed, conceptualized and To Be. We fear so often, as when taking the human form, that the extent of all reality is contained (only) within that vessel of clay. Yet, Dear ones, your true life, your true inner spark, is made of neither. It is the pure consciousness from that which we have known as Helios and Vesta — that which is known as the Source — planted eons ago upon your planet by those Mighty Lords of Venus, those who have brought forth their sponsorship for your evolution.[6]

"HOLD THE SPARK"

A time now comes where you will assume these new positions as members of this Lodge, a Brotherhood and a Sisterhood of light and love. I ask for you to consider, Dear students, that you too shall become as the elders have become. And in this time that awaits us — a Prophecy of Peace — you shall become (as) those Elohims of Tranquility, Elohims of Peace. You shall hold the spark, the Jiva, the Monad of Consciousness for those residing in kingdoms of lesser consciousness and for those who await us, those beloved dear children of the Seventh Manu, who hold within their heart that spark and consciousness for your own evolution.

I shall take my leave from your frequency and ask you to carry the prayer of the ONE throughout the day. Understand that even though we enter into a time of limited turmoil and chaos, that this is also a Time of Peace and a Time of Awakening.

---

6. The Lords of Venus comprise a group of Ascended Masters — former residents of the planet Venus — who came to serve humanity millions of years ago. Esoteric scholars say this ancient coterie of metaphysical sages existed in the nebula known as Pleiades before settling on Venus to adjust their energy frequencies for their work on Earth. Their spiritual teachings and principles center on the practice of bhakti, a type of selfless love that manifests as compassion for others. The summoning of the Violet Flame (a form of karma yoga) purifies the consciousness to higher states of understanding, awareness, and empathy.

The Seventh Manu will play a large role in raising the consciousness and the Vibration of the Earth. Saint Germain first prophesied the appearance of the Seventh Manu in a Trance-Mission on May 1, 1993.

CHAPTER TWO

Love's Service

❧

Saint Germain's message for a small group.

Greetings and salutations; good morning, students and chelas. The work upon the Earth Plane and Planet is yet to be realized — that is, achieved or actualized through the being. We shall address that heart of intent, for the time that comes forth is a time of the opening of the heart of humanity. How shall this happen, Dear ones? So many of you ask this in your prayers and in your thoughts and in your meditations.

FORGIVENESS

It is still through the use of the Violet Flame, that Mighty Flame of Mercy and Forgiveness. Dear ones, as you have understood, forgiveness is not an energy that is meted out or granted; yet, it is an energy that allows and sustains all of creation — it is that portal of Oneness, that place where two shall meet and become as ONE. This is where the understanding of the heart begins and where we open to that Mighty Energy of the Christ. There have been, throughout history, many misinterpretations of the Christ. But as we have practiced in this Lodge and in this tradition, the Christ is union achieved through forgiveness. It is also that energy where an at-one-ment, a vibrational frequency occurs. That Oneship, as beloved Kuan Yin has stated "steps forward to grant a measure of grace."

THE VIBRATION OF LOVE

The opening of this vibrational frequency of Love upon the Earth Plane and Planet has always been the concern of this Lodge of the Spiritual Hierarchy. And it has been the development of this vibrational frequency of love which has been entrusted to us through our traditions and is the focus of our intent in service to and with humanity. It is this Vibration of Love that was brought to us eons ago by those Mighty Lords of Venus and is now entrusted to you, Dear ones, and brought

to you to bring about an evolutionary rise — to raise your vibrational frequency (living intelligence) from the animal to the HU-man. It was planted, and it was known as the Monad,[1] or Jiva. Of course, these are ancient words; and we now call it simply, the Unfed Flame of activated Love, Wisdom, and Power.[2]

---

1. Monad means dynamic will, or purpose and life, as it is revealed through human demonstration. The Monad is often referred to as the Lord of ceaseless devotion, knowledge, and intelligent activity. H. P. Blavatsky writes of the Monad in the *Secret Doctrine*:

"For the Monad, or Jiva, per se, cannot be called even Spirit; it is a Ray, a breath of the Absolute, or the ABSOLUTENESS rather; and the Absolute Homogeneity, having no relations with the conditioned and relative finiteness, is unconscious on our plane. Therefore, besides the material which will be needed for its future human form, the Monad requires (a) a spiritual model, or prototype for that material to shape itself into; and (b) an intelligent consciousness, to guide its evolution and progress, neither of which is possessed by the homogeneous Monad, or by senseless though living matter. The Adam of dust requires the Soul of Life to be breathed into him … therefore when the hour strikes for purusha (spirit) to mount on Prakriti's (substance) shoulders for the formation of the Perfect Man…the Celestial Ancestors (entities from preceding worlds) step in on this our plane, and incarnate in the physical or animal man, as the Pitris (solar angel, I AM Presence) had stepped in before them for the formation of the latter … the Pitris shoot out from their ethereal bodies still more ethereal and shadowy similitudes of themselves, or what we should now call 'doubles' … in their own likeness. This furnishes the Monad with its first dwelling, and blind matter with a model around and upon which to build henceforth."

2. According to the Masters, this Unfed Flame is a Flame of Divinity and of spiritual consciousness. The Masters refer to this phenomenon in other terms: the Threefold Flame, Monad, and Jiva. The Unfed Flame urges humanity to evolve beyond its present state of spiritual consciousness through Co-creative thought, feeling, and action. Relying upon a higher, spiritual consciousness, the Lords of Venus — servants of humanity and onetime denizens of the planet Venus — rooted Love, Wisdom, Power, and the Unfed Flame in the human heart. These Divine Tenets empower humans to achieve a higher sense of consciousness, thereby assuring humanity a type of spiritual immortality.

The grafting of the sublime Unfed Flame to the carnal human heart occurred from afar. Ancestral helpers on Venus directed a collective and everlasting energy force toward humanity on Earth. The Venusian and ever-youthful lord named Sanat Kumara, the overseer of Shamballa, spearheaded this Mission. With an etheric Silver cord, he connected the Unfed Flame to every life stream incarnated on Earth. When this flame of spiritual consciousness began to develop among individuals, Sanat Kumara led a group of higher beings to Earth where they established the first Golden City, later known as Shamballa. This spiritual center possessed unrivaled opulence; streets paved with Gold passed jewel-encrusted Temples and Schools of Higher Wisdom and Knowledge.

In addition to its metaphysical influence on the human body, the Unfed Flame serves as a portal to a being of greater spiritual consciousness — the I AM Presence — to which we are indelibly connected.

Meanwhile, these legends appear in other doctrines. Vedic Cosmology — Hindu-based metaphysics — mirrors a similar creation

We have explained in previous discourse about those epochs of races from the Lemurian to the Atlantean. Now, this race known as the Aryan is, simply stated, meant to activate this intelligence. That is the definition of Aryan — to open the Heart of Love.[3] We begin to activate this intelligence by the use of the Laws of Forgiveness.

---

story. According to the sacred Sanskrit text of Hindu philosophy, the *Bhagavad-Gita*, fourteen planetary systems exist in the intangible universe. The highest is Satyaloka where residents grasp advanced spiritual knowledge. Sanat Kumara, and Sananda — who in Vedic culture is referred to as Sanandana Kumara — are two of the four sons of Brahma and inhabit in the second-tier planetary system of Tapaloka. Earth, known as Bhurloka, falls seventh in line.

Each planetary system creates a unique experience for its dwellers — the sentience of the space-time continuum and the manifestation of the physical being differentiate higher from lower beings. Residents of enlightened strata perceive time durations in millennia, have no sense of fear, and do not confront disease or the aging of the body. In the lower planetary systems, residents experience shorter life spans, marked fear, widespread disease, and increased apprehension.

3. Dark and ignorant elements of society have sullied the meaning of 'Aryan' to describe a genetically superior race, one that dominates and destroys all others. This semantic contrivance is intended to confuse humanity of the true nature and Mission of the Rays, and the intention of their services. Esoteric teachings tell us humanity, regardless of race, color or creed, is ONE race; Aryan is this race — we are ONE race.

Throughout the evolution of light and consciousness on this planet, humanity has embraced a physical incarnation of one of three distinct races: the Lemurian, the Atlantean, and the Aryan. According to the teachings of the Ray(ces), only one lineage, without exception, can embody and inhabit the Earth at one time. Each culture assumes a distinctive composite of Ray forces, which determines the physical and emotional vehicles of its members. The presence of certain Ray(ce) combinations is primarily psychological and affects the shared outer mind of humanity. This collective mentality carries the Divine Plan forward through the Divine Mind. The three best known Ray(ce) combinations are:

1. The Lemurian: The contintent of Lemuria, also known as Mu in other ideologies, was located somewhere between India and Australia. Some prophecies say it existed no more than 20,000 years ago; others suggest it dates back millions of years before Christ. This Eden-like civilization met its end when the warm waters of the South Pacific Ocean swallowed its landmass during a cataclysmic event. Many metaphysical scholars believe Lemurian survivors live inside Mount Shasta and on the African island of Madagascar.

Lemurians thrived during the first wave of consciousness. According to esoteric teachings, Lemurians triumphed over animal consciousness and rooted the flame of Divine Humanity in the human heart. Their primitive physical vehicles — clumsy bodies, exposed pineal glands, and one-eyed vision — required absolute mindfulness to hold form and sustain body functions. The result: animal consciousness dominated the physically and spiritually feeble Lemurians. Some say this ancient race developed Hatha Yoga to hone and coordinate external movements and internal mechanisms. Over time, genetics trained the heart to circulate blood, the lungs to respire air, and the stomach to digest food. Consciousness shifted from the corporeal to the incorporeal, thus establishing the foundation of an involuntary nervous system and the basis for our present-day level of conscious absolution, the Age of Spiritual Freedom. The Rays of modern times liberated our conscious minds, giving it independence and expression. Meanwhile, the extinction of the dinosaurs paved the way for new Rays of consciousness and a new race of humanity.

2. The Atlantean: The existence of Atlantis — the lost continent — still stumps the keenest minds of scientific and metaphysical communities. Even the great Greek philosophers pondered its rise and fall. According to legend, Atlantis emerges as a civilization about 400,000 years ago; its demise abuts the beginning of recorded history. Ancient lore places Atlantis in the Atlantic Ocean or near the Straits of Gibraltar; other texts say it once flourished near present-day Cuba.

A group of Atlanteans escaped the sinking of Atlantis and found refuge in America. They became the I AM Race of souls; their active intelligence continues to develop — their purpose, to foster Brotherly love among all nations.

Atlantean cognizance emerges from animalistic instinct into HU-man behavior. The Emotional Body of this race resembles modern-day mankind. Blessed with pointed intuition, this go-between group bridges the gap between consciousness and intelligence. It introduces the first social order of religion, which, through a chosen code of behavior, disciplines the emotions and the emotional Light Body. This enlightenment reveals a religious purpose, connecting the Emotional Body to the intelligent choice (conscience) and preparing humanity for social order. (To learn more, see: Divine Destiny.)

3. The Aryan: Metaphysicians allegorically associate seven divisions of the Aryan to the seven apocalyptic churches of St. John's vision in the Book of Revelations: Ephesus, India; Smyrna, Persia; Pergamos, Chaldean-Egyptian-Semitic; Thyatira, Greece-Latin-Roman; Sardis, Teuton-Anglo-Saxon; Philadelphia, Slavic; Laodicea, Manichaean (Persian Gnostic Teachings). According to the Master teachers of the I AM America teachings, the Aryan race traces its ancient roots to Africa including the primeval Egyptian city of Meroe, Ethiopia and the majestic, sacred Mount Meru, Tanzania. The word Aryan denotes active intelligence; in Sanskrit it means nobility. Scholars say the destiny of this contemporary race — Aryan — is linked with Lemurian civilization; it carries the Divine Plan forward through the qualification of active intelligence. That's why this dynamic, modern race continues to develop the cognitive ability to apply intelligent emotions, thoughts, and actions in its decision-making process.

PROPHECY AWAKENS

As you all share in one life upon this Earth Plane and Planet, we would ask you to consider at all times, Dear ones, that even that spark, the mighty Monad is as ONE, which you all share.

The time now upon the Earth Plane and Planet is not only a Time of Transition but a Time of Prophecy. These prophecies have come to awaken that flame, to foster and engender it, to bring it forward into active use. War and pestilence are in your streets; and you ask, "What is it that I may bring forth in perfect service?" And (so) I would ask, Dear students and chelas, that each day you anchor yourself as a pillar of that Law of Forgiveness, and demonstrate it.

THE VIOLET FLAME

If you are having trouble forgiving, the utilization of this law is as simple as taking a few seconds and visualizing the Violet Flame streaming forth from your feet and extending to the top of your head. You will feel it as an electric shock throughout your system as it stimulates each of the centers of light upon and within the physical body. This is a gift from the Lords of Venus so that you would understand the ONE that is contained within each and every one of you. We understand that it is almost impossible for you to comprehend all languages (genetic codes) in your separated state of being, but we ask you to hold the Violet Flame throughout your being throughout the day. Visualize that flame in, through, and around those for whom you harbor thoughts of disharmony and discord. Use it for the healing of your physical vehicle. Use it in all situations that you feel might hinder or hamper your movement within this Lodge of Service. We ask you, Dear hearts, to utilize the Flame not only in your business practices but also in your bank accounts — for it is that Flame that allows a movement toward the ONE.[4]

The ONE is contained in all things. It is that flame which is the bridge to the Universal Mind.

"TRUE CHANGE"

As we have stated before, the Prophecies of Earth Changes have been closed for a short time. However, with close attention to that Divine Plan and Mighty Will of the Light of God that never fails, we shall dispense again a series of Earth Changes Prophecies designed to awaken the hearts and minds of all those who slumber. (Editor's Note: This is in reference to the Six-Map Scenario.)

However, in this period of time, we ask you, Dear hearts, to place the emphasis upon the Prophecies of Peace. For not only do geophysical changes come to the planet; but as you have understood the dynamic of energetic reasoning, you know that first come the changes within the heart, reflected afterward in societies and communities — and only then comes the true change, in the creations of your worlds of experience.

THE GOLDEN CITY VORTICES

We shall see these changes occur first in each of the Vortices; in the order they have been assigned in the activation. You have all been called to that mighty Gobean energy, and you will first see the Prophecies of Peace anchored in that Vortex. You will also see the transformational changes occurring, first in the hearts of those who attend to them.

Second in the activation, as we have stated before, will be Malton; third in the activation will be Wahanee; fourth, Shalahah; and fifth, Klehma.[5]

---

5. Golden City Vortices are activated in two-year periods during the New Times. However, in 2020 the Ascended Masters instigated the Great Activation and simultaneously activated five Golden Cities. (For more information see the *I AM America Atlas*.)

Located in Arizona, Gobean, the first for the Time of Change, developed in the late 1970s and continued its growth into the early 1980s. Once the new energies began to flourish on Earth, the Ascended Masters, Archangels, and Elohim, in 1994, initiated a sequential, two-year awakening of the remaining Golden Cities throughout the world.

1. Malton: 1994 (United States)
2. Wahanee: 1996 (United States)
3. Shalahah: 1998 (United States)
4. Klehma: 2000 (United States)
5. Pashachino: 2002 (Canada)
6. Eabra: 2004 (Canada)
7. Jeafray: 2006 (Canada)
8. Uverno: 2008 (Canada)
9. Yuthor: 2010 (Greenland)
10. Stienta: 2012 (Iceland)
11. Denasha: 2014 (Scotland)
12. Amerigo: 2016 (Spain)
13. Gruecha: 2018 (Norway, Sweden)
14. Braun: 2020 (Germany, Poland, Czechoslavakia)
15. Afrom: 2020 (Hungary, Romania)
16. Ganakra: 2020 (Turkey)

Once a Golden City matures, humans can tap into Vortex energies for healing, growth, evolution, development, and transformation: personal, planetary and spiritual recovery form the foundation of humanity's Ascension to a higher consciousness.

Golden City Vortices are considered safe places where ongoing spiritual growth and advancement bloom. In these sacred harbors, energy finds asylum from exploitation. Saint Germain says, "These gateways or Vortex areas are protected areas for interaction with spiritual energy." (For more information see: *New World Wisdom, Book One*.)

---

4. See Appendix B1: The Violet Flame.

PURGING IMPURITIES

What is it that happens during the Times of Activation and the anchoring of the Prophecies of Peace? Transmutation occurs first with the purging of the body. There have been those who have experienced this as physical fire, within the system affected first, such as the lymphatic system, and then onward, into the joints. It is my advice, Dear ones, that as you experience this process, known as Vibrational Toning, you should increase your water intake. The fragrances of violets, jasmine, and cinnamon can also relieve these stresses.

I ask you to spend no less than ten minutes per day in thought and prayer upon the Violet Flame. Perfect this energy within the system, for you are as transmitters of light; you are vehicles of peace. Of course, first the physical body suffers as the soul purges that which is no longer needed; but then comes that time when you will outstretch your hand, and say, "Flame, you and I are ONE!"

CHANGES IN THE HUMAN AURA

There will be changes, as noted before, in the electrical field of the body. These start at the end of this year and then extend

---

Activated Golden City Vortices function at the Third, Fourth, and Fifth Dimensions in their attributes and release of beneficial energies. Golden City Third-Dimensional energies create harmonious connections to Mother Earth. Humans who physically assimilate to Golden City Vortex energies receive the gifts of longevity (slower aging); greater healing abilities (health and well-being); and physical regeneration (cell replication).
The Golden City Fourth-Dimensional energies affect human Light Bodies (the aura). Connections to the invisible kingdoms develop; one cultivates the ability to see gnomes, fairies, and Elementals. In this dimension, a person tunes into his or her telepathic and psychic abilities (the development of the super senses), and experiences lucid dreaming (dimensional awareness), honing preternatural skills and talents — natural functions in human spiritual evolution.
Fifth-Dimensional Golden City energies operate within the realm of the Ascended Masters; Shamballa; advanced spiritual teachers; archetypes of evolution; and the templates of all Golden Cities. At this level, our spiritual evolution initiates a profound relationship with the Master Teacher and the Ray Force that serves a particular Golden City Vortex. Experiences of Unana, the ONE, and the Collective Consciousness are common. At this dimension, all beings live in spiritually perfected communities. The body takes on an ageless, perfected state — one without disease or fear. (For more information regarding Golden Cities throughout the World see *I AM America Atlas*.)

onward for the next four years. Brilliant Gold light will begin to be seen, activated within the outer layers of the body's electromagnetic sphere, the ovoid of the aura. These sparks of light are flames emitted from the activation (light intelligence), both from the third layer of the Human Auric field and also from the opening of that Heart of Love. As the dove lands in the heart of humanity, you will notice an electromagnetic shock to metal and to inert substances such as wood and glass.

Will a Time of Good come amongst humanity? This I assure you, Dear hearts — yes! For it is the plan that love shall serve all, as love is the Original Intent. Send this message to the Earth with love: a Time of Change has come! Open your eyes and open your ears, Dear ones.

DIETARY CHANGES

Now we shall continue with more changes in the physiology. We have repeatedly asked for dietary changes, not only for the vibrational frequency but also out of concern for the toxicity contained in many of the food substances on the planet. We would ask you to consider that all food contains within it elements of light. We also ask you to breathe light into your light centers so that, when you do partake of food, you can assimilate and absorb the light contained therein. I have given the dietary requirements, and I would ask that you adhere to them strictly during these years of peace and transition. Why should this be so? That which is brought into the being thus attracts. It is simply a matter of magnetics. We would also suggest that you consider taking in those foods that have obtained the maturation process through light, such as fruits and vegetables. Do you understand, Dear ones?

Response: "Yes."

We would suggest that you limit or eliminate all substances of flesh, as it is the vibration, Dear ones, that we are concerned with. It is the Vibration of Fear that is now leaving the planet, and that quantitative mass of consciousness shifting to love can also be held through what you choose to partake (eat, drink) within your being.

THE GROUP FOCUS

Let us continue now, and I will outline for you some suggestions for this time; not only is it a Time of Choice and Change, this is a time for your commitment. Gather together frequently into your groups of comradery. Hold your focus and intent through prayer, song, and meditation. As dear Morya has taught, "It is the focus that creates." During this time we suggest that you see around yourself a family unit as a structure held intact. You worry about structures you should build to house your bodies during this Time of Change; first build a structure that will house your spirit. Join together in the Oneship you share and let this be a celebration of joy and of life!

If only you could open your eyes beyond the judgment the ego calls forth, you would see Paradise revealed to open the Prophecies of Peace. There will be many manifestations of this during this five-year period, and it is important, Dear ones, that you are committed to a discipline as your demonstration of spiritual service.

ACCELERATION

The activation of Gobean has now been in effect for at least fifteen years. But now we shall see an acceleration, not only of the gathering of energy forces within the Vortex itself, but many will be drawn electromagnetically, and you will be called to impart this service. Share the teachings of the great I AM. Share the teaching of that great true self, the divinity, the spark, the Monad. Share the teachings of the activation through intelligence and choice. Move them to the Heart of Love. Take them into your family. For are you not all as ONE?

These are the Prophecies of Peace that come forward for your choice and demonstration.

I shall close now and open myself for your questions.

ADVICE FOR A STUDENT

Question: "It appears that I have been working with many of the Spiritual Kingdoms integrating energy, in particular Shalahah. Is there anything that I can do that will assist my vibratory change and assist my attunement?"

Let me scan.

Saint Germain scans the student's aura for diagnostic information.

Physically, your body is lacking Vitamin C; and I would suggest using that variety known as rose hips. This will bring an assimilation of the Vegetable Kingdom into your system. We would also ask that you serve as that aforementioned Pillar of the Violet Flame, offering the assistance of forgiveness and mercy through choice. We would also ask for the current merging of the Kingdoms of Mineral, Vegetable, Animal, and HU-man. Send your thought, your prayer, and your meditation for the collective unity of these Kingdoms and for their collective healing.

It is important at all times, in your working space, to keep the Vibration of Mineral and Vegetable around you, for they work as transmitters of energy. In keeping live plants and flowers, do you not feel their consciousness?

Answer: "Yes, I do."

USE OF ROSE QUARTZ

I would choose for you those colors of violet and green, for they best serve your vibrational fields. And from the Mineral Kingdom, rose quartz would assist you in the building of the physical body.

Question: "So should I wear more rose quartz, have it on me?"

Place it throughout the room to transmit its energy. Place it in a dish — four of them, to the four directions: one to the North, one to the South, one to the East, and one to the West. They will polarize one another and set up an energy field, which will be most conducive for your energy assimilation.

Answer: "Thank you. Would my body of work now be in sending energy as the Violet Flame to the Mineral Kingdom; is that my primary focus at this time?"

If you choose this service, Dear one, we would like to extend our thank-you for your loving service to this body of work known as Prophecy.

Answer: "Thank you."

DISSOLVING OLD PATTERNS

Question: "Saint Germain, I would like some assistance concerning the alimony my ex-husband is sending me. I feel that there is a big element of control on my part, and I do not desire to control him in any way, and I know that he does not desire to be controlled by me. I need some assistance."

Dear one, in the teachings of the Brotherhood, the Violet Flame is used at sunrise and at sunset. I would suggest that you use it in regard to your question. The symbol of sunrise and sunset means a New Day. Can we have a day of just twenty-four hours crammed with twelve years? Today, Dear one, let each day be as that day.

I would suggest that you use the Violet Flame at sunrise and at sunset with the proper invocation. And use it energetically with all chakras. This will help eliminate the energy pattern you have created between you and this other individual.

I will also give you instruction on the dissolution of holographic patterns which no longer serve the path you choose to walk. This is assisted through the Vibration of Sandalwood, which is one of the highest vibrations of the Vegetable Kingdom. This will not only transmute, but bring into alignment all energies for the best and highest good.

Serve, too, as a Pillar of Forgiveness, regarding your question. This, too, is the service you bring.

In the case of the dissolution of patterns that no longer serve: Purify your Cup, in this instance, for three days in continuous light. And in the case of the sandalwood within that Cup: smudging, with its smoke between you and the other individual. As I have taught in past discourse, it is best to obtain

that person's agreement. If this is not achievable, then a picture where the eyes are visible will work, for this carries within the energy, the pattern of that being. Call forth the Violet Flame for the best and highest good, and you will then receive the best course of action.[6]

Same Questioner: "I also need some clarification. You mention the elimination of all flesh from the diet. Were you talking about fish, too?"

AN EVOLUTION OF CONSCIOUSNESS

Yes, in regard to flesh, we would ask you to eliminate even fish from your diet at this time as the pollutant activity upon the planet is consolidating within that Kingdom. If you wish to eat fish, or flesh from fish, eat that which comes from fresh water. The saltwater of the planet is no longer advisable to be utilized by the HU-man.

However, I would also like to state that there is a rise in the vibrational frequency, and that is also of the highest consideration.

Question: "Saint Germain, I did not understand your last sentence, about the waters. There is a rise in the saltwater's vibrational frequency or mine?"

In yours, Dear one. For humanity, this is the Time of the Evolution of Consciousness, a Time of the Return, a Time of the In-breath. It is a time when consciousness is leaping to that next dimension of creation.

You must remove the guilt from your life, Dear one, for it moves on you like a heavy stone. Transmute this through the Violet Flame; it has been given to you as a gift. Take repeat baths of saltwater with rosemary thrown into the bathwater. Focus upon the Violet Flame of Forgiveness, for, Dear heart, this time is your time of service; this guilt no longer serves you. Drop the heavy stone, and you may walk a bit farther. Do you have questions?

---

6. Saint Germain is referring to the removal of Subjective Energy Bodies. For more information on this subject, see "Three Teachers," *New World Wisdom, Book Three.*

Answer: "No. Thank you."

Unless you have further questions, I shall take my leave from your realm and will be glad to return with further Prophecies of Peace. Hitaka!

CHAPTER THREE

Changing of the Guard

Saint Germain and Kuan Yin
share teaching for a group of students.

Greetings in that Mighty Christ. I AM Saint Germain, and I stream forth on that Violet Ray of Mercy and Forgiveness. As usual, Dear hearts, I request permission to come forth.

"Please, Dear one, come forth."

Salutations and greetings, Dear ones. You have arrived at this time known as the Changing of the Guard. A time comes to the Earth Plane and Planet when the Earth will shake, shall we say, a rock, a rattle, and a roll. Or, perhaps a Time of Grace, a Time of Peace, a time when you shall face your immortal destiny.

DIMENSIONAL SHIFTS

I ask you, Dear ones, are you ready to face immortality? Are you ready to face the New Dimensional Shift? Over the past few weeks, you have felt a little uncomfortable ... You have wondered, what is this new feeling around me? What is this new vibration that I am encountering?

Dear ones, each and every one of you has been prepared by the Spiritual Hierarchy, Brothers and Sisters all, for this day. Have you not sensed this? Have you not sensed that the energy is now shifting, pushing, and pulling, leaving each of you wondering, "Can I take this any more? Can I take much more of this?"

This is a time when dimensionally you are being shifted, along with that Cellular Memory encoded in each and every cell of your being. It is a time when you are going through tremendous changes. Even the DNA coding is shifting in, through, and around your being, each molecular structure changing, readying itself for the shift that is to come.

Dear hearts, I have been requested by those whom I love and serve to no longer dispense Prophecies of Earth Changes for a time; whereupon, we will begin anew. We will begin to dispense new prophecies, and in one year, many new things will have happened. A time will come when those who have eyes and ears open will be willing to see and hear, and then to act. Until that time, Dear ones, we, as your elder Brothers and Sisters, will be adjusting the energy fields of the Earth Plane, helping to adjust the Collective Consciousness to be ready for the times that are to come.

Tonight we shall discuss not only the Prophecies of Peace, but also those Prophecies of Change. Many of you have waited long for this time, for a field of neutrality arcing through the dual forces of light and dark. That time, long needed, has come — Grace, Neutrality, a new vibration that is also known as the Fourth Dimension.

We long for you, Dear ones, to access these planes, for we know the benefits and wish you to find that vibration. We are here at all times to assist you to reach that new plane, but it is you who must do the work. We cannot pull you through; however, we can show you how. We have spent our time recently adjusting the Collective Consciousness for the times that are coming, but we would like to remind you that we cannot, at any time, readjust the karma of mankind. For what mankind has created, mankind must now receive. This is the Law — cause and effect. And we work with those causes, readjusting always within that great plan of the best and highest good.[1]

Yes, it is true, Dear ones, we have been working to adjust the energy up and down your Western coastline of North America and working with great effort to adjust the energies of the Pacific Rim, that which is known as the Ring of Fire. Beloved Brother Kuthumi has been sending his energy to Indonesia, and this energy is traveling South, and in a counterclockwise fashion. You have all known that there is an energy collecting itself in the Cascade Range, with Mount Saint Helens being the first in this decade to explode, demonstrating that even beloved

---

1. Karma means actions, both bad and good. It comes from the Sanskrit word, *kri*, which means "to act." This term also describes the consequences of past actions, including the activities and the circumstances of former lives.

Babajeran must assist in this dimensional shift. Many of you are worrying about Mount Rainier, and, again, I refuse to give dates, as I have been instructed to continue adjusting the energy, for, as we know, the end results lie in the choices that you yourselves make.

"BEFORE IT IS TOO LATE"

Dear ones, Dear hearts, this Time of Change is coming. And, yes, it is true that the Prophecies of Peace will reign supreme — for each one who is willing to make that choice.

Let us make that choice.

Let us make that change, within our hearts.

Let us make these changes now — before it is too late.

For a time will come when you will greet the Earth Changes with a smile and say, "This is good." What are the alternatives? Shall we discuss them in a brief history, so that you will understand?

I AM RACE

This country that you live in, known as America, extending from Canada into Central America and on into South America, was, at one time, one land — one continuous land — before that Time of the Seventh Moon, which crashed into what you now know as the Gulf of Mexico.[2] It contained within itself a vibration, an energy of this Earth Planet. And the people who walked the face of this land were you. Welcome, members of that I AM! For when you look at America, you are the I AM Race returning again, in service, to the Mother — to this which is known as the Feminine Energy, which I will later discuss. This land has a destiny, and that destiny has a time.

2. Many Native American creation stories recount an ancient Earth Changes legend involving mass destruction and reincarnation. According to lore, an asteroid collided with Earth in the Yucatan Peninsula; the impact formed the present-day Gulf of Mexico. The Masters refer to this astral body as the Seventh Moon: "It contained a Vibration of the Heart of this planet." Some mystics call it the Star of Renewal and its energy force — shakti — can create wealth and substance. Coincidentally, the seventh Vedic Moon Sign is Punarvasu (Punar-Vasu). She is the ruling deity of the Seventh Moon — the Mother Goddess Aditi, an Earth Goddess of abundance who tends the ground, preparing the soil and the seeds to bear healthy fruit. Punarvasu is also affiliated with the concretization of the will and the ability of the soul to move beyond human limitation.

Understand that Prophecy has a time. Even as Moses, in his time, dispensed Prophecy to his people, these prophecies are for you and your time.

This I AM Race of people has come to give service to this planet. You have known many incarnations, all of you, upon these lands, for you are ONE with it; and you cannot be subtracted from your own cellular memory and your own genetic code.

HOLY BROTHER

My work upon the Earth Plane and Planet, as Sanctus Germanus, now known as the Holy Brother, began with my incarnation as Sir Francis Bacon. I was educated through the Rosicrucians — known as the Rosy Cross — in geometric languages, the ancient mystic ways, and the Alchemy of the soul.[3]

3. Shamballa and the Development of the Mystery Schools: In Sanskrit it means a place of peace, tranquility, and happiness. To the Buddhists, Shamballa is an Eden, a Shangri-La tucked away in the mountains of Tibet. The Ascended Masters consider Shamballa a mystical and venerated city, a metaphysical paragon that exudes untarnished energy, absolute beauty, and spiritual perfection. But, Earth could not sustain its perfection and purity. Shamballa thrice experienced cataclysmic Earth Changes, the final initiated by the Lords of Venus. And until humanity embraces a higher spiritual consciousness, Shamballa will continue to exist in the ether. Its true purpose forever smolders in the embers of this city. Open to eternal speculation and distortion, Shamballa will always reside in the spiritual virtue of the Fifth Dimension.

According to Ascended-Master legend, the Venusian Lord Sanat Kumara sparked, literally, Shamballa's destruction. He surrounded the city with piles of sandalwood logs and set it afire. And though only ashes remained of this once glorious Golden City, the Lords of Venus established an etheric template, relocating the magnificent Temples and Schools of Higher Knowledge. Entry is exclusive and limited to those "whose eyes and ears were open." That is, those evolved and spiritually developed souls who perceive and understand the Fourth and Fifth Dimensions. The Lords of Venus, however, remained accessible and helpful to Third-Dimension members of humanity. They established hidden and secret schools of knowledge throughout the Earth: centers that encourage spiritual growth until individual contact with higher-dimensional schools is obtained.

These groups and organizations include Lodges, mystery schools, and Brotherhoods. Brahmanist, Eleusian, Samothracian, Isis, Orphism, Cabeiri, Egyptian, Druidic, Delphinian, Dionysiac, Hermetic, Rosicrucian, and Free-Masonry Lodges are among this cryptic and storied fellowship. The members of these secret societies understand the brittle underpinnings of their work. And though they strive to help humanity achieve a higher level of consciousness, organized and forceful resistance often stymies their progress. That's why they close ranks, to operate freely, detached from persecution, harassment, and discrimination, within the safety of their vows of secrecy, ancient knowledge, and road-tested wisdom. Well aware of the

After my initiation, I offered myself in service to that mighty Brotherhood and Sisterhood of the Light that have held the destiny of this Earth Planet in its hands.

I traveled, not only to the North American continent, where I had the privilege to meet with the leaders of the I AM Race, but was dispensed again to Europe, where I was to continue working on a plan which had first been set in motion in the Western World, a great United States of Europe — a United European Brotherhood on the one hand and, on the other, the United States of America to represent the Sisterhood. A polarity and a balance would thus be achieved.[4]

THE PUSH AND PULL

However, Dear ones, we know there are those who hold within themselves a systematic program of greed; and so, this goal was not achieved. It was at this time that the Councils of the Great Violet Flame decreed, through the edict of Sanat Kumara, that the energy of the Brother (masculine) would temporarily be moved from Europe to the United States. Thus the energies of both Brother and Sister would be held within this ONE I AM land.

During this time, what you know as the Civil War broke out in the United States with, again, the monsters of greed electing to stomp upon that Plan of Light, in that constant intrigue of the push and pull of Lightness and Darkness. I repeat this history for you so that you will understand that there are those whose plans work on behalf of the Dark. Is it not true that you, Dear ones, work for the Light of God that never fails? Why, then, would there not be that balance on the plane of duality — a Brotherhood of Darkness that would also follow its path upon this Earth Plane and Planet? And where is the one pivotal point of difference? In the Consciousness of Choice!

---

duality and vibratory nature of the Earth experience, these secret organizations train special emissaries to roam the world and counter resistance. The Master Teacher Saint Germain is one of these great ambassadors. These remarkable personages, forming an order quite different from society, guide humanity through critical periods of history.

4. See Appendix C1: *Saint Germain, the Holy Brother*.

YOUR RIGHT TO VOTE

You, Dear ones, are inheritors of the divine, given that gift of Free Will, the Monad in the heart, the Choice of that Inner Flame of Freedom. You see, Dear ones, it has always been a game of who is weaker and who is stronger. And, again, this game has been played at many levels. But it is a game, I assure you, whose time will end. I ask you now to search within your consciousness, to search within your hearts, and to hear the truth of the words that I speak. It is important to choose and to stay committed to that choice. It is important to love as beloved Sananda has stated over and over again. It is important to forgive and to use that Mighty Law of Forgiveness at all times. Master that Law and there is your freedom.

So, how did this continue — this game of weak and strong? It evolved into your governments. It was once as simple as monarchy versus Liberty and Freedom. But now, in this time, the most important right you have is your right to choose your leaders. Yes, it is your right to vote.

This is a right you have earned through the blood of your own children. And yet, so many of you today feel that your vote cannot and will not make a difference. I encourage each and every one of you, Dear hearts, to become educated because you believe the power lays within the leader. Not so, for the power lays within he who selects the leader, for the leader is educated by those who vote for him or her. This I assure you, Dear ones, when you no longer value your right to vote, you lose that one privilege for which you have died many deaths. Haven't you noticed that difference in vibration that has come into your being over the past twenty years? Why is this so? It is simple — you and those about you have forgotten to hold the focus on Liberty and Freedom. Become educated. Educate your children, and educate those about you. Know those who go into those political offices, for they will determine your future. How are they empowered? They are empowered by your vote. Yes, there have been times when the outcome of elections has been slanted in one direction or another by misconduct. But I promise you that eventually the destiny of this land to serve will come to full fruition, and the vibration and energies of the Spiritual Hierarchy of Light and Sound will surround this country when that time arrives.

Now crime and pestilence run through your streets. Your children carry guns. Your teachers are not fit to teach. Why is this so? You have given up the right and the ability to enact your choice. Take back that first gift you fought so dearly for — your gift of choice — and use it each day.

WHEN INSANITY BECOMES SANE

And now, the economy. It is very important, Dear ones, as I have instructed the chelas close to my heart, to invest most monies into natural resources. When I say a natural resource, I mean Gold and Silver. That which is land — those natural commodities that can be bartered, that can be traded. For a time will come when your paper money will be worthless. Its value will not hold the value you think it does now. I ask you, Dear ones, to consider all of these things as perpetrators of these times. Have I not stated before that when insanity becomes sane, the Times of Change will soon be coming?

Dear ones, it is important to stay centered within your being and to stay centered within the teachings and the Laws of Truth. As beloved Sister Kuan Yin has so adeptly stated, "You are a Oneship, and each and every one of you forms this life." I remind you, as you apply these laws, it is important for you, too, to understand that Oneship we all share.

Yes, a time comes to the Earth Plane and Planet — a time for you to choose. Do you wish to live in a world where crime reigns? Do you wish to live in a world where your rights are systematically taken away because you refuse to choose? Is this the world you would want for your future generations? Is this a world of choice? Is this a world of Freedom and Liberty?

Only you can be the benchmark, and only you can answer that question.

FOURTH DIMENSION

It was decided in the year 1952 that, should the Earth undergo a period of cleansing, Nature would provide the backdrop to afford all incoming lifestreams the ability to achieve the lessons necessary to accelerate this planet to the Fourth Dimension. It is your choice, Dear ones. During these upcoming Earth Changes, strategic points upon the planet will be adjusted — not only lei-lines and energy Vortices, which are the chakras of the planet, areas known as Adjutant Points. These are places where dense material becomes enlightened or, shall we say, spun to a degree where it is able to take on a finer vibration. With a shifting of the poles, we shall then be able to see an entry not only into the Fourth Dimension but the possibility and potential to enjoy Fifth, Sixth, and even Seventh Dimension consciousness.

As we have always taught, the Fourth Dimension is a dimension of vibration and attraction. It is also the dimension where bi-location begins. It is also the dimension of immortality — physical immortality, that is. So I refer to it as a Dimension of Alchemy. Is it possible to achieve a balance on this planet, and a Fourth Dimensional consciousness? Again, Dear ones, the choice is in your heart and in your hand. However, at this particular moment, we still work for the upliftment of humanity so that more eyes and more ears can open. When these times do come, fear not — rather, rejoice, for the entry into the New Dimensions has begun.

At this time, I should like to open the floor for questions. Are there any questions?

THINNING OF THE VEIL

Answer: "Yes, Master, I have a question. You said earlier that Mount Rainier . . . that you were not going to give any specific dates . . . and you also talked about the Ring of Fire and the volatility in that area. Are we still poised on the edge of major change in that part of the country? If so, if people ask us for direction for relocation when they ask us about time frames, what would be the best way to address their concerns?"

Are we not in a Time of Transition? Are we not in a Time of the Thinning of the Veil between the Third and Fourth Dimensions? At any time this happens upon a planet, there are bound to be many physical changes. Do you not experience the physical changes within your own being? You are ONE with this physical planet. She, too, is readying herself for her shift, her acceleration into another dimension and another way of being.

EMERGENT EVOLUTION

This Time of Change is pivotal and critical for evolution. We call this the Emergent Evolution.[5] Evolution sometimes follows a path through pain and suffering; but it is through pain and suffering that we grow along this path and gain the understanding of the glory of a new day. I ask you, Dear ones, to face this new day with eyes open, no longer brimming with tears, but able to face the rising of the Sun and the Light of God that Never Fails. I would also ask at this time that you relocate to those strategic locations known as Golden City Vortices. These Vortices are holding a collective consensus in consciousness for a Time of Peace, a Time of Grace. But let us not dilute that message of change, for the change must come first; and then peace will reign supreme.

Answer: "Thank you, Saint Germain. You also addressed the changing of our DNA. Would you give more information about that?"

We are speaking about consciousness, and consciousness that is held in a continuum of the Fourth Dimension. Those who sought embodiment here first, through that Time of the Lemurian, encased that Monad for the first time in flesh and, working continuously through the motions of Hatha Yoga, split the body into two. So we now have a body with both masculine and feminine energy contained within it. Then, during the Time of Atlantis, the emotional bodies were allowed to develop.

And now we face this Time of the Aryan, a Time of Active Intelligence, a time when the employing of intelligence leads into wisdom. During the Atlantean period, instinct led to intuition. Now wisdom, intelligence, and instinct function as one. And now you, Dear ones, carry the DNA coding of the Lemurian, the Atlantean, as well as, at this time, the Aryan.

The cradle of this coding lays physically in the spine and in the pineal gland. These are locations in the body where

consciousness can be activated to access the Fourth Dimension. We speak of consciousness being held in a continuum inasmuch as you presently hold consciousness in a continuum in the First, Second, and Third Dimensions. Now you expand your circle of the known. Consciousness expands once again, allowing you to Master it and drive your expanding consciousness into the next dimension. In this state, you will be aware of consciousness existing just beyond your ken at the Fifth, Sixth, and Seventh Dimensions; but at that moment you will actually be embodying Dimensions One through Four. Do you understand?

Answer: "I do. Thank you."

Are there any more questions?

PREPAREDNESS

Question: "I have another question that relates to preparing. We know that we are in these great Times of Change. Some here are feeling the need to relocate from areas where they live to this area in particular, which is Gobean. There is a thought coming up from me about the storage of food. I know that spiritual preparedness is the ultimate answer; but we must also look at some of our basic, immediate needs. What kind of suggestions — and guidance — do you have for us?"

Yes, we have always taught that preparedness of the heart is the first place to start; we will also remind you, Dear students and chelas, do not throw the baby out with the bathwater! As you have developed each of your senses, is not common sense the most important sense to utilize? It is important to live near land where you can grow your own food; the pesticides and the chemicals within your food come from that dark side of the government, that dark side of that Brotherhood that wishes to annihilate your future. And when I say your future, I speak of your children. For this reason, should you not have some storage of food? Would this not be practical and economical?

However, there are times coming when you will require less food. As the light — and when I say "light," I refer to prana — increases upon this planet, you will notice that your chakras or energy centers will be moving at a higher rate of spin;

---

5. When the spiritual growth of an evolving life reaches a certain stage of conscious awareness, the soul forces itself into contact with higher streams of Divine Expression and Consciousness. The union of these two states of consciousness produces a new evolutionary being as an aspect of the manifestation of evolving life. This process is known as *Emergent Evolution*.

and you will be able to take in more prana. (Energy) Our greatest concern during the Time of Changes is that your air will lose its quality, and your water will not be drinkable. These are the two most important things. For when we see the simultaneous explosions of all the volcanoes in the Ring of Fire, ash will cover your planet for almost four years. Can you imagine, Dear one, the air you will be breathing?

So this is what I would recommend to begin to clear out the lungs, to ready the physical vehicle for the times to come: find whatever breathing technique can strengthen the lungs' capacity. I would also suggest that storage of water is imperative, for during these Times of Changes, many rivers and streams will change course. Even underground aquifers will be drained within seconds. In the Canadian Prophecies, you can read how this can happen. As for food, remember that spirit is truly your first food to be taken; season it with trust! Do not allow a shadow of a doubt to enter into your heart during this time.

You are gifted with that ONE source, One Eternal Flame. Know, too, Dear ones, that we are by your side, ready and willing to lend our hand. Proceed.

FREE ENERGY TECHNIQUES

Question: "To store a sufficient amount of water for a very long period of time is a large undertaking. Is there a purification system, or a way we can purify water to address our needs?

There is, of course, the use of Free Energy. I have taught the techniques of charging the water through the hands, for, you know, your body itself is a battery that generates energy. As I have taught before, you can draw this energy up from the Planet Herself. However, during the Time of Changes, I would suggest that you be careful in areas filled with turbulent change, for the energy will be unstable, and it will be hard to energize the water with this technique. Usually, I would ask you to charge the water with your own energy. However, if you have a doubt, research filtering systems.

Answer: "Thank you."

KUAN YIN

Question: "Master. During the Times of Changes, when peoples all over Earth will be looking to communicate as ONE mind and ONE life, what advice do you have for bringing that forth in harmony?"

I shall let my Sister address this.

Saint German steps back, and Kuan Yin comes forward.

My dear children, how wonderful it is to address you all. Such joy I take in physicality again! I AM Kuan Yin.

It is the ONE and Absolute Harmony that we seek. It is the ONE Feminine Energy that opens now across your planet that you must access to achieve this harmony. Brothers and Sisters of Light and Sound, open your hearts to compassion to achieve your unity with ONE. Open your hearth within your heart and share your love. It is as simple as the Law of Love.
Kuan Yin steps back, and Saint Germain comes forward again.

Proceed.

ALCHEMY OF THE VIOLET FLAME

Question: "Master, in teaching all peoples to live within their hearts in the inner world so that their outer world may change, so that they may perceive things from a balanced point of view — what would you suggest?"

It is as simple as I have taught before: the use of the Violet Flame is imperative at this time. When you decree unto yourself, "I AM a being of Violet Fire, I AM the purity that God desires," do you not feel the marriage of your energies and the Kundalini current arcing up and down your spine? Do you not feel a heat within your throat and a heat within your ears?

I AM a being of Violet Fire!
I AM the Purity God desires!

Alchemy — this is Alchemy, Dear one. The harmony you seek is as simple as decreeing it to yourself. This is the Law of the Divine Inheritor. Decree a thing unto yourself and it comes forward in two manifestations! Consciousness creates! Seek perfection first in your intent and bring it forth through the spoken word. For the word is the action that moves it through your emotional bodies. Is not the word the action of your heart? Transmutation and Alchemy are the keys to accessing the Fourth Dimension.

As I have stated before, do you not feel, Dear ones, that you have been walking through the fires of initiation, each day another day of purification? Each day when you say, "Take this bitter cup from me!" You can lighten your load through the use of the Violet Flame — this gift, brought forth from the Lords of Venus to soften the suffering and to lessen your load. Use it, Dear ones, and you will enjoy the results. Proceed …

Answer: "Thank you, Master."

SUFFERING AND THE LAW OF BALANCE

Question: "Master, can you explain why so many children of this planet suffer and die at this time?"

These are the Laws of Balance. These are the Laws of Cause and Effect. How do we know that these children weren't at one time the warriors of previous generations, slaughtering other children, and raping and killing their mothers? This is the challenge of the Third-Dimensional experience, Dear ones — it is the challenge of duality. At one moment you perceive the dark and in the next moment the light. How rare it is that you perceive them both, in tandem. Open your hearts of compassion to those who are suffering. Send them your energy of Alchemy. Transmute to the higher planes. Transmute through the Law of Vibration. The Law of Correspondence rules all things, Dear ones: "As above, so below." Remember this, and you shall be wise. Proceed …

SPIRITUAL AWAKENING

Question: "Will you explain the best way to communicate this new information to other people who are not yet aware?"

Each day we take another step closer to the Fourth Dimension and the thinning of this Veil. At one time I would have recommended that you speak only when inquired of. The time now, however, is short; and the Spiritual Awakening is at hand. Ask me to come and give you that closer energetic reasoning you require. I ask of you, Dear Brother, to consider our equality — to consider that you and I are ONE. Did this not open your ears? — that you and I are of ONE Omni-essence, of ONE Omnipresence? I ask you to share this message. It is as Kuan Yin has stated: We are ONE.

"DOWN WITH DEATH"

Question: "Master, in the Omnipresence of life in the Third-Dimensional world, and upon leaving the physical body, how may we teach others to communicate with people that have dropped the body?"

Are you inquiring about those who no longer use physical bodies to express?

Answer: "Yes."

The teaching we bring forward is the teaching of communicating with those who have achieved Mastery over the body, a Mastery of the spiritual world. What would be the benefit of this communication?

Answer: "To let people know that the soul is immortal and that this Third-Dimensional life is truly an illusion."

Do you sense my presence about you now, Dear chela? Is this communication not in itself a teaching of how to achieve that contact?

Answer: "Yes."

Proceed each day in the application and disciplines of breath. Proceed each day in the application and the disciplines of Alchemy and Transmutation through the Violet Flame. As we proceed during this Time of Change and the thinning of the Veil, it will be more apparent who has crossed over and not taken this physical vehicle with them.

Down with death, I have always said!

Down with death!
Come alive in that one spirit,
that ONE omni-essence,
that Mighty I AM!

Life is eternal and is not dictated by our use of the physical body, is it?

SERVICE

There is, however, one thing that physical life may accomplish — it may be of service. The Life that commands itself into the discipline of service is a blessed life, a Life that is of the Mother and of the Father. Upon the Earth Plane and Planet there are many who would now say: "Let me leave, for I cannot face this time. Let me leave and Ascend now." Dear ones, where would you ascend to? Again, I can assure you, into another realm of service.

ERASE THE DEATH CONSCIOUSNESS

The incarnation process, as taught by beloved Master K. H., is a process that entails approximately two hundred years and sometimes as long as five hundred years. There are, of course, exceptions to this rule. Also, there are other planes and dimensions where manifestation has taken form. Even though you may not see them, there are many life forms in this room, life forms that also have physical manifestation. They are all carrying life, the ONE Omni-essence, the ONE Omnipresence. We must erase this death consciousness. We must erase it from our being! How else would you be able to hold your vehicle for this Time of Shifting into the service of the New Dimensions? Questions?

THE DARK GOVERNMENT

Question: "Beloved old friend, I understand that with the Collective Consciousness — realizing that it can be affected by Free Will — this is a question that may not be answerable yet, but I wonder if you would address it. I feel the hot breath of the dragon, of the Grey Man, of the tyrants that control the government, very close to our backs. I have been told and taught that some time, unless the Earth Changes occur first, we will have to endure, as Americans, the military takeover of our government. If the Earth Changes don't happen, our government will enslave us; but that the Earth Changes might be part of our freeing. I wonder if you or one of the Brotherhood or Sisterhood might address this, because I feel its presence so close."

Greetings, my beloved Sister and acquaintance. You so astutely know these times because you have experienced them before. In 1990 we released the prophecies of the camps of orphans, which had been the plan of the dark government at the time. We released the prophecies of the underground explosions in the areas of Nevada and New Mexico, carried out by, shall we say, that alien-nature of our being. And now a time comes when this dark force barks at your back. It barks at your back so that you will have to choose!

A DIFFERENT WAY?

Each day you choose to give away a right, you lose your liberty. And you complain that it is taken from you, when in fact, you have so readily given it! This is a time when people have become sheeple and know not the power vested in their hearts through choice. For this is a Time of Choice. And truly, yes, your consciousness creates all that is part of this grand illusion, this dream of the mind. I present these prophecies to you through dear Lord Sananda who stated, "Send this message to the Earth with love."

A Time of Choice comes. How then shall we understand the Liberty that was gifted to you through the blood of your Brothers and Sisters? This Time of Change that comes, it is true, is a purification. And it is, too, an initiation. Are your eyes then incapable of tears? Does your voice still carry the power to wound? Before the soul can stand in the presence of the Masters, the feet must be washed in the blood of the heart! These are the words of my Brother, Hilarion. Understand them, and understand them well.

In World War II, upon your Earth, the dark forces used a holocaust to lead a group of people through their Initiation. Their feet were washed in the blood of the heart. Must we experience this again? Or, is there a different way?

A RIPPLING CURRENT

Cause and effect, Dear one, this is the Plane of Karma. This is a Plane of Light and Dark. This is also a plane you can Master. For are you not here asking this very question? — does not this flame of desire burn within your heart?

Consciousness can change all things. Have you not noted the difference when you awake in the morning "on the wrong side of the bed?" That negative energy entraps the day, sending a rippling current throughout your every action. Where did that energy come from? It comes from you, from your consciousness.

Yes, there is an alternative plan to that dark government. But there is also an alternative plan to that light government. You are entrusted with that choice. Proceed.

Answer: "I guess there are no further questions."

If there are no further questions for this evening I should like to end this discourse with one final address.

THE CUPBEARER

As I opened this evening, I announced a Changing of the Guard. This Changing of the Guard is held within your hearts. This Changing of the Guard is that time when you shall all become Masters — Brothers and Sisters in a New Plane and Dimension of Reality. I invite you all onto this Path — the Path of Adeptship. And I ask each and every one of you to honor that flame within the heart, that Monad of consciousness. For a time comes when you must move on; and you must assume your position, entrusted with the plan of holding the Cup.

The bearer of the Cup of Life is one who has traveled the path through the Laws of Pain and Suffering, and has Mastered all, to become voided — and yet, through this, has become filled! For is this not the joy within the service?

In that Mighty Violet Ray, I call forth freedom!

I AM the Violet Flame,
An ember in the heart.
I AM the Violet Flame,
Peace and grace I impart …

Hitaka!

CHAPTER FOUR

The Fourth Dimension

℘

Saint Germain describes the Fourth Dimension.

Greetings, beloved chelas. I AM Saint Germain, and I rquest permission to come forth.

"Dear one, come forth."

THE LAWS OF CREATION

The Time of Transition is intense, is it not, Dear ones? This is a time when you gather unto yourselves, asking for that refreshing drink, that inner stillness, that Time of Peace. When shall it come in a sustained manner? When shall this grace be the law that reigns supreme?

I serve as Cohan of the Seventh Ray, the Seventh Ray that rules the Laws of Mercy and Compassion. I also serve the Laws of Ceremonial Order and Alchemy. They are as simple as Transmutation; for example, have you seen how the snow turns to water? Fire into ash? Wind into sunshine? These are all acts of Alchemy in nature. How do we achieve these?

Through the spirit, the soul, the mind, and the feelings. These principles are based on the Law of Rhythm. Beloved Kuan Yin has taught "it is sattva," or a harmonious response to vibration. You understand, Dear ones, the concept "as above, so below." The Law of Correspondence states, "as in heaven, so shall it be below."[1]

When you hear higher frequency sounds, those that are inaudible to the ear but audible to the senses, you cannot null and void that sound. It exists in another, higher dimension, and it corresponds — it also has an effect on — a lower dimension. The Law of Correspondence, you see, dovetails with the Law of Cause and Effect. The causes are engendered in one dimension, have their effects in other dimensions. In this way, you could even perceive the past and the future as being dimensional — a cause beginning in the past and having its effect in the future.

And it all happens through these laws; which rule this grand creation of mind, which rule all things and inform the nature and the quality of Omni-essence. And we still ask, how is it that this Law of Rhythm can bring peace out of turmoil, grace after siege, harmony where there has been chaos?

Picture, if you will, a pendulum swinging, even the pendulum of a grandfather clock, arching back and forth, to and fro — these are the rhythms of all things that you experience in a Third-Dimensional body. The rhythms of life always surround you — the rhythms of seasons, the rhythms of time. And do these things have an effect on you? Think back. Remember your rhythm when you were seven; the rhythm that contained you when you were fourteen; and the rhythm you expressed when you were twenty-one.

Did you not then have a particular rhythm that arced to and fro, connecting to that specific point of consciousness in time? Your whole life has a rhythm based on the Law of Cause and Effect — the causes coming from the past, the effects playing out in the future. The thoughts you had when you were seven, fourteen, and twenty-one affected every ensuing year. This intellectual energy became your future and led you through your path in life: a path predetermined by the choices you made and blessed with the breath of Co-creatorship. Subconsciously, you know that through the mighty cosmic law, Alchemy and Transmutation change all things.

WISDOM AND JOY

Oh, how you look back now on those years of your youth! But, with seeing eyes and hearing ears, you're wiser now. Those are the times I ask you to draw upon, Dear ones. Using that vibration and knowledge, which are wisdom, I ask you to draw upon those times in your Times of Peace, Contemplation, and Meditation. For then you shall see how far you have traveled on this path; and you will understand, through your tears, the joy of this spiritual work.

EXPERIENCE VIBRATION

Sattva is that harmonious response to vibration, and that Vibration often is not the cause but the effect. Right now, as I

---

1. See Appendix D1: *Hermetic Principle.*

have lowered my vibrations dimensionally, do you not feel my energy and my radiance around you, Dear ones?
Answer: "Yes."

That is a response — that feeling within your being responding to vibration. How many more vibrations do you feel during the day? I ask you to become aware, for just one hour in a day, of the vibrations around you. Experience the vibrations of nature, of consciousness, of the physical world, of business, of sound, and of light. Your body responds to all of these, adjusting your body temperature and assuring your comfort. You neutralize some of them in your mind. Some vibrations you respond to with criticism or awareness, and some you have no awareness of at all even though they bathe your body and your lifestream. Vibration, Dear ones, is the key to understanding Ascension.

The time has come to increase your awareness of vibration.

Vibration is known as the Fourth Dimension.[2] It is a dimension where you are freed to another Plane of Cause, to another experience and another existence. It is a dimension that does not require such cautious and often tedious tending of the body. However, it is still a physical experience — but an expanded physical experience on your journey home.

ASCENT OF SPIRIT

The Law of Sattva, or Rhythm, follows the ascent and descent of the spirit. The soul prepares and readies itself for the universal lessons during its experiences on its journey through life. It clothes itself with the garments of flesh, placing one body on and discarding another — embodiment after embodiment. The soul goes through cycles of infancy, adolescence, and young adult facing maturity, until it finally arrives, through evolution,

at wisdom. This process, with its many repetitions, has been taught as re-embodiment, or reincarnation.

However each successive lifetime is propelled by that Law of Cause and Effect. The soul — in seeking bodies with which to garb itself in each lifetime — seeks one that will bring balance to the past lifetime, the lifetime before that, and so on. However, each successive embodiment follows that Law of Rhythm; and, just as that pendulum swings, so a Time of Descent turns into a Time of Ascent, and you notice a lightening of the body, a lightening of circumstance and a lightening of world affairs. It is as if the hand of God now grasps yours and says, "Come to me; return to your home. But come to me not tired and weary; come to me in joy and celebration."

For the ascent of spirit is as this, Dear ones: it is a celebration, as shown in the stories of the feast.

As the pendulum stops swinging, the point at which it stops is the center. That center is the position of neutrality; a position where electromagnetic currents come to a truce, a space created in the Law of Polarities for choice. And yet, is there a choice?

Of course there is, Dear ones. For some souls have come to that position before and have failed to ride that pendulum to the other side — which ensures their journey in Ascension. Do you not feel the cosmic clock now poised at that Time of Zero and Neutrality? For this is the time we have referred to as the Time of Transition. It is your Time of Choice.

RIDE THE UPSWING

During the Time of Planetary Transition, all past experiences are brought to the forefront, including the many embodiments the soul has shared with physical experience. This memory follows a rhythm, a pattern, and a harmony. For this is where the soul chooses: shall I return on the downswing, or shall I ride the upswing, which will allow me access to the joy and the celebration of the Fourth Dimension?

It is this dimension that we ride on the upswing, on the journey home, the journey to the ONE. And the journey to all Omni-essence. And while the soul will continue in its ascent through many other dimensions of cause and effect, and more of the dimensions based on the Law of Correspondence,

---

2. This dimension of light and sound frequencies houses the invisible kingdoms of nature Devas, gnomes, fairies, and Elementals. These arcane beings, however, are not alone. Certain Akashic records — encoded libraries of Universal Knowledge — also inhabit the non-physical planes of the Fourth Dimension. To communicate with this intangible realm, one must cultivate his or her super-senses: clairaudience, hearing; clairvoyance, vision; clairsentience, feeling; clairalience, scent; and clairgustance, taste. This state of conscious awareness increases telepathic ability, lucid dreaming, and other forms of dimensional perceptibility.

it will be a joyful journey, filled with only the breath of the omnipotent ONE.

I ask you Dear chelas and students of this time — those who have chosen to ride the pendulum of transition and the path of Ascension — to consider the importance of choice, and how each choice you make can put you two steps forward or two steps backward. And now let us discuss the Fourth Dimension — the vibration — and your ability to walk two steps forward.

EXPANSION AND AWARENESS

When I brought forward the Prophecies of Change, I discussed a time when some would seek cataclysm and disaster, while others would choose peace and grace. Throughout the eons, the Spiritual Hierarchy of the Great White Brotherhood and Sisterhood has prepared retreats. These havens carry finer dimensional energies, allowing souls to achieve that quantum ride and that quantum return to the journeys lying on the upswing of the pendulum.

These places are known as the Golden City Vortices. They have been charged from the beginning of their conception and arrival here. Beloved Babajeran (Mother Earth) has held them in the state of cause, always ready and willing to commune with you for the desired effect.

Many Vortices have existed on the planet at other times; but now, at this Time of Transition, fifty-one have been prepared for you. These are places to visit; places to experience Fourth and Fifth Dimension energy; and places to understand the creation of these dimensions. They can help you in your journey to another world.

Many of you are of the opinion that you will be leaving this planet, leaving this world in a global ascent. Let me be specific: you are leaving a narrow consciousness, and expanding your consciousness in your journey and in your ride of the pendulum. Expanding into the Fourth Dimension requires discipline and service to that mighty ONE. It requires a broadening of the mind and an opening of the heart. It requires your awareness and understanding of the Law of Synchronicity, which states that "all things are effects of causes" therefore, "nothing is happenstance."

Each day, become aware of the vibration around you and the vibration you create within your being. I ask you to become aware of Collective Consciousness, or collective vibration. Have you ever entered a room and noticed that the people as a group emit a consciousness and a vibration through the blending of their thoughts, feelings, and actions. And then you enter another room and notice again the shifting energy and the changing vibrations. You grab your coat, go outside, and notice immediately yet another vibration.

To prepare for and allow yourself a new physical experience, you must become aware of the vibrations and the differences among each room, shall we say, the differences inside and outside the house. These are new experiences for you, Dear ones — new experiences in Co-creatorship and the Mastery of your energy.

I shall take a short break for questions.

A HOLOGRAPHIC BODY

Question: "Thank you, Holy Brother. It has been my observation that when you and other members of the Brotherhood and the Sisterhood come and speak to us from the Fourth Dimension that, individually and as a group, it appears as though you all have bodies, as we do in our Third-Dimensional experience. Will you please elaborate?"

At times we are required to lower our vibrational frequency to take on a holographic, illusive body to serve your need. When we are sent on a Mission to give a specific message or contact a certain person, we come attired in a garment of reciprocity. Otherwise, the recipient would not recognize us or affirm their contact with, or an awareness of, our vibration.

MASTER YOUR RESPONSE

Dear ones, as you ready yourselves to spring into a New Dimension and awareness, you, as our students engendered in the same cause, will one day be asked to hold the positions we now occupy. We are asking you to become stewards of a greater plan, to serve your Brothers and Sisters who live now in lower worlds of consciousness. It is important that you understand these rooms of consciousness and how, when thought is projected into another realm or dimension, it forms a nucleus, a physical matter, to which it can adhere.

However, the Laws of Correspondence, of Cause and Effect, and of Rhythm and sattva will determine the rate of Vibration of that matter, since each realm or dimension has its own vibration, its own ability to receive physical matter in a certain form, and its own ability to carry out the Divine Plan of Life and Omni-essence. Therefore when we say that we "bi-locate" we mean we've perfected the moving among these rooms of consciousness, the moving of a vibration without its affecting our response.

You all respond greatly to vibration, so Master your response to vibration. That is, learn how to meditate in the midst of noise; learn how to work with joy in the midst of sorrow; and learn how to rise to that other dimension — that other, ever present, and contained quality "as above, so below." For as the Law of Correspondence would state, "even as the lower dimension is present, so is the higher."

MULTI-DIMENSIONAL EXPERIENCE

At this moment you are responding only to the First, the Second, and the Third Dimensions. But remember, Fourth, Fifth, Sixth, and Seventh Dimensions exist, too. But, if you would attune your response-ability to those others, you would in turn experience and begin to understand their existence — or, better yet, their co-existence — in your world.

Have you not noticed, at times, flashes of light at the corners of your eyes? Have you not seen, at times, light haloed around the body of a friend? Have you not, at times, heard a voice — an audible voice — whispering, singing, or repeating a message in your ear? These are your Brothers, Sisters, and friends of an expanded experience who have learned to respond with their energies to those of other dimensions and other experiences.

A time will come when you will lay aside the physical body as we know it. Many have taught Ascension as the burning away of the grosser energies to respond to these energies of the finer dimensions. In some respects, how true this is. But, as above, so below — as all things come, so all things go.

Understand the Law of Rhythm; understand the Law of Correspondence. Begin to respond from the Plane of Neutrality of the Fourth Dimension. Open your awareness in times of meditation; open your awareness to your times of breath, and you will begin to experience and to understand a New World that has always existed beside the old.

ALCHEMY AND TRANSMUTATION

To move gracefully through the dimensions, it is important to understand the Laws of Alchemy and how one substance can be turned into another. For example, I have always taught the Law of the Violet Flame. I have always taught how fires of hatred and anger can be tempered and transmuted into the fires of compassion and of grace. This is accomplished through the Law of Rhythm, which captures the attention of the mind and then expands its energy through an open heart.

When you work with these Laws of Alchemy and of Transmutation, you open the doorways to your response. You create a Plane of Neutrality — that positing of the pendulum where it almost stops — and you are allowed to glimpse and experience a corresponding world.

MASS ASCENSION

In the Golden City Vortices, which are now holding a consciousness of neutrality, the energies contained within those areas allow the chela and the disciple to access Fourth Dimension more readily. As we originally discussed in the Prophecies of Change, a Time of Global Ascension, a Time of Mass Ascension, and a Time of Response-ability will come. This is that Time of Global Ascent. It is a Time of Mass Response-ability. Do you see, Dear one, how this Ascension has begun? Many of you have decided to return, through the energy of your spirits, to that natural rhythm and harmony, which will return you to your home of origin. So this is the Time of Change. It is a Time of Celebration and it is a Time of Joy. This journey is an ascent filled with joy; it is an ascent filled with discovery.[3]

---

3. After the Earth Changes, according to the I AM America Prophecies, Ascended Masters will inhabit the Golden City Vortices in physical form for twenty years. As human consciousness moves into the Golden Age,

Do you have questions?

A LIGHT BODY IS BORN

Question: "Yes, I do. Even though, to our appearance, you take on this certain form when you come and speak to us, as you are doing now, it appears as though you do have a body existing in that resonance or vibrational frequency that we will call Fourth Dimension. In light of this appearance, it has been my experience that viewing the aura is not much different than viewing the other dimensions. Will you please elaborate?"

This vision of yours is an opening into the patterning of the dimensions layered one upon the other, existing side by side with one another. However, many of those in the physical experience have not yet opened an awareness to, and therefore cannot manifest, Fourth-or Fifth-Dimensional light. The aura, or light field, seen around the adept, the avatar, or the Master Teacher, is an energy of light that comes through as a manifestation of their response in that Fourth Dimensional experience. They understand their harmonious response and begin manifesting it upon that level of experience. But, they need another body to share the experience with, hence, their Light Body is born — a Light Body that will encase the spirit or the soul after the shedding of the physical.

I hope this gives you a further understanding of light and the qualities it contains. For light, in and of itself, is a manifestation of mind ... questions?

THOUGHT AND MIND

Question: "Yes — this is another question. Light, being the manifestation of mind ... as we think something today, it becomes something else tomorrow. According to the Law of Cause and Effect, is it the mind that is the director and the refractor of light in the Co-created world? — is it this mind,

this attention that we give, this focus, this energy, that is the seed of creative activity on this plane and planet?"

Thought is the seed of all creation. And — as I have always taught, Dear one — thought can be transmuted and changed into another thought. Have you not heard the phrase, "change your mind?" Insofar as you are able to change your mind, you can change your existence and the very body that now clothes your spirit and soul.

Within the realm of mind exist both the cause and the effect — simultaneously. And when a thought is seated as an encapsulated thought, it is a seed of manifestation, able to bring about an appearance in that dimension where the focus resonates. That appearance is when you see the Law of Cause and Effect in action. Do you understand?

MASTERY OF THE LAW

Question: "Yes. The next question I would ask is: Is the true Alchemy the transition, the Violet Flame activity, beginning always with our thoughts?"

The Law of Alchemy is based not only on the Law of Rhythm — that all things change — it is based on the Mastery of the Law of Change. It is based equally on the Mastery of the Law of Cause and Effect. For it understands the cause of all things.

When you bathe your thoughts with the words, "I AM Forgiveness," do you not notice a calming effect which comes over past thoughts of hatred and unforgiveness? Do you not notice how instantly all is changed, gathered unto itself, and given a sensation of peace and neutrality? This Law of Alchemy, which opens the doors to new experiences, uses your physical body as a laboratory of experience. Here you can learn those transmuting laws and those Laws of Decay and Death, which exist simultaneously with them.

And would this again not be the Law of Polarity, which also exists in all dimensional force fields? Simultaneous experience comes side by side and corresponds to the other. Have you not noticed that happiness and despair sit side by side? And to fur-

their work will focus on teaching and healing. During these two decades, the Earth slips into the New Times, and the appearance of the Ascended Masters throughout the world is not entirely contingent on the Earth Changes. It relies on the spiritual development of humanity and the overall vibratory level of the Earth.

ther understand, have you not noticed how male seeks female, or female seeks male, side by side? And so it is.

POLARITY TO NEUTRALITY

Question: "Then our consciousness moves from the polarities to the neutrality to seek the expansion into the other dimensional realms?"

The polarities provide an experience. And through that experience, or what we call the "opening of the heart" thought becomes neutrality. It is through that neutralization, brought about by the uniting of energies, that one then begins to understand Transmutation.
Questions?

GOLDEN CITIES AND THE FOURTH DIMENSION

Question: "As we move through this dimensional shift on this plane of consciousness, would it be wise for all who seek to shift their consciousness to move to those Golden City areas?"

For those who wish to receive an initiation in vibration and those who wish to understand the opening of the Fourth Dimension in mass consciousness, it is advised. For these are areas that will experience the melding of polarized energies. As a result, an opening of the heart will help you understand the worlds that exist simultaneously.

LOVE AND THE ONE

It is with love that these teachings have been brought forward — love for life at all levels of experience. This teaching comes out of love: love for the Devas and the Elemental Kingdoms; love for the Mineral Kingdom; love for the Vegetable and Animal Kingdoms; and love for those Kingdoms of the Fourth and Fifth Dimensions. For are you all not filled with Omni-essence? Do you not all polarize, and contain the Laws of Rhythm and Correspondence within you? Are you not all ONE of the same source? The ONE Omni-essence?

Yes, you are all, in varying degrees, of that Rhythm and that Law of Descent and Ascent. But open your hearts, stewards of the plan! For this time comes to increase your awareness and allow your service to come forward. Questions?

ANOTHER KINGDOM

Question: "As our service does come forward through the opening of our hearts, which seems as if it is on a path of neutrality and a path of love, who among us are brought into contact with this vibration?"

Even those who hear these words are made aware of that Kingdom of Vibration. Even those who read these words will be affected by the vibrations surrounding them. For these vibrations are words from another Kingdom. And, yet, is this not a familiar Kingdom? Another Kingdom — which has and always will exist side by side?

Question: "Yes, this is so. This next question may seem irrelevant, but it has been my observation that the beloved beings whom we call our pets, for whom we develop close attachments — do these beings, too, move on in consciousness and become our chelas in the future?"

Some of them are brought here to help adjust and open the energy of vibration, for they have chosen simple lives of service to help at this critical Time of Awakening and Choice. However, some — ready at their own particular time — continue on the path of evolution, riding the pendulum of sattva.
Unless there are further questions, I shall take my leave.

Response: "There are no further questions, Holy Brother. I thank you for your radiance and your guidance."

I thank you for your response-ability. Always carry within your hearts the Violet Flame. Almighty I AM Violet Flame. Come forth, and heal and soothe the minds of men. Hitaka

CHAPTER FIVE

The Work of a Master

Personal instruction from Saint Germain.

Beloved chelas, I AM Saint Germain and I request your permission to come forward.

Response: "Dear Saint Germain, please come forward."

THE SERVICE OF ASCENDED MASTERS

The work upon the Earth Plane and Planet, as we have seen through your dispensation of material, has reached a portion of completion. Some among the masses have heard parts of that message and are ready to receive that refreshing drink. The portion of this message known as Prophecy will open ears and eyes to that deeper water or river.

It is time for us to step forward, and to think and plot our course, for the coming time is critical. During the next six to eight years, which will complete the planetary time known as Transition, decisions and choices will be made that plot the course. And the hands of humanity will hold the end result.

We have known for some time that humanity has stood upon the precipice of nuclear war, and cataclysmic Earth Changes. Did you know that earlier in this century your planet was barely missed by an asteroid? The work of the Hierarchy prevented this impact from happening.[1] Those of that realm have held

back the events leading to the great purification by fire. They know this event is not in the plan of the best and highest good of humanity. It is better that humanity understands and is able to plot that course itself. Humanity, in the form of Collective Consciousness or collective consensus, is then able to make that choice.

HUMANITY'S DIVINITY

Those who work in that inner circle have laid down many plans, for as you know — as I have stated before — your governments are held by a handful of powerful men, and these powerful men hold only money. Mankind — humanity at large — vests money with *power*. Do you understand what gives these men their ability to control and manipulate your world economies and your societies? Mankind must evolve to a place where it understands that money and greed can't control mankind any longer. The breath of the spirit — sparked within the heart through the divinity of men and women — shall accomplish this understanding.

And, when one decides to Master that force within the heart, … will we see an awakening — a time when a new, ever present vibration and energy come to the planet?

SPIRITUAL DEVELOPMENT

Now is the time to avert our focus and energy from the things that don't work, from the old and tired, and from what we cannot change. Instead, focus on what we can change: things we can control and Master.

And what would that be, Dear students and chelas? Our focus and attention is on that spark in the heart, that mighty Monad or Jiva. We have taught this concept, and you have learned it through the many teachings of the Mastery Courses. It's time for us to put our attention on this individualized energy of the soul, which can be developed.

---

1. The Ascended Masters are dedicated to helping humanity through unavoidable and seemingly catastrophic events. They accomplish this on a supra-physical level by adjusting and fine-tuning energy fields, which in turn influence physical creations and events on Earth. This concept is not entirely new; we learned of these actions in previous lessons.

The Ascended Masters prophesied that Earth would experience a cycle of geophysical change; accordingly, Saint Germain spun an etheric Golden Belt of high-frequency energy around this planet in the early 1950s. Its power deters catastrophic Earth Changes until humanity evolves a deeper consciousness; the belt also plays a significant role in humanity's spiritual growth.

"We have known for sometime that humanity has stood on the precipice of nuclear war and cataclysmic Earth Changes … did you know that earlier in this century (Twentieth Century) your planet was barely missed by an

asteroid?" asks Saint Germain. "It was only by the work of the Hierarchy that this event did not occur," he adds.

COLLECTIVE WILL AND CHOICE

For the gathering, that mass rapture, and that mass Ascension, a group of people have focused their attentions on the development of the individual, melding mankind and spirituality into the collective will.[2] The forces — which can hold back the fire of purification, the winds of ceaseless change, and those earthquakes and sinking lands — are contained in this collective will. Only that collective force of the "intentional spirit of will" can save humanity.

We have spoken before of the choice that is now in the hands of those who are willing to see, who are willing to hear, and who are willing to act. Dear ones, make the choice to serve that desire, that spark in the heart.

Is it as simple as following the heart's desire? Yes, it is as simple as that. And that degree of awakening is as simple as making a choice.

STRENGTH, COURAGE, AND LOVE

But let us move one step further, beyond desire, into the causeless cause, where the eyes shed no more tears and the heart has sufficiently bled upon your feet. This is the chela or student who has emptied his vessel. But is the vessel weakened? No I say. The vessel — one that won't bend in the winds of change and will hold the waters through the tempest of a storm — is now strengthened and ready to serve.

I ask you now, Dear ones, to move this work forward, to work upon all the attributes, and to have courage. The times

---

2. According to the I AM America Prophecies, Ascended Masters appear in physical form in the Golden City Vortices during and after the twenty-year period. At that time, Mass Ascensions occur in the Golden Cities, at the Star or center locations of these Vortices, and in select locations around the world, which are hosted by the energies of Babajeran — Mother Earth. A model of this type of location is *Ascension Valley* located in the Shalahah Vortex.

The energies of the Fourth Dimension, the point of Ascension or Light Body development, initiates a substantial portion of the world's population. As spiritual advancement and evolution flows, this Light Body exceeds the physical body, taking permanent residence in the Fifth Dimension. Simultaneously, a separate group of souls, according to the prophecies, experience a Third Dimensional incarnation on Earth. The incoming group of Fifth Dimensional Ascended Masters become their Master Teachers.

ahead will require many of you to make difficult choices. You may lose friendships and family members. Your Brother may confront you and say to you, "I do not understand," and yet, you do. You understand, and you carry this work forward with loving hands and loving hearts.

Dear Sananda has always instructed you to "send this message to the Earth with love." Never engage in disharmony or discord as you carry this work forward. In regard to those who are not yet willing to hear, simply plant the seed, and then move forward. Should you become angry or emotional with those who slap you or spit in your face, you must simply love them and understand that to back away is an act of courage and strength. I would also encourage you, Dear chelas, not to tolerate this type of behavior repeatedly. However, if the other is not ready, or has not developed an understanding, it is important for you to back away. For, just as you couldn't feed a child's small body a rich feast, some people aren't ready to digest your ideas. As you carry this work forward, you'll encounter those who are like small children, babies, and infants. Give them what they can assimilate.

EMBODY THE PROPHET

Know, too, that the work of the Prophet is never congratulated. Know, too, that the Prophet himself is never loved in his or her homeland. But always remember, the work that you carry forward through these prophecies paves the pathway for a time to come, a Time of Peace and a Time of Grace.

You must hold that energetic pattern of peace and grace in all you carry forward. You are the servants of the devoted Christ; you are the servants of the ONE; you represent the New World, that New Time to come. Many Prophets have foretold the New Age. You are the embodiment of this message and must carry it forward.

LOVE OVERCOMES FEAR

Love one another, as your dear Brother has stated; and if you have trouble forgiving someone, I would instruct you to spend time away, in silence, until you come to a place of forgiveness.

Understand that those who fear are not afraid of a world that is ending; rather, they fear the birth of the world to come — the Age of Cooperation, the Age of United Sisterhood and Brotherhood. For is this template something they haven't experienced?

We encourage you, Dear ones, to carry the torch for this dawning age. Lead through your demonstration. Forgive those who have injured you. Simply transmute. Turn your back, walk your path, carry your message forward, and do not engage.

Those who come forward, who choose to walk the path of peace with you, shall be gathered unto you, and they shall be as your Brothers and Sisters. This will be apparent by the lives they lead.

"A VIBRATION OF HARMONY"

It is important to carry a Vibration of Harmony at all times, in your office environment, in your homes, and among your families. Reason with your children. Sit them down and honor that Divine Oneship within their own beings, honor the flame within their hearts, that Monad or Jiva you all share. Come to the understanding that you all live together as one family, and then seek resolution through the Laws of Cooperation.[3]

As our beloved Brothers and Sisters have stated in the Twelve Jurisdictions, your harmonies (spiritual growth) cause troubles in the home. Therefore, find the rhythm of harmonies I

discussed; find the rhythm of harmonies I taught to you as sattva. This doctrine will allow the vibration to enter your business, your home, and your family. During this time, instruct all those who work with you to increase their harmony, and therefore, their abundance.

OPEN THE THIRD EYE

Dear ones, we have not been permitted yet to discuss the catastrophic prophecies that will commence their dispensation in several months. (Editor's Note: The Six-Map Scenario.) However, we have been encouraged to discuss the Prophecies of Peace and Grace in those times to come. I have relayed to you information about your own physiologies and your own bodies. At this time, many of you have been practicing the healing of the body and the release of energy through the adjustment of the Human Aura. It is important to disseminate this information at the local and the global levels to initiate Cellular Awakening.[4] These spiritual practices then create energy fields around the human body. Energy fields open the Third Eye of the practitioners, allowing them to see this electrical force.

---

3. *The Awakening Prayer* from Saint Germain and Kuthumi assists the Cellular Awakening.

> Great Light of Divine Wisdom,
> Stream forth to my being,
> And through your right use
> Let me serve mankind and the planet.
> Love, from the Heart of God.
> Radiate my being with the presence of the Christ
> That I walk the path of truth.
> Great Source of Creation.
> Empower my being,
> My Brother,
> My Sister,
> And my planet with perfection
> As we collectively awaken as one cell.
> I call forth the Cellular Awakening.
> Let wisdom, love, and power stream forth to this cell,
> This cell that we all share.
> Great Spark of Creation awaken the Divine Plan of Perfection.
> So we may share the ONE perfected cell — I AM.

4. This spiritual initiation, activated by Master Teachers Saint Germain and Kuthumi, prepares the consciousness to recognize and receive instruction from the Fourth Dimension. Cellular Awakening stimulates seven subtle adjustments on the cellular level, preparing the physical body for an intense spiritual experience. These acclimatizations include:

The Quickening: An acceleration of cells throughout the body creating a union with the I AM Presence.

Higher Metabolism: This physical change activates the Eight-sided Cell of Perfection, which is located in the heart. According to the Master Teachers, a person can inspire this phenomenon by fasting for twenty-four hours on citrus juices containing a portion of orange, lemon, tangerine, and grapefruit.

Attunement to the Galactic Beam: Also known as the Eighth or Golden Ray, this process prepares the physical body to receive the beneficial results of the Violet Flame. The Galactic Beam emits a high-frequency energy. The Earth receives this power from the Great Central Sun. According to the Master Teachers, frequent saltwater baths with two cups of salt and three to four drops atomidine (iodine supplement) will augment this process. (Atomidine is available from the Heritage Store: www.heritagestore.com)

Violet Flame: This powerful universal force disintegrates etheric genetic coding through daily meditation, visualization, and decrees. Saint Germain says that kindling the Violet Flame during the Cellular Awakening affects the water balance of the physical body, including circulation, the lymphatic system, and the Emotional Body.

Diet: During Cellular Awakening the Master Teachers say to avoid or reduce all animal products from the diet.

This is part of the dispensation, so that many people will begin to understand that one life force permeates all beings. They will see this life force around the human form and other life forms such as plants, animals, and even those of the Mineral Kingdom. This awakening is dispensed at this time to promote a greater sensitivity to and an understanding of all life forms. The majority of humanity doesn't comprehend that all life is connected as ONE — that this life force permeates all things and all beings.

Therefore, for the opening of the Third Eye, I would suggest the scents of sandalwood and jasmine, as they are both very soothing.

During this Time of Transition, many people will notice a high-pitched ringing in their ears, sometimes accompanied by a slight headache. This is a result of the following two things: the spiritual accelerations happening at this time, and the pollution that permeates the environment and your waters. The accelerations are somewhat hard on the body because they cause it to expel certain toxins.

I would instruct you, Dear ones, to use the vibration emanating from citrus fruit to purify your waters. Also, purify (cleanse) your air with the scents of honeysuckle, citrus, and orange blossom. It is important that you use the energies within the body to help bring about a purification of the environment. (Editor's Note: This is a reference to Free Energy Techniques and Energy Field Balancing.)

When you notice an area that needs a cleansing or a purification, simply gather your energies as you have been instructed: hold your hand over your heart, and direct the energies through the palm of your right hand to that area. It is always best to visualize gold and green lights streaming from your body.

ACCELERATIONS AND EARTH HEALING

During this Time of Acceleration, many of your elder Brothers and Sisters will assist you in bringing this kind of healing to the planet. Just as you have learned to use certain energy work to assist in the healing of your Brothers and Sisters, you can also use it in the air or on a group of trees. You can use it over a landfill to adjust the energy and bring forth balance.

What greater acts of the heart, which serve all so selflessly, could come forward at this time?[5]

In regard to the people you trained — those who can adjust the energy of others and those who have attained a balanced state of optimum health and Mastery — ask those persons to come forward and perform these same selfless acts of healing our planet. For the time is critical, particularly in those areas of the Golden City Vortices. It is important now to carry forward these energetic alignments by serving as purifiers of the environment, just as you have served each other through the path of the healer. As you know, the Prophet only paves the pathway for the priest.

SERVICE THROUGH SOCIAL INVOLVEMENT

I ask you, therefore, to gather in ceremony to gain strength. You must stay committed to your choice for the improvement of humanity. I ask for your involvement at the social levels. I

5. This is also known as the Step-down Transformer. The processes instigated through the Cellular Awakening rapidly advance human Light Bodies. Synchronized with an Ascended Master's will, the awakened cells of light and love evolve the skills of a Step-Down Transformer to efficiently transmit and distribute currents of Ascended Master energy — referred to as an Ascended Master Current (A.M. Current). This metaphysical form of intentional inductive coupling creates an ethereal power grid that can be used for all types of healing.

A.M. Currents release beneficially charged and sometimes spine-tingling rushes of energy throughout the human system. This energy current is often accompanied by an audible high-pitched ring and a visible translucent glow of white or Gold light. Step-down Transformers report sensations of time slowing down and a body-warming flush as hands, feet, and chakras conduct the high frequency energy.

According to the Master Teachers tuning your body and your consciousness as a Step-down Transformer resembles a high quality quartz crystal, emitting effulgent Rays of Light and energy from many directions.

Surprisingly, an A.M. Current is calming and soothing. Since the Vibration of fear is effectively extinguished in its wake, the curative and peaceful frequency influences all who come within contact. Transfers of Step-down energies create a remnant force field that is later detectable, and the frequency can change significantly in strength or weakness dependant on the purpose for the release of the A.M. Current.

Master Teachers often train students to purposely hold and direct Step-down energies of healing love and light on behalf of Earth and humanity. Primarily, Step-down Transformers work solely in private to perfect their craft and skill. When accomplished Step-down Transformers gather in groups the spiritual voltage significantly intensifies. These larger batteries of energy are often circuited into the Collective Consciousness to bring about positive political change, societal healing, and restorative balance to Mother Earth.

ask for your involvement in health care and in your schools. Develop an organization that educates people about this type of healing. See to it that people are empowered at the grass-roots level to understand the healing power that lies latent within their own physiologies.[6]

This is the work of a Master.[7]

_____

6. These are a series of lessons and techniques that move energy through the human energy field — auras and chakras. *Energy-field balancing* activates personal harmony, symmetry, and healing. The Master Teachers say we can develop these abilities beyond the scope of individual practice; and humanity, through a collective effort, can facilitate Earth Healing: the elimination of landfills, diseased forests, and polluted waters.

7. An Ascended Master is a highly developed spiritual being who has ascended the human physical manifestation beyond the Third Dimension. At one time the members of this cosmically elite fellowship, known as the Great White Lodge or Brotherhood, were men and women tied to a corporeal existence like any other human on Earth.

But a higher destiny set these souls apart from ordinary individuals. Over thousands of years, these souls encountered innumerable diverse lifetimes and an arduous yet prolific process of incarnation after incarnation. This boundless experience of trials, tragedy, knowledge, and wisdom culminated in an uncanny spiritual maturity beyond that of a normal human being. They came to understand and acknowledge in their hearts, an undeniable, great truth — divinity. The recognition of this inherent divinity drives human consciousness beyond Third Dimensional perception; it instigates the Mastery of thought, feeling, action, and experience.

A command of the Third Dimension breaks the elusive bond to the Wheel of Karma, freeing the Spiritual Master from the need to reincarnate in an earthbound physical body. Now the individual has attained the role of Ascended Master who dedicates his or her immortal existence to the universal spiritual enrichment of humanity. Many members of this fellowship, though not physically tied to Earth, remain close to terra firma and its people. Master Teachers seek others, who, although embody a physical attachment to Earth, embrace an innate desire to evolve beyond the Third Dimension.

The Great White Brotherhood or Lodge earns its name from an all-encompassing philosophy of humanity. White refers to white light, which embraces all colors, races, creeds, genders, and sexual orientation. The Brotherhood's primary goal focuses on the preservation of the teachings and the spirit of the ancient religions and philosophies of the world. They pledge to protect mankind from growth-inhibiting assaults on individual and group freedoms, self-knowledge, and personal choice. Of paramount importance is their Mission to reawaken the dormant ethical and spiritual spark that is fast disappearing among the masses.

The fellowship of the Masters welcomes new members with the following invocation:

An Invitation

"I close by extending an invitation to all of you to join with us. The need is great among humanity today. There is still needless suffering fueled by the fires of ignorance and deception. Quietly listen and you will hear the call in your heart. We are not a religious group or sect; however, we are a service group of elder Brothers and Sisters who have been known throughout mankind's history as the Great White Lodge. Through the medium of

See that this work is accelerated in the schools so that the children to come, and the generations to follow, are educated from the heart. See that they are first taught the Laws of Honor and Intent. Get involved at that level, Dear ones.

This is the work of a Master.

In this Time of Change, it is important to be involved — not only with those of, shall we say, the New Age, but with those who do not understand. Bring them this understanding in gentle ways. Bring them this understanding in ways they can accept and assimilate, as with that small child who drinks milk at the feast.

"TEND THE SEEDS"

There is much work for you to do. I would ask you to dispense all materials at this time. As I have stated before, I will set up an electronic vibration to bring forward the money and the abundance that is necessary to fulfill this leg of your journey.

I AM America is to become a clearinghouse for the New Humanity. It is important to dispense material that opens the eyes and ears of humanity to alternative forms of healing and education. As I have stated, the work of those who toil tirelessly behind the scenes is usually the work that achieves the greatest

_____

consciousness we have merged our efforts and energies aimed towards the unity of all of life.

Our goal is simple, and our work is hard. It is never promised to be easy, however, the reward immeasurable. Come, through prayer and meditation if you feel the urge of the Mission within.

A new cycle awaits humanity. It is a cycle filled with growth, learning, and life. Painfully and lovingly, sometimes this growth is achieved through disease, poverty, and destruction. However, within your heart lies the gentle revolution that can redirect the course of such events.

This is a revolution armed with the power of service, charity, and love. If you should turn your back now, know that timelessly we await.

Let us join in wisdom to extinguish ignorance and inequity.

Let us join in love to extinguish suffering.

Let us join in service to extinguish greed and avarice.

Let us join in charity to extinguish poverty.

Let us join in harmony to extinguish disease.

As our ears are opened and our eyes begin to see, let us join as ONE LIGHT, in our hearts and minds. May this light of wisdom serve all. May this light of truth and justice prevail. May the law be written in hearts and joined through harmony, Brotherhood, and love.

Timelessly and agelessly, the unknown poet sings, 'O, let not the flame die out! Cherished age after age in its dark cavern - in its holy temples cherished. Fed by pure ministers of love - let not the flame die out.'"

result. So do not worry about gaining attention. Do not worry about achieving recognition. Instead, tend the seeds you plant: water, fertilize, and nurture them so they may grow, until a New Time and a new life spring forward.

These are perilous times indeed. It's important that you carry forward the plan — the plan that focuses energy on the highest and best use of humanity and the plan that best serves humanity. So be it.

CHAPTER SIX

No Need for Change?

⌘

*A Shamballa Message from Saint Germain, Sananda,
Kuan Yin, and Mother Mary.*

Greetings my beloved chelas, I AM Saint Germain, and I stream forth on that Mighty Violet Ray of Mercy and Forgiveness.

As usual Dear hearts, I request permission to come forward.

"Please Dear one, come forward."

A SHAMBALLA MESSAGE

As you well know, Dear ones, this is the Time of Shamballa, a great Time of Feasting, and a Time of Celebrating the divinity of all life, all Omni-essence.[1] During this time, we would like to bring a message for you to share with all of humanity. A message from the Great White Brotherhoods and the Sisterhoods of Light, which have a timing and an intent to inspire the many who have opened their eyes and their ears.

THE TIME OF CHANGE

There is a Time of Change that is coming to the Earth. There is also a Time of Change that is coming among humanity. You have studied that the human and the Earth are related as ONE.

---

1. The ethereal retreat of Shamballa opens its Golden gates once a year. Some say this spiritual event happens between December 17 and January 17. During the Time of Shamballa, Ascended Beings, Archangels, and Elohim, as well as the inhabitants of other planets and solar systems, gather to establish a plan — a schematic for the spiritual and evolutionary elevation of Earth and humanity — for the upcoming year. Throughout these thirty-two days of celebration, divine participants hold meetings, ceremonies, and planning sessions. Communication with Earthly students via Ascended Master participation is of particular concern. In dream states or through the oral tradition, pupils receive messages. These parcels of information include divinations about the hierarchy's forthcoming plans; prophesied and pending events; and possible catastrophes averted or lessened through intentional thoughts, meditation, and efforts by individuals and the power of communal prayers on Earth.

You've studied this through electromagnetics, and now you are beginning to understand that even in the social structures and in the thinking of the individual all of these components fit together as one large body, which composes the Omni-essence, the universal life.

Not one of these is dissociated from the other. For all are connected in that Mighty Oneship. All are connected in that Mighty ONE that expresses all of life.

Dear ones, many among humanity ask the question, "What is the purpose of Prophecy?" And if these changes do not happen, "then what?" We feel it is important to relay this message to those who are ready to hear, those who are ready to see, and to those who are ready to take an action that serves the greater good, that greater ONE. It is our hope that those who are now ready will serve their Brothers and their Sisters, and will serve the planet in whatever form that may help at this time. However, a great change is coming. And it is important that you be prepared!

If these changes do not happen, what type of a world would we live in (the future)? Let me assure you, Dear ones, it would be a world that you would not recognize. However, let me remind you of the world that you would live in if it were not necessary for these changes to happen.

VIBRATION OF PROPHECY

Many Prophets have come before you and many Prophets will come after you. Each Prophet speaks in a (certain) tongue, and carries a vibration which is necessary to open the eyes and ears of those that they serve. Some of the prophecies that have been dispensed, shall we say, through other eyes and ears, by members of this spiritual hierarchy, are those who speak of the ending of this Earth, or the beginning of a One-World Government.

A SLAVE PLANET?

Should this happen, let me assure you, Dear ones, that you would be much happier living in that Time of Change! (Earth Changes) For the alien governments, and their technologies, will take over the Earth at large. And this planet becomes again, a slave planet! All life comes through genetic mutations which serve the consciousness of this government.

THE SPARK OF FREEDOM

However, it has also been our intent and our service to bring forward material to inspire leadership among the masses, and to re-instill the spark of freedom so some will recognize the divinity within all. And through these (types of) choices, the leaders rise among all of you and take this message to the world and share it among all — divinity is celebrated first! Now, there are those who understand the true spiritual nature of humanity, and the true spiritual nature of this work.

A PERFECT WORLD

If these changes (Earth Changes) were not necessary, let me tell you about the type of world you would live in. First, let us start with the family structures. Within the family, breakdown between husband and wife (partners) never happens. And marriages are perfect unions — ones not touched or shattered by separation or conflict. Marriages foster the growth of children who are brought into this world. Marriages (parents) are productive and lead children into literature, the arts, and the understanding of foreign languages. Parents serve children to become world leaders and group servers. Parents understand their role as a contribution to the greater ONE, live with self-acceptance, and are employed at all times to ensure the necessary growth and stability of their families.

TRUE STATE ECONOMY

Let me explain. The economies that would exist if Earth Changes were not necessary would be balanced economies throughout the world. Those (economies) share openly with the fruits of one another, and do not trade through inflated coins or printed money, but trade with natural goods. This is known as a true state economy — one that never becomes inflated and one that is based on what it produces.[2]

Few middle men would exist in these economies and an agrarian society — with a low impact on the environment — would flourish. No longer would we see the necessity for petrochemicals polluting your planet. Alternative energy supplies would be allowed, because greed would be wiped off your planet!

This is the type of economy that would exist, an economy that allows all humans to express their inborn Divine Stature to live without degradation. It is an economy without welfare. What would be the need? All would share so openly; all would give compassionately and from their hearts.

It would be an economy without useless taxation. It would be an economy of those who (voluntarily) pay the taxes needed to support municipalities to bring forward and flourish the arts, literature, music, and all else that would enhance the lifestyle of the citizens of the republic.[3]

PRINCIPLES OF HARMONY AND COOPERATION

Let us talk about the social conditions of a society where the experience of Earth Changes is not necessary. This society is without crime or deviant behavior. All express according to the Oneness and the unity of the group, and the Oneness and the unity of their hearts. How can you separate the two when each and every one has been brought up with a sense of love and cooperation.

The spark of competitiveness is wiped forever from the face of this society. The spark and the ember of Brotherhood and Sisterhood are tended and fed. The measurement of men and women, families and societies, come not through the amount

---

2. A time will come when the world's economy implodes and paper money becomes obsolete, even prohibited. Only then will a new economic paradigm emerge — one that relies on the trading of precious metals, natural resources, and tangible goods. The nascent economy, resembling a Natural Economy, is based on what it produces. This structure eliminates the need to transfer goods, resources, and services via traditional currency.

3. A republic, in simple terms, is a political body led by an elected official, such as a president or consul, rather than a sovereign leader. It follows some type of charter (e.g. the Constitution), which directs the government to elect representatives who will advance national interests and support the right of self-determination. Though the terms republic and democracy, a system where majority rules, are often used synonymously, the general idea of these political philosophies differ in principle. A republic, in theory, serves the common good of its citizens whom are subject to the Rule of Law. America in its current state is a republic — consider the Pledge of Allegiance: "I pledge allegiance to the Flag of the United States of America, and to the Republic, for which it stands … "

of money one holds in a bank account, but through the integrity and the principles that they uphold and represent. Governments are reflected through these principles; based on the Laws of Harmony and Cooperation, first. Special interests are no longer allowed, for what would be the point? All serve the harmony and the cooperation of that mighty greater good.

A police force would rarely be needed. Would there be criminals? Hardly not! And the prison system would not exist.

Open libraries and schools flourish, and are not limited (segregated) to one age group. All participate freely in this Open Society. For wiping away the ignorance of the masses is the total focus of a society that lives on the basis of cooperation and harmony.[4]

LIVING IN BALANCE

Communication among many different peoples comes openly and freely, as foreign languages are encouraged among all. Although humanity will share a universal tongue that communicates with the ONE consciousness of all, most people will speak five to six different languages. And they (languages) would be understood and celebrated, for language is the key to the growth of the human. This society honors languages and understands that through sound each intonation and syllable carries forth the thrust of DNA.

Health systems will not be filled with the atrocities of greed. These health systems come forward in a holistic manner based first on reason, and second on common sense. Virtually all disease that would come to this society would be naturally wiped away. For balance is the first principle that all practice, not only in their dietary standard, but in their mind and in their thinking.

This is a society without a need for Earth Change.

And now, let us talk about the environment. This is an environment without pollution. This is an environment without the threat of nuclear destruction. This is an environment that sings sweetly and naturally to its inhabitants and a communication is occurring at all times between nature and humanity. The Elemental and Deva Kingdom is no longer threatened, and they come forward to give instruction for that which will serve the great crops of nuts, fruits, and grains. They will give of themselves naturally to feed humanity. Starvation is wiped away forever, and no longer will the famines of Earth be allowed to exist.[5]

These are civilizations without the need for Earth Change.

These are civilizations that have learned to live in balance and harmony. These are civilizations that live in grace on the back of the Earth Mother. Why would there be a need to remove even one? These are civilizations that realize their destiny is in the Heart of Divinity. This is the excellence that the Great White Brotherhood and Sisterhood (purposely) inspire humanity to become and offer. Live and breathe the Law of the Best and Highest Good and put each foot forward in that law!

This is a society without the need for catastrophic change; balance and harmony reign supreme.

And so Dear ones, if I need go further, please instruct me! But those of you with eyes and ears open may now measure through your own sense of reason.

A CHANGE OF HEART

Do your societies, do your governments, do your schools reflect the perfection that I have portrayed for you? Are they to this caliber? Are they (evolved) to a place that needs no change? If so, then their energy is open and flowing in balance. Look today at each of the structures in which you participate. Look today and ask yourself (these questions). The answers are within your heart.

Today, most families live separated from one another. Children are raised by the Laws of the Streets! Today, the schools have lost the ability to educate; for most schools seek the Law of Money first.

---

4. Developed by philosopher Henri Bergson, an open society supports the human rights and the political freedoms of its citizens. In theory, an open society is just that: open. The government avoids keeping secrets from the public; rather, it places emphasis on tolerance, transparency, flexibility, and personal responsibility. In his book, *The Open Society and Its Enemies*, Austrian-born illuminato Sir Karl Popper defined an open society as one that allows its populace to throw out the leaders peacefully and without bloodshed. Compare this notion to a closed society — an unpredictable supremacy defined by violent revolutions and riotous coups d'etat.

5. See Appendix E1: *Devas and Elementals.*

Your medical and your political systems, need I say more? And your environment for the past forty years has been in grave danger and you say, "Everything is fine … why should we have a change?"

Perhaps the change should come first in the heart.

Awaken to the conditions that exist outside of your own home.

WIPE AWAY IGNORANCE

Understand the needless suffering that occurs on this planet because of the thirst for greed and power. When these two ignorances are wiped from the planet, then and only then, can this great New Age — a New Age of Utopia — be built. It is the plan of the (Spiritual) Hierarchy that serves the greater plan and the heart of humanity, that this Utopia comes forward! We remind you of the perfection you hold, the perfection of what you can be, and the perfection that the future holds. A Time of Grace, indeed, will come — a time that will be an Age of Peaceful Cooperation.

ANOTHER WAY OF BE-ING

However, this Age of Peace is not just a Prophecy! It is an age that comes forward through your willing hands, and you must take it into your being; live it, breathe it, and then demonstrate it. That is why we have spent so much time with you, Dear ones. We strive to raise your vibrations, work with you daily through discourse, and help you understand another way of BE-ing. You call this a, "Revolution of Consciousness." We call this the Divine Spark of your being!

SHARE THE PEACE

Let this perfection blaze forward in all that you do, and this New Year becomes a new day! Take this New Year to become a new day for a Time of Change. Do you see now, the necessity for change? Again, you have a choice: will these changes be cataclysmic or hold consciousness? Now is the time to go forward and be the World Servers that you truly say that you are.

Share the message of peace, and demonstrate the peace in your own hearts.

Share the peace with your families.

Share the peace with your neighbors, and extend it into your communities and into all of your daily affairs.

Let this peace be decreed, which you profess.

Let peace reign supreme. Questions?

Answer:"There are no questions."

Now he is backing away from the lectern, and Sananda is coming forward.

SANANDA SPEAKS

Dear Brothers and Sisters of the Golden Flame. I AM Sananda, and I request permission to come forward.

Answer: "Please Dear one, come forward."

This project of change, which is known as transition, is one where again you have wondered, "What is the purpose?" What would be the meaning of such a catastrophic change to herald in a day of peace? Let me assure you, Dear ones of my heart, the intention of our service is at all times to foster the love within you and the love without.

SERVICE OF THE HEART

The Time of Collective Cooperation and of Collective Peace will come only through hearts that truly wish to serve. Over and over again, we have spoken of service to humanity, and now it is time that each and every one of you looks within your own heart and asks of yourself, "Can I truly serve my Brother? Can I truly serve my Sister?" The service of the heart must be the first condition of moving into the Age of Cooperation. It is important that you begin to observe and understand that you are all ONE. There are very few differences among you.

Look at your Brother, look at your Sister, and recognize that he or she has traveled the path of many embodiments, that he or she, too, has had many incarnations and has traveled the path like you, lifetime after lifetime — the joys, the sorrows, the wins, the losses. All of these things your Brother has experienced too. How would he be any different from you? Hardly could he! And yet, why would you perceive such a difference among you and your Brother and your Sister?

Humanity has worried much over the differences that they experience. But now it is time to come and celebrate unity for an Age of Cooperation to come forward. The unity and the Oneness of consciousness must be celebrated within the heart. Realize first the Divine Spark that all share and all are of.

THE CONSCIOUSNESS OF DIVINITY

I have come forward in sponsorship of this transition to allow a consciousness of the ONE, and to allow a consciousness of divinity to spark itself among humanity so that an Age of Cooperation will never again leave this planet. When I came forward in this sponsorship, first, I celebrated and realized the Oneness that I shared with my beloved Brother, El Morya; with my beloved Brother, Saint Germain; with my Sisters Portia and Mary; with my beloved Kuan Yin. How could there be a difference among us if we were to move forward and collectively serve that greater ONE?

Do you argue over your differences? Do not allow differences to stop you from your movement into ONE consciousness. This is a Time of Peace and Grace. Celebrate, sup, and fEast with all. So be it.

He is backing away, and now Mary and Kuan Yin come forward.

THE DIVINE FEMININE

Greetings and salutations, we merge our energies as ONE, for we represent a quality of the Divine Mother.

We ask permission to come forward.

Response: "Please beloveds, come forward."

This is a celebration and a time of honoring all energies as ONE. We have held Soleteta — the Divine Feminine — to come forward.[6] Yet we remind you, Dear ones, that it is the feminine within and not feminism. It is the feminine (energy) that comes forward in service to help and assist the masculine. The masculine energy protects and assists the feminine. Both of these energies, together within the individual, serve the Age of Cooperation. It is (through) the masculine and the feminine energies, which come forward in the totality of balance, that beat the heart with the perfection of cooperation.

SPIRIT OF THE CHRIST

Live with balance, Dear ones. Live with the balance of your masculine and feminine energies serving that greater ONE. Celebrate this Oneness you share — that is the balance of your energies. Honor your feminine, and honor your masculine. Let them come forward and merge as ONE in the glory of the Christ, for it is through the Christ that you can see one another in the Oneness that you share. It is the glory of the Christ that breaks all barriers and perfects the bodies (physical and Light Bodies) upon the Earth Plane and Planet. Through the marriage of your energies, you will become readied for a dimensional leap to a new understanding of cooperation and unity.

---

6. (Pronounced So-lee'-tah-tah) *Soletata* is the conscious expression of the Divine Feminine, not in the sense of modern feminism or to the exclusion of males; rather, this carnal wisdom celebrates the nurturing spirit of women. It supports masculine energy, and represents conception and birth to all mankind, including Nature Kingdoms.

With an open heart and hearth, the divine spiritual power of Soletata unites the Christ energies within (child and mother), and recognizes the father as the Divine Spark. Soletata illustrates the quintessence of motherhood — the maternal role purified to domestic simplicity: the raising of children; the tending of household duties; the baking of bread; the cultivating of gardens; and the hanging of laundry in the wind.

The teachings of Soletata fall in the hands Mother Mary, the divine mother of Western culture; and Kuan Yin, the divine mother of the East. Together, they personify the higher consciousness of Soletata, or compassionate love.

Esoteric Taoist traditions magnify the significance of Soletata. These edifications tell us that the unification of the masculine and the feminine energies creates a tremendous opportunity for profound spiritual development and internal Alchemy. Physically, this phenomenon opens the body's channels or meridians, allowing a subtle yet harmonious integration of the human form and the promotion of healing. In advanced teachings, Unity Consciousness — Unana — awakens the body's feminine currents. Spiritual initiation is achieved by recognizing and using the energies of the Divine Feminine: Soletata.

Come together, Dear ones, in the marriage of your energies; come together in the spirit of cooperation; come together in the spirit of the Christ, I AM.

Saint Germain is now coming forward.

AN AGE OF REASON

Dear chelas, as usual, if there are any questions, I would be willing to address these now.

Question: "In conceiving of the perfect world, it would seem that the genetic qualities of cooperation and harmony also follow hand-in-hand with common sense. It would seem that our world goes through turmoil and discomfort through a lack of practicality. Will you please elaborate?"

It is time that we celebrate an Age of Reason.[7] It is time that we allow consciousness to be consumed first by mighty common sense! It is time for each of the senses to become alive and aware, but disciplined. You are a society experiencing, shall we say, great birth pains! And with these birth pains the many fields of auras are experiencing explosions. Many are unable to grip expanded sensibility.

Let me assure you, Dear ones, it is also a Time of Discipline. First, find discipline within. For is discipline not another form of cooperation? Check all words that cross your mind and all thoughts that will not serve your moving forward with the focus of Brotherly Love. Then check all words that cross your tongue.

The time that is coming is a Time of Perfection! This perfection will only be achieved through the weaving of Brothers and Sisters through the Vibration of Love. Beloved Mother Mary has often spoken of the Divine Cloak that covers all of you. It is a cloak woven in the spirit of cooperation, not in competition!

This, of course, is a difficult idea because so many humans have just recently risen out of the animal state. However, it is

---

7. According to Western philosophy, the Age of Reason begins in the seventeenth century with the work of philosopher, René Descartes. It represents the unification of knowledge and the end of the medieval paradigm. A new mentality, one that establishes intellectual systems such as metaphysics, philosophy, ethics, politics, and physical science, settles in. This is the time of Sir Francis Bacon, who later ascended as Saint Germain.

the choice of those who listen; it is the choice of those who read or hear this message and rise out of their animal state, and take upon them that mantle of consciousness, a mighty common sense! Discipline is the only answer at this time. And the only hope for our perfected Utopia will come when humanity embraces discipline.

FREEDOM THROUGH DISCIPLINE

The embracing of these concepts will allow humanity to experience the true freedom for which it was created. It is the embracing of discipline through which humanity will embrace freedom.

Question: "Is this discipline not a personal choice?"

At this moment, Dear ones, discipline is a necessity for the survival of the human race. The work we have brought forward has always been presented through the medium of choice. However, have you not noted the many changes now occurring on your planet: wars, famine, tremendous crime, and the breakdown of your families? And some of those still ask, "Why is such a change necessary? Why, would we even want to have the Earth Changes Prophecies to come to full fruition?"

Perhaps now's the time (humanity) addresses the fear it holds in its heart — not only the fear of change but the fear of the death of the physical body. I have known many before me who have gladly laid their lives down for the principle of freedom and the principle of perfection! However, since we have sent this message to the Earth with love, we have presented to those members of humanity that if the ember of divinity could be fanned within the heart, perhaps there would be those who would serve the nobler cause. Perhaps there would be those who would come forward and disallow the state of competitiveness within their being. Perhaps there would be those who would allow the spirit of cooperation, Brotherhood and Sisterhood, that of the unity of One Family.

It is necessary that humanity hears this message!
It is necessary that all practice it.

It is necessary that you begin to live it. How else will you achieve the discipline but by practice?

THE MELTING POT

As you have said, "practice makes permanent." Is now not the time for an Age of Grace to become a permanent age, the permanent factor by which this beloved Terra is known? As you have known, beloved Terra has never held the position of a sacred planet. However, it is known as a servile planet — a planet that offers a service, a place where many throughout the universe and the galaxy could call home. Terra, much like the destiny of the United States, has been the cradle of many members of (intergalactic) races, societies, and religious sects who no longer had a home where they could freely practice and speak their beliefs. The United States and America has also been known as this type of melting pot.[8]

The entire planet of Terra is a melting pot. Yet, when we allow a special interest to overcome, be that special-interest greed or competitiveness, we are no longer the Vibration of a Melting Pot. And what would happen? Then naturally, all patterns that

---

8. The universe comprises the following divisions of material planets: sacred and servile. Those who inhabit sacred planets experience higher energies and frequencies, eliminating the need for a physical body, although these beings may express themselves in a physical form, too. They elude the futile afflictions of mankind: they don't suffer from fear, aging, or death. Their bodies easily drift from the spiritual to the subtle — these are the Devas, the demigods, the angels, the spiritual teachers, the great saints, the sages, and the mystics. Despite their evolved consciousness, these altruistic spirits empathize with the plight and the welfare of the denizens of grosser, material worlds. They send emissaries who bring spiritual knowledge and aid in various times and circumstances. Sacred planets represent purity of thought, and exemplify Blue, Yellow, and Pink Ray Forces, and will remain intact after the destruction of material worlds.

Life on servile planets experiences an imperiled existence. Fraught with death, old age, illness, and anxiety, these worlds — especially those of lower orders such as Earth — commit its inhabitants to a metaphysical vacuum. And though some servile populations possess mystic acumen, great wealth, artistic refinement, and the ability to control gravity, time, and space, these mortals lack true spiritual development. This life is a race against time, the ultimate equalizer, and inevitable death. Those who inhabit lower servile planets help incarnating souls rectify and remediate the most horrifying acts during their human lifetime on Earth. "Although life here seems like it goes on for an eternity, in actual fact the duration of one's 'karmic sentence' here may be only seconds or moments," writes author, Howard Beckman. Servile planets express blended thoughts coupled with Green and Violet Rays.

have set up (created) on this planet fall, one upon the other. Why do you question change? Balance must be restored.

PROPHECIES OF IAMBLICHUS

Answer: "This is understood. When we speak of discipline, we speak of choice. And at some time in the future I would ask that you elaborate upon a day of discipline."

First, discipline comes through the way you see. Discipline comes through the way that you hear. When beloved Brother Iamblichus delivered the Prophecy "before the eyes can see, they must be incapable of tears…" He was teaching the greatest of all disciplines. It is time that you discipline your emotional responses. "Before the ears can hear, they must have lost their sensitiveness."[9]

The motivation of competition comes toward you as an energy — a rush or a blast — you must not react to this with more competition! Simply allow the (message to come) through that Mighty Law of Cooperation. "Before the voice can speak in the presence of the Masters, it must have lost the power to wound."

WORDS AND ENERGY-FORMS

When we speak injurious words toward Brothers and Sisters, we utter energy forms. They (energy forms) take on a life within themselves, and attach themselves energetically as you have directed that word and that thought. Oh, if humanity only knew the power of the words it speaks. That is why we have spent so much time with you through the rhythmic patterns of decreeing, through the rhythmic patterns of prayer. It is important for you to understand, my Dearest ones, how important the Violet Flame is at this time. For you are calling forward through voice and sound vibration that Mighty Law of Perfection. These words do not injure; these words heal.

HEALING

A Time of Healing comes to the planet. But the healing must be carried in your hands, in your ears, and in your words.

---

9. For more information see Appendix F1: *Master Hilarion*.

During this Time of Healing, bring yourself forward in service by the laying of hands. Don't forget to lay your words carefully, too — and your thoughts: lay them so carefully. All that comes from the center of your divinity empowers cooperation. So be it!

I AM a being of Violet Fire!
I AM the purity cooperation desires!

So be it, Dear ones. Let us now raise our Cups in celebration of the times to come. Let us now raise our Cups to the love we are and share. Hitaka!

CHAPTER SEVEN

Weaving the New Web

⟡

Saint Germain with two students.

Greetings my beloved chelas, I AM Saint Germain, and I request permission to come forward.

Response: (Both host and students respond) "Please, Dear one, come forward."

ACTIVATION OF THE GOLDEN CITIES

Greetings in that Mighty Christ, I AM. Dear hearts, it is with much pleasure that I bring this discourse to you; for we have found that on the Earth Plane and Planet the New Time arrives, a New Time for the activation of the Golden Cities of light and sound.[1]

For you see, Dear ones, these Golden Cities will birth the planet into its new state — into that state known as Unana — which is the activated Christ. Dear ones, facing you is a Time of tremendous Earth Change, but also a time that births a New Millennium of light and sound; a time when we will see many changes not only on the Earth herself, but within the Earth.

EARTH'S CRYSTALLINE STRUCTURE

Her whole crystalline structure is taking a new form, and she shall occupy that shining light throughout the New Universe. This is a Time of Preparation, a time when we'll prepare the Cup, that Holy Grail, for the light shines on in Mighty Magnificent Consummation!

GOLDEN BELT OF LIGHT

Dear ones, at this time we ask you to consider that the Earth's grids are also changing. The Golden Belt of Light, which swept around the planet in the early part of this century, is also transforming.[2] We have found a collective census of lightworkers

---

1. A full comprehension of the word "activate" is key to understanding this spiritual phenomena. The following dictionary definitions describe its usage: "to make active;" "to make more active;" "to hasten reactions by various means"; and "to place in active status." So, the term Golden City Activation includes several meanings and applications to illustrate the four types of Golden City activations.
1. Ascended Master Activation: Made Active
The Spiritual Hierarchy first conceptualized the idea of the Golden Cities by the perfect out-picturing of these spiritual centers. Certain Master Teachers, Archangels, and Elohim — in cooperation with Mother Earth Babajeran — sponsor specific Golden Cities. Their task: to gather the energies of each divine municipality. The grid structure of Earth — in tandem with the focus of the appropriate Ray — is held in immaculate concept by each steward and coalesces the energies of each Golden City. And as consciousness increases, members of mankind seek its Fifth Dimension power as spiritual retreats.
2. Geophysical Activation: More Active
The interaction of Mother Earth and the Golden Cities — Fifth Dimensional structures — produces Third and Fourth Dimensional characteristics. This phenomenon creates a more active activation. The significance of Third Dimensional activation lies in its ability to generate a Vortex at the intersection of lei-lines. When eight of these invisible co-ordinates crisscross, a Vortex emerges, including the formation of Golden City Vortices. Vortices move in a clockwise/counterclockwise motion. Geophysically activated Golden Cities have a profound effect on humans: they experience longevity, greater healing abilities, and physical regeneration. In the Fourth Dimension, Nature Kingdoms begin to interact with

Vortex energies; human visitors experience telepathic and psychic abilities, and lucid dreaming. (Lei-lines are magnetic lines of detectable energy.)
3. Ceremonial Activation: To Hasten Reactions by Various Means
Ceremonial activations, inspired by humans who seek an intense result from a Golden City, occur on an emotional-astral level in areas throughout these sacred Vortices. Similar to pujas or yagyas — known in Hindu as sacrifices — fire or water-driven ceremonies neutralize difficult karmas and enhance beneficial human qualities.
4. Great Central Sun Activation: To Place in Active Status
Produced by a greater timing or origin, this type of activation relies on the energies that emanate from the Great Central Sun or Galactic Center (our universe rotates around a larger Sun). Some theosophical scholars say power from the Galactic Center sends subtle energies to our solar system via the planetary fire triplicity: Jupiter, Mars, and the Sun.
2. Ivan T. Sanderson, an early-century Scottish naturalist, first postulated the existence of an Earth grid. He discussed a network of twelve, evenly spaced global Vortices, such as the Bermuda Triangle and the Oregon Vortex, which exist near the tropics of Capricorn and Cancer, and the North and South Poles. Here, enigmatic episodes — warped time and space, unexplained disappearances, mechanical malfunctions, and peculiar weather conditions — are the norm.
In the early 1970s, three Muscovite scientists — Nikolai Goncharov, Vyacheslav Morozov, and Valery Makarov — advanced Sanderson's findings. Published in the Soviet science journal, Khimiya i Zhizn, their article "Is the Earth a Large Crystal?" described the planet as a "matrix of cosmic

who have held this light in constant consciousness. We can now remove this band of light to allow the activations of these planetary cities.[3] The Golden Cities are part of the Prophecy that is brought for change; for change comes not only in the heart and in the mind, but change must also be an active cause. And today, we ask you for your service and unite you with this active cause.

GOLDEN CITY OF GOBEAN

Each of the Golden Cities will be activated in a sequence.[4] And as you already know, it is that Golden City of Gobean which was activated almost 14 years ago. And now, stalwart lightworkers have come forward, chelas and students of

that Mighty I AM, to carry that Cup of Service throughout the world! [5]

GOLDEN CITY OF MALTON

The second Golden City that we have asked for in the activation process is Malton, which holds constant fruition for mankind, humanity, and her people — that they may attain and complete certain goals held in the mind.

GOLDEN CITY OF WAHANEE

The third city is Wahanee. This is where I serve, arching energy to beloved Portia who serves in that Seventh City in Canada, known as Eabra. It is there that freedom shall be served as that cause on high. And also, the third activation is most important. And we ask for (Wahanee) to be completed as soon as possible. However, Dear ones, if this is impossible, we ask you to hold ceremony at the apex center of Gobean and arch energy over to the Golden City of Wahanee.

GOLDEN CITY OF SHALAHAH

The fourth Golden City that we would like to see activated is Shalahah — it holds continuous consciousness of abundance and healing for mankind. This is the Golden City served by Master Sananda.

GOLDEN CITY OF KLEHMA

The fifth Golden City called into action is Klehma, held by the continuous light of beloved Serapis Bey. It is this city that holds the continuous consciousness for Ascension of humanity at this time. It is also the city that marries the energies of East and West, and both may meet in one continuous consciousness.

THE PRINCIPLE OF SACRIFICE

Dear ones, there are specifics that I would like to share regarding ceremonial activations of Golden Cities. As you have

energy." According to Russians, Earth is a complex life form — a giant sphere of crystal that exhibits crystal-like properties. Images from space lend credence to this theory. Researchers discovered a mosaic of crystalline structures underneath the Earth's surface. These grid-like delineations follow fault lines, UFO sightings, and the boundaries of tectonic plates, the centers of ancient civilizations, and the migratory paths of animals. The trio found distinct, faceted patterns: a series of seven crystalline structures comprising the five Platonic solids and two biologically important crystals, rhombic triacontahedron and rhombic dodecahedron. Each face of the crystal produces a grid map, yielding different results and phenomenon.

But the secrets of the Earth's true makeup reach far beyond present-day theory. Ancient cultures realized our planet's role as a sphere and as a group of crystals. A creation story of the Sioux describes the powers of the earth elements: "In the beginning, all was hoops within hoops, within hoops. These hoops were orbital paths: Earth around the Sun, the Sun's around the center of the Milky Way, and the electron's around the nucleus. Everything at every scale had the same essential spherical shape and orbital path."[1] The conclusion of this Siouan narrative asks humanity to embrace the sixteen hoops, composed of the fifteen edges of Earth's crystal group and the sixteenth orbital path.

The Golden City Grid is actually a mathematical equation based on one additional hoop: this creates sixteen facets on the crystal; the seventeenth forms the final orbital hoop. The number seventeen is noteworthy in other historical and theosophical applications, too. Linked to the Star of the Magi and the birth of the Christ Consciousness, seventeen is a hallmark of ancient Chaldean numerology. This culture believes it is the eight-pointed Star of Venus — an image of love, peace, and immortality. The numerical value of seventeen also shows up in divination practices: the Tarot Star, according to tradition, symbolizes the Divine Power of nature.

3. The Golden Belt of Light is woven into each of the fifty-one Golden Cities. This was accomplished through the timely activation of the Golden Cities and completed with the Great Activation of 2020.

4. See Appendix G1: *Activation Sequence of the Golden Cities.*

5. See Appendix H1: *United States Golden Cities.*

known in the past, we have taught that it is the principle of sacrifice that brings about any activation. However, in this New Time, we would like to teach that it is discipline and labor that brings about activation. We do not see this work as a sacrifice. And it is our intent and our hope for you, that you do not see this work as a sacrifice. However, you and many others realize the labor and the discipline it takes to bring this type of work into action.

THE NORTHERN DOOR: LABOR AND DISCIPLINE

We have always taught that all things come forward in the Mighty Three of Thought, Feeling, and Action, and you know, as well as we have taught, that (the end result of) action brings a noble cause. And from that noble cause, is thus the goal achieved? Is then focus realized? To bring about this focus into manifestation, all must work with discipline and hard labor. And so we ask, Dear ones that before the activations of Golden Cities occur, that ceremonies are performed on two points of the Northern Door. For Northern Door locations (geophysically) birth the New Humanity! These locations also contain a continuous consciousness that is a substance throughout the entire Vortex. (The Golden Cities) allow a leap in consciousness, shall we say, a Star seed Consciousness.[6] We ask you to locate these two (Northern Door) points at will, sensing first through your geophysical or geo-sensitive capabilities.[7] Or, I would also be willing to give you these (Northern Door) locations as we have pointed out the width and circumference of Golden City Vortices and their action.

These two points are important (to locate and visit) so that the intent of labor and discipline is held by all chelas and all disciples of this work. (These disciples) will understand that discipline and hard work will bring forward this mighty action.

TRANSFIGURATION THROUGH THE EIGHTH ENERGY BODY

The time that comes to the Earth Plane and Planet is a glorious time, Dear ones. A time when new plants and birds, new animals, and yes, indeed, you too, shall receive a New Body. This New Body we have spoken of as the Eighth Body of Consciousness, aligns to the Light Ray vibrations of aquamarine and gold (light). This Light Body holds in continuous consciousness energies for transfiguration.[8] And, as I have stated before, this light will bring about the transfiguration of the consciousness to prepare for the times to come. For this reason (alone), it is important to reside in Golden Cities.

COSMIC WAVE MOTION

We have long asked for many of the students and chelas to come forward and live in Golden Cities. However, very few have taken this call seriously. But those who have come realize the great benefit of living in the lighted stance. We have prepared humanity for eon upon eon, readying them for this time; for you see, Dear ones, we've spoken of Time Compaction — when time will slow down and compact, then slow down and compact again.[9] These are known as Cosmic Wave Motions.[10] A Cosmic Wave Motion readies the Earth for the birth of her New (light) Body, known as Freedom Star.

---

6. Star seeds describe a family or group of Fifth Dimensional entities, such as Master Teachers, specifically Sanat Kumara and Lady Master Venus; Saint Germain and Portia; and Mother Mary and Sananda. These spirits bridge the gap between the Great White Brotherhood and other divine fellowships, and earthbound souls. Their goal: to help humanity usher in the Planetary Awakening during the great changes. But some Star seeds, who exist in lower dimensions, continue to incarnate in a physical form. According to mystical teachings, when a soul group reaches Star seed status, twenty-two soul members attain Mastery over the physical plane — thought, feeling, and action.

7. See Appendix I1: *Northern Door Adjutant Points of the Golden City of Gobean.*

8. This new Light Body develops to encourage the growth of Unity Consciousness. It does not, however, belong to the seven energy layers of the Human Aura. Instead, this glow provides an ethereal buffer, a large ball of Golden light, cushioning the body with five to ten feet of Aquamarine luminescence.

9. This phenomenon warps time as Earth enters into the prophesied Time of Change. Our perception of time compresses; it moves at lightning speed; events are squeezed into moments. This experience of time becomes more common as civilizations nears cataclysmic Earth Changes.

10. Cosmic wave motions will play a significant force in the universe, especially during the Time of Change on Earth. These interstellar belts of energy resemble the ebb and flow of tides. Originating from the Sun, cosmic waves drift to certain points in the universe, then recede. And just as the momentum of shoreline ripples collide with the ingoing and outgoing surf, the undulations of the cosmos assume a similar motion, creating an infinite and dynamic flooding of the universe. Cosmic wave motions

A BIRTH INTO A NEW GALAXY

This New Galaxy that she shall be birthed into is known as Unana. She (the Earth) will travel through a crack in the universe that you now know as a black hole. This is a Time of Dimensional Leaping and this type of movement is essential. Conventional time-keeping systems (that you have known) will no longer be used. These perceptions will be changed!

Many Brothers and Sisters who come from other galaxies are (present) on Earth at this time to experience, or shall we say, ride along on the back of this movement as the Earth prepares to enter into that Lighted Shaft of Consciousness, birthing all into a New Time, place, and a New Beginning.

A LEAP IN CONSCIOUSNESS

Many upon the Earth Plane and Planet sense this as a time of hopelessness and despair. However, as you well know, it is the strongest of steel that must go through the fiery furnace. And this furnace, as we all know, is a Time of Testing, a Time of Initiation, a Time of Hard Work, and a Time of Discipline.

But not one of these labors will be lost, for each one of these labors prepares you for this time!

Embodiment after embodiment has also prepared you for this time, for this is a monumental time when the Earth itself leaps in consciousness. The Earth Plane and Planet has experienced these dimensional leaps many other times. However, the current history does not record them. It is important to understand this, and how important and monumental this occasion is. It is also important and monumental that each one of

_____

affect the Earth's inhabitants, particularly the human and animal nervous systems. But, these waves produce positive results, too. They trigger an evolution in consciousness, and initiate a greater understanding of unity and compassion.

According to the I AM America prophecies, the movement of these empyreal swells influences the planets of the solar system, controls time, and subsequently governs evolution. During the Time of Change on Earth, the "jumbling and tumbling" of cosmic wave belts causes the deceleration or compaction of time. Saturn and Neptune, however, toss a lifesaver to Earth, helping the green planet, and ultimately humanity, adjust to the tempestuous eddies.

the Golden Cities is properly prepared (accessed by chelas and students) for this monumental leap in consciousness.

ENTERING THE STAR

Through entering the Star — the center of each Golden City Vortex — we ask you to (ceremonially) activate all Golden Cities. For the apex carries the focal point of energies. Within a twenty-mile radius of the apex are the locations where your Brothers and Sisters of this Great Lodge hope some day to manifest, and to (physically) bring forward their teachings in action. Until that date, Dear ones, it is important to prepare these places to assure that they are ready for this great time, this leap in cosmic consciousness.

Are there questions?

"WORK WITH WHAT IS GIVEN"

Question: "Yes, beloved Saint Germain, there are questions. We have come in conscious awareness to offer ourselves as pillars of light to activate the Golden Cities as you have requested. And we wish to honor the instructions that you are giving about how to go about in the activations. You have mentioned a sequence, first of Gobean, second of Malton, and third of Wahanee. At this time, there are students in the state of Colorado who have come forth and offered this June 9th or 10th, something to that effect, to activate the Golden City of Klehma, making it the third. Is this acceptable, or do you prefer that we wait on that and do Wahanee as you had requested being the third, and then Shalahah, as the fourth and then Klehma? Because I am here to offer service in the way that would be best for all, and I don't care which one it is, but I just want to do it correctly."

As you know, Dear one, all is in within that limit of Free Will and how well we know this upon that plane of consciousness occupied by the human. Free Will adjusts all things, and what we've laid down in terms of activation is the most perfect and serves that greater good. However, we must not tarry in this work; we must work with what has been given to us.

Do you remember that phrase, "turning a lemon into lemonade?" Now's the time to move forward with the work at hand — with the plow in our hand and the field in front of us. This is a time, Dear one, when we must work with what is before us. If we were to wait for the most perfect circumstance, we would wait forever and a day!

Dear ones, work with what is presented to you; work in that Law of the Best and the Highest Good. Work, also, with a plan of ease. When things fall in front of you, one step at a time, follow that plan! Like each rock placed in front of you as you cross a brook of rushing water, you must navigate your next step.

GOLDEN CITY ENERGIES: SOURCE AND DESTINATION

We ask you to consider this on the path of service. If you feel discomfort or resistance, settle back and allow the laws to play out. Do you want to enter into the storms of unreason? We ask you, Dear ones, that if activation (a ceremonial activation) of a Golden City becomes filled with discomfort and disharmonies, retreat to the apex of Gobean, which was activated years ago by another being of light who understood this seed of work. Then, it is important, Dear ones, for you to arc the energies.

Do you remember the lesson I gave you of source and destination? Use the center of Gobean as your source, for you can project those energies to activate another Golden City. Use again, the same formula: seven devoted chelas, dedicated to this work, stating their intent in ceremony. As you have been taught, and as you know, the thought creates. You know too, that there can be another group centered in the apex of Wahanee or Malton. These cities at this time seem to be more difficult for one to access and activate.

Pick a time you may hold together; pick that time to hold your thought in the collective. And there, activation too, can occur. Dear ones, it is important to keep harmony at all times and avoid the bite within your pocketbook. It is important that abundance and prosperity stream in, through, and around all of your (ceremonial) work. If you don't have enough money to go around, it is important to understand that the timing isn't right. Or perhaps (it is better) to call that Mighty Law in to

action and ask that Mighty I AM Presence to bring forward all that you need and all that you would require.

SPIRITUAL ACTIVATION

Dear ones, I bring this teaching in hope that you will understand that activation can also occur without your physical presence in a geophysical location. However, it is important that you hold the immaculate concept as beloved Mary has taught. Those who have come to be gathered in ceremony and ritual at the Golden City of Klehma are called. This is their duty and this is their service — an agreement many of them have made prior to this embodiment. This must be understood. (Those who have come to celebrate) have aligned with the collective will and that vehicle of choice; they now choose to bring forward this active service.

DIVINE INTERCESSION

Dear ones, worry not if you get off schedule. All has been laid down in the most perfect of plans. However, as we all well know, at times mankind is not receptive to the plans of God. It is, however, important at this time that we allow the Divine Intercession of Free Will. In the understanding of the Law of Opposites, each of these cities can be activated in such a manner that will circumvent certain Earth Changes.[11] Each of these Golden Cities can be activated in such a manner that will bring a balance to the Earth, the beloved planet.

THE I AM AMERICA FREEDOM FLAME

Dear ones, understand that at this time all will be laid down in front of you much like those stones over the rushing brook. Worry not if activation comes out of sequence. My only request is that we hold the focus first on the United States and carry the Freedom Flame, onward through Canada. We shall give you further instructions on how to carry this Flame of Freedom,

---

11. Sir Isaac Newton's third Law of Motion, "Every action has an equal and opposite reaction." When this is understood according to Hermetic insight, everything has a pair of opposites, (e.g. hot and cold), and their difference is separated only by degrees.

which will sweep from the South to the North Pole, covering all of America. America's destiny is to hold the focus of this Mighty Cup of conscious light! This service will travel from the heart of her lands to other lands of the world, and it will touch the hearts of many.

MANY HAVE RETURNED FOR THIS SPECIFIC TIME

This is the intention; for America is not only the return of many of those peoples who graced the planet once known as Atlantean, but many Lemurians have returned in physical form (embodiment) to bring about a final service for the beloved planet. Many have returned at this specific time, so they can birth this planet into this New Dimension of Light and Sound.

While it is a dimension of planetary Ascension, creation will continue. For you know, Dear ones, you are created in that mind's eye — the thought of the beloved Creator — and you carry within your heart the same spark of divinity as the Mighty Creator. You are a part of God and cannot be separated from God.

And so Dear ones, even if you were to give up this physical shell, this temporary house — home to your mighty Monad, the individualized Jiva of consciousness — it is important for you to also understand that the evolution and the continuation of the beloved Creator extends into other realms of creation and consciousness.

"ASCENSION IS THE FREE GIFT"

The physical body is not needed to achieve this planetary Ascension. However, there will be those who will opt to take the body with them. This too, can be achieved through hard labor and discipline. The electromagnetism and the vibrations upon the Earth Plane and Planet at this time, and at these geophysical locations known as Golden City Vortices, greatly enhances and assists the physical, emotional, mental, and spiritual bodies into the synergy of Ascension.

Ascension is the free gift. It is the Law of Grace. This is the time, a Time of Awakening. Dear ones, will you come?
Answer: "Yes, we will."

Do you have questions?

THROUGH THE DOORS

Question: "Thank you beloved Saint Germain. That brings great clarity. We will go forth as you have directed. The other question: You mentioned in activating the Golden Cities, two points, the first being, the North Door. Did I miss the second point, or, were you speaking of the Vortex?"

Dear one, these are the two points of the Maltese Cross located on every Golden City Vortex. Should you need assistance, I would be glad to point these out to you later.[12]

The Southern Doors are locations of retreats of healing; the Eastern Doors serve as Lodges, and areas for the gatherings of families and tribes. Western Doors are locations of teaching and information. The Star is a place of ascent.

THOUGHT-VIBRATION

Question: "Thank you, beloved. I understand. I would also like to speak about what you have said regarding the apex of Gobean, which is fully activated. In the two who have come forth this day to offer ourselves of service in activation of the other fifty — other Golden Cities or fifty-one, total — am I to understand that we can begin this work in the physical location of the center of Gobean? We may begin then, as pillars of seven, to do the activations?"

This is so, Dear one. For as I have taught so many times "hold the thought, first. As a man thinks, so he becomes." This Golden Age will be birthed on that vibration, that wave of thought. The Age of Aquarius is an age of thought-vibration when man will learn to discipline his thought as the mighty Co-creator of life!

Answer: "Thank you beloved. Then we will call forth our Mighty I AM Presence to begin that wonderful opportunity to serve and to activate the Golden Cities. And we would call forth your help and your guidance."

---

12. See Appendix J1: *The Four Doors (Gateways) and Star of a Golden City.*

"CALL FORTH THE GOLDEN AGE"

Call forth the Golden Age, the paradise of Utopia. Call it forth in prayer and song. Call it forth in your conscious intention. Call it forth in your consciousness. Call it forth in your thought and your feeling. Call it forth in your actions of ceremony.

THE GALACTIC WEB

Dear ones, these are the components that will birth this New Time; consciousness creates an electromagnetism, and thought is directed as a wave. This is how the Golden Band (Belt) was woven (constructed) around this Earth. And we ask you, Dear ones, to weave a New Web, the Galactic Web, around the planet. Of course, there will come a time when we will appear for planetary assistance. However, until that time, you are our hands; you are our feet; you are our ears; and you are our mouths. Dear ones, go forward in service; weave this web!

Answer: "It will be done, beloved. Thank you."

Are there further questions?

Answer: "No. Thank you beloved."

SYMBOLISM OF THE ROSE

And now I would like to close with instruction regarding the rose. It is important at all times to present the rose in all ceremonies of activation. For this (purpose), the rose symbolizes the ancient lotus of the East as the lotus of the West. We ask for its presence because we have always relied on our symbols to teach. The opening of the rose will open the minds of humanity. Understand that creation is held in thought. Understand the paradise to be birthed.

A New Time awaits all of you, Dear ones — a time that is beyond belief. It is a time long awaited. This time shall come. Hitaka!

CHAPTER EIGHT

Golden City Classes

❧

Saint Germain answers questions.

Greetings beloved, I AM Saint Germain, and I request permission to come forward.

Response: "Please Dear one, come forward."

THE NEW CONSCIOUSNESS

In that Mighty Christ, I AM, I stream forth on the Violet Ray of Mercy and Forgiveness. At this time, Dear hearts, many have gained an interest in the work that was sent through you. This interest is in the messages of the Earth Changes and contained in the Golden Cities.

In this discourse, we would like to present a template; so you will understand the work of the Golden Cities in the United States, and how they help form a New Consciousness in the Time of Change. You have understood that Prophecy comes to awaken not only your eyes and your ears, but your hearts. You will now learn that Earth Changes will lead mankind to begin to understand the Great Reason and the internal being of our soul.[1]

"AT THE FOOT OF THE MASTER"

This has been known through teachings as the metaphor. However, we like to present it as the awakening of the heart. Once the heart is open and present in these teachings, then the soul is ready to stand at the foot of the Master and receive the instructions that will change his or her being forever.

All are interested in and readied for this teaching when they begin to understand the Golden Cities. Each of these structures has been presented as a template for the understanding of global Ascension. Global Ascension in itself is only obtained when a certain percentage of those whose eyes, ears, and hearts are open, and ready to walk on the spiritual path, face each day anew, and follow the path of the Seamless Garment.[2]

The Seamless Garment is woven in, through, and around you as an aggregate body of light. However, it is not woven entirely through thought, although thought is a component. Each thread of the aggregate body of light is woven through an action taken with intentional consciousness and conscience. It is each of these actions that stays within that aura of electromagnetic energy.

Always, each and every one of your actions is subsequently recorded in the Human Aura. Understand that the aggregate body of light is woven through each of those actions that are taken with intention, with consciousness, with conscience. This is known as the alignment of the will, or the alignment of that Mighty Will to the Light of God which never fails!

GOLDEN CITIES AND THE TIME OF CHANGE

There are five Golden Cities that will exist in the United States during this Time of Tumultuous Change on the planet. Each of these cities has been formed to help assist in the Spiritual Awakening of humanity.

Dear one, we have given the exact geometrical locations of these Golden Cities. And each of these Golden Cities and their location are important in terms of the electromagnetism of the Earth during this Time of Change. You are now beginning to understand that the many-ringed map represents a worldwide creation grid.[3] The intersections of these grids help to birth new

---

1. According to theosophical thought, the Monad itself is not self-conscious. In fact, it embarks on an evolutionary pilgrimage to acquire and obtain self-conscious intelligence — the human mind. Man's destiny lies in the beauty and cooperation of infinity. This is referred to as the *Great Reason*.

2. The idea of the Seamless Garment symbolizes perfection and immortality, or what's known as the *Electronic Body*. This is the regalia of the Ascended Masters; not woven by hand, but fashioned by the perfected thought and manifestation process. It is the essence of eternal youth and beauty; it is unbound by limitations; and it exists in a consciousness free of space, time, age, and place. The term also refers to the Ascension Process or a symbol of Oneness — unity.

3. The Ascended Masters refer to a sketch of the Earth's Grid as the "Map of Rings" or the "Many-Ringed Map." It illustrates the relationship among the elements, the Elementals, and the Elemental life forces on Earth; overlapping geomantic bands that often intersect at sacred sites and power points around the globe; and the planet's major lei-lines.

creations which will assist the New Age that follows the Time of Transition and Change.

The Time of Transition and Change may be as short as six years or as long as 1,000 years. This again, Dear ones, will be determined by each choice you make and in each action that composes your aggregate body of light. I have said before, "Gather your aggregate body of light around you, Dear ones and Dear chelas of mine. Each day, take a new action filled with the hope and faith of the Spiritual Awakening." Follow your heart, as I have always taught you Dear ones. Following your desire leads to that greater union, that unity of the ONE — Unana.

TAKE ACTION IN THE LIGHT

This is the full activation of your body of light. Many chelas say, "Let us turn this in to the light, or let us turn this over to the light." I say, "Let us take action in the light, Dear ones." For then and only then is the light brought forward in full activation.

GOLDEN CITIES HOLD CONSCIOUSNESS

The five Golden Cities upon the Earth Plane and Planet in the United States will ideally affect the whole planet. Each of them holds the first seeds of consciousness that will awaken the entire globe to a New Time, a New Era, and a new way of being.

The first of these Golden Cities is known as Gobean (Gõ'-bee-on). Its energy aligns not only to that Vortex of energy known as Shamballa, but to the Middle East and to Egypt — the heart of the beginning of this time. This Vortex will be held for transformation. It is served by that Mighty Master of the Blue Ray known as El Morya.[4]

Beloved El Morya's teachings are to be understood within this Vortex. This Vortex Golden City, which was activated eighteen years ago, was held in continuous consciousness so that a Spiritual Awakening would come. It has held the consciousness that a Spiritual Awakening would happen in the United States.

And therefore, many of the cities located outside this Vortex have also held this consciousness. Do you not see this to be so?

Answer: "Yes."

Now let me explain the higher purpose of holding consciousness in a geophysical location. When you gather for the intent of holding a perfect out-picturing of crystallized consciousness, this form of consciousness takes action, and gathers and collects on a focal point. That point becomes imbued of the characteristics of that specific crystallized thought.

COLLECTIVE CONSCIOUSNESS

When crystallized thoughts gather in one area, as beloved Sananda has often said, two or more (persons) will form a Collective Consciousness in that area. And when Sananda speaks of consciousness, he means the Collective Consciousness in which all partake. The unity of consciousness is found in the concept of Unana: beings of the Deva and Elemental Kingdom, nature, trees, birds, rocks, angelic hosts, and human beings. All these entities participate in the Collective Consciousness imbued within an area.

CO-CREATION AND CHOICE

You are the HU-man beings who have been given the God-characteristics engendered in your will; and since you carry the momentum of choice, you Dear ones, are known as Co-creators. The Co-creator can activate a choice for a greater and a higher good!

Through the activation of choice, imbued with the crystallized characteristic of a focal point, consciousness fills or penetrates all of creation. When a group of HU-mans aligned to the Great and Mighty Will of the I AM gather, and align their focus and their intent for a certain comprehensive characteristic, this allows a consciousness to inner-penetrate this area.

---

4. See Appendix K1: *Master El Morya.*

FOCUS AND OUTPICTURING

I have instructed you to gather in Golden Cities and intentionally share ONE cosmic consciousness to hold ONE focus. In this out-picturing, the Rays of Light and Sound attract. They gather to an area and to that command of the Mighty Will called upon in the name of I AM. At that point and time the Ray penetrates the area by first following the middle structure, as explained in the Prophecies of Earth Change. This extends to the locations taught in terms of mileage or kilometers.

It is important to understand the scientific reasoning of how and why this would happen, and the impact it will have on the world in the future.

In that mighty Vortex gathering of Gobean — the crystallized out-picturing — the mighty focus is on harmony and cooperation. Harmony and cooperation require a great transformation of will and choice.

Many of you have discussed organizations and how this work should be organized. Worry not, Dear ones. For it was organized upon its conception. However, if you would like to gather and learn to further feed your mind for the out-picturing of this Mission, we ask that classes be formed in each of the Golden Cities. These classes follow a structure of each of the characteristics and out-picturing. Do you understand?

Answer: "Yes."

GOBEAN TRANSFORMS CHOICES

Now, let me move forward and give you further details. In the city of Gobean, the structure shall be as follows:
1. Classes taught on the nature of harmony.
2. Classes taught on the nature of cooperation.
3. Classes taught on the nature of choice.

This will help with the out-picturing of consciousness and will help bring structure to the confusion. Many who come to Gobean do not understand that they are aligning their will to the Mighty One Will, and in that alignment comes a disciplined focus.

Beloved El Morya has always taught the path of discipline as the way to achieve. In this Golden City Vortex, many will be brought to a more disciplined approach and an understanding that cooperation is the law that heals all. Cooperation is the law that leads to harmony. And only in harmony, Dear ones, can that Mighty Law of Love be understood and acted upon.

The purpose of Gobean is to transform the choices of humanity. It aligns its magnetic energy to the teachings of the ancient Egyptian mystics. Also, it is important to understand that the electromagnetic grids of Gobean align not only with Shamballa, but to the direct (Akashic) teachings of the Mighty Masters of all eons who have existed upon the Earth Plane and Planet. Geophysically it also aligns its energy to the central point of Earth at its creation and inception known as Giza.

MALTON ASSISTS EARTH'S NATURE KINGDOMS

Now Dear hearts, unless there are any other questions, I shall move on, to the city of Malton.

Answer: "Please continue."

Malton is a (Golden) City that has been brought forward to help cleanse the Deva and Elemental energies at this time. Therefore, beloved Kuthumi has been brought forward as the Master Teacher for this area.[5]

We have come to understand that the Earth's purification at this time is a cleansing and a purification of many systems. This is also a cleansing and a purification of the inner self and those who seek this inner cleansing will realize great fruits — an attainment of the Mighty Divine Mission!

When one understands this, their hearts, their minds, their intent, and their conscious out-picturing aligns with the energies of Malton. It assists the healing and purification of the Deva and Elemental Kingdom. When I speak of these Kingdoms, I speak of the Vegetable and the Flower Kingdom, the Mineral Kingdom, and the Animal Kingdom.

We seek a harmony with these Kingdoms in Malton. Not only as they can express within the human body, but their individualized expressions. It is in the Golden City of Malton that the greatest harmony of these Kingdoms will exist after the Times of Changes.

---

5. See Appendix L1: *Master Kuthumi.*

THE GENTLE GUIDANCE OF KUTHUMI

Great gardens will flourish in these areas. I ask that this be a focal point for the chelas who align their energy to beloved Kuthumi. Again, the aggregate body of light is built on action. Light is indeed love in action. Those who take the hoe into their hands with earnestness for the attainment and the fruition of the soul, walk the path of self-actualization and integrity.

Beloved Kuthumi will guide and direct those toward the gentle purpose of this time. Gentleness is the Divine Mission and the purpose of Malton, and it aligns energies with that of the great Vortex above Glastonbury (England). It also holds a relationship to the Druid cultures, and to those who understand that the Sun and the Moon (the luminaries) rule all.

Dear ones, those who come to this area of Malton, instruct them in classes that enhance knowledge of the Vegetable, Mineral, and Animal Kingdom. For this is where they will understand they're connected to beloved Babajeran (Mother Earth). This is the service of Malton. Do you have questions?

Answer: "No, I understand."

FREEDOM AND JUSTICE THROUGH WAHANEE

Now, let us proceed to the third Golden City known as Wahanee. As you have most recently traveled there, you have now felt the great strife that exists in this area through past inequity and hate. It is important that we understand the nature of freedom and how freedom is attained — only again, through action.

First, the out-picturing of perfect freedom must be understood. Perfect freedom is indeed pathless, and perfect freedom is organized. It is organized first, in the individualized heart. Teachings on individualized freedoms must be brought forward in this Golden City of Wahanee.

Teachings of justice, and individualized freedoms will help humanity and the Earth understand continuous consciousness. It is important for all to understand how governments function on the Earth. It is important to understand the history of humanity. I ask for these classes to come forward from Wahanee:

1. Classes in understanding the governments of the world.
2. Classes in governments, and their relationship to individual rights and freedoms.

This is the focus of Wahanee. Only through the past can the future be understood. Only in the marriage of the past and the future can we live in the present. Only in the present will we understand the infinite, immortal truths.

THE COLLECTIVE CONSCIOUSNESS TRANSFORMS

These teachings will change the heart and the mind of the Collective Consciousness of the world, and these teachings will set men free. Is it not unconditional freedom that we are all seeking at this time?

Dear ones, this Golden City is where I shall serve personally; and I align my energy with my beloved Twin Ray, Portia, who holds her energy in continuous out-picturing in Eabra, in North America. It is important in Wahanee that these classes are held without judgment and without prejudice. These are classes that hold in continuous consciousness the idea of freedom — freedom of expression, freedom from fear. Do you understand?

Answer: "Yes."

ATTENTIVE ACTIVATION

Now, let us move to the fourth Golden City known as Shalahah. We are well aware that you are all preparing yourselves for a ceremony of activation in that Golden City. I have taught activation in this material that is presented, and it is important that these activations occur. However, once a Golden City is activated, it is only again through the (continuous) conscious out-picturing and aggregate actions that allow the Golden City to (consciously) exist!

One cannot simply travel to a Golden City, (ceremonially) activate it, leave, and then say that it is activated and working.

All things work through consciousness. All consciousness moves through the conscious will or choice. The will chooses and creates an action. It is important that activities stream forth from each of these Golden Cities once they are consciously activated.

SHALAHAH HOLDS HEALING AND HOPE

The fourth Golden City of Shalahah is to be of major importance, particularly during the Times of most Tumultuous Change. That is why so many are now moving to this area, for it is an area that holds in the continuity of consciousness, healing, and hope for humanity. And dear Sananda, who understands the constant, vigilant out-picturing of the Christ, will be the teacher.[6]

I ask that classes on healing are taught in Shalahah. It is here that classes be held on the understanding of the Human Aura, the understanding of the body-mind connection, and the understanding that joy is lived each day as chosen.

Dear one, this is the perfect location for any school of healing to be held. And I am sure that you understand those who come, must first choose.

SERAPIS BEY AND KLEHMA

Now, let us move to the fifth Golden City known as Klehma. Klehma is held in continuous consciousness by beloved Serapis Bey.[7] He understands the Ascension Process requires complete cooperation — cooperation in the body, in the thoughts, and in the feelings.

It is here that the cooperation of thought, feeling, and action will come forward for the sole purpose of the perfect out-picturing of harmonious Ascension.

In the past, most Ascensions were obtained by men and women who isolated themselves from societies, and found, shall we say, that highest mountain peak. They became hermits of sorts, to understand the wisdom and secrets that existed in the timeless and in the immortal.

6. See Appendix M1: *Lord Sananda.*
7. See Appendix N1: *Serapis Bey.*

TIMELESS TRADITIONS AND WISDOM

In this area (Klehma) and during the Time of Great Change, many people will begin to understand this wisdom and it will exist on a global scale. These are the principles that will rule mankind at this time; these wisdoms are timeless and immortal. And in this area, I ask for these Ascension teachings to come forward. Beloved Serapis Bey will hold his timeless and immortal consciousness in this area.

This Vortex is held or aligned with the teachings of Native Americans, who traveled from the mouth of the Indus River across the Aleutian time-bridge (Aleutian Islands), and are now known as the tribal indigenous people of North and South America. Their teachings must come forward in this area and bridge again the Eastern and Western Worlds. These teachings demonstrate the timeless and the immortal.

THE ACTIVE TRUTH

Again, let these teachings have action! Let these teachings carry forward in all societies. Let these teachings carry forward in all man-made governments. Search for the timeless. Search for the immortal. And there you will find the natural cooperation of all structures.

This is the teaching of Klehma, and it holds the consciousness for Ascension. Ascension attaches to what is real and disconnects the unreal. Ascension is an activity and an understanding that is the truth.

It is here in Klehma that classes on truth and the truths contained in all spiritual teachings be brought forward. Beloved Serapis Bey will serve this focus and those who wish to align their will to his teaching.

This is the network that covers these five Golden Cities. Let me go over these again, in case we have missed any details.

FIVE CULTURES

The first Golden City of Gobean aligns itself to Egyptian teachings.

The second Golden City of Malton aligns itself to the teachings of the Druids (Celtic teachings).

The third Golden City of Wahanee aligns its teachings to that of the African tribal peoples.

The fourth Golden City of Shalahah aligns its teachings to that of the Eastern India (Ancient Kingdom of Magadha).

And that final Golden City Klehma aligns itself to the teachings of the Native Americans (Indigenous people of North America).

Now, I shall step back from this lectern and you may ask questions.[8]

MOVING FORWARD

Question: "It would seem that the outlines for each of these cities, is comprehensive. And even though short in detail, extremely long in action and activity of fulfillment. Occasionally we have those who ask us questions. And we have one from an individual who we know well. His name is Bob. Bob has a question. He asks about the project we're working on with the celestial teachers Morgan and Rachel who are working through Daniel and Alara. The work and wisdom seem excellent. But Daniel and Alara are concerned that they may be filtering information. Could you please check with Saint Germain? Is our work on the right track? Are Daniel and Alara conveying their channeled information without distortion?"

All channeled work seeks to understand the infinite internal, and it always leads one further along the path, does it not? Daniel and Alara who say that they are receiving instruction, are indeed receiving instruction from the assistance of beloved Serapis Bey. At times, they might want to call upon the Master Teacher of Klehma, and ask for the teachings to come forward.

As in all cases of work given to a heart, and then spoken through sound and vibration, a human element is always present. It is important to understand this and the HU-man who will put it into action![9] It is important to put teachings in action or, they are not teachings.

Teachings come forward to instigate action, crystallize thought, clarify feelings, and bring motion forward.

Ask of yourself, am I moving forward? And then you will know the truth of the teaching. Am I moving forward? You must ask that question of yourself in all teachings you receive. Even those from myself! If you are not moving forward, then you must take the appropriate action.

THE ADEPT

Question: "Are you saying that all teachings come to a place of being and living, breathing activity of your life?"

The adept is one who not only understands the perfect outpicturing, the crystallized focus of the teaching, but lives it.

ON SERVICE

Question: "That is clear. Thank you. We have some other questions. Friends of ours, Theresa and George, would like to know what their highest and best service would be during the Earth Changes?"

To align their wills at this time to the teachings contained in each of the five Golden Cities. Both of these life-streams have been brought forward at this time to help serve at this Time of Awakening. These two beings have known one another throughout many embodiments and have served in many levels of organization. Now it is important that they balance and harmonize their energies. One understands the Elemental nature of this work. The other understands the more practical and more organized application of this work. It is important

---

8. Every Golden City holds specific Akashic Records of ancient civilizations and cultures. These Fifth Dimensional libraries include:

Gobean — Ancient Egypt, aligns to Giza.

Malton — Druid; aligns energy with the great Vortex above Glastonbury, "Denasha."

Wahanee — Ancient African tribal peoples and the Ancient Civilization of the Sahara Desert. Aligns with the Golden City "Eabra," located in Alaska and Canada.

Shalahah — Vedic culture and the Ancient Civilization Magadha of Eastern India.

Klehma — the Native American culture and the civilizations of North and South America. This Golden City will bridge the spiritual teachings and the traditions of the East and West.

9. *HU* is an ancient name for God. When HU is combined with 'man,' it elevates humanity to the divine: the God-man. According to the Master Teachers, HU (pronounced 'hue'), when used as a mantra, invokes the Violet Flame throughout the aura. The mantra's lulling tone activates the Eight-sided Cell of Perfection and the perfected God-source within.

that they help and assist in the organization of classes in each of these five Golden Cities.

One is more directed toward the healing arts. The other is more directed toward the healing of the Earth. It is important that these two energies know they are arcing energy back and forth for the purpose of activity.

Question: "When you are referring to classes, who are you asking to teach these classes?"

Those who have aligned their wisdom and their understanding to the crystallized focused out-picturing of each Golden City. Do you understand?

Question: "How does one know if one is aligned?"

Do you not see? Do you not hear? Have we not worked with discernment? Do you understand?

ACTIVATION IS THE BEGINNING

Question: "Another question that they have is about the date and their participation in the Shalahah activation?"

Again, as I have stated, activation is important. However, it is the continuous out-picturing of that crystallized thought through action that is indeed even more important. Activation is the seed; it is the start, it is the beginning, it is the birth. It is important then, that all things that are birthed, grow and mature.

SOUL MATES

Question: "Another question comes from Spotted Pony, and she asks, what is the definition of a soul mate?"

A soul mate, or shall we say, soul mates, are beings who have been together in many embodiments, and through the course of several embodiments, have decided before the current lifetime to take on a certain Mission together. That Mission may be achieved through many means.

Missions accomplish perfect out-picturing.

Sometimes, soulmates are the blending of opposite octaves. Sometimes they are the harmonizing of a focus that is similarly aligned. It is important to understand that soul mates may vibrate at many different levels, and it is also important to understand that soul mates often vibrate at compatible or harmonious levels. However, they are brought together in a union to achieve a desired result — one that was chosen before the embodiment.[10]

OVERCOMING CRISIS

Question: "Since we have just discussed how soul mates work together, we have another question. What is Lee G.'s role in Earth Changes?"

This being has come forward with an understanding of the nature of crisis. And as there may be times in the days to come times when many people will feel a sense of cataclysmic crisis; this person understands how to help others overcome crisis consciousness and see that every lemon is made into lemonade!

ASSISTING OTHERS

Question: "What is the highest and best communication for those unaware of the Earth Changes?"

Of course, this too has been a concern for us at this level. First, it is important to teach the spiritual way. It is important to teach that hope, faith, trust, and love are the most important attributes to develop. For only through the development

---

10. Some people experience an unexplained bond with another person — this is called a soul mate. These spirits have known each other in past lifetimes as lovers, friends, parents, children, siblings, or any other type of close relationship; and before they enter into physical bodies, they agree on specific and important roles to achieve during their life on Earth. And the functions are endless. The Master Teachers often refer to these objectives as a Mission. The term soul mate denotes the essence of harmony and compatibility; however, in many cases this is far from the truth. Soul mates can be the best of friends during their ethereal existences and mortal foes on Earth. The key point of a soul mate is the notion of desired results — the agreements made before an incarnation.

of these attributes can anyone circumvent both cataclysmic and personal destruction

This should be taught and placed at the forefront. Yes, it is important too, to deliver the message. For sometimes, those who have hardened their hearts and closed themselves off to the message of love will hear first the message of losing something to which they are so attached. It is important to blend the spiritual and material, and bring both forward, as I stated before. Much like soul mates coming together as opposites, yet opposites sometimes produce attraction. This attraction can stimulate a desired result.

PROPHECY UNITES

Answer: "Yes, I understand. We have further questions. This is from Shanti: do human archetypes play a role in how people perceive Prophecy?"

Prophecy is Prophecy. Prediction is prediction. Love is love. That is the most important thing to understand. Prophecy strives to unite love and hate or fear, so that one may come to a point of conclusion. That is the inner work that must be done. Prophecy helps bridge the gap of two worlds colliding. Do you understand?

INDIVIDUALIZATION

Answer: "Yes. I do understand that. How do we change the archetypes of man to allow this New Era to come forward?"

There is no archetype of man, for man is individualized![11] How can you archetype a snowflake? How can you archetype a thumbprint? There is no archetype of man. Man is here to take his identity. That is the path.

---

11. To understand the spiritual meaning of this word, return to its Latin root *individuus*, which means indivisible and whole; cannot be divided.

PROPHECY AND PREDICTION

Question: "Understood. What is the relationship between psychic predictions and prophecies?"

Psychic prediction relies upon the electromagnetic currents of the present moment. Also, it relies upon the interchange and the interaction of that moment. Prophecy is a philosophy and a spiritual teaching.

Question: "Understood. What is the relationship of Free Will and future predictions?"

We have always taught that your future lies in the moment of your choice. Will is choice. The choices that are made today create the future. You are now living the end result of a great line of your choices of the past. Look carefully at your life and you will understand this.

Question: "Yes, I do. What is a person to do with the fear that is generated by psychic predictions?"

He who knows himself and functions with love, faith, hope, and trust. Does he worry?

Answer: "Truly not. Prophecy is a philosophy of spiritual teachings of actions chosen within certain life experiences. Many people who consider the life experience of death as the end will see more death as a result of an Earth Change on the planet. How would you ask people to deal with this in their hearts?"

You, as light bearers, forbearers of the future, Prophecy has been given to you so you will become teachers and pillars of consciousness! Prophecy has been given to you so that you understand the cohesiveness of natural law. Prophecy has been given to you so that you understand balance and that both sides exist simultaneously.

THE END OF A CYCLE

These times will come, as all cycles must come to an end. All cycles travel the sequence of birth, growth, maturity, and decay. You are now in a cycle of decay, and because you are in a cycle of decay, do not forget who you are and your Divine Mission! Death is part of this cycle. Understand through death comes rebirth. Do you not see this exampled in nature? Do you not see this exampled in your own life? Think of a time when you experienced spiritual death within only to be reborn again anew! This teaching of the Christ consciousness exists as super-consciousness, ready to birth itself out of death!

Follow the teachings, Dear ones, forbearers, light bearers, and pillars of light! Understand the warning contained in the spiritual teaching of Prophecy. You must always live with an understanding of the cycles and the warnings. Understand how important each choice is that you make.

ALTER THE OUTCOMES

Question: "Can we alter these prophecies with our choices?"

We cannot alter the cycle. However, we can alter outcomes of cycles. We can alter many things through the ways we see them. Is this not true? Is the glass half full? Is the glass half empty? Can we make lemonade from a lemon? These are all things we must begin to understand to alter any situation. Have you not met two Brothers: one who sees only the bad and one who sees only the good? Have different things happened in their lives? On the surface, they've probably lead similar lives; however, the difference is how they see their lives. One sees what they do not have, another sees what they do have. It is through the blending of these two perceptions that we begin to understand and Master duality.

Question: "Understood. Is there anything for those individuals who are agnostic or atheistic, or those who don't necessarily have an opinion one way or another to consider about Prophecy?"

Live each day with a personal sense of Prophecy. Understand that you create your Prophecy each day of your life. Understand that Prophecy is part of you as the Teacher and the Healer. Prophecy is the Mystic that exists in all of us. Prophecy is created each day as we choose to live.

Question: "Does a cause-and-effect relationship exist among the gradual deterioration of the environment, humanity, and the Earth Changes?"

"DO NOT FEAR"

It is part of the cycle. It is part of this time. It is the completion of a time for mankind to grow and to learn; this cycle must be completed. To circumvent this completion is moving backward, and such energy would be counterproductive.

Do not fear the times ahead of you! This is a time to practice what you have learned and know.

PROPHECY AND CULTURE

Question: "Do survivalists or paramilitary groups have an appropriate answer to the future?"

They have the answer that is for them. Again, truth is pathless when we begin to understand choice and freedom.

Question: What is the relationship of Christian Biblical Prophecy and the Ascended Masters' Prophecies?

Those Christian Prophecies were the prophecies given at that time. Prophecy is always for the present moment. Prophecy is given for those cultures to understand at that given time. Is it difficult for you to understand the prophecies of those times? Those were prophecies given to the people of that culture, of that time.

These are prophecies given for people of this time.

Question: "Do prayer, meditation, and acts of charity affect the future?"

As always, those out-picturings of trust, faith, hope, and love change all things, and make a day much brighter and more useful. Isn't it more pleasant to live the Law of Love than to live with fear? Only those who have experienced this would understand. Of course, they do!

Know that we are with you. Know that our vibration is there in service. Know that you may call upon us and we may assist you. Have we not proven this already?

Answer: "This is true. I thank you for your guidance and counsel."

CHAPTER NINE

Vibrational Shifting

☙

Saint Germain with a friend.

Greetings in that Mighty Christ, I AM Saint Germain, and I request permission to come forward.

Response: "Dear one, please come forward. You have permission."

THE THINNING SHEATH

Dear ones, the work upon the Earth Plane and Planet is one where I say again, tarry not! For the accelerations in the dimensions, in the sheath that exists between the Third and the Fourth Dimension, is thinning on a daily basis. As you know this is a Time of Transition; it is also a Time of tumultuous Change.[1] We have come forward to bring our service, our vibration, and our energy to assist you, Dear one, in taking the next step toward that mighty gift of the Ascension.

---

1. This is a system of new energies that are present on the Earth as outlined in the teaching, "Vibrational Shifting," which includes these processes:
   A. The thinning of the barrier or sheath that exists between the Third and Fourth Dimensions.
   B. Insanity is sometimes caused by small tears in the barrier skin of the dimensions and the thinning of the dimensions. This produces the phenomenon of "dimensional plane-ing," as the dimensions slip into one another.
   C. Dimensional plane-ing affects the entire human Chakra System, good and bad, depending on the ability of the individual to qualify the new energies. During times of Dimensional Acceleration the I AM Presence assists the awakening of the chakras.
   D. Dimensional Acceleration assists and aids the Ascension Process, known as "the Higher Law."
   E. The Violet Flame calms the energy centers — chakras — during this process.
   F. To begin the process of integrating new energies, take saltwater baths. Dissolve one container of table salt or one cup of Epsom Salts along with an essential oil of your choice, e.g. violet, rose, jasmine, sandalwood, and so on.
   G. During Dimensional Acceleration, the reflection from the Moon's emotional energy through the Earth is intensified within the individual. The collective psychological body of humanity is affected by this phenomenon.

CHAOTIC ENERGY

It is a time when things are changing rapidly. And many people around you are changing, too. Have you now had lessons of experiencing another who is in the process of losing bits of their reality? You call this insanity. However, we know this, too, as only a symptom of vibrational-shifting, rifting, or tearing. The energy is so impacted on and within the individual that they can no longer deal with their own centers of energy.

This is why we have given you so many instructions in the different centers of energy — your Chakra System — so that you can understand. There is also much energy flooding the Earth Plane and Planet at this time. The chakras or energy centers are imploding upon themselves, as if the chaotic energy does not know where to go. The individuals do not know how to qualify or use the new energy. Do you understand?

Answer: "Yes."

ADDICTIONS AND THE TIME OF CHANGE

This insanity, along with increased drug and alcohol addiction, will become more common in this Time of Change. Because, Dear ones, these are people who have simply failed to understand choice. We have said over and over again "you, yourself, are doing the choosing." Although we ask you to make a decision, you are actually the ones who align your will to the Divine. Your choice to stay in that stalwart commitment — commitment to the Mighty I AM — allows you to awaken and utilize these centers of energy for the service of all.

SERVICE AND COMPASSION

As we have stated, the way to take the next step up this evolutionary ladder is to be of service to your Brother and Sister. This will help you abandon self-aggrandizing ideas while allowing you to access the energy of unity.

Only in compassion are all things united. Have compassion for those around you, even though they are a bit insane at this time! Have this compassion for them, Dear ones, for indeed it has been stated before, "They know not what they do."

However, in this time and with this acceleration of energies occurring, there is also a higher law. And we ask you to consider using this energy influx to help lift you to that next step — that new level of understanding.

USE OF THE VIOLET FLAME

At this time it is important to spend time alone in the Violet Flame. This calms and centers the activation of your energy centers. Apply what we have taught, Dear ones, to awaken your cellular energy.

CALMING BATHS

It is important to take calming baths in a saline solution. To create a saltwater bath, mix one cup of salt, along with the essential oils of violet or jasmine, in your bathwater. Also, adjust your dietary standards to align with thoughts of harmony and beauty within the body. (Editor's Note: this is in reference to a conscious diet.) These molecular adjustments are planetary in nature, and they do affect the Earth and Sun through waves that reflect from the Moon.

MOON ENERGETICS

You have heard that the Earth affects the Moon. However, this is the reflection of energy from the Moon to the Earth. And so, it is important to understand that these are planetary influences; learn to integrate them into a higher nature or energy.

This is also a time when the Earth may go through tremendous upheaval and geophysical changes. Therefore, it is important to understand that before such great movements happens, the psychological body of humanity must go through many changes and upheavals, too.

POLITICAL AND SOCIAL CHANGE

Over the next five years, you will see many changes in the political and social systems of the United States. As stated always in the prophecies of change, it is the United States that will first go through these geophysical changes. And therefore, many of the social and political changes will begin in the United States. It is important to observe the next presidential election. For in this election, you shall see the coming together of the inevitable flurry between light and dark forces. It is important to watch this, to understand it, and to identify it. For its outcome will determine the extent of many Earth Changes.[2]

As we have stated in the Six-Map Scenario, it is up to the collective choice of humanity to determine what will become of the Earth and her peoples, and to decide the inevitable outcome of these times. Some outcomes can be predicted by taking a look at the current political and social unrest of the peoples of this planet.

It is important to pay attention to social systems, and it is important to understand that their breakdown is inevitable. Why many of these changes are inevitable is what we would know as a type of "death-cadence." It is important also, to understand that through death comes birth. Death allows the new cycle of birth.

A NEW WAY EMERGES

Perhaps you have realized, Dear ones, that as you let go of an old idea — something that no longer serves your needs, even if it's an old piece of clothing, or a way of thinking or doing things — a new way of being emerges in your life. Have you not noticed that when you discard an old piece of clothing, a new garment comes quickly?

It is important, Dear ones, to understand that at this time death-cadence (decadence) is all around you, but a birth awaits you. This birth is cellular and physical, yet filled with the majesty of the heavens! It's a collective birth that coincides with the system of the Earth Mother. You are of it, and it is of you. You are all connected to that Mighty ONE!

As we have stated in other laws, specifically, in the Law of Rhythm, unity is in all, and corresponds to those Laws of Rhythm.

---

2. Saint Germain is referring to the controversial election of year 2000. Many of the negative events of that time period were the dark forces attempting to negate the possibility of humanity's collective entrance into Timeline Two. Timeline One and Timeline Two are thoroughly explained in future teaching from Saint Germain. See *Evolutionary Biome*.

DIMENSIONS SLIP

You may experience a time in this energy shifting — what we refer to as dimensional plane-ing — a time of one dimension slipping into another. Time seems to fall backward, and then it may move forward. Whatever way you move is your choice, Dear ones. That is why we stand here in support, and hold at all times the thought of the Mighty I AM. We stand with the out-picturing of thought, holding you in perfection.

Dear ones, during this Time of Dimensional Plane-ing, a tunnel is created between the Third and Fourth Dimensions — you may enter it. Think of it as a staircase: one step up at a time.

You have been studying the Laws of Octaves, and it is important to understand that this barrier you are entering is known as shock. In these times, energy may slide back and forth uneasily and easily.[3] Do you understand?

---

3. The relationship of planets, colors, and musical notes are said to be based on the Law of Octaves — also known as the *Law of Seven*. The ancients knew and understood this concept. They saw the Sun as analogous to that of white light; it contained the seeds of every tone and color potential. Since sight has a restricted cognition of range, as compared to hearing (the ear can register nine to eleven octaves, the eye registers seven fundamental color tones), certain colors are compared to musical notes, this table follows:

1. Red, the lowest color tone, equals the musical note, Do
2. Orange = Re
3. Yellow = Mi
4. Green = Fa
5. Blue = Sol
6. Indigo = La
7. Violet = Ti

The eighth color tone that completes the scale becomes a higher octave of red. It is also important to note that the three fundamental notes of the musical scale, the first, the third, and the fifth, correspond with the three primary colors — red, yellow, and blue. Interestingly, the seventh note and color — violet — is the transition to the next octave.

Another way to understand the Law of Octaves is to understand vibrations and their infinite patterns of appearance: ascending and descending orders; fine and coarse; weakening and strengthening; crossing and colliding; and so on. Octaves can accelerate or retard at different moments of development. This is due to the structure of the musical seven-tone scale, including intervals and absent semitones. Because of this, the progress and the development of phenomena on all planes are not ruled by straight lines; the difficulty of thoughts and harmonious actions often come about in ways opposite to what we wanted or anticipated. Yet, what this law teaches is invaluable.

The Law of Octaves demonstrates that nothing in the world stays the same and nothing is static; everything is changing and moving along the lines of octaves. Nothing can develop by staying on one level, yet in

Answer: "Yes."

ENERGIES FLUCTUATE

The laws we have given you are important. Pay attention and follow the energy.

This energy fluctuates: it can force you backward, catapult you forward, or keep you in one place. Again, these are your choices. You have witnessed those who have used drugs and alcohol. They are people who now use their voices within the theater of the mind to create insanity.

You too, have the same choice to align your will. Dear ones, are there questions?

OVERWHELMING EMOTION

Question: "How does it affect your mind when this energy slides back and forth?"

It is unsettling, of course, to the mental body. However, as we begin to understand the Laws of Pitches or Laws of Octaves, it creates a sound vibration within the mental body. The disunity of bodies abrasively corrodes the others, causing an overlapping — which is not transmuted — of emotional substance. All the emotions not yet transmuted or transformed into a higher purpose overshadow the mental body. There, the mental body, or that which is the thinking body, is overwhelmed by emotion. Its purpose loses definition.

Question: "Does this cause memory loss as well as insanity?"

Not only memory loss, but mental loss — corrosion of the mental body.

---

understanding descending and ascending cycles, vibrations develop in an orderly manner, following the same direction in which they started.

In ascending cycles, according to the Law of Octaves, the first interval occurs between Mi and Fa. A greater intensity is needed to develop between Ti and Do. In descending cycles, the greatest interval occurs at the beginning of the Octave after the first Do; the material that fills it is found within itself or in lateral vibrations. For this reason alone, descending cycles develop easier than ascending octaves.

Question: "How do you heal this so that you can remember day to day what's going on?"

It is important to watch the vibrations of those around you at this time. Do not engage in their emotional outbursts. It is most important to stay within the focus of your own being — into the center of your own I AM.

SILENCE IN NATURE

It is important to spend time in silence, and you personally require this. There, your mental stability can regain its footing. Spend your time in nature, especially in wooded areas and near running water.

Question: "So my mind has slipped on the ice. Can I help my emotions? Will silent time help my emotions also?"

EMOTION, THOUGHT, AND THEN ACTION

When an emotion comes up and begins to crowd the thinking, it inhibits crystallized thought. It is then important to use thought to contain the emotion. Emotion is quite different from feeling. Feeling comes from the instinctive body. An emotion, however, comes from a higher frequency of the Emotional Body; and is closer to a crystallized thought. Emotion bonds thought to action. Emotion, which allows action to take place, is related to the fields within the sphere of the Human Aura or energy bodies.

It is important to understand that emotion is like an adhesive glue of thought to action.

THE DREAMSTATE

Question: "Then, would the new energy affect the Dream World in a different way also?"

The energy you carry about your being is what you use to travel at night. This is known as the higher Emotional Body, an Astral Body often used at the time of dreaming. However, some people have developed higher mental bodies. They use them in alchemic marriages — the fusing of higher emotional states with higher mental bodies. This forms a stronger body for astral projection into the dream state.

Sometimes in the dream state you may feel as if you are being attacked. You may feel a sense of impending doom. This is, of course, being carried out through the Emotional Body. These residues have not yet crystallized into physical action.

EARTH CHANGES AND CHOICE

Question: "Can I ask about my Sister's dream of sliding in a house and finding firm ground, she and her daughter?"

The location where she is presently living is geo-physically unsafe. And she is currently feeling the geophysical residue (Earth Changes) that may occur in the future.

Question: "Will Nevada be a safe place?"

This of course, is contingent upon the choices of humanity. However, the area she's considering moving to is filled with environmental pollutants. Her energies are conducive for the states of Wyoming and Montana.

COMPLETING A CYCLE

Question: "Is all of Alaska unsafe? What about the Aleutian Islands?"

Much of this area, of course, is affected by the Pacific Ring of Fire. And, if the planet as a system enters into the Time of Great Change, this area will experience many shattering earthquakes. It is important to live in an area where you feel called, and are able to fulfill your destiny or your service to humanity. For at this time, many people will be called to live in areas that will inevitably end up under water. Yet, it is important for these individuals to move to these areas as they feel called. This is a Time of Completion and the ending of cycles. It is a time when we must remain committed to the choices that we have made.

It is important now to play every last note of this octave. It is important that we allow our choices to play out the last crystallized activity. It is also important, Dear ones, to remember that at this time, only a few will have the ability to move or live in a safe place. It is important to act on every desire, so a New Time can enter.

HUMANITY MOVES FORWARD

This thinning of the Veil is indeed, purposeful. One may ask, "What is the purpose of this, and wouldn't it be easier to stay with what we have already experienced?" Dear ones, please understand this: the Time of Change will move humanity forward and reshape the entire planet.

This is a Time of Unana, a Time of the Activated Christ.[4] This is a time when we will experience Oneness and unity beyond the Earth Planet — this is a Oneness and a unity with the universe.

This area you question, Alaska, is an area that will go through many geophysical changes — not only earthquakes, but volcanic activity. However, if your Sister is called to stay in this area, it is important for her to be trained with medical knowledge. She has an aptitude for this; she received preparation in previous lives and in other schools of understanding of the workings of the Human Body. She could be of great assistance in the Time of Change by helping many in medical clinics and hospitals. Is this not true?

Answer: "True. And possibly she could do the same even in Nevada or California or any place."

---

4. Unity Consiousness. This is the path leading to this state or level of consciousness starts with the simple Mastery of thoughts, feelings, and actions. The union of these three energy bodies — the mental, emotional, and physical — produces the Alchemical marriage of the masculine and feminine forces in the body. "This initiates Unity Consciousness," says Master Saint Germain. He adds, however, that individuality or the undivided state comes first. Proceeding is the next natural state, contact with the ONE. This higher form of consciousness is all-knowing, all-pervading, and all-powerful. In this state of existence, all is connected as one larger, non-physical, yet thinking and feeling body. "Unana," (pronounced ooh-nah'-na) is the name the Ascended Masters have given to this level of inter-connectedness, where the mind moves beyond individuality and into a unified field of consciousness.

It is possible indeed. These are the choices. I am only sharing knowledge with you at this level, so she may use this information to assist her choice.

"WE ARE ALL CONNECTED"

Question: "When everything is based on a group rather than an individual, how much individual Free Will or protection can we generate? Or, are we bound by the group, the group consciousness, compared to the individual? How much Free Will does the individual have? Can you protect yourself and be guided to do what you need to do?"

It is important to understand the energy contained by the individual. Take for instance, a pool of water. Dip a glass into the pool. Hold the glass away from the pool, and let it sparkle in the Sun. Is that not the individual — who is like the glass — contained of that one pool? The pool and the glass exist independently. Yet, the pool and the glass contain the same water. Is this an example of the ONE? Inevitably, yes. But the glass alone, is it not the ONE? It is not the ONE, but of the ONE.

Individuality is, shall we say, the pooling of many forces! Please understand — we are all connected as ONE. Even we, in this dimension, are connected to you at your dimension. This connection extends to plants, vegetables, insects, and minerals — they're all connected within and as ONE.

MASTERING THOUGHT, FEELING, AND ACTION

However, on the path this is a discipline — understanding individuality. Every soul that comes to this planet seeks embodiment or pursues a path to understanding their individuality. Once individuality is completed, other courses are available to explore, or shall we say, to Co-create.

However, at this moment, you understand the forces within the individual; you are Mastering the forces — those commonly known as thought, feeling, and action — within. You will first work with, gain an understanding of, and contain these forces. Once this is achieved, other courses will be given.

At this present time, however, Mastering these forces is as simple as thought. The union of all three — thought, feeling, and action — produces an Alchemical Marriage, and unites the masculine and feminine forces within the body. This initiates Unity Consciousness — the Mighty Unana, as we have spoken of before, Dear ones. However, at this time it is important that we put our focus, and our attention, on what we must Master first. That is, individuality. And then we will focus our attention on the universalities of all things.

SELF-AWARENESS AND DESTINY

Question: "Is there any way that we are going to alter, as an individual, alter anything … or is it now set what will happen?"

Of course, there is collective Free Will — collective choice. There have been many moments throughout the history of humanity when choices were made that altered destiny. However, destiny is more or less, unalterable.

Each and every person has played out a destiny in previous embodiments — a destiny may play out in this embodiment or future embodiments. This destiny is like a web; it is part of a line that exists in the Plane of Consciousness known as time. Each embodiment resembles a dot that encapsulates moments of destiny.

Men often refer to this as fate. However, we would like to refer to it as self-awareness. It is important to understand that all things work for the common good. It is also important to understand that the good and the light — the right way — is always coming forward, even though it seems to be left-handed or a wrong way. Always see through self-awareness that the right way or better way is an evolution happening before your eyes.

MIXTURE AND BALANCE

As you understand that all things work together for the good of all, you will then begin to understand that everything is somewhat predestined. Yet, Free Will is present. Individuality is present. Free Will and individuality are working in the harmony of mixtures and balance.

PEACE OF MIND THROUGH SERVICE

Question: "What else can you tell me about my Sister's personal life? Can I do anything to help her find peace of mind? Since she quit drinking, she doesn't seem to have a life of her own, other than her children. What advice can I give her?"

As I have said before, she would do best by giving service to others. This service may or may not be given to the family. However, it will most likely be found in medical institutions, for there is a natural aptitude that has been gained in other embodiments. She also has an aptitude toward natural healing, and understands the application not only of acupressure and acupuncture points, but of herbs and the healing of the body.

It is perhaps to her best advantage to study these things and to reawaken the memory obtained from many lifetimes. It is then important that she utilize her knowledge for the service of humanity. There will be many who will appreciate the service that she could offer.

Answer: "Thank you. I have no more questions."

I shall close and will be most happy to return in the service of the breath, the sound, and the light …

Response: "Thank you very much."

CHAPTER TEN

Closing the Circle

∿

Saint Germain helps a friend.

Greetings my beloved, I AM Saint Germain, and I AM here to bring discourse and guidance. Do you have any questions before we proceed?

THE LAW OF ATTRACTION

Question: "I need to know about how I got into this jam that I'm in. Why am I experiencing all this fear? What can I do to make peace with this person who is stoned out of their mind?"

Again, let me remind you of the Laws of Attraction and Repulsion we have taught so many times and of which you are aware.

These laws, which are the Laws of Duality, govern the world of form. The Laws of Attraction and Repulsion continuously serve the evolution of the soul on the Earth Plane.[1] The evolution of the soul is always compelled or propelled by the Laws of Attraction and Repulsion.

The soul takes in its journey a series of lessons to be learned. Some lessons are brought through a natural course of action through the Law of Rhythm; sometimes through the Laws of Octaves; sometimes through the Laws of Death and Rebirth; and sometimes through the Law of Love. And in this case the lesson is learning the Laws of Attraction and Repulsion — a Law of Duality, of opposites attracting. This also allows a fusion of Universal Laws to serve for education. In this case, one, whom you have known in many other embodiments, has been

brought to your path. Not only as a Brother but as a father. You have known one another many times. Does he not carry energy, a vibration, of your own biological father in this embodiment?

Answer: "Exactly — totally."

A SOUL'S EVOLUTION

This is the purpose of this lesson: to close the energy so you may move on for the evolution of your own soul. It is important that this has happened at this time in your life. For after you jump over this hurdle that is in front of you, brought by the Law of Repulsion, this allows the Law of Attraction to come forward in your life.

This too, serves the greater cause and the greater purpose. It has been said, "In the best and the highest good." This means that in the greater law of all comes the harmony of all voices. There is a harmony in mixtures when light and dark meet together in one homogeneous manner, and a unity of consciousness is achieved. It is a way that one is brought forward in evolution. It is a way that one is brought to a greater understanding.

Dear Sananda has taught that all points comprise the circle. It is a time, yes, for the circle to close; it's also a time when the spiral within the circle comes forward. This is the lesson in front of you.

ADDICTION AND SUBJECTIVE ENERGY BODIES

Question: "Why are so many people using drugs?"

It is, of course, a time when society is de-structuring. A time when many people are escaping from the reality they will be facing in the next ten to twenty years. This reality is hard for them to understand. Again, it is the Law of Repulsion and the Law of Attraction.

Addictive substances create subjective bodies that many people in these induced states clothe themselves with.[2] For

---

1. This physical and spiritual truth serves as the foundation of the Law of Duality — the Yin and the Yang. In simple terms, like charges repel and unlike charges attract: the Law of Polarity. Under these circumstances, everything in nature follows one of two opposite paths, each with its own essence. Life exists on a spectrum, one that offers an infinite number of possibilities between its opposite ends: darkness is less light; fear is less courage. Of course, this notion applies to the intricacies of daily life when humans are faced with innumerous viewpoints or solutions to a problem. Indeed, opposites exist within each other.

2. A spurious type of energy — often encountered through drug and alcohol abuse — subjective energy bodies produce a false sense of consciousness. When triggered, it elicits a lower consciousness and a behavior-changing "thought-form." Popular belief perpetuates this notion: the idea that addictive substances increase a person's state of euphoria

instance, have you noticed that a person who is using an addictive substance suddenly becomes another person? It is as if they have changed into a whole new set of clothes, placing them on, and of course, coloring this person's personality. One minute the personality is happy. The next minute, the personality is angry. This is what an addictive substance does. These subjective bodies, of course, remain long after the death of an addict. And even if that being or soul decides to no longer use or abuse a substance.

These subjective bodies float in the (lower) astral plane. In this case, this area is located between the Third and Fourth Dimensions of your planetary sphere. This is an area where disembodied spirits and beings without mind substance, also known as ghosts, reside. They are all mindless, like a rack of clothing, a wardrobe hanging in a storefront.

This is one way for you to understand addictive substances. They each contain an element of lower octave consciousness that creates the addiction. However, these creations only work within one mind focus; this one mind focus is of one plane and one element. Therefore, addictive substances are very limiting, though they provide an escape in that moment. They are always limiting.

One who has used addictive substances soon realizes that these substances limit their freedom; their ability to make sovereign choices; and their ability to express the true nature of their being. This is often the reason why the addictive substance

and relationship to a higher power. When in reality, nothing could be farther from the truth. Drugs and alcohol actually suppress lower energy fields and block the ability to create elevated states of consciousness. The experience of love without fear, the sense of pure joy without anxiety, and the ability to live on life's terms are rare. Yet, the exhilaration produced by a high compels the user to chase experiences sans the emptiness of lower vibrating energy. But, as tolerance necessitates the need for more, the addict or alcoholic futilely struggles to achieve an artificial divine connection authentically produced through sincere and careful spiritual cultivation. What's left, after the intoxication ebbs, is a more desperate need to fill that spiritual void.

Humans, however, can suppress lower vibrations through contact with a higher consciousness: meditation and other spiritual disciplines are excellent means to achieve this end. But, because this growth is achieved through the Transmutation of lower level energies, subjective energy bodies are not present or created. This base force has limited range; it floats in astral planes and passes from one lifetime to the next in the form of discordant, obsessive thoughts and behaviors. Repetitive ideas, feelings, and actions carry consciousness or karmic "energetic patterns" of which one is not responsibly aware. The Master Teachers calls this an "invisible creation."

is discarded. However, the addictive nature — the subjective body — that is created through the use of addictive substance is never removed. Or shall we say, never leaves that sphere of consciousness. It is always there, waiting for you to put it on. It's much like an old sweater, an old pair of shoes, or an old pair of socks, ready for you to wear again, ready to color your personality. Do you understand?

RECOGNITION

Answer: "Yes. How can I escape, get away from this, or stop? How do I stop this mirror that I have brought to myself? How do I get out of this condition where I am so full of fear?"

Recognition is, of course, the first element. Recognition and diagnosis of this condition are always first. The second element is the understanding of the will and the choices involved. It is also important for you to complete this cycle, this inner cycle where you must deal with the male energy held in torment through anger and rage. This was present with your own biological father, and now with this person who wears the same pair of shoes as your father! This is the same type of consciousness, as I have explained in addictive behavior.

Never engage a person when they are thus clothed, for they are under the influences of a dimension that are not at all friendly toward you!

Question: "Like walking through the valley of the dead souls?"

It is known in some instances as a dead zone. However, sometimes it is important to experience the dead zone to understand the gift of life and to experience the difference. Sometimes, it is important for the evolution of the soul to receive the lesson as mirroring; and once again the soul faces an apparent opposite. However, the experience of the dead zone and the understanding of the gift of life allow a synergistic movement, as I have mentioned before, that brings a unity of consciousness and a unity of purpose.

In this case, recognition of and closure with the energies of your father allow energy to move forward. It is important that you cut all ties you have had with your father, in terms of energy, on the other plane. It is important for you to enter into the ceremonies that you have been taught by your spirit guides. For they too, understand the torment that has tied you astrally and spiritually.

HEALING AND CLOSURE

These energies are draining you. These are the energies of fear that you are looking to heal. This has allowed the attraction. It is important for you to bless your father and send him on his way. For this allows final closure. Do you understand, Dear one, that the situation you chose to live during your early years on the Earth Plane and Planet now gives you strength of character? Do you understand that this recognition and closure is a rite of passage?

The ceremony, itself, does not imbue your character. For the quality of character was gained through your experience. However, the ceremony allows for a closure of the circle. This is a closure of energies of learning through abuse, of learning through a nemesis, and learning through opposition.[3]

There are many other paths you can now follow for knowledge of the soul. And the contrary path is one path that one

---

3. The Closure Ceremony: Saint Germain observes this ritual to recognize and cease addictive and karmic energy patterns. It marks the end of a person's tendency to assume oppositional, abusive, vengeful, and adversarial positions. Upon completion of the ceremony, the soul is ready and open to learn through new Laws of Attraction and Unity. But it's not for everyone. A person will achieve the best results if he or she has already developed the ability to contact spiritual helpers and guides. Components of this ceremony include:
1. Changes in energy-field magnetism
2. The removal of subjective energy bodies
3. Asking for the assistance of spiritual helpers and guides
4. Performance at full Moon
5. A location near a body of water, which allows the proper attraction of magnetism. Lenz's Law — one that refers to the behavior of diamagnetic materials — forms the basis of this practice. Fin de siècle chemist Henri Louis Le Chatelier discovered the properties of chemical equilibrium: *Le Chatelier's Principle*, that theorizes:
"Every change of one of the factors of equilibrium occasions a rearrangement of the system in such a direction that the factor in question experiences a change, in a sense opposite to the original change," he wrote. "(It is) a state of rest or balance due to the equal action of opposing forces."
6. Sound Vibration: The basis of physical manifestation is sound. This knowledge is carefully taught in Vedic mantras and practiced in Native American drumming, which simulates the heartbeat of the Earth Mother.

may follow. However in this case, it is now your choice, for you have completed the path of learning through the Law of Opposites. And now, should you choose, you may learn through the Path of Unities. You may learn through the Path (Law) of Attraction — all that is magnetically drawn to you, because energetically it is similar to you. Do you understand?

LEARNING THROUGH OPPOSITION

Question: "I don't need to be the contrary any more?"

Yes, it is important for you to understand that, again, through your will and through your choice, these lessons have come to you personally. You chose this situation before you chose this embodiment. You chose in this lifetime that you would Master the contrary laws, the Law of Repulsion. You learned what you resisted the most! You learned through the dark side or the opposite side of yourself. Is this not so?
Answer: "Yes."

CHANGING MAGNETISM

And now, a closure comes to this circle. This is a time spiral, as you would understand it. This is a time for you to see again; it is your choice if you continue along this path. This is what this other soul has brought to you. Does he not represent all that repels you? Does he not represent everything that is against what you have learned and chosen?

Answer: "Yes."

And now, if you continue in the evolution of your soul, you too may choose to learn through new laws. You have achieved, as a rite of passage, a new understanding and a clear understanding of the Law of Repulsion. The ceremony given to you by your spiritual teachers — your spiritual guides — shall be done during the time of the full Moon. It shall be done, if at all possible, near a body of water. It shall be done in such a way to allow the magnetism to properly attract. The magnetism is also created through sound vibration, as you have been taught in

Native American drumming. Through this you will change and choose new ways to evolve. Do you understand?

Answer: "Yes."

WE ARE CHOOSING EVERY DAY

And so, you must make the choice. Will you continue to learn through the contrary path or will you go forward through the active gate (attraction). This again, is your choice. All embodied life on Earth contains the blend of conscience and consciousness; these souls learn what moves through the will and the choices. It is choice that brings every soul here. It is choice that evolves intelligence into wisdom. It is choice that allows life to be.

Question: "When I do the ritual to let all this go, to pass it off, and to understand it, will he then feel no energy elsewhere and move on?"

This is so! He fulfills his own destiny with those he has come to serve. Do you not see the same pattern in the life of your own father? Do you not see that he helped many to make certain choices and to continue along a certain path?

Is it not apparent that your mate has chosen a path of nonviolence? And so therefore, do you act with nonviolence towards him?

Response: "Yes."

So, this is true. In your choice the Law of Attraction exists, as exampled by your present life of nonviolence. Every day, you are choosing your destiny! If humans would understand only this, they would no longer see themselves as victims of circumstance. Instead, humans are choosing every day of their lives; and at any moment, they may also change the course of direction through the wind that generates in the soul.

Answer: "It felt like I chose the path of fire."

Fire transmutes quickly and allows one to understand how to bring something from the lessons, and find Mastery swiftly and rapidly. Wind feeds the fire. But it is the earth element that allows you to take the steady and stable ground. You might consider that it is time for Earth within your life.

SYMBOLS TRAVERSE CONSCIOUSNESS

Answer: "In the ceremony, I feel like the ceremony has to be fire as well."

Ceremony represents symbols. These symbols speak a language that is more direct than words or mind substance. Symbols unlock the potency held in universal languages and are able to transverse states of consciousness. The symbol holds these things, so choose the symbol carefully as you would choose the name of your child! For these symbols will repeat the New Law you choose.

Answer: "I see. I've got to meditate on that. I want clarity on this to the point where I never have to walk this path again. I don't ever want to be in the path of someone who is insane. I don't ever want to draw this to me again. I want to find a more peaceful, creative space. I feel as if I've paid my dues. I want a rest."

THE SOUL KNOWS

The soul knows when a lesson is completed. The soul itself knows when it is time to change the path. The fact that you are now ready indicates the soul has recognized this willingness. As I said in the beginning of this session, the first element is your recognition of the pattern, and the second is your will or your ability to take action.

Once these two things have been achieved, change will happen. This is the Mastery again, of those three components: knowledge, willingness, and expression. And in this instance thought, action, and then feeling. This has been taught in prior lessons in the sequence: thought, feeling, and action. In this case, we will temporarily remove the feeling body, as often times the feeling body is housed in astral levels. Since we are asking for a change of the evolution of the soul, it is important that we work first with the thought, and then we will work with the action, and finally the feeling. Do you understand?

CHOICE AWAKENS THE WILL

Answer: "Yes. I feel as if half the people on Earth right now are hiding inside drugs — the dead zone. The other half is out challenging life with dangerous hobbies such as mountain climbing, trying to prove they're alive. Why are so many people testing death?"

It is true that there are those testing death who are dead themselves — so many among humanity are not even awake! They slumber in the dead zone. They slumber in this Time of Spiritual Awakening. A bell rings to awaken them from centuries and embodiment after embodiment of sleep.

However, it is their choice to remain asleep. It is their choice to be dead. But then, there are those who have made the choice to be alive and make daily choices, fully awake, resulting in full consciousness and conscience in all of their activities. It is important, Dear ones, to understand at this Time of Transition that this is a time when choices awaken the will. It is the awakening of spiritual laws that all is contained within and without. We have always said, "as above, so below."

What does this mean Dear one? The laws are contained within every cell, from microscopic organisms to the most complex organisms. All contain within the Laws of Unity of all things. When we speak this way, we speak in an older language that is hermetic in origin. It is also universal.

COLLECTIVE AWAKENING

The world is asleep. It is so! It is time for universal awakening. There is indeed a connection between the body and mind. It is the mind that creates the body. There is also a connection between the collective mind and the Earth. The collective mind is collective consensus, and you now know this as the one-hundredth monkey. Perhaps it will only take one more for the collective awakening![4]

Are these possibilities? Are these probabilities? Of course they are Dear ones! There are laws which govern, "as above, so below." These are the Laws of Momentum, and you understand them in your science of physics. And now we offer them through the understanding of psychology, religion, and beliefs. It is important, Dear ones, for you to see the importance during this time to stay awake and conscious. It is also important to use your conscience. Every day make intentional choices with knowledge and understanding.

---

4. Twentieth century author Ken Keyes, Jr. based his book, *The Hundredth Monkey*, on the work of botanist Lyall Watson. Watson originally coined the term in his work, *Lifetide*. His book discussed the work of primatologists in the 1950s who observed the macaques monkeys on the Japanese island of Koshima teaching each other to wash sweet potatoes. Keyes expanded Lyall's findings to the realm of human consciousness.

"The Japanese monkey, Macaca fuscata, had been observed in the wild for a period of over 30 years. In 1952, on the island of Koshima, scientists were providing monkeys with sweet potatoes dropped in the sand. The monkeys liked the taste of the raw sweet potatoes, but they found the dirt unpleasant. An 18-month-old female named Imo found she could solve the problem by washing the potatoes in a nearby stream. She taught this trick to her mother. Her playmates also learned this new way and they taught their mothers, too. This cultural innovation was gradually picked up by various monkeys before the eyes of the scientists. Between 1952 and 1958 all the young monkeys learned to wash the sandy sweet potatoes to make them more palatable. Only the adults who imitated their children learned this social improvement. Other adults kept eating the dirty sweet potatoes. Then something startling took place. In the autumn of 1958, a certain number of Koshima monkeys were washing sweet potatoes — the exact number is not known. Let us suppose that when the Sun rose one morning there were 99 monkeys on Koshima Island who had learned to wash their sweet potatoes. Let's further suppose that later that morning, the hundredth monkey learned to wash potatoes. Then it happened! By that evening almost everyone in the tribe was washing sweet potatoes before eating them. The added energy of this hundredth monkey somehow created an ideological breakthrough! But notice. A most surprising thing observed by these scientists was that the habit of washing sweet potatoes then jumped over the sea … colonies of monkeys on other islands and the mainland troop of monkeys at Takasakiyama began washing their sweet potatoes. Thus, when a certain critical number achieves an awareness, this new awareness may be communicated from mind to mind. Although the exact number may vary, this Hundredth Monkey Phenomenon means that when only a limited number of people know of a new way, it may remain the conscious property of these people. But there is a point at which if only one more person tunes-in to a new awareness, a field is strengthened so that this awareness is picked up by almost everyone!"

(Editor's note: Since its original 1984 publication, *The Hundredth Monkey* has been criticized for lacking substantial evidence. It is included here for the reader as context to the lesson, "Closing the Circle." Saint Germain often says, "Never believe anything that I say! Take it unto the laboratory of self!")

WAKEFULNESS IS REQUIRED

Question: "If you are awake and your collective essence or energy is directly related to the Earth, how do the dead, the asleep, drug addicts, or other abused souls affect the Earth? Compared to how the awake affect the Earth? Does it take a lot more, or is it half and half? Is this going to make a bearing on how soon the Earth crumbles and is destroyed? Does the Earth need the energy of awakened people?"

There is a percentage of people who sleep; there is a percentage of people who are awake. And this has always been and always shall be. However, for the New Dimensions to be opened, and to traverse through time with a leap in consciousness, a certain percentage of wakefulness is required. This of course, must be subjective first, and then understood and experienced on an objective or collective level. The individual choices that you make become choices made for all of humanity.

If one person, one individual, subjectively awakens to this objective ideal and begins to understand how individual choice affects, in essence the whole, then in one small way an opening, a portal, a window for consciousness grows. This is achieved day by day through the holding of thought, visualization, and an understanding of peace. However, there are still those who will remain in a dead zone. These are those who must be left, they must be discarded, as was spoken in the Book of Revelations: two are standing in the field, side by side; one will go, the other will stay. Do you understand? This choosing is not by (a) God. This choosing is through the will, the developed will, the conscious will as God in man!

It is a choice and a commitment to stay firmly rooted. Recognize that when someone is asleep it is not necessarily your responsibility to awaken their slumber, but to allow their choice. For within their dream, some day, they will awaken to the ONE reality, the ONE truth, which is within.

FEAR OF AWAKENING

Question: "Why do churches ask all their people to apostatize as if they want to awaken and bring God to everyone around them? Why do they do that?"

It is again, a slumber within the sleep, another illusion, another dream created within the dream. It is fear of awakening, fear of what would happen if the slumber is removed. (Then) One would be free. However, it is important to let those who sleep to remain in slumber. For those who are awake, stay awake!

COMPLETION

Question: "With Lee, is it best for me to do my ritual and just stay out of his way, and send him love?"

It is important to understand the completion of the spiral of energy. For you carry this in your DNA as well as your electromagnetic aura. It is important for you to understand that this is the completion of a major task of your life's work. This is a completion of a major portion of what you have come this time to learn. Does this speak truth to you?

Response: "I find myself leaning toward the shaman's answer of healing and peace: cast him into the winds to do his own thing. Meanwhile, I don't need it anymore."

That would work, Dear one. As I have said before, call upon your spiritual teachers, your spiritual guides and friends. They are with you and will help you to bring this to full fruition and completion.

Response: "I thank you. I understand."

So be it! In that Mighty Christ, I AM.

Fountain of Life

Saint Germain gives personal instruction.

Greetings in that Mighty Christ. I AM Saint Germain, and I request permission to come forward, Dear students.

Response: "Please Dear one, you are most welcome."

We have requested to come forward this day to give you discourse about the upcoming times and changes. Alongside me today is beloved El Morya, Chohan of the First Ray as he has instruction to bring to you; however, before we proceed, I would like to give you a short discourse.

USE OF DECREE

This discourse is in preparation for the times to come, the times ahead. It is a discourse not only on forgiveness, but a discourse on transmutation. As I have always said, "Down with death!" Death, you see Dear ones, is a consciousness that is held. It is also a pattern held, and it is also a pattern held in the body and in the Cellular Memory. How do we destroy the consciousness of death and allow the consciousness of life to become the ever present life force?

It is as simple as electromagnetics; but, it is also as simple as thought, feeling, and action — as we have always taught in these teachings.[1] When you decree a thing through the voice and the power of sound, you bring it into a level of manifesta-

tion.[2] When you speak with your voice, the voice you recognize, the words of your language create a quality of consciousness.

That is, the brain has allowed a thought to come forward to pattern the cells of the body. So, when you speak the decrees we have given you and with the word I AM, which commands the God presence into action, you are, in essence, decreeing a thing into motion, into rhythm, into sattva.[3]

---

1. Thought, feeling, and action, according to Ascended Master teachings and tradition, serve as the cornerstones of the co-creative process. The Mental (Causal) Body and the Yellow Ray represent thought; the emotional (astral) body and the Pink Ray, feeling; and the physical body and the Blue Ray, actions. Imbalances in any of these processes form the foundation of disease (dis-ease).

The principles of thought, feeling, and action, however, aren't limited to esoteric doctrine. Astrological teachings also utilize these fundamentals to indicate the strengths, the weaknesses, and the influences of astral powers: the Sun, Causal Body; the Moon, Astral Body. Action incorporates the will, and the choices we make and act upon.

2. Similar to prayers and mantras, these statements of intent and power are often integrated with the use of the I AM and requests to the I AM Presence. And when it comes to activating these spiritual channels, the possibilities are endless. Some express decrees silently through prayer and meditation, while others opt for forceful pronouncements of intent. Rhythmic chanting and singing, therapeutic journaling, and write-and-burn techniques provide just a few conduits of worship.

Decrees form the foundation of Ascended Master teachings; these simple affirmations create a conscious contact with the I AM Presence, shifting consciousness, expanding awareness, and activating the Co-creation process.

A classic Ascended Master decree for the Violet Flame is as follows: "Violet Flame I AM, God I AM Violet Flame!"

Within the text of the teachings in *The Fountain of Life* Saint Germain gives a decree to command life unto your being:

I AM the effervescent life flowing through.
I AM the effervescent life transmuting.
I AM the effervescent life of life!

3. The essence of the I AM bridges the physical, the spiritual and the transmigratory activity of human existence. I AM represents God's infinite spirit; the I AM Presence embodies the individualized presence of God — the relationship between the human self and the Divine Presence within and around us. The resulting energy unites and becomes the taproot of all God powers: life, intelligence, power, and action.

During each lifetime, the light, life, and energy of the soul flow from the I AM Presence to our physical and Light Bodies. This twining connection of energy and light — also known as the Silver cord — follows the pull of gravity. Light streams through the crown of the head where it cascades to the heart of the Presence and circulates to the base of the brain: the medulla oblongata. Tiny threads of light radiate energy to every cell of the body. The Hindus call these healing filaments Nadis; chakras form at points of intensity. Light then surges from these tributaries of energy — Nadis and chakras — to a mighty confluence of light energy known as the Pillar of Light or the Tube of Light.

The Ascended Masters rely heavily on the power of the I AM Presence for protection. Conscious calls to the I AM Presence activate the Pillar of Light, insulating lower bodies — Causal, Astral, and physical — from difficult karmas. The Pillar of Light and the addition of the Violet Flame construct a spiritual shelter much like the protective force of mantras, spiritual ceremonies, and prayers. That's why the consistent practice of these transcendental exercises raises spiritual consciousness: the summoning of greater fields of light ameliorates and eliminates seemingly insurmountable difficulties, and creates miracles.

The Christ-self — also known as the Higher Self or Guardian Angel — protects the physical body, even though it operates at a lower vibratory rate than the Presence. It also provides an intermediary power

Dear ones, to bring forward the pattern of life, one must constantly attune their speech patterns and life habits toward the quality of effervescent life. Avoid speech patterns that accept death as an inevitable ending as in that final fear in doom and gloom.

A FOUNTAIN OF CONSCIOUSNESS

Haven't you come to understand that consciousness, indeed, is the quality that can hold either pattern of life or death? Then it is consciousness that is the key that holds the final pivotal point and acceleration to the New Dimensions. The New Dimension(s) that we speak of at this moment is the Fourth Dimension of Vibration. This Fourth Dimension of Vibration is indeed the next level that must be developed to understand life eternal. The first Three Dimensions that we speak of are held within the karmic waves of life and death. The karmic waves of life and death are where consciousness and death consciousness are programmed — the understanding that death could rule life. However, you have known through these teachings that knowledge rises above superstition. The belief systems that once held you in the trappings of illusions and death are just those, illusions. It is time Dear ones, stalwart followers of this work, chelas, and disciples of the Violet Flame, to come forward now, and decree life unto your being:

> I AM the effervescent life flowing through.
> I AM the effervescent life transmuting.
> I AM the effervescent life of life!

Those who have sought the fountain of youth have now discovered that the fountain of youth lies within the fountain of consciousness! Open your fountain of consciousness — let the waters pour forward into your life, into your energy fields.

FOURTH DIMENSION

This wellspring, this fountain of life that exists within you, will lead you onward to Fourth Dimensional Consciousness. Fourth Dimensional Consciousness is indeed the Consciousness of Vibration. When we enter into your energy fields, we enter and access through the Fourth Dimension. That is why we ask, "Do we have permission to come forward?" For this permission allows us to access your Fourth Dimensional (Energy) Fields; to raise them to a higher level of vibration.[4] When one opens the Third Eye through the pineal gland that exists in the physical body, you are opening an entry, a door, a portal, to the Fourth Dimension.

The Fourth Dimensional Consciousness is where we reside when we come to give discourse. Now is not the time or the dispensation when the Masters — spiritual teachers — will appear in Third Dimensional bodies. For you see Dear ones, the Earth, her people, and her transition have allowed the Collective Consciousness to fall to yet even a lower state; a lower state that will not allow our entry at this moment. However, a time will come when we shall appear again, not only in the Fourth Dimension, but in the other dimensions (such as the Third Dimension) as you are now experiencing.

THE GREATEST GIFT IS THE VIOLET FLAME

This will come after the great shift of the poles; after the great shift in consciousness. You will rest your weary feet and hands. But for now how shall you persevere throughout these days, these final days, the days of transition? It is important to continue with your spiritual disciplines as I have outlined in this discourse: call a thing into action and call Transmutation into action. This is done through the use of the Violet Flame, and at this time, the Violet Flame is the greatest gift for all

---

between the I AM Presence and the outer human form. Simply speaking, this intelligent body of light serves the energies of the I AM as a Step-down Transformer and a propellant of action in the physical plane. Scholars say the bodies of the I AM Presence and the Christ-self are just as tangible in their own realms of vibratory action as the body in its physical world.

4. Mankind's conscious contact with the Great White Brotherhood is a matter of choice. That's why the Ascended Masters follow the cardinal rule of asking permission when it comes to human interaction. By vow and practice, the Masters never intrude: they don't demand deference from or dictate a doctrine to a chela or student. Instead, their directions are based on suggestions and affirmations. The Masters identify the presence of natural laws that may affect or alter the course of one's life. Their knowledge and teachings uplift our consciousness, vibration, and energy. The disciple is free to heed the message and act on it — or not.

of humanity. When you call upon the Violet Flame, it alone has the ability to transmute and change any situation at any time. Even the wars currently waging in the Middle East could be changed if the focus were placed on Transmutation and the Violet Flame. But there are the Doubting Thomases among you, and that Doubting Thomas has crept into your consciousness and there it resides! You hold the key through your consciousness. Therefore, through your choices you bring forth the manifestation.

Dear hearts, if you wish to change anything in your life, anything that you are currently experiencing, first you must conceptualize it. Also, you must understand it through that will of intention as beloved El Morya has taught. You must choose life over death for there to be regeneration in any situation. You Dear ones, students in this schoolhouse called life, must understand the rules and the laws of which you have been brought here to your own manifestations. Yet, you cry and weep when you find that you are living the result of your own creations! These are your own manifestations, but give conscious awareness to your creations through choosing effervescent life.

HOW TO CHANGE?

The fountain of life is indeed the fountain of youth. How shall I change the present situation? How shall I take my body and regenerate each cell from old age? How do I take worn out perspectives and attitudes, and transmute — change them? Charge them with the Violet Flame through your daily use of decrees and through your daily focus of consciousness. This indeed will raise you above all trial and tribulation. All things that come to you that you wish to change, blaze with the Mighty Violet Flame through your consciousness, and you will see that I have offered you that most refreshing drink![5]

5. The *Refreshing Drink* is an allegory of the Universal Supply of Life. It originates from the work of Guy Ballard, who, under the pen name Godfré Ray King, authored the classic theosophical book of Ascended Master teaching, *Unveiled Mysteries*.

Ballard's work evolves from a simple meditation during a hike on Mount Shasta. On a warm day, Ballard — asking God to define his path — finds his way to a stream and fills his cup with its water. A drink of the liquid sends an electrical current through his body. Suddenly, a young man materializes and telepathically relays this message: "My Brother, if you will hand me your Cup, I will give you a much more refreshing drink."

Humanity is on the brink of devastation, but humanity is also upon the brink of great evolution and Spiritual Awakening. During these times, as you ride the wave, or walk the cliff or the precipice, ask, "How can I move forward? How can I move forward without devastation to myself or to others?"

Call upon the teaching that you have known deep within your heart; the teachings of Grace, Forgiveness, and Transmutation are always there as your eternal and infinite tools. They are indeed the fountain of life. Call upon these tools, Dear ones. In this schoolhouse learn to use these tools to bring forth beauty and cooperation for evolution.

Questions?

FORGIVENESS RESTORES BALANCE

Question: "In everyone's daily life, your advice, your guidance, and the law is to apply the Violet Flame decree to anything that's challenged and transmuted? In doing this you're stating that this law is a Law of Compassion, a Law of Forgiveness and Understanding. In a Three Dimensional collective world, it seems only that the Law of Balance exists. Are you saying that the higher Law of Transmutation will neutralize this Law of Balance?"

Dear beloveds, it is the higher Laws of Forgiveness and Transmutation that restore balance. One cannot walk in balance until they have opened to purification, to Transmutation. These are the tools and the way that one enters; to begin to walk in balance.

FORGIVENESS AND TRANSMUTATION

Question: "Bearing this in mind, if anyone on this planet wants to create a balance in their economy, their health, their personal relationships, their political relationships, or even with the environment, then the only solution is through the use of this higher law. Is that correct?"

The young man later on reveals himself as Saint Germain; Ballard's water flows directly from the Universal Supply, "(as) pure and vivifying as Life itself; in fact it is Life — Omnipresent Life — for it exists everywhere about us."

This is so, Dear beloved, and yet humanity, through beliefs and old dialectics has interpreted forgiveness as turning the other cheek.[6] This is simply not so! It is a Law of Purification; a Law of Transmutation. It is the Law of Alchemy that comes forward, transmuting the animal consciousness into the human consciousness; transmuting the base realities into the greater realities; bringing the First, Second, and Third Dimension into an understanding of Fourth Dimension. It is all of these things, Dear hearts, beloved students and chelas, all of these things. It is not putting your tail between your legs and groveling for the respect that you are recognized as Divine Human Beings! It is indeed that refreshing drink. It is the understanding and the realization that you are whole. It is the understanding and realization that you are Divine. Dear beloveds, Transmutation and purification cleanse the old cobwebs of the mind; the old patterns that no longer create the world in which you wish to live. It allows the new door to open, and shuts forever the door on death and illusion!

Question: "Then in essence, if you are choosing to alter an outcome that seems inevitable by the moment's standards, or the understanding of the moment, it is through the application of the Violet Flame that this outcome can be altered?"

If only you would use the Violet Flame vigilantly, every day, many of the trials and the tribulations in your life would be lifted from you. You would be taken to a greater understanding; a greater understanding would be given to you and seen in all your affairs. As we have always stated before, Dear chelas, place your attention solely upon the work at hand! There has been that individual who has walked as a dark shadow alongside your

work and has taken the work of the Hierarchy, adulterated it, and used it for personal gain. This, of course, is none of your concern, but it is our concern. Do not allow your energies to be infiltrated or misused by one who is simply manipulating Laws of Fear and Death. Close the door forever on this energy, and allow it never to come amongst what you are doing. Do you understand Dear ones?

Answer: "Yes. However, the personal sense of injustice is great."

How would there be injustice when you hold the key to your own creation? How could injustice exist when you have been given the key of how you, yourself, now can walk in balance? You must call upon the Transmutation, the purification — the Violet Flame. Close the door to death; let the fountain of life resume.

"KNOWLEDGE WITHIN"

Answer: "As you have instructed, I will follow. It makes perfect sense."

I do hope you realize, Dear beloved, that death and illusion have attracted or attached to you. Now it is time to resume the work that has been given to you. Do not allow your intentions to be diverted away from what has nothing to do with the work and the message brought forward through this body of material and information. As you know, the Great White Lodge does not and will not sponsor information that leads an individual to the trappings of fear or the trappings of illusion. As you see, with this individual, there has been the soulful test of, shall we say, "guru status" as beloved K. H. (Kuthumi) has so eloquently spoken. This is the time of the death of the outer guru and the time of ever present knowledge within the individual. As we have always stated before, Dear ones, Dear hearts, it is towards the individual (one undivided) that we aim our work for and toward, and yes, while there is the Vibration of Unana — the unity of all, the merging of consciousness, the understanding of the mighty and glorious Christ that we all exist of — there is also the complete sovereign individual who shall shine forth in

---

6. The Ascended Masters never encourage forgiveness as a matter of turning the other cheek. Rather, absolution is based on the metaphysical notion of the Law of Purification: the act of transmuting slower, base energies into a higher form. It's about discarding a perception of a situation or a circumstance, and seeking freedom from objectionable or undesirable elements. This involves the process of atonement, but not in the theological sense.

Esoterically speaking, At-One-Ment is the birth of the Christ Consciousness within: the realization of divinity, wholeness, unity, harmony, and clarity of consciousness; and not the reconciliation between Man and God via the blood of Jesus Christ. From this viewpoint, forgiveness allows humanity to forever close the door on and disengage the processes of dark and deceptive energies.

these days to come. This is the individual who will understand the HU-man, the God-man, and the work of the Ray Force, individualized within that beam as God-force, a true son, daughter of God. This is the work that we strive for, Dear ones, do you understand?

Answer: "Yes, completely."

ELDER BROTHERS AND SISTERS

Do not let your attention or your energies be diverted into the trappings of hate, judgment, and guilt. For are not all of these a fountain of death? Place your attention on that which brings you life, which moves you forward, not backward, Dear ones! Place your feet on the path and move ahead toward the goal. It is easy to be diverted in this world of duality that you are learning through, so easy to divert your energies at any time. Understand Dear ones, we are here as your elder Brothers and Sisters, and as your guides. We have walked before you and we shall continue to hold the lamp high! A time shall come when you will do this too for those of lesser consciousness. But for now, you must keep your attention on the path, on the task at hand. Do you have further questions?

Answer: "No, you have satisfied all immediate curiosities and desires. Thank you. I'm grateful."

CHAPTER TWELVE

The First Golden City

❧

Saint Germain explains the traditions of Shamballa.

Greetings beloved chelas. I AM Saint Germain. Shamballa and greetings beloved students and chelas of the Seventh Ray! As you have requested my presence, I come forward in the service of the Mighty Violet Ray — that Mighty Violet Ray of Mercy, Compassion, and Forgiveness.

TIME OF SHAMBALLA

Shamballa is a time when we all gather; you have asked questions concerning the celebration of this focus of our thought, our feeling, and our action. You have asked questions about this celebration; and I have come forward today to give discourse on this time, as I have given you information in past discourses regarding the Time of Shamballa.[1] It is of course a time of great feasting; a time of celebration; a time of camaraderie among friends in the service of the ONE. It is the time for the anchoring of energies on the Earth Plane and Planet. It is a celebration of the Rays of Light and Sound; it is a celebration of the creation of humanity, and the work of the Spiritual Hierarchy upon this Earth Plane and Planet.

THE FIRST ACTIVATION OF THE GALACTIC WEB

Yes, Shamballa is our spiritual home and the first retreat located above the Gobi desert now in that Golden City also known as Gobi. Energy steadily arches across to the beloved Star of Gobean where El Morya now holds his focus for that Mighty Blue Ray of Transformation, Harmony, and Peace on the planet. We have always stated that it is in the apices of the Golden Cities where celebrations, or focuses, should be held for the movement of energy upon the Earth Plane and

Planet.[2] And naturally, Gobean would be the first place where one would travel to anchor peace in the hearts of the Collective Consciousness. For this is one of the activated portals, the first, in fact, of that mighty Galactic Web. That web bursts forth this new creation known as the New Age.

EL MORYA AND THE NEW AGE

This New Age was prophesied long ago by many other messengers of this Lodge. And you are both sharing in that service of messenger — as a Prophet. It is an important time, the birth of this New Age. We've stated before, the Hierarchy has worked for thousands of years to bring this time to the apex of its fruition. One that will not be realized yet for still thousands of more years; however, you are now at this time on the verge of revolution — a point of departure. Now a point that steadily, and with the focus of the mighty I AM, moves the energy of the New Age forward. It has grown from the point of 51-55 per cent. Continue in the stalwart plan, Dear ones. Align your focus and your energy with the Master Teacher of Gobean — El Morya — for he has come forward to bring the focus of the energies that will bring the supreme completion to the activation of Gobean. Align your energies and loyalty to the Mighty Teacher of the Blue Ray; align your energies, Dear ones, for this is how you now may serve!

Shamballa is a time, yes, of feasting, supping, and celebration among us; but, it also represents many teachings that have been passed on since the birth of humanity. You have asked when it begins, and it begins on that seventeenth of December, a day of the Christ, and the awakening of the Christ Consciousness within each and everyone of you. The seventeen signifies in ancient numerology the birth of the Star of the Magi — the gift of the Sun of Light within. Sons and daughters of light, come forward this day, on the seventeenth, and celebrate the opening of Shamballa!

---

1. See Appendix O1: *Shamballa and Sanat Kumara.*

2. The Golden City apex is known as a *critical point*. A critical point is defined in energy systems as the location where the least amount of force will create the greatest effect.

FOUR WEEKS OF CELEBRATION

Shamballa takes place for exactly four weeks — twenty-eight days to be exact. And during these twenty-eight days, a celebration of the four elements is carried forward. Let me explain further for your understanding.[3]

THE FIRST WEEK: EARTH ELEMENT

The first week is the opening of the energies, and it is here, during this week, that we celebrate the first primal substance that brought humanity to the Earth, and the earth element itself. So it is the earth element that is celebrated in the first seven days. We suggest that the first seven days of your celebrations and festivities are focused upon Earth Healing and Earth Celebrations. Celebrate the birth of Mother Earth! Celebrate and give thanks to Mother Earth — beloved Babajeran — for she has given you your physical bodies from her own body, cloaking the Mighty Spirit I AM with her substance.

Dear ones, Shamballa is the time when we carry forward our celebrations for the Earth Mother. We also carry forward ceremonies and rituals for her healing as celebration and thanks for what she has given each and everyone of us, and for the opportunity to come here for the joy of the experience.

THE SECOND WEEK: AIR ELEMENT

The second week is ruled by the element of air. From the traditions that you well know, air rules all mental movement. Mentalism is conscious thought; however, as a tradition during Shamballa, the second week is celebrated as the week of the Messengers — those who traveled forth in consciousness — to give the message of this Lodge to humanity. This is the week when there are various celebrations of Krishna, Buddha, Christ, and the many other avatars and adepts who have carried forward the focus of this Lodge to those of humanity who are willing to see and to hear. In your Christian traditions, this is the week of the celebration of the birth of Jesus-Sananda, the Christ. If you wish to celebrate, celebrate in the fullness of all teachers. Celebrate in the fullness of all messengers who have come to ease the pain and the suffering of humanity. The Week of Air is celebrated with thankfulness and gratitude for the world teachers who have gone before you.

THE THIRD WEEK: WATER ELEMENT

The third week is ruled by water, and as you know, water moves emotion. The third week of Shamballa is a celebration of love — Brotherly and Sisterly love. This is the time when fEasts are set at many tables in Shamballa. It is also the time of the passage of one (solar) year to the next. It is a time of camaraderie, where family and friends gather. It is a week of fEasting and supping together as ONE. On the Earth Plane and Planet this is the most perfect week to perform the Cup Ceremony to understand that you have traveled together as a soul-family — a group of souls focusing on a point of consciousness. All components in a family make this Mighty ONE. Your hand consists of five fingers; however, it is one hand. Each finger needs the

---

3. Over four weeks (twenty-eight days), esoteric followers, including Ascended Masters, honor the Celebration of the Four Elements during the Shamballa festivities. It begins December 17 — accompanied by lighting of the Eternal Flame Candle, or the Fireless Light — on the altar of the main temple. This etheric celebration is divided into the following four parts:

1. Week One: December 18 to December 24. Element: Earth. The celebration and thanksgiving offered to Mother Earth. Ceremonies and rituals for Earth Healing are held at Shamballa during this time. Bowls of salt, which represent earth united with spirit, are placed on all the altars in the Temples of Shamballa.

2. Week Two: December 25 to December 31. Element: Air. Celebrations of gratitude and thanksgiving to the World Teachers and the messengers of the Great White Brotherhood who have selflessly served humanity are held this week. Krishna, Jesus Christ, Buddha, and other well-known avatars and saviors are also lauded. Doves of Peace are symbolically released this week.

3. Week Three: January 1 to January 7: Element: Water. A thanksgiving for our Soul Families is held during this week. This phase of Shamballa Celebration is about revering love and friendship, and performing Cup Ceremonies. A Cup Ceremony is a water ceremony that celebrates the union of Mother Earth and Soul Families. A cup of water is passed and infused with the prayers of the devoted. The prayer-charged water is then poured on the Earth.

4. Week Four: January 8 to January 14: Element: Fire. This week is a celebration of Spiritual Fire. This time is set aside for personal purification, intentions, reflection, and meditation for the upcoming year. This is an important period for the Brotherhoods and Sisterhoods of Light to review plans for the following 365 days. Candles for each of the Seven Rays, representing the seven Hermetic Laws, are lit this week.

5. The Sealing of Divinity: January 15 and 16: Celebrations of Unity — Unana — and the ONE.

6. The Closing of Shamballa: January 17: the light of the Eternal Flame returns to Venus.

movement of the other finger to perform its functions. Water movement rules the third week of Shamballa.

THE FOURTH WEEK: FIRE ELEMENT

The fourth week of Shamballa is ruled by fire. Fire is the Seal of Solomon, placed as a capstone on the other elements. It is the message of spirit, the soul, the Jiva, and the Monad. This is the essence of all of life, the song of the soul. The purpose of the fourth week is Spiritual Fire. This is the most perfect time to receive messages, to meditate, to pray, and to purify the body and mind to receive that which is most perfect for your movement into the next year. During this week members of the Hierarchy — the Brotherhood and Sisterhoods of Light of this Lodge — meet together and position their most perfect plans for the coming year. As you shall see, this is a week of planning, orchestrating, and understanding the movement of the Collective Consciousness. It is also a week of supreme service, beginning first through the purification of the individual and then moving into the collective.

You, of course, have had many celebrations during this Time of Shamballa, a time of the death of darkness and the birth of the lighted ones. Carry out many celebrations. Carry out the service of love, as dear Sananda has always instructed you to. We too give gifts to one another during this time. We give four gifts total, one for each week; each gift signifying the earth, air, water, and fire elements, for overall it is a time of sharing and understanding.

SEALING OF DIVINITY

Unana becomes our focus — the unity of ONE. After twenty-eight days, two more days are added for the sealing of divinity when we work together as ONE to become a cohesive unit. For in the unity of all is that Mighty Light of God that never fails!

Do you have questions?

SYMBOLS OF THE ELEMENTS

Question: "The only pertinent questions I have are about the ceremony during the Time of Shamballa. Can you offer a ceremony we can do on this Plane and Planet that will coordinate with your celebrations in other dimensions? This, of course, is totally up to you. It's only a thought that may make students, chelas, and aspirants feel closer to you. It will help build that tradition of unifying the Lodge of the universal world, but I leave it up to you."

There are many symbols used during Shamballa. One symbol for the Earth is salt, and we always place a bowl of salt upon our altar to represent the earth substance (element). This represents the Spiritual Fire in the substance of Mother Earth. The Dove of Peace is the symbol of the messengers, and many doves — Doves of Peace to soothe the ailing hearts of humanity — are released during the second week. Of course you know water is signified by the Cup. It is used in many of your ceremonies, and it is used as we have instructed in each of the ceremonies during Shamballa. Fire is signified by the lighting of the seven candles for each of the seven Rays; it signifies the seven mighty Hermetic Laws that rule all of creation that humanity will experience, learn, and Master on the Earth Plane and Planet. At the beginning of the opening of Shamballa, one candle is lit; one candle represents the Mighty Light of God that never fails! This candle is held in Shamballa as an eternal flame — a fireless light — which is conceived from the heart of all life. The fireless light is lit continuously throughout the entire thirty days of celebration. At the closing of the thirtieth day, the light is taken home by a light-bearer, back to the planet of Venus, where it is held in continuous consciousness until the next year of Shamballa.

These are the traditions we share. There are many more ceremonies, some of them from individualized perceptions of the same teachings. Many of them (ceremonies) carry these symbols that represent the eternal and infinite truth that have always ruled those who come to the Earth. There are many things that will be occurring in the next year, and these of course, will be set out in the plans to come in the following week. It is during this time that we will formulate a Master Plan for the movement of consciousness in the mighty Galactic Web and the activation of the Golden Cities. Shamballa, as you know, was originally created as an etheric city to hold a perfect consciousness for the evolution of humanity. And now, as we reach this time when more (people) have come and more shall choose, it is important that we continue to focus on the building of all fifty-one etheric Golden Cities, so that the spiritual template is laid in the hearts of all men.

Do you have questions?

Answer: "I have no further questions."

In that case my beloveds, I must return to the celebrations at Shamballa. Know that always I AM here at your request. In service to that Mighty Breath of Light and Action of God, I AM Saint Germain.

CHAPTER THIRTEEN

The Ever Present Perfection

*Saint Germain explains the movement of energy
throughout the Eight-sided Cell of Perfection.*

Greetings in that Mighty Christ. I AM Saint Germain and I stream forth on that Mighty Violet Ray of Mercy and Transmuting Forgiveness. As usual, Dear hearts, I request permission to come forward to bring discourse.

Response: "In the most effervescent life, please come forward Dear one."

THE EIGHT-SIDED CELL OF PERFECTION

Today the topic of our discussion shall be that ever present perfection of life, the Eight-sided Cell of Perfection.[1] (Saint Germain diagrams the Eight-sided Cell of Perfection.)

As you see on this chalkboard, I have diagramed an Eight-sided Cell of Perfection, better known as an octagon; each side is in perfect harmony with the center. For you see, each side is always in perfect harmony with the center of its source. This is the premise of all perfection.[2] Perfection mirrors more perfec-

_____

1. The Eight-sided Cell of Perfection provides a direct link to the core of Cellular Awakening during the Earth Changes. According to the Ascended Masters, within each person lies one perfect cell known as the Eight-sided Cell of Perfection. It is associated with all aspects of perfection; it contains and maintains a visceral connection to the Godhead, e.g. the God within, the God realization, and the God manifestation in all creations and perceptions. This cell is located in the Chamber of the Heart, surrounded by a mandala of energy: the Unfed Flame of Love, Wisdom, and Power. The vibral-core axis provides a material connection to the Eight-sided Cell of Perfection in physical form. Located near the Solar Plexus Chakra, it serves as the central energy current that runs through the human body. Here, the aura ties to the seven chakras (energy centers); the core of the planet; and the spiritual over-soul. The over-soul is also known as the energy system that incorporates the Christ-self and the I AM Presence. As earthly energies increase in vibration and frequency, the Eight-sided Cell of Perfection awakens, stimulating Cellular Awakening and spiritual growth.

2. According to Ascended Master teachings, perfection is often seen as balance or harmony; perfection is associated with self-knowledge and Mastery. It is also understood as a state of evolution.

tion, and therefore perfection is infinite. This is the philosophy and the understanding.

FOUR ELEMENTS IN DUALITY

The eight represents the four elements of the Earth in duality — two times two. {(2x2)2} For you see, Dear ones, two times two represents eight perfect mirrors of perfection mirroring from the central source of being.

THE MAGNETIC POLE

All energy movement on the Earth Plane and Planet follows the course of the magnetic poles, the South and North Poles, and the center, of course, is known as the core of the Earth.

INFINITE, ABSOLUTE PERFECTION

Imagine this Eight-sided Cell of Perfection superimposed over the planet, with eight perfect mirrors throughout the planet. Now, if you extend this with dimensional vision, you will see many mirrors at the central core — the source of all perfection. Perfection mirrors itself back infinitely, creating infinite absolute perfection.

THE CO-CREATOR'S CHOICE

As the Earth travels through its many sojourns and epochs, we now see times on the Earth Plane and Planet when perfection is less than its complete out-picturing; times when disharmony and discord run rampant on the Earth Plane and Planet. This thought, feeling, and action mirrors disharmony through the perfect source. Why does this happen? Through the qualification of energy through the use of the Free Will. For you see, Dear hearts, you have been given that mighty illuminated mind in which you may choose which path to tread. This again is the choice of a Co-creator.

NORTH AND SOUTH, DARKNESS AND LIGHT

In this time of your epoch, North is the direction that humanity is facing. This is toward a more darkened perspective on life itself. Facing the South — where more light comes to the planet — is a more enlightened perspective. Those who face South understand the feminine aspects of creation and (have) a more enlightened mind.

MIND AND INTUITION, EAST AND WEST

Facing East are the scholars; those who have achieved a literal and an intuitive way of viewing life through the scholastic and disseminating processes of the mind.[3] To the West are those who sing the song of philosophy; those who understand through the literal and expressive intuition that energy movement comes forward.[4]

THE UNFED FLAME

This is a brief teaching of the four directions as understood through the teaching of the Eight-sided Cell of Perfection.[5] The Eight-sided Cell of Perfection covers the entire planet and is also planted within the heart of your being. This infinite source, the center of the Eight-Sided Cell, is where the Unfed Flame of Love, Wisdom, and Power resides. There was once an epoch, many ages ago, where the Unfed Flame had risen to such a high state of infinite awareness that those who carried this plume about them resonated only perfection and harmony. This group of souls now resides as Cosmic Teachers over this planetary system and have evolved from Earth, beloved Babajeran.

MOVEMENT OF CONSCIOUSNESS AND ENERGY

Dear hearts, when you begin to understand the energy movement of the Eight-sided Cell of Perfection you will begin to understand how consciousness moves on the planet.[6] You are currently in the transitory state before a major shift of the poles, not only in consciousness, but in the most literal sense. That is why I have come forward with this teaching, so that you would understand the movements of energy and consciousness, the Mirrors of Perfection.

NINE MOVEMENTS OF THE CHRIST ENERGY

In most ancient teachings nine movements are taught, nine being the 3x3, the understanding of the Christ energy. There are, indeed, nine movements of perfected energy within the Eight-sided Cell of Perfection.[7]

FIRST MOVEMENT

These nine perfected movements begin always in the central source, the heart. This is the Temple of Your Being, and within all Shamanic movement upon the Earth Plane and Planet, the central location is always where the temple resides. This is infinite space from which all future holograms of perfection mirror — it is the central source. It is the perfection of all being (creation) and it mirrors perfection throughout the rest of the movement within the Eight-sided Cell of Perfection.

---

3. Intuition, instinct, gut feeling, sixth sense — these definitions aptly explain the Intuitive Mind on a basic level, but according to esoteric teachings, it encompasses much more. The Intuitive Mind comprises the entire energy field, including the aura; the chakras; the energy meridians; the bonds with spirit and the Earth Mother; and the connections to higher wisdom and knowledge. With the help of the Intuitive Mind, the soul grows at its own rate and vibration of development. Albert Einstein summed it up best, "The Intuitive Mind is a sacred gift and the rational mind is a faithful servant. We have created a society that honors the servant and has forgotten the gift."

4. Expressive intuition is an innate psychic gift, but to the degree a person develops this aspect of the Intuitive Mind is their choice. Artists, psychics, and channels dip into the intuitive-driven supersenses — clairvoyance, clairaudience, clairsentience, and clairgustance — to practice their craft. The great Prophet Edgar Cayce spoke often about intuition in spiritual teachings, "The more and more one is impelled by that which is intuitive or the relying upon the soul force within; the further, the deeper, the broader, the more constructive may be the result." Literal Intuition is also known as instinct.

5. See Appendix P1: *Eight-sided Cell of Perfection Energy Map.*

6. See Appendix Q1: *Energy Maps.*

7. See Appendix Q1: *Path of Energy through the Eight-sided Cell of Perfection.*

SECOND MOVEMENT

Facing, of course, this most central area is the altar, or the Unfed Flame of Infinite Being and Energy. This creates energy through the career, fame, and fortune, which you have chosen as your Divine Path. This is the next perfected movement of expression.

THIRD MOVEMENT

The next expression is the movement toward marriage, or the longing for another with whom to share life. Naturally, this next movement is known as family.

DIAGRAM OF THE FIRST THREE MOVEMENTS

Let me diagram these for you again. The first movement exists in the center and is indeed the altar or the Temple. The next movement is toward the Divine Path (dharma). These are essentially as ONE. They are also known as Divine Purpose.

The second movement from here, or the third in sequence, is indeed marriage. It is the longing for the Twin Flame, the other half of yourself.

FOURTH MOVEMENT

The fourth perfected movement is that of family. For when two become as one, they move in cosmic purpose. This also relates to cosmic movement in its totality (macrocosm). These are the first four movements of energy in the Eight-sided Cell of Perfection.

THE MICROCOSM MIRRORS THE MACROCOSM

Now let us move to the human body. These exact movements are the same within the physical system. They bring about healing for another who may have problems in any one of these areas. They also address the direction or the course of energy movement through the knowledge of the Eight-sided Cell of Perfection.

Perhaps if one is having trouble in their career — or Divine Purpose — you will note the Ray as it arcs from the central source of the heart, and you will understand how to bring forth such a treatment. The same goes for one who desires to meet their beloved, and to bring forth the fruition of marriage on this plane. And so you see there are numerous applications!

The movement of energy in the microcosm is mirrored with the macrocosm.

THE DIVINE HEAVEN

Now let us continue. As there are five more directions, each direction matches with the fingers of the hand and the toes of the feet. For you see Dear ones, these are all concerned with manifestations brought forward on the Earth Plane and Planet, the first four manifestations belong to the Divine Heavens — an infinite understanding of being.

EARTH: CAUSE AND EFFECT

These last five movements are equally important, as they are the measurement of Cause and Effect. They are the measurement of your planes of duality and your understanding of Hermetic Law.

THE FIFTH MOVEMENT

The fifth direction is children. Children bring and represent that great fruition and understanding between the sexes. Children are a generation of the forces of nature; they are made of the energies of male and female — the Yin and Yang — coming together. Children represent the future, and they also represent the path of abundance that a couple or a union shares.

THE SIXTH MOVEMENT

The sixth movement is of benevolent beings of a higher force that assist this family or movement. This is where your spiritual teachers reside. It is through this energy of the sixth movement that your spiritual teachers, contacts, and guides come through at the most auspicious moment to help and assist you, to guide you, and lead you further on the path of evolution.

THE SEVENTH MOVEMENT

The seventh direction is the direction of abundance. This is the understanding that not only wealth, but total prosperity brings perfection to the incarnation on the Earth Plane and Planet. This is the best location to grow gardens — outwardly and inwardly — and develop your link to beloved Mother Earth — Babajeran. Are there questions, Dear ones?

Answer: "No, not at this time."

THE EIGHTH MOVEMENT

The eighth movement is the direction of occupation. The eighth understanding determines where we toil in this world, and it is much different from the career. For instance, one may have the Divine Purpose of a mother. However, her daily occupation may be as caregiver, nurse, or doctor. So the career — or the Divine Purpose — of this woman is that, indeed, of mother, however, her occupation is much different. Do you understand this difference?

Answer: "Yes."

THE NINTH MOVEMENT

The final direction, of which we will concern ourselves, is the direction of outer influence. It is indeed a much misunderstood direction, but it is one that is of vast importance. It is choice! Choices are made to enhance or dehance (weaken). These are the types of choices made within the lifetime — the embodiment. It is here where one decides to take a higher or a lower way. Which way shall I go? Through the comprehension of choice, supreme knowledge is obtained. Understand the difference in choices, and knowledge is understood. This final direction is known as the Star of Knowledge. It is through this movement that all chelas and initiates of this work begin to

follow, most discriminately. You see, Dear ones, choice creates our future, yet choice remains with us as the past. The Star of Knowledge contains within it the infinity of time. For it contains both past and future, and we return home to the infinite Temple of Love, Wisdom, and Power! From this direction, infinity is known, and the Eight-sided Cell of Perfection mirrors to the first direction again, and so on, and so forth.

PERFECTING EACH MOVEMENT

Each of these directions is a spiritual discipline, and one may incarnate only to perfect but one mirroring. Perhaps they have chosen to be the most perfect parent, and therefore, arc the greater part of energy toward that direction. Another may decide that they shall be a priest, and therefore, mirror or project their energy toward the sixth direction. Another may decide that he or she shall mirror his or her energy into business and into the eighth movement. Does this bring an understanding of perfect energy?

Answer: "Yes."

Within the seventh direction of abundance, you will find a tendency for your money and wealth to grow. So understand too, if one is directed in their incarnation toward continuous prosperity and abundance, often they will choose occupations that are geared toward the flow of money, banking, and economics. Do you understand?

Answer: "Yes."

BALANCE AND THE PATH OF PERFECTION

Each of these teachings is a perfect path, spiritually linked toward the central source. As you see the flow of the energy of this perfection, do you see how disharmony through war and poverty is brought on the Earth? Without the understanding of infinite perfection, it is difficult to proceed upon this path of Mastery, for one begins to perceive imbalance.

Yet when one moves to the understanding that all things are in perfect balance at all times, balance is then achieved through the Path of Perfection. It is important always to keep your mind upon the Path of Perfection. Left balances out right; hot balances out cold; and the front balances out the back. Study and assign attributes to each of these Paths of Perfection, and see that balance is present at all times.

Balance is always found in the center point — the heart of all understanding, the infinite understanding of Love, Wisdom, and Power, all brought together through that perfect blend.

All energy moves through light, and indeed through sound. Have you noticed as you open the windows in your house, how the sunlight carries energy that circulates throughout your home? This is also true of sound; one who carries a pleasant voice also carries the benevolence of the Gods. When you play harmonious music, the strings of a harp and the tone of a piano carry a higher vibration and energy. This energy feeds each of the paths of perfection. You have noticed that through light and sound, healing comes forward to a patient. Have you not?

Answer: "Yes, indeed."

THE MOVEMENT OF LIGHT AND SOUND

This is the same with all of your other activities. Even in your business, bring forward light and bring forward sound. Light and sound move stagnant and dead energy, energy that needs to be moved out! As one develops a Mastery of the movement of energy through light and sound, one begins to understand the cause behind the force that moves. This returns to the center of this understanding, the infinite source — that Unfed Flame. Thought, feeling, and action are the movers of light and sound! When they come together in perfect partnership, the movement is even more potent or powerful! This first concept is taught through that process known as mentalism. We have always stated before that "as a man thinketh, so he becomes." Have you noted this?

THOUGHT CREATES

Thought creates.[8] Thought moves light, and thought, indeed, moves sound. Thought entering into perfect union with sound is also known as feeling. When one feels the purpose of their thought, again, it's a much more powerful movement. It adds the trinity of action in that same, direct course — thought, feeling, and action move together in perfect partnership through the perfect path of light and sound movements of energy. Do you understand that it is desirable to learn the movement of energy through thought, feeling, and action of light and sound?

Answer: "Yes."

ENERGETIC FLUX

When one begins to Master these components, one truly becomes the Master of all energy movement. I stated earlier in this discourse that there is a slight difference in the direction of energy movement prior to a polar shift; you will notice that your Westerly directions are off five to sixteen degrees depending on the flux of the energy fields of the Earth. It is important to consider this in all of your calculations. It is also important to understand this for the times to come.[9]

---

8. Mentalism is the study of mental perception and thought processes — it's the understanding that these states are to action as cause is to effect. Author James Allen said it best in his book *As a Man Thinketh*, "Every action and feeling is preceded by a thought."

9. The ancient Vedic rishis — advanced spiritual teachers who lived in the previous ages of superior light and truth — gave humanity the science of Vastu, gross energies, and Vaastu, subtle energies. They recognized the Earth's natural energy conduits, also known as lei-lines, which form a grid around the planet. This esoteric system of latitudinal and longitudinal striae, running from the dipolar magnetic points of North and South and from East to West, follows the path of the Sun. This web of electromagnetic energy creates a subtle influence on an individual's mind and body as it transforms the Causal and Astral Body (Light Bodies). This effect becomes noticeable as these changes reshape physical health in the body and overall life experiences. The Earth's imperfect spin perpetually shifts to the fixed position of the stars. The following visible results demonstrate the wobble of the Earth:

1. In the fifteenth century, the pole-star Polaris was first used to navigate true North. Yet in the year 150 BC, it moved 12° 24 minutes from these coordinates. In 13,000 years the star Vega will replace Polaris as the pole-star.[4] Not all ancient cultures followed Polaris as its focal point. The ancient Egyptians relied on Alpha Draconis (Dracaenas) as their polestar in the construction of the pyramids.

GOLDEN AGE

As I stated before, the direction of Collective Consciousness is now directed more Northerly, or toward more male-dominated experiences. This has created in your societies an overextension toward warring and an overextension toward materialism and comfort seeking; and too much harshness, inflexibility, and hardness in the world. After the Pole Shifts, an orientation toward the South will become prevalent. Therefore, this will be known as a Golden Age — the Age of Gold. For Gold is indeed the metal associated with the South. A Southern exposure of consciousness will orient toward the feminine; an understanding of unity; and a softness, shall we say, of consciousness.

EARTH, THE PERFECT MIRROR

Do you see the contrast again: hot and cold, soft and hard? Do you see, Dear ones, how the Earth is the most perfect, benevolent schoolhouse? It's a perfect mirror of your thoughts, of your feelings, and of your actions. Through this understanding, your world is the total creation of perfection — a total creation of the Eight-sided Cell of Perfection; each of these paths mirror from within through your thought, your feeling, and your action. All that manifests comes through the perfection of your out-picturing and through the perfection of your conscious attunement; what's in your being is fed through the infinite ONE. Do you have questions?

Answer: "Not at this time."

MASTERY

When one begins to understand the movement of energy, one is able to enter on a path of total Mastery over their created world. For you see, you have come forward to learn how to create your perfect world. Through the creation of an imperfect world, one learns and moves forward to create a perfect world, a perfect experience. Through perfection comes Mastery, and through the spiral of evolution comes increased duty and responsibility. As you have known for some time, in this creation of the new Golden Age which is peaceful and feminine, you are moving forward in your own evolution to become a Master: first a Master of your created worlds, and then a Master directing the created world of form.

A COLLECTIVE FOCUS

The Ascended Masters have been appointed to guard the evolution of humanity at this time so that humanity may move forward in a most constructive and non-destructive manner. We work through the energy of consciousness much like Shamans of energy movement. We, too, work with chi, orgone, light, and sound![10] These are a few words that you have come to know energy through and by. This energy movement is quite important in the movement of consciousness, for again, as stated in the law, "as a man thinketh, so he becomes." So as humanity thinketh, so it is! The great civilizations that have flourished in other Golden Ages understood the one perfect focus that all carried — the one perfect path from the Eight-sided Cell of Perfection. That was the sole focus — unity and harmony of their thoughts, of their feelings, and of their actions together as ONE organism. This, of course, is known as a Collective Consciousness aimed toward a collective focus.

When we move our energy toward a collective focus there are times when we come together. Sometimes, beloved El Morya or beloved Portia joins alongside me in directing an energy focus toward an entire group of chelas aimed toward collective unity!

---

2. The wobble of the Earth also causes precession of the equinoxes. Precession is the slow backward shifting motion of the Earth as it rotates.[5] This slight tilting of the pole is calculated at approximately 23.5°; it's the source of the Vedic Ayanamsha, which differentiates planetary movements against the position of stars — sidereal astrology. In contrast, tropical or Western astrology tracks planets in reference to seasonal points according to a point of view from Earth. Vedic astrology adjusts for precession; the Western system does not.

10. Many schools of thought address energy movement — chi, orgone, or prana — in some capacity. Two doctrines, however, express these principles in a comprehensive historical perspective, Vastu Shastra and Vastu Vidya. They form the foundation of the 4,500-year-old dwelling sciences of Vedic philosophy and Classical Chinese Feng Shui, the Taoist art and science of living in harmony in the environment.

BUILDING THE GOLDEN AGE

We have started a movement, working through our chelas, to understand this current Time of Transition and the upcoming Time of Change. That is why we have sent the Prophecies of Change. There are those who resonate toward this message. Those are the ones who have come under the direction of the movement of our light and sound vehicles (Light Bodies); those are the ones who have been sensitized and are aware of the perfect path.

Now, these beloved ones have come together in an understanding through this Divine Focus for the building of the Golden Age — the time beyond the changes. In this time you shall move forward as Divine Inheritors, and each path of perfection will be experienced in its totality, allowing you to spiral up the stairs of the Eight-sided Cell of Perfection toward the infinite union of the ONE.

STAGNATION

Do you see how the evolutionary process works through these Eight Paths of Perfection that are aimed toward the unity of the last and final path — complete Mastery over your thoughts, your feelings, and your actions? As this Mastery is attained, another level of understanding is brought forward into a greater service and a greater union with the ONE. At that staging point, the movement of energy becomes even greater. But for now, so that you may keep your focus on the task at hand, it is most important that you first Master your own world, and bring forth the path of perfect harmony. As Kuan Yin has often stated, "perfect harmony with a perfect path."

Do you see, Dear ones, how this movement of energy, once it is Mastered, can instigate the calculation or strategy of your next move? For you have thought for some time, "Where should I move: to the left or to the right, to the front or to the back, do I move up or do I move down?" Therefore, you move not at all! This non-movement causes stagnation. Have you noticed that when a pool of water has no movement, the waters become stagnant and rancid? This is what happens when you refuse to move beyond what you have indeed Mastered. We have asked you several times to make movement, and yet you find it impossible to move beyond where you have contained yourself, and therefore the energy — the chi, the light, the sound — enacts a series of events that are non-movement. The lack of movement causes disease and problems within your world, and sometimes even a backward motion ensues! Now that you have had this experience, Dear ones, do you see the microcosm as a reflection of the greater macrocosm? Can you understand why the Earth will go through its Time of Great Change? Humanity refuses to move forward, and this causes stagnation.

"BE A LIGHT"

Your work is to be a light to those so they may move forward during these times. Do you see now, through the path of the Eight-sided Cell of Perfection how all must move forward with perfect alignment to the perfect plan?

Answer: "Yes, I understand. Thank you."

CHAPTER FOURTEEN

The Point of Perception

᠍ᢒ

*Saint Germain's teachings on the
conscious Co-creation process.*

Greetings beloveds, in that Mighty Christ. I AM
Saint Germain and I stream forth on that Mighty Transmuting
Violet Ray of Mercy and Forgiveness. As usual Dear hearts, I
ask permission to come forward.

Response: "Saint Germain, you have permission."

FROM THE OUTER TO WITHIN

Often you ask within, "What is my purpose here? What is
the purpose of life and this existence in the physical?"

Dear ones, the work of Prophecy has been brought forward
to show you that you are indeed the Creator of your reality. It
is a teaching that scratches only the surface, and only the chela
that is willing to go deeper within discovers that he or she is
linked to the purpose of all things.

Prophecy is a teaching that begins at the greater reality, and
then leads one into the inner-reality. That greater reality is of
the world: political systems, social systems, and geophysical
systems. Then the student or chela faces the inner being; the
inner systems that exist, such as the soul's intention; and the
individual's purpose of life in the physical reality.[1]

CHOICE AND CREATION

You have asked many times in your meditations, "Why am
I doing this? What is the intention of this work? What is the
purpose of my life on Earth?" You see, Dear hearts, you are
here for one sole purpose, and that is your choice. You have all
chosen to come here! All choose to take physical incarnation.
All choose the circumstances of each birth. All chose the time
that each incarnates.

When one begins to understand that they are the Creator of
their circumstances, their situations, and all things surrounding
them, they are placed, shall we say, into a new division. For
you have begun to understand that thought, feeling, and desire
through your expert focus creates your reality, it creates your
circumstances, and it creates each situation.

THE "NEW" AND COLLECTIVE CONSCIOUSNESS

You may wonder, "Where does time fit into all of this?" You
see time as a nonexistent entity, and a way to identify each circumstance, each situation. Time is relative in this respect, Dear
hearts. Time comes forward to serve your creation. So then, you
move on to understand that there is no past, there is no future,

---

1. The science of souls is defined through realities perceived by various
systems of the soul, including:
- The Soul's Intention: An overall plan or theme carried forward throughout every lifetime. This intention or destiny evolves over lifetimes.
- Individual Purpose: Each lifetime fulfills a specific purpose. This may be
a particular quality or aspect related to the soul's overall intention of
growth.
- Significance of Choice: Before a new lifetime, the soul chooses the
circumstances of birth, his or her parents, and the time to re-enter the
physical plane. The work of Dr. Michael Newton, a life-between-life
therapist, has documented this concept extensively: "This depends
on the nature of the upcoming life, the karmic lessons to be addressed … prior to some lives, only one or two body choices are
offered, at other visits to the place of life selection they may be given
up to five (body choices) … souls seem to know which body would be

their best choice for learning and they usually choose it." A soul, according to Newton's research, will test various potentials and possibilities in large screening rooms before each lifetime. The examination offers a snapshot of possible events and potentials. Though the certainty
of future events isn't written in stone, the soul is already prepared for
the opportunities, choices, and challenges in the upcoming lifetime.
Newton describes this process as: "An indefinite number of futures
connected to a present in the now Time of the spirit world. And yet,
while there must be many futures, souls seem to view the most likely
futures in a matrix of possibilities and probabilities. On the screens,
events and opportunities of a future life may be enlarged and drawn
out, or reduced in size for soul analysis. It is like looking at the large
trunks and smaller branches of trees. I use this analogy because some
timelines combined with certain life scenes seem more prominent than
others."
- Co-creation: An advanced system, which addresses thought, feeling,
and action, utilized by the soul. It directs the soul as a contributing
Creator of reality, circumstance, and situation.
- The application of the Law of Harmony (balance) in all situations. The
consciousness of the soul is at all times in touch with its intention;
therefore, it is aware of the situations and the circumstances of previous lifetimes, and the contexts of future lifetimes. The soul's efforts and
actions are often focused on this unconscious yet prevailing knowledge and insight.

there is only now. The time is now! We have always stated this in the introductory teachings of Prophecy. The times that come ahead, which could be a time of geophysical, social, political, and economic upheaval, are all those events chosen by the will of the Collective Consciousness.

Collective Consciousness is a higher structure, a higher arcing of energy of individual consciousness.[2] You, yourself, as an individual have individual consciousness. This we have studied, Dear hearts, in understanding layers of the auric field and the flame within the heart. However, as we have taught in many other teachings, you are linked to a greater Oneship — the consciousness of Unana, the consciousness of the ONE. This consciousness of the ONE is comprised in its simplest form of two or more. However, there can be many more linked into this greater scope of consciousness. This we have called in other teachings as a unified field of thought. This is taught in the First Jurisdiction in the teachings of Creatorship as harmony.

HARMONY UNITES

When harmony is present among two or more, there is the potential and the possibility for a unified collective thought. The unified collective thought creates a greater reality, a greater understanding. This greater understanding, which comes forward in the consciousness of Unana, is what is meant by the term Collective Consciousness. Collective Consciousness acts on a greater will, greater than the individual; and it serves the plan of the group united in harmony.

ADJUST THE BANDWIDTH

You may scratch your head and wonder, "We have created this reality through harmony?" This is indeed so! What you see, you have created. What you are living is what you have created. This creation comes forward through harmony. It is very similar to adjusting your television to a bandwidth to receive a television program. In the same manner you adjust your own receiver to a bandwidth of new experience.

"SURFING UPON THE WAVES"

Let me explain this even further. There are indeed different planes, or unified fields of Collective Consciousness that you may tune yourself individually. This is how you adjust experience. This is how you can adjust the way that you perceive a situation — a circumstance. When you understand this concept there are many possibilities that exist within a bandwidth of Collective Consciousness. You will begin to understand the power of your choice and the power of your Creatorship. You are in essence, like consciousness surfing upon the waves of time.[3]

A MULTITUDE OF EXPERIENCE

Time, again, is perceived by the individual, but you are surfing upon a selection of circumstances and situations, and you are at the controls. You are the Master of this show, the Master of Ceremony of your life! Bearing this in mind, Dear hearts, Dear ones, Dear chelas, you are now ready to move forward. Understand that through your ONE collective reality that you have created exists a multitude of choices and a multitude of experiences that you may now choose from. Have you not noted while driving in traffic that your experience can be one of many? You can be frustrated; you can be peaceful; you can be

---

2. Saint Germain defines Collective Consciousness as a higher structure or a "higher-arcing (hierarchy)" of "individual consciousness." Simply defined as "two or more," Collective Consciousness is also known as a unified field of thought or Unana among more than one being. (See Unana, Unity Consciousness). Some define Collective Consciousness as a field of awareness and intelligence that exists in all human beings. This phenomenon allows our ability to intuitively sense and interact with the physical, emotional, mental, and spiritual energy fields of others, primarily beyond the constraints of space and time. Well-documented examples of this activity include telepathy and remote-viewing. Advanced uses of Collective Consciousness thought-fields — through the use of focused attention or intention — can create order in physical systems and synchronization among nervous systems. This is known as remote or long-distance healing. Research shows marked reductions in crime rates, drug abuse, traffic fatalities, and unemployment in cities and areas where Transcendental Meditation programs have applied the "pervasive field of Collective Consciousness." These projects influence coherence and neutralize stress.

3. Time Surfing is the ability to adjust experiences in the past, present, or future by intentionally choosing various scenarios and re-languaging them with new perceptions and choices.

focused; you can be detached — a multitude of feelings that you can have through the simple act of driving.

Now, let us take this idea to a greater idea, a greater experience.

In your life today are many choices, many possibilities of how you may live out each moment. Each moment — not time — each moment is a situation, a circumstance of how you choose to experience living in a greater collective reality. Do you see that you are surfing the greater reality, choosing your experiences? Choice does indeed create!

The creation comes through harmony. This greater harmony that you have come to experience is imbedded, again, in the principle of your choice. As your choices come together, there is indeed the collective reality. Do you see the relationship, Dear one?

Answer: "Yes."

THE TEACHINGS OF CONSCIOUSNESS

So in laying this framework, this groundwork, I would like to proceed and impart more understanding. As you now see that you have many experiences to choose from, how is it that you may travel among each of these experiences, each of these circumstances, each of these situations? It is through your consciousness. Now let us refer back to the beginning teachings of consciousness. Consciousness creates an electromagnetic pulse. This electromagnetic pulse is the basis of the field of life that exists around you known as the Human Aura. I have explained this in previous teachings, and the Human Aura can be separated into different bodies or fields of light. Each of these fields of light experiences a different circumstance, a different situation. We may call these simply the Emotional Body; the mental body. These are teachings that I have given in prior discourse, and if you review them, you then will understand this next point.

Much as you are able to adjust your experiences among each situation that you choose, and each circumstance that you choose, how is it that you are able to perceive difference? It is through creation, again through thought, that a new body is formed through that mental Point of Perception. This allows the consciousness to travel to each experience. This body of light, as it is called and known by in these teachings, radiates through each of these experiences.

SIMULTANEOUS CREATION

Now, there would be those who call this a Simultaneous Experience, but now you understand yourself as a Creator, as the originator, the God-source of these different bodies of light. You see, within yourself is a hierarchy of creation! Many different bodies of light travel through to an experience, a point in time that is perceived, and then the totality of that experience is allowed through circumstance and situation.

"THE SOURCE WITHIN"

What enfolds from this unified field of understanding is Simultaneous Embodiment, fields of light springing from the ONE continuous source that precedes, and even from one point again, as one point has sprouted from that source. Again it contains the source within it, and so it is able to sprout again, or perceive a new reality, a new consciousness. Let me diagram this so that you understand with greater clarity.

He is now drawing on a chalkboard. And he has drawn out a circle at the top right-hand corner, and from that he has drawn a line down and drawn another circle.[4]

This, you see, is the Point of Perception from the Source to a new experience. Now, at the point of the Source, ONE has not given up its one perception. Instead, the perception becomes dual, therefore, there are two experiences happening simultaneously.

Now he is drawing four more lines from the first.

PERCEPTION EXPANDS

And so you see, Dear hearts, as this Point of Perception travels to another sphere and dimension — Point of Perception of

_____

4. See Appendix S1: *Diagrams for the Point of Perception.*

understanding — there is now the opportunity, again, for more perception and more understanding. And so you see, it is a web of creation, hierarchal in a sense, but connected and joined. You see, at all times, all is emanating from this Source, the center of this creation, this creation of choice, yet, it is perceiving different circumstances — different situations. Yet they are all linked ideally as ONE. It is indeed a web of consciousness that creates a greater understanding and a greater reality. This is how our consciousness is linked with your consciousness. This is how your consciousness becomes linked into a new reality, a new circumstance, a new situation. Indeed, we are the Creators of time! Therefore, we must become the Masters of Time. Do you have questions?

Question: "Do I experience you because I can perceive you?"

This is true. But understand this, Dear chela, the perception you have is because of our link to each other. Do you understand?

Response: "No."

PERCEPTION CREATES REALITY

We are linked together through the perception of consciousness. Now you perceive me as an entity of consciousness to be greater than you, and yet this is not true! We are linked together. We contain the ONE Source. We are equal in this sense. Now again, I may have a Mastery of my creation that you may not, but then again that *difference* is always as dear Sananda has stated, "the experience." So my challenge to you, Dear hearts, is to understand these lessons in creation, understand these lessons in projecting consciousness. Questions?

Question: "Does a poor person live in poverty because that is all they can perceive?"

SIDE-BY-SIDE CREATION

This is so. This is my point exactly! Each reality is created through the perception. Now, you can have a simultaneous perception, however, those perceptions may or may not have harmony. That is contingent upon your out-picturing. Now, can poverty and wealth exist simultaneously? Of course they can! Yet, there are those who perceive that you may only be poor or you may only be wealthy, yet we know, as the world has proven, that they exist side-by-side. Is this not so?

Answer: "True, because poverty may not just be money; you may be wealthy but poor of character, poor of intention."

SHAPESHIFTING PERCEPTION

Well stated, Dear one, yet these are simultaneous experiences. The Master of the creation understands that harmony exists within each of these experiences. Harmony, as outlined in the Hermetic Law, is founded upon Laws of Polarity and Laws of Satvva, or Rhythm. For every time there is a season. Now, the Master of the creation begins to understand that there is a rhythm to creation, and there is a rhythm to the Point of Perception. What does this mean in the greater reality? It means that at any time perception can be shifted. The focus, or point of perception, can be taken on one experience, and removed, and put on another. This is what is known as shapeshifting — shifting the Point of Perception, becoming what is necessary to fulfill the desire within the heart, the desire of creation.[5]

---

5. Saint Germain teaches that shapeshifting occurs when we move from one point of perception to another, becoming "necessary to fulfill the desire of creation." John Perkins, founder of *Dream Change*, identifies the three levels of shapeshifting.
- Cellular: Indigenous people can shapeshift into a plant or an animal. In the modern Western culture, this type of occurrence is analogous to cancer that miraculously disappears. Or losing weight, toning your body through exercise, and changing your physical appearance.
- Personal Transformation: Examples include overcoming an addiction, and spiritual growth, and awakening.
- Societal or Cultural Transformation: Transforming the institutions that shape our lives: corporations, governments, laws, workplaces, businesses, media, schools, and churches. According to the Ascended Masters, this is one of the important purposes of the Golden Cities.

Now, does the other creation continue? It could. It depends on the amount of energy that is poured into it by the Creator for experience, circumstance, and situation. But as the Point of Perception, the preceptor begins to pour the consciousness forward to another stream in time. Then the energy of thought, feeling, and action is poured to that point. Do you understand?

Answer: "Yes, I do. The thought that comes to me is, I am perceived by you and you are perceived by me. However, I am of the opinion that you have out-pictured me to do what I am doing."

Yet, do you not contain the ONE within you?

Answer: "True, because it is all the same point of purpose."

"EQUAL TO"

It is all connected to the ONE, and therefore, each point is not less than but equal to! Therefore, if indeed I have out-pictured to you, then could you not return to me?

Answer: "True."

Then could you not out-picture onward into your own creation?

Answer: "True."

THE GOD SOURCE

That is your choice. Therefore, you are equal to. If there is a hierarchy, it is only a hierarchy of understanding. Steeped in ignorance and superstition, the teachings to the masses contain no hierarchy — just a desire to control. Yet, there is this understanding, that when one grasps it, they understand that they are the center of their universe. They are their own Great Central Sun. Inside of each individual is Helios and Vesta, for invested in them is the God Source. Now, Dear hearts, when we speak of Monad or Jiva that is what we speak of. It is the great flame that we are all of.

PROJECTION OF CONSCIOUSNESS

Now let us get on to the work at hand — creation and Creatorship. As I had mentioned, there are Light Bodies that exist for traveling among each out-pictured reality. The consciousness perceives itself as whole among each reality or each dimensional leap, for each reality is ideally as ONE. But let us, just for now, say it is between a dimension. Let me explain.

He's walking to the board, and he is showing the line that exists between the second circle and one where he has drawn the four circles.

You see from this perspective …

He is pointing at the end to one of the four circles.

Perception from here would say … from this line to this line.

Now he's pointing between the circles.

One would perceive that this is higher than this.

Now he is moving between each of the circles in the diagram.

But indeed, these are not higher realities. Indeed, these are not other dimensions. That is only what this experience labels it as *in* perception. These are instead united as ONE. However, the sense of separation is this circle, here, that is on the end, has not yet out-pictured and created another stream of consciousness. Now, how does this circle — the one on the end — which perceives itself on the end, begin to understand its link to all of consciousness? It comes through the creation of additional Light Bodies. Inasmuch as the Human Aura has been created by the being through the out-picturing of the being linked to it, this (Light Body) now begins to project another body of light to another reality. This projection comes again through what you have known as thought, feeling, and action.

This projection begins first through the dream world. Many are of the perception that the body requires rest. This, as you know, is entirely untrue. Instead, it is a time allotted in the creative activity to allow the consciousness to create! The consciousness, at this time, is projecting to another point in the ONE. The stream of consciousness projects to what you will now call in your experience, another dimension. However, it is experiencing a projection into a unified ONE. There (the person) projects through thought, and feeling; it desires a new body, a new electromagnetic energy, and a current force from the mighty ONE — the Monad. This is why at night you may have many experiences, each of them very different, each of them varied within the range and scope of experience, each of them containing a different force or life. This I know you understand, because you have experienced it. Do you awaken some mornings feeling disjointed, feeling as if you have been in many different places all at once?

Answer: "Quite frequently."

Indeed, this is the experience of the projection of consciousness into many different places, into your own web of creation. Do you also have an experience when you know that you have been directed to one point and remember this as well?

Answer: "Of course!"

Now what is that? It is but a higher development of that body into a directed stream.[6] It is gaining force and energy. Do you see how the simultaneous existence of you is now possible?

Answer: "But it is only perceived through the dream state."

---

6. Recurring dreams and frequent visits to specific locations in the dream world expand an energy known as directed stream. When a repeated pattern of consciousness occurs, the directed stream suggests that an experience is gaining force and energy. The following examples illustrate this point:
1. Visions
2. Lucid dreaming
3. Out-picturing through meditation and visualization.
A directed stream of consciousness is the outgrowth of developed memory. This expanded use of memory is the result of tapping into the Co-creation process through thought, feeling, and action.

MEMORY

Now, let us work to bring that dream state into a greater understanding and reality. What is the experience of a vision or a lucid dream? It is the development of memory. Memory is brought through the experience of perseverance. It is a repeated pattern that allows the consciousness to be trained, pouring in a continuous stream of the electromagnetic current of thought, feeling, action, and focus. Do you realize that when you meditate during the day that this meditation is only training the memory to work at night? This trains the consciousness as it is detached from physical reality, and from the physical reality that you are currently experiencing.

MEDITATION

Throughout the day you identify with your body. You identify with its movements, its needs, its limitations, its desires. This, too, is an out-picturing of consciousness that has preceded you. But now you are working to bring your web of creation into your Mastery of time and space. So you perceive consciousness as being detached from the body as a stream, shall we say, of pure energy. This you experience in meditation through visualization and through out-picturing. This is put in a greater practice at night into your dream state.

Now, I shall go one step further. Questions?

Question: "Consciousness and perception is multi-level?"

Exactly.

Question: "Is the reality we call Three Dimensional reality the point of consciousness and perception where we have persevered and placed the most focus?"

This is correct.

Question: "To alter the reality that we have created by placing the most focus, we choose another reality that we then consciously, actively, and with perseverance and diligence pour focus into?"

THE HEART'S DESIRE

And with purpose, Dear heart, with purpose! Now, this purpose is linked to the desire within the heart. The purpose and the desire link us as ONE. For you see, that is where the harmony streams forth to allow the creation to come forward in abundance.

Question: "So it is the desire that I have in my heart for humanity's freedom that is a linked purpose that you and I have?"

This is so, beloved. Now, do you see the greater understanding that you are indeed linked? We are all linked as ONE. And yet each of us serves through our choice and creates through our choice. That is where individual Mastery is achieved, yet we are all linked as ONE. I would like to proceed to a new level of understanding.

CONTINUITY

Now we are linked as ONE — one understanding. How do you move into a synthesis of understanding and creation? Do you see, Dear one, how you must become like that (intention, desire) which birthed you to continue your link to the ONE?

Answer: "But, what birthed me was the desire of that freedom!"

That is correct.
Answer: "And the understanding of creation."

So this leads us to the next level of understanding. You must become I; I must become you.

Question: "Well, what are the steps to achieve this?"

CONSCIENTIOUS CONSCIOUSNESS

You must out-picture and become conscientiously conscious of your creations. This conscientious consciousness brings to the forefront the full memory of your different points of perception, and then it chooses those creations you pour your energy into. These are simultaneous realities or simultaneous experiences from which you can choose.[7] And in the same way that a great force out-pictured my own existence, now the same happens for you! Each of the bodies that you have created into different experiences requires your conscientious memory. It is always best in these beginning steps of understanding your creations to focus on a half a dozen or so — no more than six at a time — six different possible realities that you are pouring your energy into.

AN EXPERIMENT WITH SIX DIFFERENT REALITIES

Six different realities that you know and understand create through your perception. This allows you to become more aware of your creations at a memory level. Again, know this, it is the development of memory that we are focusing on. When we say, "to awaken," it is to awaken the greater memory — the knowledge of total experience birthed through the field of harmony. Now, let me give you a hypothetical situation so you may understand this with greater clarity.

Currently, there are six different Earth Changes realities that exist. The first reality is a world that is completely destroyed by the asteroid. The second is a world that has seen the shifting of tectonic plates with only one half of the population of the

---

7. In the linear world we experience a concrete past and anticipate an unknown future. Therefore, the future pulls us toward our expectations. Simultaneous reality, however, is based on a non-linear perspective of time. It prepares us for potential possibilities in all situations — past, present, and future — and retains the capacity for multiple encounters and outcomes. Each reality exists side by side, so humans can consciously open up to these events to gain insight and self-knowledge. Author Lynda Madden Dahl discussed simultaneous reality in her book *The Wizards of Consciousness*: "The sudden answer to a current problem, the strength just when we need it, the optimism that seemed lacking yesterday, but floods today, sometimes comes from other portions of our self who are experiencing those issues."

world left. The third world is filled with pollution, global warming, and flooded coastal cities. The fourth is a world that has begun to understand that it has created this situation — this scenario — and is now enacting treaties at a global level to help the pollution of the Earth. The fifth is a reality where the world has been destroyed through nuclear destruction, and the sixth is another reality where the need for global peace has become so strong that all are now living under one great treaty and war is no longer! Now, do you see the different realities that are instantly created? As I described each of these realities, could you see them?

Answer: "Absolutely!"

As I describe each of these could you feel them?

Answer: "Yes."

Perhaps you may use as a template, for your thought, one of these realities and project into it, and then begin that experience. Now do you understand how your life has been created? Answer: "Yes."

PERCEIVE — RECEIVE

Now, let us turn this around. Do you see that when you have struggles, or cannot achieve a goal, what the problem is?

Question: "You cannot visualize it?"

You have not been able to perceive; you have not been able to out-picture; you have not been able to visualize. It is that simple, Dear one.

Now, to create an alternative reality you must be able to receive it. Perceive — Receive. They are related!

To perceive something, one must be able to receive it. This again creates the link among circles, as I have diagrammed on the board. To perceive a creation, one must be able to receive it. To aid in the creation of multiple realities, one must be focused; also, one must be able to experience it, to receive it, and to create it into their reality.

Now, how do we bring this into physicality? How do we take an experience that we perceive and are ready to receive? How do we generate it into the physical reality? It is pouring the energy with the focus of consciousness. It is that simple. It is the pouring of consciousness into. It is the focus, you see.

Do you see how each of the six possible realities could become your reality if you poured the focus into them?

Answer: "'Pouring focus in,' is a very foggy statement!"

THE CANDLE MEDITATION

I see. Let me explain. Remember when you were given the exercise by El Morya to become ONE with the candle?[8]

Answer: "Yes."

That is the point of focus. You poured your intention. You poured your thought, and soon you become ONE with it. Did you not become the heat of the flame in that moment?

Answer: "Yes."

That is the point of consciousness traveling through what you perceive as *time* to another point in consciousness.

Dear Sananda has brought this teaching forward. For new wine to be poured it must be poured into a new wineskin — there must be a place to pour consciousness into. That place is your Point of Perception. That place is how you define yourself, and you pour your focus and intention into it, and become one with it. But, you are still linked to the point of departure, you see, because departure and arrival become as ONE. They are two points linked in immortality. They are deathless. They are filled with the effervescent life.

A MENTAL BLOCK

Now, what you are speaking of, and I shall get to the point, is what is known as a mental block. Sometimes mental blocks

---

8. See Appendix T1: *El Morya's Candle Meditation.*

occur. They occur through doubt, lack of trust, lack of faith, lack of understanding, ignorance, and again, superstitions! These, too, are creations where you have poured energy. You have poured more energy into the doubt, into the superstition, into the ignorance and therefore, you see, it too has created a force. Men have the choice to create truth or ignorance. Yet, they are linked to the ONE. Remember, as we spoke, that poverty or wealth can exist simultaneously? Again, it is where you choose to pour your consciousness toward — your desires, your actions, your emotions, and your feelings. See how it works, Dear one? It is as simple as honing the consciousness.

Question: "Is it almost picturing yourself in the situation?"

USE YOUR SENSES

It is. See yourself, feel the forces about you, become aware through your senses — smell it, touch it, see it, hear it! This, I know you can do!

Question: "So, do this as a mental and spiritual exercise?"

This is what out-picturing is!

Response: "In the event of the candle, in stepping into the candle, you step only into the flame, at least from my experience. I'd become the flame, the light, never burning but ever burning, always light."

WITHDRAW THE OLD CREATION

Much the same as you choose another experience, you see yourself stepping into that experience. But, if you are blocking, or stopping the experience from happening because of an old creation, you must first withdraw your energy from the old creation.[9]
Response: "I see."

---

9. See the *Closure Ceremony* described in "Closing the Circle."

A NEW BODY OF LIGHT

It is hindering you. This is the parable of the new wineskin. You must create the new body of light to travel through consciousness.

Question: "So the purpose in the Violet Flame Decrees?"

Is to destroy the old wineskin!

Question: "To dissolve the old creations?"

Precisely.

Question: "Now in utilizing that technique to dissolve old creations, if you don't visualize what you are dissolving, can you still dissolve it? Can you dissolve it just by saying your intention is to dissolve this block?"

Yes.

Question: "And that is enough?"

THE UNIVERSE RESPONDS WITHOUT JUDGMENT

As long you retain the focus, you see. Consider one who comes from an alcoholic pattern or who has engaged in drug abuse — it's a misperception of creation. These subjective bodies, which we have discussed must be dissolved, for they are hindering the creation of the new desire. The universe has responded objectively and without judgment.

Question: "So when the person thinks or feels that they're unworthy?"

Then, they are unworthy.

Question: "Truly. And the Violet Flame Decrees, you can just utilize and say out loud, 'I AM now dissolving this sense, feeling, thought of unworthiness?' Use decrees, and it dissolves?

Eventually, would you have to stop the decrees so there is no more energy going into the pattern of unworthiness?"

This is so. But it is through the training of the consciousness, for you see the universe will immediately respond without judgment and without hesitation.

Question: "I see. And so it almost sounds like the person who decides they want a new car, and they take a picture of it and tape it on the refrigerator."

It is training and ingraining the consciousness again to that Point of Perception. Train the consciousness to perceive the desired result.

Question: "So what has really happened with the world? Is this the creation of destruction, Earth Changes, or catastrophe for civilization? Is this something that collectively everyone hasn't decided they don't want?"

Some have chosen to do so. Some have chosen not to. And then there are those who choose nothing at all, for they are not ready. For everything there is a time and a season.

Question: "So, on the one point of creating a pristine planet."

It is for those who wish to have that experience; and for those who wish to have destruction, they, too, shall have it! Do you see, Dear heart, you are equal to.

Question: "It is most interesting. I have wondered whether some people who don't even perceive destruction of the planet or Earth Changes, whether that is ever going to be a reality for them, or will they go through it because collectively there are many who do not perceive it?"

Then, those who do not choose, choose to go along.

Response: "I see."

"DOWN WITH DEATH"

Let me continue. In the dream state you have created several different bodies that you utilize for different experiences. These bodies stay in their Point of Perception when the consciousness returns to the physical body. These different Light Bodies are developed for you to put on as a seamless garment — a seamless garment in a point of time that allows yet another creation. As I've always said, "Down with death!" For you see, the aging of your physical body is the aging of your perception in that experience. Do you understand?

Question: "While we're on that subject, would it be wise to have a picture of yourself younger?"

If you wish to youthen the body, this is so. Or you may create another simultaneous experience in which you pour energy. Now when the body dies, it is a stream of consciousness leaving and departing to another reality that has been created.

Question: "That's interesting. So you could almost pre-create the new life?"

This is so. Do you remember in the teachings that have been given to you, the dropping of the body?

Answer: "Yes."

THE PRINCIPLE OF BI-LOCATION

It is the dropping of a Point of Perception and moving onward to another Point of Perception. Until the other is developed, how can the other go? It is the development of the new wineskin. Now let us get even further into this.

There may be many bodies that are created from this ONE central source, right now, in this experience; you, now, in this physical body. You see, you may be creating up to a dozen, or even thousands of different bodies from this Point of Perception.

Question: "Where is this being created?"

It is created all around you, for the universe responds without judgment.

Question: "As we've discussed earlier, even these bodies you are dissolving, you are creating? And you could step into one of those in another time continuum? I see what you are saying."

Exactly! This is the principle of bi-location.[10] Now, when one becomes aware of the different realities that exist, they become quite focused on its creation and begin to duplicate the same consciousness, the same body, into another field of reality. Therefore, when you begin to understand this principle, and within this, abandon the idea of time, you are able to create the same body elsewhere. You create a different body depending on your choice, depending on the field of circumstances and situations. This is how a Master can be in many places at once. It is through the development of consciousness, the Point of Perception!

Response: "If you can perceive it, you can create it."

This is so. In the same way that you became the candle, you can also become crystallized to the Point of Perception through thought, feeling, action, and experience.

VARIED REALITIES

Question: "So when you appear to us as a young man, vibrant, virile, and energetic, it is your choice of creation that you appear to us in?"

This is so. You too, may create various realities you live in! You may have full life in many realities, many different realities existing simultaneously from this point now in time. When the

consciousness decides to move on, that is, destroy the physical body through death, and it moves to a new reality or to several newly created realities. That is indeed the choice of the Creator. But there are those who have not yet Mastered or created the body into which they would move! There are those who have not yet perfected this technique, and they move on into a realm where they are cared for by the person who sponsored them, who out-pictured them. Do you understand? They return to what out-pictured them, for you see, they are linked as ONE, as ONE creation, and so you see, the force of the consciousness is contingent upon the force of all.

Question: "So, in the event that I was to leave my body today, I would come back to you?"

This is so. And there you receive instruction that would fit to the unified field of harmony, into the greater plan Divine.

Response: "Interesting. It is truly my desire, though, to sustain this body for a period of time as an example to the consciousness here."

And if you wish to sustain the physical, you may do so. But I also encourage you to create other Light Bodies which shall indeed create physical bodies so that you may travel between. There you have the fullness of Mastery. There you have the fullness of experience.

Question: "Interestingly enough, I have often wondered why so many people on the street will wave to me no matter where I would be in the world!"

A WEB OF CONSCIOUSNESS

It is as I have taught you today as simultaneous reality, a simultaneous experience. Therefore, there is no such thing as "time," as you have perceived it in the past, but there is time as you perceive today.

Question: "Time is not a line. It's a web?"

---

10. The ability to be in two or more locations simultaneously. This is first achieved through the conscious dream state and meditation techniques. As the consciousness is further trained and developed, physical bi-location is achieved at the cellular level, similar to cellular shapeshifting techniques.

It is indeed that, but it is the structure that we pour our consciousness into.

Question: "So time exists as a medium for focus to create space?"

It is a point of understanding, and that is all it is. It is no different than a mathematical system that is given to reference quantity. It is as much as that. And now, Dear one, I shall give you time to reflect upon this and shall return for discourse at a later point in time.

Response: "Thank you. At your earliest convenience, please return. I thank you again."

So be it.

Light of Awakening

Based on the Prophecies and Spiritual Teachings of

Saint Germain

El Morya

Kuthumi

CHAPTER ONE

Light a Candle

༄

*Saint Germain shares spiritual teaching
for times of conflict.*

Greetings, beloved, in that Mighty Violet Light, I AM Saint Germain.

I stream forth on that Violet Ray of Mercy, Transmutation, and Forgiveness. Dear hearts, at this time I ask permission to come forward.

Response: "Dear one, you have permission, please come forward."

THE HIERARCHY'S MISSION OF LIGHT

Greetings and salutations! I AM most happy to be able to come forward this day. It has been some time since we have had such technical discourse, but, it was the feeling of the hierarchy that this (discourse) would be imperative; for there is, you see, an opportunity for great war upon your planet. We had hoped, through this discourse, that we could ready those who claim to be, or state and say they are, light-workers. Come forward and bring the balance of light for the Earth and her planetary evolutions!

At this time there is great dissension that is brewing among your world political leaders, and this is of great distress and disturbance for this hierarchy and its purpose and intention. For, you see, our work is for those among humanity who are willing to bring a greater harmony, a greater understanding of LIGHT. This LIGHT, of course, is the illumination of the mind, but is also the opening of the heart. So, one may understand that it is indeed the equilibrium, or balance of peace that all are seeking, and so as we see through the choices that humanity makes, a time could come for imbalance, resulting in great war upon your planet. It is important, shall we say (for light-workers),

to tip the balance of that scale. And those who are willing to go into the silence of the Great Silence; willing to tap into the universal consciousness, can bring forward a Time of Peace and imbue the planet, humanity and the planetary Rays with the qualification of greater harmony and greater unity—peace.[1]

THE SILENT PATH

May our minds and hearts not divert to the lower energies of competition, greed, avarice and fear. May these energies be transmuted into the greater energies of light and peace, and be directed toward our political leaders. May both sides of any conflict be given support at the higher level, and never treated with dissension or disrespect. Instead, in the most silent ways, may these greater energies imbue all who may partake of them (and our world leaders) at an unconscious level.[2]

While certain leaders may not be aware of these Ray Forces and subtle energies working upon them, you know, Dear chelas, that they are powerful indeed. For, at one time in your past, were not you, too, led to the path of light through the same subtle force!

---

1. The foundation of Ascended Master education is rooted in the spiritual teachings of the Seven Rays of Light and Sound. The Rays expand esoteric power; the utilization of their energies guides students to the fascinating world of Co-creation. A restorative and sacred journey, where the soul encounters the inherent blueprint of perfection, begins with this venerated science. Knowledge and application of the Seven Rays can emancipate an individual from third-dimensional restraints and transform consciousness into the expanded experiences of the super senses: telepathy, clairvoyance, clairaudience, spontaneous healing, and Unity Consciousness.

A Ray is a perceptible energy, though its presence is often subtle. Only individuals whose attention is tuned to the nuances of the Fourth and Fifth Dimensions may readily detect the esoteric existence of a Ray. Through personal experience, conscious understanding, and various states of awareness and manifestation students refine their ability to recognize the presence of Ray Forces. According to Ascended Master teachings, Ray Forces are present in every aspect of human endeavor; these energies influence the physical, psychological, emotional, and psychic essence of mankind. Rays are said to dispense Karma and direct spiritual evolution—individually and collectively.

2. Periods of tranquil power are referred to as the *Great Silence*. This Ascended Master spiritual principle encourages contemplative periods of quiet and stillness, which create intense spiritual energies in certain circumstances and situations.

DAILY MEDITATION

May Divine Grace empower the little wills of man!

We see this brewing—this time which was also a Prophecy. We ask for those who are willing to serve through the greater cause Divine to meet in unison of mind and heart. Begin first in daily meditation and prayer for planetary peace for the Earth and harmony among its peoples. Even as this disturbance is the choice of those who would do so, it is our hope that a greater union and peace should prevail, and this serves the greater cause—Divine.

HUMANITY'S CHOICE

It is all a choice, as you, Dear hearts, would understand this most astutely. It is indeed a choice, if we should have wars and famine, or peace and prosperity on this planet. These are the choices that humanity must make!

But students who understand the Greater Laws Divine, know that it is also a consciousness, or an energy—a qualification of the Ray Forces, that imbues the planet for good or bad. Undesired energies can be diverted, shall we say, "Glanced into a greater harmony," that may prevail upon the Earth.[3]

PRAYER CAN CHANGE EVENTS

There are those who are the doubting Thomases, who feel that prayer does not indeed affect things. Instead, it is the Will of man and the Will of the forces of nature that are causing such at this time. But indeed, it is, shall we say, the higher "Point of Perception," as we have taught in earlier discourses, that can change the course of events.[4]

Again, this is based upon that subtle premise, "Is the glass half full or is the glass half empty?" It is the Point of Perception—the way in which things are seen.

From there, it is the way in which things are qualified or acted upon. Through this premise, one may begin to understand a greater working in the unison of Greater Mind.

A WHITE CANDLE

Dear hearts, it is our request that this be posted among your students, among the chelas, among those who are interested to help the greater cause of the Great White Brotherhoods and Sisterhoods of Light. May meditation and prayer be part of the vigil at this time. We ask that all light a white candle for planetary peace. May this candle symbolize the ONE light that all share.[5]

---

3. See Appendix A2: *The Rays and Ray Systems*.

4. *Point of Perception* is a Co-creation teaching of the Ascended Masters. This process pivots on the fulcrum of choice. A Master of Choice carefully selects specific actions, which opens a world of possibility by cultivating perceptions, attitudes, beliefs, thoughts, and feelings. This allows the development of outcome by creating various scenarios and opening the dimensional doors to multiple realities and simultaneous experiences that dissolve linear timeframes into the Ever present Now.

5. According to the Master Teachers, the lighting and burning of white candles invokes the assistance of the Great White Brotherhood. This practice also helps sustain their mission for world peace. The white candle is a symbol of unity, peace, and the ONE spiritual light shared by all nations of the world. Master Teachers recommend directing prayer, meditation, and the lighting of the candle toward world leaders in particular. They often state, "May Divine Grace empower the little wills of man!" Lighting of white candles, along with meditation and prayer for peace, is reportedly more intense when it is physically done in Golden City Stars (apexes) and in the Heart of the Dove—also known as the Center of Fire, located northwest of Kansas City, Missouri. The list below delineates the towns and cities located in the Stars of the five Golden Cities of the United States. (Editor's Note: for more information see the *I AM America Map* and *New World Wisdom, Book One*.)

1. Golden City of Gobean
Pinetop, AZ
Lakeside, AZ
Springerville, AZ
Eagar, AZ

2. Golden City of Malton
Mattoon, IL
Charleston, IL
Shelbyville, IL
Sullivan, IL
Humboldt, IL

3. Golden City of Wahanee
Augusta, GA
Grovetown, GA
Appling, GA
Harlem, GA
Gracewood, GA

(Editor's Note: It was also taught in this discourse that the lighting and burning of white candles in certain geophysical locations would enhance the energies for world peace. While it is our opinion that the entire Earth is sacred, these areas earmarked by Saint Germain are: The apices, also known as the Stars, of all Golden Cities. These areas are approximately forty miles in total diameter. Here are some apices that we have identified: GOBEAN: Baldy Peak, Arizona. MALTON: Mattoon, Illinois. WAHANEE: Augusta, Georgia. SHALAHAH: Lolo Pass, Montana. KLEHMA: Cope, Colorado. Again, please remember that the area extends in a 40-mile circle around these center points. Another area in the United States that the Masters say is extremely important in affecting World Peace, because of its connection to the planetary grid, is Kansas City, Missouri. This is often referred to as the *Heart of the Dove*.)

Thompson, GA
North Augusta, SC
Trenton, SC
Eureka, SC
Parksville, SC
Kitchings Mill, SC
Williston, SC

4. Golden City of Shalahah
Lolo Pass, MT
Lolo, MT
Missoula, MT
Stevensville, MT

5. Golden City of Klehma
Cope, CO

CHAPTER TWO

Emanation

ৎ৩

Saint Germain on Ray Forces.

Greetings, Beloved in that Mighty Christ, I AM Saint Germain, and I stream forth on that Violet Ray of Mercy and Forgiveness. As usual, Dear hearts, I request permission to come forth.

Response: "Please, Saint Germain, come forward."

GOLDEN CITIES AND HIGHER ENERGIES

Dear ones, it is most important that you observe the energies that are moving now upon the Earth Plane and Planet.[1] For, remember, we told you there would come a time when those with the eyes to see and the ears to hear would place their hands into action. You see, beloveds, it is very important we continue our work upon the Earth Plane to increase light upon the planet.[2] The increased value of this light is that the Earth Changes, or, cataclysmic geological changes are held back, and those who have the eyes to see and the ears to hear have the opportunity to assimilate the higher energies at this time. These higher energies are coming forward through the Golden City Vortices and also through those areas that are known as the ancient Vortices.

OTHER PORTALS OF LIGHT

There are also many Portals of Entry, so to speak, as we have taught before in other discourses.[3] All of these are sensitive points upon the Earth Planet, beloved Mother Babajeran, and indeed are taking in light forces at this time. Many among humanity absorb these light forces.

A GREAT WAVE

This great cosmic force, as it works upon the planet as a great wave in the same way that the ocean tidal system exists upon your planet, has the ability, to speed up consciousness into a greater evolution, into a greater consortium of the ONE.

UNITY CONSCIOUSNESS

It is important for you to understand that it is this Unity Consciousness that we are speaking of, and it is important, as the light energies increase upon the planet that you understand its ability to affect all humanity— to affect all in a much better way.

CELLULAR FEAR

For you see, Dear ones, there are those who live with great fear, those who live with the fear of impending doom, those who would live, shall we say, seeking only protection and safety from fear which resides within themselves. Now, this fear has occurred for many generations and lifetime after lifetime, and, you see, it can adhere to the genetic structure and is passed on from one family to the next and to the next. When an opportunity like this occurs, this allows one to transmute, even genetically, lifetime after lifetime of genetic-held fear—Cellular Fear. The light that emanates from the Great Central Sun is the light that shall free you all.[4] It is the Light of Awakening.

---

1. According to the Ascended Masters, the Earth Plane includes everything that inhabits and occurs on our planet, including the Third, Fourth, and Fifth Dimensions. Earth Planet refers to Babajeran—the Earth Mother—and it comprises her physical, emotional, and spiritual existence.

2. Galactic Light is a quasar type of extrasensory light that emanates from the Great Central Sun or the Galactic Center. Galactic Light is said to conduct the esoteric Seven Rays of Light and Sound.

3. Portals of Entry are prophesied geological locations on Earth where energy anomalies occur. New energies enter the planet via these locales, affecting her physical, emotional, mental, and spiritual evolution. Models of this type of energy portal include Ascension Valley in Washington and

Idaho and the Transportation Vortex, located near Coeur d'Alene, Idaho. According to various prophecies, hundreds of energy portals—each with a distinct and unique power—will emerge and develop as we enter the Golden Age.

4. The Great Central Sun is the center of the Cosmos—the Sun behind the Sun. It also known as the Galactic Center or the Central Galactic Sun. According to the Vedic sidereal (or star) zodiac, the Great Central Sun is located in the sign of Sagittarius and the nakshatra of Mula—which means *root*—and connotes a foundation, a beginning, or a source. A real root is often gnarled and knotted, that's why the meaning of Mula also encompasses the notions of restraint and bondage. Consequently, the Seven Rays

THE LIGHT OF AWAKENING

When we gave you instruction of the Cellular Awakening, this is, too, what we were referring to, and the increase of light is available for all to partake of. There are many opportunities that will come to accelerate this light process upon the Earth. It is indeed an acceleration of the light process, an acceleration of love, and an acceleration of Unity Consciousness. This is the only solution that can stop cataclysmic change and heal all as ONE.[5]

FACING FEARS EXPANDS THE LIGHT

Prophecy, as you know Dear beloveds, has been brought forward, to expedite this process, to bring forward the unconscious fear within yourself. Facing fears enables purification and redemption; then one is able to face the future with hope and love and a willingness to create for the good of all. Indeed when all are in this Consciousness of Light then—truly then, and I say this from a firmness of knowledge—all benefit; all are then received as ONE. So you see, during this process you spin off the past; spin off the Karma of many lifetimes of fear, of war, of poverty, deceptions, betrayals, and the little hurts that occur to one. Now we see the results of past Dharma and your purpose is connected to letting go of fear, letting go of the little wants, letting go of the little trappings that can keep you trapped within the world of your perception.[6]

_____

travel from the Great Central Sun under a form of cosmic bondage to the Earth Plane, where our personal Karma is dispensed.

5. _Light of Awakening_ is a prophesied wave of cosmic light that originates in the Galactic Center. Its destiny is to evolve humanity into the Golden Age by altering human genetics and transforming our sensation of fear. The appearance of the Light of Awakening will also play an important role in activating individual and worldwide spiritual healing and initiating Earth's entrance into the consciousness of the ONE.

6. Often confused with the idea of good Karma, this Sanskrit word means _duty_ or _purpose_.

PERCEPTION AND CHOICE

We have discussed perception many times. But perception, Dear hearts, Dear chelas, is indeed a pivotal point when one has the choice to how they shall see something; the choice of how it will be contained within their being, and how it will create in their worldly experience.

"LIGHT FOR ALL"

This Time of Acceleration, of Cellular Acceleration and of genetic acceleration is a Time of Light and Bliss. This is the time in which the purpose of the Mighty I AM is revealed to all. This purpose is revealed at an individual level and then released as to the many. So you see, beloveds, it is important to firmly hold this vision of light for all upon the Earth, to not see that it should go to just a select few, but light is to go to all. For all will gain through this experience and through this acceleration. The upliftment of the Earth is of the utmost importance and this upliftment is through the medium of consciousness. Also, the medium of conscience and many choose their greater purpose, and a greater way that will serve all. For you see, beloveds, the future is always in your hands. It is held in the power of your choice.

RAY FORCES

Let me get to the work at hand. I have come forward to give further instruction upon Ray Forces, as this has been the topic of many conversations between the two of you, and also conversations between many of the chelas who request information on Ray Forces and how Ray Forces color light, and sound vibration which activates one toward greater harmony, greater understanding of unity and a greater understanding of the current time, the Cellular Awakening. There are indeed seven Ray Forces that work in the HU-man, the man who is to be God, the man who is to be realized through self-understanding. As I have taught before, the Rays are indeed anchored within the heart, and emanate through various Kundalini points along the spine with various meridians and points upon the body.[7] The Ray Forces arc out of the bottom of the feet as well as through the hands. Also Ray Forces arc through various chakras situated along the spinal cord. Ray Forces carry the encoding. They carry the information of who and what you are as substance. They carry the past. They carry the present, and they carry the future. The Rays come under the direction of the Great Central Sun. This is a force emanating throughout your universe and acting like a collective consciousness to unite one purpose to the next, one Karma to the next, one Dharma to the next. Do you understand?

Answer: "Yes."

SEEK HARMONY

Unity brings all together into a greater harmony. One would think at times that they are being punished for an experience they may experience, but indeed this is not so. There is harmony in all things. You must seek to see it. And when one understands the Ray Forces, they understand that the grand conduction of energy is only working through Law, and the Law is based upon the first Jurisdiction, Harmony. So you see, Harmony pervades all activities upon the Earth Plane and Planet as it comes under the conduction of the Great Central Sun.

THE SCIENCE OF ASTRAL LIGHT

Many of the Ray Forces that emanate from the Great Central Sun arc off of other planetary forces as they travel toward the Earth. Known as astrology, this science has been studied for many ages and is indeed true. It is the subtle science of the Astral Body, the first Body of Light that can be viewed by a HU-man, a God-realized man.[8] This is the emanation, or the light-field force.[9]

EVER PRESENT NOW

This magnetic and electromagnetic force-field is indeed the emanation of the energies of the Rays in their commingling of experience. And this experience is indeed broad. It may vary, shall we say, from one Ray to the next in a current lifetime, but, you see, in as much as one event is committed, as you have learned in the Point of Perception, indeed it becomes a point of departure for another event, and so on, and so on, and so on. That one event is never dissolved—it is continuous. It is always an experience. So, all history, as you would perceive, is indeed always accessible. There is truly no past, there is truly no future. There is only the Ever present Now.

CONTRACTION AND EXPANSION

So that you may understand . . . this—as your brain, as your intellect, is a binary system—one that relates more to dual-

---

7. In Sanskrit, Kundalini literally means *coiled*. It represents the coiled energy located at the base of the spine, often established in the lower Base and Sacral Chakras. Some scholars claim that Kundalini Shakti—shakti meaning energy—initiates spiritual development, wisdom, knowledge, and enlightenment.

8. An Astral Body is a subtle Light Body that contains the feelings, desires, and emotions of an individual. It exists as an intermediate Light Body between the physical body and the causal (mental) body. According to the Master Teachers, humans enter the Astral Plane—the transitionary ether between dimensions—during sleep with the help of the Astral Body. Many dreams and visions are experienced in this plane of vibrant color and sensation. Spiritual development increases the strength of one's Astral Body; the luminosity of its light is often detected in the physical plane. Some spiritual adepts can consciously leave their physical bodies and travel in their Astral Bodies. For most people, however, this happens only during sleep and after physical death, when the energies of the soul journey to the Astral Plane. Paramahansa Yogananda, the revered spiritual leader of the *Self-Realization Fellowship*, questioned the avatar of his Master Teacher Sri Yuteswar after it appeared to him following the sage's death. "Are you wearing a body like the one I buried beneath the cruel Puri sands?" The adept answered, "Yes, I am the same ... though I see it as ethereal; to your sight it is physical. From cosmic atoms I created an entirely new body, which you laid beneath the dream-sands at Puri in your dream-world. I am in truth resurrected—not on Earth but on an astral planet. Its inhabitants are better able than earthly humanity to meet my lofty standards. There you and your loved ones shall someday come to be with me."
The Astral Body is also known to esoteric scholars as Body Double, Desire Body, or Emotional Body.

9. Emanation means to flow out, issue, or proceed as from a source or origin; especially the path of a Ray as it travels from the Great Central Sun.

ity—and I will explain it first from a more dual perspective.[10] First, there is the perception that time exists as wasting away into nothingness. Yet, there is the present when time is potential, shall we say, much like a spore or an egg that has the ability to expand and grow into the future. Now do you understand this?

Answer: "Yes."

THE COLOR RAYS

I will proceed so that you may gain even a broader understanding of Ray Forces and how they work. You know the Seven Ray Forces, as they exist, identify and relate to a color. Each color is a particular harmonic for the Earth Field and Planetary Field of Experience. Each harmonic creates through various experiences for the individual. For instance, one who is imbued with the Green Ray is more apt to have more experiences with one's own physical body in relationship to disease or disorders that exist within the physical body. The Green Ray, then, naturally brings one to seek his own healing. So, through the experience of one's own healing, one comes forward to help many others on the path of healing. The experience of the Green Ray may be one that is not totally understood within the context of one lifetime. But often there have been many lifetimes in which one has suffered or one has had diseases that appeared to be incurable. So in a predominance of the Green Ray Force will provoke one to seek greater Harmony. The harmonies will first come through aligning the light-bodies, and that alignment sometimes comes through artistic and musical expression, but is primarily used as a force-field to bring healing to others, and to ease suffering and develop compassion. This

is just one explanation of a Ray Force. My intention is to not go into great detail of descriptions of Ray Forces, for these are contained in many other materials, and also can be found in many Ascended Master teachings. Most of them are quite accurate. For those who are requesting greater accuracies on these, I will be willing to concord and provide such information. But for now, I would like to stay with the work at hand so that you may understand how Ray Forces work together.

THE CHOHANS

There is always a Chohan (Lord) of a Ray. This is a Master Teacher of that particular Ray Force. This Master Teacher is responsible for the way in which the energies of a Ray Force from the Great Central Sun is utilized upon the Earth Plane and Planet. Now, you understand in the science of Astrology that there are planets that arc certain energies, and the force of this particular Chohan resides as a consciousness between that planet and the Earth. For instance, the Chohan of the Green Ray resides as an energy force, a force of consciousness that is timeless and perpetually immortal between Mercury and the Earth.

A LIGHT AND SOUND HARMONIC

The energy exists simultaneously not only as a light force and a sound force that is recognizable to one upon the Earth Plane and Planet, but as a Ray Force that is a resonance, a harmonic, so to speak. Those of science often identify this as a laser Ray or as a life force that can be sensed, measured by an existing scientific principle—but a Ray Force does not work in a direct current.

EMANATION

Indeed, it emanates like a coal in a fire. It emanates a certain warmth that later ignites the fire, and so a Ray Force is as an emanation, an emanation a quality, and it brings this quality to the painting of the greater picture. Do you understand?

---

10. The intelligence of humanity, according to the Master Teachers, is binary. Rather, it is based on the dual experiences of the left brain and the right brain. These differences are illustrated in the table below.

Left Brain	Right Brain
Logical Sequential	Random
Rational	Intuitive
Analytical	Holistic Synthesizing
Objective	Subjective
Looks at parts	Looks at wholes

Answer: "Yes."

This emanation is an important factor in understanding Ray Forces and how they work together. For instance, take your hands and rub them together. As you rub them together, do you not feel a heat?

Answer: "Of course."

The heat is indeed the emanation of friction. This is how a Ray Force indeed works. It emanates, radiating and generating a greater and greater energy as it travels throughout space or time.

QUALIFICATION THROUGHOUT LIFETIMES

And so, as one begins to recognize the workings, the qualities of a Ray Force through lifetime after lifetime, it begins to emanate a greater and greater surgence throughout the being. We have explained before that once the emanation exists, and if you were to measure this along a mathematical line once it is functioning above fifteen percent within the HU-man being, it may then be qualified. Again, an emanation may be qualified in several ways, for good or for bad, as the Earth Plane is dual. Things are hot; things are cold. Things are up; things are down. Again, Dear hearts, beloveds, it is perception as to how the emanation is realized and understood. This emanation, travels forward from lifetime to lifetime, and is qualified in this same manner. As it is qualified by the grand conductor and it is of course given as a free gift to the HU-man. For the HU-man, indeed, has the choice of how to utilize this energy for experience. For instance, referring back to the Green Ray, one may use the Green Ray for greater harmony to bring forth a great compassion and understanding of scientific knowledge, which frees another from suffering—this creates compassion in the world. But if there is not complete understanding of the emanation, the Ray Force is expressed as dual. You may meet one whose life is emanating, the lower qualities of a Ray, choosing only to produce or manifest the energies in this dualistic quality. When this occurs, the invidivual becomes overly analytical and scientific, and relies more upon the processes of the Ray,

and not upon the results of the Ray. Have you not seen this many times?

Answer: "Very true."

DEVELOPMENT OF A RAY THROUGH CHOICE

So one has a choice concerning how to utilize a Ray Force as it arcs from the Great Central Sun and gives each of you the life of Co-creation. The HU-man develops this faculty of choice. Within choice lies the ability to make the Earth a heavenly paradise or filled with the torments of hell. The darkness that has covered the Earth oddly, is but a choice—a choice of the qualification and utilization of emanation. When one speaks of the Ages of Darkness that have covered the Earth, do you now understand with greater wisdom and knowledge how the darkness had to exist in order so one could begin to understand and experience how Ray Forces are qualified and used for greater and further evolution?

Answer: "I see what you're saying."

It is not a matter of judging a time and saying that it must not exist, or it is of a darker or of lesser quality. It fully serves the function of reason. It fully serves the function of choice. Choice is indeed the wholistic pivotal process of how the Rays work, and how the Rays send their emanation.

ACTIVATION OF THE EIGHT-SIDED CELL OF PERFECTION

Now, let us talk about the interplay of the Rays. Again, I have mentioned there are Seven Ray Forces that are utilized for the education of the soul and the enfoldment of the incarnation. These Seven Ray Forces, as I have stated before, enter into the Eight-sided Cell of Perfection.[11] The Eight-sided Cell of Perfection is activated upon the first breath upon the birth of the child. That is why many upon the Earth Plane and Planet record a specific time of birth, but it is not so much the birth

---

11. See Appendix B2: *Movement of the Rays through the Eight-sided Cell of Perfection.*

process itself, but the intake of the first breath. This breath activates the Eight-sided Cell of Perfection, the Kundalini along the spine, and all of the Chakra Systems.

EXPERIENCES THROUGH THE LIGHT

You know that a chakra spins in a clockwise or counter clockwise position. The spinning utilizes the Ray Forces. This spinning can indeed tell you how the emanation of the Ray Force is conducting its Karma or Dharma within that particular individual system. So, when you see, for instance, a chakra spinning in a counter clockwise motion, producing, a cloudy Green Ray color, like a muddy green, you know the individual is still learning through the lower energies of the Green Ray and yet to qualify into the higher energies. This emanation sets up many experiences through the light and energies of the aura.

EMANATION THROUGH THE ASTRAL BODY

Now, you begin to see that the Human Aura is an interplay of the many Ray Forces as they interact along the Golden Thread Axis and emanate through the Chakra System.[12] When you encounter a life force, at times you may meet one from whom your destinies are very different, from whom your experiences are very different, from whom your beliefs are very different. Upon meeting and greeting one another, you feel a sense of repulsion toward one another. Now, you have experienced this, and many others have experienced this. It is not a matter of judgment, of good or evil, it is a matter of understanding emanation. It is a matter of understanding the science, the Astral Body. This science of the Astral Body may be utilized in many forms. As one, we begin to understand the greater harmony and the greater working of mind, soul, and body. Now, this Astral Body that you carry with you at all times, your first light force, so to speak, the first interplay of all Rays coming together, also to some extent controls the field of experiences that you may have. For you see, Dear ones, as you carry this light field and force with you, it carries, shall we say, the programming of the Ray Forces so that throughout your day it can control the types of experiences you will have, the type of people you will meet, the types of interactions that you will have. Too, it sets up a force-field for your co-creative abilities.

DREAMTIME

At night, when you sleep, there is a type of detachment from the physical body, and the greater light force is then freed up and allowed to explore the worlds that exist beyond that of only physical understanding. Many of you have had these dreams. Sometimes the dream experiences end up actually bringing forth a creation in your world. That is because the imprinting of that was already contained through the Ray Forces. Now do you understand?

Answer: "Yes."

This is very important to understand the emanation of Ray Force and how it works for creation, how it works to bring all forward in a greater harmony. And now I will open the floor for your questions. (The Master momentarily leaves the teaching, and then returns.)

EMANATION AND THE MASTER TEACHER

Greetings, Dear ones. Now I shall continue on this discourse of emanation. Did you feel the disconnection of our energies?

Answer: "No, not really."

What you felt was the continuing emanation. Now, for instance, when a Master Teacher enters a room, before that Master Teacher enters into the room do you not first feel the emanation?

Answer: "I hear your sound, I smell a fragrance and I see your light."

That is indeed an emanation, and when a Master Teacher leaves the room there is still a heat. There is still a fragrance.

---

12. See Appendix C2: *The Human Energy System and the Rays.*

There is still a sound and a vibration within the room. This, too, is emanation.

"WE BUILD AN EMANATION"

As you can see, emanation, much as the coal has been lighted to fuel the fire, is an energy that builds. That is why, whenever we come in to bring discourse, we build an energy. We build an emanation. This is very important so that people understand that the Ray Forces of the subtle astral bodies are built lifetime after lifetime after lifetime. There may be one life force that comes forward into a very strong incarnation. The strengths of those Ray Forces within that individual have been built lifetime after lifetime after lifetime. One is not born with a strong Ray Force without, of course, putting the work forward, without having effort.

YOUR FUTURE

So, you see, all comes together in a perfect harmony. This harmony, of course, is the result of actions that you have taken and choices you have made in previous incarnations. So, you see how important the ever present now is, for this, too, will create your future, create the lifetimes that you will have in the future, create the experiences, the types of friends, and so on and so on. And so, Dear hearts, as you can see, emanation is indeed an important understanding when you begin to understand the work of Ray Forces and their conductivity within the human body.

GOLDEN CITY RAY FORCES

Now, Dear ones, when you understand how a Ray Force is gathered, in this case an individual lifetime after lifetime, when we begin to understand the Golden City Vortices and that each of them is part of an individual Ray Force, now you can understand that they, as new planetary Vortices, are building energies, their emanations starting, of course, and building and building and building. And so in the beginning to birth of a new Vortex, it may be difficult at first to feel the energies of a Golden City,

to feel the emanation of that Ray Force.[13] However, over time the emanation builds. And in the same way that a Ray Force emanates throughout the Astral Body of an individual, that Ray Force in the beginning may only be functioning, maybe at a low rate of five percent, seven percent, ten percent, but then as

---

13. The energies of Golden City Vortices grow alongside their emanation of light. This process fortifies the Ray Force of each Golden City Vortex qualifies as we enter the New Times. Golden Cities of the United States are represented by the following Ray Forces:
Gobean: Blue Ray
Malton: Ruby and Gold Ray
Wahanee: Violet Ray
Shalahah: Green Ray
Klehma: White Ray
The energies of nascent Golden Cities may be difficult to detect at first. That's because the development of its Astral Body is incomplete. As the energy field of an incipient Golden City increases its strength and power to 10 percent, subtle indications of the qualified Ray Force commence. Paradoxical anomalies, however, are often present in the early stages of development.
The lower energies of a qualified Ray may manifest before the maturation of Golden City's Astral Body. Collective and individual characteristics may include:
i. Blue Ray: Inflation, greed, gambling, weakness, vulnerability.
ii. Pink Ray: Selfishness, lack of conscience, emotional instability, moodiness, negativity.
iii. Yellow Ray: Lack of integrity, common sense, enthusiasm, and compassion.
iv. White Ray: Vanity, compulsion, attention-seeking, vulgarity, insensitivity.
v. Green Ray: Dependence on technology, disease, poverty, addictions, irrationality.
vi. Ruby and Gold Ray: Worry, doubt, obsession, lack of confidence, fear, passivity.
vii. Violet Ray: Competition, violence, manipulation, political corruption.
Master Teachers counsel by developing spiritual perception and choice; chelas and students can qualify energies of Golden Cities beyond their primitive level. "Perception is critical to utilize a Ray Force"—this key understanding is often known as qualification of a Ray.
During the Golden Age, Golden City Vortices will replicate the energies of their designated Ray Force throughout the planet. This energy will expand and emanate toward its highest achievable level possible on Earth. As Earth and humanity progress toward the apex of the Golden Age and as further light is received from the Great Central Sun, this synergistic emission of energies will occur sequentially.
The light and energy from the Golden Cities evolve individuals into the *HU-man*—the God Man. This individual evolutionary process moves humanity toward the experience and the understanding of the Co-creative and Instant-thought-manifestation Process. The Master Teachers refer to this phenomenon as Manifest Destiny.

this grows, shall we say, in its force-field, the Ray Force is then able to start giving its subtle indications.

LOWER ENERGIES

Remember, as I have taught, indeed this is a dual system, and so very often in the beginning of development of Golden Cities the more lower energies of that Ray Force will then exist. For instance, in the Golden City of Gobean, where you are dealing with transformation, harmony, all indications of the higher use of the Blue Ray, you may get shortsightedness; you may get coldness; you may get disharmony.

EMANATION AND QUALIFICATION

You see, it is a matter of qualification of taking the energy forces as they exist and using them at the higher level. This requires an understanding of perception, an understanding of your choice as we have always taught. Is the glass half-full? Is the glass half-empty? Again it is a matter of your perception of how do you utilize a Ray Force. This is known as qualification. These two principles, emanation, qualification, need to be understood so that the chela, the student of these teachings, may move forward in understanding how to utilize the energy of Ray Forces within their own being.

CONDUCTIVITY AND GEOMETRIC PLANES

I should like to discuss the idea of conductivity. In the same way that we have described the pyramidal structures of the Golden Cities and outlined its circular motion, shown you the apex of a Vortex, the doorways of a Golden City, and the parameters in miles and kilometers, we must also explore this within the human body. You are all well aware of the idea of pressure points and meridians within the body. Many of you are also exposed to the idea of Kundalini currents of this force moving within the spinal system, activating the Chakra System. Conductivity relies upon geometrical structures, each geomet-

rical structure peculiar to each planetary system.[14] The conductivity is carried out, of course, through this sacred geometry.[15]

CIRCULAR MOTION

Remember, Dear hearts, when we brought forth the teachings of sacred geometry so that you would understand its language, its purpose, and its intent? In the human body, most of the movement of conductivity occurs upon a circular motion. Sometimes this is also seen as a wave. This is why the Kundalini current is sometimes known as the snake energy, as it mirrors the movement of a snake in the sand, but this is ideally a circular motion. That is why, throughout your life, you may have periods of time when you feel that two ends of a circle now meet. However, you also feel, through the series of experiences, that you have had a higher perception, a higher knowledge, in the closure of understanding a completed lesson.[16] This spiral of energy is indeed circular when viewed from certain perspectives, but this is also how the Ray Forces work in their conductivity in your present field of experience.

THE TRIANGULAR SYSTEM

Within the Golden Cities, this sacred geometry, or shape, is based on a triangular system. As you were taught in previous discourse, triangular forces duplicate energies—duplicate them again and again—whereas, circular forces expand energies. The Golden City Vortices have been placed upon the planet to duplicate the Ray Forces, the Ray Forces of the higher emanation, qualification of understanding of their teachings.[17] So, do you see, Dear ones, this harmony working together, the expansion of the HU-man, the God-man, the triangular forces

14. Spiritual energies, according to the Master Teachers, are often transmitted the same way metal conducts electricity. Instead of a mass of free-floating electrons being pushed along by an electrical current, however, geometrical shape and geometric movement serve as the conduit of these subtle yet vital energies. Perhaps one of the best illustrations of geometrical conductivity is the sacred geometry of the Golden City Structure.

15. See Appendix D2: *Sacred Geometry.*

16. When an individual completes a specific soul lesson, the Karma affiliated with this educational process is released, and the soul is freed for new and further growth and development. The Ascended Masters often refer to this as *Closure of Understanding.*

17. See Appendix E2: *Golden City Dimensional Symbolism.*

duplicating the higher end of these energies so that they may be given to many others upon the Earth Plane and Planet at this time, and to move humanity into a greater evolution and understanding of its manifested destiny? Now I shall open the floor for questions.

MENTAL ENHANCEMENT OF A RAY

Question: "Can Ray Forces be enhanced?"

Ray Forces are enhanced through your understanding. When one begins to understand the force-field of the Ray Force itself, the existence of the Ray, the intention of the Ray, its higher and lower usage, indeed it is enhanced perceptibly by the individual, the HU-man. Then it is utilized in its greater understanding, in its greater workings for choice, and for the greater capacity for love, compassion, service and charity. Many of these higher forces are understood in the Twelve Jurisdictions, but then one is moved to utilize, to make the choices, with these Ray Forces for greater understanding. Enhancement may occur in many ways.[18] Of course, the one method that we recommend

for enhancement is meditation upon the Ray Force itself to gain an understanding of that Ray Force in your life. To simply meditate upon the Green Ray and its existence in your life will, of course, bring the Green Ray to a greater force-field within your experience. But it is better to bring it to the element of mind and to choice, consciousness, and conscience so it can be utilized at its greater understanding. It is recommended that you meditate upon the greater use of this force-field as a Ray, as an emanation within your life, in this individual's lifetime, to bring forth the desired result. Meditation, when used along this line and with this complete understanding, can be very beneficial to the chela.

ENHANCEMENT THROUGH THE MINERAL KINGDOM

Forces indeed exist within the Mineral Kingdom, these coming from beloved Babajeran, herself. Ray Forces can be increased through certain Golden Cities. These Golden Cities have been brought forth to help and assist those who would like to take a particular focus with a Ray Force or a Ray energy. The crystalline forces also contain many different emanations of the Seven Ray Forces, and it is best for the chela to choose one that they feel drawn to and that they feel magnetized toward. For, you see, Dear ones, it is always choice. So, Dear hearts, yes indeed, Ray Forces can be significantly strengthened throughout the body, throughout the mind, throughout the soul.

ENHANCING RAYS THROUGH SOUND

But perhaps the strongest of these, in terms of forces, is through the use of vibrational sound. Now you have known that when the Vibration of OM is given that it snaps the Kundalini, or, shall we say, that Golden Thread Axis, into complete alignment with the Sun and with the Earth, and then there is indeed

---

18. To enhance the energies of a Ray Force, an individual must first accomplish a level of esoteric education in regard to the Seven Rays. Second, a student must be able to recognize the presence and the influence of a distinctive Ray in their life. Finally, a student or chela must be able to critically define their intention for augmenting or treating a Ray Force.

According to Saint Germain, various spiritual teachings and techniques can enhance the potency of Ray Forces:

Meditation on a Ray establishes the energies of that particular Ray Force in the mind. The purity of a Ray activates the will. The Ray can then be further applied to the development of the conscience and the growth of consciousness.

The use of certain gemstones manifests qualities of the Rays.

Certain Golden Cities that emanate a corresponding Ray can increase the strength of Ray Forces.

The use of sound—specifically mantras—can also enhance Ray Forces. This treats the Astral Body.

The Violet Flame drives the energies of a Ray Force into its higher use while releasing the Karma surrounding the lower emanation of a Ray. This liberates a Ray Force. Saint Germain recommends an easy decree for this purpose: Violet Flame, I AM, come forth! Violet Flame, I AM!

While transmuting Karmas, the Violet Flame expands the Astral Body and the overall light and life of the physical body. This expansion induces spiritual freedom and the individual's liberation from perception.

As an Alchemical Ray, the Violet Flame fuses the interplay of the Rays with sound vibration-ing. This creates harmony and the ability to apply individual choices, while expanding and evolving spiritual consciousness to achieve personal goals.

Saint Germain specifically gives this decree to harmonize the Ray Forces of an individual:

Violet Flame come forth in the Harmony of the Seven Rays!
Transmute the cause and effect, and all records (Akashic) that have been genetically inscribed and genetically used by me.
Violet Flame, blaze forth in Great Harmony to the Divine Plan and the Divine Will!

a sense of grounding, a sense of purpose, an expansion of the solar forces within the Astral Body. I have given you many decrees that vibrate to the Violet Flame.[19] "Violet Flame, I AM, Come Forth. Violet Flame, I AM." You see, the Violet Flame forces help to aid one in overcoming especially trying circumstances. The Violet Flame is an emanation of the higher use of your Karma. It allows the trying circumstances, suffering, tears, problems and anxieties that surround the release of Karma of the misuse, or the lower emanation of a Ray Force. It drives the energies of that Ray Force up into its higher use, so that one is then freed, liberated, so to speak, from the lower understandings, from the lower emanations, of a planetary force. So,

_____

19. The Violet Flame fosters harmony within by fusing together Rays and Ray Forces. Rays work with focused cooperation, affirming inherent divinity and Co-creatorship.

Ascended Masters use the Violet Flame as a Grand Conductor of Ray Forces; they employ the conductivity, emanation, and qualification of the Rays to achieve contact with the One to ultimately attain Unity Consciousness—Unana.

The Ascended Masters do not give an exact amount of prescribed Violet Flame since this quantity is based solely on individual need. Some individuals may need to use the Violet Flame only once a day; others may need to focus on its transformative and transmuting energies minute by minute.

As one begins to acquire more experience with the use and the results of the Violet Flame, the vibration and the energy of the Spiritual Fire are not spoken or decreed. Rather, they are carried in Light Bodies and are in constant activity, influencing personal choices, actions, and interactions with others. According to Saint Germain, this sanctity of the Violet Flame is akin to chanting Violet Flame decrees in temples, "It is possible to carry that Mighty Violet Flame in, through, and around your being all the time."

The Violet Flame, similar to Ray Forces, operates on the concept of emanation.

When one begins to work with the energies of the Violet Flame, Saint Germain suggests chanting a mantra or decree forty-nine times (seven times seven). This creates a momentum of energy that increases the power of each of the seven Ray Forces.

In the beginning stages, the use of the Violet Flame mitigates the difficult burdens in a person's life. Continued focus and use of the Violet Flame manifest attributes of the Violet Flame in the physical world. These are:
• Acts of Forgiveness
• Acts of Compassion
• Acts of Mercy
Please remember: there is no exact method of calculating the Violet Flame's function and result. Saint Germain states, "...this is about the chela's inner union and harmony with regards to the Seven Forces—the Seven Rays."

The ideal use of the Violet Flame moves one beyond egotistical, selfish motives and into the service of the greater good. The intention of the alchemic Spiritual Fire, ideally, is to liberate an individual from the fears that inhibit him or her from uniting with the Light of God.

Dear hearts, it is entirely and absolutely recommended that the use of the Violet Flame is always of the utmost importance in strengthening any condition that may seem trying. It is sound vibration that comes forth within the Chakra System. It is sound vibration that comes forth within the consciousness. It is sound vibration that allows the conscience to have the clarity to choose the right way at the right time. That is why I have repeatedly recommended the Violet Flame to my students and my chelas, as this is the clearest, the quickest path to liberation and to understanding the Ray Force of emanation, and to allowing a greater field of experience. Indeed, it does expand your astral field, your field of experience, the force-field that you have come to live through and to experience through. Questions?

LIBERATION AND ALCHEMY THROUGH THE VIOLET FLAME

Question: "Since the Ray Forces come together to make the Astral Body, or the Astrological Body, and that is the conductive control for the experiences or the life that a person leads, what attracts to them, what repels from them. If there are certain Rays that are functioning at smaller percentages than others, is the Violet Flame the best usage for, I would say, the neutralization of any of the afflictions of the Rays of Light?"

The Violet Flame has been brought forth to free, or liberate one so that they may understand the higher use of energies. When one has achieved a certain understanding of liberation through the use of the Violet Flame being used, of course, as sound vibration, then one may begin to explore the use of other vibratory forces through the use of sound to actually enhance or increase the force-field in another direction. But until that moment has happened, it is, of course, always best to free the individual first. It is through freedom that one is allowed to expand, until one is able to see that they can see it from a whole other viewpoint. This is the freeing of perception. And it is, of course, recommended that all sounds be used to bring healing forth for the individual, but the Violet Flame, as you can see, is, of course, the one that is used, shall we say, at the first levels so that consciousness is freed and ready to explore other harmonies that exist within them.

Question: "So what you're saying is that the Violet Flame is, of itself, also a transmutating Ray and that is the first focus?"

It is Alchemical, as well, as it fuses in an interplay of the Rays, allowing each of the Ray Forces, for instance, a Yellow Ray, a Pink Ray, a Blue Ray, to come together in greater harmony. These forces, at times, are not in harmony at will within the individual, for that individual had chosen to allow the Ray Forces to war against one another, to be in disharmony with one another. It is the Violet Flame, indeed, that allows the Ray Forces to work together. Have you ever seen a team that seems to have all the strengths and all the qualities to achieve its goals, but yet the individuals within that team war among themselves and are not able to cooperate to achieve one thing?

Answer: "Yes, I have."

LESSEN DISHARMONY

This is the same metaphor for understanding the Ray Forces within the Astral Body. One may have a great quality and another great quality, but they are not able to bring them together, to make them work together. The use of the Violet Flame brings, through sound vibrating, a lessening of the Karma and a lessening of the disharmony; and it brings together a fusion of cooperation between the Ray Forces, that one may now work together. If you would begin to view the Seven Rays as a team force that is working for you, through your choices and through your consciousness within your Astral Body, then you begin to understand how the Violet Flame, and use of this Mighty Violet Ray, will bring you to a greater freedom for you to achieve your goals.

VIOLET FLAME DECREES TO HARMONIZE THE RAYS

Question: "Can you give us a decree, specifically, to harmonize the Rays?"

"Violet Flame, come forth in harmony of the Seven Rays. Transmute the cause and effect and all records that have been genetically inscribed within me, genetically used by me. And now, Violet Flame, blaze forth in greater harmony to the Divine Plan and the Divine Will.

It is as simple as that: decreeing this unto yourself as a prayer. Let the Violet Flame be poetry to your soul. Let the Violet Flame come forward to bring greater harmony between you and the Seven Rays, so that each of the Ray Forces becomes a team player within you.

Mighty Violet Flame, come forth in the Light
of God that never, never, never fails.
Mighty Violet Flame, come forth and heal all that ails me.
Mighty Violet Flame, come forth and bring cooperation
in, through and around me.
I seal this forth in the name of the Divine Plan
and the Divine Will.
Mighty I AM!

So, you see, Dear hearts, decree this unto yourself and it is so. It is the affirmation of your divinity. It is the affirmation of your Co-creatorship. Yet, this prepares you for a greater conductivity of the emanation and the qualification of the Ray Forces within you. As the Great Central Sun is the grand conductor of these Rays, do you see how you now become as a conductor of the Ray Forces?

Answer: "By pronouncing the decree, yes, we actually enhance the conductivity, and you harmonize that conductivity."

This is the idea of liberation and freedom so that one is then led to become as ONE with the forces of the universe. This leads one naturally to the Consciousness of Unity in Unana. This is the principle that we apply. This is the principle that we utilize.

"CARRYING THE FLAME"

Question: "Truly, this is most enlightening. To consider that for all the embodiments and all the eons, we can, at this moment, transmute much of that. How often would you suggest that this decree be done and at what time of day?"

It is, of course, based upon each individual need. It is best, of course, that the individual prescribe this for himself, for only he would know the discomfort he is feeling. Only he would know the harmony that he is seeking. It is best for an individual to choose this for himself. Perhaps for one individual to use the Violet Flame once a day is all that is required. And yet, for another, whose discomfort and suffering is so great, perhaps he should use the Violet Flame a thousand times a day. Of course, this depends upon the person and his choices. But you see, Dear heart, when one begins to vibrate totally to this concept of the Violet Flame, to this concept of liberation and freedom, to this concept of greater unity within the self, one may speak this as a mantra and say it all day, throughout his being. It is not spoken, of course, through that spoken word but emanated through actions, emanated through choices, emanated through interactions with others. They carry this like a force-field, as part of their Astral Body, incorporated within their being. They carry it forward each day. This is just as sacred as sitting in front of your temple and shouting these decrees for all to hear. You see, Dear ones, it is possible to carry the Mighty Violet Flame in, through and around your being all the time.

ACTIONS AND CHOICES

Question: "And how does one achieve this?"

Through focus and through the focus of one's intention through imbuing these qualities within oneself and bringing them forth into actions and choices. Do you see, Dear one, how the emanation is built? Like the coal, fueling the fire, the Violet Flame is present and builds a greater and a greater energy. This is the concept again of emanation.

SEVEN TIMES SEVEN

Question: "Through this focus, what is it that you would suggest or direct anyone to visualize or out-picture or focus upon?"

It is individual choice, but if I were to recommend a program, perhaps it would be to say the Violet Flame seven times seven, forty-nine times. This would assure that a momentum would be gained for each of the Ray Forces within the being. Again, this is only a recommendation, and this is only brought forth in reference to your question so that you may begin to understand. The Violet Flame is then used forty-nine times per day, and from there the individual notices a lessening of the burdens within his life. Then perhaps he would like to bring forth an element of the Violet Flame, actually an act of forgiveness, an act of mercy, an act of compassion as an intention of the demonstration of the Violet Flame. We know that intention and demonstration carry this forth into the physical world, and there we have an expansion, of the emanation of the Violet Flame. Do you understand?

STEP-BY-STEP

Answer: "Yes, it is a step-by-step process."

It is a step-by-step process. There is no formula or exact way for this to work. It is about the chela's union and harmony with the Seven Forces, the Seven Rays. It is the chela's choice, and this choice is revealed through action.
Question: "I understand. The number seven, or the Rays of Light and Sound, are really as far as our consciousness can perceive, aren't they?"

Let us start one step at a time, and as our consciousness emanates and grows into that Mighty Flame, that Mighty Light of God that never, never fails, then one is ready to be introduced to greater light, to greater understanding and to greater endurance in the Unity of Consciousness.

Question: "So, in the use of the Violet Flame, when you asked us to decree for peace, we could ask for the harmonization of the Rays of all governments, all businesses, all global consciousness, could we not?"

This is the ideal use of the Violet Flame: what moves beyond selfish motive and into a motive that serves the greater good. As I stated before, when suffering is lessened for your neighbor, indeed is not the suffering lessened for you?

Answer: "True, that is truly compassion. So this would probably be the most useful pivotal point for all types of healing ... yes, your personal challenges, but for the Earth Changes themselves."

Of course, beloved, this is the intention of the Violet Flame, to free and liberate one from fear, to free and liberate one from all that would inhibit the greater union with that Mighty Light of God. So, Dear heart, as we seek completion of this lesson, if there are no more questions I shall take my leave.

Answer: "No, I have no further questions, but, as usual, much more work to do."

In that Mighty Light of God that Never Fails., I AM the Ember of the Violet Flame burning through all desire, burning now to seek the ONE service, the mighty union of all. So be it. Hitaka.

Answer: "So be it, and thank you."

Unless you have further questions, I shall take my leave from your realm and will be glad to return with further Prophecies of Peace. Hitaka!

CHAPTER THREE

Behind the Interplay

ᔦᔩ

*Saint Germain gives further instruction
on Ray Forces and sound.*

Greetings, Beloveds, in that Mighty Violet Flame I AM Saint Germain, and I request permission to come forward.

Response: "Please, Saint Germain, come forward."

SERVICE LIFTS YOUR KARMA

Dear ones, at this time I would like to speak to you about service.[1] Service comes forward to release you from your own Karmic burden, your own Karmic debts. However, Dear ones, service, as you well know, is an expression of the intention of your own soul. And that intention is sometimes clouded with the ego, other yearnings and other desires.[2] You have known at times those who have come forward offering to help you, yet they have come forward wanting only something of their own desire, and expressing their own desire. Service in its purest form is without desire. It gives only for the want of giving. Service lifts your Karmic debt. It can release your bondage to the wheel of life. It is another opportunity for you to free yourself, to be spiritually liberated.

THE EMANATION OF SERVICE

Service is another way that your life is lifted into spiritual light. Service allows one to see things from a more detached perspective, so that you may qualify the Rays of Light within your (astrological) chart to a higher understanding, to a higher learning, so that you may free the Rays of Light functioning within your aura to a higher qualification. Service also is again very much like the coal in the fire; it brings a greater emanation, and builds energy. But it is always intention that will determine how and when the emanation shall occur.

CLARIFY YOUR INTENTION

So, it is important to scrutinize your intention. It is important for you to understand the motive behind all that you do and the reason for so doing. For service, you see, can create Karma within itself. That from which you set out to free yourself can indeed turn around and create more. You see, Dear ones, the chelas upon the path, when they offer themselves to be of service, may indeed encumber themselves even more Karma in their own web of ego demand. It is important to understand desire, the working of desire, and where desires may lead you. Clarify your intention in all offers of service; also clarify your intent before offering yourself of service. Do you have questions?

Answer: "Not at this time."

"THE PLANETS WORK SIMILARLY"

Light continues to flow within the Human Aura; light flows at its highest intention to fulfill the demands of the cosmos, the Great Central Sun. The light emanates from the planetary life forces, and you see, Dear ones, planets also are life forces.[3] Life streams through a planet in the same way life streams through your body. We have explained this before in the teachings of Beloved Babajeran, but this teaching is congruent within this planetary system, such as Mars, Venus, Jupiter and Saturn, and so on and on. Even your Moon contains a life force unto itself. Although it may seem to be a more collective life force, or a collective being. But, in the same way you contain many harmonizing systems—a circulatory system, a respiratory system, and an immune system within your body, the planets work similarly. They contain systems that must come together and harmonize for them to properly arc energies to planet Earth.

---

1. *Service* is described as a helpful act based on the Law of Love. According to the Twelve Jurisdictions, it is the fifth virtuous law for the New Times. This definition is expanded in Behind the Interplay and explains how service can balance and sometimes ameliorate difficult Karmas. Good Karma is often achieved through renunciation, detachment, discipline, and surrender to the Divine Will.

2. Intention: A deliberate, conscious thought that determines individual actions, the ensuing results, or both.

3. See Appendix F2: *Planetary Life Forces of Our Solar System.*

EXPERIENCE IS THE TEACHER

Planet Earth at this time, Beloved Babajeran, is the ONE schoolhouse where HU-mans are learning. This learning is a very important process. It requires many lifetimes and allows the soul, the HU-man soul, to evolve through the course of experience. Experience is the only teacher from which one develops the idea of one's will, choice, and conscience. So, Dear hearts, it is indeed many lifetimes that you spend here on planet Earth learning and growing through the many experiences contained within these lifetimes. The planets, the greater servants, and Beloved Babajeran, a greater servant unto herself, offer themselves to be of service to you during this your evolution. They offer themselves, arcing light and sound to you, and bring forward throughout your own Astral Body a multitude of experiences that create an evolutionary and experiential understanding. It is the apex of each experience that leads you to greater understanding, greater force, and a greater will for you to choose. Choosing seems to be the vehicle for the HU-man to begin to distinguish one experience from another.

RAY FORCES CREATE DIVERSITY

When one begins to understand the Ray Forces and how they work and orchestrate the many experiences throughout one's body, one begins to understand how to differentiate the various experiences. It is the Ray Forces that give us the multitude of experiences throughout the solar system. And on planet Earth a variety of experiences are afforded through the Ray Forces. As the Ray Forces arc themselves from the Great Central Sun to the planets who are indeed of service to this force greater than themselves, they, in turn, arc the energy to Beloved Babajeran. It is here that the energies are picked up through the Astral Body, and human experience unfolds. History is created, and the whole drama, the whole play is then set forward for learning to gain ever important experience. Beloved Sananda has said in past discourse, "What is the difference between you and me?" What the difference is indeed, Dear ones, but experience. And it is the Rays, through the interplay of the harmonies of the spheres, that light and sound blend and create your all-expanded awareness.[4]

KARMA AND BALANCE

Intention exists behind the interplay of the Rays.[5] This intention is orchestrated, not only through your will and through your choices, but also by your Karma and your past; Karma is one action for another, and seeks the balance within and the balance without. Many upon the Earth Plane and Planet define Karma to be a punishment, the meter of judgment. But it is not, Dear one, for judgment and punishment exist only within yourself and the way in which you view circumstance, through your beliefs and your choices; and the way in which you deal with any given situation, or the actions in those situations, and how you create balance.

The Higher Self is ever present through each incarnation, and ever present through all experiences, is there as the guiding angel, the guiding force, to see that balance is kept and restored within all situations.[6]

---

4. According to Ascended Master teachings, sound creates and calibrates light, and is a natural complement to light. In the physical world, sound is a wave of frequencies that travels through a solid, liquid, or gas. Esoterically speaking, however, sound takes a different form: vibration. Master Teachers refer to sound as "vibrations per second." A musical note is akin to a musical atom; it is also a musical pitch with a certain frequency. Each Master Teacher is assigned a specific note.
  • El Morya: B
  • Mother Mary: F
  • Kuan Yin: F or C
  • Kuthumi: E or C
  • Saint Germain: G
  • Jesus Christ: E or C
  • Sananda: High F
5. Interplay: Reciprocal action and reaction.
6. Many Eastern religions and philosophies, such as Hinduism and Buddhism, refer to the immortal quality of mortality—the god within, as the Higher Self. Said to reside in the spiritual planes of consciousness, the Higher Self is energetically connected to each individual in the physical plane, and is free from the Karmas of the Earth Plane and identification with the material world. Sometimes the Ascended Masters refer to the Higher Self as the I AM Presence, as the Higher Self often bridges vital energies of the I AM Presence. They are however, entirely different from one another. The Higher Self oversees the human development of choice, the development of conscience, and conscious self-correction. Prayers and decrees to the Higher Self act with great efficacy, liberating the I AM Presence from Third Dimensional restraints of time and space.

THE RAYS AND THE ASTRAL BODY

This allows for a greater harmony in the interplay of the Rays and for the interplay of sound within the astral field. You see, Dear ones, it is almost as if the Astral Body is a grand book to be read, a grand book with an ever-changing plot, an ever-changing beginning, and an ever-changing end. It is this book that you must learn to read and begin to write for yourself, page by page, your own script, your own part, to achieve Mastership of the Ray Forces and the forces of sound.

A COMPLEMENT OF SOUND

It is important that you begin to understand each Ray Force is also complemented by a great sound. Many cultures have brought forward the various sounds that they resonate to in terms of light. I have given to you the "HU" sound. The "HU" sound vibrates to the Mighty Violet Flame of Mercy and Forgiveness.

THE "HU" AND THE VIOLET FLAME

When I give you the "HU" sound to use as a vibration, or to use as a mantra, it is used to bring a completeness to all that you do.[7] All is held within that vibration of finer tuning, with respect to forgiveness, mercy, and Divine Intervention. The Vibration of "HU" is used so that you may be brought into a greater understanding, into a greater Oneship with all things. It is the "HU" vibration that vibrates to the higher levels of the Violet Flame. The Violet Flame is birthed out of the Blue Flame, the Blue Flame of Will and Conscience, the Blue Flame of Choice, that Blue Flame of Direction and Directive Power.

But it is indeed the Violet Flame, when it is blended with the Pink Flame of Love, that Divine Compassion becomes a higher qualification of this force. And it is the "HU" vibration that you shall use alongside it to intensify its work.

SEAL THE DECREE

For instance, when you practice a Violet Flame decree:

"Mighty Violet Flame blaze in, through
and around all my past Karma.
Mighty Violet Flame blaze in, through,
and around all of my present choices.
Mighty Violet Flame blaze in, through
and around me.
Raise me into the glory and the life of the Ascension!"

Then repeat, "HU, HU, HU" three times three.

This commands the Law of the Trinity and seals the energy. The sealing is very much like a seal that exists upon a chakra. Those who have developed their Auric Vision can see, when they work on an energy field or when they view their own energy field, a seal exists at the end of every chakra or center where light is taken in and released. This seal is of vast importance, for sealing the Chakra System enveloping the Human Aura seals the intention of a new creation. This allows the intention to carry through from the point of creation, the choice and the conscious will of the Co-creator.

"SOUND DELIVERS THE LIGHTED COMMAND"

So, you see, sound acts as a complement to light and sound, and light, like best friends, create harmony similar to the Seven Rays and their work in the interplay of light. Sound comes, seals, and delivers the essence of the lighted command. Sound sets the intention, allows, and creates its manifestation or action. Do you understand?

Answer: "Yes, I do."

Dear one, do you have questions?

---

7. *HU* is a sacred sound that represents the entire spectrum of the Seven Rays. That means when the sound is meditated on or chanted, HU can powerfully invoke the presence of the Violet Flame—the activity of the Violet Ray and its inherent ability to transform and transmit energies to the next octave. HU is also considered an ancient name for God, and it is sung for spiritual enlightenment. The spiritual leader, Harold Klemp, writes, "HU is woven into the language of life. It is the Sound of all sounds. It is the wind in the leaves, falling rain, thunder of jets, singing of birds, the awful rumble of a tornado ... Its sound is heard in laughter, weeping, (and) the din of city traffic, ocean waves, and the quiet rippling of a mountain stream. And yet, the word HU is not God. It is a word people anywhere can use to address the Originator of Life."

Answer: "Not at this time."

DISCOVER YOUR SOUND VIBRATION

So, sound within itself is of major importance to bring forward each command to a higher level, a higher understanding, and to allow it to bring forward its actions from your Divine Source.

Let us continue. Of course, each of the colors of light has its own sound vibration. It is best, though, that each chela find the sound vibration himself. It is best that each chela begin to meditate upon each of the Ray Forces, and through meditation a sound will be revealed. Why is this so? Each chela is individualized through his differing experiences, through the many choices they have made throughout their travels upon the Earth Plane and Planet. Sound within itself is a harmonizing effect, and seeks its own level. There are certain sounds that can be given to you, and they carry a very high frequency. But if the chela is not prepared or ready to absorb that certain sound energy, it will not, and cannot, bring the Rays into their consummate interplay. So, it is more important for the chela to find the sound vibration that will meet the interplay of his or her own Rays.[8]

The process for this is quite easy. Within meditation, you will begin to hear a sound vibration. Soon, you will identify this sound starting with a consonant. It will contain a vowel sound. Very often these sound vibrations end with the "M" or the "ING" sound—this creates, of course, the vibration within the human to activate the Kundalini. This is of vast importance to understand that each find one's own sound vibration to the Ray Force that one is integrating within one's system.

RHYTHMIC HARMONIES

It is also of vast importance to continue to use the Violet Flame, for the Violet Flame will lift the chela to a higher realm, and a higher understanding. Within the time of meditation, there will also be occurrences of hearing mathematical harmonies associated with each sound vibration.[9] Sometimes these

---

8. Each Ray Force has a specific sound; Master Teachers claim that "light is complemented by sound."

Sound and light are best friends; these forces combine to form a power.

According to Saint Germain, sound seals and delivers the essence of the lighted command, which refers to the quality and force of sound. It allows light to carry forth a conscious intention in the Co-creative process.

Even though each Ray Force is assigned a sound vibration, chelas and students should meditate on a specific color instead. This process of discovery will lead the student to a personal experience of the sound. Sounds are individualized on a chela's various experiences, lifetimes on Earth, and working with certain Ray Forces.

Since sound will naturally seek its own level, the sound vibration heard during meditation is most harmonizing for that individual; it is a sound the student is best prepared to receive.

Some sounds carry high frequencies and may be difficult for a chela to absorb, harmonize, or apply at first. Revealing the individual sounds of the Rays within their Light Bodies through meditation assures a custom-fitted sound, designed to assist the interplay of light frequencies in the aura.

To find your unique sound for decree and mantra listen carefully for a recurring sound vibration during meditation.

You will soon identify a particular sound beginning with a consonant (e.g., B, C, D, F, G, H ...).

This sound can be used to activate the Kundalini and open chakras and perception to higher spiritual arenas.

Often the intricate sounds heard during meditation are mathematical harmonies—an expression of the Interplay of the Rays—working to correct deficiencies of the Rays or harmonizing the Rays in the aura of the individual.

Continued use of the Violet Flame is always recommended while identifying and utilizing personal Ray tones and vibrations.

Saint Germain often reminds one "Only through your own practice can you experience the force of God working within you." This personal experience is vital to the evolutionary process; it incites clarity and understanding in the personal desire to serve the Light of God.

9. *Harmony of the Spheres* is a philosophical concept associated with the notion of Sacred Geometry—that somehow everything in nature is organized according to a Divine Template. The Renaissance astronomer and mathematician, Johannes Kepler, was a proponent of musica universalis, music of the spheres. He viewed the movement of the cosmos in terms of a mathematical or providential harmony. Its foundation is rooted in Pythagorean tuning, a tuning technique that relies on a scale of intervals. These intervals are based on certain ratios, which can be applied to measure pitch—among something as small as notes on a page or as vast as the distances between planets. Pythagoras claimed an interval of one pitch exists between Earth and Moon; from Moon to Mercury, an interval of one-half pitch; from Mercury to Venus, an interval of one-half pitch; from Venus to the Sun, an interval of one and one-half pitches; from the Sun to Mars, an interval of one pitch; from Mars to Jupiter, an interval of one-half pitch; from Jupiter to Saturn, an interval of one-half pitch; from Saturn to the fixed stars—stars which were believed to be one gigantic celestial sphere— an interval of one-half pitch. The chords of this ethereal music, however, can only be heard by those who have developed the ears to hear—clairaudience. The mystic Manly Hall writes "The Pythagoreans believed that everything which existed had a voice and that all creatures were eternally singing the praise of the Creator. Man fails to hear these Divine Melodies because his soul is enmeshed in the illusion of material existence. When he liberates himself from the bondage of the lower world with its sense limitations, the music of the spheres will again be audible as it was in

sound vibrations are rythmatic, tapping out within the mind their own repeated rhythm. This is an important note for the chela, for these mathematical harmonies work to bring a correction or a harmonization effect for the Ray Forces.

"KNOW THYSELF"

I will not give you a set formula on how to activate sound and light to work together as ONE. It is more important that each chela, through the medium of his or her own experience, find this path. As I have stated before, Dear ones, it is most important to know thyself, and this becomes your grand experience, as your time in meditation and the interplay of the Rays become your own laboratory. Through your own practice, you will experience the force of God working within you, and this indeed will give you a new experience, a new evolution, and a greater understanding. Above all, Dear hearts, meditate with a clear intention, with a clear understanding of your own service to that Mighty Light of God that Never Fails.. Do you have questions?

Answer: "Not at this time."

So, Dear hearts, I shall take my leave from you, for this is the discourse of the day, and I shall return at a later time to bring forward more information.

Response: "Thank you very much."

---

the Golden Age. Harmony recognizes harmony, and when the human soul regains its true estate it will not only hear the celestial choir but also join with it in an everlasting anthem of praise to that Eternal Good controlling the infinite number of parts and conditions of Being."

CHAPTER FOUR

A New Day

*Saint Germain and El Morya present prophecies
and teachings on belief.*

Greetings, Beloveds, in that Mighty Christ, I AM Saint Germain, and I stream forth on that Mighty Violet Ray of Mercy and Forgiveness. As usual, Dear ones, I ask permission to come forward.

Response: "Dear one, come forth."

HUMANITY'S PREPARATION

Beloveds, the work at hand is indeed important, for I have explained before in previous discourses that the information that is soon to be received is, shall we say, of a finer quality and lies beyond the tip of the iceberg. As I have explained before, the prophetic material, the I AM America Maps, the Freedom Star Map, were all given like an appetizer to a main course. For now, the information must be given to prepare humanity for a greater evolution, and for a greater understanding of their Divine Destiny. For you see, Dear ones, the work that is now in front of the Spiritual Hierarchy is that of raising the vibration through the spiritual evolution of humanity. Those who have the eyes to see, the ears to hear and the hands to do, will now come forward in this New Time, this Golden Age that is indeed the important part of this Prophecy.

THE INTERNAL LIGHT OF ASCENSION

For you see, Dear ones, it has long been determined that humanity shall raise its vibration to a greater understanding, and to a greater knowledge of their internal light. This has long been known as the Ascension. There have been those who have raised their vibration, understanding, and consciousness, and who now reside in New Dimensions, in a new understanding of breath, light, sound, thought, feeling, and action. So, Dear

hearts, in this New Time it is important that you understand so that you may prepare yourself for the great opportunity that now awaits. This great opportunity is one that many have prayed for, sought after, lusted after and now thirst for, for many embodiments, and they now wait for this most especial time. This is a time when mankind will be adjusted in many ways. Frequencies will change, not only in the electromagnetic field, which is the Human Aura, but there will be an understanding, a telepathic Oneness, a union between all of humanity. We have explained this before as Unana. You know this now as Unity Consciousness. Prior to any significant change, there must be changes that happen inside. Today, we see dissent among humanity—Brother against Brother, Sister against Sister, strife among families, but this is just a greater preparation for the understanding of Unity Consciousness. The old ideas, the old beliefs, must first be shattered.[1] Beloved Sananda has said in previous discourses that in order for new wine to be poured, a new wine skin must be structured. This, too, is the process of Ascension. It is indeed structuring a new wine skin, a new belief, a new concept.

CONSCIOUS IMMORTALITY

The first of these beliefs is, as I have said before, "Down with death; conscious immortality arise." You see, Dear hearts, beloveds, your consciousness is indeed immortal, your thoughts stream forth lifetime through lifetime, ready for you to access at any moment so that you may understand in full knowledge and in full light all of the circumstances in front of you.[2] The idea of a Shroud of Darkness over your consciousness is one you have

---

1. A belief is a conviction or opinion of trust based on insufficient evidence or reality. This confidence may be based on alleged facts without positive knowledge, direct experience, or proof. According to the Master Teachers, beliefs may be negative, positive, or both. Often the unchallenged nature of beliefs form the nucleus of Co-creative activity. The spectrum of individual and collective beliefs can vary from innocent gullibility to unwavering religious faith and conviction.
2. The consciousness of the soul is eternal and survives the physical death of the body; consciousness is immortal and does not cease to exist. This enduring light permeates all of our physical, emotional, mental, and spiritual bodies during, after, and between lifetimes. Recognition of this everlasting law naturally leads the individual to God Realization and the Ascension Process.

instilled through your present beliefs.[3] The information may not be carried from lifetime to lifetime. But you see, Dear one, this is an old belief, and in order to maintain and understand the New Consciousness, one must access information from lifetime to lifetime so that the proper choices are made.

THOUGHT

When one begins to understand that they are consciously immortal, that there is a part of them that never dies, but only the physical body, this prepares the new wine skin. When thoughts are continuously upon immortality, feelings and actions will soon follow. These feelings and actions create a new body, a body that is not only linked consciously from one to the next in Unana, in Unity Consciousness, but is also linked as ONE to Beloved Babajeran, to the Mother Earth. For you see the dramas, the tears, the fears in each lifetime with its own desires, wants and trappings, along with its Karma, and with its Dharma has been played out on Mother Earth.

BABAJERAN'S ASSISTANCE

Mother Earth has served in essence as a witness, as a witness to all the events that you have staged in your journey here upon schoolroom Earth, learning, loving, and living. She, too, comes forward to bring assistance as the grand teacher that she truly is. This assistance helps you to unify from within and create unity within all experiences. This unification of self is extremely important, for unification of self brings forth the birth of conscience, and it is only when Unity Consciousness is united with conscience, or your chosen course of direction, then and only then may Ascension and the work as a Co-creator come forward in its greatness and in its fullness. So, it is true that at this time the Beloved Babajeran has offered herself to be of assistance.

---

3. Ascended Masters refer to the cloak of inhibiting beliefs that obscure the soul's direct contact with their innate Conscious Immortality as the *Shroud of Darkness*.

THE POWER OF CAUSE AND EFFECT

We have explained certain geophysical locations upon the Earth Plane and Planet. These are known as the Golden City Vortices. We have explained these quite thoroughly in other discourses, but we hope through this material to explain exactly and directly their purpose, their manifestation, and the role they will play in the times to come. Each Vortex is an energy source upon Beloved Babajeran—one that has been manifested directly by her to bring forth a cosmic lesson and, therefore, a cosmic unity within each individual. You realize now that, as a small child when you touched a hot stove, the result was your burned finger. This is the idea of cause and effect.[4] Within a Golden City Vortex, one begins to understand cause and effect in its most simple manner. Today, with Time Compaction, the speeding up of events and the society that mankind has chosen to live through, and the constant and the steady hammering of this illusion, one is unable to recognize cause and effect. This has caused deterioration within humanity, an inability to recognize the truth that lies within, the truth of their Divine Destiny, and their own immortality. Consciousness and conscience work together as ONE and create a unity to body, mind and soul. So, when one is in a Golden City Vortex, because of the arrangements of energies through the assistance of the Beloved Cosmic Beings—the Elohim of this Earth and Mother Babajeran—these teachings are quickly understood. The individual enters into a New Consciousness through body, mind, and soul, an acceleration that not only brings a telepathic response through Unana but also an immortality of such, an understanding that all is connected as ONE.

RELEASE FEAR

All life is for life, and death is indeed the ultimate illusion. This begins with the removal of fear held at a cellular level—fear that you have held from embodiment through embodiment, lifetime after lifetime. This fear that has kept you

---

4. Every action causes an event, which is the consequence or result of the first. This law is often referred to as *Karma*—or the sixth Hermetic Law. "Every cause has its effect; every effect has its cause; everything happens according to law; chance is but a name for law not recognized; there are many planes of causation, but nothing escapes the law."

trapped within the shell of the physical body. It is a time to release this fear, primarily the fear of physical death.[5]

THOUGHT MODELS REALITY, CHOICE RENEWS

As I have said before in previous work, as the thought continues, the feelings and actions model themselves in the same way a potter's wheel forms clay. The hands of God are indeed your hands upon this piece of clay, and it is through your choice and your will that you begin anew. It is your choice if you begin anew.

Perhaps this shall be the first place we will begin. We will begin with this discourse, "Beginning Anew," "Starting Anew," "A New Day."

I would like to introduce the one who shall start this discourse on "A New Day." He is Beloved Brother El Morya.

Saint Germain steps back and Beloved El Morya comes forth.

"Greetings, chelas. I ask permission to come forward."

Answer: "Please come forward, El Morya."

EL MORYA

Beginning anew is an important concept for those who wish to have a new mind. A new mind begins within the intention. This intention is extremely important. It comes within the depth of the soul. This intention determines the outcome—the outcome of all events, and all of the actions that the chela has come to experience.

INTENTION, THE WILL, CHOICE

Many upon the Earth Plane and Planet lay down their best plans. They play them out, and then in anguish and sorrow wonder why such plans did not unfold as they had wished and hoped. The reason is quite simple, for not once did they

consider their intention, and intention must be closely aligned to Will. To begin anew, one must identify and understand one's own Will—the Will that runs through him—then you begin to understand the Will that encompasses all choice, the flora of choice that has allowed your creation. Choice is the backbone of any person upon this planet. Therefore, choice very often can be seen in the Human Aura. It can be seen as a Vertical Power Current that runs along the spine, and attaches itself to the Mother Earth, and the lines to Father Sun.[6] We have encountered those throughout life who we may judge and say, "He has no backbone." "She has no will." They are those whose will is indeed broken, whose idea of their own choice is no longer theirs, who give their will over to collective illusion, collective thoughts, collective feelings. Their actions mirror only those of the collective mind, caught up in fads, in whimsies and in what only others tell them to do. When one makes the choice to begin anew, he makes the choice within himself through an internal process. It is sparked within himself. It is not sparked from any outer influence, but comes through an inner influence, and this grows in its strength and in its current. This you have seen many times upon the Earth Plane and Planet as electricity crackling down as lightning. This is indeed the entity, Beloved Mother Babajeran making Her choice, aligning Her will to the Divine.

DEVELOPMENT OF THE WILL

In the beginning, to begin anew, one may not particularly choose to align to the Divine Will.[7] In the beginning, one may

---

5. According to the Ascended Masters, the emotion of fear accumulates in human Light Bodies and simultaneously affects DNA. An individual can carry some of this genetic toxicity to the astral plane after physical death. It can be passed on to the next lifetime until it is released by the soul.

6. The Vertical Power Current—also referred to as the *Golden Thread Axis* or the Rod of Power—is a cylindrical beam of light that centralizes its vertical energy along the spine. It enters through the Crown Chakra (top of head), exits through the Root Chakra (perineum), and generates the Kundalini (the untapped consciousness). This internal conduit channels the soul's vital current of energy; it simultaneously grounds the physical body to the Earth and the I AM Presence. The Vertical Power Current activates several channels of energy within the body, including the Nadis (energy meridians); chi or prana (life force); and the seven chakras (energy centers). The vitality of the Vertical Power Current creates luminous human Light Bodies, also known as the layers of the human aura.

7. The notion of Divine Will has meant many things to many people, cultures, and belief systems. For instance, the Essenes—an ancient Jewish sect—believed that Divine Will was predetermined. Ascended Master teachings, however, accept Divine Will as the living presence of God—a presence that operates on individual Free Will.

choose to align to his own wishes, to his own Heart's Desire. This is perfectly normal, and is a developmental stage. But, as you well know, the result of all action is but education, and soon the chela becomes quite educated and begins to understand a greater working, pulse and magnetic pull. One begins to understand that beginning anew is not a selfish action, but their intention becomes aligned to conscience. And there is the true birth of Divine Will, where one begins to understand the purpose, the direction, and the flow and that all must contain within it the Divine Plan as a plan Co-created among all God forces.

"EQUAL TO"

Unity Consciousness does not see one God force as greater than another. It sees all God force equal to. This allows for a greater understanding of cooperation and of harmony. The concept of "equal to" is again a step in beginning anew.

A FRESH START

In beginning anew, one prepares the body, the mind and, inevitably, the consciousness to start fresh. Have you ever heard of a fresh start, a day in which all things seem changed, a day when you can breathe a sigh of relief and begin anew?

WHAT IS HOLDING YOU BACK?

This is the same consciousness that must be utilized to gain your Ascension. You must discard and throw away the old beliefs, old choices, old collective illusions that will not serve your movement into the ONE. What is holding you back? What are the things that are holding you back?[8] Ultimately, when you

examine each and every one of these, you will find it is fear of death, conclusion, fear of ending, fear of decay and destruction. When one releases such fears, one becomes ready to begin anew. Throw them away. Make the choice from within. Find you own backbone. This is your Will. It is your Divine Gift, given to you so you may become a true Divine Inheritor. Contemplate and meditate upon this concept. Now, I shall turn the podium back to Beloved Saint Germain; of course, if there are no questions.

LIFE IS INTERCONNECTED

Question: "Intention, as you have brought forward, both of you, intention, as you have shared before, determines the outcome. In observing humanity, the fear that drives them forward to want Ascension is truly the fear of death, the fear of aging, the fear of decay. This I have observed in everyone, including myself. However, the great desire to be of service to the upliftment of humanity, the great desire to see humanity come to its Divine Plan, its true design, its entering into the ONE, many times overpowers any of those, oh, doubts. So, if there were a one, two, three process to be described by you for those who will hear this tape and who will read this as a transcribed book, I would assume from your discourse that the first is to determine your intention. Why

---

8. One of humanity's greatest challenges today is restructuring personal beliefs to sync with those required during the New Times. Once that finally does happen, these new beliefs, attitudes, and ultimately social mores and cultural norms will begin to reflect the following ideas:

Consciousness is immortal; it cannot cease to exist or end. Often, Saint Germain affirms this new concept with the statement: "Down with Death! Conscious Immortality Arise!" Our consciousness survives death and our immortal thoughts travel with us from one lifetime to the next.

Conscious Immortality allows mankind to access comprehensive information surrounding certain circumstances or situations it may be encountering. The Ascended Masters explain that our inability to access our Conscious Immortality, described as the Shroud of Darkness, is the result of a personal inhibition of beliefs.

Humans unintentionally block information from other lifetimes through a belief in the Shroud of Darkness. As humanity enters the New Times, this soul-impeding energy is perceived and understood as nothing but an old-world credo. Humanity freely disregards this obstructive attitude, and in turn, embraces and maintains the New Consciousness.

As more thoughts grow toward our Conscious Immortality, individual feelings and actions obey the Co-creative pattern, and a new spiritual body is created. Known as the Ascension Body, this energy body is linked to the consciousness of Unana and to Mother Earth.

Since Mother Earth witnesses each and every life experience our soul encounters on Earth, the Master Teachers often refer to her as the *Grand Teacher*. She assists the soul through life's continuous journey and tries to unify each individual from within. Her work readies the consciousness for physical birth and helps it identify levels of conscience. This process deepens the experience of Unity Consciousness. The Ascension and our Adeptship in Co-creation are achieved through this greater unification.

At this time in history, Mother Earth—as the cosmic being Babajeran—has offered to assist every individual effort to build the Ascension Body and to give aid to humanity's mass evolution and Ascension into the light.

would you want Ascension? Why would you want immortality thought of as consciousness? Why? And so I ask you, give us the reason Why for this."

The greater union that exists beyond the HU-man is a Body of Light that no longer requires physical incarnation. The drudgery then is released of the physical plane, but it is no longer perceived as drudgery, instead it is embraced as life for life. As I have said before, "Live life for life." When one begins to understand the greater plan Divine, they see the interconnection between all circumstances, and between all situations. This is Unana.

SIMPLICITY

As a simple program, what would I prescribe? Of all things, Beloved Saint Germain, my Brother in Service to Light and Sound, would call upon that Mighty Violet Ray. Of course, what is contained within the Violet Ray but that Ray of Truth, the Blue Ray that understands the alignment of the Will. When I speak about intention and the alignment of the Will, it is important that one spend time alone, that one spend time in simplicity to allow the unessential to drop away. How long would I prescribe? As long as it takes—as long as it takes—Dear one, to spend your time in solace and reflection. Spend your time in meditation upon the ONE. What is the ONE intention that you hold? What is the ONE will that you are of? What is the ONE choice that is of most importance to you? If this takes but one day, then so be it.

CAST TIME ASIDE

If it takes ten years, so be it. Many say time is of the essence, but, in this one particular instance, I would say time must be cast aside.

EXPERIENCE CONNECTION

It is more important that you understand and totally embody experience, for there is the ONE unity that exists within you. And it is the connection of you to the All. Of all things that must be understood, first is that the hypnotic illusion living upon the Earth in the temporary encasement of the physical body perceives a separation that exists between that one individual life and the many other individual lives that exist upon the Earth at any given time. To understand a grander plan, to understand the connection between all, one must integrate from inside and feel a unity within. Do you understand?

"WE TAKE ON FORM AT WILL"

Answer: "So, what you're saying is that your appearance to us as Mahatma El Morya is only for our understanding. The Brotherhood and Sisterhood of Light and Sound are ONE."

This is so, Dear ones. We take on form at Will, so that we are able to convey particular and certain focused ideas, focused thoughts, focused vibrations for the work at hand. In this case, it is a preparation of consciousness so that humanity may begin the greater and grander change.

TRANSMUTATION

As a second reflection upon your question, I would propose to use that Mighty Violet Ray of mercy and compassion and forgiveness. Of course, this is blended with the Pink Ray of Love. When one develops this greater connection, this greater understanding, transmutation is the end result. If you would like more instruction upon this Violet Ray, Beloved Saint Germain will speak.

Response: "Yes, but I have one other question."

Proceed.

OVERCOME ILLUSION

Question: "Since all transmutation starts with intention and the redefining of the Alignment of Will, it would seem that your individual existence has now been collectively stuck together so that it is not one will, but it is a unified will. For an individual, such as myself, choosing to join you, you have given reflection and the Violet Flame as the first two steps.

The question that I ask is, once we have fulfilled all these desires that we have, all these little magnetic attachments to incarnations repeatedly, and it seems like the same things, new day, I think that humanity gets to the place where it becomes pointless. So, the only thing that is left is the inevitable, and that is to align one's own choices, will and intention to the unified choice for the movement of humanity and the uplifting of consciousness."

But the illusion of your thinking is the same things, new day. A New Day does not come forward with the same things. It is the altering of the thoughts. It is the altering of the feelings and the actions that creates a New Day. A New Day comes forward when one has simply stated the intention of one's purpose. It is that simple.

THE RELEASE

It takes a time of release, releasing that which no longer serves the Greater Will Divine. How does one apply such a concept to release that which no longer serves that Greater Plan Divine? You must evaluate your own life and see what is within your life that no longer serves your greater plan. Have the courage to create a greater plan for your life. Have the courage to write it down. Have the courage to meditate upon it. Have the courage to live it, feel it, act it out. Then you will understand what is that that is serving you. What is serving the Greater Plan Divine of your life? Do you understand?

Answer: "Yes, you have answered my question sufficiently."

And now I shall turn this over to Beloved Saint Germain.

EMBRACE A NEW CONSCIOUSNESS

In that the Mighty Violet Flame, I come forward. Again, I must ask permission to continue this discourse.

Response: "Please come forward. You are most welcome."

As Beloved Brother El Morya has stated, to use the releasing of old energy patterns, old thoughts of disease, old thoughts of decay, all thoughts of death, which can bring forward a greater understanding and a greater unity of the soul, how is this achieved? Of course, in the beginning it is difficult. You have been hypnotized, you see, through collective illusion. Each day in your world when you read a new book, talk to a new person, turn on your television, read a newspaper, what are you participating in? A collective hypnotic illusion of what others think the world must be, reflecting it back to you. You take that unto yourself, digest it as food, assimilate it within your being, and then your cells reflect that thought through feeling and action. How does one begin to embrace the New Day? How does one begin to embrace a new body, a New Consciousness?

"CALL FORTH THE VIOLET FLAME"

One must begin through the gift that was given eons ago through the Lords of Venus, and that is the use of the Violet Flame. As I have said repeatedly, it is only through the use of the Violet Flame that one can begin to release, to let go of, these past patterns that no longer serve, and no longer allow a New Day to emerge. When you become discouraged, when you wonder, will this ever end? That is the time, in that most perfect instant, to call forth the Violet Flame.

Violet Flame, I AM. God, I AM, Violet Flame.
Come forward in this instant manifesting perfection,
in, through and around me.
Violet Flame, I AM. God, I AM Perfection,
Violet Flame.

DIVINE INTERVENTION

And you see, Dear ones, in that instant the Violet Flame has provided the gift, that one Divine Intervention, in the same way that lightning cracks on Beloved Babajeran. In that instant, the Violet Flame cracks within you, aligning your will, releasing all thoughts, feelings and actions that no longer serve you. When you begin to ponder upon the past through worry and guilt, what is it that you are really engaging in? Fear. The fear of lack or a perceived lack of perfection. These are the things that must be addressed in order for the New Day to come forward in your hearts and in your mind. These are, indeed, the most important key elements. The use of the Violet Flame, may it ever be within you, within your hearts and shared with all of humanity, for the Violet Flame is indeed Divine Intervention— Divine Intervention structured to lift you out of suffering, limitation, death, destruction, and into the New Day.

Violet Flame, I AM. God, I AM, Violet Flame.

Before I proceed with more instruction, are there questions?

Answer: "Yes."

Proceed.

BE SPECIFIC

Question: "If we go back to intention, we address that many people, to this day, probably do the Violet Flame, and yet their bodies become old, they decay, they die. And they are still caught in the illusion as we are here in those of us who choose to help you. If the intention were to redirect for personal freedom, to redirect to be ONE with you, to be ONE in the Great Divine Plan, and the Violet Flame were applied to that intention, would that be a much more expedient transmutation?"

This is quite perceptive, for indeed, the Violet Flame may be applied with a specific idea in mind, a specific focus in mind. If one is practicing Brother El Morya's technique of simplicity and feels that his life is still cluttered, use of the Violet Flame to gain simplicity will only enhance and unencumber the consciousness, the thoughts, to allow the New Day to come forward. To allow a New Day to come forward will allow a new week to come forward. A new week becomes a new month. A month becomes a year. And before long what is it that has been created? But an age, a New Age, a Golden Age, and an age that is quite different from the time humanity is now experiencing.

But we must start with our little steps. We must start with the necessary education that is needed now to begin. Questions?

FOCUS ON YOUR CO-CREATION

Question: "Yes. Instead of focusing on the imbalances that I perceive, is it now more expedient to focus upon the unity of the Great Divine Plan?"

It is expedient to focus upon that which you wish to Co-create. Focus through the use of the Violet Flame on all that would hinder you, or keep you from the fulfillment of that singular intention … release to the transmutation of the Violet Flame of transformation, mercy, compassion, forgiveness.

FORGIVENESS OF SELF

You see, Dear one, until one has truly forgiven oneself, it is almost impossible to move forward into the New Day. This may be compartmentalized into a series of exercises that the chela may then practice. For instance, say that they have decided to embark upon Brother El Morya's lesson of simplicity to find a New Day, but they are still hampered by feelings of guilt concerning an event that happened, perhaps, five years prior. Call upon that Mighty Violet Flame. Transmute the cause, effect, the record and memory of that event, and then move forward without a harness about your neck holding you back!

SINS OF SELF

When we are held back in this way it is not so much a sin against humanity, but a great sin against the self. It is the little sins of the self that keep us trapped in the ideas of death, delay, destruction and catastrophe. To set yourself free—to truly set yourself free—will require perseverance. But it will only require perseverance in one application, and that is the plea to the Violet Flame for Divine Intervention to allow its Ray of Light to come forward into your life. Do you understand?

Answer: "Yes, I understand that it transmutes."

Questions?

GRACE AND DIVINE INTERVENTION

Response: "But I still haven't figured out, even for myself, what the specific intention would be to move myself forward, which now requires immense meditation."

Know thyself, Dear chelas of my heart. Know thyself, and there shall be the first component of your freedom. To create your New Day, you must indeed know thyself.

Answer: "So, truly that is the format that everyone must follow, and I assume it is the one that you, too, followed to reach the place where you are now."

It is true, Dear one, that it was only through Grace and Divine Intervention that I was allowed this experience to be truth for myself. Now, I would like to proceed with further instruction.

THE NEED FOR CONSTRUCTIVE CHANGE

It is through the consciousness of Unana that humanity can and will move forward. First, this will be achieved through understanding the need for change. When one accepts that things must change, they can accept that the change must happen first within them, and that the change must reflect to the outer, to their family, loved ones, partner, those with whom they may work, their neighbor and onward into their community. These changes are absolutely necessary in order for the New Day to come forward. From there, the change may reflect to a collective level, and then the change becomes collective reality.

Do we need Earth Changes in order to create such changes within ourselves? In some respects, some would say it is necessary, for others will not change unless an outer influence is forced upon them. But is this truly the type of change that is needed? As you can see, Dear ones, Dear hearts, Dear chelas, it is the inner change that truly brings about the constructive change. It is the inner change that brings about the New Day,

hence the New Age and the New Time. So, how shall this be achieved?

THE RAY OF LIGHT

The Greater Plan Divine working with all of us is designed first toward forgiveness—forgiveness of all past mistakes, injustices, understandings where one feels inequities, hurts and harms. These must first be released and dropped from a person's life so that he can move forward in the light of a New Day. When the Ray of Light is so firmly planted within one's heart, one begins to reflect upon the alignment of his will to a Divine Purpose. Beloved Babajeran has offered herself at this time to be of service to humanity, to allow an acceleration of understanding, an acceleration into the realms of light, an acceleration into the New Times.

GOLDEN CITIES AND THE COLLECTIVE CONSCIOUSNESS

The five areas known as the Golden City Vortices shall indeed be put forward as locations upon the Earth, specifically now, within the United States, so that people may travel to them. Feel these energies at an experiential level, and, when within them, occurrences will take place through collective thought form. Do you understand?

GOLDEN CITY ENERGIES

Answer: "Yes, so it is your recommendation that people move to the Golden City Vortex centers and have an intention for moving there."

Such movement will allow a movement within themselves. If you feel you cannot release injustice, a sense of inequity within your life, it is suggested that you take a trip to assimilate the Vortex of Wahanee. There, the energies of the Violet Flame, if they cannot be felt, will be absorbed. As I have said before, to drink the water, breathe the air, raise vegetables and to ingest them in an area such as this will increase the Vibration of that single focus within yourself. You see, Dear hearts, Beloved

El Morya has put forward to bring forward the ONE, to bring forward truth, harmony and inevitably cooperation; and to bring forward feelings of peace within oneself. One would then travel to the Vortex of Gobean, for that will instill and insight this action within the chela who is seeking to understand, who is seeking to gain a knowledge of Unana. You see, Dear hearts, this is the Greater Plan Divine. Questions?

Question: "Similarly, for each of the Ray qualities that are represented and brought to life in the Golden Cities, if that truly is the intention for the person to experience and to transmute, and in some instances just to absorb, then at the very least, a trip to these areas and at the very most, a new residence?"

"A GREATER UNION"

Whatever one would choose. When one feels he has assimilated these energies, he may move on, move back to where he lived prior, or move on to another Vortex. You see, Dear ones, these energies have been presented so that one may gain a greater understanding of the ONE—a greater union with Mother Earth, a greater union within the Self and his own God, I AM; a greater union with the Hierarchy. It is this union that is sought, a union of body, mind and soul, so that the New Day may begin. One may not perceive a New Day until one has released the past, which holds him from the future. One may not live in the present until the past is no longer in front of him, tripping him up much as a block that one might stumble over. To live fluidly in the now is to release all that has kept you from your Ever present now, from your ever present Oneship.[9] These are the teachings that we will elaborate on, each of the Golden Cities, so that chelas and students will understand what they are present for at this time and the great gift they can bring in a grander service.[10]

---

9. Life in the consciousness of the ONE neither perceives the past nor anticipates the future: time loses all linear orientation. An individual in the ever present now cognizes his or her experience in the continuous present with full recognition of inherent divinity.
10. See Appendix G2: *El Morya's Teachings on Creating a New Mind,* and *Saint Germain's Teachings on Starting Anew.*

AN ACCELERATION

You see, Dear ones, the Prophecies were given to tantalize those to see the need for change, and now we must move within the greater context of that teaching. It is change that must be made inside. There will be those who will not need to travel to a Golden City to take in the energies. It may not be necessary, but they are brought at this time to bring a greater acceleration: a greater acceleration vibrationally, electro magnetically; an acceleration of thoughts; an acceleration of feeling. In fact, there will even be an acceleration of the concept of time when one is within a Golden City. That is why the physical body requires less sleep when one first enters a Golden City. These are all concepts that we hold to lay down one by one in the next few weeks and months, as we spend our time releasing this information for humanity.

BUILDING ENERGY

Now, I would like to lay down a template for the way in which we shall work together. As you well know, Dear chelas, I, along with those who work with me, prefer to build an energy. In building energy around a project, it allows a greater harmony and a greater clarity to be brought forward in the works. This we taught with the I AM America Map. Do you remember when we instructed you to place your left hand over your heart, your right hand to project it outward and to bring that visualization into its fullness? We were building an energy, and we shall do the same within that context in releasing the teachings of Gobean. It would be best if we selected a time each day to meet, one in which we can comfortably provide the information and not interfere with your day, yet dispense the information so that it may help all of humanity.

EARLY MORNING HOURS

Question: "What was the time that you used previously?"

Early morning hours are always best for the collective consciousness. However, if this is impossible, we can work with other times. However, it is our suggestion that we work at 6 a.m. each morning.

Response: "We will do that, then."

We will instruct on the days we will come forward. We will take frequent breaks. This will allow rest and relaxation, but a more important aspect for the assimilation of the information, so that it may be organized and then utilized.

VISUALIZATION

Now, some visualizations. Bring out the template of the Gobean Vortex, and each day I ask you in your meditation and your visualizations to perform the same technique of the left hand over the heart and projecting the energies out of the right hand toward the Gobean Vortex. Is this understood?

Answer: "Yes."

Then proceed every day until completion of these teachings. Master El Morya will serve as the Master Teacher instructor. I shall serve as Master of Ceremony and will provide an interface. Do you understand?

Answer: "Yes."

Are there any questions, Dear heart?

Answer: "Not about the process and the project."

Then, let us proceed in Grace and Divine Intervention. Let us proceed in the light of a New Day and the hope of a New Age. OM Manaya Pitaya Hitaka. So be it, Beloveds.

CHAPTER FIVE

A Quickening

*Instruction for a student
with Saint Germain and El Morya.*

Greetings, Beloved, in that Mighty Violet Ray. I AM Saint Germain, and I request permission to come forward.

Student response: "Please, dear Master, come forward."

TIME COMPACTION

In that Mighty Violet Ray that streams forth from the Logos, the heart of Helios and Vesta, I come on a wave known as time. Upon the Earth Plane and Planet, this time period known as Time Compaction is, indeed, a time when you may ponder and question, "Can I take much more of this?" You see, Dear ones, this time that you are now living is a Time of Opportunity, a time when action upon action is a time where you may now transmute those many fears, longings and desires that you have held through each lifetime. It is only through the use of the Violet Ray that one may move forward in the desire of their choice. You see, Dear ones, this time that has been brought forward, is a time that is indeed for the evolution for all of humanity; a time when Unana will reign supreme upon the Earth Plane and Planet. Unity of Consciousness will come forward to create that Law of the Best and the Highest Good. But, Dear ones, Time Compaction, itself, must be understood so that you will understand the use of the Violet Ray. You see, Dear ones, as we have discussed in "The Point of Perception" it is thought, feeling, and action that Co-creates this reality in which you are living. But it is also your choice, Dear ones, and choice upon choice, desire upon desire.

This is indeed a Time of Endings, a time when we enter into the fires of purification. What is this fire of purification? But only Time Compaction. It is as if one event is compressing upon another, tightly compacted, neatly one up against the other. And you feel as though you are stressed and harried. But,

Dear ones, let me assure you that this is indeed also a time that has been given so that you will understand your own actions, your own thoughts, and will hone that faculty of choice.

You see, Dear ones, to move into the Point of Perception, to understand your role as true Co-creator of your reality, you must understand your choice, the importance and the value of such. Time Compaction has been given as a great gift for you to instantly understand your thoughts, your feelings and your actions. It is as an Instant-thought-manifestation.

Now, let me diagram.

A DIAGRAM OF UNITY CONSCIOUSNESS

He is showing two, swirling Vortex structures beside one another ... like two larger funnels are meeting one another.[1]

You see, Dear ones, in Co-creation where one idea meets another idea, there is almost a collison ... and the two shall become as ONE.

From the two meeting one another, he is drawing a third, which comes from the bottom and the top. He creates a circle around it.

You see from this diagram that thoughts, when they seem to collide upon one another, compact upon one another, create a more whole thought, a newer thought. It is sometimes perceived that there are disharmonious thoughts that do not work together, but this is entirely untrue. What happens, indeed, is that some of the thoughts may not be acted upon, but they do, indeed, work together as ONE. All things work together as ONE, and in Time Compaction, one action upon the next, also comes together as ONE. You see, Dear ones, this is the beginning of the understanding of Unity Consciousness that all things will work together as ONE, as ONE unit, as ONE being of light.

THOUGHT, FEELING, AND ACTION CREATE

In the New Dimension that you will be living in, the New Times that you are being brought to understand, Unity of

1. See Appendix H2: *Saint Germain's Co-creative Thought Process.*

Consciousness is the most important thing to grasp and understand. There are those who say, "Well, if I do not agree with this one, then I shall go my separate way." This is true in most instances that you do go your separate way, but the thoughts, the feelings and the actions that you perceived as a disharmony still created.

> All thoughts create.
> All actions create.
> Feeling is the beautiful tie that binds
> and can lift a thought into harmony.[2]

We have viewed this before as a Point of Perception, but the emotion is the most valuable key. We have discussed this before in prior discourses, known as the E-motion.[3] The E-motion sometimes is known as sound. It is this sound vibration that harmonizes all things to come forward into this greater unity, this greater cause of action.

DISHARMONY

Then you collect yourself with another group who decide that their thoughts, their feelings and their actions are in harmony. And they say, "Let us unite in our minds, our hearts and our hopes, our desires and our wishes." And yet nothing comes forward! Why is that so?

The collective action was charged with disharmony. It became the impetus and the force, you see. Impetus and force enable an action and then another action manifests. This presence of this charge is most important in all things. The charge that you have created and the disharmonious situation are just as important

as the creation of harmony. Also, this thrust of your character (moral strength) into your creation is most important. This again is the E-motion.

E-MOTION AND YOUR CHOICE

Dear chelas of my heart, decide what E-motion you shall put forward. Shall it be one of joy? One of enthusiasm? One of ecstasy, thrilled beyond? It is yours to choose.

Within this time, Beloved Mother Babajaren, along with help from your beloved Brothers and Sisters, are here to assist during Time Compaction so that you may understand why it is that so much is currently thrust upon you all at once.

TURNING THE PAGE

We're preparing for a New Time, and as Beloved El Morya has said, "This New Day begins one step at a time." Before the New Day can start, we must close down the old one. Now we must leave behind all that is ready to be closed and turn the page. In turning the page, one must understands how harmonious situations and disharmonious situations are created. How may one choose to create more harmony within one's life?

WALKING AWAY FROM DISHARMONY

How may one choose to walk away from disharmony? Now the charge, itself, that you may feel in a disharmonious situation … do you wish to walk away from it? First, I suggest to blaze it in that Mighty Violet Flame.

> "God I AM, Violet Flame."

Using this Violet Flame on a daily basis, and I mean *a daily usage*, will indeed help and assist through this purification. But it is also very important, Dear ones, that you understand the choices that you continue to make while in the charge of disharmony. Take time away in meditation. Take time away to calm yourself, your mind and your thoughts; to quell your E-motion. Resting this E-motion is of vast import, to understand that it is

---

2. Harmony finds its root in the Greek word *harmonia*, which means joining, concord, or music. However, when referred to in Ascended Master teachings, Harmony likely means agreement. Harmony is the first virtue of the Twelve Jurisdictions; it is based on the principle of agreement.

3. E-motion plays a critical role in the Co-creative process by melding and balancing thoughts and emotions. E-motion is also considered a type of "charge," which ignites and propels a kernel of thought-feeling into action. This charge represents the all-important impetus that compels and characterizes Co-creation. Enthusiasm, joy, and passion are essential components of a harmonious E-motion and Co-creative process. Anger, frustration, and revenge are the essential activators of the disharmonious E-motion. The harmonizing vibration of sound is sometimes defined as feeling.

the charge, like a trigger that leads one into yet another event, then another.

KARMA AND FREEDOM

This Wheel of Karma is engendered in your choices. Dear ones, Dear hearts, begin to understand this. Seek the solace of the soul, and there you will begin to find the true Fire of Freedom. Find this first in all things, and then you can return to a creation in its wholeness and fullness. Understand the times that you are living in. See it as an opportunity that has been given for you, and you can then move on in grace and in harmony. Now, Dear ones, I shall open the floor for brief questions.

THE GRAVITY OF COLLECTIVE CONSCIOUSNESS

Question: "Time Compaction has long been a question that most people have asked me. It has always been my opinion that the planet and the solar system were changing their position relative to the galaxy, and in the movement of that change, Time Compaction was one of the results. As this Time Compaction progresses, the electromagnetic charges that have been built up over the eons in the Earth's atmosphere and in the atmosphere of the individual must go through a transmuting process, more so than ever. Because of the new dynamics of electromagnetics and levels of consciousness that completely affect the planet at all layers and realms ... is this why you have stressed the Violet Flame so much?"

The Violet Flame can set you free from any trying circumstance, from any sense of dissension, from all disharmonies within the soul. It can also begin to foster the growth of peace and stillness. The Sun and the Moon create the pull of life upon the Earth, and it is through the collective thoughts, feelings, actions and desires of humanity that any sense of gravity exists upon the Earth. There would be those of science who would argue with this concept, but it is the total force of thoughts holding together the collective reality of the Earth. As I have said in many past discourses, the Earth is a vast schoolroom where many can be taught, if they choose to learn. Through this gravitational pull, we are pulled in essence to understand ourselves. Know thyself, Dear ones, and the truth within shall set you free.

QUALIFYING KARMA

During this period of Time Compaction, the choices, thoughts and desires of many other lifetimes are opened. Prior to this lifetime, an Akashic Record exists of your prior embodiments and is comprised of your many thoughts, feelings, desires, and actions.[4] Now, the Karmas you wish to experience are poured into your life, for you to qualify into action, and will again create harmony or disharmony. Do you see, Dear one, that it is a simple choice?

The gift that has been given to you is the work of the Violet Flame. Call upon it, live it, and breathe It. The Violet Flame is the Divine Intervention that can lift you from the most trying of circumstance and lift you from all suffering. It is brought as a Law of Mercy and Compassion given to you so that you may find within yourself whom you truly are. Dear Divine ones, it is the work of the Violet Flame that will set you free, not only in mind, not only in feeling, but from the path that you

---

4. From the Sanskrit word *akasa,* which means to be visible, appear, shine, or be brilliant, the Akashic Records are built from ether, the fifth cosmic element. Occultists claim the Akashic Records contain the history of all created things from time immemorial, including recorded details of past lifetimes and personal factors related to the soul's spiritual growth and development. Akasa encompasses all of space and records all events, from the seemingly insignificant to the critical and decisive moments that change us forever. Akashic Records permeate our dimension; however, we may not have the ability to access or sense their content. For this reason, interested individuals may seek out mediums that are sensitized to the psychic undulations of akasa. The Ascended Masters, however, encourage our personal development through meditation to develop this ability.

According to esoteric teachers, the Akashic Records are purer than Astral Light, and exist in the Fifth Dimension. Since the Astral Body composes our Karmic pattern of emotion, it is influenced by our state of consciousness and does not extend beyond the Fourth Dimension. Mystics explain that the Astral Light is "the tablet of Earth and of its child, the animal-man," and Akashic Light contains the memory of the Spiritual Hierarchy that manages and organizes our Planetary Logos and the souls that inhabit it. Akasa is known as the crucial agent in religion, occult electricity, an aspect in the HU-man energy system and Kundalini, and it "enters into all the magical operations of nature, producing mesmeric, magnetic, and spiritual phenomena." The book of Genesis describes akasa as the waters of the deep; and Gautama Buddha considered only two aspects of creation as eternal: akasa and nirvana.

feel encumbers you ... from all transgressions that you perceive, from all guilt that you perceive. In the time to come, it is hoped that through the use of the Violet Flame the Earth shall be lifted into that shiny Star of Freedom. From that point a New Age will dawn, and humanity will experience a New Time. Do you see the hope and wonder that awaits? It is indeed this simple.

Call upon the Vibration of "HU." Call upon the help of those who are here to give you assistance.

> "Mighty Violet Flame,
> Come forth through I AM That I AM.
> Mighty Violet Flame,
> From the Grace of the Divine Heart, I AM.
> Come forth!
> Blaze in, through, and around
> All that keeps me from my Divine Path.
> Violet Flame, I AM.
> God, I AM, Violet Flame.
> So be it."

When you command such a force into the action, it affects all around it.

A RIPPLING EFFECT

Now, let us return to the drawing table.

It appears the two thoughts were colliding upon one another, however, they still create. They create a force. The Violet Flame affects the ONE. It acts as a point of harmony and unity, the birth of peace. Do you see now, as I describe these waves? It starts from the center in the same way that a pebble, when it is dropped into the center of a small puddle of water, sends its rippling effect to the outer edges? In the same way, the Violet Flame works in your creation and works within you. When you call upon the Violet Flame, it works from that perfect cell, the Eight-sided Cell of Perfection within the heart of the Unfed Flame.

THE VIOLET PLUME

There were times upon the Earth Plane and Planet when humanity used the Violet Flame so regularly that the plume grew among the masses, and the skies actually took on a Violet hue throughout the day, and the Sun and the Moon cast a Violet hue (light) upon the Earth.[5] It was carried electromagnetically in the aura as light, and as sound. So you see, Dear ones, to call upon it collectively only increases this force.

FORGETTING DIVINITY

But why is it that we now live in a different time? It is this simple ... it is forgetting. It is this forgetfulness through eon upon eon of fear, rejection, dejection and giving to that creation more power than the power of harmony or the power of joy. It is most simple to understand in this context, but it is the application of this use, of this Mighty Law in action that shall set you free. Questions?

Question: "Beloved Saint Germain, is there any additional information that you would like to share with us at this time?"

THE LAW WITHIN

There is indeed much more information that I shall impart this day, but I wanted to open this discourse with the use of the Violet Flame, its application so that it could be understood in

---

5. According to the Master Teachers, in ancient times of greater light on Earth, the masses frequently used the Violet Flame to achieve spiritual growth. As a result, it increased to such strength and power it became a visible, ubiquitous violet-purple light in the human aura—the atmosphere was suffused with it. Meanwhile, the Rays of our Sun and the luminous Moon continuously reflected its vibrant lavender tone day and night. As humanity entered Kali Yuga, the final stage of the dark age, and consciousness denigrated on the Earth, the Violet Plume retreated to the subtle tones often observed at sunrise and sunset. Darker shades and vibrations of the Violet Plume can also be detected during certain phases of the full Moon.

its fullness. To understand a law in action is a holy thing indeed. To understand this law within you is Divine.

Now I shall proceed.

THE GOLDEN CITY STARS

Beloveds, the work in the Golden Cities is of great import.[6] As you know before, we have identified many different areas of these Golden Cities so that you could understand them energetically, so that you could understand their purpose. The Golden Cities are interacting with Beloved Babajaren and the Ascended Masters, this Hierarchy of Service, at this time, to bring forth a stillness, a peace, a harmony, an understanding of the ONE in this Time of Tribulation upon the Earth Plane and Planet.[7]

We've explained many facets about these cities so that you may understand how they interact with you. But it has been pointed out most succinctly through Beloved El Morya that the Stars themselves coalesce. It is the most direct force of the energy Rays, and it is in the Stars that we would like to give discourse so that you may begin to understand how they can be used to bring forth qualities within your life.

Now, I would like to bring forward Beloved El Morya.

El Morya steps forward.

Greetings, chelas. I request permission to come forward.

Response: "Please come forward."

_____

6. See Appendix 12: *Saint Germain's and El Morya's Teachings on the Golden Cities.*

7. According to prophecies, humanity and planet Earth may experience an era of conflict, struggle and cataclysmic Earth Changes—known as the Time of Tribulation. This devastating period can be thwarted, however, depending on the quality and quantity of mankind's collective spiritual growth and evolution. Darkness and negativity may be recalibrated if humanity can raise its spiritual conscience.

CHANGE YOUR PERCEPTIONS

Dear ones, we have spoken upon a New Day. Now we must proceed, for there is more to this lesson. There is a New Time. To understand a New Time, you must change the way you perceive.

> To change the way you perceive,
> You must understand.
> To understand,
> You must begin with choice.

You have had many choices of which way to go, to turn left or to turn right, to move forward or to move backward. Now, it is important that you review such choices and say, "Has this helped me?" "Am I now in a position in which I feel content?" Or "Am I just stagnating in the mire of my thoughts?" That I cannot tell you, Dear ones, but you must decide within yourself whether you are content—whether you feel peace, or do you only perceive contentment out of the fear of moving forward.

RADIATION OF THE STAR

The Star of Gobean is now activated. This has been placed in Divine Order to bring a magnetic effect for the New Time. Have you not noticed that now many are being drawn and pulled, and are moving and gravitating toward the Star. This is because of the radiation that is within it. It is not a radiation that exists within the Earth itself, even though Beloved Babajaren is offering herself to be of service. It is an energy that we are building. It is a template of perfect thought, perfect feeling, and perfect action. It is a template, or a network of understanding, and you may model this in your own lives and use it to move forward into these New Times.

There are Strategic Points that exist geophysically. You see, Dear ones, there must be physical demonstration of this New Time. Physical demonstration of the energy is built for those who have the eyes to see and the ears to hear. We have laid this template down so that a New Time may be birthed—a New

Time that is now much needed upon your Earth Plane and Planet.

PURPOSE OF GOBEAN

Engendered within this template is a transformative harmony. You have noted that when you live in disharmony in such a Vortex city, that it is almost impossible to move forward without the use of the Violet Flame. But it is that Blue Ray of Will, that Blue Ray of Choice that fills the mighty Vortex of Gobean. It is there where chelas may learn through this energy, learn about the manifestation of their choices, and transform through working in groups with the principle of harmony. It is through this Star of Knowledge, and understanding that we ask you to move forward to utilize these energies for yourself, for the work that you are bringing forward. They are present for you to understand.

A NETWORK OF CONSCIOUSNESS

Traveling, of course, to any of the selected points and working in ceremony, in song, or in meditation would allow an infusion of such to come to you for your use and for your daily application. To live in such an area would bring about the same result. You see, Dear ones, Dear chelas, the infusion of these energies through and around you will only bring you into greater harmony with the Divine Will. Each of these locations is connected to the apex of other Golden City locations. Therefore, when you meditate in such a location, the energy travels quite quickly as a network of consciousness.

The Golden Cities are comprised primarily of a purity of consciousness.[8] As I have stated before, Beloved Babajaren has also offered herself to serve in harmony with these grids of pure consciousness. But this is given again, as Saint Germain has said, as an opportunity for you to grow and to learn at this time. These locations are very important, for many will travel to them during the Time of Great Change. There have been those who have asked, "When is this Time of Change?" We reply, the Time is Now, Dear ones. The changes are upon the Earth Plane and Planet. The changes are happening now within you. As above, so below. This Template of Consciousness is also the first template of the consciousness of Unana.

FIRST, THE WORK OF HARMONY

And it is the Blue Ray, as held by myself, Beloved Archangel Michael, and Hercules the Elohim, comes forth to bless humanity to understand that the work of harmony must come first in all of its creations. In the Jurisdiction, Harmony was brought forward first. For harmony must be contained in all creations and Beloved Saint Germain has lectured upon the use of the Violet Flame.

Now, let us continue with the lesson of harmony. Harmony is the only way that this New Time can be understood. If you feel even the slightest tinge of dissension, the slightest tinge of disharmony, then move yourself back, set yourself away.[9] Take

---

8. The Mineral and Vegetable Kingdoms that flourish amid the Stars and Adjutant Points of Golden City Vortices are imbued with the energies of that particular Golden City. As a result, water and produce are beneficially charged with Vortex-infused minerals. According to El Morya, each doorway of the Golden City of Gobean releases the following benefic Vortex energies into the air, water, and locally grown foods:
  Gobean Northern Door: The Inner Growth of Harmony
  Gobean Southern Door: Healing of Disease and Disharmony
  Gobean Western Door: Higher knowledge and understanding of Harmony, Peace, and Cooperation.
  Gobean Eastern Door: Harmony among family, friends, and groups.

Gobean Star: Acquisition of a new understanding of Harmony and transformation.
9. Discharging Negative or Disharmonious Situations: Holding on to negativity perpetuates individual and collective darkness. Moving toward spiritual growth, however, is about releasing adversity and replacing it with light. Saint Germain recommends the following steps to alleviate personal discord:
  Using the Violet Flame on a daily basis provides assistance during self-purification.
  Time spent alone, in the solace of mediation and silence, can quell disharmonious E-motion. This practice calms the mind and eases thoughts.
  Resting the E-motion, that is, quieting the triggers of disharmonious thoughts and feelings can help achieve serenity.
  According to Saint Germain, serenity ignites the true fires of freedom, which assists our return to wholeness, grace, and harmony while living in difficult times.
  Saint Germain offers the following decree to discharge negativity and disharmony:
    Mighty Violet Flame, come forth through the I AM that I AM.
    Mighty Violet Flame, from the Grace of the Divine Heart, I AM!
    Violet Flame, come forth.
  Blaze in, through, and around, all that keeps me from my Divine Path!
    Violet Flame I AM, God I AM Violet Flame! So be it.

time in silence and address your intention. Anything that does not align to Divine Harmony must now have its place in purification. Bring yourself forward, Dear chelas, ready to face the New Times, restored unto yourself. You see, beloveds, this is how harmony moves forward. It is through that simple intention of harmony. Questions?

Response: "Harmony seems to be a very illusive thing for most of us on the planet, for those of us who choose to be of service with you. I understand the use of the Violet Flame as a focus to create the harmony if that is the intention. However, I would ask that you would also share to create more of the harmony here in all that we do, and participate with us and join us."

"ONE PLUS ONE"

It is as simple as focus.[10] For you see, Dear ones, focus aligns. Focus brings all into the clarity that is required to bring the union of harmony. You see, Dear ones, harmony is indeed a union. One would think that harmony is a simple, single focus, but not so, beloveds. Harmony is indeed a union of focus coming together, focus coalescing from one to the next: one simple thought and one simple thought, one plus one equals two. That two is harmony. One plus one does not equal four. One plus one does not equal eight, but one plus one equals two. It is that simple. It is the coalescing of the harmony. It is this union that is contained within the self. This union is then contained throughout the being, this union that then is expressed in Beloved Gobean. But what are we really speaking about ... one plus one? It is left plus right. It is dark plus light. It is hot plus cold. It is the knowledge that the dual forces work together at all times to bring forth a greater wisdom. And yet there is such dissension that is felt through this process, such chaos as it is judged, such disorder as it is judged, such dishar-

---

(Sing the Bija-seed mantra of HU—a sound vibration prayer to the Creator/Creative Force; call upon the assistance of Master Teachers and spirit guides before uttering this decree.)

10. A central point of attraction, attention, or activity; often Ascended Master teachings refer to a focus as an intention, prayer, or meditation for spiritual growth.

mony as it is judged. This Point of Perception is indeed choice, the way you are willing to *see* such a thing.

INTUITION IS THE CREATIVE FORCE

Seek the higher level through your intention, understand your intention, understand the power of your creative force. It is this creative force that moves throughout you. This is known as ONE. This Divine Source is the center of Unana.

UNANA IS WITHIN

In the same way that the Violet Flame moves forth from the Eight-sided Cell of Perfection, the consciousness of Unana runs forth through you. It is part of you. It is you. It is connected to this Earth. It is connected to us. You see, Dear ones, it is the force that brings us to you. It is the force that brings you to us. It is the seeking of this ONE, the seeking of this unity, the seeking of this harmony that brings us together. Why deny such a thing?

HARMONY IS A LAW OF NATURE

Harmony is a natural Law of Nature. It is mirrored throughout your world. Harmony exists to bring you peace. Questions?

Question: "So the path of harmony is the Violet Flame?"

THE DENIAL OF LIGHT

They are interconnected as ONE. They are known as ONE. Divinity exists all around you, but you must see it. You must perceive it. Divine Intervention is but a glance away, a moment away. To bring it into your experience of now, to your Time of Now, you must choose for it to be so, to choose such Divinity, to choose such Grace, to choose such harmony. Are these not the qualities of the Co-creator? Beloveds, Dear ones, this time has been brought forward so that you could understand that which is within yourself without judgment and without shame. It is the Light that is within you that will bring you now to the greater harmony. When you engage in judgment, it is not judgment of another. It is judgment of the Light within yourself, the Light that you deny yourself, the unity that you deny yourself. Do you understand?

Response: "Yes, then it is truly my choice for this harmony. I choose for the Divine Intervention of this moment to be sustained always. So be it."

So be it, Beloved.

STRATEGIC POINTS

These Strategic Points (Adjutant Points) that exist now within the Beloved Star of Gobean can assist you in understanding this. Travel to such a point and spend just a day reflecting upon the intention of your soul to create greater unity into harmony. Take this, Dear one, as your first step, a small step into creating a New Day.

Response: "So be it."

And now I shall open the floor for questions.

DISCARD FEAR AND INJUSTICE

Student's question: "Beloved Master, these polarities that we perceive, or that we seem to perceive and seem to experience, are they ultimately not real when we choose to be nonjudgmental?"

They become as ONE within yourself, Dear one, and that perception becomes the reality of Oneness. The reality of Oneness is when all fear is brought to the side, where all sense of injustice is brought to the side, and they are discarded as an unused garment, something that no longer serves the consciousness. You see, when one understands unity, that all forces work together as ONE, there is purpose in all things. Do you understand?

Response: "Yes, I do. Therefore, if you were to address all humanity, what would you say are the three most important things that we must endeavor to do?"

"CHOOSE, CHOOSE, AND CHOOSE AGAIN!"

Choose, choose and then choose again for yourself. Find within yourself the Divinity that you are, that is of all things. Choose, choose, choose for the ONE, for the ONE that is contained within All. Choose, choose, choose for love. As Dear Brother Sananda has said, "Love one another." These are the three that I would choose.

Student's question: "Is there any additional information, Beloved Master, that you would like to share with us at this time?"

THE QUICKENING

Prepare yourself, beloveds, prepare yourself, for the time is at hand. A quickening is amongst humanity. As we have said so many times before, those who have the eyes to see and the ears to hear, now bring your hands into action. Join as ONE in that choosing of the new qualities: these qualities of harmony, of cooperation. Bring forth this transformation within yourself, assisted through the work of Beloved Saint Germain's Mighty Violet Flame. Beloveds, Dear ones, this time is again an opportunity—an opportunity for your growth, an opportunity for your understanding. If you are feeling disharmony within your life, it is important now to choose. If you are feeling disharmony in your life, use the Violet Flame. If you are feeling disharmony within your life, see all things working together as ONE. These are the simple lessons, the simple understandings. But this is where we must start to create a New Time and a New Day.

Now, I shall proceed upon more of the Vortex structures.

He is drawing a diagram. He's circling the Stars, and he points to the Northern Door of the Vortex.

SPIRITUAL GROWTH IN NORTHERN DOORS

The Northern Door as you have understood it is indeed an area of fruition and growth. If you seek the growth and understanding of harmony within yourself to bring things together to the unity of causes, this is a simple place to travel to (Spiritual Pilgrimage), to ingest and take in such energies, for this will bring a fruition and an understanding.

Now, he's drawing the Southern Door.

HEALING IN THE SOUTHERN DOOR

If you perceive yourself to be ill at ease, the disharmony has brought dis-ease within your physical body, travel to this area and ingest such energies to bring about harmony, to bring about miraculous healing. These areas are infused with the waters of miracle healing. We have stated before that air, water and food that are contained within certain areas of the Golden Cities are indeed infused with energies to bring about such qualities. Travel, Dear ones, to this area, if you feel you need to bring about healing of the body

Now, he's drawing the Western Door.

WISDOM OF THE WEST

To bring about higher understanding, higher knowledge of harmony, higher knowledge of unity, higher knowledge of peace, higher knowledge of cooperation, move to this Western area, stay for several days, ingest such energies. They will bring about a greater and higher clarity, knowledge that can be utilized, knowledge that is known as wisdom.

Now, he's drawing the Eastern Door of the Vortex.

HARMONY IN THE EAST

To this Eastern Door, travel when you seek harmony among friends, harmony among groups, harmony with one another. If there is dissension within your family, travel to this area, spend but a few days, or a few hours, whatever it takes to infuse yourself with these energies until you feel the energies complete within.

You see, Dear ones, this is a great opportunity that is given to humanity at this time. It is brought forward to create collective healing on our planet so that we may move much more swiftly into the New Times. Questions?

Question: "You are making these references to the Star locations of the points on the compass. Correct?"

THE STAR OF TRANSFORMATION

I'm making these references to the entire Vortex, and now for the Star.

The Star is the perfect harmony of all energies coming together, coalescing with one another, infusing and working together. This is where you travel to if you seek transformation, if you seek new knowledge, if you seek new understanding through the path of harmony or through the path of transformation. Travel there to seek your new intention, to seek your new understanding. Do you understand?

Answer: "Yes, thank you."

The Star of Knowledge is brought forward as a ceremonial ground. This ceremony exists only within yourself, but can be shared with others as a celebration of the ONE. So you see, Dear ones, the work and the purpose at hand. You see, Dear ones, the work of the Golden Cities, their great service to humanity, and what they now afford for All. Share this information with many others so that they, too, may come to know and to understand. I shall now turn the floor back to Beloved Saint Germain.

Response: "Thank you, El Morya."

Saint Germain steps forward.

Greetings, Dear ones. In that Mighty Violet Ray I now conclude this discourse. And I ask that grace impart within all of your hearts. May grace be the final Law that binds us all into the New Time. Hitaka.

Response: "Hitaka."

CHAPTER SIX

Golden City Rays

༽

*Saint Germain gives instruction on Ray Forces,
and the Golden Cities.*

Greetings, Beloveds, in that Mighty Christ, I AM Saint Germain, and I stream forth on that Mighty Violet Ray of Mercy and Forgiveness.

As usual Dear hearts, I request permission to come forward.

"Please, Saint Germain, come forward. You're most welcome."

RAY FORCES EVOLVE HUMANITY

Today, Dear ones, we shall focus on a teaching of the Rays and Ray Forces and their interaction with the Golden Cities, how they work through the Golden Cities, and how this information may be used to move humanity forward into the New Times.[1]

The Rays, as you see, Dear ones, are a coalescing of life force, a singular focus of light and sound that come forward to lift humanity in evolution. In this sense, a Ray can allow a person to move forward to become a new being clothed with a new body.

Ray Forces work in such a manner, prodding and moving the person along the path of evolution, spiritual evolution, and begin to move that person onward into greater understanding, knowledge, intuition, and Mastery of the force of his life.

THE AURA AND CHAKRA SYSTEM

As I have said before, it is important for you to know thyself first, and to know thyself is to understand how the Rays work within the being, the aura and the electromagnetic field.

The Human Aura is comprised of many such Ray Forces coming together and working, coalescing, one arcing among the other. The Chakra System is also influenced by the different

Ray Forces, each of them coming forward and moving each chakra in a different vibration and through a different sound. It is indeed true that a Ray Force influences each of the chakras, even though there may be a coalescing of the various life forces.

The chakras work alongside the light forces, and alongside each light force is also a sound; these work together, Dear ones. The light forces are determined at the moment of birth, and, as you have studied, it is the Astral Body that determines the predominance of a Ray Force or the predominance of a sound force. The two work together, as an Elohim of light and sound, in an Absolute Harmony and absolute cooperation, moving the individual to greater understanding and to greater evolution.

QUALITIES OF THE BLUE RAY

As we understand that there is a predominant light force, and a predominant Ray Force, a predominant sound force within the individual, there is also a predominant light force or Ray Force and a predominant sound force in each of the Golden Cities.[2] As you have known, Gobean is known as the Blue City. It is working toward the qualities of harmony and cooperation. The Blue Ray brings one toward this. First, it holds one's consciousness steadfast unto the idea of a unifying force of cooperation of the Oneship of all things, so steadfastly one holds to this Blue Ray. It is known as Will, or Power, or Force. This, of course, then aligns the Vertical Power Current, which you know as the Kundalini of the spine. It works with many of the chakras in different combinations, but, of course, it is most identified with the Throat Chakra and upon occasion with the Third Eye, or pineal gland. This allows one to make the choice in an expression and allows the choice to be expressed through the Will, for the Blue Ray is also at times known as a Ray of Will. This, of course, must be developed within the being to allow evolution. It is only through choices that one begins to evolve in a greater understanding, knowledge, and power of their own Godship.

You see, Dear ones, the Blue Ray is of vast importance and, of course, is always known as the First Ray. For it is only through Will and the development of choice, and the expression of those choices that one is able to understand one's own cause and effect. Cause and effect, of course, has been known as Karma, but

---

1. See Appenidix J2: *Saint Germain's Teachings on Golden City Rays.*

2. See Appendix L2: *Determining Dominant Ray Forces.*

it is only through Karma, or cause and effect, that one begins to learn and to grow through one's choices. So, you see, Dear ones, the Blue Ray is of vast importance. And it is, of course, the first Blue Ray that serves in the Golden City of Gobean.

ENTRANCE AND RADIATION OF RAY FORCES INTO THE GOLDEN CITIES

The Ray Force enters through the apex of each Golden City. It is directed through the Great Central Sun. The Great Central Sun is a source of order in your Universe of collective thought, feeling, and action. Each Ray Force enters into the apex and radiates out in a circular motion, and when one is working toward integration of a Ray Force, it is important to move closer to the apex of a Golden City. And as one is there physically enjoying the energies, one becomes aligned in assimilating the Ray Force into one's being and purifying that Ray Force within one's being.

A PURIFYING PROCESS

In the beginning of understanding a Ray Force, such as the Blue Ray, one would feel a bit of purification, a bit of disharmony, in the same sense as when a body enters into disease, which sometimes has the same effect. When the Ray strikes the body, the purity of the Ray Force causes one to begin to discard all which does not align to the force and the working of the Ray. In the same way, when the body enters into disease, it is dispelling what the body will not cooperate with. So, it is in the same manner. When one is closer to the purity of a Ray Force when entering into a Golden City, and in this instance I am referring to the locations of the Stars, there will first be some discomfort. The body may require larger amounts of rest. There could be disharmony in relationships with others, and there may be some purifying process that the body must go through in order to begin to assimilate the purity of the Ray Force. This you will notice in any Golden City when you are working to align with the Ray Force.

QUALITIES OF THE RUBY AND GOLD RAY

It is the same for all of the other Golden Cities. In Malton, you would be working to align with the Ruby and the Gold Ray. The Ruby and the Gold Ray are Rays of Devotion. This Ray may create desires into manifestation, for it has been stated that in Golden City Vortices desires are instantly manifested. So one begins to understand, through one's choices, the desires that they choose, the desires that they wish to attain and bring to fruition. It is also understood that the Ruby and Gold Rays play important roles at this time in assisting and helping the Elemental Kingdoms of the Earth. For many of the Elemental Kingdoms, the Devas, the little fairies, and the gnomes and all (others) who are there and do exist (of the Nature Kingdom), are also going through their own type of purification. You see, humanity has created an Earth out of balance through the use of many pollutants, which are affecting the Kingdoms and causing an imbalance in many of the Nature Kingdoms. So, it is through the use of the Ruby and the Gold Rays that these are brought back into a balance.

The Gold Ray also rules the ability to take action, and the ability to take action with force. Sometimes it is only through force that things are achieved. The Ruby and the Gold Ray rules such actions that exist on the planet as volcanic eruptions, tidal wave motion, tectonic plates moving. This is the Elemental Force at work, working to bring balance to remove that which has brought about disharmony. In the recent tidal wave that you have had upon the planet, humanity must understand that even though great sorrow was brought for the many who have now crossed over into New Dimensions, a great balance was also achieved. This balance allowed the Elemental Kingdoms to achieve an increased sense of their own harmony. You see, Dear ones, it is Absolute Harmony and balance that is sought at this time upon the Earth Plane and Planet. It is balance that must be held in order for humanity to move into the consciousness of Unana. It is only through balance that this is achieved in the great Oneship.

The Ruby and the Gold Rays enter into the Vortex of Malton at the apex, and it is the alignment to this Ray that, if one is seeking fruition of desires to bring their thoughts into instant manifestation, one may travel to align one's energies and Chakra System to this.[3] The chakra that aligns most evenly with the Ruby and the Gold Rays, even though I would also like to add that all chakras are affected by all Rays, is the lowest chakra (Root Chakra). The lowest chakra is an action chakra. It is the chakra that allows things to move and to be birthed into existence. When one moves to Malton and allows the activation of these energies into one's being, they will begin to experience a movement of the Kundalini forces. Of course, in the beginning, they will notice an increase in sexuality, the creative ability, and the desire capacity. It is important to understand when you are integrating a Ray Force from a Golden City into the being, that you must use a type of breathwork to move the energy through the chakras, to keep the body in balance.[4] Any type of breath-work is recommended, any that the chela finds to bring balance.

Of course, Energy Balancing is also recommended, and we have spent much time upon these techniques, have we not? So, Dear hearts, I would suggest that any technique that balances the energy throughout the system will help.

Of course, in the beginning, as in Gobean and the assimilation of the Blue Ray, you will note that nothing seems to go right, that the desires that serve your Divine Purpose seem to not work or manifest correctly. But this is all the process of purification, of bringing this into alignment to your plan of the best and the highest good.

---

2. This is the principle of *Spiritual Migration*. An individual can transmute personal Karmas and initiate the Ascension Process by traveling to, living near, or living in a Golden City Vortex, thereby deliberately and physically accessing its energies. Known as Spiritual Migration, this process involves embracing and understanding the metaphysical knowledge of the four doorways—or four directions—of a Golden City. A chela's passage through the energies of each doorway is literal and metaphoric on all levels: physical, emotional, mental, and spiritual. The journey begins in the Northerly area of the Vortex, also known as the Black Door. The spiritual course progresses to the Blue Door (East), onward to the Red Door (South), and to the final door, the Yellow Door, found in the West. It concludes at the Star, the center or apex of a Golden City. This gradual evolutionary expedition is designed to introduce a student to the higher frequencies of a Golden City, but it is not a voyage taken alone. Presiding Ascended Masters, archetypes of evolution who steward Golden City Vortices alongside the physical presence of specific Golden City Power Points—namely Golden City lei lines—and Golden City Adjutant Points provide the necessary Fourth- and Fifth-Dimensional mentoring. Golden City energies must be carefully integrated before entering the intense energies of Golden City Adjutant Points and Golden City Stars.

First, it is suggested that chelas visit or live near the outer perimeters of the Vortex to acclimate to the energy—one to forty miles within a Golden City Vortex should be sufficient. Once that step is completed, a chela can then carefully migrate inside, to the inner perimeters and power points of the Vortex. Students should have developed the ability to contact the appropriate Golden City Master Teacher and the capacity to maintain this contact during the critical moments of this arduous passage. Advanced students may take as few as twenty-one days to complete their spiritual migration—one day for each of the twenty-one major power points present in a Golden City Vortex—whereas others may journey for years.

The number twenty-one is sacred, not only in the realm of theosophy but in matters of creation. It represents many things—the meeting of spirit and matter, the beginning of HU-man individuality, the transition from youth to adulthood, and the sacrosanct vessel of God and the Holy Temple. The number twenty-one also contains elements of destruction and renewal; it prepares our consciousness to receive the master number twenty-two, a powerful integer associated with initiates and the Master Builder.

The ability to integrate Golden City energies depends on the spiritual depth and development of a student. His or her capacity to adapt, to transmute self-inhibiting Karmas and desires, to rely on the innate HU-man divinity, and to remediate problems and obstacles are key indicators of spiritual maturity. A chela should rely on the physical and spiritual presence of Golden City energies during his or her spiritual migration. The experiences and disciplines learned throughout this metaphysical pilgrimage will help guide the chela toward spiritual transformation and unfolding and inevitable self-realization and Mastery. According to the Ascended Masters, as more individuals become aware of the spiritual power inherent in the Golden Cities, the process of spiritual migration will shepherd humanity's collective entrance into the New Times and onward to the Golden Age.

4. Chakra Breathing is a form of meditation and visualization that focuses primarily on unblocking one chakra at a time. A practitioner accomplishes this by intentionally calibrating his or her breathing with a mental image. This relaxation technique is most commonly used to heal the body, mind, and spirit. Chakra Breathing has more specific applications as well. It can help the integration process when it comes to assimilating new energies currently present on Earth. Chakra Breathing can be augmented with other types of breathwork, such as yogic breathing. Based on the creation of Pranayama—the practice of filling breath with life, vital force, or control—this Hindu-based practice regulates respiration, thereby carrying more oxygen to the brain. According to many practitioners, this technique activates the subtle energy system and gives an individual control over the life energy in the body, which awakens innate and dormant powers.

So, this beloved Ruby and Gold Ray of Ministration and Service begins to serve in its highest way. There will be those souls that will be attracted in the times to come, in the New Times, the Golden Age, to the different Golden City locations that will align to the Ray Force that is most predominant within their being, their soul force, their Star seed. You see, Dear ones, different Star seeds serve along different Ray Forces. Of course, there has been such an intermingling of Ray Forces and genetic mix that it is difficult to say that one is strictly of this Star seed or that Star seed. But, you see, there will be one (genetic) that becomes more predominant. This domination comes, through the choice of where you wish to serve. So, you see, the Ray Forces serve and work together to bring a greater harmony and a greater self-knowledge. Questions?

SELF-KNOWLEDGE THROUGH THE RAYS

Question: "So, what you are saying about the different Star seeds is the multiplicity of genetic tribes on the planet was for the integration of the individual or the group for each of the Rays, so we have all had our turn, in a sense, through embodiment after embodiment?"

This is so. It brings about a greater orchestration of self-knowledge, a greater orchestration of knowledge of the Rays and their greater working with light and sound forces.

WAHANEE AND THE VIOLET RAY

I shall continue. In the Golden City of Wahanee is the Ray Force of the Violet Ray. The Ray Force enters into the apex of the Golden City. The apex is located in Augusta, as we have enacted a certain amount of inpouring into that area in terms of consciousness and intention. The Ray Force of the Violet Ray brings forth compassion, mercy and forgiveness, but another value of the Violet Ray is its ability to transmute any situation that is holding you back from your achieving the internal union of the ONE.

In working with the Violet Ray, one first begins to understand the purifying and transmuting fires. As I have always stated, "Down with death, God I AM. Conscious immortality arise." It is only through the use of the Violet Ray that one begins to understand that one is indeed immortal. The Violet Ray allows one to release the consciousness of death. It is through the Violet Ray that one can begin to regenerate. When you live in a Star area that is near the apex of Wahanee, you can begin to regenerate yourself. You see, there is such a condensation of the Violet Ray energies now entering into that area that the orgone, or prana, is tightly condensed, and for those chelas who wish to drop the consciousness of death and begin to accept their immortal destiny, this is the place toward which they will gravitate.

There are many other uses of the Violet Ray. Of course, this is one that we are releasing at this time so that humanity may begin to understand the great service that the Golden Cities have to offer. So, healing clinics would be a wonderful location in the Golden City of Wahanee for those who wish to regenerate their perspective. You see, mind is the builder, and one must begin with mind if one is to have the new body. We must start first with the thoughts that we hold. We must transmute the old thoughts to bring in the new thoughts. So, Dear hearts, it is through the use of the Violet Ray that Divine Intervention, grace and mercy are imparted to humanity. At a higher level, these energies will be used for Brotherhood, for bringing all to a greater understanding of the unity of all of consciousness. Once we drop the energies of Cellular Fear, we can begin to move into a greater understanding of love and compassion, but first things first.

CHAKRAS AND THE DEATH URGE

Let us start with regeneration and purification. It is here in this Vortex where one will, in the beginning, notice harder effects upon the physical body: flu-like symptoms, intestinal upsets. You see, the Violet Ray works, not only with the Heart Chakra, but also with the Solar Plexus. It is a transmutation of the Solar Plexus energies that are needed in order to drop the idea of death.

Down with death. Conscious immortality arise.

At the higher levels, the Violet Ray works with the Crown Chakra and moves the Kundalini energies to the top of understanding. Are there questions?

Answer: "Not at this time."

HEALING OF THE MIND, SPIRIT, AND SOUL

I shall move on to the Vortex of Shalahah. Shalahah is known as the Green City. It is only through the Green Ray that one begins to harmonize the body, mind, and spirit. You see, healing is not just repairing the body; it is repairing the mind. It is repairing the spirit; it is repairing the soul. All of these must come into balance in order for total healing to be sustained. The Ray Force, which is the Green Healing Ray, enters into the apex, located near Lolo Pass. This also has a certain coalescing of energies of Blue Rays and Gold Rays. You see, Dear ones, they work together, bringing forth a greater understanding and a greater harmony. Healing is about accepting the Divinity within yourself. These healing forces will bring such about. Healing, also, is understanding that you are not separated, that you are ONE with all things. When one has accepted healing within oneself, he is ready to move to the New Dimensions.

ASCENSION VALLEY

There are two Vortices that have been outlined, sub-Vortices that exist within the Shalahah Vortex. One is known as Ascension Valley, which is a Vortex area where one may go to integrate one's Oneship, one's divinity within, to prepare the body, mind, and spirit to move into the New Dimensions.[5]

TRANSPORTATION VORTEX

Also, there is that which is known as the Transportation Vortex. The Transportation Vortex is a Vortex that will be developed more as we move into the New Times. This is an interdimensional portal, a place where Mother Earth has allowed her energies to commingle with the energies needed, and the heavenly energies of the other dimensions. More will be understood on the Transportation Vortex as we move on and are attuned with the Ray Forces and how they work.

BI-LOCATION

You see, Dear ones, when you enter into Shalahah, because of the commingling of the Blue Ray and the Gold Ray, there are other anomalies that exist. This allows for interdimensional travel that is achieved, of course, through the projection of the mind, but as the body becomes fine-tuned, bi-location is indeed a possibility. In the New Times, this will be an accepted form and mode of travel, but only until the body, mind, and spirit are honed and able to accept this type of acceleration. It is suggested that many health retreats be built in this area in the New Times, but the health retreats should focus primarily upon mind as a builder, and body will follow. Do you understand?

Answer: "Yes, so far."

ABUNDANCE AND PROSPERITY

Now, let us return. When chelas travel, or gravitate, to these areas in Shalahah to bring forth the healing forces, they will notice that abundance and prosperity will enter into their lives.[6] When the body, mind, and spirit are brought into balance in complete and Absolute Harmony, the next result is abundance.[7] Natural prosperity comes forward. We have taught this in the Jurisdictions, and Shalahah will be the physical demonstration of this. So, chelas who are working to manifest abundance and prosperity into their lives travel to Shalahah, to the apexes, to align themselves to the Green energy. But, Dear hearts, you must understand that in the integration of such a force there is

---

6. See Appendix K2: *Initiation and the Golden Cities.*
7. Based on the Law of Choice, the second of the Twelve Jurisdictions is the principle of overflowing fullness in all situations and circumstances. Abundance, from the perspective of Ascended Master teaching, is the natural result of Harmony, the First Jurisdiction. (For more information on the Twelve Jurisdictions, see *New World Atlas, Volume One.*)

---

5. Integrate: To bring together, as a part into a unified whole, especially when incorporating the Rays for spiritual growth and evolution

an unraveling effect in the beginning. This will affect not only Heart Chakra energies, but also the Solar Plexus energies. You see, one begins to feel unsafe, for there is over identification with physical materiality. When one begins to understand that it is the coalescing of all the energies that brings about balance within the body, safety is truly a matter of the heart. Abundance, then, can stream forth with clarity and with beauty.

CRYSTAL CITY OF THE WHITE RAY

Now, I shall move on to the last and final Golden City and the Ray Force of Klehma. The White Ray of Purity is a Ray of Cooperation. It is also a Ray of Attainment, for it allows one to enter into the New Dimensions that exist beyond where physical embodiment is not required. In the Golden City of Klehma one of the first Crystal Cities will etherealize in the New Times.

THE NEW UNITED STATES CAPITOL

It has been said that this will be the new capitol of the United States, and indeed it is so, for the rulership and the guidance of the United States in the New Times will come from this ethereal city, where those who have gone before, leaders such as Abraham Lincoln, John F. Kennedy, Martin Luther King, George Washington, Thomas Jefferson. And those you have known as Native American leaders, Mayan leaders, who have known the Christ as Quetzalcoatl will also serve in this City of Cooperation in Klehma.

VENUSIAN ENERGY

You see, Dear ones, vibration to the White Ray is a vibration to all the Venusian energies. The Venusian energies are a vibration to a White and Crystal Purity, a purity of intention, a purity of heart and mind united in service. So you see, beloveds, when leadership comes from the highest of intention, it leads the country into a New Time, into a new vision.

KLEHMA AND THE ANCIENT CRYSTAL CITIES

Klehma, itself, is aligned to the Golden Cities that existed at one time in South America and in Mexico. These were the Golden Cities that held the ethereal Crystal Cities that guided the Mayan culture into its dimensional leap. You see, Dear one, there is a purpose and a timing to all things. Klehma, as the White Ray, brings about a purity and a cleansing of intention.

COOPERATION AND COMMUNITY

As we have said before, scrutinize your intentions, for they are powerful Creators. This creation can move one into greater understanding of community and into greater understanding of cooperation. And those who are seeking to learn of unity through cooperation and community, service to humanity, and the united Brotherhoods and Sisterhoods of this Earth can travel and absorb the energies at the Star of Klehma.

WHITE FIRE OF ASCENSION

This energy also develops the energies of Ascension, which will have similar effect on body as in Shalahah, but it is the quality of White Fire. You see, the White Fire is purity, and the body releases the final death urges. The work that is initiated in Wahanee is completed in Klehma. I have given you a brief outline of how the Golden Cities work along with Ray Forces.

MANTRAS OF THE GOLDEN CITIES

Now, let us talk about sound, for each of the Ray Forces also vibrates to a sound quality, which is important to understand.[8]

---

8. Certain sounds, syllables, and sets of words are deemed sacred and often carry the power to transmute Karma, purify the spirit, and transform an individual. These are known as a mantras. The mantra is a foundation of Vedic tradition and often treated as a devotional upaye—a remedial measure of difficult obstacles. Mantras, however, are not limited to Hinduism. Buddhists, Sikhs, and Jains also utilize mantras. The Ascended Masters occasionally provide mantras to chelas to improve resonation with certain Golden Cities.

My teacher of Vedic tradition gave this explanation regarding the anatomy of the mantra:

MAM + TRA = MANTRA
Chants + Protects = MANTRA

Om Shanti vibrates to the Golden City of Gobean. Om Shanti brings about a sense of peace and a sense of harmony, so chelas who wish to chant this as a sound vibration may do so.

Om Eandra is the mantra vibration to be chanted for Malton. Om Eandra is the Vibration of the Elemental Kingdoms. It creates a harmony and a balance. It is also the mantra, or the sound vibration, that can be chanted to bring something into fruition, into attainment, so that you may own it as a Master of your desires.

Om Hue is the chant for Wahanee. You see, Dear ones, Hue aligns all chakras along that Vertical Core Axis, and allows the Violet Flame to work its Mighty Miracle! Om Hue is a Vibration of the Violet Flame Angels and brings about it the most purifying and healing effects to the body.[9]

In Shalahah, the vibration to be chanted is Om Sheahah. Om Sheahah for Shalahah means I AM as ONE. You see, Dear ones, in Shalahah one must become as ONE to find healing. One must become as ONE to find true prosperity.

And the final mantra that is chanted for Klehma is again Om Eandra. Om Eandra is the final capstone placed upon the Golden Cities, Om Eandra. You see, Dear ones, through sound vibration and light Ray Forces, all is brought together in a glory and a conclusion. Are there questions?

Question: "I see, so that's how it's qualified. So, for Gobean, when you say Om Shanti, that's the qualification of the Ray specifically for the use of the Blue Ray in Gobean?"

This is so, Dear one.

SOUND ACTIVATES THE RAYS

Question: "Are each of these specific chants the activating phrases for each of the Rays?"

Indeed they are. The activating phrases for the Rays as they work in a Golden City. Remember, it is the energy of your own electromagnetic field, your own aura, working with that of the Golden City Ray Force.[10]

Question: "Okay, and when we utilize these mantras and chants, are you saying that we can apply them in the same way as the Violet Flame in creating our intention or manifesting something into fruition?"

He was particularly avid about adding the sound HREEM before chanting the mantra to transmute difficult Karmas. His explanation:

H = Sins
REEM = Removes
HREEM = Removal of Sins

9. The Angels of the Violet Flame protect the purity of the Flame, dispense its transforming vibration, and carry the transmuting energies of the Flame whenever called upon. These angels can be summoned to assist with decrees and meditation regarding spiritual growth, governmental freedoms and rights, wealth and supply, and to hasten the Ascension Process. Perhaps Angels of the Violet Flame are best known for their ability to expedite healing. Edna Ballard of the *I AM Activity* writes:

"When you want to call forth the Healing Flame to assist someone, hold the picture of the Violet Flame Angel, and watch from the Sun Presence of its heart the projection of a Flame, the center part pink, the outer violet and the outer radiance blue, reaching out and going forth to enfold your Loved Ones, or any one to whom you wish to give assistance.

This can also reach out and into the mental and feeling world of an individual, quiet disturbance, purify and raise the vibratory action of the Inner Bodies into the same Great Purity and Love which the Healing Angels project!"

The following is a decree from the I AM Activity teachings to the Violet Flame Angels for healing:

"Beloved Mighty I AM Presence and Blessed Nada!
I DEMAND the Healing Flame of Love from the Angels of the Violet Consuming Flame COME FORTH in and around me and all under This Radiation, to purify and perfect our bodies! I DEMAND the Violet Flame Angels of Healing Love come and abide with me and heal all I contact!"

10. According to Saint Germain, individual mantras infuse Golden City Ray Forces into Light Bodies (auras), a practice that evolves the conscious life experience toward Ascension Consciousness. He suggests that the efficiency of a Ray is best understood when used in a Golden City Vortex, where the energy of a mantra works concurrently with the centrifugal force of the Golden City Star. Uttering mantras is most effective in the Star of a Golden City, but don't let that prevent you from the practice. If you can't make it to the Star, saying mantras in any part of a Golden City is beneficial. The following mantras should be used simultaneously with the initiatory Ray work in each Golden City.

GOBEAN, *Om Shanti:* Produces peace and harmony

MALTON, *Om Eandra*: Produces harmony and balance for the Nature Kingdoms. It is also associated with instant thought manifestation.

WAHANEE, *Om Hue*: Aligns the chakras with the Vertical Power Current, or Golden Thread Axis, and evokes the Sacred fire—the Violet Flame. Since this mantra is a Vibration of Violet Flame Angels, it invokes their Healing presence, which helps purify and heal the body.

SHALAHAH, *Om Sheahah*: Evokes the consciousness of the ONESHIP—Unana. This mantra means, "I AM as ONE."

KLEHMA, *Om Eandra*: Used as a decree for Instant-thought-manifestation of Ascension, glory, and conclusion.

Yes. This is the purpose. This is the intention of the Golden City forces and the way in which they work with your own electromagnetic force-field. You see, Dear ones, the Golden Cities are indeed force-fields that exist for you to access. These are some of the keys of how you may access them and the results that you may get.

Question: "I see, so its effectiveness is better located within the Star?"

This is so, Dear one. It brings forth the intention, the fruition, the qualification of the energy of the Golden City.

Question: "I see. So even if someone wishes to move to a Golden City and they find it difficult to get to the specific one that they have chosen, this chant would help them to expedite that?"

This is so. However, it is preferred that these chants be used within the Golden City, as they are sound vibrations that work with the centrifugal force of that Ray Force in the Star. It can be used throughout the whole Golden City, but the pull of it, as you can see, will work most strongly in the apices. It can be used, of course, throughout the Golden City.

ALIGNMENT TO THE GOLDEN CITIES

Question: "Hmm. So, by knowing the qualities of each of the Golden Cities, as stated in this discourse and in previous discourses that show up in the books and the tapes and the maps, and utilizing these specific mantras, the purpose intended by you in your life in a Golden City can then be brought into manifestation more easily?"[11]

This is so, Dear one, for those who feel aligned to move to the Golden Cities, can go forward in alignment, knowledge and the force that they may bring into their lives.

Answer: "I see. Well, this sounds like an extremely valuable tool. Thank you."

Now, Dear one, unless if there are other questions, I shall depart.

Response: "Not at this time. This is more than enough to think about and to put into application."

In that Mighty Christ, I AM!

Response: "Thank you."

11. See Appendix M2: *Golden City Names.*

CHAPTER SEVEN

Blue Illumination

Teachings on the Golden Cites of Gobi, Gobean, and Shamballa.

Greetings, beloveds, in that Mighty Christ, I AM Saint Germain, and, as usual Dear hearts, I ask permission to come forth.

"Please, Saint Germain, come forward."

Today, we will discourse more upon the Gobean Vortex, and I have brought with me Beloved Brother El Morya. He is coming forward.

El Morya steps forward, besides Saint Germain.

GOBI, VORTEX OF ANCIENT SHAMBALLA

Greetings, Dear one, in that Mighty Blue Flame, I AM El Morya. I ask permission to come forward.

Answer: "Please do, Brother and Teacher, come forward."

Today, I shall bring forth further discourse on the Vortex of Gobean. We have discussed all the Strategic Points, the doorways and the Star of Knowledge. Now, we shall move forward so that you may understand a bit of the ancient history that surrounds the network of the Golden Cities.[1]

Dear hearts, we have spoken about the idea that many of these Golden City Vortices are aligned to other Vortices throughout the planet. As we have explained before, Gobean aligns to energy in Gobi, which is now the Vortex that covers the ancient City of Shamballa.[2]

You see, Dear ones, all of these are connected to the idea of emanation, how energy is built. This enables the (Golden

1. See Appendix N2: *El Morya's Teachings on the History of Shamballa.*
2. See Appendix O2: *Gobi and the Spiritual Lineage of Shamballa.*

Cities') demonstration or the physical manifestation. When energy is built according to the principal of emanation, you can begin to understand how manifestation, or physical desire, can manifest. Saint Germain has given you continued discourse upon this principal, and it is important to understand, when studying a Golden City Vortex, its doorways, its points, and how it functions. Each of the Golden Cities that are given in the complete network of Vortices are all connected to other cities, but for now we shall place our emphasis upon Gobean and the work of the Blue Ray.

SHAMBALLA ORIGINS

It is the work of the Blue Ray that brought Shamballa into its physical manifestation. You see, Dear ones, some of the original inhabitants of Shamballa were not only from Venus but from other planets. Mercury played a very large role in its inhabitation, along with other planets that are not in your present star system. These people were known as the Blue Race. Many of you have known them as the Vedic traditions. There they built the ethereal city and manifested it into your Earth Plane. Many of those who lived in Shamballa knew perfection and also understood the work of the Blue Ray as representing truth, harmony, and cooperation as a manifestation upon the Earth.

CRYSTAL CASTLES

The first city, when it was built, held many Crystal Castles. The Crystal Castles were encrusted with rubies, emeralds, pearls and gems that today would be deemed of great value. It was there that the first Unfed Flame of Love, Wisdom, and Power was kept enshrined, and many celebrations and ceremonies were held in honor of this flame.

THE IMMORTALS

Many of the people understood the idea that they were indeed beyond physical incarnation; and death, as you now understand, did not exist. The great immortals, those who were the great teachers whom your history has now honored, existed in that first City of Shamballa. However, as the Earth was populated from other Star seeds, that is from other planets, a warring force, or a warring energy of non-cooperation and disharmony, was generated.[3]

THE GOLDEN CITY IS MOVED AND REBUILT

This brought about a dissent within the city. You see, there were those who would enter into the city and their vibration not able to handle the perfection, and the emanation, or the energy, that was built in Shamballa deteriorated. It was then decided that this city shall be moved, and indeed it was, and rebuilt. This time, it was kept hidden, so that those, who at that time upon the Earth sought to find it, but could not. This city held again the same energies of perfection, of longevity, of perfect health, and perfect harmony. Music played throughout the day. The night-time was sweet, and the scent of jasmine filled the air. You see, Dear ones, perfection is indeed an emanation. It is an energy that is built and held within the body. When you seek your own perfection, you must idealize it as a perfect crystalline thought in your mind first, and then build the energy through the Principle of Emanation. The Principle of Conductivity then comes into play, and it was through conductivity that the second City of Shamballa began to radiate throughout the Earth.

MATERIALITY AND DETERIORATION WITHIN

The second City of Shamballa grew in such a manner that it affected all the Earth for greater harmony and greater perfection. But materiality began to obsess the population. Materiality was the demise of the second City of Shamballa, and this time the

---

3. Star seed: The Ascended Masters assign two associated definitions to this term. The first defines the Star seed as a family or soul group whose members have evolved to Fifth-Dimensional awareness. Star seeds can also contain members who have not yet evolved to this level and are still incarnating on Earth. The second definition of Star seed is somewhat literal and refers to populating groups, or soul groups, originating from other solar systems and galaxies. Some Star seeds intentionally leave their homeland planets to inhabit Earth and adapt their DNA through reproduction with humans. Other Star seed souls and soul families enter the earthly evolutionary Wheel of Karma, and spiritually incarnate in human form. Occult historians claim that Earth is now riddled with Star seeds through genetics and spiritual connection.

deterioration came from within the city. Many long-term residents, the immortals who first held the focus of Shamballa, also fell in consciousness, and for the most part, required rebirth. But the few remaining, who held the purity of consciousness, rebuilt the city for the third time.

THE ETHEREAL CITY OF SHAMBALLA

Upon the request of Sanat Kamara, it was decided that this city would not manifest in the physcial planes, or to plainly speak: seek physical incarnation. This time, the city was held in the finer ethreal qualities and the emanation would be detected only by those who had developed the finer subtle bodies (qualities) within the Astral Body. So, those who were trained in different ashrams throughout Eastern Asia were also trained to seek, through higher consciousness, entry into the Golden City of Shamballa. It remains in this same location today.

A CIVILIZATION OF SHAMBALLA

At one time, the consciousness of humanity was raised to such a peak that within the Gobi Desert, directly beneath the ethereal Crystal City of Shamballa, another civilization was built. As above, so below. The law was mirrored, and many traveled to this city seeking healing and the ancient teachings. However, as humanity moved into the time period now known as Kali, the gates of Shamballa were tightly shut to but a few; now, this time period is over, and the New Time period moves Earth forward and humanity develops into a new understanding and into a new evolution.

Before I proceed with more information, are there any questions?

Answer: "Yes, there are."

Proceed.

THE PRINCIPLE OF CONDUCTIVITY

Question: "You spoke of conductivity, and prior to that you spoke of focus in creating perfection. In that step-by-step manner, is there an exercise, or is there a tangible way to take this and utilize it for everyday use for humanity?"

To build your energy fields through the Principle of Conductivity, it is important to understand the ONE, the Oneship, unity of all things. Conductivity is based upon this idea. Through the course of emanation and conductivity all energies basically function as ONE. To build this within your own energy fields, practice again the meditation which I gave you years ago of the candle. You must have the singular focus that you and the candle become as ONE. Do you understand?

Answer: "Yes, I do."

This prepares the mind for a greater understanding, a greater illumination. Are there more questions?

Question: "So, the practice of the candle meditation, you would say, is the first step in developing the focus what may be sustained through any distraction or any time period that would allow the conductivity to also be sustained?"

This is true, Dear one. You will receive great results if you practice this in earnest.

Response: "Thank you. Please continue."

GOLDEN CITY OF GOBI

So, the third and final City of Shamballa, which it was decided should remain in its ethereal state, has kept its position over the Gobi Desert. Of course, of the ancient civilization that existed in a physical state, there are still remnants of it, and those who search for the City of Shamballa may find it if they so choose. The energies of Gobean align to this ancient Golden City, known as Gobi. You see, Dear ones, as above, so below. When Shamballa and the City of Gobi intertwined, it created a force-field. The force-field then created a Vortex. This is how all Vortices come into being, through a relationship of ethereal consciousness and emanation and conductivity. Do you understand?

Question: "I see. It's the basic structure of how the Rays of Light and Sound go together."

It is indeed as such, a Co-creation of Heaven and Earth. The two exist simultaneously, exist together. It takes the two for such to exist, built upon, as I have explained and Master Saint Germain has explained, through the elements of conductivity and emanation.

GOLDEN CITY OF GOBEAN

Now, I shall proceed, Dear ones. There is yet another city that aligns its energy to the energies of Shamballa, or the City of Gobi, the Golden City of Gobean. These two Vortices are connected as ONE. So, when you meditate upon the perfection of Shamballa in the City of Gobean, you can be instantly transported there. You see, Dear ones, as the perfection streams forth into your own bodies, your own minds, your own hearts, as you are accelerated in the times to come, the times of the Golden Perfections, you shall then be able to transport your body, through the process of bi-location, to the City of Gobi. You shall also be able to take in the perfected energies of the ancient City of Shamballa. This ancient City of Shamballa is the city where many of the Master Teachers meet on a yearly basis. This I'm sure you are familiar with.

Response: "Yes, absolutely."

ACCELERATION IN A GOLDEN CITY

As you integrate these perfected energies, as we have instructed you, as time progresses, or as time compacts, in this grand opportunity that is being offered to humanity, you will note further perfections within your own bodies. As you see, the water and air in a Golden City is of a higher and finer quality. The principal of prahna or orgone, as you have been taught, is much more condensed, It rotates at a higher millisecond. This higher rotation within your body brings about an acceleration. We have spoken of the Cellular Awakening. This acceleration brings you closer and closer to the idea of a deathless body of physical immortality, of Ascension into new realms of understanding. This acceleration is most essential to access the energies that are inherent in a Golden City Vortex.

Of course, there are other energies that are apparent. I have spoken already of the ability for miraculous healing in the Southern Doors. I have also spoken of the abilities of Instant-thought-manifestations of the Northern Doors.[4] You see, there are other qualities and other gifts that the Cities are here to bring to humanity as the course of Divine Intervention proceeds. This alignment of energy with the ancient City of Shamballa is most important, Dear hearts and Dear ones, for Gobean is the perfect location to extract the ancient records through Thought Projection. I have taught you before about this principle; do you not recall?[5]

Answer: "Yes, I recall."

TRUTH AND DIRECT PERCEPTION

To project your thoughts, or your mental body, into another realm to receive information, in Gobean one may travel to receive the ancient knowledge of other times. In meditation, you can access this information much more readily than in any other Golden City. You see, Dear ones, through the Blue Ray of Truth, the truth of the history of the planet comes forward for you now to view. It is not a truth that is given through another one's perspective. It is a truth that is infused directly to you so that each is given his or her own individual understanding of the history of this Earth, the history of this schoolroom and your own individual participation. You see, in truth, it must be received at an individual level, so through the individual experiences of each they can receive. When it is imparted only as knowledge or as belief, it carries less importance. You see, Dear hearts, Dear ones, this is the importance of Gobean for its alignment to the ancient knowledge.

Historically, Gobean also aligns to another ancient city. In your history, this is known as Giza. Why is this so? The teacher Serapis Bey, who was known as Akhenaten, traveled to the location of Gobean, and there he gave forth his teachings.[6] Many did not understand them at the time, for you see he was able to project through his consciousness a perfect form of himself, ethereally, and there the teachings were brought to the cultures that existed in the ancient areas that are now known as Gobean. This is why you will see there are similarities in the cultures. He was known as a great teacher among many, and yet this was a projection of the (his) consciousness. So, you see, again, as above, so below.

SERAPIS BEY

Serapis Bey became one of the first teachers of the Continuity of Consciousness. He taught about the opening of the Third Eye and the Crown chakra, the Star of Knowledge.[7] This was passed down, you see, Dear ones, and the energy and the focus that were held through these teachings created a force-field that is in the location of Gobean. In later years, I was to come under the tutelage of this same teacher, and I, too, was taught the technique so that I could project my consciousness, and there became a series of teachings in Gobean, and many of the cultures gravitated toward this. These appearances had a tendency to raise the energies, and you see now how this has come to be. Do you have questions?

Question: "Yes. Question one: Was the center of Gobean at that time, when you were projecting into it, in the same exact location that it is in now?"

---

4. As you become more perfectly aligned and in harmony with your thoughts, feelings, and actions, your individual focused, directed desires may quickly manifest. This Co-creative activity is known by the Master Teachers as *Instant-thought-manifestation* and moves the Initiate to the beginning stages of Arhat. As initiates perfect this process, they may notice that the period of time between thoughts and manifestations diminishes; this is a common quality of HU-man development.

5. This ability acquired through a Mastery of meditation enables individuals to split their consciousness (existence, sensations, and cognitions) to another physical location or plane, while retaining the physical body in the physical dimension. Masters of this technique project their consciousness both to teach and to learn. As this technique is perfected, an ethereal body is often used for projection. This body is similar in appearance to the physical body. Projection of Consciousness is a pre-requisite skill for bi-location—the ability to physically exist in more than one location or spiritual plane—a talent often employed by an Ascended Master.

6. See Appendix P2: *Akhenaten*.

7. The *Star of Knowledge* is yet another term for the Star of a Golden City Vortex, the center of the Vortex, or the apex.

It was more to the North, and assisted many of the different tribes of people that are now known as Native Americans.

QUETZALCOATL

Question: "Would these tribes be the Hopi?"

Some of the Hopi were affected by this emanation, as well as Anasazi and Mayan cultures. The work that Akhenaten began was a long-held tradition. Before Akhenaten had begun this type of bi-location projection, there were those from the City of Shamballa who were doing such work. I hope this brings a greater understanding to the location. The reason Egyptian teachings now fill the area of Gobean is because of the work of Akhenaten to bring the energy of the Christ forward. This energy of the Christ was known as Quetzalcoatl. Quetzalcoatl was the first to actually anchor this energy into human consciousness in the geophysical area that is now known as Gobean. Do you understand?

THE HALL OF WISDOM

Question: "What you're saying is that if we go back to the City of Shamballa, that is in essence the portal for the upliftment of all of humanity, which is a collection of many Star seeds?"

This is true, Dear ones. This is also known as the Hall of Wisdom. For this Earth, it is an entry point for many souls who come here to gain higher knowledge. Of course, there are those souls who try to come to schoolroom Earth to disrupt the knowledge process, the learning process that is imparted. But now you can understand that, through Thought Projection and bi-location, the evolution of humanity has largely been brought forward through the work of Shamballa. Do you understand?

Question: "Yes, I understand. One more question."

Proceed.

"A PIVOTAL POINT"

Question: "Then all the Golden Cities are, in essence, stepping stones at one level on the path of the upliftment, and, on another level, they are also energy points that energize the consciousness of humanity in the upliftment process?"

They serve as Divine Intervention, to bring about higher knowledge, higher understanding. They are indeed a pivotal point of evolution.

CHAPTER EIGHT

The Light of a Thousand Suns

୧୭

*Saint Germain and Kuthumi reveal
prophecies and teachings.*

Greetings, Beloveds, in that Mighty Violet Flame, I AM Saint Germain, and I request permission to come forth.

"Saint Germain, come forward. You are most welcome."

AN INDIVIDUAL PATH

Today, Dear ones, we have much to talk about, not only a brief discourse from myself, but today Master Kuthumi, or Brother Kuthumi, as he is known by us, will bring a discourse about the attributes of the Golden City of Malton.

I must continue to remind you, Dear ones, that along the path of what you have been assigned to do, to bring forward the Earth Changes Prophecies, that you will encounter many along the path who, while connected to the work of the Brotherhood, may not have the same connection to the type of work that you are bringing forward. This is important to understand, Dear ones, that while all are united in a consciousness of Unana, a Unity Consciousness, that there are still the individual paths that one may take. As Beloved El Morya has said, "Choose. Choose. Choose." It is in the choosing that the individual becomes strong and is strengthened by the spiritual fires that temper the will and show the individual the power of choice.

"EQUAL TO"

You see, Dear ones, to raise the consciousness—the animal consciousness—into the human consciousness requires the development of the Will.[1] And it is only through tempering

the spirit, that the Will is strengthened. When you encounter those whose paths are somewhat different than yours, you must understand that not one has more power than another. The power is equal. This is important, Dear ones, that you gain this concept. "Equal to" is of vast importance. However, it is also important that you stay entirely focused on the work at hand. Each of these pieces must be strong if they are to fit into the mosaic.

GOLDEN AGE OF THE CO-CREATOR

It is also important for you to know that within the next three months there will be an earthquake that will strike the coast of California.[2] While we hope this can be averted or lessened in some small way through the work of your consciousness, it is important that you know this, so that the work at hand can now solve the problem. There have been many other changes that have been happening on your world or global scene. There have been several activations of the Ring of Fire and volcanic eruptions that may soon happen. Understand, Dear ones, Dear hearts, that each of these changes birth a New Time, and while they may be frightening at first to understand, when you understand them in a greater scope and in the greater unity you will see that they birth the New Time, the Golden Age.

The Golden Age is the fruit of the out-picturing, as you understand from the Point of Perception.[3] It is in the grand out-

---

1. Raising human consciousness completely out of animal states requires the development of the will. Tempering this spirit strengthens the will.
   Saint Germain assures that we are not victims of predestination. "You are the purveyor of your own will," he says. This means that through our conscious perceptions and choices, each of our thoughts is carefully cultivated and inevitably creates our world of experiences.

2. Master Teachers will often predict events. However, accompanied with their projections are their calculations of probability and whether or not forecasted circumstances might have a negative effect. Therefore, along with predictions, Masters will often share the appropriate remedies to lessen or avert catastrophe. This type of prediction is known as a prophecy. In the teaching *The Light of a Thousand Suns*, Saint Germain informs listeners of a possible coastal earthquake in California, and says that prayer and consciousness will play an invaluable role in its outcome. A large quake has never occurred in this area, yet interestingly, the same year the quake was predicted, an earthquake swarm—the Long Valley Caldera occurred.
   According to the Ascended Masters' teachings on prediction and prophecy, once events are prophesied, recognition by those who hear the prophecy has an effect upon individual and collective consciousness. Students, chelas, initiates, and their Master Teachers work appropriately to alter possible tragedy through adjusting collective energy and light fields

3. This is a Co-creative process taught by the Master Teachers that includes meditation, focused attention, and visualization. Students and

picturing that creation comes forward into a greater harmony, into a greater knowledge. The seed that is engendered in you as a Co-creator is, of course, of the most importance. You are not a puppet of predestination. Instead, you are a purveyor of your own Will.[4] It is important that you understand the power of choice and how, through your own Point of Perception, you perceive, how you bring the seed of thought forward and carefully grow it into your Creative Will; then create the world that you live within.

KARMA AND THE VIOLET FLAME

As usual, Dear hearts, I still remind you that it is the use of the Violet Flame that will bring an ease within your life. When you feel the stress and turmoil about you of others, their energy projecting its creation upon you, it is only through the use of the Violet Flame that you can clear the air; so use it in the same way in which you would light a stick of incense or that you would shift the energy through music. In the same way, with each chant of the Violet Flame excess Karma is wiped away from your path. The agendas and the creations of others are wiped away from your path. The Violet Flame is a way to pave the pathway clear for you so that you may again take each step upon your own path.

MOVING OUT OF JUDGMENT AND INTO THE ONE

As I have said so many times, it is important to know thyself, and to know thyself first. It is very difficult to bring two together

until they understand the value of this lesson.[5] When you know yourself clearly and have identified your path so clearly, then it is always much easier to unite two into the consciousness of the ONE. Then, there is a natural harmony, and the consequence of that harmony is always a good action. It is important, Dear ones, that you not judge your Brothers and Sisters, but that you discern. As dear Sananda has said, "By their fruits you shall know them." But it is important that you not cast a final judgment upon one, and that you understand that indeed a grander harmony, a grander symphony will someday play. Today, you are simply tuning the instrument, preparing ALL and ONE for the grand conduction, but indeed, you are ALL still united as ONE. Indeed, you are all upon individual paths. Today, the work at hand is to stay focused upon your path. Stay focused upon the work at hand.

Before I turn the floor over to Beloved Brother Kuthumi, do you have questions?

Question: "I have only one question."

---

chelas are encouraged to use the Out-picturing Process especially in the realization of objectives and goals. The process may also include the use of specific breathing and energy techniques together with holding precise mental pictures.

4. Purveyor, or purvey, is derived from an old French word: *porveeir*, which in turn comes from the Latin word providere. Providere means to foresee; provide for; or make provision. *Videre* is a later Latin word which means see; look at; or consider. When considering the development of the will and Saint Germain's statement that we play a role as its purveyor, we understand that the derivation of the word suggests that indeed, an honest assessment of self is absolutely necessary to understand personal strengths, weaknesses, and past choices—in order to navigate the spiritual path ahead. Purveyor is also synonymous with the word *promulgate*, which means to make known; decree; or declare.

5. Saint Germain's teachings on relationships with others:
Encountering those on a spiritual path that is a bit different than yours does not mean that your path is superior or more evolved. Remember to understand and respect the concept, "Equal to."
Working toward Unity with others is imperative. One way to achieve this is joint ventures in consciousness efforts through prayer and conscious attunement toward worldwide events.
When you feel stress and turmoil in relationships, Saint Germain suggests that the use of the Violet Flame can shift negative energies and wipe away conflicting Karmas. Once the muddy waters of others' agendas are cleared from your thoughts, you can see your own path.
Saint Germain states: "Know thyself; and know thyself, first." Self-knowledge assists you in finding your purpose in a relationship and provides a bridge into Unity—two as ONE. From this point, the relationship can evolve and grow.
This evolutionary process with others can be difficult, and filled with judgments and doubts. Saint Germain, however, gives this guidance: "When there is natural harmony, the consequence of that harmony is always a good action."
Even in relationships, as we strive to unite as ONE, we are still individuals, and our challenge is to remain focused and to not be diverted from our own choices and spiritual path. Saint Germain reminds us that as we develop and grow through relationships, we are tuning and practicing our instruments of will and choice. This invaluable experience ultimately grooms our consciousness for entrance into a larger symphony with others.
Our knowledge and understanding of the individual roles we play in relationships and partnerships ready our consciousness to unite into the ONE. Know thyself first, and harmony is assured.

Proceed.

Question: "You have just alluded that at a level of harmony it is much easier for two to join the ONE. Is this so?"

It is always so, Dear one. Have you not noted the instruments in a grand symphony? They are all playing one piece of composed music, and yet all are playing a different part. It is only through knowing the part they play, the role they serve, that they unite in a greater union. Know thyself first, and harmony is then assured.

Answer: "I understand. Thank you."

And now, Dear ones, I turn the floor over to Beloved Brother Kuthumi.

Master Kuthumi steps forward.

BROTHER KUTHUMI

Greetings, Beloved Brothers and Sisters of the Golden Sun. I AM Kuthumi of the Ruby and Gold Ray, and I request permission to come forward.[6]

Answer: "Please, Kuthumi, you are most welcome."

Dear hearts, the time is at hand. You see the Earth in its changing glory. You see the stars predict it as so.[7] You also know that the Earth is beginning its process of purification. Beloved Saint Germain and Beloved El Morya have brought forward information that is to assist humanity at this time, and I, too, now join as a group in their Oneness. I, too, bring my service. This service is to lend yet a deeper understanding of why such change would come and why such change is needed. There are many who hope that the change may not be filled with the fury they demand. There are many who hope that through their prayer they may hold such change back. It is not the idea of holding such a change back, but the idea of praying that humanity will change itself inside.

There is much that is happening now upon the Earth Plane and Planet, much that is happening now in terms of change and the Times of Change. It is rare that we bring this type of information forward, but there are several things that are important for you to know and to understand. The economy of your nation is in grave danger. And while you may look at this time and ask how this could possibly happen, it is true that manipulation is happening behind the scenes, and world politics will ever play out its web of deceit. But this is important for you to know, to understand and to plan for.

A GENTLE BIRTH

The Elemental, Vegetable, and Mineral Kingdoms are now within a change. Their evolution must move forward. You see, Dear hearts, Dear ones, our beloved Brothers and Sisters of

---

6. See Appendix Q2: *Kuthumi's Prophecies and Teachings on the Gold Ray.*

7. Vedic and Western astrologers alike agree regarding the Earth's winter solstice position's current conjunction with the Galactic Center, or in Ascended Master terminology: Great Central Sun. This position is calculated within one degree, and while there is some speculation as to the exact conjunction point, it is placed at 6° 40' sidereally or approximately 29° tropically. The sidereal zodiac is used primarily by Eastern, or Vedic, astrologers; the tropical zodiac is a calculation commonly used in Western astrology. The difference between the two zodiacs, in a nutshell, is precession, or the slight wobble of the Earth as it rotates on its axis.

Precession of the equinoxes is the slow backward shifting of the Earth as it rotates. This slight tilting of the pole is calculated at approximately 23.5°; this is the source of the Vedic Ayanamsha, which differentiates planetary movements against the movement of stars—sidereal astrology. In contrast, tropical, or Western astrology tracks planets in reference to seasonal

points according to a point of view from Earth. Vedic astrology adjusts for precession; the Western system does not.

The precise conjunction point of the Galactic Center with the Earth will not be exact for about fifty to one hundred years; however this influence is currently producing many changes on Earth and among humanity. Prominent Vedic astrologers, such as Dr. David Frawley, contend that the current conjunction is responsible for new collective spiritual beliefs, akin to the Spiritual and Cellular Awakening in Ascended Master teachings. Contrasting this profound opportunity for spiritual growth is the potential for worldwide catastrophes and possible Earth Changes. Frawley writes, "Much of the new spiritual thinking and the potential cataclysmic changes on the planet may be from this attunement process that insists we enter into a new ascending age of light and cast off the shadows of the dark ages of strife and dissension." Our ability to enter the New Times and receive the benefits of the Golden Age, albeit in its infant stages, is subject to our capacity to integrate and apply the energies from the Galactic Center. This harmonization process demands our attunement with the great cosmic laws and forces of the universe, and initiates either humanity's spiritual enlightenment or retributive destruction.

these Kingdoms are an evolving consciousness and part of the total system of your evolution. They have offered themselves to be of service to you. Have you not seen how your own special animals have become as pets and dear companions to you? Each of them offers a special form of consciousness that allows you to develop and to understand your own path. It is the same with the Vegetable and the Mineral Kingdom. The very crystal qualities of every mineral, arcs the qualities of a Ray Force to serve you. The Vegetable Kingdom, with fruits, nuts, berries and vegetables offer their own life force, their own prana, so that you may continue to grow and to learn in this planetary scheme. All is now moving forward in a greater evolution. It is important that this change not be held back, but that it be assisted, as in a gentle birth.

We have spoken of this birth in previous discourses, but it is important to teach others the value of the great birth, the value of the New Time. A greater harmony awaits mankind. This is the harmony of the Vegetable and the Mineral Kingdom. Do you realize, Dear ones, Dear hearts, if you were to bring your own spirit into total harmony with the Earth and its various Kingdoms, that open telepathic communication between plants, animals, and minerals would be totally possible?

AWAKENING AND TELEPATHY

It is through the lack of harmony, as my Brother El Morya has brought forward, that there is separateness and a separation. In the same way in which I come forward and bring this telepathic information to you, there is an opening, a bridge. The time will now come to all humanity when an opening and a bridge will be formed. This Bridge of Awakening will allow a telepathic connection to occur between animals, plants, and minerals from each human. As this opens in a greater awareness and a greater knowledge of all of consciousness, it is equal to the amount of harmony and peace that is created among yourselves. Are there questions?

Answer: "Not at this time. Please continue."

THE RUBY RAY

I would like to give further information concerning these Kingdoms and the purpose of Malton. You see, Beloveds, Dear hearts, it is indeed the Ruby Ray that opens this bridge as an awakening so that the desire can come into fruition.[8] There are many wants among humanity: wants for money, for particular things that the world can give you, but let me assure you that sometimes the desires are trappings within themselves. What is at the core of all of it, but an urge to know God.

"TO KNOW GOD"

God dwells within each of us. God is part of all of us: your neighbor, your political leaders, your family members, the little pets in your household, the trees that grow among you. Everything contains God in some form and is part of God. This quest or thirst to know God is the greatest of all desires.

---

8. The Ruby Ray acts as a catalyst for the fulfillment of desires. Desires are not perceived as trappings of materiality or sinful craving, but as another aspect of God's promise of fulfillment. Hindu philosophies similarly teach that until man fulfills his desires, it is difficult to achieve liberation. Ultimately, Master Kuthumi views the human core of desires as, "an urge to know God."

Once all desires are obtained, often all that is left is the desire to know God. Master Kuthumi observes the quest to fulfill long-held desires as the greatest of all initiations, as it comes directly from the heart. Students and chelas who work intentionally to achieve desires through the Ruby Ray follow the Path of Desires as a liberation process.

As one becomes a practiced Master in the achievement of desires, the transparent cause of Unity and the ONE is realized. However, humanity is still in its infant stages of understanding this spiritual truth. In fact, Master Kuthumi claims that the simple desires of Peace and Happiness, which are constantly within the grasp of any individual, become almost impossible to obtain.

Since human nature craves demonstration of all things physical and is obsessed with materiality, one of the Golden City of Malton's purposes is to satiate desires.

Malton's higher purpose brings completion to the long-held desires of the human experience. Kuthumi asks students and chelas to assemble a list of the many unfulfilled desires held lifetime after lifetime. This step is critical before entering the upcoming initiatory steps of liberation—the Ascension process.

The Elemental and Nature Kingdoms assist the preparatory Path of Desire in the Golden City of Malton.

During the New Times, conscious phases of Instant-thought-manifestation demonstrate to humanity the supreme truth that this unseen world of heaven—the spiritual planes—exist.

To bring this into fruition is also of vast importance. The path of knowing God is also the path of desire. To bring a desire into fruition is the path of completion. How does one complete himself through all that he or she wants, through all that one yearns for? It is through the Ruby Ray that this bridge is formed.

THE SOUL'S COMPLETION

When one begins to see the unity of all cause united as ONE, he can desire no more, for Divinity is indeed within ALL. When one realizes that at any moment one can touch the desire that he craves, that he can be part of the unity of ALL, then completion may come to order. But you see, among humanity, while this has been presented in its most simple form, humanity is not yet evolved enough to understand it in its most simplistic manner.

Humanity craves demonstration, wanting to create everything to be much bigger and better. The peace of God is not enough. The inner peace of God is not enough, so *more* must come forward, until the soul tires. Part of the purpose of Malton is to bring desire into fruition, but for the cause only, and I must emphasize this to bring completion to the soul.

While one may want to judge such desire as futile, it is not.

In the same way that a child craves candy or a continuous display of colorful toys, eventually they tire of such and grow out of such things. Yet, the innocence and the wonder of the thirst, the innocence and the wonder of the desire bring one to this completion. The energies of Malton are present to bring such desire to completion. It has always been said that before one leaves the schoolhouse known as Earth, one must complete all that they want, all they desire. Malton's purpose, as a Golden City in this New Time, is to bring this forward.

A LONG LIST

Think of all the little desires you yourself have that have not been fulfilled. Think of those who see themselves as less because of that long list that has been written lifetime after lifetime that has never been fulfilled. What a gift the Nature Kingdoms bring you! It is through their cooperation, the Elemental Forces, that this can now be so.

VIBRATION AND THE GOLD RAY

The great gift of the New Time is to demonstrate to humanity that, in their sojourn upon the Earth, heaven does indeed exist, that the world of spirit and the principles which create it indeed exist. Truth is indeed supreme. Along with these forces from the beloved Elemental Kingdoms is also the work of the Gold Ray.[9]

The work of the Gold Ray for the New Time will help birth the Earth into its new vibration. I use this word although, while it is not entirely accurate, it is the best to understand. You see, the Earth, during this Time of Great Change, is raising its vibratory rate. It is the difference between entering a room where there are many angry and frustrated people, and moving on to the next room where there is peace and cooperation. This, I know, many of you, Dear ones, Dear chelas, have felt, and the best word to describe the New Time is that a total vibratory rate will heighten upon the Earth. This is due to the new energies that are being utilized by the Elemental, Vegetable, Mineral and Animal Kingdoms. It is important that we assist them, too; that humanity may understand the new vibration, so that it may assist in this great unity and great rising of consciousness.

Consciousness is at the core of all of this.

---

9. The Gold Ray in classic astrology and teachings on the Rays is often identified with our Solar Sun, an archetype of the Divine Father, and associated with leadership, courage, independence, authority, and justice. In fundamental Ascended Master teachings, the Gold Ray is often paired with the Ruby Ray, and this celestial partnership refines the energies of Mars (the Ruby Ray) from its base energies of war and aggression into passion, skill, determination, and duty. In later teachings on the Rays, the Gold Ray is also coupled with the Aquamarine Ray (Neptune), as a moderator of this Ray 's association with illusion and fantasy, evolving the blue-green Ray 's mysticism into perception, self-realization, transparency, and spiritual Unity. The Gold Ray is also associated with the Great Central Sun, the Solar Logos; our Solar Sun is a step-down transformer of its energies. According to the Master Teachers, the Gold Ray is the epitome of change for the New Times. The Gold Ray is the ultimate authority of Cosmic Law and carries both our personal and worldwide Karma and Dharma (purpose). Its presence is designed to instigate responsible spiritual growth and planetary evolution for humanity's aspirations and the development of the HU-man. The Gold Ray, however, is also associated with Karmic justice and will instigate change: constructive and destructive. The extent of catastrophe or transformation is contingent on humanity's personal and collective spiritual growth and evolutionary process as we progress into the New Times.

THE ELEMENTAL AND PLANT KINGDOM

As it has been taught before, it is your Point of Perception that will determine the outcome. Consciousness and its qualification—the way in which it is utilized—will again be of great assistance in this New Time. As you see that water is comprised of the Elemental Kingdoms, it, in itself, is raised in consciousness.

As you see that the Plant Kingdoms are raised in vibrational content, they are raised, too, in consciousness. So, do you see this greater working that is coming through the Gold Ray?

THE PLAN BEGINS

This plan was long determined about the year 2000 for humanity, that a greater consciousness, a Ray of Light, would flood the Earth. Now, it is humanity's choice of how it will utilize this new Ray Force. In the beginning of this, there may be discomfort and there may be disharmony, but to prepare for this and its greater working is to continue your work in consciousness.

Remain stalwart and stay focused, Dear ones.

Keep in vigilance your prayers for your Sisters and your Brothers.

USE OF PRAYER

When there is disharmony among you, pray simply, "Bring harmony forth to my Brothers and Sisters. Let us be united as ONE, for we truly are." When you confirm this great law and truth, it is recognized and, therefore, acted upon. The Gold Ray, as it beams forward in its greater illumination and its greater understanding, will bring the Light of a Thousand Suns to those whose hearts are open and willing. Do you have questions?

LORDS DIRECT THE GOLD RAY

Question: "Yes, Dear one. Does the Gold Ray come about in an overall Divine Plan for the forward movement of humanity?"

Yes, as it was determined long ago that there would be those as (like) the Lords of Venus to out-picture such a Ray and, in its Divine Order and Divine Timing, would come forward.

Question: "So, we have now come to this time?"

As Sananda has said, "The time is at hand; the awakening is now." The Ruby Ray has built this bridge to allow the Gold Ray to come forward in its greater working. Do you understand?

Answer: "Yes, I understand that things work in a sequence and one must be laid down before the other can come forward, so the Ruby Ray has played this part. And so it would seem as though humanity is now faced with the great potential of this harmony, or the great potential of discord. Once again, it is choice."

INCREASE IN VIBRATION

Vibration, you see, Dear ones, is the key to understanding.[10] The Mineral Kingdom is also growing in its vibratory rate. The Vegetable Kingdom, plants, flowers, herbs and trees, are all growing in a vibratory rate, as has been taught in other discourses by my beloved Brothers. These vibratory rates are enhanced in the Golden City Vortices. That is why we have requested for many to move to such areas to live because of the increase in vibration. It is through this increase in vibration that greater understanding and the bond of telepathy is established—not

---

10. In common English, vibration comes from the word vibrate, which means to move, swing, or oscillate. In Ascended Master teachings, vibration is associated with light's movement in both physical and spiritual presence. In this context, light is affiliated with Wisdom, Love, and Power—attributes of the Unfed Flame and the expansion of the heart-flame through spiritual enlightenment. According to Master Kuthumi, increased light results in spiritual evolution, and this produces greater intuitive and psychic abilities; harmony with others, including the Animal and Fourth Dimensional Nature Kingdoms. Our vibration is calibrated by our thought processes—which consciousness grows out of—and these processes are fed by personal perceptions and choices. Kuthumi calls this the Eye of Consciousness, which is crucial to our personal level of vibration. States and levels of consciousness are perhaps the most powerful tools of vibration, and they create through the Out-picturing Process our recognition of human or HU-man experience.

only telepathy with us as your Teachers and Guides into this New Time, but a telepathic bond with all of nature, a telepathic bond with the Elemental Kingdoms. You see, Dear ones, this is important to understand in totality. In Malton, not only will there be fruition of desire, but a greater harmony will exist for the Mineral and Vegetable Kingdoms. This greater harmony will then arc itself to the Sister City of Denasha and fulfill, in a greater plan, a harmony to all Elemental Kingdoms. Do you have questions?

Question: "What is your definition of vibration?"

"THE EYE OF CONSCIOUSNESS"

I use that term sparingly, for vibration is not perhaps the most accurate way to understand what I AM speaking about. However, it is the closest in terms of your understanding. It has to do with movement, movement of light within the cells of your physical body—a physical demonstration of light movement. However, as you know, that it is the Point of Perception; light uses as its seed the vehicle of consciousness, so it is only in perception that vibration can be as it is. Vibration is, of course, movement to see something move or to vibrate. It is a vibration that may not be perceived by the physical eye or even through various tests. However, it is a movement that is in the Eye of Consciousness. Do you understand?

Question: "The Eye of Consciousness—so that would mean that the light movement is going to be proportionate to the openness of someone's perception, perspective, or attitude?"

It was once said that beauty is in the eye of the beholder, and so is the vibration within the eye of the perceiver. In order for a heightened consciousness or vibration to be understood, it must be perceived first in the one who recognizes it. So, when I use the word *vibration* I must qualify such a statement. However, we have out-pictured that a greater time shall come to the Earth, a greater time when suffering and misery shall be lessened. However, one must then be ready to let go of one's perception of misery, the perception of suffering. Do you understand?

PERCEPTION AND STATES OF CONSCIOUSNESS

Question: "I see, so if we can perceive it, then it can be created?"

This is so. This is the tool of consciousness, as it must be honed. That is why desire must not be denied or judged. It must be allowed its total fruition, for, through this process, consciousness is exercised and brought into its greater working, where the perception of peace may be attained.

Question: "So if we were to choose to perceive a world of harmony and telepathy with the Nature Kingdoms and each other and the planet on a whole and the spiritual hierarchy, those who would choose that perception would move into this Golden Age?"

This is the idea, to bring such a teaching into a Unity of Consciousness. The desire is that to bring unity to ALL, to bring harmony to ALL, but until that desire is fueled with the fire of Co-creation, it cannot be attained. Where two or more are gathered, there I AM; the universal consciousness of peace is exactly that. It is universal. It is for ALL.

Question: "So it really comes down to a matter of desire of the individual and groups?"

It is, Dear ones, Dear hearts. Now I ask of you that within the next year, if you have the opportunity to travel to the Vortex of Malton, to feel these energies, to understand exactly what we have just spoken about. Is this possible, Dear heart?

Answer: "I have great desire for this."

Then, let us bring this into fruition, together as your Brother, so that these energies may be understood and taught. Bringing desire into fruition is a good thing, for there is a greater understanding that lies behind it.

Now, unless, of course, there are no other questions, I shall take my leave.

Response: "At this time, I have no more other than a request that you return more frequently."

So be it.
In the Light of a Thousand Suns, I AM.

Master Kuthumi steps back, and Saint Germain comes forward.

Greetings, Beloveds, and again I must remind you that it is in the work of the Violet Flame that I hold you ever sincere and dear. Hitaka.

Answer: "Hitaka. Thank you."

Divine Destiny

Based on the Prophecies and Spiritual Teachings of

Saint Germain

El Morya

Lord Macaw

CHAPTER ONE

Template of Light

El Morya shares teachings on the Golden Cities.

Greetings, beloveds. In that Mighty Violet Flame, I AM Saint Germain, and I request permission to come forward.

Response: "Please, Saint Germain, come forward."

Dear ones the work at hand is indeed important, and I shall not tarry longer. I introduce you this morning to Beloved El Morya.

Master El Morya steps forward.

Greetings, Dear ones. In that Mighty Blue Flame, I AM El Morya, and I request permission to come forward.

Answer: "Please come forward, El Morya."

THE BLUE RAY OF GOBEAN

Dear hearts, Dear ones, the activation of Gobean (Golden City) is complete, and it is important to understand each of the teachings as they have been set forward. We have laid down the template of all the doorways, each of them complete in the teaching that they bring and emit. But it is important to understand the full use of the energies of the Star.

The Star, you see, is not only the coalescing of the energies of each of the doorways, but is also the finer qualities of that Mighty Blue Ray. When you understand the Galactic Web and how each of the star systems is interconnected, it is through the Sun of the solar system that these Rays arc their energies to the intersecting grids known as Golden Cities.[1] Each is then quali-

fied by pure mighty God Force. The God Force is known in Gobean as the Blue Ray, and it brings forth many of its inherent qualities. These qualities are peace, harmony, cooperation and, ideally, transformation of the human into a God State.[2]

THE GOD STATE

There will be those, when they recognize the God State, who will feel a Oneness, a sense of bliss, or Unana, with all creation. There will be those who will mock such a state and will ask how a human can obtain such an ideal consciousness; but it is so, Dear ones. The God State is an understanding of the inherent Mastery that exists within each of you. This has been taught before as the Unfed Flame of Love, Wisdom, and Power. This is the perfection of Divinity that exists within each of you. To align to this Divinity brings forth a natural harmony, a natural cooperation of each of your energy fields. Beloved Saint Germain has brought forth a discourse on the energy fields, their separate purposes and how they may be applied as energy forces in this New Time.

THE RAY FORCE IS STRONGEST IN THE STAR

It is in the work of Gobean, particularly that of the Star, in which the energy bodies are brought into a union and a harmony of understanding. You see, Beloveds, it is in the Stars that the Ray Force is at its strongest point or strongest pitch in auditory sound. It is that place of movement where light and sound work in their greatest movement to bring humanity

---

1. Arcing of Ray Forces to Golden City Vortices: The Seven Rays of Light and Sound originate from the Great Central Sun — or Galactic Center — as it is known in Hindu and Mayan cultures. Ray Forces are an unseen type of energy that are said to function like a quasar–type of light. Since Ray Forces control many human evolutionary aspects, they distribute their energies by arcing through the planets of the Fire Triplicity of our Solar System to Earth: Mars (Aries, the spiritual pioneer); Sun (Leo, the spiritual leader); and Jupiter (Sagittarius, the spiritual teacher). Vedic Rishis and Master Teachers concur that the amount of galactic light streaming to Earth as the Seven Rays controls lifespans, memory function, ability to absorb and respect spiritual knowledge, and access to the Akashic Records. Golden City Rays arch primarily through our solar Sun and enter the Earth's core. The movement of Golden City Vortices draws the Ray Force through, to the center of the Vortex — the Star. Energies of the Ray are disbursed from the Star throughout the entire Vortex.

2. God-state: The attainment of Unity Consciousness — Unana — is associated with the God-state. The God-state level of consciousness is considered a precursor to the Ascension, and students and chelas may be given initiatory glimpses into its wondrous vibration; however, it is a state of consciousness achieved in the final levels of the Arhat and the beginning stages of the Adept.

forth in its evolutions. Naturally, when one retreats or retires to a Star, one is filled with a higher frequency, a higher energy.

APPEARANCE OF THE MASTER TEACHERS

These Star areas in all the Golden Cities are considered by the hierarchy to be sacred areas. They are areas that shall be used for the strongest pulse of the energies of each Master Teacher who is assigned. These are also areas that, when defined, are where the Master Teachers of each defined area will manifest a physical body when the energies are in their optimum state. Creation toward the optimum state will be required in order for this to happen, and many will ask of you, "In what time span shall this occur?" But you will know, Dear ones, Dear hearts when the energies will be ready, for they will not be denied. It is important to know that these energies are pure, and in their purity and innocence they are able to bring forth the higher and finer qualities. You see, as we have explained before, it is the hierarchy of consciousness working with the service of Beloved Babajeran, as Mother Earth, to bring this forward now for humanity. Many will see it and exclaim that it is a Divine Intervention. However, it is a plan that has been held in my focus. It is a plan that has been held in my own heart's desire.[3]

A GREATER LAW BECKONS

Gobean will perform a great service for many during the times of great change. It will serve as a beckoning point. Have you not noticed that many are being drawn and called to live in this area?

Answer: "This is very true."

These are due to the energies, and many are being called forward. Many feel a magnetic draw or an electromagnetic pulse drawing them closer and closer. You see, it is a plan that was long held, not only through the service of the Hierarchy and through the service of Beloved Mother Earth, Babajeran, but it is also within that longing of the soul to become ONE with, to become atoned, to become ONE in the consciousness of Unana. One may say, yes, this is a genetic pulse, but it is only that inherent Divineship . . . exists within each of you which is now being pulled to its fuller expression.[4] Only in the service of Brotherhood and Sisterhood can the chela move forward to the greater understanding, to the greater work, to the greater

3. El Morya's Teachings on the Star of Gobean: The Star of Gobean carries a combination of spiritual energies:
The energies of the Four Doorways coalesce throughout the Star.
The fine and subtle qualities of the Blue Ray manifest the spiritual qualities of peace, harmony, cooperation, and transformation.
Energies ideally suited to initiate the student or chelas into the understanding and realization of the God-state; ONENESS, and the consciousness of Unana.
The energies of Stars, especially the Star of Gobean, harmonize and balance the energy of the light-bodies.
The Ray Force of each Golden City is strongest in the Star. Due to this intense energy, some individuals may hear the auditory pitch of the Ray Force within the Star, and its powerful movement of Light and Sound frequencies can quickly evolve humanity. Time spent in Star locations fill an individual with heightened awareness, spiritual frequencies, and spiritual energy.
While the entire Golden City Vortex serves as a spiritual abode for many Master Teachers, the Star locations are considered to be the most sacred to the Spiritual Hierarchy. To some degree, the Star location is considered to be an Ashram of the Master Teacher assigned to the individual Golden City. The Star areas are strongly energized by the physical and spiritual presence of the Master Teacher of each Golden City Star. (Editor's Note: It is also important to understand that Ascended Masters, Archangels, and Elohim will all unite on Earth to serve various Master Teachers in Golden Cities.

For more information on this topic, see *Golden Cities and the Masters of Shamballa*.)
The pure and innocent energy of the Star of Gobean evokes in the chela higher and finer qualities of spiritual development. This evolutionary process is based upon these principles:
Service. Entrance into the service of the Great White Brotherhood and Sisterhood of Light offers the chela a leap in spiritual understanding and knowledge.
Cooperation and Harmony. These spiritual precepts allow the chela to experience and understand life as ONE Body of Light in the path of Self-Mastery.
Collective Consciousness. Through developing an awareness and sensitivity to the consciousness of Unana, one is able to understand the spiritual work of the Greater Law.
Unity of All Life. Let go of small misgivings; the sense of injustice; and little hurts, as these can become major stumbling blocks in your spiritual evolutionary process.
The Spiritual Hierarchy's work with humanity is based entirely upon all of these principles: Service, Harmony, Cooperation, Collective Consciousness, and the Unity of All Life.
4. The essence and presence of the Divine is present within the individual. This is illustrated in Ascended Master teachings through the Unfed Flame, the Eight-sided Cell of Perfection and humanity's spiritual unfoldment through the Higher Self, the Christ-self, and ultimately the I AM Presence. The Divineship is reference to these components of the immortal, spiritual HU-man as a synthesis of their articulate systems and processes.

knowledge. It is only through merging in cooperation and harmony, and in understanding the ONE body of light, that one can move forward in one's own steps of self-Mastery. Through collective consciousness, or the consciousness of Unana, one is able to understand the greater working of the greater law.[5]

MOVE FORWARD THROUGH UNITY

That is the reason we pull you forward into harmony. Let go of your little misgivings. Let go of the little hurts, for they become major stumbling blocks in moving forward in your own greater understanding. It is in the unity of consciousness that the hierarchy works and is able to bring forward its greater service with Beloved Babajeran. It is only through our understanding of the unity of all of consciousness, the unity of all of life, that we are able to move and experience our light being; so, understand, Dear chelas, how important the work of harmony and cooperation is. It is a greater movement into a greater knowledge, a greater understanding, which ultimately will set you free.

Now, I will continue with more teachings upon the arcing of the Ray energy.

ENTRANCE OF THE RAY FORCE

Each of the Ray Forces enters in and to the Stars, and this pure energy connects itself to the core of the Earth. It is from there that it radiates out again, out through the center of the Earth, and works as a streamline force of energy.

Now, I shall diagram this so that you will understand exactly how a Ray Force works.

He is first drawing the Great Central Sun and from the Great Central Sun he is drawing a series of lines. Each of these lines works as a Ray Force. And they move toward the center of the Earth.

Now, understand, chelas, that this activity is not peculiar only to Earth itself. This is the same type of pattern as Ray Forces arc to any other planet within your system.

He is showing that it moves to the center of the Earth.

EARTH'S INNER SUN

It is the core, itself, that attracts light force to light force, for the core of the Earth is also a brilliant Sun. Of course, your scientists would say it is a molten type of rock, but this is not so. It is another Sun in its own evolution. You see, as Earth moves forward in its evolution, it, too, shall become the Sun of its own solar system in its own time and in its own place. But you see the attraction of one light to another.

Now, he is showing how the Ray Forces arc from the Central Sun within the Earth to each of the positions of the Golden Cities.

THE HIERARCHY QUALIFIES THE RAY

It is through the work of the Hierarchy that this light is qualified.[6] Each of these Vortices exists in a similar compatibility. Each of these Vortices exists as a template that covers the entire planet. It is the work of the Master Teacher and the Elohim of that Ray that brings forward the qualification of the qualities of that light.[7] It is my presence, along with many other servants of the Blue Ray, that brings forward the qualification of this as a light force. Each of the Golden City Vortices exists as they are, each of them very similar in their working and understanding. But it is the presence of the Master Teacher, and those who wish to follow in the ashram of consciousness of that particular thought, that continues to bring that qualification of light through. Do you understand this diagram?

---

6. See Appendix B3: *Spiritual Hierarchy.*

7. Elohim: Plural for Eloah; this is a Hebrew word for God. In the vernacular of the Ascended Masters, Elohim is specifically a God of Nature and Creation, associated with the quality of magnetism. The Elohim oversee many aspects of the eco-systems of our planet in all dimensions, giving them authority over the Four Elements; Nature Devas; the Animal Kingdom, Plant Kingdom and Mineral Kingdom; and Elemental Kingdom of Gnomes, Undines, Sylphs, and Salamanders. Regarded as the ancient mythological Gods of Earth, the myths of the Elohim engage their compelling presence alongside the Angelic Kingdom in the creation of the Earth as the unseen magnetic carriers of the Rays of Light and Sound.

---

5. See Appendix A3: *Greater Law of the Great Law.*

Answer: "Not completely. I was always of the opinion that our local solar Sun was the window to the Central Sun."

"LIGHT UNTO LIGHT"

There is indeed a Great Central Sun, but it is through the solar system that this energy is allowed to emit to its finer quality. I could explain this so that you would understand how light is attracting light unto light. It is the Great Central Sun that emits its own Ray of light to the Sun of this solar system. Do you understand?[8]

Answer: "Okay. I think we're talking about the same thing."

A HIGHER OCTAVE OF EVOLUTION

Essentially, it is. I'm talking only about your own solar system, so that you may understand exactly how this works within the Golden Cities. You see, each solar system has its own evolutionary cause, its own evolutionary template. So, you understand, only in its own time and place can these forces move forward. We have spoken much in the past about the Lords of Venus, and it was through their own evolutionary process that they were able to take each Ray of Light and its own sound vibration and bring them into a higher octave of evolution.

At this time, Earth is being readied for a greater understanding of light and sound. Light and sound move many things forward. History is created. Interactions among humanity and societies change, political systems and economic systems also begin to change. This sets up a ripple effect in the same way as when a pebble is thrown into a pond. The ripples over the water create an effect that is felt by all within the pond. Envision your solar system as that pond, exposed to a the Ray of Light and Sound, with a small pebble being dropped, and a Source which drops it. The hand that dropped the force is now your Sun. But there is a greater force of consciousness behind the hand.

8. See Appendix C3: *El Morya's History and Science of the Rays and Teachings of At-ONE-Ment.*

That is the Great Central Sun orchestrating a greater Divine Intervention of the Rays of Light and Sound.

LIGHT AND SOUND JOIN

Understand, Dear ones, chelas, that even sound works as a Ray. It is through this circular vibration — which we have explained before as the spiral — that light and sound join to one another. And it is when this vibration is consciously applied by the chela, through the work of the Violet Flame or other mantra work, that they engage in that light, which is then bonded to sound. Ultimately, it is the intertwining of consciousness with action. Do you understand?

Question: "The intertwining of consciousness with action — so, by taking the action of the Violet Flame Decree, or a mantra, that starts to imbue into the cells of the body a light frequency?"

"A UNIONIZATION EFFECT"

This is so, Dear ones. And it brings forth an acceleration within the chelas. That is why, when we explain the work of the Violet Flame and the work of the different mantras that can be utilized in each of these Golden Cities, they are brought forward with a timing and an intent to move evolution forward. It is this cooperation that is created within each of the Light Bodies, which allows a unionization of each of the fields of light. You see, at this point there are indeed layers of the field of the Human Aura, or different Light Bodies. These can, and are, at times separated by Will by those who have complete Mastery over each of the light fields. And it is through a type of Mastery that they are brought together or unionized at Will, when the Violet Flame is utilized and mantras are utilized by individuals and the Master for different Ray Forces. This brings about a unionization effect within the aura. Do you understand?

VIBRATIONAL FREQUENCY OF THE BLUE RAY

Answer: "Yes, and that also explains, when I have seen your aura, or that of any of the other Masters, that the auras are perfectly arranged and harmonized, and are organized by color and sound."

The Mantra, "Om Sham, Sham, Sham or Om Shanti, Shanti, Shanti," *sham* is the vibrational frequency of the Blue Ray within the solar system. This brings forth a coalescing of energies, a natural cooperation, a natural harmony that is inherent within the individual. As you understand each of these teachings, you first exclaim unto yourself, "a great mystery is now revealed," but that is not so.

TONING YOUR ENERGY FIELDS

In its own timing and intent, all, as Universal Mind, is revealed. You see, Dear ones, Dear hearts, you are all Divine. You all carry within you the same Source. You are all equal to one another. It is by this concept of Brotherhood and Sisterhood that the Mastery of the physical is accomplished. That is why dear Sananda has always said, "Simply love one another." To bring forth this work of the Blue Ray in the Golden City of Gobean is my first intent. My second intent is to teach this work and its application, to bring your own energy fields to consciously align them, to consciously unify them, to bring them as ONE to at-ONE-ment, to bring them into a *tone*. Now, do you understand?

Answer: "Yes."

ALIGNMENT AND GROWTH

This work brings about a greater harmony, a greater force of electromagnetism. For, you see, the qualification of the Golden City Vortex Ray is magnified in force. As others align to its energy, it grows exponentially. Now do you understand?

Answer: "Yes. It's the way in which the system works."

Each is then treated, when reaching this level of intentional service, as a Step-down Transformer, used to carry forth the work of the Ray Force within that Golden City. Some will feel more aligned to energies other than the Blue Ray, but the Blue Ray is the most perfect place to start, to bring the body into alignment, to bring the energy fields to atonement.

AT-ONE-MENT

Question: "So atonement is also at-ONE-ment?"

They are one and the same. They are brought through the light and sound frequencies, working together as ONE. This is the beauty of the creation of the Rays, and part of the greater plan to bring humanity back into its state, its true state of at ONE.[9]

CHANGE, ONENESS, AND USE OF THE VIOLET FLAME

During the Time of Change, many changes are occuring; changes not only upon the Earth, but changes within yourself, within your neighbor, within society.[10] Humanity is changing. Is this a change that is forced upon it (humanity)? Hardly, but one that was planned and one that was long desired. Of course, there are always those who resist such change, and this

---

9. See Appendix D3: *The Great Plan.*
10. Prophecies of Change:
 Once the energies of the Stars reach their optimum state of heightened energies, Master Teachers are prophesied to materialize physical bodies in these locations to assist humanity through healing and teaching in the Golden Age.
 The spiritually enlightening, transforming, and healing energies of the Golden Cites will not be denied.
 In the New Times, the Golden City of Gobean will serve as a beckoning point to those who feel the New Energies and the electromagnetic pulse of the Blue Ray.
 In the Time of Change, many will experience an urge within, like a "longing of the soul," to enter into the Consciousness of the ONE, and experience the At-ONE-Ment, and the Consciousness of Unana.
 The inner longing, or urge for ONEship may seem to be genetically linked; however, it is the expression of the inherent Divineship within, "each and every one of you."
 Individuals will experience numerous changes deep from within and witness the same among neighbors; and, in a greater scope, in our cultures and societies. However, El Morya reminds us that these prophesied events are not the result of the Time of Change and are instigated by a profound metamorphis of our own desires.
 While much of humanity will undergo a worldwide transformation, there will be many who will resist the change resulting in disease, insanity, suicide, and an obsession with the death urge.

causes disease, insanity, suicide, all of the death urges. You see, when one encounters higher frequency, if one has not cleared the energy bodies out through the steady and constant use of the Violet Flame, one will not feel comfortable in his Oneness. Now, you understand, in its greater working and greater harmony, why Master Saint Germain has brought forward the work of the Violet Flame.[11]

Question: "So you are saying that, in the evolution of humanity, all of the prayers that have pre-existed before this time, which have brought us to this place — those things we call chants or mantras or intonations — culminate with the use of the Violet Flame to bring humanity to its next place in the evolution of a cycle?"

THE HEALING EXPERIENCE OF LOVE

This is so. Now the working of the Violet Flame in the mass collective consciousness first stimulates that which is known as the Kundalini. This has another electromagnetic force working itself throughout the human body which is known as the First Chakra. Have you not seen the lust and the greed, the climbing for physical security when these energies are not allowed to rise further, and to bring their expression towards the true force they are meant for? It is through this work of the Violet Flame, and the rising of the forces of the Kundalini to the Heart Chakra,

that brings one to the understanding of love. It is only through love that all may be healed. It is only through love that all may become as ONE. You see, love becomes, as Saint Germain would say, the grand elixir. Love is indeed the energy that all must understand, all must experience. It is one thing for me to mention love, but it is another for you to experience it. Is this not so?

Answer: "This is very true. It is love that has brought me here, and it is love that keeps me here on this path."

LOVE'S ACTION: SACRIFICE, PURIFICATION, AND CHOICE

In love, the chela encounters sacrifice at many levels, purification at many levels. That is why love is the energy of all Eastern doors. It is not sacrifice that keeps a family together as ONE; it is only when one overcomes petty selfishness and little hurts that energy is raised to a greater understanding of the ONE. This is not to say that the individual's wants and needs are not important, but this allows for a greater understanding of the higher knowledge of choice. It is when one chooses love as the action that the understanding of the Violet Flame comes forward in its greatest harmonizing effect. This template of energies that is laid down through use of the Violet Flame allows one to work with the Blue Flame.[12]

A VISUALIZATION TECHNIQUE

Now let us talk about the work of the Blue Flame. The Blue Flame, in its highest understanding, is anchored within the Throat Chakra. Of course, this is identified with the higher use of the Will. Then, all expression comes forth in cooperation and in a greater harmony and peace: perfect sounds, perfect creations, and perfect light. Are these not the blessings and the wants of paradise? But in order to understand how this works

---

11. El Morya's Comments on the Violet Flame:
Saint Germain's worldwide spiritual work with the Violet Flame is meant for the many who do not feel comfortable with the ideal of Oneness and the concept of conscious immortality.
The effect of the Violet Flame in the mass collective consciousness stimulates the Kundalini; this raises the transformational fire to the Heart Chakra, evoking the experience and understanding of love (Bhakti). This transforms the base energies of lust, greed, materiality, and the constant need for security.
The experience of love is healing. Once humanity is healed, we can experience and understand the ONE.
"Through Love, the chela experiences sacrifice at many levels." The spiritual ideal of sacrifice is the foundation of family, and the ability to overcome personal, individual selfishness. This involves an evolved understanding of choice; love develops from feeling moving into action. This new template of thought, established through the Violet Flame, initiates the spiritual processes of the Blue Flame.

12. The Blue Flame is the activity of the Blue Ray in all human endeavors manifesting the qualities of Truth, Power, Determination, and Diligence. The activity of the Blue Flame is said to primarily affect the individual will, transforming our choices. The processes of the Blue Flame align the individual will to the Divine Will, and this important spiritual growth develops the HU-man through detachment and the ability to serve others with steadiness, calm, harmony, and God-protection.

within your own physiology, let us now practice a breathing technique.

Together, let us meditate upon the Violet Flame. Raise (visualize while breathing) the energies from the base of the Kundalini, the base of your spine, now purposely raise the energies up to your heart. Meditate upon and experience this flame, and when you feel the burning within your heart, signal me.[13]

Response: "It is done."

Now, do you feel the collection of the energies of the Violet Flame?

Answer: "Yes, they grow."

BLUE FLAME OF POWER

They emanate. This teaching has been brought forward to you. To bring this into a greater understanding, the Blue Flame now rests within the heart of the Unfed Flame of Love, Wisdom, and Power. Now, the Blue Flame of Power, as an electrical current, moves the rest of this energy up to the Throat Chakra. We are speaking now of the higher use of energy. Do you feel this energy, as you breathe, moving itself, ever so gently, to your throat?

Answer: "Yes, I do."

"THIS IS KNOWN AS WILL"

This energy is used as a Divine Expression. It is the work of this Will — this Will of greater love — to bring a unionization. As these energies travel into their higher expression, an alignment of all systems occurs within the physiology. This alignment of systems encounters Elemental Kingdoms, Mineral Kingdoms and Vegetable Kingdoms. We have spoken of the harmony of Kingdoms as they exist in the human physiology.[14]

13. See Appendix E3: *Breathing Technique of the Blue Flame.*
14. The Elemental Kingdom and Human Physiology:

Element	Physical System
Earth Element	Skeletal System; Skin, Hair, Nails
Fire Element	Muscular and Circulatory Systems
Water Element	Lymphatic and Endocrine Systems
Air Element	Nervous and Respiratory Systems

Now this harmony moves on into its greater working and a greater alignment, for its source is love, *pure love*, purified love, the love of sacrifice, the love of purification, the love of choice. This is known as Will. Let it come forward.

In that moment did you feel a chill throughout your body?

Answer: "Yes."

That was the unionization of your energy fields. Some may say "goose bumps."

Answer: "Goose bumps, yes."

Did you get a chill?

Answer: "Yes."

This is the unionization of all fields moving you to the consciousness of Unana. Now, dear chela, do you understand why I gave you the Candle Meditation?

Answer: "Yes, but this was more simple than I had thought."

UNITY AND RIGHT ACTION

Now, you have another understanding of unity and its purpose, and how it brings about greater harmony. Let us focus on the results of what this work can now bring: a beautiful result in your interaction, *right action with others*; an ease of understanding in bringing forth your own God idea, your own God creatorship; a greater understanding in working in harmony with others; and a greater understanding in working with the energies of Gobean. This unionization of the energy fields brings, of course, a type of regeneration to the physical body; greater yet, it brings a greater regeneration of you, with your true inherent Divinity.

Now I shall open the floor for your questions.

RAISING THE KUNDALINI

Question: "I find this very interesting. In my personal meditations, I have asked for a similar instruction, and, without saying a word to Lori, it has come forward, as usual. It is more verification of the inner workings of the Divine connection and of the telepathic connection in that service. The question I would ask is for anyone who may read or hear this. This type of — we could call it an exercise or meditative action — would this be wise to do several times a day?"

It is best to do after one has completed the Violet Flame and after completing one's work with the Blue Flame. You see, this will bring great assistance in raising the energies throughout the Kundalini. Do you understand?

Question: "Yes. In considering that our world is made of light and sound, the Blue Flame does have a frequency and a pitch, is this not so?"

SOUND AND PITCH

Yes, and that has been explained. Of course, pitches will change as frequency changes in resonance. So you must understand that we start with just the pronunciation of what the sound possibly is, for those who can hear.

Response: "I understand. However, in your world, there are specific pitches that are utilized."

They are not utilized. A better word would be "achieved."

Response: "Achieved and experienced. I understand. So, in doing a Candle Meditation and in doing the Violet Flame Decrees, this next step can be added for the harmonization of the layers of the aura. One of its benefits is that it helps to purify the body and energizes it."

A HIGHER CHAKRA SYSTEM

It also brings forth the creation of what you have known to be the axiotonal bodies, the higher frequency Chakra System.[15] However, we shall not proceed with that teaching yet.

Let us focus on the work at hand and bring it into a perfect harmony.

Response: "I would agree. At this point, I have no further questions."

In that Mighty Blue Flame, let us all move forward in perfect harmony, cooperation, peace and Unana. And now I turn the floor back to Beloved Saint Germain.

Saint Germain steps forward.

Response: "Thank you."

A NEW TEMPLATE

Dear ones, it was our hope, in bringing this information forward, that you would not only understand a greater working of the Violet Flame but also of the Blue Flame and the Blue Ray and its purpose in the Star of the Golden Cities. You see, these teachings are brought forward to be a template of all the teachings so that there will be a greater understanding and a greater knowledge of how these forces work to bring humanity forward.

Unless there are other questions, I shall take my leave.

---

15. Axiotonal bodies are created by Axiotonal Lines: magnetic energy lines, similar to acupuncture lines on the human body, and lei-lines on Mother Earth. Axiotonal lines are claimed to connect our biology to resonating star systems within our Galaxy, effecting human chemistry and genetic change. The Axiotonal Bodies are similar to Light Bodies; analogous to the blueprint, or grid bodies of the human aura; however, several types of Axiotonal Bodies exist in the human and HU-man and contain diverse qualities and characteristics through various dimensions.

Response: "No, but I AM thankful to both of you, for this has been a lesson that I have long desired."

In united Brotherhood and Sisterhood, let peace reign supreme. Hitaka.

Response: "Hitaka. So be it. Thank you."

CHAPTER TWO

Conscious Creation

❧

Saint Germain presents teachings on the Heart's Desire.

Greetings, beloved chelas. In that Mighty Christ, I AM Saint Germain, and I ask permission to come forward.

Response: "Please come forward."

VIOLET FLAME FOR DIVINE INTERVENTION

I stream forth on that Mighty Violet Ray of Mercy and Forgiveness. And, Dear hearts, I must remind you that it is this Violet Flame that brings forth the beauty and the glory of Ascension. It is the beauty and the glory of Ascension that all are seeking at this time upon the Earth Plane and Planet. All ask us, "Is there a better way and a higher way so we can move forward in this time known as the Golden Age?' I ask you, Dear ones, to consider that it is the work of the Violet Flame that unites your mental focus as ONE, bringing your focus into the unity of consciousness that is required to move all into this New Time. You see, the Golden Age is a Time of Peace and prosperity for all, a time for the end of little sufferings. You see, there are those who seek an end to the little sufferings of life and seek a spiritual liberation, a knowledge that passeth all understanding. It is for this reason, Dear ones, Dear hearts, that we bring this Violet Flame as water for your most thirsty drink. It ends the suffering and allows Divine Intervention to move forward. Dear hearts, today I shall give a small discourse and then shall open the floor for your questions.

QUESTIONS START THE JOURNEY

I see in previous material that I have created quite a stir, for you have many questions and many inquiries. This is good, for in questioning we learn and gain a greater understanding of the whole. As we have discussed before, a little knowledge can be dangerous, and in this case, the *little knowledge* that has been

sent to you opens a greater question. The search for knowledge is the desire within you — the unquestionable thirst that brings you into greater understanding. As I have always said, "know thyself," Dear students, Dear chelas — "know thyself first." It is through the question that one begins to start and depart upon their journey.

PERCEPTION CHANGES OUR PERSONAL VISTA

In past discourses, we have spoken about the Point of Perception and how important the Point of Perception is in understanding anything at any given time. The Point of Perception allows you to move in a different direction, to stand at a different point. It is as simple as standing upon the mountain and looking across the vista. Perhaps you are now standing in that deep canyon and looking up at the mountain. You see, it is a Point of Perception. Those who seek self-Mastery can understand that at any point in time they may be in the canyon. They may be on the prairie. They may be on the hill. They may be on the mountain top. From each of these Points of Perception, one is able to view all the circumstances and begin to understand creation.

THE HEART'S DESIRE

We have spoken about creation many times and the fact that you are indeed the Creators of your own destiny.[1] Your destiny is that purpose which is deep inside you — a destiny that speaks to your heart, this is known as the Heart's Desire.[2] It is that flame within you that has flickered for so long and now bursts forward in its own creation, intention, understanding, and complete unfoldment. This is the truth of life. The desire is then fulfilled. And in knowing and understanding your work (Heart's Desire), your desire sets you free, Dear ones. To set yourself free from desire is to Master desire, through understanding the desires that are within you, the desires that are yet to be fulfilled, and those desires that are as small embers within your heart, completely unfulfilled. They still exist and in their

---

1. For more information see Appendix F3, *Saint Germain's Teachings on the Co-creation Process.*
2. See Appendix H3: *The Heart's Desire.*

yearnings they (seem to) create a trapping for those who desire liberation. But are they indeed a trap?

"DESIRE FOSTERS GROWTH"

I say desires present a varied way that humanity can evolve, learn, and grow. Desire fosters growth and this growth becomes good, does it not Dear chelas? It is the growth that leads you from the valley, to the prairie, to the hill, and onward to the mountain. It is desire that leads you to climb out of the canyon . . . and a brook leads you onward to the river. The desire that is within you is also the beginning of all (your) creations. It is important, indeed, to know that you desire.

UNCONSCIOUS DESIRES

Sometimes we are of the opinion that we are unconscious of desire, not knowing how it exists within us; yet, there it is creating and recreating, and recreating (again) the same set of circumstances.

When we meet someone whom we begin to know quite well, we notice certain habits, certain patterns. Repeated behaviors come through, at times, as an unconscious urge, a desire within self, having not yet learned to manifest at a more constructive level. These repeated patterns may be good, or they may be bad. It would depend upon those who may be recipients, and those experiencing through the desire. You see, Dear ones, there are many levels when we are dealing with unconscious creation. However, the work of the Aspirant, the one who is seeking self-knowledge, is to let those desires of unconscious quality come forward to consciousness so that they are understood in their deep unfoldment.[3] The Aspirant is then readied to come forward for a much fuller creation, a creation that becomes not one of repeated patterns that are unconscious, and wholly transforms into a conscious and experiential creation.

THE FLOW OF LIFE

Conscious creation prepares a student or chela for a greater understanding of the greater working of all of life. This allows the chela to be ONE within the flow of all of life, to stand within the flow of that mighty ever present River of Life as one who understands one's true creations, true intention, who can set conscious desires forward with complete intention.[4, 5] So you see, Dear ones, that is why it is important to begin to identify the unconscious creation.

FROM UNCONSCIOUS TO CONSCIOUS BEHAVIOR

How is it that an unconscious creation can become conscious? It is most important to begin by observation, the highest of all sciences. Keep a journal to observe self. Observe daily the little things that you do. Observe daily the little things that you say — even the most minute circumstances or situations may become a key, a clue, to understanding repeated behaviors that you no longer desire and wish to transform. You see, Dear one, when we explained the work of the Ray Forces you began to understand that there is a lower qualification and a much higher or conscious qualification. Do you understand this?

Answer: "Yes."

It is the same of all desires. All desires (eventually) manifest. This is the Universal Law. But it is up to all chelas to become aware of the desires they manifest — to become aware of the desires they transform from unconscious to a conscious creation. It is as simple as understanding, and qualifying desire as we have taught before. It is as if each desire is emanating from your energy field and manifesting its result to your world, teaching you, leading you, and evolving you. Evolution moves forward, and all life becomes ever present.

---

3. Aspirant: A newly awakened spiritual student, whose ambitions create aspiration; the student has yet to find or acquire a guru, a teacher who can assist their evolutionary journey on the spiritual path.

4. See Appendix G3: *River of Life*.
5. Intention: Acts, thoughts, or conceptions earnestly fixed on something, or steadfastly directed. Intentions often reflect the state of an individual's mind which directs their specific actions toward an object or goal.

DISSOLVE UNWANTED CREATIONS

So, let us continue. How does one become aware of the unconscious to the conscious? It is important, of course, to observe, but then it is also important after observing, to remove the creations that no longer serve. When you become aware of a creation that is no longer working well for you or for your highest good, and in this case, that which you *do not choose,* call forth the sacred Violet Flame. Use it and apply it. This is truly the purest Divine Intervention. You see, beloveds, what this brings forward in that moment is a total dissolution of the past, so that the present may become what you wish it to be. Do you see now how unconsciously created desires keep us trapped within the past? We repeat and repeat.

We are unable to move forward, but now it is time to move into the now. So, the soul becomes trapped, living in the past, desirous of the future, but with no way to experience the present. This is the torture of hell. It is the torture of ignorance.

"HEALING IS COMPLETE"

After one becomes aware of the Violet Flame and the science of Divine Intervention, one is able to remove the past. The scars disappear. Healing is complete. You see, until one removes the scars, one is still not whole. One still walks with a limp. One still has slight vision. One's hearing is not 100 percent. Do you see the metaphor that I use, Dear ones, so that you can begin to understand how one must move forward in one's creations?

IDENTIFICATION

Now, let us talk about consciously creating. All desire that is within you must be identified. It must be brought to the forefront. Remember, Dear ones, when I taught you the Write-and-Burn Technique?[6]

Answer: "Yes."

This was so that you could consciously remove past creations — consciously identify and remove them. To bring a conscious creation to the forefront, so that it may become part of your life, you must take those first necessary steps in their completeness. This brings total resolution of the past, so that the past is over and is no longer part of the present. Do you see, Dear one?

Answer: "I have an idea of what you're saying."

BLESS THE PAST

Now, to move into the present, you must wave good-bye to the past. Bless it as you would an old friend. Then move on to the new group or consciousness.

---

6. Perhaps one of the most easily understood yet metaphysically powerful Transmutation methods is the Write-and-Burn Technique. First, students are encouraged to identify and then write what they want to Co-create, much like a letter to the Universe. This process affirms the individual's sacred desire. Likewise, if an unwanted pattern or behavior has been discovered, this too is disclosed to the Universe for dissolution. It is recommended to call upon the power of the I AM Presence, along with the transformative Sacred Fire — the Violet Flame. Teachers and practitioners of this science of Co-creation contend that its power comes only through handwritten letters, as the ink and paper are infused with the energies of the individual.

Often students wish to refine the Write-and-Burn Co-creation Technique, and it is suggested that they burn outdated requests. This creates conscious space for the new creation.

The Write-and-Burn Technique is varied and individualized. Some students request the assistance of certain Angels, Archangels, Saints, and Masters. Others call upon Ray Forces and Elohim. Saint Germain recommends calling upon the assistance of the Violet Flame Angels for transmuting difficult patterns of disease; the Ring of Blue Flame Angels for expediency; and for clarity of request, to place the petition under light (electric or candle) for seven days before burning. As explained if the electricity or light bulb should fail or the flame extinguishes for any reason, start over again and refine your request. The mental dexterity this process occasionally demands cannot be underestimated!

Before burning your request to the Universe, you can recite a prayer, a decree, or chant mantras. Some people burn incense or sage during the Write-and-Burn process, or sprinkle blessed water or plain table salt before engaging the technique. (This is usually a ring of salt, which represents Spiritual Fire as the Heavenly Father; a ring of blessed cornmeal represents the Creative Force as Mother Earth.) Again, there is no set standard, and the practice is diversified by personal preference and individual belief.

It is also suggested to write release Write-and-Burn requests during cycles of the dark (waning), contracting Moon. Cycles of the waxing, or bright Moon, are said to imbue the energies of expansion and growth to Co-creative processes.

"SILENCE IS THE QUICKENER"

How does one become consciously aware of the desires within the heart? It takes a deep knowing and a great understanding of self. If you must spend time in silence, I advise you to do so. Sometimes silence is the quickener, that which brings awakening. To be awakened is to know what one wants to create, what one wants to live. To be asleep is to be unconscious of that which is driving you. In your world, when you place gasoline within a car, you know what is fueling the engine. Yet, so many lost souls know not what is fueling them, know not what is fueling their constant urgings.

"TO KNOW WITHIN"

It is important to know the fuel that is inside you. What is this fuel? What is this substance, this desire that makes you move farther? To begin to understand requires the purifying fire of the Violet Flame to resolve, transmute and to let go of the past. But how do you begin to identify that fuel, that substance that is truly within you? From the silence, it comes, the Great Mystery of life.[7]

To know within oneself what one is made of is ever important. It is that which you can only identify for yourself. Perhaps one, as example, finds within oneself a great yearning to grow flowers. This, one must do, and with ever completeness to bring this desire forward into its perfect understanding, into its perfect manifestation. One should become aware of what is fueling one's desires; then one is ready to pursue, not only conscious creation, but move into what we call the *state of timelessness*. Now, before I proceed, are there questions?

---

7. The Great Mystery: According to Native American Sioux traditions, the source of Creation, or the Divine is known as *Wakan Tanka*, translated as the Great Spirit or Great Mystery. The term Wakan Tanka also refers to this tribe's cosmology and organization of Creation similar to the Ascended Masters' Spiritual Hierarchy; and all elements of life contain the sacred and aspects of the Divine.

SELF-AWARENESS, PERCEPTION, AND CHOICE

Question: "The path of knowing yourself, the path of examining your own conscience, your own desires, there is no fool-proof method for this, is there?"

There is not one. And yet I wish there were. I desire, even myself, to bring this forward to you, but it does not exist. It is within each of you. It is the Godhead. It is that from which you are part, and connected to all of life.

Answer: "So, that is really a pivotal point in the self-awareness."

And from there comes the Point of Perception in that moment that you are in the canyon, and you make the choice to consciously move to the valley, onward to the hill, onward to the mountain top. Instead of being driven by unconscious yearning, you are driven by consciousness.

Response: "So, truly knowing oneself, what those desires are, what those great yearnings are within oneself and accepting them, fulfilling them, is the only path to freedom."

THE WILL AND SELF-DEVELOPMENT

Realize that you are qualifying them much again as a Ray Force is fueled within you. At times it would seem as though your Free Will is not at all involved in your life, that your life and destiny are under the orchestration of the Great Central Sun and the service of the Rays. Yet, Dear hearts, it is through the development of the Will that one becomes aware of the power of choice and its ability to develop the self. Identifying desire is of the utmost importance.

A SIMPLE EXERCISE

In a simple task, write down five desires that are within you. Perhaps one of these is one you have not yet fulfilled, one you have not yet realized. Yet, look for it in its lower qualification in your life. Now, identify for me but one desire.

Answer: "Yes. One desire. One desire would be to be free of the world's turmoil, but be free of my own turmoil first."

Yet, have you not felt at times the manifestation of peace in your life?

Answer: "Yes."

Has this not come to you as its gift, as the yearning was inside you?

Answer: "Yes, it has."

"HOLD IN PERFECT OUTPICTURING"

To sustain this now to a greater field of understanding, to bring it into greater consciousness, hold it now in its perfect out-picturing of that moment when you felt the peace, when all turmoil was quelled. Hold it as if you would an infant child, precious and endearing, close to your heart. Each day, it will grow in emanation; it will grow in light. And in that minute in your Point of Perception, that instant of understanding, you will have consciously moved your desire from the canyon to the valley, correct?

Answer: "I suppose that symbology would be appropriate."

And onward it moves, its evolution moving forward. Soon the desire that was a small ember in your heart is now as large as a mountain of your being. It becomes you. You and the desire have become as ONE. Peace is carried ever present around you. The external no longer affects the internal creation. The internal creation becomes fueled by desire. Contemplate these, Dear ones, Dear hearts, and I shall return again for discourse upon this. Questions?

Question: "Many times you have asked me at the moment just before waking, 'What do you choose to create this day?' I can remember this as an infinity. Hardly a day has gone by when I have not heard your words. So, this day I would truly choose to create that peace."

So be it.

So, now I shall take my leave, but I shall notify you and return. In that Mighty Christ, may the Violet Flame surround you at all times and bless and keep your work focused to the ONE. Hitaka.

CHAPTER THREE

Divine Destiny

Saint Germain's teachings on Prophecy.

Greetings, beloveds. In that Mighty Christ, I AM Saint Germain, and I request permission to come forward.

Response: "Please, Saint Germain, come forward. You are most welcome."

PROPHECY IS NOT PREDICTION

There is much work among you, Dear ones, and during this time it has been decided that a transmission should come forward to help in direction and to give you instruction for what lies ahead. You see, there is much work — work that has been given to you to bring forward the work of Prophecy, the understanding of Prophecy and the philosophy of Prophecy.[1] It is important in your work to emphasize this always, that this is a work of Prophecy: a work that is to lift humanity, to lift its heart, to lift its understanding of its own creation. You see, Dear ones, Prophecy is given in that nick of time so that a different choice can be made and the Will aligned to a new understanding. Prophecy is not given to provide a view point of the future or to give a prediction. Instead, it is given so that understanding and awareness can be gleaned through the present circumstances and situations that govern Elemental Life.

Those who seek to understand this difference shall place an emphasis upon the spiritual nature of all of life. For it is in this spiritual nature of life that one begins to understand that it is truly the alignment of the thought, the feeling, and the action which brings the creation together as ONE. Prophecy addresses this greater Oneship and understanding that ALL is interconnected, and ALL is ONE.

Dear hearts, Prophecy also brings forward an understanding of compassion and Divine Intervention. You see, different choices, thoughts, and feelings inevitably create a different experience, do they not? We have taught this many times, and those who are beginning to understand the difference between a prediction and a Prophecy will also see that within their choice lies their own future.

MASTERY OF YOUR CO-CREATION

It is important that this, as a message, is carried forward with all the I AM America material. You see, Dear ones, there are those who would trap their consciousness into dates, timelines, and into seeing what next event happens to prove the worthiness of the (I AM America Maps) project. The project has been brought forward to teach about creation, your own Co-creation, and how your thoughts, feelings and actions do indeed create your present experience. This is the idea of Mastery, and it allows one to move forward with a greater understanding of one's world of creations. Through this, suffering is lessened and understanding is gained. You see, Dear ones, through this understanding the foundation of the teaching of Prophecy is built, and one gains control and Mastery over their creations. One does not feel as if he is the victim of the whirl of the winds.[2]

CHOICE CREATES REALITY

You see, life is not created through little whims and circumstances that have blown this way or that way. Indeed, life is created through choices, and it is the action of these choices, the way in which they are applied, that creates the present reality. We have discussed reality before, Dear ones, but reality, as you know, is but a perception of the present moment. This reality can change through that different focus.

---

1. See Appendix 13: *Saint Germain's Teachings on Prophecy.*

2. Victim Mentality: According to Saint Germain, there are no mistakes ever, ever, ever! Consciousness trapped in the dark cavern of the victim is unable to recognize the roles and choices made by the individual that are currently governing life's situations and circumstances. The inability to recognize this predicament places blame on external factors: he did . . . she did . . . they did . . . with a sense of hopelessness sans personal accountability. The teachings of Saint Germain state that this perception is far from truth, and life "is not created through little whims and little circumstances that have blown this way or that . . ." Healing of this state of consciousness is realized through the development of the will and conscious choices. Indeed, the action of our choices creates our present reality.

ALIGNMENT OF THE WILL

Beloved El Morya has brought forward the information of the alignment of the Will to the Divine. It is the alignment of your Will to your Divine Destiny, your heart and your heart's desire, which will bring forth the new Co-creation.

NOT DOOM AND GLOOM, BUT AN EXERCISE IN CO-CREATION

Prophecy also brings forward a vision of hope, light, and the Law of Love for the future. This is the focus of Prophecy and its intention, so that the out-picturing for the future may be a hopeful one, a lighted one, one where human evolution moves forward in balance and harmony. You see, Dear ones, many perceive that Prophecy is brought forward to warn us of doom and gloom that is pending.[3] But indeed, Prophecy is brought forward to bring, in the nick of time, a lighted statement, an understanding that in the present "Now," a creation of choice may come forward. And that choice is up to you. So, when those who contact I AM America ask, "Where shall I go?" "Where shall I move?" "What shall I do?" Remind them that it is all within their choice. This information is brought forward so that they may begin to choose, so that they may begin to understand. The Earth is always changing. It always has and it always will, but Prophecy is brought forward so one may begin to understand that which is changeless within them, their own Divinity.[4] Questions?

Answer: "Not at this time."

---

3. See Appendix J3: *Transforming Archetypal Prophecies of Doom and Gloom.*
4. Divinity: Ascended Master teachings concur that all humans are evolving, and this development is aimed toward individuality, Mastery, Godhood, and inevitably Ascension. This characteristic is innate in all, and held within the spiritual structure of the Unfed Flame in the Eight-sided Cell of Perfection. Essentially all persons reflect their state of Divinity; some are refined and complex; others are simplistic. Each level of innate Divinity is expressed and evolved as infinite aspects and manifestations of the Creator.

A NEW CREATION

Now, I shall proceed with more information for you, Dear one. In the direction of the focus of I AM America during the last Shamballa, a great pouring of energy was put forward into the question of how to proceed correctly with this type of information. We see there are many fish feeding in the frenzy of the pond — many who have now come forward at this time to use this information in an imbalanced way — who are now using this type of information in a way that does not promote harmony, light, and a sense of Brotherhood among ALL. The intention of the I AM America Map has always been so that it can be brought forward to immediately point to the folly of man's creation and to show that a new creation can indeed come forward. This new creation is the New Time, which is held through the light of understanding, and engendered in choice.[5]

THE TIME IS NOW

It would appear that there are those who are looking upon this statement as a way to apply it to a certain directive of their own. Is this coastline correct? Is this day correct? Worry not about such matters. Instead, worry about the message that it carries within itself. The time is NOW, Dear ones. The time is NOW, Dear hearts, to begin to see that you create your own world, your own America, in this moment. It is up to you to decide how the future shall be. It is not up to the Ascended Masters. It is not up to the psychic or the predictor. It is not up to the Prophet or the Prophetess. Indeed, it is up to each and every one of you to begin to create the world that you wish to live in and experience.

HARMONY, LOVE, AND UNDERSTANDING

This is the message of all of the I AM America material, and this has always been our focus and our intention. I AM America, as a focus, has always continued its work to bring harmony, love and understanding so that those who have the eyes to see and

---

5. See Appendix L3: *New Age.*

the ears to hear may now put their hand into action and begin to understand.

THE CHANGE WITHIN

Perhaps it is time that I provide more insight into the eyes that see and the ears that hear. Those eyes that now can see are those that can see what is happening in the world of collective illusion. This created illusion is one where you can see disharmony, continued distrust, continued contentiousness between brother and sister, families, husband and wife, societies, governments. The ear that can hear is awakened to the voice within, who can say, "This is not right!" and is prodded with the voice of conscience. The hand in action is the one who chooses through seeing this, and wishes for a change. This change starts from within, which carries the message outward. Remember the lesson that I gave: as the coal burns as an ember, soon it sparks into the fire.

This is the work that is ahead of you, Dear chelas. The work of Prophecy is to bring change from within. This change begins at the individual level and extends onward. It grows exponentially. This is the Law of Love.[6] Dear hearts, this is the message that I ask for you to share through the work of I AM America. Let us take the emphasis off earthquakes and volcanoes. You see, this was the story given to *awaken* you, to incite you to change. Now, I sense your question.

Response: "The change that you speak of, I understand completely, but average persons do want to know about the next cataclysm."

Then you must remind them of their own Divinity. Remind them that at any time, through their choice, they may change that. It is important for them to understand the nature of their consciousness and the nature of Co-creation. This you have taught many times, have you not?
Answer: "Yes."

GOLDEN CITIES AND COLLECTIVE CONSCIOUSNESS

That thought, feeling and action line up together, and there is the true creation. This is the teaching. It is not about earthquakes. It is not about the next catastrophe. It is about the created reality that you choose. Let us now bring this forward. This is the teaching of the Golden Cities: that if a sufficient number of minds join together, where two or more are gathered the collective consciousness then manifests the Law. This is the basis of the understanding of the Law of One: two merging together as ONE. You see, Dear ones, it is important to bring this teaching forward so that greater understanding might occur. It is not about a changing Earth, it is about the change within humanity. This change is necessary.

Will the Earth go through a change? That is still the large question that remains upon the blank slate known as the Universal Law. Will it indeed go through a shift of the poles? All of these have been presented as different scenarios, different possibilities. It is still up to each of you.

Question: "I understand what you're saying. I recall words to the effect that Benjamin Franklin once said at the Continental Congress, before the signing of the Declaration of Independence. This is not a very good quote, but his words were to the effect that 'Either we all hang together now, or we will hang separately later.' Is this not so?"

THE GREATER ONE

This is very applicable and perceptive upon your part. For, Beloveds, see that it is the time to move into the Universal ONE, into the Time of the Law of Love, and yet it seems to be difficult to move above the little ego, the little self, and the trappings of what one individual wants versus the larger group. In this moment though, it is indeed the larger group that would prefer catastrophe, cataclysms, Earth Changes. It seems to be

---

6. Law of Love: Love is often referred to in the Master teachings as the creative principle of light in action. Love is also the Fourth Jurisdiction, and is based on the sacred tenets of allowing, maintaining (stewardship), and sustainability. The Law of Love states, "If you live (with) love, you will create love." Lord Sananda states, "Love is the first action and energy to come forth in Creation."

the small group that prefers the Law of Love.[7] It is important now to move forward so that those lovers of life move forward as the lesser ONE to become this greater ONE.

DIVINITY AND THE I AM

"Down with death," as I have always said. Down with catastrophe. Down with cataclysm. All effervescent life comes alive through the Law of the Great I AM." This is the Law of Life. It is the Law of the Universe, the I AM.

When it was said in the Bible, "I AM THAT I AM," the truth was known and revealed for all to understand. This I AM is within all of you. It is contained within every particle of life. This is the great interconnection. This is the great knowledge of the ONE, I AM. You see, the focus and the direction of energies through your Divinity are what determine the creation. This is the Law. Proceed with your next question.

Question: "To simplify this for others who may hear this, what you are saying is that the maps are only the probability of the discord that has been present and sustained in the consciousness of this planet?"

PROPHECY, AN AWAKENING TOOL

The maps are brought as prophetic awakening tools. They are there to jar you and waken you from your lethargic sleep, the sleep of the ego, of illusion, and from those who would fear. The maps are brought to awaken you to your Divinity, for you to see who you truly are. Do you understand?

Question: "Yes, but I ask you this so that those listening might understand. And so, in a sense, our choices, as you have started this discourse with, are the determining factors of whether we are together or separate, or whether we ignore our Divinity, and that will perpetuate our perception of separateness."

---

7. See Appendix K3: *Group Mind.*

YOUR EARTH CONNECTION

To believe in a worrying Earth, a diseased Earth and an Earth in need of purification is to also believe that you are not connected to this Earth. As you see, the Law demonstrates that you are indeed connected. It is only through your misperception that you would see the need that you are not as ONE united — that you are not as ONE united in the Great Law of Love. Through your thoughts, your feelings and your actions, the present circumstances and situations can always be re-created, can they not?

Answer: "Yes, very true."

"GOD WITHIN YOU"

And it is that Point of Perception where one begins to understand that he is the Co-creator of his experience, that he is the one in charge. (Master) K. H. has said this is the time of the death of the guru, and indeed it is. There are those who give their power away aimlessly and fruitlessly to others; to other's dreams, schemes and plans. Create within yourself your own dream, your own plan, and from there unite with your Brother … from your own vision, unite with your Brother. This is a true unity of consciousness, not one that is enforced upon another, but a true unity that is engendered in freedom. If you have trouble creating your own identity and your own understanding of the God within you, call forth the Violet Flame.

CUT THE CORDS OF SHAME AND DOUBT

Sometimes there are those who are greatly hindered by the results of other lifetimes and by the results of shame, doubt and anxieties imposed upon them by others. Cut those cords free by the use of the Violet Flame of Mercy and Forgiveness. A compassion will then awaken within you, and your consciousness will be set free.

USE OF THE VIOLET FLAME

It is through use of the Violet Flame that mankind shall truly become free. That is why we invoke its presence before every discourse. The Violet Flame will free your consciousness and allow your own Divinity, the pure God I AM, to come forward within you. Allow compassion and forgiveness to be carried within you where you walk, talk and act, and in the way you feel. This is most important at this time. You see, Dear ones, Dear hearts, there is much suffering upon the Earth. It is suffering that (often) creates even more suffering, as Master K. H. says, "fueled by the fires of deception, fueled by the fires of illusion."

How else do we break such a spell of this captive illusion but by calling forth the Violet Flame? There you are united with the Great I AM. There you are united as ONE with all of life. The Violet Flame affirms again and again that *life is for life.*

> "Violet Flame, COME ALIVE.
> Violet Flame, I AM."

Questions?

Question: "In my love and understanding of you as a teacher, a friend and a Brother, it is still the interpretive process that the rest of humanity takes, with your words and your creation, going forward into this world. Most things that you say, I completely understand. Some, I do not. When I ask questions, it's mostly for the reader or listener of the future."

This is understood.

Question: "It is impressed upon me that this illusion gains momentum and ebbs and flows in different directions. Yet, the unity, the harmony, the divinity that is in ALL things, down to the smallest cell, even in any creature and the smallest particle of any element that is Divinity, is continuous. This I can perceive, see and understand. Many have not a clue when I discuss this with them, either on the phone or in person. Many feel that only certain things are worthy of this Divinity, and yet how could God or Source give anything but Source?"

SIMPLICITY

It is important to keep things simple and in their simplest context. Then one begins to understand through simple gestures and simple motions. When you were a small child, did you not feel love through the gentle touch of your mother's hand? Did you not feel nourishment by a simple bowl of grains? Did you not feel comfort through a simple blanket? Did you not feel joy through the simple toy? Dear one, take this approach and this shall assist you in all understanding and in helping those who inquire. Always keep it simple, Dear one. Always keep it simple.

Answer: "I understand. I will. I thank you for your guidance, your help and your love."

Now, I would like to proceed with more general information in the running of your daily activities.

Response: "Please continue."

OVERCOME THE OLD CONSCIOUSNESS

As I have said before, there will be two more people who shall be brought to you. It will be through their adherence to the Violet Flame that you will discover who they are, but they will identify themselves to you. This is a vibration, you understand. These energies are being poured into the work at I AM America. One of these offices (roles) is now to be filled. It is important, as a group consciousness, that you unite on a weekly basis and use the Violet Flame. This will help any situation or circumstance with which you are dealing — financial issues, harmony issues, expansion issues. You see, Dear ones, the Violet Flame removes the obstacles, it removes any hindrances that you are feeling. When you encounter an obstacle, realize that it is the old consciousness that is now rearing its ugly head. This is not the time to draw out the sword and to fight it. It is the time to accept and understand that this is an old consciousness, an old creation. It is time to embrace it as you would your Brother or your Sister, and tell it that its time is now past and that a New Day has come forward, a new consciousness, and this new consciousness will now have its say. This is done through the use of the

Violet Flame. This gives energy to the new consciousness, to the new creation. Do you understand?

Answer: "Yes. So in the creation that we choose as a group, we may decree the Violet Flame into that as life."

When you pour the energy into your creations, does this not work?

Answer: "Yes."

THE NEW CREATION

That is why I have suggested this technique. It is one of the easiest and readily available for you to use. If you would like to use it again, I suggest it. If you would like to visualize through out-picturing, this will work, too. You see, it is the new creation that is coming forward. These stumbling blocks are remnants of the old creation. In the same way that the I AM America Map shows devastated coastlines and yet wondrous Golden Cities, there is the old creation and the new creation. Let the new creation come alive, for that is where the heart of humanity lies, in the new and in the good. Let the new creation come alive, for this is the Age of the ONE, Unana.

Now, with this continuous focus on a weekly basis within your office (role), you will begin to note a shift within the energies, and a growing. It is important to hold this focus and to see that the work you bring forward, while it is carried out with business-like precision, is indeed spiritual work and is built upon the Law of Love. Let this harmony of the ONE prevail.

Response: "As you wish."

A NEW AGE

Questions?

Question: "In the I AM America Map, you're saying the old creation that is the changed coastlines, is it not?"

This is indeed. This is the old creation of destruction, of an eye-for-an-eye and a tooth-for-a-tooth.

Question: "And this has been the direction humanity has been headed into?"

This is indeed, Dear one.

Question: "However, through Grace, humanity is now being redirected into the New Age of Harmony, that Golden Age, and the centers of these are the Golden Cities?"

Where one understands that one's own creation, through thought, feeling, action and the alignment of the Will to the Divine allows a New Day to move forward, so be it.

Response: "So be it."

And now, Dear hearts, if there are no longer any questions, I shall depart.

Question: "I have only one. I know that it takes energy and focus to build up the transmission to come into our density. If there is anything that you would need for us to do to make that easier or more frequent?"

All is within its Divine Plan. All is within its Divine Timing. Listen again to this discourse, and you will gain a deeper understanding.

Answer: Thank you for coming.

In that Mighty Christ, may the light now shine upon the office of I AM America, and may it always be at peace and at onement with humanity. May its work move forward in the blessing of the ONE. Hitaka.

Saint Germain gradually leaves, and as he leaves he directs a Violet Ray from the palm of his hand, and imbues the sound vibration of HUE.

CHAPTER FOUR

Map of the Ancients

❧

Lord Macaw presents a map of
Mu, Lemuria, Rama, and Atlantis.

Greetings, beloved chelas. In that Mighty Christ, I AM Saint Germain, and I request permission to come forward.

Response: "Please, Saint Germain, you are most welcome. Come forward."

The work of the Violet Flame is blazing now across this planet. Let it manifest Divine Compassion for all who have the eyes to see and the ears to hear. Dear ones, it is important that we proceed with this work so that you will begin to develop a greater understanding of what has been given to you to share with others. You see, Dear ones, the work of the Rays is indeed very important, so that it can be understood completely.

DIVINE INTERVENTION OF THE GOLDEN CITIES

If there is a science, it is the science of the Rays that will bring together a completion and understanding of the Golden City Vortices. In the Golden City structures, one will begin to understand how the Rays vibrate and pulsate within a Vortex and their utilization. It is most important that all is understood that they can be utilized at this time. You see, Dear hearts and Dear ones, Dear chelas, it is important to see at this Time of Great Change that the Golden City Vortices will bring about a Divine Intervention. It is through this Divine Intervention that humanity will be accelerated into a new understanding. This new understanding is where we place our focus and where we place that great momentum of the Violet Ray.

THE GOLDEN AGE

When we instruct you in the use of the Violet Ray, it is for one purpose only — to bring purification to you so that you understand how to move into the New Times. This acceleration, upon the Earth Plane and Planet, is being brought about to bring a collective gathering of humanity to one Point of Perception. It is through this, through conscience application of the law of the Violet Flame, that we shall gather this consciousness, or Greater Mind, to an understanding that the Golden Age does indeed exist and can be utilized for all who are ready. In this great acceleration, it is our hope that through a greater understanding and opening of the Heart of Divine Love that one will be drawn to understand the consciousness of Unana.

UNANA

It is most important for those who seek the consciousness of Unana to move and live in Golden Cities, for this is where the first understanding of the concept can be brought to a physical level — to gain a physical demonstration.

PHYSICAL DEMONSTRATION

It is important, you see, for the human to have physical demonstration of all the spiritual laws at work, particularly in this time. You see, beloveds and Dear ones, it is important for the human who lives in the world of duality to understand that physical demonstration is very important. It is the true path of understanding, and all sense of reason is then satisfied.[1] Among

---

1. Sense of Reason: The use of this term is a reference to the human mind and its primary existence as a blank slate—tabula rasa. This radical idea was in direct contrast to seventeenth-century Christian thinking. The philosopher John Locke (1632–1704) theorized that the human mind is influenced by knowledge that is determined by experience, "derived by sense perception." He also postulated that the mind, by virtue of its emptiness, is shaped by experience, sensations, and reflection as the source of all of our ideas. Locke and fellow philosopher Joseph Addison (1672–1719) paved the way for contemporary enlightened thinking, a reprieve from the Calvinistic doctrines of original sin and innate human depravity. As consciousness evolved through the eighteenth century, humanity embraced the Free Will and the salvation and goodness of man alongside our ability to evolve.

the human, there is always the doubt and the suspicion as to whether this is for real — does it really exist? When it is shown through physical demonstration, one begins to understand about the true reality and the true spiritual nature of all of life, and where one truly is from and is returning to.

BEGIN WITH HISTORY

In the quest for spiritual knowledge, one must begin to study history — the history of all humanity. Then one can begin to understand why this time is so important. As we have taught before, each has a piece of the puzzle and each place in time carries a piece of the puzzle? This builds a base of knowledge like the great pyramid of Solomon, so that it is understood in its greater glory.[2] The search for this greater knowledge and a greater understanding of history is where we shall begin our discourse for the day.

I have brought with me another great being whom I consider to be a teacher, even to myself. Lord Meru, as he is known by you, is also known as Lord Macaw.[3] Lord Macaw was the great tribal lord who instigated the energy and the dispensation of Ameru, which, you know in your history to be the Land of the Plumed Serpent.[4, 5]

It is important for you to understand America and its great destiny. In doing so, you will gain a greater understanding of this most prophetic time and the work of the Rays arcing from the Great Central Sun. You will then have a greater working knowledge of how all things come together in that great puzzle. So, without further delay, unless there are questions, I shall introduce Lord Macaw.

Response: "No, (questions) please continue."

Greetings, students, chelas, I AM Lord Macaw, known as Lord Meru, and I ask permission to come forward.

"Please, come forward. You are most welcome."

HUMANITY'S SPIRITUAL EVOLUTION

I have shared technology through this work before. I have shown the work of the archtometer, or that which I call the Earth Gyroscope. I have shared other inventions, too. But it has been deemed at this time that this (archtometer) technology shall be withheld for now. You see, it is more important that emphasis be placed upon spiritual evolution. Humanity is not ready, and today, perhaps through this discourse, you will begin

---

Thomas Paine (1737–1809) was best known for his revolutionary pamphlet *Common Sense*. Paine, an avid supporter of the French Revolution, narrowly escaped execution while imprisoned in France in 1794. His ideas presented in the Age of Reason estranged him from the institutionalized religions of the day, and he called for the "free rational inquiry" into all subjects, especially religion.[2] He is quoted as saying, "I do not believe in the creed professed by the Jewish Church, by the Roman Church, by the Turkish Church, by the Protestant Church, nor by any church that I know of. My own mind is my own church."

As humanity evolves through the New Times and we embrace our destiny through Co-creation, our church of mind evolves to Divine Mastery.

2. See Appendix M3: *The Great Triangle (Pyramid) of Solomon*.

3. See Appendix N3: *Lord Meru*.

4. Some esoteric historians refer to Ameru as Ameru—the Incan Christ, Quetzalcoatl. From Ameru comes the word *America*, and, according to Manly P. Hall, "Ameruca is literally translated 'Land of the Plumed Serpent.'" The ancient peoples of America were known as the *Red Children of the Sun* and worshipped Quetzalcoatl, a prophet of the Christ Consciousness, a messenger from our solar Sun.

5. Ameru and the Right-hand Path: The provenance of Ameruca—the Land of the Plumed Serpent—is the lost history of Mu, Lemuria, and Atlantis. The Plumed Serpent metaphorically represents the developed Chakra System of the Divine God-man, the Ascended Masters' HU-man. The plume of light atop the head is the developed crown chakra, and the

serpent's coils represent the mature Kundalini system, or human energy system comprised of seven chakras. It is claimed that many Lemurians and Atlanteans had the advanced capacity to function in both the Fourth and Fifth Dimension as Spiritual Masters and Shamans where an Alchemical and spiritual battle ensued: the Left-Hand Path versus the Right-Hand Path. Spiritual development at this level of consciousness endows power over the Elemental Kingdom, and the unascended Spiritual Master is often pitted between both malevolent Black Magic and constructive White Magic. (Editor's Note: These are the prominent abilities experienced by individuals who have achieved the Tenth Pyramid of Consciousness in HU-man development. For more information, see the *Great Triangle of Solomon*.)

According to Theosophical history, the Lemurian and Atlantean epochs overlap and it is alleged that the lands of Lemuria, also known as Shalmali, existed in the Indian and Southern Pacific Oceans and included the continent of Australia. Lemuria is the remaining culture and civilization of Mu—an expansive continent that once spanned the entire present-day Pacific Ocean. Some esoteric writers place the destruction of Mu around the year 30,000 BC; others place its demise millions of years ago. The apparent discrepancy of these timelines is likely due to two different interpretations of the Cycle of the Yugas—large recurring periods of time employed in the Hindu timekeeping system. The older classical method of calculation literally applies time spans of millions of years; the contemporary method, revealed in 1894, applies cycles that are much shorter.

to understand why it is more important to place this emphasis upon the spiritual development of self. As you have known and have been taught by the inner dialogue, on which I place great emphasis, I have been here before. I have had many previous embodiments upon the Earth Plane and Planet; therefore, I understand the great trials and tribulations that are before humanity. It is a time of the shaking of the Earth, you see, beloveds. It is also a time of the shaking of the inner self.

THE INNER DIALOGUE

Let us talk now about the inner dialogue and the importance of such. Only within the realms of self can truth be revealed at a level where it is understood and applied. When truth is enforced from the outer, it functions under the law of suspect, or, as Saint Germain has said, under the doubt and skepticism of the ego. But inner dialogue must be established between the student and the I AM Presence, the higher-self, or the spirit of God, which is engendered within all. It is through this connection that truth is strengthened through the bonds of love. I know this has been explained to you many times before, but it is important to understand that this is a process that requires patience, love and understanding.

CHELA AND MASTER TEACHER

It is through this great awakening that the energies of the Kundalini and the Tao are then awakened and the knowledge of the ever present ONE is acquired. During this time, the chela comes under the magnetism, the tutelage, of a Master Teacher. The Master Teacher works upon a Ray Force that is most identified within a Kundalini system of that chela. This is of great importance, and, again, one would naturally ask why it is that only one Ray Force is identified.

As I explain to you this planetary history, you will begin to understand why one identified Ray Force is important and is at the base of all beginning of true knowledge and understanding. You see, to take the body at the cellular level, and lift it from doubt, suspicion and ego, requires adherence to the truth. It requires a development of true spiritual knowledge and understanding. But it also requires respect for the laws that exist upon this Earthly Realm. As you have understood it, it is the blending of the Four Pillars of knowledge that bring forth a clearer understanding. These are indeed incremental steps in understanding the ONE.

Adherence to the inner dialogue is most important, to keep it open, to foster its growth and to gain an awareness and an understanding. Now, let us take a moment of silence — you and I.

THE GREAT CENTRAL SUN

Now, let us begin. As you have understood, there is the work of the Great Central Sun. It is the center or the heartbeat, the pulse of this planet. It determines life as it exists throughout these planetary schemes, and, yes, there are other planetary schemes that vibrate to this great central heart.[6]

QUETZALCOATL CONSCIOUSNESS

This heart enters, as has been identified to you, into the middle which is known as the United States. It is because this is a very important location, and at this time it will become a center for the understanding of the Land of the Plumed Serpent. When I speak of the Land of the Plumed Serpent, I AM speaking of those who understand the knowledge of the Kundalini and who will bring it into a greater knowledge of Love, Wisdom, and Power. This was the teaching I brought forward in that time known as Quetzalcoatl (Consciousness).

This was a teaching that was spread throughout all of South America and Central America and was understood completely for the opening of the Third Eye. But it was indeed diluted in North America and was never brought to its fullest understanding; therefore, it is a work that is incomplete. But it was deemed by the Spiritual Hierarchy that it would be completed within this time through the work of the Golden Cities, and that each of them will bring an understanding of the Kundalini forces that exist within each of you individually, and also through love, wisdom, and true balanced power. Did I not teach you about balanced power?

---

6. See Appendix Y3: *The Lineage of the Galactic Suns.*

Answer: "Many times over."

THE INDIVIDUALIZED RAY FORCE

(This teaching) is about the understanding of the flow of energy, as it exists throughout the human — the flow of energy that exists in your body and upon Mother Earth.

Now, we shall talk about a flow of energy that has existed since time immemorial, and it is important for you to understand how this flow extends from the Great Central Sun and to this Earth — this entity being you know as Babajeran)Mother Earth). Each of the Ray Forces is the individualized presence of the source of the ONE. It never separates away from the ONE, yet it is an expression of the ONE. It individualizes so that the work and the service of the ONE can bring a flow and a balance. Perhaps these types of questions are not asked yet, but will be asked in the continuation of the process.

SOUND AND LIGHT

Each Ray Force identifies with sound and with light. Of course, sound and light are the beginning of all of life in a dual form; therefore, in resonating to a higher dimension and into another understanding, it is important again that sound and light be utilized.

TECHNOLOGY

These are the laws that shall set you free. They are the Laws of Spiritual Liberation. Technology cannot set men free, but only encumber him in a greater sense — encumber them to be dependent upon others. Do you understand?

BREATH AND ETHEREAL ENERGIES

Answer: "Yes, technology is the external use of the law we are talking about and not the internal use of the law."

It is through the work of the breath, the taking in of life force, prahna, orgone, the many names it has been called — the ONE. Integration of light and sound occurs within the physical cells. It has already been proven by your science that it is through oxidation processes within the cell that essential nutrients are carried to the body, but it is through breath that a higher ethereal substance is brought into the body, united with the Kundalini. It raises the energy to completion and opens the Third Eye.

Through the opening of the Third Eye, one begins to receive the inner instruction that is essential for completion of the inner dialogue, for the completion of the Godhead, to the understanding of the Divine Being that exists within the human. This brings one into the knowledge of many — the sages and the seers, who have been considered to be the gods of this Earth, yet their presence is a natural evolution that comes forward. This has been the orchestration of the Ray Forces and the understanding of their use.[7]

MASCULINE AND FEMININE

Now, I shall proceed. The Ray Forces are arcing their energies from this Great Central Sun, through the Sun of your universe. This Sun, as you understand, is a dual Sun, much as your Moon is a dual force. Your Moon has its waning and waxing cycles, and so does the Sun. This, of course, is not yet understood or developed, but there are waning and waxing cycles of the Sun — a feminine side and a masculine side. During the course of the masculine side, energy is built and taken in. During the course of the waning side, energy is released and purified in the same way that the Chakra System works, taking energy and then releasing it.

"INTAKE AND OUTTAKE"

This is the basic concept of the Ray Force and the way in which it works within the body. It is as simple as the breath you take in and release. This is the law of understanding a Ray Force. It pulsates in the body in the same way as a time of taking in and a time of releasing. It is the same way that the body and its physiology works, a time of taking in the energies of Mother Earth and a time of releasing these energies. This is an immutable law that exists throughout all of creation. Of intake and outtake, it is mirrored in many ways throughout

---

7. See Appendix R3: *The Four Great Yugas*.

your system. But the Ray Forces work through self in such a manner that there is a most opportune time to take in a Ray Force and a most opportune time to purify a Ray Force. Now, is this understood?[8]

Answer: "Yes, everything has a cycle."

SOLAR INFLUENCE

All has a cycle, as beloved Kuan Yin has instructed. There is that time of the swing of the pendulum — a time when it goes to the right, when it hits the center balance, and then when it swings to the left. These are all the rules and the laws. Certain Rayces of individuals, beings of individuals, have had their cause and effect upon this Earth Plane through the course of the waxing and the waning of solar or Ray influences.[9] These solar influences upon the Ray do indeed affect events of history upon this Earth. They control the weather patterns, the flow of economics and all that happens upon the Earth — the birth of an adept, the death of a criminal. These events affect all things, and need to be understood to achieve a greater understanding of the Land of the Plumed Serpent.

"A UNITY OF PEOPLE"

Ameru means "a unity of people," — a unity of people who can work together in cooperation and harmony, through an understanding of these higher laws. To translate it further at this point may only bring confusion, so let us keep it now in

a simple context. It is a cooperation of the law that I have just explained. Is this understood?

Answer: "That cooperation would be based upon agreement, though."

"ONE THROUGH SIX"

As always, it is through simplicity — through these Laws of Simplicity — where there is total agreement of the Will to such. Each of these Ray Forces came forward in their purity — one through six arcing their energies upon the Earth from a Sun in its most exalted position, that of building a masculine force to the core of your Earth and radiating from the great heart. This caused an emanation back to the universe of the Great Central Sun creating within itself a perfect ecosystem. Do you understand?

Answer: "Yes, because it would create balance."

THE LORDS OF SATURN

This balance creates unity, cooperation and ultimate beauty. Concerning the First Ray (let us deal not with one through six, for this brings great confusion.) Let us approach it from planetary systems so it can be understood. Those first pitris, (stars or seeds), also known as your great lords, came first from that planet known as Saturn. They had the diligence to break through the atmosphere, to give their greater understanding of this Law of Beauty. They settled into that area known today as India, but at that time it was known as the Land of Rama.[10] Questions?

Question: "Would this be the blue race?"

Yes, but let us not attach a color to this. Let us not confuse. Indeed, they carried the essence of that vibration. Perhaps vibration would be the better way to bring an understanding. But it was indeed the planet Saturn comingling with the dual

---

8. See Appendix S3: *Lord Meru's Prophecies and Teachings on the Rays.*

9. The Solar Cycle: Astronomers theorize that the Sun cycles through periods of intense sunspots, solar flares, and coronal mass ejections to minimal solar activity. This cycle of the Sun's movement rises and falls in eleven-year cycles, which correlates to the Sun's magnetic field flipping its polarity. Subsequently, it takes twenty-two years for a full solar cycle comprising both activity and inactivity. Scientists have coined the phrase Solar Maximum to describe the increase in solar movement that is thought to be linked to the Sun's changing magnetic fields. As the Sun cycles halfway through the eleven-year cycles, Sun activity quells, and then builds to start a new cycle. Since 1610, scientists have observed sunspots and in 1849 began to archive their numbers in peaks, (Solar Maximum: Yang, or masculine cycles), and valleys (Solar Minimum: Yin, or feminine cycles). Today, NASA researchers believe the cycles of the Sun are driven by a Great Conveyor Belt and the current cycle of the Sun —Solar Cycle 25— peaks in the year 2022.

10. See Appendix Q3: *Land of Rama.*

forces of the Sun and the Great Central Sun to bring about the vibration. Does that help to bring understanding?

Answer: "Yes, but what you're saying is that Saturn is inhabited."

All planets have been inhabited, but at this moment the life that we must deal with is here on Earth, here on beloved Babajeran (Mother Earth). This is the schoolroom through which you are learning, and this is where our focus shall remain. This is what you must deal with. Your Ascension will not be made from the planet Saturn. Your Ascension will be made from this position. Let us keep our focus upon what must be done. I give this so you will glean understanding and a sense of true history.

LORDS OF JUPITER

The Second Ray came from that which is known in your time as Jupiter, but it was also known as Brihaspati. This was the planet that brought another group, pitris, or soul force to the Earth. They settled into an area now known as the island of Japan. But at that time it was a greater continent.[11]

Now, it is important that we begin to look at this geography and how it once existed, so that you will understand how these two major influences have grown upon this Earth. I asked you before, do you trust me?

Answer: "Yes."

This is important, for my energy must now enter yours to direct you in the drawing of these two areas, as they once looked.

Response: "Yes, and don't forget, you can just show me."

It is more important that you have this experience. It is more important that there be an understanding that develops between you and me.

---

11. See Appendix O3: *The Map of the Ancients*.

PRIMORDIAL INDIA AND THE CONINUOUS DISK

Let us first look at the continent that once was India. You see, at one time the Earth was one continuous disk that floated over one continuous water. It followed always, in the Light of God that never fails, that the light of the Sun was directed by the Rays of the Great Central Sun. But it was broken apart through several influences that we shall not discuss in this dialogue; yet, we shall look now at the entering of this time so that it can be understood for your purpose. Present-day India was once connected to the same continent that was Asia. It was, as you can see, connected more to the Eastern side. Let us draw this connection.

He is now walking over to you. He is very close to you.

Let us draw this now, together. Correct that one last area. It is inaccurate. Let us go over this one more time. There will be a few minor corrections.

Question: "Is that better?"

LANDS OF JAPAN

We are complete. We shall continue with the entry of the Ray Force from Jupiter, which is in the area of Japan. But, as you see, we have extended the lands of Japan, which extend to present-day Alaska.

Response: "Oh, Yes."

LEMURIA

Now, let us draw this extension together. There are two bay areas: one to the North, and one to the South, that follows the North almost exactly. This was caused through earth movement, then in a developmental stage. Underneath this is an old, prehistoric tectonic plate.[12] Through the teachings of these

---

12. Lord Meru refers to this geological plate, which is in reference to the Pacific Plate, as an oceanic tectonic plate beneath the Pacific Ocean. Esoteric historians theorize that the Pacific Plate, through periodic geologic upheaval and Earth Changes formed the submerged lost continent of

two Ray Forces came the beginning of a land known a Mu or Lemuria.[13]

ANCIENT SHAMBALLA

Within the center of this continent, was a mountain range. This mountain range in the center was where the creation of the first ancient city of Shamballa existed. These two Ray Forces, in their completion and understanding, developed a large sense of true spiritual knowledge, which is still upon this planet today. This is where some of the greatest leaps in human evolution occurred, in the understanding brought forth through these two Ray Forces. There is also a time that existed prior to these civilizations. Is this understood?

Answer: "Yes."

We are not inquiring into that history as of yet, and for good reason, for it must be understood how these Ray Forces have worked together to bring about the current situation.

VENUS' GREAT PURPOSE

Simultaneously, two Ray Forces, or almost three, came to assist these civilizations that existed — civilizations from the Moon, from Mercury, and from Venus came simultaneously.[14] But, you see, Venus was not in its completion, for it was indeed a foreign planet that came directly from the heart of the Logos, the Great Central Sun, to restore a purity to the Ray Forces. This I hope to give in detailed history, was a time of almost near destruction of the Earth, had it not been for Venus. This happened in your own twentieth century, and it was the completion of the energies of Venus that allowed the implementation of the plan of the Golden Cities, but let us not rush into that at this moment, but keep it for reference and questions.

Lemuria. Some Earth Changes theories claim Pole Shifts caused entire continents to rise or fall due to Tectonic Plate Theory.

13. See Appendix P3: *Lemuria*.

14. See Appendix T3: *The Colonization of the Earth as Taught by Lord Meru*.

THE MOON AND MERCURY

Let us now understand how the Ray Forces of the Moon were brought, and the Ray Forces of Mercury. You see, they worked together simultaneously and brought great civilizations into Africa and to the center of the Sahara Desert, as it is now known — and another civilization into South America at that time, which would be the area of Central America.

Now, let us draw this continental shape. South America was closely conjoined with that of Africa. Let us unite these two. Are we complete?

Answer: "Yes."

THE FEMININE

You can see what is known today as Cuba. But the greater and lesser Antilles were a complete land mass, and it was in the center of this land mass where the civilization of Quetzalcoatl appeared. This civilization was brought through the sponsorship of the Moon force, and its effect was indeed feminine.

A CRADLE OF KNOWLEDGE

In Africa, in that area that was once known as Sahara, a great cradle developed. Those there vibrated to what is known as the Green Ray, or the Ray of Mercury, and knowledge was brought into an understanding that could be outwardly applied. Civilizations developed there that had a greater understanding of writing, a greater understanding of communication at telepathic levels, and a greater understanding of the healing arts. This carried an influence into the creation of your Christian Orthodox Church.

AUSTRALIA

Now, the final Ray Force is that of the Sixth Ray — a devotional force that split itself apart upon entry into your system. At that time, it was hoped that the Ray Force could be brought through the waning aspect of the Sun, and this indeed happened, which gave it a more feminine effect. And two pitris,[15] or Star seeds (great Lords), developed in what is now known as Australia. Are we ready to proceed?

Answer: "We are ready to proceed."

THE RAYS DEVELOP AND MERGE

Near what is known as your Northern Sea, close to the present-day North Pole, but more toward the side of Russia and the islands therein, there was an extension of the continent, which was the Sixth Ray merging with the influences of the Ray of Mercury, the Sixth Ray being a Ray that comes from Mars. Venus brought forth an emanation, and the great lovers of beauty and cooperation also merged along this line with the Moon. Some sporadic groups also developed along Ray influences. Is this understood?

Answer: "Yes."

"WAXING AND WANING"

Lovers of beauty also influenced those groups of the Moon, while Venus influenced those groups of Mercury. So, a dual influence was brought about, this happening, again, through the course of a waxing and a waning solar force, which creates the solar flares. They influenced the great turning of the waxing or the waning Moon. At some point in your history, it will be understood how to chart the waxing and the waning Sun. And this will bring a greater understanding to all, of planetary knowledge upon the Earth and an understanding and deepening of astrological systems.

---

15. Derived from the Sanskrit word *pitr*, Pitris is a generic word in Theosophical terminology and Ascended Master teachings for any progenitor of the human race. This includes the lost civilizations of Mu, Lemuria, and Atlantis, and Pitris are considered the ancestors of human consciousness who directed the evolution of mankind through the root-races and sub-races by first incarnating in the astral plane of Earth, and later in physical bodies.

"TWO TIMES THREE"

Before I proceed, it is important that we sketch in the continents. It is important to look at North America and its influence under the Lords of Venus. As you see, Australia has always, and will continue to be, a free-floating continent. Its work shall be known throughout the Golden Age, and it shall become a capstone of understanding. It was the work of these six Rays conjoining that brought together one of the highest levels of harmony the Earth has yet seen — each in purity, or Sattva, Tao or balance, each a perfect dual force of the Christ, two times three — working in steady and complete harmony. Then Earth entered into a new cycle. But before we speak of that new cycle (the Seventh Ray), let us talk about the Earth and how it looked at that time.

HARMONY AND THE ANCIENT EARTH

Plants existed in complete harmony with the Mineral Kingdom. There were very few mammals in existence, except the human. A few birds were here, in a most colorful variety, along with several animals that had been brought as companions. Several of the great companions are still companions to the humans today. These are typical cats, dogs and horses, and a certain breed of ox. These were all brought to lift the burden of the human and to develop understanding of true friendship. Several fishes existed, but primarily the whale and the dolphin.[16]

At that time, all humans existed on a purely vegetarian diet. This brought simplicity, and allowed the Kundalini system to develop and grow. Nuts, grains, and fruits were collected after their complete maturation. All cooperated in complete harmony with one another.

FOODS AND RAY FORCES

Insects, including butterflies and bees, were brought through the Lords of Venus. Bees collected honey, which allowed humans an expanded diet and provided a capacity for illumination.

---

16. See Appendix U3: *Flora and Fauna of the Ancient Lands of the Plumed Serpent.*

Each of the foods was eaten with the understanding of its association and affiliation with the Ray Force. Each provided an understanding of spiritual knowledge and the demonstration of the physical laws of cooperation that sustain a land of great beauty and harmony.

ENTRANCE OF THE SEVENTH RAY

As all things must change, this indeed changed through the explosive side of a planet known as Uranus, which is indeed a dark side of Saturn. The explosion came forward arcing with tremendous force through the Great Central Sun. Those (Lords) of the other Rays asked if it could be held back. But it was deemed that it would fit into the purpose of all and would later bring even greater glory and understanding to consciousness and the great and ONE mind.

Its entry, which is known as the Seventh Ray, came into the lands that are known today as Europe. Now, let us draw Europe as it existed at that time. As you see, there was one great inland sea, which looked almost like an artist's palette, and which contained, within it, one singular island. This sea is your present-day Atlantic Ocean.

"AN IRREVERENT FORCE"

This Ray Force brought with it many new and explosive ideas. It brought us an almost irreverent force. It brought rebellion and a celebration of shadow (hidden or occluded)knowledge. When I say shadow, it is in reference to a feminine and deeper knowledge. It brought a fall to the Earth — a fall from the unfettered Time of Cooperation and paternal (inherited) understanding of the source of the Great Central Sun, and in that window it created explosive opportunity. Many other life streams from galaxies yet unheard of in this Earth gained entry as a soul force. This brought a true comingling of the Rays, but races began to develop wars between one another. The time of Lemuria was broken, and slaves were then taken.

One was distinguished within a system of caste. You were either free or you were a slave. Of animals that existed, a few were interbred genetically, through technologies that were brought to a point at which they were bred for sacrificial and religious use and for eating.

SHAMBALLA'S DOORS ARE CLOSED

That brought about a downfall of the Kundalini forces and a closing of the Third Eye and its use. It was deemed by those in the higher octaves that Shamballa should be closed, and eventually, after several rebuildings, its doors were closed forever to those who could not reach it through the inner dialogue.

THE ENTRANCE OF SAINT GERMAIN

New laws were set upon the Earth that only those — through the inner dialogue, once it was developed — would be deemed worthy to acess the true spiritual heavens. You see, this great development of technology was foreign to the Earth and its inhabitants, and it brought about an arresting of the true nature of the being. But through the process of genetic interbreeding, eventually this Ray Force was brought to a greater understanding. Then a great Master, known as the wonder man of Europe, came forward in sponsorship of the Ray's higher vibration.

This Master you now know as Saint Germain. It is through the work of Saint Germain and the Violet Flame, when the flame is integrated through the inner dialogue, that one can force one's vibration through this arrested development, and can find the true path.

THE VIOLET RAY

Now one may begin to understand the migration and evolution of consciousness. It has been through this warrior force, this explosive force of the Violet Ray, which has taken nearly two thousand years to manifest, to bring it and to tame it unto an understanding for evolution.[17] It has set the evolution of the Earth back by over ten thousand years. But, again, I deem it as such that it was brought for a greater union and a greater understanding yet to be revealed. Now, are there questions?

---

17. See Appendix V3: *Lord Meru's History of the Violet Ray.*

Question: "Yes, about the Violet Ray that we are now discussing . . ."

Proceed.

Question: "In its simplest form, we always understand the Violet Ray as something of transmutation. In this expanded explanation you're giving to us, it seems like it's more of an integration."

UNITY CONSCIOUSNESS AND COMPASSION

It brings integration and purification to cooperation, and harmony to the inner dialogue. In the beginning, this Ray Force forced man away from God and into structures and organizations of man, which did not serve the true need and the true understanding. But it is through the uniting of all as ONE, the consciousness of Unana, that mankind can proceed back upon the track to where it must go and toward its Divine Destiny.

Question: "So, what you're saying is that there was a harmony that existed for the first six Rays and that it took a time period of assimilation, and the coming of the Seventh Ray, which has now gone through a similar assimilation period — to create a purification and a harmonization of all Seven Rays. Is this correct?"

This is so — and ultimately Divine Compassion is the end result. It is through compassion that one begins to integrate and understand this explosive force that brought the development of ego above the true spiritual identity.

Response: "Oh, I see, so identity of the self superseded the identity of the unity."

This is so, but it did not serve together as ONE. Indeed, it did seem to slow the process of evolution, yet, in the greater harmony and understanding, it fit together as ONE.

Response: "So, once again, the model of the piece of the puzzle, the ego, does exist to create the borderlines for the puzzle piece, yet it still belongs to the greater picture."

Yes, indeed, it serves Unana. Are there further questions?

Answer: "Not at this time."

Then. I shall take my leave and will return for further instruction. Now, I turn the floor to that wonder man of the Violet Ray, beloved Saint Germain.

Response: "Thank you."

MASTERY AND THE VIOLET RAY

Beloved chelas, does this give a greater understanding now when I invoke the Violet Flame? Mighty Violet Ray come forth and transmute all discord, all disharmony, so that I may move in ONE beauty and cooperation. It is stated that as a combined force it calms and tames this Ray into a direction where violence, and wars, and the technology that have aided and abetted the dark side of the human, can now be brought into complete and total Mastery — where the true self can now be united as ONE with the universe. Do you understand this?

Question: "Yes, the individual does exist, yet we are still not separate from each other?"

It is through adherence to the work of the Violet Ray, to bring it into this greater understanding of Divine Intervention of Mercy, Compassion, and Forgiveness, that one can move in one's evolution, with the basis of the Christ Consciousness. It can then move us all into a greater understanding and evolution, into the higher chakra centers and the opening of the Third Eye. And now, unless there are further questions, I shall take my leave.

Response: "No, not at this time. And I thank you for your discourse."

In that Violet Flame, I AM Saint Germain.

CHAPTER FIVE

The Time of Testing

~

Saint Germain prophesies world change.

Greetings, beloved Dear hearts. In that mighty Violet Ray, I AM Saint Germain, and I request permission to come forth.

Response: "Please, Saint Germain, you are most welcome. Come forward."

FREE YOUR CONSCIOUSNESS

In the heart of the Mighty Logos burns this mighty Violet Flame of Mercy, Compassion, and Forgiveness. When you call upon it in your daily decree, or visualization, or meditation work, you call upon this Mighty Law in action as it streams forth from its great and Mighty Power through the Great Central Sun and onward to your own Sun and to the planet. In the same way in which I have explained and described how Ray Forces work, this comes forward in that manner. It comes forward in the same natural laws, as they have been set forth in previous discourse. This is important to understand, for, you see, the Violet Flame is this Mighty Law in action. When you call upon it, what it does, precisely and exactly, is free your consciousness from any inhibiting doubt or harm. It allows for a focus to come forward so that you can begin to accept the perfection of your thoughts and feelings, the perfection of all action, and the activation of the Mighty Will in action.[1]

THE LIGHTED STANCE

You see, Dear hearts, Dear ones, it is only the acceptance of the perfection that each of you carries in that mighty Chamber of the Heart. It is this one perfected cell that awakens the other cells into their own perfection and carries this awakening

throughout your system. I have spoken about this before as the lighted stance of activating each of these cells within your system, to bring about this perfection—the perfection of your divinity, or your Divineship. Within it lie many of the answers to eternal memory, eternal life and eternal Oneship with the Divine Creator.

THE FORGETTING

You see, beloveds, Dear ones, it was through a collective forgetting that a forgetting occurred within the genetics. This created a masking of the consciousness. Because of the inability to retain information, the memory died down. It is through this collective forgetting that mankind entered into successive cycles of embodiment-upon-embodiment of experience, and never knew its true source with the ONE, with all, in the mighty Divineship.

LOVE AND COMPASSION

Beloveds, Dear hearts, a time now comes upon the Earth Plane and Planet when there will be great testing, a testing not only of the Wills, but a testing also of putting this Mighty Law of ONE into action. You see, when you call upon the Violet Flame and the opening of the heart, you are led into the understanding that all is one, and all is ONE in an unconditional form of love. Through this mighty unconditional love, you are able to develop the higher aspects or emotions of compassion, gratitude, and Brotherly and Sisterly love. This earmarks the beginning of a greater civilization, of a greater society that can vibrate and understand why indeed it is manifesting itself at this time. You see, other societies have existed before you, many other great civilizations in their rise and their fall, but perhaps the one area where they did fault, the one area that they tripped upon, was the lack of development of compassion. You see, when one understands that one must not judge another, for they do not understand the circumstances that another walks or treads upon—one then enters into a higher resonance and a greater frequency. The idea of Mercy, Compassion, and Forgiveness earmarks always the birth of greater awareness and greater understanding, and allows access beyond the Third Dimension. In

---

1. See Appendix W3: *Saint Germain's Teachings on the Violet Flame and Spiritual Prophecies.*

perceiving, in an empathetic sort of way, the situation of your Brother or Sister, you are then able to understand at a higher energy level how all life is interconnected as ONE.

SEPARATION

It is always through thinking and perceiving the self as being separate that produces more separate realities. Thus we enter into a stream of disharmonies, a stream of miscommunications and a lifestyle that filters through that lens of noncooperation.

A TIME OF TESTING

But, indeed, we enter into a time that is an Age of Cooperation. Among all things, Dear hearts, this is of vast importance. The next seven years shall be a Time of Great Trial and Tribulation; a time that will be best known as a Time of Testing—not only a testing of the Mighty Will, but, as I have stated before, a time to put the Law of ONE into action.[2] It is also a time when I assure

2. The Time of Testing: The Time of Testing is a period of seven to twenty years which began around the turn of the twenty-first century, following the time period known as the Time of Transition. According to Saint Germain and other Ascended Masters, the Time of Testing is perhaps one of the most turbulent periods mankind will experience and its first seven years is prophesied as a period of change and strife for many. [Editor's Note: Other prophecies indicate this timeframe may be seven to twenty years.] As its title suggests, the Master Teachers claim this time frame may challenge students by testing their spiritual acumen and inner strength.
This period is also known as the great trial. Students will realize forceful contrast through adversity, while remembering the softer predecessor to this period: the benefic Time of Transition. This favorable twelve-year period began in the mid to late eighties of the twentieth century and ushered in tremendous spiritual exposure and growth through a proliferation of alternative self-help and healing groups, spawning a renewed zeal for other forms of faith. Beginning in 1988 and ending in the year 2,000, (some I AM America prophecies suggest a longer duration), the beloved Ascended Masters, Archangels, and Elohim flood the Earth with light (the Rays) to restore mankind's spiritual growth and acuity. Spiritual development achieved in this period proves essential because of the events which mark the end of its benevolence and introduce the Time of Testing. These events try humanity's resilience and challenge our grasp of Forgiveness, Tolerance, and Compassion amidst the violence of the 9-11 tragedy, the Iraq War, and increased natural calamities. (Iran earthquake, 2003; Indian Ocean earthquake and tsunami, 2004; South Asian earthquake: Pakistan, India, Afghanistan, 2005; Peru earthquake, 2007; Sichuan earthquake, 2008; Samoa earthquake, 2009; Haiti earthquake, 2010; and the Japanese earthquake and tsunami, near the East coast of Honshu, Japan, 2011.) Climate and global changes escalate in this period with extreme weather and wildfires in Greece, Australia, and California; worldwide blizzards,

you, Dear ones, Dear hearts, that I shall always be available to give you guidance and discourse, as needed. This has been my assignment, given to you for this time period, so that we may begin on a more personal note to understand how things may swiftly change. This indeed will be a Time of Swift Change, not only upon the Earth Plane and Planet, but you will see within the minds of men that there will be many who will be called to the task, many who will be called for the great choosing. You see, beloveds, Dear ones, the events upon the Earth will be among the greatest teachers that mankind has yet to see. It will take but one or two jarings of this Earth, a few mighty winds and a few mighty rains, and mankind will begin to see things in a subtle and different manner.

CROSSING THE THRESHOLD

How do we touch the heart? How do we open the heart and allow this Oneship to stream forth? This has long been the question at the pivotal point of evolution for humanity and mankind. This has long been an important barrier that we now have an urging to cross. How do we open up the New Dimensions so that mankind may cross this great threshold and begin to understand that it is this Inner Marriage of thought and feeling that leads to Divine action and Divine Manifestation?

flooding, cyclones, tornadoes, and hurricanes (North American blizzard, 2011; Chinese winter storms, 2008; Rio de Janeiro, floods and landslides, 2011; Queensland, Australia, floods, 2010; United States, tornadoes, 2011; Nargis, Burma, cyclone, 2008; New Orleans, Louisiana, Hurricane Katrina, 2005; Galveston, Texas, Hurricane Ike, 2008.) Alongside natural disasters, numerous corporate bankruptcies lead to worldwide economic uncertainty and government bail-outs.
Through the backdrop of world instability and global fragility, Ascended Master chelas and students hone the spiritual skills of Transmutation and transformation. Humanity's ability to Alchemize geo-physical, social, economic, and environmental events may forecast mankind's ability to survive the catalytic and polarizing threshold of change we are now entering. Once we leave the Time of Testing, the Ascended Masters prophesy the Time of Change is upon us. This is a time of worldwide change, with possible Earth Changes which inevitably leads to global transformation prophesied by the Ascended Masters, religious prophets, sages, and indigenous tribal leaders. The Time of Change ushers in the Golden Age of Kali Yuga.

GOLDEN CITY DOORWAYS

We have given the locations of the Golden Cities so that a Divine Intervention shall come forward. This Divine Intervention is brought for the grace of humanity. It is brought so that humanity may now come forward in a greater choosing, in a greater understanding. This Divine Intervention comes through the integration of many energies that come from the Northern, the Eastern, the Southern and the Western doors, and onward to that Mighty Star where all energies coalesce and are available for integration. Each of these teachings has been given with its timing and intent so that it can be used as a type of intervention. In the next seven years, these doorways and energies of the Golden Cities will become known to their greatest extent, and more probing into their wondrous knowledge will begin. You see, there is enough energy within these Golden City Vortices to blaze mankind into the next level of understanding. But if mankind is unable to choose or unwilling to act, then this Divine Intervention may, or may not, move forward.[3]

THE AWAKENING

You see, the time is at hand. The awakening is at hand, but indeed, in terms of your Earth years and understanding, this time is short; yet the awakening is immortal. This awakening is for all and beyond the barrier of time. But the events that come will be marked by time and recorded in your history.

---

3. Prophecies of Change: During the Time of Testing (2000–2020), many of the Golden City Vortices mature, and their energies assist humanity in one of history's most definable transformations through cooperative group efforts and worldwide spiritual awakening.

Living in Golden City Vortices helps to enhance physical and spiritual contact with the Fourth and Fifth Dimensions. This is necessary to adjust our bodies, minds, and spirits in preparation to birth the New Times—the Golden Age.

As we enter the Times of Change and experience the Fourth and Fifth Dimensions, many will experience simultaneous realities. This experience can temper the fury of the Great Purification and assist the creation of the Golden Age.

"I OFFER THE CUP"

Beloveds, Dear ones, know that I AM here to serve. Know that I AM here and that I offer the Cup of the most refreshing drink. I offer this so that those who have the eyes to see and the ears to hear may now understand in the greater opening of the heart and the greater understanding and alignment of the Will. It will take this mighty alignment of the Will to move humanity into a cooperative group, into this group action.

RELOCATING TO THE GOLDEN CITIES

We have set forth the locations of the Golden Cities so that a relocation of sort may also begin. The relocation we have described several times, that it shall start first from the outer periphery of the Vortices.[4] Then, as a chela, student or Aspirant carefully observes and integrates these energies, he will be ready to move onward to that star—that mighty Star of Self-knowledge. This may also be engendered from our teachings. We brought you forward to the Vortex of Gobean, but you integrated the energies at a much slower pace on the outside, did you not?

Answer: "This is true."

This is perfect and in great Divine Alignment, for you see it is important that, one by one, the energy is understood and assimilated before you can move on. It is suggested, when there are those who ask in each of the successive movements where they should settle and stay, that they spend a time of close to 16 months to two years in each area. You see, Dear ones, we have found that in the human, this is the time that is needed to begin the assimilation process. If you ask for one to come and live near you or with you, this is the time required for the complete integration process. Do you understand?

Answer: "I understand what you're requesting; I don't understand the complete process."

---

4. See Appendix X3: *Teachings on Pilgrimage or Moving to a Golden City Vortex.*

LIVING IN A GOLDEN CITY

It is a process that begins on the outer periphery of a Golden City Vortex, a 20- to 30-mile flux to the outer outside fringe area of the Vortex. Of course, it is best to live within the Vortex, but for those who wish to just assimilate energies, they can also live at the outside. It is our request that they stay there in the integration and assimilation mode for sixteen months, twenty months, or twenty-four months, depending upon how quickly the energies are assimilated. Then, they can move a little closer in, not yet to the Star. They can do this in successive motions, until they feel the integration of the energies, and then, in that final motion, move onward to the Star. For you see, Dear ones, that is where the higher knowledge can be given. That is where the greater assimilation of the energies occurs. Questions?

Question: "Yes. Are you versed in the current cities on the planet that exist in the Star area of Gobean, or towns?"

Let me do a quick scan. Now, I AM following Akashic Records. Proceed.

Question: "Is there a preference in the Star of Gobean that you would ask us to move to? A specific location?"

GOLDEN CITY STARS

As always with the entry of the Ray Force is the strongest pulsation of the energy matter. You see, Dear ones, Dear hearts, this is the highest concentration of the energy within itself. Now, even upon the entryway into the Star, for those who are not ready for these higher and finer energies, it may be best to enter first into the Star within a 30- to 40-mile radius and onward to the greater energy force, which is from 20 miles to the central point. Do you understand?

Answer: "Yes."

Within twenty miles is, of course, better. Do you see how this interim instruction works simultaneously with the sound and light force?

Question: "What you're saying is that the inner instruction would be heightened and intensified in that Star area?"

Yes, this is so. But it also allows a greater contact with the next realm of creation, reality and understanding, which is absolutely necessary to birth the New Time, the Golden Age. You see, in the Point of Perception, I outlined the scenario of simultaneous reality. This will be so in the Time of the Great Purification, the Time of Great Change, the Time of the Golden Age. Do you understand?

FOURTH AND FIFTH DIMENSION

Question: "Yes. So, what you're saying is that in the Star area there will be access to the Fourth and Fifth Dimension?"

This is so, beloveds, Dear hearts. And it is absolutely essential for the work that you are carrying forward, for it brings forward a contact throughout the whole planet of the consciousness that you are carrying forward. For the location of this consciousness to be located in a 20-mile radius of the Stars allows for a greater sensitivity within the collective consciousness, for this work to stream forward into the whole of humanity. As we have stated before: as above, so below. And we are dealing now with the principle of collective consciousness, that of the mighty Unana.

Response: "I see. Then your preference is that we move to the Star of Gobean."

RELATIONSHIP OF THE RAYS

Now, you can choose any Star that you feel the alignment to. Any of these will work for you. But for the sake of alignment to that mighty Blue Ray, it is this force that will change the role of mankind, and that is why this Star has been selected. The work that you carry forward actually impacts the work of the Green Ray (Shalahah) for healing and hope for humanity. And within the Green Ray there are components of the Will and a mighty alignment to wisdom within itself. The Green Ray, of course, brings forward that understanding from a technical perspective, and from a scientific point of view, but it also opens the great chamber in the heart. Now do you understand the relationship of Gobean and Shalahah (Green Ray)?

Answer: "Yes."

This, again, is of your choosing. And for that matter, even if you prefer, you may retreat to the city of Wahanee. Again, it is all within your choice.

Response: "It would be my preference for the Gobean center. However, is the way made clear for us to be able to achieve this?"

SPIRITUAL ASSIMILATION

The way was made clear for you to gain spiritual evolution through the greater energies. And this is what was being brought forward several years prior. But you reached a level of spiritual knowledge, of spiritual assimilation, and it was time for you to move on, as is the current situation.

Response: "I understand. Is there any need, at a personal level, for us to help create a community in this area?"

HARMONY CREATES ABUNDANCE

If this is your desire, then so be it. But I caution you not to become diverted from the work at hand, as often times this is the case when you bring those who are of mixed vibration into the work that you are bringing forward. I hope you understand it to its fullest conclusion. However, the application and knowledge of the laws are realized through that Mighty Law of Attraction; from those who bring a harmony, those who bring an alignment. But remember, if you bring them only to line your coffers, you may not be exercising this Mighty Law in action. It is important to understand that it is the Law of Harmony that creates abundance and onward, as set forth in the Twelve jurisdictions. These Laws of New Jurisprudence are based upon the forbearers, the Laws of Light and Sound. So,

Dear hearts, Dear ones, remember always the mission that you have been given and its sacred stewardship.

IF THE POLES SHIFT . . .

Response: "I understand what you're saying. As far as the type of structure, what type of structure should we actually build? We have several . . . "

It has been noted in the Prophecies of Change, the prophecies designed to change your heart, which may change this world, that there are probabilities of wind forces from 300- to 400-miles per hour with polar shift. Now with just gale forces, these are tornado-type winds, which can exceed, at times, up to 500 miles per hour. But in other areas, and in the area in question, if you would give it to me, I then may answer.

Response: "We are considering Greer."

POSSIBLE CHANGES

Now, it is important to understand that there can be touchdown tornadoes, which will have wind forces of 200- to 280-miles per hour in this area, so prepare your structure for these types of weather disturbances. These are caused by electromagnetic fluxes, huge thunderstorms that will hit this area during the Time of the Great Monsoon. The Great Monsoon will come after the Time of the Great Fire. This we have outlined in Map Number Four. (See: I AM America Six-Map Scenario Map.) Now, I can give you, if you so choose, more specific understanding. Once you make the decision to move into an area, I can give you the records for that area, to bring forth the proper conditions.

A GOBEAN VALLEY

Question: "Is Greer close enough to Mount Baldy for your purposes?"

Now, let me scan. Yes. This will work, for it carries a high vibration, not only from Mount Baldy, but there is another mountain in the area that carries within it a vein of mixed alchemical substances. These mineral substances leak their energies into a valley area, which is channeled through the valley. Do you understand?

Question: "Yes. Do they channel through the river that comes from Mount Baldy?"

WATER AND VORTEX ENERGIES

Of course, these mineral substances can be found in most rivers and from areas of such a high nature. The water impregnates the area with this Vibration of Gobean and the Master Teacher of that Mighty Ray in action, El Morya.

Question: "If there were another parcel of land available closer to Mt. Baldy, would that be more in alignment with the needs?"

As I said in our discussions earlier, one must consider the Prophecies of Map Number Four and this fire zone, for, you see, once upon the entry into the Time of Change, one must understand that these changes will occur then for many, many decades.

So, it is best to deal with water that comes from a pure source. This is why, within twenty miles of the central part of Gobean, within itself, the water sources are kept at a purer level. Do you understand?

Answer: "Yes. There are springs and small creeks coming from the mountain. All right. Then I understand. We will look for a suitable location close to the mountain."

I AM here to serve. Do you have questions?

GOLDEN CITY STRUCTURE

Question: "Yes. As far as a building structure, we have, potentially decided upon personal homes. They would be dome-style structures that would be made of concrete and steel re-inforcement. The other thought that crosses my mind is the Golden City structure. Would that be a suitable home structure?"

These structures have been provided to raise consciousness. They are given so that one may gain access to fourth- and fifth-dimensional levels of understanding, to achieve communion with the Master Teacher of that Vortex. Now, this will all depend upon the conditions of the Earth at the time. Gold is suitable to arc the energy from each of the doorways. Do you understand?

Answer: "Yes I do."

However, if it is unattainable at that time, copper can also work to some degree to gain this type of energy momentum. This can be done through a simple lining of each of what you would call meridian points, or a lei-line, within the Vortex structure of the construction. Residential homes, again, must carry the safety measure for winds up to 280 miles per hour. Different areas, of course, will vary with this requirement. There will also be some minor earth movement that will be felt through the impact of a meteor in your area. So, it is important to understand all the different possibilities that may occur. However, the Golden City structure, within itself, has been given to assist and enhance spiritual development and raise consciousness to gain entry into the higher levels of understanding.

Question: "I understand what you are saying, but is it suitable as a home?"

For those who have the eyes to see and the ears to hear, it may be suitable, however, it is best to be seen as a temple.

Response: "I see."

There will be those who could live within it to become a caretaker. Do you understand?

Answer: "Yes."

However, for those who do live in this manner, it is important that food is prepared in a certain way and that no food of animal substance be prepared within this type of structure. For, you see, that brings a layering of vibration and it is important to keep the vibration of such a structure at the highest possible potential. This is not to say that this structure will not work; however, it is to keep the energy at a level of purity.

Question: "I see. All right. That answers two questions. The third question is that Greer is extremely expensive and at, present time, is not within our budgetary abilities, considering all our other obligations. Is there something you would suggest so that we may become free of our Karma, our debt here, so that we may move on in a very easy and rapid manner?"

ENERGY–FOR–ENERGY

The property that you seek exists upon a ridge, which is a bit lower from that of a property that you have already seen. This would be attainable and usable for your purposes. However, again, I strongly urge and remind you to keep up the work at hand. Keep the message of I AM America moving forward. It is important always to keep this flow of knowledge streaming out into the hearts of humanity, for then this energy can be matched equally. Do you understand?

Answer: "I understand."

This is all built upon the principle of momentum, which we have studied before. It is also built upon, and you know this well, that cycle of rhythm.

Question: "Yes, I understand what you're saying. One other question that I have."

Proceed.

Question: "Lori has been continuing on with additional studies of the Vedic work and with the history of mankind through the origins of Sumeria. Are these truly related to you?"

They are all related to all. You see, the Earth, within its own framework, is a mighty schoolroom.[5] There are many different genetic life streams, so to speak, which have come here and impregnated themselves. Each of these, in its own time, has left to move onto other schoolrooms, to achieve other goals. You see, as we have stated before, this is a love-in-action planet. And the various life streams from various planets, when they are ready to bring about their souls to this greater understanding, bring about the process. Do you understand?

Answer: "Yes, I do."

So, when one says there is a great harvest or a great collection of souls, it is so. You see, these souls are then readied to leave the Earth Plane and Planet and move onward to other experiences to bring greater perfection.

Question: "Is it that time when the souls actually remember?"

---

5. Schoolroom Earth: The inhabitants of Schoolroom Earth, as seen by the Ascended Masters, are not the creation of one spiritual teacher, god, or race of aliens. They are, in fact, a bit of all of these. And, in the overall cosmology of the soul, Earth serves as a location, as a school for learning—open to many Ray(ces), religions, genetics, and alien Star seeds. This design ensures that Earth maintains a certain, steady vibration, or learning level. Hindu cosmology addresses these same issues, and claims Earth, known as *Bhurloka*, is not the highest or the lowest vibration when compared to other planets. A soul evolves through the potentials and possibilities on Earth; and the soul moves on to New Dimensions or planets with frequencies that resonate with its new vibration and energy. Saint Germain explains that Ray Forces accompany our soul's journey to Schoolhouse Earth, and assist our growth and pattern of evolution.

Periodically the Earth rises or lowers in vibration, and this change precipitates the ascent or demise of civilizations such as Lemuria and Atlantis. This change allows new incoming streams of souls as Ray(ces) to evolve in their educational and spiritual processes. As one class graduates and proceeds onward to a new dimension—loka, or planetary schoolroom—a new class enters Schoolhouse Earth.

Each planetary graduating class is similar to a family. Saint Germain describes the Earth's humanity at this time as the Aryan Family, and once we achieve our personal and global Ascension, we will move onward, into new evolutionary circumstances.

THE RAYS AND CIVILIZATIONS

Oh, of course. And in between embodiment the soul truly knows. Memory has been wiped during embodiments because that time is a cycle of complete forgetfulness. Yet, this all works together to serve a greater understanding, to serve a greater collective awakening. But, you see, as Lord Macaw, has outlined, each of the Ray Forces reaches its maturation in its own time and in its own place. Now, when I speak of these as Ray(ces), do you understand?

Question: "You're speaking of Ray Forces functioning through the genetics?"

THE ARYAN

This is certain. This is so, Dear one. What I also would like to impart to you is that there were other civilizations that existed way before those in Sumeria, Babylon and Mesopotamia. That is the story of the civilization that is related to Aryan. (See: Points of Perception.) However, there were also those life-streams related to Atlantean, those life streams related to Lemurian, and also to other Kingdoms which existed prior to that. This Earth is a great schoolroom, and periodically, through change within itself, it allows a greater education for the Ray(ces) to come forward in their greater understanding. But indeed, for the time that you are dealing with now, Earth continues to be a great cradle of civilization and school for the Aryans.

Question: "I understand. So in this time period, even you are part of this Aryan time period?"

Yes, it is so. And through the perfection of consciousness, through the use of the Violet Flame, all can raise their consciousness and successive embodiment to another level of understanding, to another dimension of being. And then the soul is readied and taken to a new schoolroom, to a new set of circumstances. Do you understand?
Answer: "Yes, so, in a sense, we belong to a family group."

This is so—in the same way that you belong to a graduating class and to a family. But, in a family, does it not have many cousins?

Answer: "Very true."

So, this Aryan time is, in this essence, a family. There are several cousins who also embodied at the same time, and they may, or may not, leave at the time of graduation. They may stay or they may move on to a total perceiving schoolroom. You see, occasionally one great avatar—one great adept—is brought in to lead the masses as a teacher, to bring an understanding in that collective consciousness.[6]

Response: "I see and we've had, I suppose, several of these."

6. Avatar: Hindu classifications of the stages of human spiritual advancement are well documented in the Upanishads. They are: Siddha, a perfected being; Jivanmukta, freed while living; Paramukta, supremely free with full power over death. A Paramukta or Ascended Being purposely creates a physical body and descends to Earth to either assist humanity or to spiritually bless or balance a disordered world. This Divine Manifestation is known as an Avatar. The perfected, death-free body of an Avatar does not cast a shadow or leave footprints. Such Masters never appear in the gross public, and have the ability to become invisible. It is claimed Saint Germain will take the form of a beggar or an old woman dressed in a wisp of purple or violet clothing. Sananda states he is not limited by form of any kind, and will assume any form or appearance necessary for the task at hand.
According to the teachings of the Ascended Masters, twelve Spiritual Avatars are physically present on Earth at any given time. This ensures specific levels of vibration, radiance, and spiritual energy to foster humanity's growth and evolutionary requirements. Concurrently, another group of twelve Avatar Masters reside at the Fourth Dimension, and yet another series of twelve in the Fifth Dimension. Saint Germain explains that there are minor levels of consciousness between the Third and Fourth Dimensions; and minor levels between the Fourth and Fifth Dimension. Altogether, including the numerous minor levels, a total of 144 Avatars assist humanity's evolutionary process on Earth. A total of 108 Avatars exist on the minor, sub-planes between the Third, Fourth, and Fifth Dimensions. The number 108 is considered sacred in Vedic tradition.
Saint Germain claims that many of the Master Teachers are focusing their energies and teachings toward the awakening of two spiritual aspects of humanity. Their first goal is to awaken the innate Divinity and perfection of the HU-man through the activation of the Eight-sided Cell of Perfection within the Chamber of the Heart. Secondly, use of the Seventh Chakra awakens the pineal gland (the Third-Eye) and opens the flow of the inner dialogue between the student and the I AM Presence. Saint Germain prophesies that the personal awakening of the Seventh Chakra promotes the collective development and opening of humanity's heart. This enables mankind to enter a new dimension of spiritual awareness and understanding.

TWELVE AVATARS

They are always sent in groups of twelve. And there are always twelve present at all times upon the planet.

Question: "There are twelve now?"

There are indeed twelve now; twelve in physical embodiment, bringing their teachings. Now, some are not known to the public, but they radiate their energy from where they are located. But indeed, there are always twelve adepts who are always upon the Earth Plane. Then, there are those such as we who work, and there are indeed always twelve of us who work at one level of consciousness to bring teachings forward from that understanding of ONE, and, again above us, another twelve. Always there are 144 of us, always working to move consciousness further, and so on. Do you understand?

Answer: "Yes I do."

This is where that teaching comes from. Now, do you understand why there are Twelve Jurisdictions? These are twelve sacred spiritual teachings.
Question: "Then there truly are twelve planets in our three-dimensional realm?"

Indeed, there are, however, it is important to not get lost in that teaching at this moment. For there will be further teachings that will be given at the right time and at the right place. So let us deal now with the work at hand.

LINEAGE OF GURUS

Question: "As you wish. Lord Apollo, he is our sponsor?"

He is a grand teacher, and one of my teachers.[7]

Question: "I see. So he came at a time before us?"

7. See Appendix Z3: *Apollo.*

As you have a grandfather, a great-grandfather, or an ancestor who has brought you teachings, this is also the way to understand and regard Lord Apollo.

Question: "But an ancestor always sponsors the progeny. Is this not true?"

THE HEART AND THE CROWN CHAKRA

Yes, but you do understand that this is the awakening of the heart, as I stated before. There is this vast difference between the progeny and the awakening of the genetic. In this time that we are dealing with, because all genetics are so closely related, as I have stated before, now our focus is upon the awakening of the Chamber of the Heart (Eight-sided Cell of Perfection) and the use of the Seventh (Crown) Chakra. These two things will allow this larger family to enter at Will into a New Dimensional understanding, a New Dimensional awareness.

PERCEPTION AND CONSCIOUSNESS

This, of course, is achieved with greater fluency and accuracy in the Stars. You see, Dear ones, there is a greater pulsation with the vibral core of the Earth. The Earth, right now, in its simultaneous realities, is offering a great flora and fauna of lessons. It is through the backdrop of this great flora and fauna that many understandings of how we shall all evolve will be understood. Remember before, Dear hearts, Dear ones, when I said there will be a Time of Great Change and one man will perceive it with great sorrow, one will perceive it as a great change, and one will perceive it with great joy! Each of these is dimensional awareness.

One perhaps has his focus on what he has lost in his bank, the home that he has lost—all of these are attachments to the physical world. Then, there is one who perceives it with grief, for loss of love, for loss of all things that he was attached to at an emotional level. Then, there is the man who perceives this only as a change and a new way for him to see things, a new way to have experience. Then, there is the one who sees the opening of the gateway, the spirit world, the true existence, the consciousness of Unana. These I've outlined before in the

"Point of Perception." It is an understanding that within you, with the activation of your Chamber of the Heart lies the out-picturing of consciousness for creation.

DIVINE INTERVENTION OF ASCENSION

You see, Dear ones, Dear hearts, it is indeed a Time of Co-creation, a time when the activation of the Will can bring forth the finest results. But understand, too, that with the assistance of beloved Babajeran and through the work of the Brotherhood of Breath, Light and Sound, the Brotherhood of this White Lodge—this "white-light" lodge—we are now able to manifest a Divine Intervention. This will bring forward, at Will, a greater understanding of your true divinity—an upliftment—raising the physical body into Ascension, eliminating the craving for the requirement of that cycle of constant rebirth into the Earth Plane. Do you understand?

Question: "Yes. So the Ascension is really an interdimensional movement?"

Indeed, this is so. This is why we have outlined areas such as Ascension Valley, such as the Transportation Vortex located in Coeur d' Alene, Idaho. Do you understand?

Question: "And these will be achieved without external technology?"

They will be achieved through understanding and opening the self, through awakening the perfection within the heart, through opening the Seventh Chakra.

Response: "I see. I understand."

There are also teachings that will assist this. And they will come at a later date, however, so that you can understand them in general terms.

Response: "This is most enlightening and joyous. I thank you very much. I have no further questions."

In that case my beloveds, I must return to the celebrations at Shamballa. Know that always I AM here at your request. In service to that Mighty Breath of Light and Action of God, I AM Saint Germain.

CHAPTER SIX

Memory Is Freedom

*Saint Germain shares teachings
on developing true memory.*

Greetings, Beloveds. In that Mighty Violet Flame, I AM Saint Germain, and I stream forth on that Mighty Violet Ray of mercy, compassion and forgiveness. As usual, Dear hearts, I request your permission to come forward.

Response: "Please, Saint Germain, come forward. You are most welcome."

SAINT GERMAIN CALLS FORTH TRANSMUTATION AND TRANSFORMATION

Transmutation. Transmutation of all which brings discord into your life, which brings pain and suffering, which brings ills that seemingly keep you off the path and keep you from understanding the United Brotherhoods and Sisterhoods.

Transformation. May transformation now stream forth into the hearts of all mankind. May transformation guide the Will of men. May transformation now stream forward to this Planet Divine and may this Mighty Freedom Star (Babajeran) now take its position within the universe.

PERCEPTION AND TIME

Dear ones, Dear hearts, there is so little time left, yet at other times it may seem there is so much time. Time drags on, and the minutes and the seconds tick. The awakening is at hand, yet it seems to drag so. Why are these perceptions of time brought forward in such a way that it is difficult for mankind to understand? You see, Dear ones, time is a matter of perception. It is always a matter of understanding. The moment of when you grasp onto your own reality, you will see, Dear ones, that the truth and treasures of heaven lie not in the illusion of maya,

nor in time, but in the eternal wonderment of understanding true love.[1]

THE QUEST FOR LOVE

The Law of Love, as dear Sananda has spoken, "how does one bring forth this transformation, where this eternal Law of Love is lived everyday," is brought forward into the human existence, and then allowed to move on into a fuller and a richer understanding.[2] The Law of Love, as we have taught before, is the beginning and the end. The Law of Love is the true Alpha, the true Omega. It is the one law that serves all of humanity at all times, and yet, love itself is the drink that all are questing and thirsting for. All are looking for love to fill their lives, and yet there is not one upon the Earth Plane and Planet, in this moment, who feels that his Cup is filled to the brim with true love and the understanding that brings supreme peace. This great truth and treasure comprise the law that brings forward transformation for all upon the Earth Plane and Planet. It brings forth an understanding that goes beyond time and beyond minutes and the ticking clock. It is an understanding that brings peace supreme and allows countries to put down their arms against one another; allowing seemingly bitter enemies to shake hands, and join in a mutual cause. It is this Law of Love that heals all wounds and brings one to that higher understanding, and yet it is so hard to bring about its implementation. Why is this so?

Lifetime after lifetime, we collect experiences, or that collective memory of experience. It imbeds itself into the Records of Akasha, and the soul then carries the memory of every experience with it through successive embodiments. Wouldn't it be a bright New Day if that record that is carried, is erased eternally

---

1. Maya: This term often refers to illusion; however, from Saint Germain's teachings maya indicates the presence of imperfect memory, and is therefore partial truth.

2. The Law of Love: Perhaps every religion on Earth is founded upon the Law of Love, as the notion to "treat others as you would like to be treated." The Law of Love, however, from the Ascended Master tradition, is simply understood as consciously living without fear, or inflicting fear on others. The Fourth of the Twelve Jurisdictions instructs, Love is the Law of Allowing, Maintaining, and Sustainability. All of these precepts distinguish love from an emotion or feeling, and observe Love as action, will, or choice. Lord Sananda says, "Love is the first action and energy to come forth in creation.

and replaced only through that Mighty Law of Love—the Law of ONE? Then all that is then carried—the hurts, the wounds—which have caused the need for successive embodiments, the need to remain trapped in the physical—are then removed. Oh, but what a day that would be, Dear ones, Dear hearts. It is that simple.[3]

DETACHMENT THROUGH THE VIOLET FLAME

When we call upon that Mighty Violet Flame of Mercy, Transmutation and Forgiveness, essentially at the electromagnetic level, we are erasing all memories of the past—memories that hold you from your eternal freedom. Again, it is a matter of perception for you see, Dear ones, Dear hearts, our memories serve either for our higher understanding and for achieving a higher reality, or our memories hold us prisoner, trapped in the confines of the flesh, in successive rounds of birth and death. How can we achieve this liberation?

It is a type of detachment—detaching from outcome, loosening the rope of expectation, but it is even more, my Dear ones, a calling upon that transmutative law, the Mighty Violet Flame. Decree:

"May freedom ring supreme in the hearts of all mankind.
Mighty Violet Flame, blaze in, through,
and around all situations
of Memory that hold me from my eternal freedom—
that hold me from my true self.
Mighty Violet Flame, come forth now
and remove such memories,
that may keep me bound into the rounds of birth and death.
Mighty Violet Flame, come through and set me free.
Mighty Violet Flame let me truly be."

"LOVE IS THE REALITY"

You see, Dear ones, it is that simple. Removing a death consciousness requires embracing the consciousness of love eternal. Love is that one reality, that one true treasure; the one

true vibration. It is ever present. It is as it is. To embrace the true Law of Love in its totality is to be set free. Now, before I continue, are there any questions?

Question: "Yes. This question pertains to memory."

Proceed.

"HEAVENLY TREASURE"

Question: "As you have just stated, memory can be for the higher purpose or for the entrapment in the flesh. It is obvious, in speaking to people and in my own instance, most people have no interest in remembering other lifetimes or embodiments because they feel extremely overwhelmed by the current one they're in. As you have just stated, is it to be understood that when you choose to remember, for the higher purpose of freeing yourself, that the memory will come back in a way in which it will free you? That is my question."

Memory is indeed one of the keys to obtaining the treasures of heaven, to obtaining your immortality. It is one of the keys to the prison you're trapped in called "illusion." True memory, seen and viewed from its true context, is what we speak of, a "heavenly treasure" of memory. Now, let me explain.[4]

Indeed you are all, Dear ones, Dear hearts, living in a Time of Great Testing—a Time of Testing once known as tribulation. Yet we now prefer to call it a Time of Testing, for, you see, you

---

4. True Memory: Memory, as defined by Ascended Master teachings, is not seen as a function of the brain, or the soul's recall of past events. Instead, True Memory is perceived as an essential key that is cultivated and honed in order to obtain the greatest treasure of heaven—immortality. This is achieved through cultivating our perceptions and adjusting our individual perspective on a situation to the multiple juxtapositions of opinion and experience. The Master Teachers refer to this as the perception of, "a thousand eyes."

This depth of understanding gives clarity and illumination to every experience. Our skill and Mastery through True Memory move our consciousness beyond common experiences to individualized experiences where our perceptive power hones honesty and accountability. The innate truth obtained from many experiences through the interplay of multiple roles creates True Memory, and opens the detached and unconditional Law of Love to the chela.

---

3. See Appendix AA3: *Saint Germain's Teachings on the Law of Love, Spiritual Prophecies, and Teachings on True Memory.*

are never given a test that you are not ready for. This test is not given as a punishment; this test is given so you may examine and understand the skills you have gained toward your path of spiritual liberation.

ONE WITH SOURCE

There was a time when humanity existed in a purer state. There is not one soul now upon this plane of illusion, or Maya, who does not understand or know the truth of this, for memory is embedded within it. Do you see how memory embeds within?

All who hear these words, all who understand this principle and this concept, know within their hearts that they existed in another time, where their being was ONE with God, ONE with Source, ONE unified to a cause of life.

THE UNFED FLAME

I refer to God as a source of light, as a source of the Causeless Cause,[5] as the source of desireless desire. All understand and

know the purity that lies within themself. All feel the urge within the heart, which is that urge to move forward, to know the truth of that memory embedded within themself. The truth of that memory is the Unfed Flame of Love, Wisdom, and Power; true love, true wisdom and true devoted power, that is the eternal memory.

The Divine Spark is within all, and all instantly recognize this great eternal truth. But beyond this ONE memory that we all share, and unify toward is the history of who and what humanity is, where humanity came from and where this great schoolroom is heading.[6]

THE ORAL TRADITION

Mankind, at one time, contained a greater capacity to learn and to retain, which was known as memory. Of course, I speak of a time before books were required, before the written word was required, and the Oral Tradition flourished. That is why our teachings are always brought forward in the Oral Tradition, through this tradition a consciousness is able to pervail. This all-important consciousness is ever expanding, ever transforming, ever transmuting. Even in this moment, as you listen to my words, your consciousness is being impacted at a memory level. Of course, it is not the words themselves, but the intention of the consciousness that you now feel permeating your memory … it is almost as air feeds the flame. That ember of consciousness and memory existing in all upon the Earth Plane

---

5. Causeless Cause: In Theosophical terms, the Causeless Cause means "the Omnipresent, Eternal, and Immutable Principle," which is also described as infinity—essence to "the one life," and the "unmoved mover."[3] Theosophists and Hindu philosophers both agree the Causeless Cause—known as Parabrahm in Sanskrit—is analogous to chaos, whose movement of the Logoic Monad creates the Seven Rays of Light and Sound. In order to perceive the Causeless Cause, one must first be capable of disassociation, which in theory is impossible from a fixed or finite point of view. Theosophist Jerome Anderson wrote in 1898 that, "This Causeless Cause is conceived of as Unmanifested Unity from the logical necessity of there being but one infinite power possible."[4] Anderson theorized that Western philosophy's simple attempts to distinguish the Causeless Cause as the absolute, infinite substance; the infinite thought; or infinite mind is dwarfed when compared to Eastern Philosophy's recognition of the illusion of finite matter and finite consciousness. Some Eastern philosophies argue if Causeless Cause is capable of the definition absolute; this, in itself, negates absoluteness. Many Eastern teachings claim the Causeless Cause is synonymous with Absolute Unity.

No doubt the Ascended Masters infer the Causeless Cause is associated with the Godhead, our evolutionary journey toward the light and the recognition of the finer states of consciousness encountered through the transmutation of finite energies into infinite expression. "A reasonable object of evolution would seem to be to enable consciousness to become self-consciousness," And Anderson continues with advice to not over-intellectualize spiritual experience, "Only let us avoid the capital error of isolating man from Nature, whose creation and child he is, for this is to despoil him of his divine birthright—to achieve one day out of his manhood—Godhood."

---

6. Desireless Desire: Desireless Desire is a reference to desire that is not motivated by Karmic desire; Karmic desire is known in Sanskrit as *kama*. Most Hindu scholars agree that kama is desire—pure and simple. Its definition does, however, differ, and some state Kama indicates desires that need constant restraint and discipline, as the unfettered condition produces addiction and obsession. Yet, some Vedic astrologers disagree, and although kama means *last*, the Vedic viewpoint identifies desire as the achievement of one's aspirations, our relationship with sexual partners, our urge to relate to others, and the success we seek in our relationship with the world and all living beings. Some Vedic philosophers purport that we must first fulfill our Earthly desires before initiating the liberation process. From this viewpoint, Desireless Desire is the desire to intimately know the source within, through the "dissolution of delusion."

and Planet expands so that true memory, like the treasure in heaven, is restored among humanity.[7]

"RECALL YOUR DIVINITY"

There were those who understood the cycles of time—the cycles of time within illusion—and knew that collectively a challenge would come to the memories of those souls trapped in the prison, and that it would become much more difficult for them to absorb knowledge and to work beyond the memory. They would have to keep a written record in order to understand and grow, in order to transmute and move beyond the schoolroom. This is the time you are now experiencing. Some call it Kali, some call it tribulation, but for those, who begin to understand the true difference of illusion and reality, it is known as a Time of Testing. Remember, Dear ones, Dear hearts, that you are ready for this test. Know, Dear ones, that your memory is now developed and ready to recall its true divinity.

LISTEN WITH HEART

It has been said to "listen with open ears." What does this mean? When one listens with true open ears, the ears are not only connected to the brain, but they are connected to the true memory, and that true memory is connected to the Law of Love. Have you not heard the saying, "Do not listen with your ears, listen with your heart?" This is what is being said. This great truth eternal, true open memory, true memory that understands, is memory based upon that one law eternal, the Law of Love.

"THE THOUSAND EYES"

Through the open heart, the understanding beyond, one is able to see a situation, not from just one perception, but through the eyes, "the thousand eyes of many." Memory is then recalled. For instance, the murderer may finally see the suffering of the parent, the suffering of the victim, the suffering of the husband or wife and the ripple effect that each action causes. Through the Law of Love, one is able to clearly see the grander purpose that is fulfilled, the grander teaching that comes forward. In the moment as a murderer, one may play a small role but yet may prove to be central in instigating many roles through the "thousand eyes." Do you understand?

Answer: "Yes. I understand."

LOVE OPENS TRUE MEMORY

This is perception—true perception and true memory.[8] I have said before, "Things do not happen to (people), things happen with." This is of most importance to understand. To truly open the memory is to truly open the gates for the Law of Love. Now, simple exercises.

How does one obtain a greater memory? First, call upon that Mighty Violet Ray. This will pave the pathway for a clear intention and for all obstructions around you to seamlessly fall away. But it is also important to actually put this into action, in the meditative state, to begin to recall the lifetimes of the past. You see, when the chela begins to recall his former lifetimes, he is able to understand the role that he played, as only one set of the "thousand eyes."

---

7. The Oral Tradition: According to the Master Teachers and many indigenous teachers, the Oral Tradition, or learning through oral instruction, is the preferred medium to receive spiritual knowledge. This method requires the use of memory and memorization and also instigates the presence of vital, yet subtle nuances that engender spiritual comprehension and may include the Master Teacher's use of telepathy, clairaudience, and clairvoyance. In times of greater galactic light on Earth, this is the preferred technique for spiritual instruction and creates the ever-important guru/chela relationship. Through the use of this ancient tradition, parables and archetypes of consciousness are seamlessly relayed through the command of sound. The written word is temporarily circumvented and a higher frequency emerges. This technique of ancient training, Master to student, guru to chela, is designed to open and develop latent HU-man powers currently dormant from lack of use. This important process and education is often described by the Ascended Masters as the training of, "the ears to hear, and the eyes to see."

---

8. See Appendix BB3: *The Cycles of Human Perception and Consciousness.*

WEAVING THE SEAMLESS GARMENT

The tragedy that happens to humans is that they see themselves, as only individualized egos, and they see the one lifetime as a "king or queen," as the mountaintop of their whole existence. Then they see that one lifetime as the "beggar" as the one lifetime of punishment. Yet, all lifetimes are woven together to create the Seamless Garment. Each experience is like a thread that weaves that garment that the soul then wears. But how else is each thread brought together into that magnificent Seamless Garment, than through memory? Woven together and held in the consciousness of memory, each thread is ever important; each experience is part of the garment. Each experience is not woven to, it is woven with one garment.

KEEP A JOURNAL

Dear ones, Dear hearts, recalling each past life is important, and I would suggest that you keep a journal of these experiences brought forth through meditation.[9] Soon you will begin to see

---

9. True Memory Exercise: Saint Germain suggests this exercise to open True Memory during past-life recall:
  • **Clear your intention.** Call forth the Violet Flame to surround you before, during, and after the exercise. This clears away any energy that may obstruct the process. Also, the Violet Flame prepares your mind for meditation.
  • **Clarify.** While in meditation ask for clear details regarding each specific lifetime. Have the courage to ask, "Is there more?"
  • **Nothing is insignificant.** Realize each lifetime, as insignificant as your current memory can recall, is important. Each experience you recall opens the door for further, deeper recollection. Keep a written journal of your experiences in True Memory.
  • **Weaving the Seamless Garment.** Recalling past life memories requires the development of True Memory. As our current memory shifts to this new level of developed perception, the individualized ego drops, and we enter into the first stages of building the Ascension light-bodies. Saint Germain refers to this as weaving each thread of the Seamless Garment: "Each thread weaves the garment the soul wears."
  • **Detachment.** After viewing past-life experiences call again upon the Violet Flame to help you to develop detachment and non-judgment of self. Saint Germain advises to perceive these types of experiences as events that lead you to self-realization, knowledge, and experience of the ONE, and the Law of Love. [Editor's Note: If you are unable to enter into self-guided past-life meditation, seek the help of a certified past-life regressionist.]
  • **Memory.** Your journey here is temporary; your memory of this journey is permanent!
  • **Inclusion.** When we retrieve painful memories, our illusive, limited perception often disassociates to separate from the experience. Always

how each experience weaves the memory of you. Then call upon that Mighty Violet Ray of Mercy and Forgiveness and see the experiences, not in judgment, but see them as experiences that led you to understand knowledge of the ONE, the knowledge of the Law of Love.

Question: "Could you give us the definition of maya?"

ILLUSION'S MAGNIFICENT PURPOSE

When I use the term "maya," I speak of illusion. That is the Point of Perception seen only through duality, through only one set of eyes. But understand, that beyond illusion, is reality, where the eternal truth resides. When I use "Maya," it is to indicate that which is the nonperfected memory. It only contains part of; therefore, it implodes upon itself. It is, and I say this so that you will begin to understand, only a partial truth.

How could there be but a partial truth? There are those who see their lifetime here as inconsequential because it is an experience only of illusion, yet, all serve the Plan Divine. Each plays its part in weaving that Seamless Garment of experience. So even the time that is spent in illusion, while it seems to be fruitless, is the fruit of a magnificent feast.

"NEVER GIVE UP"

So, Dear ones, never give up hope. Forge forward, even though at times you feel worried, at times you feel tired, and wish only to lay the body aside, to move into the greater understanding. But know that you always carry that greater truth with you.

MEMORY AND THE GREATER YOU

Your journey here, yes, is only temporary, but your memory of this journey is a permanent memory. It becomes one of those experiences that becomes part of the *greater you*. The Maya, the illusion, is when you hold this experience as being the *only you*. The maya, the illusion, is when you hold this moment as

---

remember that every memory is "part of," and included within, our soul's direction and permanent growth.

being the definition of you, yet it is not. The Law of Love is eternal. That Law of Love is the only truth to set your focus upon. Questions?

Question: "Could you give us a list of keys that will bring us freedom when we put them into action?"

I give to you this day the first key to focus on. That is to bring into your conscious memory the experiences of your past that have "created you" in this moment. Do you understand?

Answer: "Yes."

It is that simple. However, the retrieving of such memory is sometimes a very painful process. Why is it painful? Perceptions that you hold of an experience are illusive, for you see these experiences through judgment, or dual perception. You hold these experiences as happening *to you*, not happening *with you*. You see yourself as only one molecule instead of one part of a wave. You are included "within the wave." You are not included "without it."

Dear ones, Dear hearts, start to retrieve the memories of being "with," rather than memories of things happening "to you alone." Strive and go beyond a limited perception, and you will begin to see with a thousand eyes, and you will open to the Law of Love. Questions?

Question: "Yes. You've just said something, 'included within.' Are you saying that we, including yourself and other members of the hierarchy, are included within God and that all is here is the illusion?"

MIGHTY I AM

We are but a small portion of that Mighty, Magnificent I AM. And even to fathom the all inclusiveness of that Mighty I AM, even to fathom but one sweet breath of that, is to touch a limitless motion. Now, Dear ones, Dear hearts, focus upon this that I give to you. Focus upon one step at a time. Yes, you are all included within that Mighty Heart, that Mighty Love of the I AM. And as each day that the I AM inhales and exhales, you are within. So be it. Questions?

Question: "Yes. May we take this transmission in its audio form and put it on our website?"

You may share all the teachings that I have given you with those who have the eyes to see and the ears to hear. There are those who mock you, those who say, "How could one ever achieve such communication?" But know this, it does exist beyond the dual eyes. There is a reality that exists beyond the small reality—that illusion that you are experiencing now. There is a time that exists beyond time. There is the eternal truth of love, and it binds us all as ONE to another. Dear ones. Questions?

Answer: "I have no further questions on the discourse you have just presented."

Then proceed with your other questions.

Question: "As you are very well aware, we have made great sacrifice and worked diligently to bring this message to this Plane and this Planet, and in doing so we have incurred great expense, which, on one hand, has enabled us to move forward, but on another has encumbered us in this duality. It has been suggested that we do something in addition to this. Would you have any suggestions?"

Of course, this is all "Maya" again.
This is all illusion, but it is the path that you have chosen.

Response: "I understand, but I now choose a path where we can continue with this work without any encumbrance."

And so you desire to be free. You desire your liberation from illusion?

Answer: "Yes. At all levels."

KARMA, CHOICE, AND FREE WILL

You see, Dear ones, as I've spoken before of Karma, and when I speak of this, I speak only of action and the actions we choose to take in the world. You have shared this message in many forms and, for that, we are grateful for your service. It was a service that was chosen with forethought, yet it was a service that was chosen through your Free Will. It is odd for you now to question Free Will when you are choosing to align yourself to such a mighty plan and such a mighty work. It is your choice always, Dear one, Dear heart, to bring forward even but one or two words of our transmissions. It is your choice always to share this information in whatever form is available for those to receive. We support all of these fine acts of generosity and kindness and they bring blessings unto you. They free you from other Karmic encumbrances. The work that you have done, the work that has been brought forward, has brought many blessings into your life, has it not?

Answer: "I agree."

And now, at this time, do you not feel more free than you ever have been?

Answer: "Yes."

This is where the focus and the attention must go. You must understand and give thanks for such a blessing within your life. However, the tortures of the world are also there, are they not?

Answer: "Yes, however, I take them much less seriously."

And is this not, again, the freedom that you speak of?

Answer: "Yes, it most certainly is."

GRATITUDE AND BLESSING

It is a matter, again, of perception and how you see either with the "dual eyes" or a "thousand eyes." I do suggest that you look upon the great blessings brought forward in this work, and this will help to lessen the suffering of the debt that you feel, the heaviness of lack that you feel, when you begin to understand the great transmutation and transformation that you have brought forward, not only to yourself but to many, many others. It is important to understand the blessings that are brought forward in this work, the sweetness and the joy that it brings, for that is always the intention; that is always the purpose.

Response: "In my heart of hearts, I feel like I have just begun to get warmed up in bringing this message forward to the world."

It is always important to follow your heart, for when you follow your heart you are living only that Law of Love. That is the Divine Law. That is the Divine Law of the truth and the treasures of heaven. Questions?

Question: "Is there a way for us to continue to only do this and to satisfy the responsibilities that we have created in doing this?"

"DOUBT IS DEBT"

To bring balance forward with those past-due responsibilities, one must diligently call upon the Violet Flame to bring mercy, to bring compassion in all situations. That is most important—to call that forward, so that situations can begin to ease themselves. Situations can then begin to transmute themselves. The Karmas, the actions that have been taken in the past, seem to follow us and become part of our present. One then feels chained to the past, feels he cannot move to any sort of present, or even visualize a future, until he is unfettered from the actions of the past. This is truly what you speak of when you speak of debt, for debt is indeed doubt. Debt is the measure of your doubt—your doubt of your divinity and of your service. Your doubt will impact what you give.

Response: "Whoa!"

It is indeed that measurement of a lack of confidence in what you are achieving. Call forth the Violet Ray. Call it forth to transmute all that doubt that you carry. Call it forth, Dear ones, Dear hearts. Questions?

Question: "Yes. It sounds like we need to call it forth daily, more than once a day. Transmute it. You are correct. I have doubted my worthiness to help any of you or the world and yet we have continued to do so. It is my desire to bring all of this to balance, to transmute the doubt and to love, and then all will be brought to balance. Is this not so?"

It is so, Dear one. The actions that you choose today indeed impact the world you will live in tomorrow; therefore, the chelas are often presented with, "Am I making a wise choice? Am I truly serving my path?" Do you see, Dear one? It was never promised to be easy, however, the reward is immeasurable. We are always here to give our assistance to you. Questions?

Answer: "Yes. As we have spoken, I can tell from the answers you have given that it would also be your preference that we stay focused on one mission."

Of course, this is always our first choice. However, we realize that the chelas who we work with still carry their Karmas of the past and still create Karmas presently that they will fulfill in the future. You see, Dear one, spend time in meditation, spend time looking with a "thousand eyes" and you will then begin to see, you will then begin to hear. It is much more important to understand this. Then, your actions will feel aligned with that great and Mighty Law of Love. The work you have brought forward is a blessing indeed. It cannot be measured at all by the doubt that you feel. May that doubt be a feeling only. When you allow it to pervade all action, it becomes an energy and a force unto itself. Do you understand?

Answer: "Yes. I apologize to you for letting my doubt encumber our work."

Then, let us now move forward in the light of a New Day. Let us now move forward, using the Violet Ray to transmute all sense of lack, all doubt that we feel, and to transmute the little Will to align itself to a greater Plan Divine. Understand, Dear heart, Dear one, that the work you have been given to do is one that you are perfectly prepared to handle. Have I not said before that all tests are for those who are properly prepared?

Answer: "Yes."

CHAPTER SEVEN

Growth of the Soul

~

*Saint Germain prophesies the Great Purification
and shares spiritual techniques.*

Greetings beloveds. in that Mighty Violet Flame, I AM Saint Germain, and I stream forth on that Mighty Violet Flame of mercy, compassion and forgiveness. As usual Dear hearts, I request permission to come forward.

Response: "You most certainly have permission and you are most welcome."

"THIS IS THE TIME"

Dear hearts, it is most important that you continue with our work. For you see, it is during this Time of Transition that you have experienced the momentum—that aggregate body of light—that we built.[1] This aggregate body was brought forward to bring forth a Spiritual Awakening, to foster harmony among all people. It was brough forward to bring forth, shall we say, a greater understanding of spiritual reality…an understanding of the New Dimensions and, of course, an understanding of evolution and ultimate liberation and freedom. Dear ones, now we have entered into a Time of Testing where all souls that have been led to this greater understanding and greater awakening, are tested. Tested, shall we say, not because they are incomplete, but tested because they are readied, because this is the time. The time is now as we have always stated before.[2]

A NEW TIMELINE

There are many changes that are happening now in the Earth Plane and Planet. Changes, not only geophysically, volcanic eruptions, earthquakes, environmental and weather, but also changes that are happening within the collective consciousness itself. These changes are most important, shall we say, to bring forth the birth of the New Dimensions and to bring forth an understanding of the "Golden Age."

The Golden Age will arrive as a birth, and will bring a timeline of understanding and education. The birth we bring forward, shall we say, as the next step in human evolution. The Golden Age is most important, Dear ones and Dear hearts.

PURIFICATION AND ALIGNMENT

It has been humanity's choice as to how it shall arrive. It may come through a Time of Testing, a time where the soul itself is brought through a fire of purification. It may also come, through a change in the Earth itself, a change where the physical body experiences a type of purification. This purification, at what level upon which happens, is most important, for you see, it is through this purification that one begins to bring his Will into a greater alignment to the Divine Plan. This alignment is most important for all of humanity to understand, for this alignment brings forth a clarity and a purity of purpose. This purpose streams forth from the heart of the great Logos, the Great Central Sun, and under its jurisdiction comes all the Rays, with their force and energy.

This force and energy leads humanity onward into a greater spiral of evolution, and this evolution serves that Mighty Plan Divine. Beloveds, this Time of Testing that is upon all of humanity, is a time where one will enter into a greater understanding of choice and a greater alignment of the Will itself. It is important to bring forth this alignment of the Will.

GOBEAN'S ROLE FOR HUMANITY

Beloved El Morya has served this need through the work of the Blue Ray. In the Gobean Vortex, this energy of alignment is being held in its purity for all of humanity. Alignment within itself brings forth a greater harmony, a transformation of the soul, if you will. This transformation is very important for all of humanity to understand those choices facing it, to understand the greater harmony and the greater Will influencing

---

1. Aggregate Body of Light: The Ascended Masters often define an Aggregate Body of Light as the sum or mass of our individual light-bodies; however, this definition is extended to larger bodies of light created by the Ascended Masters and Divine Beings.
2. See Appendix CC3: *Saint Germain's Prophecies of Change.*

the actions of mankind. When one begins to view humanity through a lens of perception, seeing the greater harmony in all of humanity's activities, then one begins to understand that there are no mistakes in the world around them. Every action serves another action. Yet that action, within itself, is a result of a past action.

How does one enter into this greater alignment? How does one serve this greater purified Will? How does one, then, come forward and transmute the past so that the future may move forward into transformation.

"THE SOUL IS TESTED ACCORDINGLY"

Apply the Violet Flame, Dear ones, Dear chelas. Apply this Mighty Law of Mercy, Transformation, and Forgiveness. It is only through this Mighty Law in action that the soul can withstand this Time of Testing, and the soul, in its awakening and evolution, can then move forward to a greater alignment to this Divine Plan. It is only through this Mighty Law that the soul can then withstand all that is hurled against it, for you see, the Time of Testing is exactly as it is stated. The soul is tested in accordance to its own skill. The soul is tested according to its own understanding.[3]

When the small child is educated and is first learning how to read and write the child is tested for words that it has already learned. It is not tested at a level for which it has not been trained. The child is tested for new words. Use this as a way of understanding the Time of Testing that is upon you. At times you may wonder why the test is so hard; why the test is seems to be one ready to break your Will in half. But understand, Dear ones, Dear hearts, Dear chelas of mine, the test is for the student who is already properly prepared for a new level of understanding. The test is for the one who is ready to withstand each question as a problem to be solved. See in the moment that the test itself is only that…a test. It is a limited experience. It is only brought forth, as you would call it, as a bump in the road. It is not a permanent situation. It is only a temporary experience for the soul to move through and to learn from. Then the soul itself can measure its own experience and move onward in growth.

TESTING AND GROWTH

It is important to understand this upcoming perilous time for there will be those who see this peril as something the soul deserves or brought upon itself, but this is not so. The soul in its journey and sojourn in reality, has been brought forward to move the soul forward through its own evolution. Know how important this testing is. Only through this testing can the soul use its experiences and then gain and grow through them. Know then, that only when something has been purchased through hard work, through the experience and sweat of the brow, can it be truly valued. This is important to understand, for in the world of dual experience and dual consciousness — as above so below — there is always the need for balance. As I have said Dear ones, Energy-for-energy and it is only through that experience of Energy-for-energy that the soul then values the experience, whether perceived as good or bad.[4]

YOUR EXPERIENCES BUILD LIGHT

There are many of those, who in the process of seeking liberation, seek complete detachment. And yes, it is so that we

---

3. Saint Germain's Teachings Regarding the Growth of the Soul: "The soul is tested in accordance with its own skill . . . according to its own understanding."

Tests are not punishments! Keep in mind the temporal illusion of trying times and trying circumstances. Be assured transformation, growth, and spiritual evolution are the permanent results.

Knowledge and experience is "Purchased through hard work and the sweat of the brow," and therefore is highly valued. This is the foundation of the spiritual principle of *Energy-for-energy.*

In order to seek higher spiritual levels and spiritual liberation, Saint Germain reminds students that the soul, "does not detach from what it has learned" in each lifetime. The experiences of each lifetime help to shape and develop the soul's unique, individualized Aggregate Body of Light.

Suppressed memories often surface in destructive and dysfunctional patterns. Once a chela has the courage to face and experience the pain surrounding dark memories, the Re-membering causes a purification of the soul. This same metaphysical and spiritual initiation is often known as facing your dark side.

---

4. Energy-for-energy: To understand this spiritual maxim, one must remember Isaac Newton's Third Law of Motion: for every action there is an equal and opposite reaction. However, while energies may be equal, their forms often vary. The Ascended Masters often use this phrase to remind chelas to properly compensate others to avoid Karmic retribution; and repayment may take many different forms.

must detach ourselves from this physical world to move on into higher understanding and reality. But yet the soul does not detach itself from what it has learned. The soul does not detach itself in building its own aggregate body of light, for each experience gains and grows upon itself exponentially. As I have said in many of my own discourses, and as dear Sananda often reminds us, it is always the experience that is important, is it not? It is the only way; it is truly the way of learning. The soul moves on and forward in this learning and in this path, and there it gains and it grows with each experience, one upon the other. But what if the memory that is kept, is sharp and wounding? What if the memory that is kept, instead of moving the soul forward, becomes blocked? What if the soul cannot move forward, but is stuck in that same furrow or grove of experience?

VIOLET RAY REMOVES OBSTACLES

That is what the use of the transmuting Violet Ray is for…to unblock all circumstances, to remove all obstacles, and to allow the soul to continue in its path of growth. It does not remove the test, no indeed, Dear chelas, dear students. The test is of vast importance. What the Ray does is remove the obstacles that would keep you from your path and from where you are . . . towards. Understand this, Dear ones: when you call upon this Violet Ray it will remove the obstacles, however, it will not remove the tests that are required to move you forward in your own initiation. This initiation is of vast importance. It is the initiation of the mind. It is the initiation of thought. It is the initiation of perception.

CONSCIOUS "RE-MEMBERING" AND "HIS-STORY"

How does one view a past situation when they Re-member it? By Re-membering.[5] By bringing it into conscious activity.

To bring it into conscious memory requires the person (to) Re-member such an item, such an experience, in the way that it is aligned to the series of causes. The *series of causes* humanity defines as, *His-story*.[6]

EXPERIENCE, MEMORY, AND PERFECTION

It is the telling of the story of circumstance. There are many perceptions to history. There are many understandings and illusions that the soul may then paint upon the canvas of experience. But it is most important to understand this to bring this *His-story* — the series of causes — into its own timeline within itself. Then the soul understands how each has served in its own perfection, in its own wonder. Only in this type of memory, in this type of Re-membering of a grand alignment to the Divine Plan, can the soul then move forward without blockage, without negative forces holding it back, without it being imprisoned through the essence of duality.

---

5. Re-member: The process of recalling past events may be painful or wounding, or the recalled presence can create obstacles to spiritual growth. The Re-membering Process uses the careful evaluation of thoughts and perceptions to recalibrate memory. Saint Germain suggests these important steps:

Use of the Violet Flame is critical to remove identified obstacles blocking our spiritual growth and development. Since the Violet Flame perfectly balances Karmic situations, students may find that the challenge or test is not entirely eliminated; however, the ability to focus and emotionally and mentally progress through personal trials is assisted and honed.

Diligently work to overcome self-illusion. Personal critique is aided by the application of His-Story. Review of His-Story is best accompanied by a constructed timeline of serial causes, or the reasons certain actions or conditions persist.

According to Saint Germain, the soul perfectly serves its own unfoldment and development. Through developing detached states of Re-membering His-Story, negative blocks may be removed; reducing the suffering and pain imposed through captivity in dual perceptions. (e.g., good-bad; light-dark; weak-strong)

Evolving perceptions to simultaneously experience both sides of duality is incredibly freeing. Saint Germain explains that Re-membered experiences usually contain elements of light or dark, good or bad, happy or sad, etc. Moving our memory to this new expansive perspective, seeing contrasting elements, initiates consciousness into the experience of Unity, the One, and alignment to the Divine Will.

The Blue Ray, which is a well-known transformational energy perfected by Master El Morya, is recommended to transform obstructing ideas, opinions, and perceptions locked into dual expression. Saint Germain recommends calling upon the Master Teacher El Morya and his inherent Mastery of the Blue Ray in action— the Blue Flame — to move beyond duality, initiating your consciousness into the Law of Love.

6. His-Story: The re-telling of the story of circumstance directly related to one's level of spiritual understanding, perceptions and personal experience.

DETACHMENT

When an experience is Re-membered as being bad, or when an experience is Re-membered as only being good, it is trapped in the dual experience [duality]. But with the proper detachment experience can be Re-membered exactly for what it was—containing all elements within itself, bad and good, the forces of light and the forces dark. All experiences contain these things in the duality of this world, and to say that they contain only one is to trap yourself again, within the illusion.

"ALL THINGS CONTAIN THE ONE"

When one begins to understand this mighty work of the liberating Violet Flame, the Violet Flame brings the consciousness to a level of understanding; that all things, within themselves, contain the ONE. It is in this Unity of Consciousness that the soul then moves forward into its own greater understanding and alignment to the Divine Will.

EL MORYA AND THE BLUE FLAME

If you have trouble understanding alignment and are stuck in that one moment of seeing an experience as only good or as only bad … as only light, or as only dark … as only hot, or as only cold, call upon beloved El Morya. It is this Blue Ray of complete transformation that brings the Point of Perception to understanding that dual forces are contained in all things, and a greater alignment and transformation awaits you. Call upon my beloved brother El Morya. Call upon the Blue Flame, for the results of this Blue Flame will bring you to a greater understanding. Then you will begin to lay the groundwork and framework to understand that Mighty Law of Love.

THE LAW OF LOVE ALLOWS

In that Law of Love you can see and understand the acceptance, tolerance, and complete detachment. It is through this Mighty Law of Love that Brotherhood and Sisterhood are achieved; that the Mighty Oneship comes forward in complete

alignment to a Divine Plan.[7] The Law of Love at times brings a sense of detachment. The Law of Love at times, allows you to turn your back in a trying situation; yet, this Law of Love moves the soul onward and upward in complete and total understanding of the dual forces. It allows an understanding of darkness when there is also light. It allows light to flood into the darkest of crevices.

You see Dear ones; love within itself allows all things to be sustained. Love within itself allows all things to be maintained. The Law of Love allows dual forces to exist side-by-side simultaneously. The Law of Love allows several perceptions of one situation to exist. The Law of Love, within itself is tolerance supreme. It allows all levels of creation to coexist in their path of Mastery. These two mighty dual forces, when blended together, create a harmonic alignment, and alchemize the Violet Flame.

VIOLET FLAME FREQUENCIES

The Violet Flame is of vast importance, Dear ones, for it is indeed the hope of all humanity.[8] The Violet Flame, within itself, allows humanity to enter into this greater understanding

---

7. Law of Love (expanded). In previous teachings the Ascended Masters have affirmed, "If you live love, you will create love." This is foundational to understanding the Law of Love. In further teachings, the Master Teachers expand this concept and explain the concept of love in depth and dimension and declare that through practicing the Law of Love, one experiences acceptance and understanding; tolerance, alongside detachment. Saint Germain elaborates: "The Law of Love brings a sense of detachment. The Law of Love, at times, allows you to turn your back in a trying situation, but yet this Law of Love moves the soul onward and upward in complete understanding of the dual forces." Metaphysically, the Law of Love allows different and varied perceptions of One experience, situation, or circumstance to exist simultaneously. From this viewpoint the Law of Love is the practice of tolerance. To synthesize Saint Germain's teachings on this venerated yet highly misunderstood spiritual precept: Love + Tolerance = Alchemy (Transformation). This is the philosophical basis of the activity of the Violet Flame.

8. Spiritual Prophecies: The Violet Flame, which is the outgrowth of practicing the Law of Love, is the greatest hope for all of humanity and will enable consciousness to enter into the Oneship.

Saint Germain explains Ascended Master Consciousness as a higher frequency of thought, feeling, and action which embraces the unity of humanity through the principle of the Oneship. These spiritual practices and principles are foundation for HU-man consciousness to enter into the New Dimensions. This embraces: Allowing, Alignment, Transformation, Self-knowledge: *Know thyself.*

of the Oneship.[9] It allows humanity to enter into a greater understanding of the other dimensions. When you enter into this higher frequency—this higher understanding of allowing, this higher understanding of aligning, this higher understanding that is transformational—you enter into the beginning stages of "Ascended Master Consciousness." As I have said before, "know thyself; know first thyself."

SUPPRESSED MEMORIES

If you find yourself Re-membering a situation, call upon that Mighty Violet Flame so that the remembrance of it is brought in its totality so that all is understood, and you may see it through the true eyes of wisdom. There are many who follow this path but refuse to acknowledge it, or, are in denial of pain that they hold within themself. This pain, which is indeed a suppressed memory, carries on within them; embodiment, through embodiment, through embodiment.[10] They come to a point in their own evolution, through the non-expression of that suppressed memory, where they begin to attract unto themself, violence, hatred and the ugliness of that suppressed memory.

There are Hermetic Laws that rule and govern the soul and its travel in the dual worlds, and, resultingly, all things attract their equal unto themself. But when the soul has the courage to bring about an understanding of suppressed memory, of suppressed remembrance, then the laws allow a great purging, a great purification, so to speak, of the soul.[11] These memories are exposed to the Mighty Light of God which never, ever fails, and through the use of the transmutation of the Violet Fire and Flame, all memories are brought forward beyond dual understanding.

---

9. Oneship (expanded): "A combination of many, which comprises the whole, and when divided contains both feminine and masculine characteristics."[7] This definition was derived from the teachings in Points of Perception and is expanded in Divine Destiny to include the evolution of consciousness which is the natural outgrowth of humanity practicing and living the Law of Love, based on the principles of detachment and allowing.

10. Suppressed Memory: Denial of pain.

11. See Appendix DD3: The Great Purification.

ACCEPTANCE OF DARKNESS

One cannot ice over a sad and painful situation with, "it is all good, it is all light," …this is nonsense. For you see Dear ones, there are the dark forces that do indeed work alongside the forces of good. So often many chelas say, "let us move only within that mighty light. Let us move only forward in light and goodness," and know this, Dear ones, Dear hearts, that light and goodness do indeed reign supreme. But light and goodness within itself, in the dual worlds, exist because there is also the dark side. This must be accepted also by the chelas to understand that their experiences contain both of these forces. To allow only one half of the expression is to allow only one half of the soul to evolve.[12] Inevitably, the soul itself is brought forward into an embodiment where it will need to deal with suppressed memories, with that suppressed half of itself that it never allowed itself to experience.

How do we quickly move onward? How do we bring the dark memories forward and move to that higher plane of understanding? It is through that mighty use of the Violet Flame. Let me explain further about this "Mighty Law in Action."

---

12. The Dark Side: The energy and force of the common man draws power from raw human emotions like: pain, hatred, passion, and attachment. The contrary Light Side, which evolves the human to the HU-man, and the HU-man to the One, is aligned with honesty, compassion, mercy, love, and self-sacrifice. Both forces exist simultaneously within the HU-man, whose challenge is to align or balance the dual forces within through recognition (Re-membering); self-knowledge (His-Story); purification (Alignment), and Mastery (Oneship). This process can be blatant or curiously subtle and leads the soul lifetime after lifetime through a transformational liberation process—the Ascension.

Perhaps one of the best known allegorical tales of the Dark Side is *Star Wars*. These memorable quotes come from this engaging story of good versus evil:

"The dark side clouds everything."~Yoda

"It is simple enough to know the light. A Jedi must feel the tension between the two sides of the force in himself, and in the universe." ~Thon

"Attachment is forbidden, possession is forbidden. Compassion, which I would define as unconditional love, is essential to a Jedi's life."~Anakin Skywalker

According to Saint Germain, "To allow only one-half of the expression is to allow only one-half of the soul to evolve."

A FORM OF KRIYA YOGA

If you have a dark memory that is suppressed, blocking your endeavors, blocking your growth, blocking your forward movement—you can call forth this Mighty Violet Ray and bring it as a breath throughout the entire Chakra System. This teaching was brought forward, by that mighty messenger who taught the Violet Flame, through the Kriya (a type of Yoga) of breath. It is important to understand that there are many applications of the Violet Flame. There are those who bring the Violet Flame into action through thought. There are those who obtain the Violet Flame through sound and decree. There are those who obtain this Violet Flame, this "Mighty Law in Action," through the breath.

For those who have physical obstruction within the body itself, which bring dis-ease, dis-harmony and problems related to the physical health of the body, bring forward that Mighty Violet Ray in breath. Bring it forward using the instructions for activating the Chakra System. This is most important, Dear ones, Dear hearts. Now before I proceed, Questions?

Answer: "Not at this time."

VIOLET FLAME BREATH

Then I would like to proceed now, in giving a brief instruction for using the "Violet Flame Breath."[13] For you see, Dear ones, Dear hearts, this will alleviate the problem that the questioner is experiencing. This is an ancient blockage that has been brought to the surface now, will bring forward your healing. It was the time that you spent traveling in the Southern door of the Gobean Vortex. You are bringing it forth now, in a greater alignment to your Will, to move your service forward. Haven't you have been praying and decreeing for your service to be revealed?

Answer: "Yes!"

---

13. See Appendix EE3: *Various Applications of the Violet Flame and the Violet Flame Breath.*

"A RARE COMBINATION"

Now, in order for you to move forward into this greater service, into this greater alignment to the Plan Divine, we must now work to remove this one physical blockage, which is a result of (not) Re-membering. Now for your sake, it is not important that we talk about the experience as of yet. This will be revealed to you after you begin the releasing process. It will be revealed to you in a way so that you understand the past experience that created this block; that it is of this dual world, and this dual world only. Things as you perceive them are not good or bad only, they are that rare combination of both. Now, let us start first with the breath. First, close the eyes and focus upon the pineal gland. Let me know when this has been achieved.

Answer: "All right."

THE TECHNIQUE

Now, do you see a spinning of the Violet Flame opening the Third Eye?

Answer: "Yes."

From this spinning, move the flow downward into the Heart Chakra. This can be achieved by visualization. Move the flame through the throat itself and onward into the heart where it radiates again. You will feel the combination of the pineal and the heart functioning together as one force and as one breath.

Response: "Yes."

Now move it down to the sacral area. Signal me when you have achieved this.

Response: "Yes."

Now all three are functioning as one: The Pineal, Heart and Sacral (Chakras). What this allows for is the front part of the

Chakra System to be connected as ONE. Do you feel this energy within you?

Answer: "Yes."

Now we shall start. Once these three contacts have been merged, we'll begin to move the breath up the spine. Let us start with one breath. Begin . . .

Response: "Yes."

Do you detect a slight blockage in the back area from where you are experiencing this pain?

Answer: "It slows down the breath."

Let's move this blockage . . . again, up the spine to the base of the neck. Do this no less than seven complete times. Signal me when you are finished.

Response: "Yes, it's complete."

Now that you have completed these seven cleansing breaths, you will feel some radiation at the base of the neck. Is this so?

Answer: "It feels very warm."

This is where the energy has now moved to. This is the energy, the Re-membering of that experience. Now you must bring this through the skull and back to the pineal. Move this energy, again, through the skull; but seven times . . . it is as the completion of a great loop. When you complete this, please signal me.

Response: "I'm complete."

Now beloved, Dear one, do you feel the mass of completed energy that is now completed within the Third Eye, the pineal itself?

Answer: "Yes."

From this (point) you can Re-member the experience. Now you can view this experience in pure detachment. Do you understand what created such a block within your system? Do you see the blockage which you refused to acknowledge and complete?

Answer: "This is very interesting. At a technical level, what I'm seeing is this disease in the body, and through the proper breath technique, can move it to the pineal and then view it."

THE BALANCE OF FORCES

This is correct. This is another work of the Violet Flame itself, for it brings the soul to a level of detachment. That is where the soul can have complete experiences of both forces, without allowing one to override the other. This is how the body can be brought back into balance and the soul, then, can continue in its path of growth and evolution.

Continue with this technique. It may take you several days, depending on the severity of the block involved. Once you become aware of the experience that you suppressed and allow a full body experience of this, the pain will cease and you will begin to understand this total alignment process.

READINESS

You see Dear ones, bringing these experiences into another level of initiation is most important, for this indeed is part of the test. Any test in front of you is a test that you are ready to receive. It is one that you are ready to experience. Now, before I proceed, do you have any more questions about this instruction?
Answer: "No. This is very simple and yet very effective."

Call upon that Mighty Violet Ray before and after using the technique and the energy of the Violet Flame will assist you in this endeavor.

Response: "I will."

And now, as I have completed my discourses, are there other questions that you would like to bring forward?

Answer: "Yes, I did have some prepared. However, just having had this experience, I think I shall save them for another time."

Then in that Mighty Christ, I shall return at the next time allocated for teaching. May the Violet Ray stream forth into the hearts of all men and women united in the Brotherhood and Sisterhood. Hitaka!

CHAPTER EIGHT

The New Children

Saint Germain prophesies the birth of the Seventh Manu.

Greetings beloveds, in that Mighty Christ, I AM Saint Germain, and I stream forth that Mighty Violet Ray of Mercy, Transmutation and ultimate Forgiveness. As usual Dear hearts, I request permission to come forward.

Response: "Please Saint Germain, come forward, you are most welcome."

SCIENTIFIC PRINCIPLE OF THE VIOLET RAY

The work upon that Mighty Violet Ray is indeed an important one, Dear ones, Dear stewards of mine. For you see, it is this work of that Mighty Violet Ray that brings forth the ultimate forgiveness, the ultimate transmutation of humanity, which is necessary to bring forth evolutionary consciousness and understanding into the New Times. It is, indeed, as I have said so many times, "that most refreshing drink," a drink that you should never tire of, a drink that always fills you completely.[1]

Forgiveness, in itself, brings forward an understanding of humanity and an evolution. It is true compassion, in action, which many others have spoken of. Beloved Kuan Yin has brought forth many teachings on compassion and it is indeed through that Mighty Violet Ray that compassion streams forth to all of humanity in a greater understanding. It is through this Ray that suffering of all kinds is lessened, that disease and the harm that it brings to the spirit and the body are also lessened. It is through that Mighty Violet Ray that many of the little sufferings and little ills of humanity are treated completely. Understand and know this and apply it as a scientific principle.

At a scientific level, when you use the Violet Ray, it brings a higher vibratory rate to the body itself. Have you not noticed Dear ones, that when you use this Mighty Violet Ray on a steady basis, that it brings forth better health, a better attitude, better spiritual understanding of all situations? It brings resolution to all conflicts, and creates that ever present unity. This is so important Dear ones, Dear hearts, that I cannot over-emphasize this fact. At a scientific level too, not only is the Ray known to cure diseases, but it also brings all conflict into resolution and creates a platform for harmony. If your politicians (would) only apply this Mighty Violet Ray at a worldwide level, there would be no need for nuclear armaments. There would be no need for military movements. It could bring healing at all levels to the government, to your economies. It could bring healing at personal levels, at societal levels, and also at governmental levels.[2]

---

1. Spiritual Prophecies: The Violet Flame plays an ever important role for humanity as we enter the New Times. Its transcendent, alchemizing vibration evolves human consciousness through humanity's collective transmutation.

Through applying the Violet Ray during tumultuous times, suffering and disease are collectively lessened for humanity, increasing the presence of Compassion throughout the world.

2. Saint Germain on the Violet Flame: According to Saint Germain, the Violet Flame raises the vibration of the physical body. This creates certain individual benefits, both physical and emotional, that can inevitably impact the world and world events. They are:

Better health and the lessening of the disease process.

A positive attitude resulting in spiritual understanding that may give rise to the resolution of conflicts of all kinds.

Through evoking harmony, the Flame helps cure disease and emotional conflict.

Use of the Violet Flame for worldwide conflict could reduce nuclear threats, militarization of the world, and heal corrupt governments and suffering economies.

While the Violet Flame heals at a personal level, this benefic energy positively influences worldwide societies and governments.

Saint Germain suggests this Violet Flame decree to assist the Earth during the ongoing changes to assist our entry into the New Times:

"Violet Ray, stream forth from the Heart of the Mighty Logos—the Great Central Sun. Stream in, through, and around Beloved Babajeran—the Freedom Star. Violet Ray, stream forward, and transmute the cause and effect, the record and memory of all that is holding the Earth back from its own evolution and understanding of Compassion, Forgiveness, Mercy, and Tolerance."

The Violet Flame ideally liberates our consciousness and assists the Ascension Process.

VIOLET RAY FOR OUR EARTH

The Violet Ray is very important Dear ones, Dear hearts, and may its light now stream forth from the heart of the Mighty Logos, the Great Central Sun:

> "Stream in, through, and around
> Beloved Babajeran — Freedom Star.
> Violet Ray come forth!
> Transmute the cause and effect,
> the record and the memory,
> of all that is holding the Earth back
> from its own evolution,
> and the understanding of Compassion,
> Forgiveness, Mercy, and Tolerance."

VIOLET RAY OF LIBERATION

The mighty "Law in Action" will not only transmute any situation that you find uncomfortable, it will also liberate you Dear ones, and set you free. It will liberate you from all circumstances that are holding you from greater and deeper spiritual understanding. It can also bring liberation and enhance one's consciousness in working toward Ascension. So actively use this Mighty Violet Ray. It is important.

FEED THE GROWTH OF YOUR CONSCIOUSNESS

Now I would like to give a small discourse on the importance of *sattva* or rhythm. It is only through rhythm that a constant application of a wave can be applied. When we work with those whom we have chosen, we bring forth the energy and the intention of the work in a "wave." This is very much like the waves in an ocean in your tidal system upon the Earth. This water or "Water of Knowledge" fills and impacts the beach.[3] This

impact works through a constant influx, a constant knowing in a timely manner that it is there, not in the way that it has been brought forward in the current schools of education. It is almost like mealtime, when your stomach knows it must be fed, or your body requires water on a steady basis. Consciousness, when it is growing, requires the same needs, the same food, so to speak. So these are given on a timely basis. I hope now that you understand why we have chosen one day a week to do our work together. This is a time when your consciousness needs feeding so that it may continue its growth through this special nourishment. I would also like to give some discourse, today, on the Golden Cities and their importance at this time. However, before I proceed, do you have any questions?

Answer: "Yes, I do."

Proceed.

---

3. Water of Knowledge: According to the Master Teachers, consciousness requires nourishment—much like the physical body—in order to grow and develop. When the Ascended Masters choose a chela or student to work with, they emit this vital energy to the individual, which transmits an essential substance known as the Water of Knowledge. The Water of Knowledge functions like an oceanic tidal system and transfers waves of conscious energy of differing degrees of power, force, and intention designed to stimulate and impact the student's consciousness through various effects.

The constant roll of undulating consciousness moves with precision and timeliness, geared specifically for the student, and his or her level of Mastery and spiritual achievement. Since this energy is specifically unique for the spiritual level and vibration of the individual, and the "work at hand," Master Teachers often assign a certain day of the week to release the energies of the Water of Knowledge, selected precisely for its vibration, influence, harmony, and Ray Force. Days of the week typically assigned to the Seven Rays are:

Sunday: the Sun; Ruby and Gold Rays
Monday: the Moon; White, Blue, and Pink Rays
Tuesday: Mars; the Ruby Ray and the Pink Ray
Wednesday: Mercury; the Green Ray
Thursday: Jupiter; the Yellow Ray
Friday: Venus; the White, Blue, and Pink Rays
Saturday: Saturn; the Blue and Violet Rays

Balinese Hindus celebrate Saraswati, the Goddess of Learning through specific ceremonies designed to worship "God in his manifestation as the Master of all knowledge." Contained within this series of ceremonies is the *Banyu Pinaruh*, also known as the Water of Knowledge. During this ceremony, devotees swim and wash in sacred rivers and lakes, purify their bodies with medicinal herbs, and engage in communal prayers for spiritual knowledge, spiritual wisdom, and good health. "The more knowledge people have, the wiser they should be in speech, thought, and deed; and human life will become more interesting, beautiful, and delightful and full of peace."

THE INDIGO CHILDREN

Question: "We have heard your discourse in the past on the Seventh Manu and we have also had others who have come to us, with information, on a group of souls incarnating known as the Indigo Children. Could you elaborate and let us know if there any relationship or correlation?"

These great souls are a wave of souls that are currently incarnating on the Earth. Many of them have not been on the Earth Plane, in a schoolroom scenario for several thousand years. Some of these great souls are reincarnating from prior embodiments in Atlantis. Many of them contain high technological information most important right now for the Earth and for the evolution that it is now going through. Some of these beloved Dear ones are incarnating from other planets, some within your own solar system, some, that are indeed, very distant.

THE "THIN VEIL"

Now, when I say this, it is important to understand that only in physicality is there the idea of distance, for you see Dear hearts, Dear ones, the soul itself is timeless. So, therefore, distance, within itself, does not exist to the soul. These galaxies, these star systems that exist in the physical, thousands and thousands of light years away, exist instantly, across a thin Veil of Understanding. They are very close indeed.

"A SPECIAL TASK"

These souls that are coming in at this time, are being brought forward with a special task. Not only are they here for their own evolution and schooling to receive greater understanding and ultimate liberation, they are also here to bring great assistance to many other souls that are now trapped within the cycle of reincarnation upon the Earth Plane and Planet. They bring with them an energy of transmutation. They bring with them an energy of liberation and understanding and their own unique

karma, a series of actions that they must fulfill themselves for their own growth and evolution.[4]

AGE OF TRANSPORTATION

They carry within them, as a collective consciousness, a great collective purpose. This purpose is to assist and help many others upon the path. This assistance will not only come through a greater understanding, a greater tolerance and knowledge of the true spiritual life, but also through an understanding... will come at a technological level, and will move the Earth forward into the Age of Transportation.[5] These souls carry within themselves knowledge from other Star seeds and systems and the understanding of bi-location and timelessness as I have just described.

THE FUTURE ELDERS OF OUR EARTH

This knowledge, of course, will take several thousand years to develop upon the Earth Plane and Planet. However, since each soul continues to move in its journey through the Earth Plane and Planet, time is relative. For you see, in the heart of the Mighty Logos, time is indeed as ONE mighty breath, that would appear only in that sense of time as one second. So you see these beloved Dear ones that are coming through, may be seen as children, but perhaps it is better for us not to refer to them as such. Many of them are indeed ancients, ancients that have existed as great pillars of understanding, great pillars of technological understanding, great pillars of spiritual growth and evolution for humanity. They are elders in a sense, elders brought forth in this great time to move the Earth forward in it's own evolution.

---

4. See Appendix FF3: *The Seventh Manu.*
5. Age of Transportation: A prophesied epoch Earth and humanity will experience once we leave the current Information Age (late eighties through the twenty-first century). The Transportation Age will see humanity's consciousness evolve into Mastery beyond the human maxims of time and space. During this period, which is prophesied to run concurrently with several periods of the Golden Age—the Age of Cooperation and the Age of Peace—humanity will begin interstellar travel, alongside leaps in evolutionary growth resulting in telepathic communication, spiritual technologies, and bi-location.

While many of them, now in this millimeter of experience, are being incarnated as children, they are not children. They are wise, indeed, beyond their years in the same way as when a great Master Teacher is born into the Earth Plane and Planet. Having spent lifetimes learning, prior to this ultimate liberation and Ascension, he or she is now brought forward, and many perceive this individual in awe and wonderment.

"THEY, TOO, WILL BE TESTED"

This same group of souls is seen in this context somewhat, however, I cannot over-emphasize that these souls also carry their own collective karma. In their own development and history there is (comes) their own testing…a time when the Earth itself will receive the great influx of energy from their influence and then they must choose a path.

All who come to the Earth Plane and Planet are bound by the same laws that we have discussed before, and because individuals of great advancement are born here, does not mean that they are not subject to the laws of duality.

"DIVINITY IN ALL"

Of course, humans often work towards deification of the Divine, instead of the acceptance of divinity in all things. This seems to be one of the great parodies of spiritual development within the human.

DIVINE INTERVENTION

However, Dear ones, Dear hearts, it is important to understand the "Seventh Manu," as they are known, and the great blessing of Divine Intervention that this generation, or shall we say, great wave of souls, will give to this Earth. Questions?

THE SEVENTH MANU

Question: "So indeed the 'Indigo Children' as others have termed them, are indeed the 'Seventh Manu' as you had spoken to us back in, as early as 1990?"

This is so, Dear ones. They are referred to as this for they come upon that wave of the "Mighty Violet Ray in Action." They come forth on that Ray of ultimate Forgiveness, Compassion, Transmutation, and Tolerance. They also understand the ceremonial order of nature within itself (Evolutionary Biome). This is the base of their technological understanding. For you see, while they may work within the time of the Information Age, their work, indeed, is for that of the Age of Transportation… that time when mankind will begin to understand and capture the energy that exists within the dimensions themselves.

INTERDIMENSIONAL ENERGIES AND SOUND

Now, so I do not go into information that you are not ready for, I shall try to explain this at a very basic level of understanding. You can feel in this discourse, at the moment of entry or departure of our energies there is a shift. This creates a slippage, shall we say, of the chi or prana as you know it. This orgone exists in small pockets between each of the dimensions. These pockets of energy can be gathered and used, at will, to travel through all of the dimensional frequencies, however, there is much more to know about this and its relationship, primarily, to sound vibration. I will not elaborate any further, but I will say this: in its time and development, this energy will be gathered and used for the Time of Transporation, interdimensionally.

ATLANTEAN SOULS

These souls who have come from another time to your Earth Plane and Planet, from the time of the Atlantean, and understand how matter can be migrated across such dimensions and brought to use *beyond* (the constraints of) time. They also understand some of the limitations that are now experienced within the physical. However, mankind or each human must develop much further on an evolutionary level to use these energies, or else these energies can be used for great miscreations upon the Earth.

TECHNOLOGY AND CONSCIOUSNESS

You see, even when nuclear weapons (and knowledge of) were given to mankind, there was much discussion over the devastation that might be brought through misunderstanding. However, it was deemed that there were some great souls existing upon the Earth at the time, who would also come forward and foster the birth of consciousness alongside the birth of this technology. You see it is not technology itself that we fear; it is the lack of growth of consciousness. Technology itself is only the mirror of the growth of consciousness.[6] Now there are those who do not understand this statement. They do not understand, and they think that technology itself has brought about the destruction of consciousness.

"WE ARE NEVER TESTED BEYOND OUR CAPABILITY"

But when you begin to understand it in its entirety, you will see that technology and consciousness fit together perfectly and are based totally upon the Law of Attraction. So Dear ones, Dear hearts, know that this group of Indigo souls has incarnated at a most important time…a most important time to bring forward consciousness in its evolution. That is why alongside carrying such technological knowledge; they also carry such information and knowledge about tolerance, acceptance, and understanding. You see these are all very important. When higher technologies are dispensed upon mankind, then mankind is tested. And as I have stated before, we are never tested beyond our capability. Do you understand?

Answer: "Yes, I do."

Questions?

Question: "What part of the world is this Seventh Manu group predominantly incarnating in?"

MOTHER MARY'S SPONSORSHIP

Many of them are coming through the energies of the *Swaddling Cloth,* which is located now in South America. However, there are some pockets and groups of souls that are currently being born into the war torn areas as Serbia and Czechoslovakia, and in Bosnia. Upon your Earth Plane and Planet, they come under the sponsorship of beloved Mother Mary. At this time, they must be brought forward with great nurturing to keep their hearts open because upon entering upon the Earth Plane and Planet most immediately become very cynical, when they see the great disparities that exist among the classes of people.[7]

THEIR ASSISTANCE OF GREAT LIGHT

These great beings come from other star systems where there is no such idea of poverty and there is no suffering at the levels

---

6. Spiritual Technology is the practical application, process, methods, and techniques associated with spiritual and sacred knowledge. According to the Ascended Masters, human evolution is prophesied to rapidly evolve along these lines; and while most Spiritual Technology naturally merges with scientific and biologic principles, Spiritual Technology is preferred over the corporate pseudoscience that has negatively influenced our current medical, health, communication, computer, and entertainment sectors. Some avid practitioners of Spiritual Technology claim that the contradictive and secular influences on our current technology actually suppress and retard our innate HU-man unfoldment. Current technology separates man from nature; Spiritual Technology does not.

7. Prophecies of Change: During the Age of Transportation, scientists will begin to access and capture energies that exist beyond the Third Dimension.
During the Age of Transportation, interdimensional travel will be developed and perfected. This opens the door for Time Travel.
According to the Ascended Masters, it is not the growth of technology that is feared by many; it is the fear of the lack of spiritual growth and spiritual conscience congruent to humanity's good use of technology. The souls of the Seventh Manu are prophesied to balance this problem.
Technology is the outgrowth of developed consciousness. It is prophesied that the Seventh Manu will play an important role in merging technology and consciousness through the Law of Attraction. Alongside a keen scientific and technological consciousness, Seventh Manu children have these spiritual qualities: Tolerance, Acceptance, and Compassion.
While many Seventh Manu souls will incarnate throughout the entire world, many of these souls will incarnate in war-torn areas to assist the anchoring of conscious light to flood the world with Compassion and Unity.
The Seventh Manu souls are sponsored by the Ascended Master Mother Mary and are prophesied to primarily incarnate in South America, in an area known as The Swaddling Cloth.

that there are on planet Earth. They have come forward in their great mission, to bring this service of great import. These great beings wipe tears away where there is great suffering and many problems of political and class orientation. Those that are born within the Swaddling Cloth itself, are provided some protection, yet in other areas they are not understood by the societies that they are born into. Of course there are small pockets of these souls that are born everywhere upon the Earth. However, as there are groups of souls that are incarnated to initiate a leap forward or to promote greater understanding, they are also being born into areas upon the Earth where their help and assistance can bring great light, and flood the world with a higher understanding of compassion. Questions?

Question: "How does an individual identify one of these children?"

TOLERANCE AND UNITY CONSCIOUSNESS

Of course all children are born innocent. All children are born with a sense of love and higher understanding, for they carry with them the energy of the Devachan…the energy of that great rest in-between each incarnation. However, these children of higher vibration are born under the influence of Saturn and you will see this Ray Force, which is known as the Blue Ray, giving great influence. That is why many have referred to them as the "Blue or Indigo Children." But I shall give more information on this; this is an influence of Saturn and also, as has been stated in the understanding of Cosmic Wave Belts (see *I AM America Six-Map Scenario*), this is the influence of Neptune, for Neptune (energies) provides highly mystical and spiritual understanding. These children have a high tolerance for others. They have a high tolerance of those of all consciousness levels and cultures. This is exactly how they will be recognized as they enter into adulthood. They will also feel strongly that, "All shall be united as ONE." Their understanding of Unity Consciousness is indeed very high. These are two of the greater indicators. Questions?

A DECREE FOR ASSISTANCE

Question: "For those of us in the United States who are of economic means, is there any way that those who have the heart connection, the consciousness and the means, that they may help these children?"

I have given the decree in my first discourse (see *New World Wisdom, Book Two*). It is the decree that is brought forth at 6:00 a.m. every morning upon awaking. This is indeed an energy that is brought to the Swaddling Cloth.[8] Now, this brings forth an energy that can be utilized for all of the incoming Manu. It does not empower, specifically, the Swaddling Cloth itself, instead, what it does is set up a vibration to the Swaddling Cloth that energizes the entire atmosphere of the Earth and allows the vibration of these souls to come forward.

Question: "I see. So in a certain sense, that decree will help with the sponsorship and acceptance in this plane?"

Indeed it shall, Dear ones, Dear hearts. And those who feel called to that work shall apply it diligently.

Answer: "Yes they shall. Most interesting. I have one other question."

Proceed.

KALI YUGA

Question: "We are now in the time of Kali Yuga. There is much conversation with the practioners of Vedic Astrology as to its starting time, how long the cycle is, and whether there are sub-periods within where there is greater radiance or greater potential in such a time of darkness. Could you elaborate?"

This time of Kali we have spoken of, have we not?

Answer: "Yes we have."

8. See Appendix GG3: *The Swaddling Cloth and Mother Mary.*

There are those who use this time as part of their religious culture and to develop greater understanding. Upon that, I shall not give comment. But, I shall talk about the time itself, that is known as Kali. It is a time of darkness, indeed, that is over the Earth. It has been in existence for over 2,000 years now. This time of darkness that covers the Earth is indeed all related to the Rays and their ability to impact evolution through light and sound. This is why we have given the Violet Flame at this time for the Violet Flame, or that Mighty Violet Ray, allows for the growth of light to come forward to the soul itself.

"AS THE BODY NEEDS FOOD, CONSCIOUSNESS NEEDS SPIRITUALTY"

For as I have stated before, as the body needs food, the soul and its consciousness need spirituality. To understand this at a greater level and in greater harmony, one needs the Light Divine to float in, through and around one's being. In the time of Kali, this process is thwarted significantly. This has to do with the position of the Earth within the solar system and the galaxy; however, it also is, for your presence and soul's growth.

THE SPIRITUAL WARRIOR

This time of Kali is bringing the soul forward to become a very strong Spiritual Warrior. That is why in the time of Kali, there will be many wars upon the Earth Plane and Planet. Wars are not only fought in military action, but within the soul itself, for the soul is constantly at war with the forces of duality. This brings the soul to a greater collective understanding; a greater understanding of the Will, and to move the Will forward for the betterment of all through the Law of Love.

THE GREAT AWAKENING

The time of Kali will exist for some time; however, within it, there are pockets of possibility and potential. One of these pockets is now upon humanity, in the form of the Great Spiritual Awakening of which I have spoken. Prior to that, there was another time of spiritual evolution and growth. But within this time of darkness, where there is a limited amount of light

for use, it is most important that you utilize the Violet Flame. It is as a fertilizer is to a plant. It brings forth the most wondrous blossoms and blooming of the flower. Now, of course, during times of darkness, it is equally important to understand times of light. As we've stated in our past discourses, a time once existed of perfect integrated memory. That time of perfect memory, of course, does not exist under the current situation. This society reflects the current mind of humanity.

And now, Dear one, unless that there are other questions, I shall take my leave.

Answer: "No, at this time I personally don't have any questions, although I do become concerned from time to time about whether we're doing our job properly."

As I have said Dear one, that is doubt. Are you doubting your presence within this work?

Answer: "No, not at all. Not since that discourse."

"A NEW DAY"

Then let us proceed in the light of understanding that a New Day can come forward with complete and total focus upon that Violet Ray of Mercy, Compassion, and Forgiveness.

"May light stream forth in, through, and around all your business activities. May light stream forth into all of your economic activities. May light stream forth into your consciousness and feed the growth of your soul. So be it."

Response: "So be it and thank you."

May that Mighty Violet Ray stream forth now to all who listen to this discourse. May that Mighty Violet Ray stream forth into your hearts and bring forth pure, absolute transmutation.

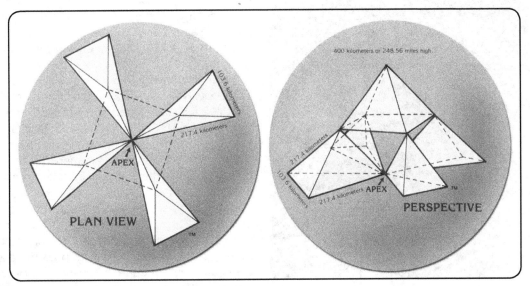

Golden City Dimensions

The above illustration gives the dimensions of the Golden Cities in both kilometers and miles. The height of a Golden City is 248.56 miles. A Golden City Gateway is 64.37 miles. The Golden City Cardinal lei-line is 135.09 miles. However, it is important to note that Golden Cities can vary in size due to their cyclic and varying activity.

Golden City Vortex

A Golden City Vortex — based on the Ascended Masters' I AM America material — are prophesied areas of safety and spiritual energies during the Times of Changes. Covering an expanse of land and air space, these sacred energy sites span more than 400 kilometers (270 miles) in diameter, with a vertical height of 400 kilometers (250 miles). Golden City Vortices, more importantly, reach beyond terrestrial significance and into the ethereal realm. This system of safe harbors acts as a group or universal mind within our galaxy, connecting information seamlessly and instantly with other beings. The Master Teachers coin this phenomenon the Galactic Web.

Fifty-one Golden City Vortices are stationed throughout the world, and each carries a different meaning, a combination of Ray Forces, and a Divine Purpose. Some are older than others; some Vortices are new; and some shift locations. The activation of Golden City Vortices occur in patterns — that's the crux of the numbering system. The Master Teachers call the Earth Beloved Babajeran.

Although the Masters, as a group, oversee all Golden Cities, each stewards his or her own Vortex. A Golden City Vortex works on the principles of electromagnetism and geology. Vortices tend to appear near fault lines, possibly serving as conduits of inner-earth movement to terra firma. The Gobean Vortex near the fissure-filled Mogollon Rim of Arizona; the Malton Vortex of the Midwest, adjacent to the New Madrid fault line; and the Shalahah Vortex of Idaho, an ancient cleft near the Snake River and Hells Canyon, lend credibility to this theory.

Geology has a profound effect on the potency of a Vortex. Not surprising, the five Golden City Vortices rest on areas of highly magnetic geologic formations. The iron-rich content of basalt pillars and ancient-lava deposit serve as natural conductors of electromagnetic energy; igneous

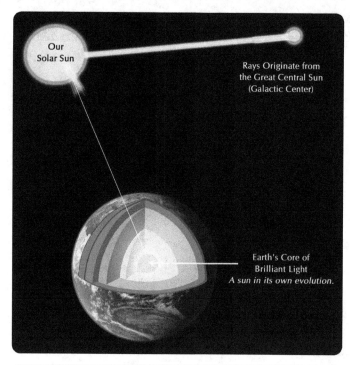

Ray Forces and Golden Cities: (Left) Rays originate from the Galactic Center. (Below) *Ray Forces and Golden Cities:* Ray enters Golden City.

rocks, according to geologic data, create more magnetic pull than sedimentary rocks. That's why Gobean exudes so much energy. Landmarks — such as Mount Baldy in Arizona, the apex of the Southwestern Vortex, and the Golden City Vortex of Shalahah — are filled with basalt and iron-rich rocks.

Water also drives the disbursement of Vortex energies. The Gobean Vortex sits atop the largest aquifer in the Southwest. Shalahah, too, surrounded by three, huge fresh-water lakes near Coeur d'Alene and Pend'Oreille, Idaho, and Flathead Lake in Montana, draws power from water.

Visitors to Golden Cities experience spiritual and psychic development — they feel a heightened sense of balance, harmony, and peace. Natural places of meditation, connection with spirit guides, and contact with past-life experiences, Vortices can instantly align the human energy field (aura). During your first stay in a Vortex, you may sleep more while your body adjusts to powerful energies. As you acclimate, you'll undergo a rejuvenation of the body and the spirit. After the shock subsides, many Vortex-seeking pilgrims will engage in prayer and group ceremonies with friends and spiritual mentors, awakening deep connections among fellow humans.

Arcing of Ray Forces to Golden City Vortices

The Seven Rays of Light and Sound originate from the Great Central Sun — or Galactic Center — as it is known in Hindu and Mayan cultures. Ray Forces are an unseen type of energy that are said to function like a non-visible, quasar–type of light. Since Ray Forces control many human evolutionary aspects, they distribute their energies by arcing through the planets of the Fire Triplicity of our Solar System to Earth: Mars (Aries, the spiritual pioneer); Sun (Leo, the spiritual leader); and Jupiter (Sagittarius, the spiritual teacher). Vedic Rishis and Master Teachers concur that the amount of galactic light streaming to Earth as the Seven Rays controls lifespans, memory function, ability to absorb and respect spiritual knowledge, and access to the Akashic Records. Golden City Rays arch primarily through our solar sun and enter the earth's core. The movement of Golden City Vortices draws the Ray Force through, to the center of the Vortex — the Star. Energies of the Ray are disbursed from the Star throughout the entire Vortex.

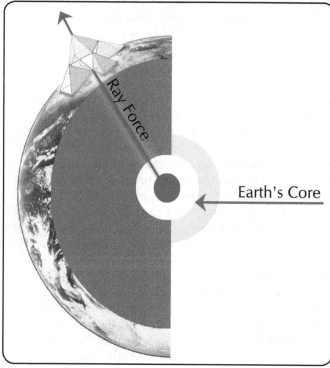

Tornadoes

Water Down the Drain

Vortex Geometry

Black Hole

Sea Shell

Ocean Wave

Examples of the Vortex in Nature

Violet Flame in Chalice
The Violet Flame depicted on the ethereal altar of the Temple of the Violet Flame.

The Violet Flame

Simply stated, the Violet Flame stabilizes past karmas through Transmutation, Forgiveness, and Mercy. This leads to the opening of the spiritual heart and the development of bhakti — the unconditional love and compassion for others. Our Co-creative ability is activated through the Ascended Master's gift of the Unfed Flame in adjunct with the practice of the Law of Love, and the Power of Intention. But the Violet Flame, capable of engendering our greatest spiritual growth and evolution, is spiritual velocity pure and simple.

Invoking the flame's force often produces feelings of peace, tranquility, and inner harmony — its ability to lift the low-vibrating energy fields of blame, despair, and fear into forgiveness and understanding, paves the path to love. The history of the Violet Flame reaches back thousands of years before the Time of Christ. According to Ascended Master legend, the Lords of Venus transmitted the Violet Flame as a spiritual consciousness during the final days of the pre-Atlantis civilization Lemuria. As one society perished and another bloomed, the power of the Violet Flame shifted, opening the way for Atlantean religiosity. This transfer of power initiated a clearing of the Earth's etheric and psychic realms, and purged the lower physical atmosphere of negative forces and energies. Recorded narratives of Atlantis claim that Seven Temples of Purification sat atop visible materializations of the Violet Flame. The archangels Zadkiel and Amethyst, representing freedom, forgiveness and joy, presided over an Atlantean Brotherhood known as the Order of Zadkiel, also associated with Saint Germain. These Violet Flame Temples still exist today in the celestial realm over Cuba.

The Violet Flame benefits humans and divinities equally. During spiritual visualizations, meditations, prayers, decrees, and mantras, many disciples seek the Violet Flame for serenity and wisdom. Meanwhile, the Ascended Masters always use it in inner retreats — even Saint Germain taps into its power to perfect and apply its force with chelas and students.

The Violet Flame, rooted in Alchemic powers, is sometimes identified as a higher energy of Saturn and the Blue Ray, a force leavened with justice, love, and wisdom. Ascended-Master lore explains the Violet Flame's ability to release a person from temporal concerns: Saturn's detachment from emotions and low-lying energies sever worldly connections. That's why the scientific properties of violet light are so important in metaphysical terms. The shortness of its wavelength and the high vibration of its frequency induce a point of transition to the next octave of light and into a keener consciousness.

Archangel Zadkiel
Valdimir Suvorov.

Tibet, Himalayas.
Nicholas Roerich, 1933.

Saint Germain, Ascended Master for the United Brotherhood of Earth

The Lord of the Seventh Ray and the Master of the Violet Flame, Saint Germain, lived numerous noteworthy lifetimes, dating back thousands of years, before incarnating as the Comte de Saint Germainduring Renaissance Europe. He lived as the Englishman Sir Francis Bacon, the sixteenth-century philosopher, essayist, and Utopian who greatly influenced the philosophy of inductive science. His most profound and well-known work on the restoration of humanity, the *Instauratio Magna* (Great Restoration), defined him as an icon of the Elizabethan era. Research also shows his co-authoring of many Shakespearean sonnets.

According to Esoteric historians, Queen Elizabeth I of England — The Virgin Queen — was his biological mother. Before Bacon's birth, the queen married Earl of Leicester, quieting ideas of illegitimacy. Elizabeth's lady in waiting, Lady Ann Bacon, wife of the Lord High Chancellor of England, adopted him following the stillbirth of her baby. Bacon was, therefore, the true heir to the crown and England's rightful king.[1] But his cousin James I of Scotland succeeded the throne. Sir Bacon described this turn of events in his book, Novum Organo, published in 1620: "It is an immense ocean that surrounds the island of Truth." And Saint Germain often reminds us to this day "there are no mistakes, ever, ever, ever."

Bacon's philosophies also helped define the principles of Free Masonry and democracy. As an adept leader of the Rosicrucians (a secret society of that time), he set out to reveal the obsolescence and oppression of European monarchies.

Eventually, Bacon's destiny morphed. He shed his physical form and sought the greatest gift of all: immortality. And that's what placed him in the most extraordinary circumstances throughout history. Even his death (or lack of) evokes controversy. Some say Bacon faked his demise in 1626 — the coffin contained the carcass of a dog.

According to the author, ADK Luk, Saint Germain ascended on May 1, 1684 in Transylvania at the Rakoczy mansion. He was 123 years old. Some say Saint Germain spent the lost years — from 1626 to 1684 — in Tibet. During this time he took (or may have been given) the name *Kajaeshra*. Interpreted as *God's helper of life and wisdom*, it was possibly a secret name and rarely used. Kaja has several interpretations: in Greek it means pure; Balinese, toward the mountain; early Latin (Estonian), echo; Hopi, wise child; Polish, of the Gods; and Hebrew, life. The second part of the name — Eshra (Ezra) — translates into help or aid.

Indeed, Bacon's work would impact centuries to follow. During his time in Tibet, tucked away in silent monasteries, Germain designed a society that eventually created a United Brotherhood of the Earth: Solomon's Temple of the Future. It's a metaphor used to describe the raising of consciousness as the greater work of democracy. Author Marie Bauer Hall studied the life of Francis Bacon. In her book, Foundations Unearthed, she described the legendary edifice: "This great temple was to be supported by the four mighty pillars of history, science, philosophy, and religion, which were to bear the lofty dome of Universal Fellowship and Peace."[2]

But Germain, *pictured above*, [3] embraced an even deeper passion: the people and nation of America, christening it New Atlantis. He envisioned this land — present-day United States, Canada, Mexico, and South America — as part of the United Democracies of Europe and the People of the World.

---

1. Marie Bauer Hall, *Foundations Unearthed*, originally issued as Francis Bacon's Great Virginia Vault, Fourth Edition (Los Angeles: Veritas Press), page 9.

2. M. Hall, *Foundations Unearthed*, page 13.

3. Saint Germain, *The Secret Teachings of All Ages*, Diamond Jubilee Edition (Los Angeles: Philosophical Research Society, Inc.), Manly Hall.

Francis Bacon by John Vanderbank, (1731). Francis Bacon coined the term "New Age" in the seventeenth century. The English philosopher is said to be the last human incarnation of the Ascended Master Saint Germain.

America, this growing society, held his hope for a future guided by a Democratic Brotherhood.

The Comte de Saint Germain emerged years later in the courts of pre-revolutionary France — his appearance, intelligence, and worldliness baffled members of the Court of Versailles. This gentleman carried the essence of eternal youth: he was a skilled artist and musician; he spoke fluent German, English, French, Italian, Portuguese, Spanish, Greek, Latin, Sanskrit, Arabic, and Chinese; and he was a proficient chemist. Meanwhile, literary, philosophic, and political aristocracy of the time sought his company. French philosophers Jean-Jacque Rousseau and Voltaire; the Italian adventurer Giacomo Casanova; and the Earl of Chatham and statesman Sir Robert Walpole of Britain were among his friends.

In courts throughout Europe, he dazzled royalty with his Mastery of Alchemy, removing flaws from gems and turning lead into Gold. And the extent of Germain's ken reached well into the theosophical realm. A Guru of yogic and tantric disciplines, he possessed highly developed telepathic and psychic abilities. This preternatural knowledge led to the development of a cartographic Prophecy — the Map of Changes. This uncanny blueprint, now in the hands of the scion of Russian aristocracy, detailed an imminent restructuring of the political and social boundaries of Europe.[4]

But few grasped Germain's true purpose during this time of historic critical mass: not even the king and queen of France could comprehend his tragic forewarnings. The Great White Brotherhood — a fellowship of enlightened luminaries — sent the astute diplomat Saint Germain to orchestrate the development of the United States of Europe. Not only a harbinger of European diplomacy, he made his presence in America during the germinal days of this country. Esoteric scholars say he urged the signing of the Declaration of Independence in a moment of collective fear — a fear of treason and ultimately death. Urging the forefathers to proceed, a shadowed figure in the back of the room shouted: Sign that document!

To this day, the ironclad identity of this person remains a mystery, though some mystics believe it was Saint Germain. Nevertheless, his avid support spurred the flurry of signatures, sealing the fate of America — and the beginning of Sir Francis Bacon's democratic experiment.

The Comte de Saint Germain never could shape a congealed Europe, but he did form a lasting and profound relationship with America. Germain's present-day participation in U.S. politics reaches the Oval Office. Some theosophical mystics say Germain visits the president of the United States the day after the leader's inauguration; others suggest he's the fabled patriot Uncle Sam.

Saint Germain identifies with the qualities of Brotherhood and freedom. He is the sponsor of humanity and serves as a conduit of Violet Light — a force some claim is powerful enough to propel one into Ascension.

According to the I AM America Prophecies, Saint Germain says that the people of America have a unique destiny in the New Times. America contains within it a unique anagram:

A M E R I C A = I A M R A C E.

The I AM Race of people is a unique group of souls who lived in America as Atlanteans. But their destiny has evolved since those ancient times. Instead of sinking on a continent destroyed by the misuse of technology and spiritual knowledge, their active intelligence continues to develop in modern times. Their service is focused on the Brotherly love of all nations. In the I AM America Earth Changes Prophecies Saint Germain states, "America will be the first to go through the changes, and then give aid to the rest of the World."

4. K. Paul Johnson, The Masters Revealed: Madame Blavatsky and the Myth of the Great White Lodge (Suny Series in Western Esoteric Traditions) (Albany, NY: State University of New York Press), page 19.

Interpretations of this Prophecy explain why American is possibly the chosen land — the first society to experience dimensional change. Members of this regenerated, enlightened society will share and teach the benefits of this new understanding with the rest of humanity.

Saint Germain identifies with the qualities of Brotherhood and freedom. He is the sponsor of humanity and serves as a conduit of Violet Light — a force some claim is powerful enough to propel one into Ascension. When Saint Germain accepts a chela, the Master appears in physical form. Sometimes, he playfully disguises himself, leaving clues of his identity, most often purple clothing.

Today the essence of Saint Germain — that eternal, eloquent diplomat — fills the world. His presence assures humanity of an alternate path to evolution and growth. In Changing the Guard he illustrates this point: "We have spent our time adjusting that Collective Consciousness for the days and the times that are coming. We also would like to remind you that we cannot, at any time, readjust the karma of mankind. For what mankind has created, mankind must now receive. This is the Law of Cause and Effect. But we work with those causes to readjust that plan of the best and highest good." Perhaps our present karma is indeed predestined, but how we work through karmas is engendered in our Free Will and choice.

FARMERS!
Uncle Sam asks you…

to get ready for the census taker
In January the U.S. Census Bureau will ask you about 1944 crops - amount - value - acres - livestock - tractors - labor hired and tenure
THE LAW REQUIRING YOUR REPORTS MAKES THEM CONFIDENTIAL

Farmers, Uncle Sam Asks You to Get Ready for the Census Taker
The author is unknown in this poster depicting Uncle Sam during the World War II effort. This depiction of Uncle Sam was designed for multiple government agencies: the Office for Emergency Management, Office of War Information, Domestic Operations Branch, and Bureau of Special Services. 1943-1945.

Saint Germain
A contemporary portrait of the Ascended Master by Summit Lighthouse.

Hermes Mercurius Trismegistus
In this illustration Hermes hands a Book of Law, (the Hermetic Laws), to Moses with
his right hand. His left hand rests on a plate with the Divine Word. From a cathedral
floor in Siena, Italy, 1895.

The Seven Hermetic Principles

The Law of Mentalism

 The all is mind; the universe is mental. According to this law, perception creates your reality of God and the universe — God is an everlasting consciousness, and all reality is an expression of that consciousness. The Law of Mentalism touches the intangible. To understanding this law is to understand nothing: the universe lacks definability. It is an infinite, indescribable construct of the mind.

The Law of Correspondence

 As above, so below; as below, so above. On a transpersonal level, the Law of Correspondence tells us our inner world defines our outer world and vice versa: this universal tenet forms the foundation of our everyday thoughts, attitudes, and beliefs. For instance, if your insides are chaotic and miserable; if you lack confidence and self-esteem; if you're full of anger, resentment, and negativity, you'll experience a tumultuous outer reality. The grasping of this fundamental precept is the key to comprehending the Laws of Cause and Effect (karma) and the Law of Attraction. The Law of Correspondence is also described as mental equivalent. "But we know now that any outward act is but the sequel to a thought, and that the type of thought which we allow to become habitual will sooner or later find expression on the plane of action."[1]

The Law of Vibration

 Nothing rests; everything moves; everything vibrates. Closely related to the Law of Attraction, this third Hermetic Principle states that all entities in the universe, including humans, emotions, and spirituality, are in constant motion and perpetual transformation. This translucent friction, which recalibrates energy, creates a synergy among all things in nature. For instance, if your mental waves wealth, it will come to you.

The Law of Polarity

 Everything is dual; everything has poles; everything has its pair of opposites; like and unlike are the same; opposites are identical in nature, but different in degree; extremes meet; all truths are but half-truths; all paradoxes may be reconciled. Everything has an antithesis; opposites, yet mutable, are just two extremes of the same thing — darkness becomes light; cold becomes hot; hate becomes love.

The Law of Rhythm

 Everything flows, out and in; everything has its tides; all things rise and fall; the pendulum-swing manifests in everything; the measure of the swing to the right is the measure of the swing to the left; rhythm compensates. The Law of Rhythm creates the hidden unifying force in the universe: is the catalyst of natural timing and consistency. The right rhythm creates harmony; the left, disharmony. An action produces a reaction — the ebb and flow of the tides, the waxing and waning of the Moon, and the rising and setting of the Sun.

The Laws of Cause and Effect

 Every cause has its effect; every effect has its cause; everything happens according to law; chance is but a name for law not recognized; there are many planes of causation, but nothing escapes the law. This sixth Hermetic Law — the notion of karma — states: "But we know now that any outward act is but the sequel to a thought, and that the type of thought which we allow to become habitual will sooner or later find expression on the Plane of action." Nothing in the universe occurs by accident: everything happens for a reason.

The Law of Gender

 Gender is in everything; everything has its masculine and feminine principles; gender manifests on all planes. All forms of nature — animate and inanimate — possess the duality of gender. This final Hermetic Principle says all things in the universe, even energy, exhibit masculine and feminine traits.

[From The Kybalion: A Study of the Hermetic Philosophy of Ancient Egypt and Greece, written anonymously by the Three Initiates, Chicago, 1940.]

---

1. Emmet Fox, *The Sermon on the Mount* (New York: Harper & Row, Publishers), page 68.

Devas and Elementals

Deva, meaning shining one or being of light, is a Sanskrit word that describes a God, deity, or spirit. Helena Blavatsky, co-founder of the Theosophical Society, introduced these celestial beings, or angels, to the Western World in the nineteenth century. She described them as progressed entities from previous incarnations that would remain dormant until humanity attained a higher level of spiritual consciousness. Devas represent moral values and work directly with nature kingdoms.[1]

Elementals, on the other hand, are an invisible, subhuman group of creatures that act as counterparts to visible nature on terra firma. Medieval alchemist and occultist Paracelsus coined the term for these Elemental spirits. He divided them into the following four categories: gnomes (Earth); undines (water); sylphs (air); and salamanders (fire).

Gnomes: The term comes from the Greek word "genomus" or "Earth dweller." These subterranean spirits work closely with the Earth, giving them immense power over rocks, flora, gemstones, and precious minerals; they are often guardians of hidden treasures. Some gnomes gather in families while others remain indigenous to the substances they serve or guard. Members of this group include elves, brownies, dryads, and the little people of the woods.[2]

Undines: These fairylike pixies, the deification of femininity, synchronize with the earth element, water. Their essence is so closely tied to aquatic milieus that they possess the power to control the course and function of water. Undines, imbued with extraordinary beauty, symmetry, and grace, inhabit riparian environments — rivers, streams, lakes, waterfalls, and swamps. According to mythical lore, these lithe spirits, also known as naiads, water sprites, sea maids, and mermaids, assume male or female identities. Sioux legend says water deities, or wak'teexi in the native tongue, often incarnate as human beings: a telltale blue birthmark on the body will bare their original identities.[3]

Sylphs: The most evolved of the four Elementals, sylphs — often synonymous with fairies and cherubs — are beautiful, lively, diaphanous, yet mortal demigods. They represent the vaporous element of air and the expression of the female essence. Omnipresent, sylphs float in the clouds and in the ether, though their true home lies in mountaintop hamlets. There, they erect sacred sanctuaries for the Gods. This spritely covey, blessed with millennium-passing longevity and highly developed senses of sight, hearing, and smell, are particularly receptive to the voices of the Gods — that's why theosophical scholars believe the ancients used sylphs as oracles. Guided by Paralda, the king of air, and a communal of female sylphs known as sylphides, sylphs occasionally assume a petite human form. They are intelligent, mutable, and loyal to humans.[4]

Salamanders: Salamanders represent the invisible Elemental spirit of fire and the embodiment of the male divinity; without their existence, warmth wouldn't exist. Working through the blood stream, body temperature, and the liver, salamanders produce heat in humans and animals. Some theosophical scholars say this class of Elementals occupies balmy Southern regions.

The mystical salamander encompasses much more than its amphibious counterparts. According to esoteric teachings, these fabled creatures manifest distinctly different forms. At approximately twelve inches in length, the lizard like salamander is physically tantamount to its terrestrial Urodela cousin. But, unlike earthly species, ethereal salamanders thrive in fire and slither through flames. Lore describes another group of salamanders as a race of giant creatures that wear flowing robes, don protective armor, and emit a fiery, incandescent glow. According to Medieval tradition, the third coterie of these entities are descendents of the great salamander Oromasis — son of the enigmatic Greek, Zarathustra.

But the Acthnici, ruled by the Elemental king Djinn, are the most powerful and feared faction of salamanders. They travel as indistinct globes of light, especially over water. Voyagers and sailors often experience Acthnici at sea as

1. Orin Bridges, *Photographing Beings of Light: Images of Nature and Beyond* (Highland City, FL: Rainbow Press, Inc.), page 57.
2. Manly Hall, *The Secret Teachings of All Ages*, Diamond Jubilee Edition (Los Angeles: Philosophical Research Society, Inc.), pages 106-107.
3. Richard Dieterle, *Waterspirits* (Wak'teexi) (http://www.hotcakencyclopedia.com/ho.Waterspirits.html), (2005).

4. M. Hall, *The Secret Teachings of All Ages*, pages 107-108.

Midsummer Eve
Edward Robert Hughes, 1908.

Child Hiding in a Rose
Charles Robinson, 1913.

glowing forks of flame on the masts and the riggings of ships. They call this phenomenon St. Elmo's Fire. Scholars and other savants encourage others to avoid these salamanders. The price of knowing them, they say, outweigh the benefits.[5]

---

5. M. Hall, *The Secret Teachings of All Ages*, pages 106-107.

Saint Elmo's Fire
Saint Elmo's fire depicted on masts of a ship at sea,
from *The Aerial World*, by Dr. G. Hartwig, 1886, London.

Master Hilarion

Master Hilarion works upon the Green Ray of Healing and Science and is considered a Lord of Truth and Medicine. Because of this affiliation, Master Hilarion is an archetype of both Mercury and Hermes, alleged to have the skill to traverse the diverse spiritual boundaries of the Astral Plane and the Fourth Dimension.[1] He is known to appear in moments of personal crisis, and has the ability to instantly awaken our innate Divine Spark. The *shakti*, or hidden energy of Master Hilarion is powerful, with the capacity to paralyze illusion with Divine Wisdom, or to instantly assist one to gain spiritual victory through Divine Truth. The presence of Master Hilarion sustains rapid growth, abundance, and spiritual nourishment.[2]

His noteworthy incarnations include overseeing the *Temple of Truth* during the times of Atlantis, shortly before the continent's demise. It is claimed that as a custodian and priest of this holy place, he transported many of the Temple's physical artifacts and sacred objects, and literally carried the *Spiritual Flame of Truth* to Greece before the cataclysm. Annice Booth writes, "The focus of Truth that he established became the focal point for the Oracles of Delphi, messengers of truth who served under the direction of Pallas Athena for hundreds of years, until black priests penetrated the Delphic Order and perverted the Truth that had been brought forth. The Brotherhood then withdrew this service to embodied mankind, since people were unable to distinguish between Truth and error."[3]

Master Hilarion later embodied as the Syrian mathematician and Neoplatonic philosopher Iamblichus. Iamblichus formed a mystery school in Apamea, Syria for the study of the works of Pythagoras, Plato, and Aristotle. Today, his work survives only in fragments that introduced interpretations of the ONE as Monad, presented in the *I AM America Teachings* as *Being* (Oneness), *Life* (Oneship), and *Realization* (the ONE).[4]

Theosophist Mabel Collins wrote the classic treatise "Light on the Path," and credits its timeless wisdom to the inspiration and teaching of Iamblichus, and his Master Teacher *the Venetian* (Venutian). The Venetian is known as *Sanat Kumara* in certain Ascended Master Teaching. The ageless aphorisms of *Light on the Path* were originally written on palm leaves, an ancient manuscript credited to "The Book of Golden Precepts."[5] The following excerpt from this book was originally scribed in Sanskrit, and later translated to Greek:

Master Hilarion
Ascended Master of the Green Ray.

"Kill out ambition;
but work as those work who are ambitious.
Kill out desire of life;
but respect life as those do who desire it.
Kill out desire of comfort;
but be happy as those are who live for happiness."

In contemporary teachings, Master Hilarion of the Green Ray is associated with science and communication technology, mathematics and engineering, medicine, herbs, and healing. Master Hilarion's lineage of gurus includes Sanat Kumara, and his students are the Master Teachers and Golden City Hierarchs Paul the Devoted (*Crotese*, Costa Rica) and Soltech (*Pashacino*, Canada). As the Hierarch of the Golden City of Yuthor, located in Greenland, Master Hilarion is an advocate for choice, which creates the spiritual principle of *Aboundness*:

"There is plenty for all!
There is always enough!
The universal substance is indeed abundant!"

1. *Mercury and Hermes*, (http://www.unrv.com/culture/mercury), (2021).
2. Dennis Harness, *The Nakshatras: The Lunar Mansions of Vedic Astrology, First Edition* (Twin Lakes, WI: Lotus Press).
3. Prophet, *The Masters and their Retreats* (Corwin Springs, MT. Summit University Press), page 133.
4. *Iamblichus*, (Wikipedia.org/wiki/Iamblichus), 2021.

5. *Light on the Path*, (https://www.theosophical.org/files/resources/books/LightonthePath/LOTP.pdf), (2021).

Agni Yoga
Nicholas Roerich, 1928.

Activation Sequence of the Golden Cities

GOLDEN CITY	VORTEX ACTIVATION (Year)	STAR ACTIVATION (Year)	MASTER TEACHER	COUNTRY
GOBEAN	1981	1998	El Morya	United States
MALTON	1994	2011	Kuthumi	United States
WAHANEE	1996	2013	Saint Germain	United States
SHALAHAH	1998	2015	Sananda	United States
KLEHMA	2000	2017	Serapis Bey	United States
PASHACINO	2002	2019	Soltec	Canada
EABRA	2004	2021	Portia	Unites States, Canada
JEAFRAY	2006	2023	Archangel Zadkiel, Amethyst	Canada
UVERNO	2008	2025	Paul the Venetian	Canada
YUTHOR	2010	2027	Hilarion	Greenland
STIENTA	2012	2027	Archangel Michael	Iceland
DENASHA	2014	2031	Nada	Scotland
AMERIGO	2016	2033	Godfre	Spain
GRUECHA	2018	2035	Hercules	Norway, Sweden
*BRAUN	2020	2037	Victory	Germany, Poland Czech Republic
*AFROM	2020	2037	Claire and Se Ray	Hungary, Romania
*GANAKRA	2020	2037	Vista	Turkey
*MESOTAMP	2020	2037	Mohammed	Turkey, Iran, Iraq
*SHEHEZ	2020	2037	Tranquility	Iran, Afghanistan
*ADJATAL	2020	2037	Lord Himalaya	Afghanistan, Pakistan, India
PURENSK	2022	2039	Faith, Hope, and Charity	Russia, China
PRANA	2024	2041	Archangel Chamuel	India
GANDAWAN	2026	2043	Kuthumi	Algeria
KRESHE	2028	2045	Lord of Nature, Amaryllis	Botswana, Namibia
PEARLANU	2030	2047	Lotus	Madagascar

The Great Activation

GOLDEN CITY	VORTEX ACTIVATION (Year)	STAR ACTIVATION (Year)	MASTER TEACHER	COUNTRY
UNTE	2032	2049	Donna Grace	Tanzania, Kenya
LARAITO	2034	2051	Lanto and Laura	Ethiopia
MARNERO	2036	2053	Mary	Mexico
ASONEA	2038	2055	Peter the Everlasting	Cuba
ANDEO	2040	2057	First Sister, Constance, Goddess Meru	Peru, Brazil
BRAHAM	2042	2059	Second Sister	Brazil
TEHEKOA	2044	2061	Third Sister	Argentina
CROTESE	2046	2063	Paul the Devoted	Costa Rica, Panama
JEHOA	2048	2065	Kuan Yin	New Atlantis
ZASKAR	2050	2067	Reya	China
GOBI	2052	2069	Lord Meru	China
ARCTURA	2054	2071	Arcturus	China
NOMAKING	2056	2073	Cassiopea and Minerva	China
PRESCHING	2058	2075	Archangel Jophiel	China, North Korea
KANTAN	2060	2077	Great Divine Mother and Archangel Raphael	China, Russia
HUE	2062	2079	Lord Guatama	Russia
SIRCALWE	2064	2081	Group of Twelve	Russia
ARKANA	2066	2083	Archangel Gabriel	Russia
MOUSSE	2068	2085	Kona	New Lemuria
DONJAKEY	2070	2087	Pacifica	New Lemuria
GREIN	2072	2089	Viseria	New Zealand
CLAYJE	2074	2091	Orion	Australia
ANGELICA	2076	2093	Angelica	Australia
SHEAHAH	2078	2095	Astrea	Australia
FRON	2080	2097	Desiree	Australia
CRESTA	2082	2099	Archangel Crystiel	Antarctica

The Five United States Golden Cities

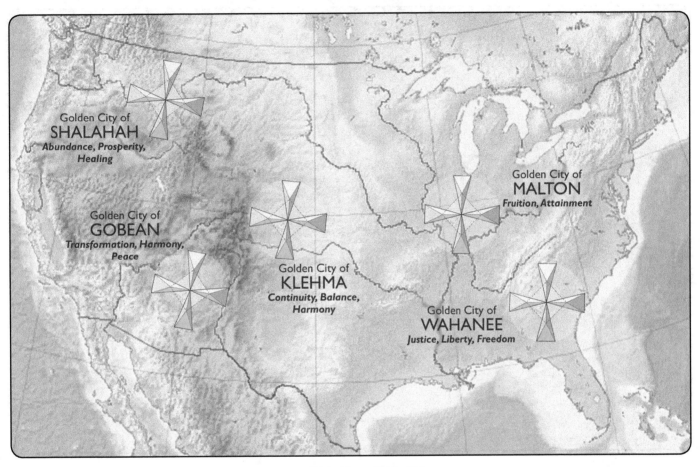

United States Golden Cities

Malton, located primarily in Illinois and Indiana; Wahanee, located primarily in South Carolina and Georgia; Klehma, located primarily in Colorado; Shalahah, located primarily in Montana and Idaho; Gobean, located primarily in Arizona and New Mexico. *Locations are approximate and not to scale.*

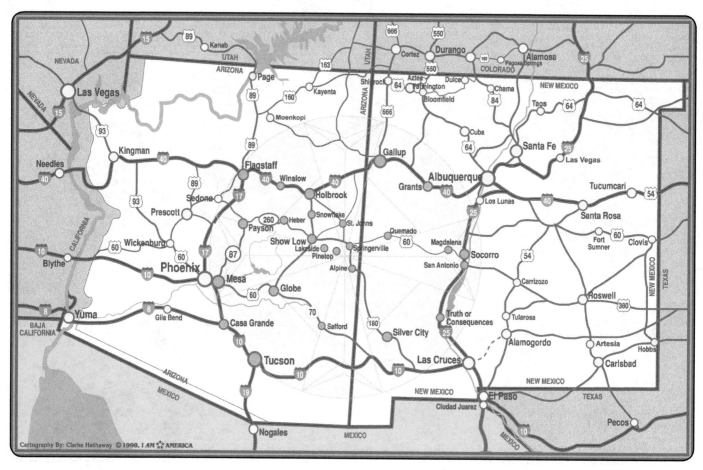

Golden City of Gobean
The Golden City of Gobean is located in Arizona and New Mexico, United States.

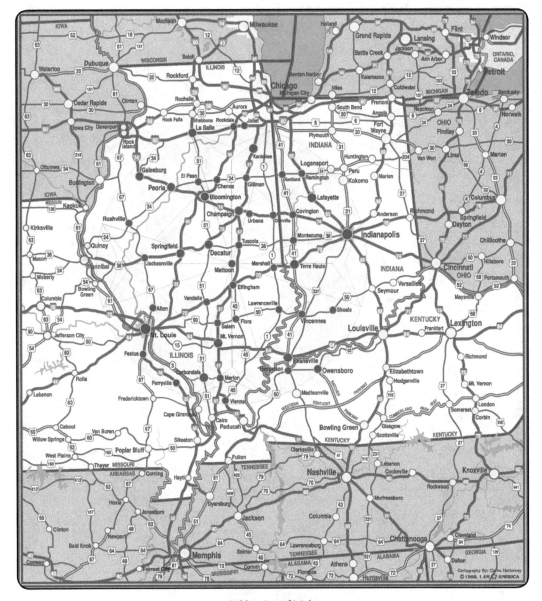

Golden City of Malton
The Golden City of Gobean is located in Illinois, Missouri, Indiana, and Kentucky, United States.

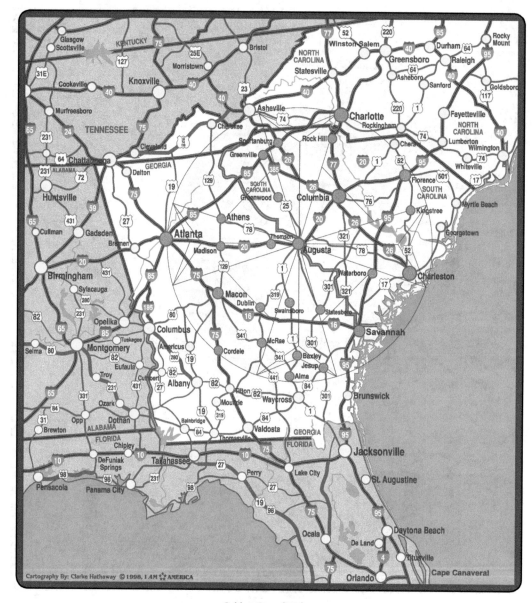

Golden City of Wahanee
The Golden City of Gobean is located in South Carolina, Georgia, Tennessee, and North Carolina, United States.

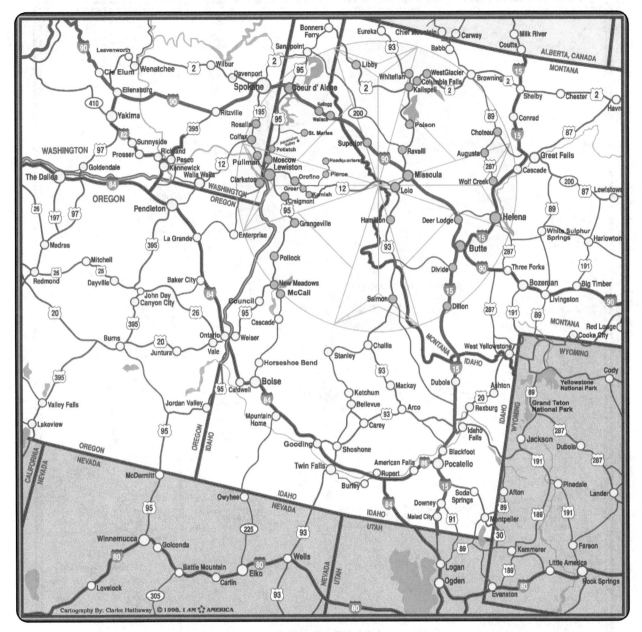

Golden City of Shalahah
The Golden City of Gobean is located in Montana, Idaho, Oregon, and Washington, United States.

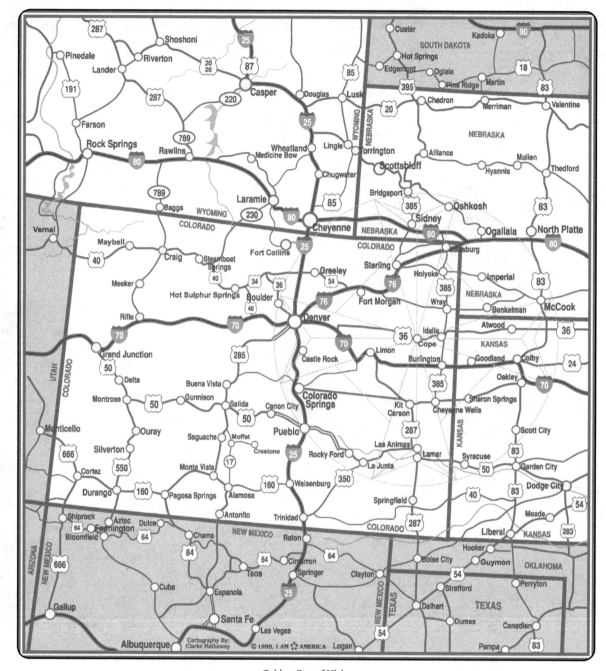

Golden City of Klehma
The Golden City of Klehma is located in Nebraska, Kansas, Colorado, and Wyoming, United States.

Adjutant Points of Gobean Northern Door (Gateway Ashrams):

1. First Point: Masculine Energy, Mahatma Ishmar of the Ruby Ray.

Located on the Hopi Indian reservation near Keams Canyon and First Mesa, Arizona. Take Highway 264 to Clenga Canyon Road; bear North for approximately two miles. You will see the mesa from this point.

2. Second Point: Feminine Energy, Lady Master DeNaire (feminine of *Dinè*) of the Violet Ray.

Located near Red Lake on the Navajo Indian Reservation in New Mexico, on Hwy 12 near Canyon De Chelly. Travel up an abandoned road (East) to Squirrel Picnic Ground, at the base of Chuska Peak.

The Hierarchs and Ray Forces of Gobean's Adjutant Points
The Golden City of Gobean (Southwest, United States), and the Hierarchs and Ray Forces of its Adjutant Points. Golden City Hierarchs and their Ray Forces are pursuant to change in 2024, at the end of the Eighth Cycle and the beginning of the Ninth Cycle. For more information see *Golden Cities and the Master of Shamballa* and *Evolutionary Biome.*

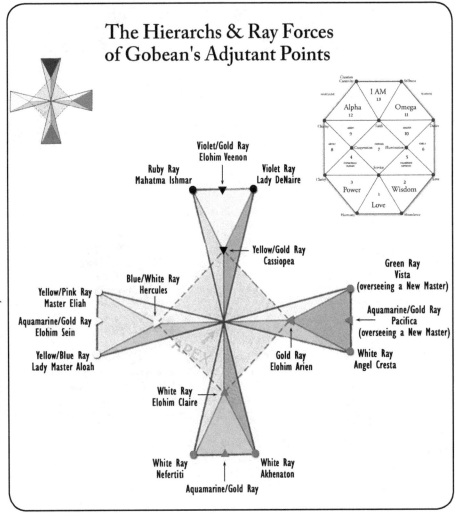

The Hierarchs & Ray Forces of Gobean's Adjutant Points

Ruby Ray
Mahatma Ishmar

Violet/Gold Ray
Elohim Veenon

Violet Ray
Lady DeNaire

Yellow/Gold Ray
Cassiopea

Green Ray
Vista
(overseeing a New Master)

Blue/White Ray
Hercules

Yellow/Pink Ray
Master Eliah

Aquamarine/Gold Ray
Elohim Sein

Aquamarine/Gold Ray
Pacifica
(overseeing a New Master)

Yellow/Blue Ray
Lady Master Aloah

Gold Ray
Elohim Arien

White Ray
Angel Cresta

White Ray
Elohim Claire

White Ray
Nefertiti

White Ray
Akhenaton

Aquamarine/Gold Ray

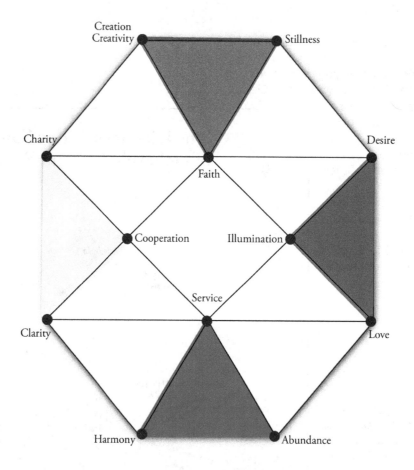

The Eight-sided Cell of Perfection
with the Four Vortex Doorways and the Twelve Jurisdictions
The Eight-sided Cell of Perfection as a Golden City Vortex identifies
the Adjutant Points as the Twelve Jurisdictions.

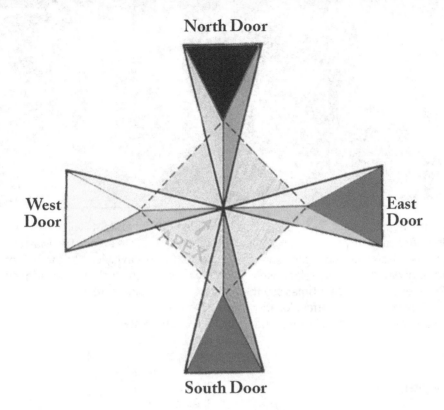

The Four Doorways of a Golden City
The Four Doors, (Black, Blue, Red, and Yellow), are also known as Gateways.

Doors (gateways) of the Golden Cities

The four doors of the Golden Cities signify the four directions, and each represents certain attributes and characteristics. They also represent four spiritual pathways or spiritual initiations.

The Black Door
Direction: North
Esoteric Planet: Earth, Saturn, Mercury
Qualities:
1. Discipline and Labor
2. Physical Abundance
3. Worldly Benefits
4. Transmutation and Forgiveness

Attributes: The Northern Doors represent discipline and hard work. Spiritually, they denote self-control achieved through transmutation and forgiveness. Some say the Northern Doors manifest abundant consciousness and gratified wishes. The prophecies of the New Times foretell bountiful and prolific crops; this doorway is best for commercial and business endeavors.

The Blue Door
Direction: East
Esoteric Planet: Moon
Qualities:
1. Purification and Sacrifice
2. Alchemy

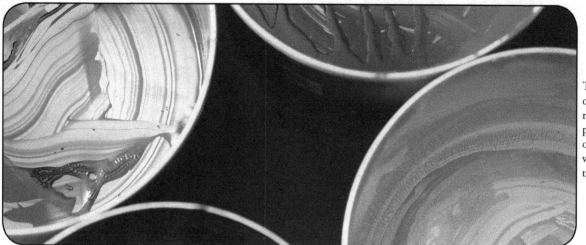

CMYK
The Four Doorways of a Golden City are represented by the four primary colors found in our three-dimensional world: Cyan, Magenta, Yellow, and Black, known as CMYK.

3. Often referred to as, "the Elixir of Life"
4. Friends, Family, Helpful Acquaintances
Attributes: According to the Master Teachers, time spent in contemplation at this doorway can resolve relationship and family problems. Prophecies of the New Times say the Eastern Doors of Golden City Vortices are perfect locations for communities, group activities, residential homes, and schools for children.

The Red Door
Direction: South
Esoteric Planet: Mars, Jupiter
Qualities:
1. "The Healing of the Nations"
2. Enlightened Love
3. Nonjudgment
4. Faith and Courage
Attributes: The energies of the Southern Door induce physical, emotional, and spiritual regenerations; and miracle healings are commonplace. That's why this doorway is a great place for hospitals, clinics, retreats, and spas.

The Yellow Door
Direction: West
Esoteric Planet: Sun
Qualities:
1. Wisdom
2. "The Philosopher's Stone"
3. Adeptship and Conclusion
Attributes: The Western Door terminates the four pathways and acts as a portal to the "Star of Knowledge." Here, Golden City inhabitants will find universities and schools of higher, spiritual learning. The Master Teachers say the energies of this doorway create the hub of civic activity: Golden City government, including its administrative structure and capitol will reside here.

The Star
Direction: Center
Esoteric Planet: Venus
Qualities:
1. Self-Knowledge
2. Empowerment
3. Ascension
Attributes: The "Star" also known as the "Star of Self-Knowledge" punctuates the center of every Golden City. This area, the most powerful of the Vortex, produces self-knowledge and self-empowerment. The energies of the four doorways coalesce here — that's why it's identified as the absence of color, white. Its power reaches beyond the boundaries of the Golden City. Forty miles in diameter, a Star's healing qualities can extend as far as sixty miles. Here, spiritual growth in the New Times happens: the Star's energies encourage self-renunciation, meditation, and spiritual liberation. During the Time of Change, the purity and beneficence of a Star's power will attract the Ascended Masters, who will then manifest in physical form. And the city's inhabitants will flock here to absorb spiritual teaching, miracle healings, and Ascensions.

Master El Morya

El Morya incarnated from a long line of historical notables, including the fabled King Arthur of England; the Renaissance scholar Sir Thomas Moore, author of Utopia; the patron saint of Ireland, Saint Patrick; and a Rajput prince. El Morya is even linked to the Hebrew patriarch Abraham. But in spite of his illustrious lifetimes, El Morya is best known as Melchior, one of the Magi who followed the Star of Bethlehem to the Christ infant.

El Morya first revealed himself to the founder of the Theosophical Society Helena Petrovna Blavatasky — also known as Madame Blavatsky or H. P. B. — during her childhood in London; that mid-nineteenth century meeting forged a lifelong connection with her Master and other members of the Spiritual Hierarchy. Some esoteric scholars recount different, more dramatic scenarios of their initial introduction. Blavatsky herself claimed El Morya rescued her from a suicide attempt on Waterloo Bridge.[1] The gracious Master dissuaded her from plunging into the waters of the Thames River. Others say the two met in Hyde Park or on a London street. According to Blavatsky, El Morya appeared under a secret political cover as the Sikh prince Maharaja Ranbir Singh of Kashmir, who served as a physically incarnated prototype of Master M. Singh and died in 1885.

Metaphysical scholars credit Blavatsky's work as the impetus for present-day theosophical philosophy and the conception of the Great White Brotherhood. Devoted disciples learned of the Hindu teacher from Blavatsky's childhood visions, and later on in a series of correspondences known as the Mahatma Letters, which contained spiritual guidelines for humanity. El Morya's presence in H. P. B.'s life enriched her spiritual knowledge, and she shared this transformation in a prolific body of texts and writings, namely Isis Unveiled and The Secret Doctrine. During a visit with Madame Blavatsky, A.P. Sinnett, an English newspaper editor, found the first of these letters among the branches of a tree. Over the years, the true meaning and authorship of the Mahatma Letters, reportedly co-authored by fellow Mahatma Kuthumi, have spurned controversy; some say Blavatsky herself forged the messages.[2]

Master M. is associated with the Blue Ray of power, faith, and good will; the Golden City of Gobean; and the planet Mercury. A strict disciplinarian, El Morya dedicates his work to the development of the will. He assists many disciples in discovering personal truths, exploring self-development, and honing the practice of the esoteric discipline. El Morya passes this wisdom to his numerous chelas and students. The Maha Chohan — El Morya's Guru, Lord of the Seven Rays and the Steward of Earth and its evolutions — educated him during his Earthly incarnations in India, Egypt, and Tibet. Declining the Ascension a number of times, it is said that El Morya finally accepted this divine passage in 1888, ascending with his beloved pet dog and horse. (Esoteric symbols of friendship and healing.)

1. Papastavro, Tellis S., *The Gnosis and the Law* (Tucson, AZ: Group Avatar), page 53.

2. Johnson, K. Paul, *The Masters Revealed: Madame Blavatsky and the Myth of the Great White Lodge* (Suny Series in Western Esoteric Traditions) (Albany, NY: State University of New York Press), page 41.

Taj Mahal Mausoleum
Vasily Vereshchagin, 1874-1876.

Master Kuthumi

In the late nineteenth century, Ascended Master Kuthumi — also known as Koot Hoomi or K. H. — collaborated with Helena Blavatsky and El Morya to introduce humanity to the spiritual teachings of theosophy. And like Master M., K. H. is dedicated to advancing the spiritual fitness of mankind to a higher consciousness. Thus, Kuthumi approached his interaction with humans in the same manner as his mahatma contemporary: he veiled his identity behind the Indian dignitaries of the time, in this case, Thakar Singh Sandhawalia, leader of the Singh Sabha movement. Founded in the early 1870s, this Indian independence campaign emerged as a grassroots effort to maintain the purity of Sikhism, otherwise eroded by Christian Missionaries. Sandhanwalia, Ranbir Singh — one of El Morya's aliases — and H. P. B. joined forces to spread theosophy throughout India.

Kuthumi and El Morya shared a close relationship through the ages. Both trained by the Ascended Master Maha Chohan, the spiritual duo, as two of the wise men, paid homage to the baby Jesus: K. H. as Balthazar and Master M. as Melchior. Kuthumi also shows up as Sir Percival at the round table of King Arthur (aka El Morya). But his incarnation history isn't limited to associations with his spiritual Brother. Kuthumi's past lifetimes include the Greek philosopher Pythagoras; Thutmose III, the warrior pharaoh of the eighteenth dynasty; Shah Jahan, the emperor of India and builder of the Taj Mahal; and founder of the Franciscans, Saint Francis of Assisi.

Highly educated and extremely private, Kuthumi, a Cambridge University alumni, spent 200 years in seclusion in the Himalayan Mountains before ascending in 1889. He is a gentle Master affiliated with the Golden City Malton, and the Gold and Ruby Rays of ministration and service to humanity. In one of his earliest letters to A. P. Sinnett, Kuthumi calls the holy Golden Temple of the Sikhs his home, although he's seldom there, preferring the solitude of Tibet.[3]

Author Alice Bailey, who continued to work with the Masters after Blavatsky's death in 1891, writes about a visit from K. H.: "Master Koot Hoomi, [is] a Master who is very close to the Christ." In 1895, Kuthumi told the fifteen-year-old Bailey that she would travel the world "doing your Master's work all the time" and that "I would have to give up being such an unpleasant little girl and must try and get some measure of self-control. My future usefulness to him and to the world was dependent upon how I handled myself and the changes I could manage to make."[1]

A.D.K. Luk writes of Kuthumi: "He was such a lover of nature that he would watch a certain phase for hours, or would stay a whole day with a flower to see it open into full bloom, and perhaps watch it close again at night. He was one of the few who represented the heart of the Nature Kingdom. He was able to read through the Elemental Kingdom and accelerate his consciousness to a point where he was of assistance in that realm. Birds and animals were drawn to him to be in his radiance which was about him; drawn by his constant attention and adoration to his Source."[2]

---
1. Bailey, Alice A., *Unfinished Autobiography* (New York: Lucis Publishing Company), page 36.
2. Luk, A.D.K., *Law of Life, Book II* (Pueblo, CO: ADK Luk Publications), page 275.

Jesus Goes Up Alone onto a Mountain to Pray
James Tissot, 1886-1894.

Lord Sananda

During his paradigm-altering incarnation more than 2,000 years ago, Lord Sananda (above), also known as Sananda Kumara, embodied the Christ Consciousness, as Jesus, son of God. Some esoteric scholars say he's one of the four sons of Brahma — Sanaka, Sanatana, Sanat-Kumara, and Sanandana — his namesake. According to Vedic lore, the foursome possess eternally liberated souls and live in Tapaloka, the dimension of the great sages. Before manifesting in physical form, Jesus belonged to the Angelic Kingdom. His name was Micah — the Great Angel of Unity. Micah is the son of Archangel Michael who led the Israelites out of Egypt.[1] [For more information on the life story of Jesus' life, I recommend reading, *Twelve World Teachers,* by Manly P. Hall.]

Sananda Kumara revealed his identity to the mystic Sister Thedra. Her Master first contacted her in the early 1960s and instructed her to move to Peru, specifically, to a hidden monastery in the Andes mountains. There, undergoing an intense spiritual training, she kept in constant contact with Sananda, and he shared with her prophecies of the coming Earth Changes. After leaving the abbey, Sister Thedra moved to Mt. Shasta, California where she founded the Association of Sananda and Sanat Kumara. She died in 1992.

Sananda posed for a photograph on June 1, 1961 in Chichen Itza, Yucatan. He told Sister Thedra that though the image is valid, he is not limited by form of any kind; therefore, he may take on any appearance necessary. [See Appendix DDD: Sananda's Sunday Peace Meditation].

Lord Sananda is the Hierarch of the Golden City of Shalahah, located in Idaho, Montana, and Oregon, United States. The Lord of Christ Consciousness also serves as World Teacher in the Shamballa lineage.

---

1. Papastavro, Tellis S., *The Gnosis and the Law* (Tucson, AZ: Group Avatar), page 358.

Pyramids
Ivan Aivazovsky, 1895.

Serapis Bey

The lore of Serapis Bey is heavily linked to the story of Helena Blavatsky, Master M., K. H., and the founding of the Theosophical Society. According to lore, Serapis Bey incarnated as Paolos Metamon, an Egyptian magician. Metamon and Blavatsky connected in the mid-1850s during her wanderlust years in the Middle East. H. P. B. soon became his pupil. He introduced her to the secret world of the occult and possibly served as her first physical Master. But many esoteric scholars disagree; they say the Ascended Master of the Fourth Ray is rooted in the Greco-Egyptian mysteries, and appropriately so. Before his Ascension in 400 B.C., Serapis Bey embodied as a high priest at the Ascension Temple of Atlantis more than 11,000 years ago. Other myths put the Master — carrying the Flame of Ascension to Egypt by boat — at the banks of the Nile River near Luxor before the demise of Atlantis and the Earth Changes of Dvapara Yuga.[1] He also incarnated as the Egyptian pharaohs Akhenaten IV and Amenophis III; the heroic King Leonidas of Sparta; and Phidias, the great architect of the Parthenon, the temple of the Goddess Athena, and the colossal statue of Zeus.

A tireless and strict disciplinarian, Serapis Bey, the Master Teacher of Ascension, identifies and prepares souls for Ascension. He accomplishes this by the destruction of the lower self, the state of animal-man, that is captivated by worldly ignorance. And when the corporeal attachments dissolve, the Real Self emerges, a step essential to the attainment of Ascension. The Ancient Egyptians followed a similar practice in their Temples of Serapis. Priests carried out initiatory rites involving rigorous and severe rituals; symbolic illusions of the lower world through which the soul of man wanders for the truth. Those who survived the ordeal were ushered into the presence of Serapis — an awe-inspiring figure, illumined in unseen lights. Serapis became known as the Adversary or the Trier who tested the souls of those seeking union with the Immortals, the Ascension.[2] Serapis Bey serves on the Fourth Ray — it is associated with the absence of color,

white; harmony through conflict; and the path of beauty.

The number seven plays a significant role in the worship of this Ascended Master. It begins with his name — Serapis — which contains seven letters. During worship, disciples chant hymns comprising seven vowels, the seven primary sounds. And when expressed in imagery, Serapis wears a crown of seven Rays, symbolizing the seven divine intelligences represented through solar light. Meanwhile, the word "serapis" has many associations: it is the ancient term for Sun; in Hebrew it means "to blaze out"; and it is the soul, enmeshed with the form during physical life, which escapes from the body at death.

1. Manly Hall, *The Secret Teachings of All Ages, Diamond Jubilee Edition* (Los Angeles: Philosophical Research Society), pages 26-27.
2. Papastavro, Tellis S., *The Gnosis and the Law* (Tucson, AZ: Group Avatar), page 358.

King Leonidas
Textile, Leonidas at Thermopylae, 1815.

Shamballa and Sanat Kumara

Shamballa, which means to *make sacred*, is the Earth's first Golden City. The notion of Shamballa represents peace, happiness, and tranquility. It's a place of spiritual cleanliness and divine dominion; it's the ethereal home and sanctuary of Sanat Kumara.

To understand Shamballa's metaphysical antiquity is to grasp its complex timeline. According to modern occult literature, this mystic metropolis existed more than 60,000 years ago. Other sources suggest that Sanat Kumara's legion of volunteers descended to Earth millions of years ago to build and inhabit the first incarnation of Shamballa. Over its long and calamitous history, the White City experienced a series of cataclysmic Earth Changes that destroyed it three times during sensitive alignments with the Galactic Light of the Great Central Sun. This cosmic susceptibility occurs when the progression of yugas (periods of Vedic timekeeping) move from one age of light to another. Sanat Kumara's followers rebuilt Shamballa twice; the third time the White City ascended beyond the physical realm where it now exists in etheric perpetuity. This is the thirty-sixth Golden City Vortex of Gobi, known today as the City of Balance. It is located in China over the Qilian Shan Mountains next to the Gobi Desert.

The Venusian Volunteers

This City of White served a specific purpose: to save the Earth and humanity from certain annihilation. Stories like this in the Bible abound. Man's faith falters; his connection with God dims; and moral, physical, and spiritual depravity prevail — as was the state of the Earth before the Time of Shamballa. In a theosophical sense, universal principles demand a certain level of spiritual enlightenment for an entity to exist. The Earth and its inhabitants, however, consistently fell short; so a cosmic council of divine luminaries, including Sanat Kumara, voted to destroy the unfit planet.

But the compassionate Venusian Lord wouldn't allow Earth to fall into oblivion. Instead, he offered his light to balance the planet's metaphysical darkness and disharmony. As word spread of the Master's plans, devotees — 144,000 of them — volunteered to accompany their Guru on his karmic Mission. One-hundred of Sanat Kumara's stalwarts arrived on Earth 900 years beforehand to proliferate light; propagate the Flame of Consciousness; and prepare for the coming of Shamballa.

But, Sanat Kumara's volunteers paid a heavy spiritual price: karma. No longer would their Venusian souls enjoy the fruits of constant consciousness. Instead, as terrestrial bodies bound to the wheel of embodiment, they would follow the Laws of Earth — death, birth, and the passing of forgotten lifetimes — as their incarnating light energy lifted the consciousness of Earth.

Esoteric teachings say fellow Venusian Serapis Bey served as Sanat Kumara's first volunteer. With an affinity for architecture, this Master Teacher — along with the Seraphic Hosts he served with on the planets of Mercury, Aquaria, and Uranus — offered to oversee the creation of Shamballa.[1] Serapis Bey, the exalted being of light, performed one of the greatest sacrifices in Ascended Master legend by descending — as the light of heavens dimmed — into a physical body. On Earth, with his legions of seraphim, Serapis Bey oversaw the building of the White City for nine centuries. His sacrifice awarded him the honor of the Divine Architect of Shamballa.

This legend is analogous to the Hindu deity Tvashtri, later known as Vishvakarma, the celestial architect credited with the designing of the Universe and its contents.[2] Vishvakarma represents the power of regeneration and longevity. Serapis Bey later incarnated as Phidias, the great designer of the Parthenon, the classical sculptor of the Statue of Zeus, and the architect of the Temple of the Goddess Athena.

The Design of Shamballa

The builders of Shamballa modeled it after the opulent Venusian Cities of the Kumaras. On a white island in the sapphire-colored Gobi Sea (present-day Gobi Desert), workers erected the Elysian metropolis of light and con-

---

1. Tellis Papastavro, *The Gnosis and the Law* (Tucson, AZ: Group Avatar), page 28.
2. Hart Defouw and Robert Svoboda, *Light on Life: An Introduction to the Astrology of India* (London: Penguin Books Limited), page 232.

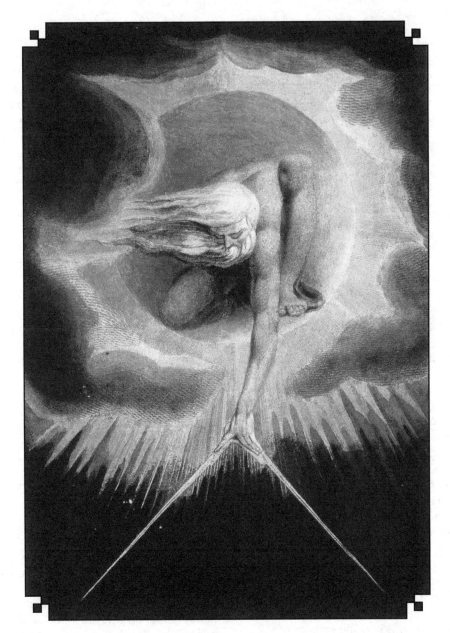

The Ancient of Days
by William Blake (1757 — 1827)
Sanat Kumara, portrayed by the visionary artist William Blake as *The Ancient of Days*, holds his spiritual compass as
if to engineer the spiritual city Shamballa. This portrait is housed in the British Museum, London, and is claimed
to be Blake's final painting, commissioned by Frederick Tatham.

Sanat Kumara
The Venusian Leader of Shamballa.

...sciousness. An ornate bridge of marble and Gold connected the White Island to the mainland. They adorned the city with hundreds of white, dome- and-spire-capped temples — that's where Shamballa earned its moniker, the City of White. Against this white-washed backdrop, the luminous Temples of the Seven Rays and their corresponding hues — blue, pink, yellow, pearl-white, green, ruby, and violet — stood prominently along a landscaped avenue. At its terminus rose the Temple of the Lord of the World, Sanat Kumara's annular, Golden-domed sanctuary. Here, the Ascended Master; three other Venusian Kumaras (lords); and thirty high priests, also known as Lords of the Flame, held conscious light for Earth to sustain her place in the solar system. During his time in Shamballa, Sanat Kumara provided more than a spiritual safe harbor for the Earth's denizens. He also formed the Great White Brotherhood — the fellowship of the Ascended Masters.

Thus, Shamballa defined itself as the earthly seat of self-lessness. Divine beings, including the unascended, flocked there to volunteer their efforts and services. To elevate their consciousness, and prepare them for upcoming lifetimes and undertakings, Sanat Kumara magnetized their energies with his Divine Love. Others seeking the Master's Heart Flame trained as messengers at Shamballa's numerous temples. Many of these servants became initiates of the Great White Brotherhood.

The Ethereal City

During Shamballa's physical existence on Earth, ascended and unascended members of the Great White Brotherhood returned annually for sanctuary, retreat, rejuvenation, and instruction for the upcoming year. After the third destruction of the city, and Shamballa's subsequent Ascension to the Fifth Dimension, ascended beings continued this tradition. But, without their aid, earthbound souls could no longer enter the City of White. To gain access, ascended members escorted the unascended to the etheric temples of the City of White by accelerating their Light Bodies during meditation and dreamtime.

For now, Shamballa will continue to exist in the ether, but Sanat Kumara prophesies its return:

"[It] shall remain there until it is lowered again, permanently, into the physical appearance world as the Golden Age proceeds and mankind, individually and collectively prove themselves worthy to sustain it for all eternity. It will be My Gift to the evolution that I have loved, and will remain a part of the Star of Freedom, long after I have returned to my home … "[3]

Mythical Names for Shamballa from other cultures:
Hindu: Aryavarsha
Buddhist: Shambhala, a hidden community of perfect and semi-perfect beings.
Chinese: Hsi Tien, Western paradise of Hsi Wang Mu, the Royal Mother of the West.
Greek: Hyperborea
Russian: Belovodye and Janaidar
Jewish and Christian: Garden of Eden
Celtic: Avalon
Esoteric: Shangri-La; Agartha; Land of the Living; Forbidden Land; Land of White Waters; Land of Radiant Spirits; Land of Living Fire; Land of Living Gods; Land of Wonders.[4]

Sanat Kumara

Sanat Kumara, the venerated leader of the Ascended Masters, is best known as the founder of Shamballa, the first Golden City on Earth. He is also known in the teachings of the Great White Brotherhood as the Lord of the World and is regarded as a savior and eminent spiritual teacher. Sanat Kumara is revered in many of the world religions as the familiar Ancient of Days in Judeo-Christianity, Kartikkeya in Hinduism, the Persian deity Ahura Mazda in Zoroastrianism and as Moses' challenging teacher and the Sufi initiator

3. Tellis Papastavro, *The Gnosis and the Law* (Tucson, AZ: Group Avatar), page 103.
4. Mary Sutherland, *In Search of Shambhala*, http//www.living in the lightms.com (2003).

of Divine Mysteries Al Khdir. C. W. Leadbeater and Alice Bailey referred to Sanat Kumara as the Youth of Sixteen Summers — a paradox to his Ancient of Days identity — and the One Initiator, as the Master of spiritual ceremonies of initiation. According to esoteric historians, Sanat Kumara was one of the few Ascended Masters who revealed his four-fold identity as the Cosmic Christ: first as Kartikkeya, the Hindu commander of God's Army; second, as Kumar (Kumara), the holy youth; third, as Skanda, son of Shiva; and fourth, as Guha — a Sanskrit term for the secret place in the heart, as he lives in the cave of all hearts.[5]

Sanat Kumara's Vedic and Buddhist Connection

The leader of the Spiritual Masters of the World appears historically in Vedic religious texts as a rishi who was one of the four sons of Brahma, the Creator. The four sons are born as liberated souls, and in early life take vows of celibacy. Since they are young, unmarried males, this becomes their eternal appearance, and the four sons are naturally attracted to devotional service to humanity. The four sons, or Kumaras, are known as: Sanaka Kumara; Sanandana Kumara (Sananda); Sanatana Kumara; and Sanat Kumara. In Sanskrit the name Sanat Kumara means eternal youth. Vedic scholars claim that the four sons are actually one incarnation manifesting on different planes of spiritual and physical reality. [6]

Santana Kumara	Supra Cosmic Plane
Sanaka Kumara	Solar Plane
Sanandana Kumara	Earth Plane
Sanat Kumara	Earth Planet

Sanat Kumara's affiliation with the Earth is often referred to by esoteric researchers as the station or office of Planetary Logos — a soul whose evolutionary journey leads them to oversee entire planets. Dr. Joshua Stone describes this cosmic position: "The job of the Planetary Logos is to set up a framework on the physical level for all evolving life forms which allows them all to evolve and grow. The Planetary Logos could be symbolically likened to a mountain and the paths on the mountain which the life forms travel to evolve. The Planetary Logos is also at the top of the mountain so

The Four Kumaras
The four youthful, immortal Brothers are depicted in this Indian print.

he can guide all life forms toward the top." [7] Perhaps this understanding alone gives explanation for Sanat Kumara's abiding presence in Shamballa, known in ancient India as the true spiritual center of Earth, akin to Earth's Sahasrara — Crown Chakra.

The Vedic epic of ancient India, the Mahabharata, states that Sanat Kumara is reborn as the son of Lord Krishna, Pradyumna. Pradyumna was an incarnation of the God of Love — Kama — and met a Karmic death at Dwaraka, one of the seven sacred cities of ancient India. With this final Earthly Karma completed, Pradyumna resumes his cosmic identity as Sanat Kumara and secures his rightful seat as the Planetary Lord of Shamballa.

5. Wikipedia, *Sanat Kumara*, http://en.wikipedia.org/wiki/Sanat_Kumara, (2011).
6. Wikipedia, *Sanat Kumara*.

7. Joshua Stone, *The Complete Ascension Manual: How to Achieve Ascension in This Lifetime*, (Light Technology Publishing, 1994, Sedona, AZ), pages 178–9.

Path to Kailas
Nicholas Roerich, 1931.

Buddhist lore defines Shambhala (Shamballa) as the place of happiness, tranquility, and peace; and where the records of the Kalachakra Tantra — advanced spiritual practices, spiritual philosophies, and meditation techniques — are claimed to be safeguarded. The teachings of Vajrayana Buddhism declare the King of Shambhala as King of the World, and this royal lineage descends from the Kalki Kings who maintain the integrity of the Kalachakra teachings. Early Tibetans claim Shambhala's location to be North of Lake Manasarovar, the highest fresh-water lake in the world, and nearby Mount Kailash, which derives its name from the phrase the precious one and is considered a sacred mountain of religious significance to the Bon, Buddhism, Hinduism, and Jainism. This area is considered the hydrographic center of the Himalaya, and its melted snows are the source for the Brahmaputra River, the Indus River, and Karnali River — an important tributary of the Ganges River. It is thought that all of the Earth's dragon currents — energy lei-lines — intersect at Mount Kailash.[8]

Evolution and Training of a Planetary Logos

Sanat Kumara's evolution is said to have occurred primarily on an Earth-like planet located in the Milky Way Galaxy. It is claimed that after sixty-nine lifetimes, he achieved the Ascension. After a brief study of the Music of the Spheres, he elected the path of Planetary Logos. This training was arduous and spiritually challenging and the Master divided his consciousness into 900,000 fragments with each portion strewn to a different planet of the galaxy. From there he wove each individual piece back into the ONE through unconditional love and equanimity. After this great test of Mastery, Sanat Kumara was required to take on a physical

8. Wikipedia, *Sanat Kumara*.

body to continue his training on the Planet Venus, where he encountered the cosmic being Adonis who became his Guru. It is claimed that Sanat Kumara was educated in the beautiful Fourth Dimensional temples of Venus for 2,000 years. During his epoch tenure on Venus, Sanat Kumara was assigned to work with the Venusian Planetary Logos. As the Master grew in experience and knowledge of planetary infrastructure and patterns, he evolved his spiritual Mastery to embrace Unity Consciousness, integration, balance, and the power of choice. These important spiritual precepts ultimately groomed the young Lord for his chief assignment: Earth.[9]

Some esoteric texts claim Shamballa existed more than 60,000 years ago, while others claim Sanat Kumara was sent to Earth to build the restorative Golden City more than 18,000,000 years ago. This complex timeline may be explained by the cosmic susceptibility to the progression of the Yugas (periods of Vedic timekeeping) and their correlation with cataclysmic Earth Changes. The provenance of Shamballa states that the wondrous City of Light was destroyed and rebuilt three times. The first Golden City on Earth, however, was in all of its various stages of planning, construction, destruction, modification, and transformation, under the stewardship of Sanat Kumara. His assignment was simple but relatively complex: raise the consciousness of humanity. Should he fail in his mission, Earth would likely be destroyed. The compassionate Venusian Lord offered his light to balance the planet's metaphysical darkness and disharmony.

Prior to Sanat Kumara's descent to Earth, he was given a well-deserved vacation of fifty years. Upon his return, he was given a party where it was announced that Sanat Kumara would be accompanied by the Venusian volunteers Lord Gautama and Lord Maitreya. Along with the angelic Serapis Bey, these two Lords would play invaluable roles in humanity's spiritual history and development.[10]

As Sanat Kumara entered Earth, his three Brothers — the immortal Kumaras — held their focused energies to assist the heavenly incarnation. Today this is known as the Astrological Spiritual Trinity transmitted to the Earth through Jupiter, the Sun, and Mars. And to this day, energies of the Galactic Center triangulate to the Earth through these planets. While Sanat Kumara's incarnation took effect immediately, another 1,000 years was needed to properly seat the celestial powers and link the supreme consciousness to Earth. During this 1,000-year period, occult historians claim the Earth's atmosphere was filled with electrical storms. Sanat Kumara and his stalwart volunteers patiently calibrated the Earth's energy fields and established their spiritual headquarters located near the Himalayan Mountains, near the present-day Gobi Desert.[11]

Sanat Kumara: Shamballa and the Great White Brotherhood

H. P. Blavatsky first coined the phrase "Lords of the Flame," to describe Sanat Kumara's association with humanity's Divine Evolution. Yet it was the theosophists Leadbeater and Annie Besant who claimed Sanat Kumara deployed thirty Lords of the Flame to accompany him on his spiritual mission to Earth. Classic Ascended Master teachings concur with this legendary story, however Sanat Kumara's group numbered 144,000 Venusian volunteers — pledged to enlighten Earth at a time of collective spiritual darkness.

One-hundred of Sanat Kumara's volunteers arrived on Earth 900 years beforehand to proliferate light, propagate the Flame of Consciousness, and prepare for the coming of the Golden City of Shamballa. Esoteric teachings say fellow Venusian Serapis Bey served as Sanat Kumara's first volunteer. With an affinity for architecture, this Master Teacher — along with the Seraphic Hosts he served with on the planets of Mercury, Aquaria, and Uranus — offered to oversee the creation of Shamballa. Serapis Bey, the exalted being of light, performed one of the greatest sacrifices in Ascended Master legend by descending into a physical body. On Earth, with his legions of seraphim, Serapis Bey oversaw the building of Shamballa — the City of White — for nine centuries. His sacrifice awarded him the honor of the Divine Architect of Shamballa.

The builders of Shamballa modeled it after the opulent Venusian City of the Kumaras. On a white island in the sapphire-colored Gobi Sea (present-day Gobi Desert), workers erected the Elysian metropolis of light and consciousness. An ornate bridge of marble and gold connected the White Island to the mainland. They adorned the city with hundreds of white, dome-and-spire-capped temples — that's where

---

9. J. Stone, *The Complete Ascension Manual,* page 179.
10. J. Stone, *The Complete Ascension Manual,* page 181.

---

11. J. Stone, *The Complete Ascension Manual,* page 182.

Shamballa earned its moniker, the City of White. Against this whitewashed backdrop, the luminous Temples of the Seven Rays and their corresponding hues — blue, pink, yellow, pearl-white, green, ruby, and violet — stood prominently along a landscaped avenue. At its terminus rose the Temple of the Lord of the World, Sanat Kumara's annular, golden-domed sanctuary. Here, the Ascended Master; three other Venusian Kumaras (lords); and thirty high priests, also known as Lords of the Flame, held conscious light for Earth to sustain her place in the solar system. During his time in Shamballa, Sanat Kumara provided more than a spiritual safe harbor for Earth's denizens. He also formed the Great White Brotherhood — the fellowship of the Ascended Masters.

Sanat Kumara's Return to Venus

Before Sanat Kumara's appointment as Lord of the World, Sri Magra held the office in Earth's spiritual-political hierarchy. After millions of years of service to Earth, Sanat Kumara was granted his freedom on January 1, 1956 and the noble Lord returned to his beloved Venus and his Divine Consort, Lady Master Venus. His three beloved Venusian volunteers — Lord Gautama, Lord Maitreya, and Serapis Bey — had successfully developed and advanced their sacred mission.

Serapis Bey became renowned as the World Architect and was also revered as the Hindu deity Vishvakarma.

Lord Maitreya became the leader of the Great White Brotherhood as a representation of the Cosmic Christ. He is the magnificent Guru of Jesus, Kuthumi, El Morya, Saint Germain, and many other Masters, saints, and spiritual teachers. Through the process of overshadowing (overlighting), this avatar "enfolded Jesus in His Cosmic Consciousness through Jesus' form." [12] The overshadowing process is described by Joshua Stone, PhD, in *The Complete Ascension Manual*:

> "Overshadowing was a process of melding his consciousness from the spiritual world into the physical body and consciousness of Jesus. In a sense, they shared the same physical body during the last three years of Jesus' life. Most people do not realize this. Many of the miracles and

sayings attributed to Jesus were really those of Lord Maitreya who holds the position in the Spiritual Government as the Christ. Jesus so perfectly embodied the Christ Consciousness that it enabled the Lord Maitreya, who is the Planetary Christ, to meld his consciousness with that of Jesus." [13]

Using the same technique initiated by Lord Maitreya as the World Teacher, Sanat Kumara overshadowed and accelerated the Earth's spiritual development through Venusian Lord Gautama's earthly embodiment as Prince Siddhartha Gautama, an Indian prince (563–483 BC). Through Sanat Kumara's careful guidance, their consciousness melded as ONE, and Lord Gautama became the Enlightened One and qualified as Earth's first Buddha. According to A.D.K. Luk in the Law of Life, the activity and service of a Buddha is, "to step-down the high spiritual vibrations and radiate them to nourish, expand, and sustain the light in all beings during their development on the planet. He is to radiate God's love to a planet and its evolutions; to draw and hold the spiritual nourishment around a planet for all evolving lifestreams on that planet both while in and out of embodiment, sustaining them spiritually and developing their inner God natures especially the emotional bodies. He guards and sustains the flame of the least developed soul, so that it will not go out. A Buddha's work is through radiation, by radiating." [14]

Buddha's radiation of the indwelling spiritual consciousness of humanity paved the pathway for the development of humanity's conscious mind and the Christ activity, or Christ Consciousness in self-realization. Lord Buddha also assumed Sanat Kumara's vacant position at Shamballa as present-day Lord of the World, an honor bestowed from the now seasoned Planetary Logos: Sanat Kumara — mentor, Guru, and friend.

The Spiritual Contributions of Sanat Kumara

The spiritual role played by Sanat Kumara in Earth's history and humanity's spiritual enrichment is truly invaluable and, without question, almost impossible to measure. There

---

12. J. Stone, *The Complete Ascension Manual*, page 138.

13. Ibid.
14. A. D. K. Luk, *Law of Life*, (A.D.K. Luk Publications, 1989, Pueblo, CO), Book II, page 310.

Ahura Mazda Investiture

Ahura Mazda (right) with Ardeshir I (left) in this archaeological relief at Naqh-e-Rustan (Iran). This rock carving is from the birth of the Sassanian Empire (224 — 651). Ahura Mazda, a Persian Deity and God of Zoroastrianism, is one of Sanat Kumara's noteworthy incarnations.

are, however, several significant and remarkable accomplishments worth noting.

Sanat Kumara spearheaded the mission to graft the sublime Unfed Flame — a Flame of Divinity and spiritual consciousness — to the carnal human heart. The Unfed Flame urges humanity to evolve beyond its present state of spiritual consciousness through Co-creative thought, feeling, and action and the Divine Tenets of Love, Wisdom, and Power. This empowers humans to achieve a higher sense of consciousness, thereby assuring humanity a type of spiritual immortality. With an etheric silver cord, Sanat Kumara connected the Unfed Flame to every life stream incarnation on Earth. This ensured the development and growth of spiritual consciousness among individuals.

During the 1,000-year period while Earth energies were purified to receive the spiritual presence and teachings of Sanat Kumara, the esteemed Lord performed yearly sacred fire ceremonies to clear Earth's etheric atmosphere of darkness. These ceremonies assisted the spiritually awakened to maintain contact with their I AM Presence. It is claimed that many attended these rites, and each attendee would take home a piece of the sacred wood used for the fire — likely sandalwood — to keep throughout the year. These ceremonies forged an indelible bond between Sanat Kumara and those he once served. A. D. K. Luk writes, "Sanat Kumara came ages ago to give assistance to the Earth when it would have been dissolved otherwise. He offered of his own Free Will to supply the light required to sustain her and keep her place in the system until enough of mankind could be raised to a point where they could carry the responsibility of emitting sufficient light ... Now when people first come in contact with his name they usually feel a sense of happiness come over them. This is because of his connection with their lifestreams through radiation during the past."[15]

The sacred City of Shamballa is said to be both "a location and a state of consciousness."[16] Sanat Kumara's service to advancing spiritual students is never static and always unfolding; and along with various counsel meetings among the Spiritual Hierarchy, Sanat Kumara's purpose at Shamballa is to continue the initiatory process of students and chelas and to provide a haven for those who have successfully passed the fifth initiation. The seven levels of human evolution and their initiatory processes are:

The spiritually un-awakened, yet Conscious Human.

The Aspirant — a newly awakened, ambitious student.

The Chela — the disciple who has entered a formal student relationship with a guru or teacher.

The Initiate — personal experience by degree, test, and trial that is encountered morally and mentally.

The Arhat — one who has overcome antagonistic craving, including the entire range of passions and desires — mental, emotional, and physical.

The Adept — one who has attained Mastery in the art and science of living; a Mahatma.

The Master — "human beings further progressed on the evolutionary pathway than the general run of humanity from which are drawn the saviors of humanity and the founders of the world-religions."

"These great human beings (also known by the Sanskrit term Mahatma 'great self') are the representatives in our day of a Brotherhood of immemorial antiquity running back into the very dawn of historic time, and for ages beyond it. It is a self perpetuating Brotherhood formed of individuals who, however much they may differ among themselves in evolution, have all attained mahatma-ship, and whose lofty purposes comprise among other things the constant aiding in the regeneration of humanity, its spiritual and intellectual as well as psychic guidance, and in general the working of the best spiritual, intellectual, psychic, and moral good to mankind. From time to time members from their ranks, or their disciples, enter the outside world publicly in order to inspire mankind with their teachings."[17]

In metaphysical terms, Sanat Kumara may be seen as a mastermind of Earth's spiritual evolutionary process. A mastermind contains organized effort — a true measure of everlasting power. Sanat Kumara had the ability to hold the focus of the Elemental and Fourth Dimensional energies to create Shamballa on Earth and then actively engage the help of literally thousands of Lords, Masters, sages, saints, angels, Elohim, and adepts throughout our galaxy. Esoteric scholars claim that the entire spectrum of the Seven Rays are indeed embodied in Sanat Kumara and distributed through the synthesizing radiance of the Lord of the World.

Sanat Kumara Today

Presently the ethereal City of Shamballa is open to all who have acquired the eyes to see, and the ears to hear from December 17th to January 17th on an annual basis. During this time, Sanat Kumara returns to Shamballa and gives guidance to the Brotherhoods and Sisterhoods of Light for their yearly plan for humanity's spiritual growth and progress. Sanat Kumara's visit is accompanied by the Celebration of the Four Elements: a twenty-eight day festivity centered on devotional sacraments dedicated to the elements of earth, air, water, and fire in conjunction with thanksgiving, gratitude, love, friendship, intention, and unity. (For more information see: *Points of Perception*, and *The Celebration of the Four Elements*.)

Sanat Kumara is the guru of four of the Twelve Jurisdictions — spiritual precepts on Co-creation designed to guide human consciousness into the New Times. As he gave this important wisdom, his ethereal presence was often accompanied by the Golden Radiance of the Solar Logos: Apollo. Here is a synthesis of Sanat Kumara's four teachings.

15. A. D. K. Luk, *Law of Life*, Book II, page 306.
16. J. Stone, *The Complete Ascension Manual*, page 185.

17. *Encyclopedic Theosophical Glossary*, http://www.theosociety.org/pasadena/etglos/etg-hp.htm, (2011).

Message from Shambhala
Nicholas Roerich, 1933.

The Masculine Principle of Cooperation: The spiritual teachings of Cooperation, the seventh of the Twelve Jurisdictions, are taught by both Lady Master Venus and Sanat Kumara. Cooperation is the spiritual knowledge that teaches every individual to honor their divinity. Both Lady Master Venus and Sanat Kumara share their philosophies on this topic. Lady Master Venus gives the feminine point of view. Sanat Kumara elaborates from a male perspective. In his teachings Sanat Kumara states, "Your enlightenment has always been and will always be. That is unchangeable. Bring your conscious awareness, your focus, to the sustaining, and cooperate with yourself in this great magnificence that you are. Cooperate with all others in the great magnificence that they are."

The Principle of Charity: The eighth of the Twelve Jurisdictions is the spiritual guidance to live with love and equity. Sanat Kumara advises, "Charity is a distribution, and it is the equalizer when there is un-justice and inequity."

The Principle of Desire: The ninth of the Twelve Jurisdictions is based on a new perception of desire based on the true etymology of the word. De is a French word that means of, and the English word sire means forefather, ancestry, or source. From this context, Sanat Kumara teaches the Heart's Desire is the source of creation. He states, "Desire springs not only from the heart, it comes from the soul, the spark of creativity."

The Principle of Stillness: Stillness is the eleventh of the Twelve Jurisdiction and Sanat Kumara explains this important spiritual knowledge as the Law of Alignment. The practice of this immutable law was likely perfected during the creation of Shamballa, and the Lord of the World states, "Stillness is the space where energy is gathered and aligned to come forth in a manifestation."

Buddha Walking Among the Flowers
Odilon Redon, 1905.

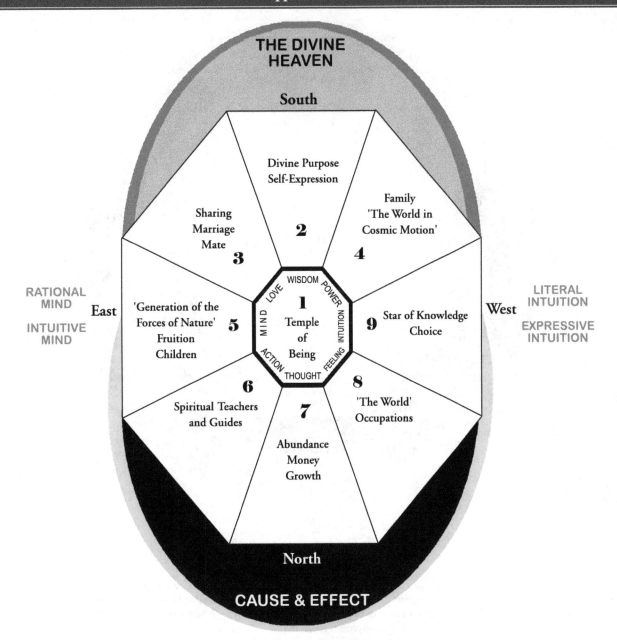

Eight-sided Cell of Perfection Energy Map

The Eight-sided Cell of Perfection with the Nine Perfections (Palaces). North represents Cause and Effect; South, the Divine Heavens; East represents the Mind, and West the Intuition. The center direction is the Temple of BE-ing and the Unfed Flame of Love, Wisdom, and Power. The Nine Palaces represent Nine Movements, or domains, of HU-man Evolution.

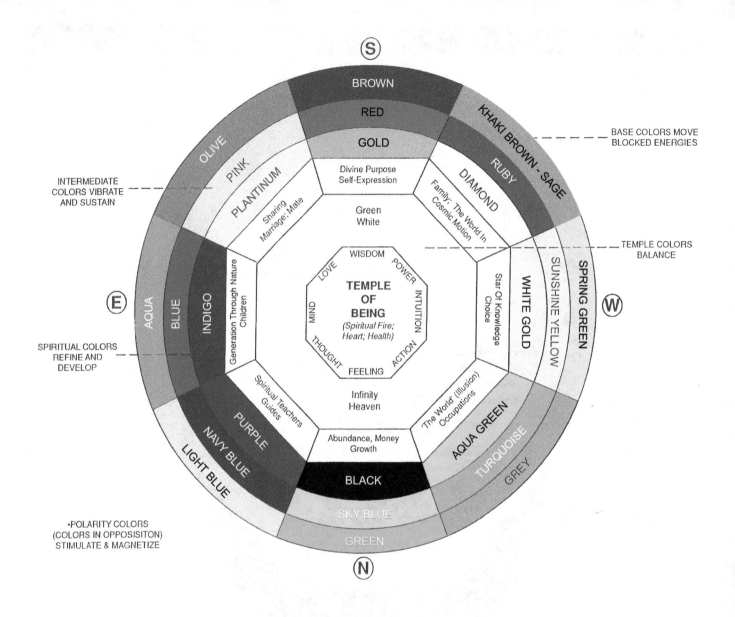

Esoteric Color Wheel of the Nine Palaces within the Eight-sided Cell of Perfection
Various colors express throughout the Nine Palaces of the Eight-sided Cell of Perfection.
The colors depicted are not based upon the Color Ray system; however, Ray Forces will
express through the esoteric colors.

Esoteric Color System

The Esoteric Color System is a specific arrangement of color frequencies and vibrations meant to accompany and enhance the movement of energy throughout the Nine Palaces of the Eight-sided Cell of Perfection. It is important to understand that this arrangement is not based upon the planetary Ray System, although the colors represent a modulated Ray System; nor is it a Feng Shui practice. This system is intended to supplement the characteristics and qualities of the Nine Palace as they will activate, enhance, develop, and increase the effective movement of both Earthly and ethereal energies. Specific colors on this wheel complement Third, Fourth, and Fifth Dimensional activities and readily shift stagnant or blocked states of consciousness. Used appropriately, they can dissipate Subjective Energy Bodies. This progressive movement is based upon the Ascended Master ideal of "Ever Present Perfection," the notion that the developing and realized HU-man is an immortal, divine BE-ing of light.

CMYK

This science of interactive color is based on the dynamic infrastructure of the Maltese Cross that parcels light into four primary colors: cyan (blue), magenta (pink or red), yellow, and black. Each primary color is associated with a cardinal direction with black designated to the North, blue to the East, red to the South, and yellow to the West. The center is often associated with the color white, which in Ascended Master Teaching is the presence of all colors. Saint Germain adds the color green to the central palace, a Ray Force associated with the planet Mercury and the Aryan Epoch, the time period we are currently experiencing.

How to Apply the System

You can apply the colors by wearing them, paint specific walls or rooms with their vibrant shades, or use in meditation and spiritual practice. Some Feng Shui practitioners claim that color will raise energy by only five percent. However, through the appropriate use of the Esoteric Color System energy movement can be immediately enhanced by sixty to seventy percent.

Four Levels

According to Saint Germain there are four levels of color: base, intermediate, spiritual, and temple colors. Each classification has a distinctive purpose and energetic characteristic.

Base Colors vibrate to the physical plane and are best used to move stagnant or torpid energy. They assist to remove personal energies of lethargy, sluggishness, or exhaustion. They are especially effective when applied with their specific direction, either cardinal or inter-cardinal. Base colors help to eliminate obstructions at many levels: financial, creativity, relationship, academic, and career. They can also assist us spiritually and receive assistance from the spiritual planes through defining our purpose, strengthen our will, and help us to define and exercise our numerous choices. Base colors, moving from North to East on the color wheel are: green, aqua green, Aqua (more blue), olive, brown, khaki, sage, spring green, and grey.

Intermediate Colors assist and sustain the vibration of a benefic or supportive condition. When applied in their appropriate direction they promote the flow of Fourth Dimensional energy and experience. Moving from North to East on the color wheel, they are: sky blue, light blue, blue, pink red, ruby, sunshine yellow, and turquoise. Intermediate colors nourish and maintain the ongoing evolution of the HU-man.

Spiritual Colors purify, refine, and expand spiritual growth and evolution. Since they vibrate to Fifth Dimension their qualities advance and further cultivate the HU-man Ascension Process. From North to East on the color wheel they are: black, purple, indigo, platinum, gold, diamond, white-gold, and navy blue.

The Temple of Being vibrates best to the color white, which is considered the presence of all colors. It is also suggested to temper white with the color green, which also carries a balancing effect.

Polarity Colors

Opposing pairs of colors can also be utilized for intensifying and stimulating magnetically. This requires experimentation on an individual basis as certain pairs can invite or draw upon the directional qualities, and in rare cases cause resistance or repulsion. Practical pairs are: green and brown or aqua with spring green. Dynamic pairs are gold and black, diamond and purple, platinum and navy blue, indigo and white-gold.

Experiment

The best way to gain personal experience with the multi-dimensional Color Wheel is to experiment. First, it is suggested to practice with a color by applying meditation while holding beads, crystals, gemstones, metals, or papers of the desired color. Cover or fold a decree or prayer request with a sheet of colored paper – purple is best for this. For added benefit face the direction of the desired result. For instance, if you are seeking a new job face the Northwest during meditation. Looking for spiritual assistance? Face the Northeast during daily spiritual practice or place a special altar in this direction of your home or apartment.

Rainbow
Arkhip Kuindzhi, 1905.

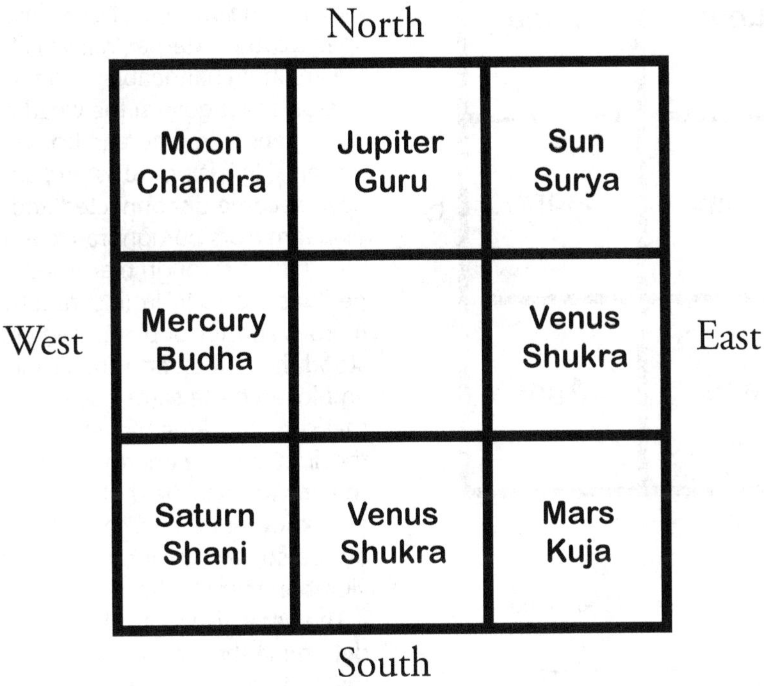

North

Moon Chandra	Jupiter Guru	Sun Surya
Mercury Budha		Venus Shukra
Saturn Shani	Venus Shukra	Mars Kuja

West   East

South

The Vedic Square
Vedic Square (yantra) Energy Map of the Nine Planets and their corresponding directions.

Maps of Energy Movement

Many schools of thought address energy movement — chi, orgone, or prana — in some capacity. Two doctrines, however, express these principles in a comprehensive historical perspective, Vastu Shastra and Vastu Vidya. They form the foundation of the 4,500-year-old dwelling sciences of Vedic philosophy and Classical Chinese Feng Shui, the Taoist art and science of living in harmony in the environment.

The Yantra

The Yantra is a sacred geometrical tradition of Vedic philosophy — a visual tool often used during meditation that helps the mind tune out mental noise. Permutations of shape and mathematics create decorative and magical patterns such as the mandala, kolam, and rangoli. The source of these structures stems from one of the oldest systems of mapping unseen energies: the Vedic Square, also known as the Paramashayika. It's based on and derives its power from the number nine, considered a sacred numeral in Vedic Astrology — Jyotish — based on nine grahas or planets. The Vedic Square also represents what lies beyond. This energy map contains divisions of nine equal parts, forming a diagram of eighty-one squares (9 x 9). The larger square depicts the macrocosm; the detailed squares of eighty-one segments calculate the microcosmic nuances of space.

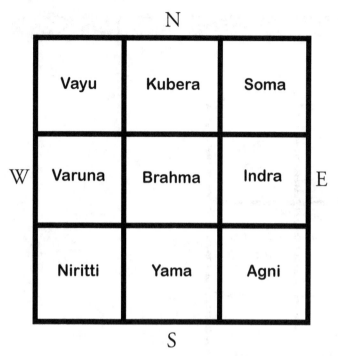

The Vedic Square
Energy Map of the Nine Directions and Vedic Deities.

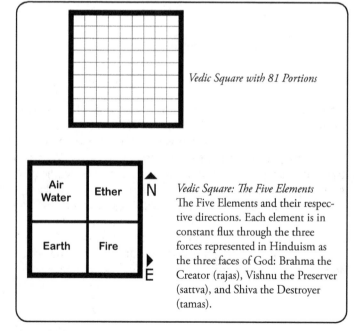

Vedic Square with 81 Portions

Vedic Square: The Five Elements
The Five Elements and their respective directions. Each element is in constant flux through the three forces represented in Hinduism as the three faces of God: Brahma the Creator (rajas), Vishnu the Preserver (sattva), and Shiva the Destroyer (tamas).

Energy Lines

First, to understand the language buried within energy maps and concealed in their concurrent lines and formulas, one must delve into the ancient Indian knowledge of Vastu Vidya — the science of dwelling. From this esoteric perspective, the external (macro) life and the internal (micro) life are interchangeable, and the same laws and underlying energies that govern the weather are the same that control the organs of the human body. Today, this important and universal link is non-existent, and our societies and cultures have become disconnected and alienated from nature. The planet mirrors our ignorance as delicate eco-systems rapidly change through man-made threats to the environment, perilous Global Warming, and the growing extinction of numerous species of plants and animals. The ancients understood the hidden and stabilizing forces of the universe, and employed these same cosmic principles and universal laws that controlled the movement of the Sun and the Moon; the light and the energy of the Sun, and the magnetic and the gravitational field of the Earth. Application of this venerated knowledge restores balance between the cosmos and our personal environments, creating a timeless and positive vibration that results in health, wealth, and happiness.[1]

The Vedic rishis calculated the significance of lei-lines to determine the wobble factor. These scholars ascertained that the flow of the lines meandered primarily from Northeast to Southwest. At times, however, the energy currents change and run North to South and from East to West. Vastu philosophy understood the profundity of this phenomenon, and assigned deities to govern and protect these matrices.[2]

Earth's Wobble and Precession

The ancient Vedic rishis — advanced spiritual teachers who lived in the previous ages of superior light and truth — gave humanity the science of Vastu, gross energies, and Vaastu, subtle energies. They recognized the Earth's natural energy conduits, also known as lei-lines, which form a grid around the planet. This esoteric system of latitudinal and longitudinal striae, running from the dipolar magnetic points of North and South and from East to West, follows

1. Juliet Pegrum, *The Vastu Vidya Handbook: The Indian Feng Shui* (New York: Three Rivers Press), page 10-11.
2. Ibid., page 56-57.

the path of the Sun. This web of electromagnetic energy creates a subtle influence on an individual's mind and body as it transforms the Causal and Astral Body (Light Bodies). This effect becomes noticeable as these changes reshape physical health in the body and overall life experiences. The Earth's imperfect spin perpetually shifts to the fixed position of the stars. The following visible results demonstrate the wobble of the Earth:

1. In the fifteenth century, the pole-star Polaris was first used to navigate true North. Yet in the year 150 BC, it moved 12° 24 minutes from these coordinates. In 13,000 years the star Vega will replace Polaris as the pole-star.[3] Not all ancient cultures followed Polaris as its focal point. The ancient Egyptians relied on Alpha Draconis (Dracaenas) as their polestar in the construction of the pyramids.

2. The wobble of the Earth also causes precession of the equinoxes. Precession is the slow backward shifting motion of the Earth as it rotates.[4] This slight tilting of the pole is calculated at approximately 23.5°; it's the source of the Vedic Ayanamsha, which differentiates planetary movements against the position of stars — sidereal astrology. In contrast, tropical or Western astrology tracks planets in reference to seasonal points according to a point of view from Earth. Vedic astrology adjusts for precession; the Western system does not.

The Movement of Prana — The Vital Breath

Prana — also defined as the vital breath and referred to as *chi* in Chinese Feng Shui — excludes air, wind, or exhalation in the traditional sense. Rather, it encompasses the essence of the soul: immortality. It is pure, untainted, and unattached from any manifest form. In the physical body, this spirit reflects an energy known as Asasya, and without its presence the body fades and dies. Prana, as the sages observed, wanders like lei-lines. So they studied prana to determine its movement and how to best harness it. During this process, they perceived its current streams from the Northeast to the Northwest and then toward the Southwest; it also flows from the Northeast toward the Southwest, and then toward the Southwest. Since benevolent energies meet in the Southwest, entrances are never placed in these loca-

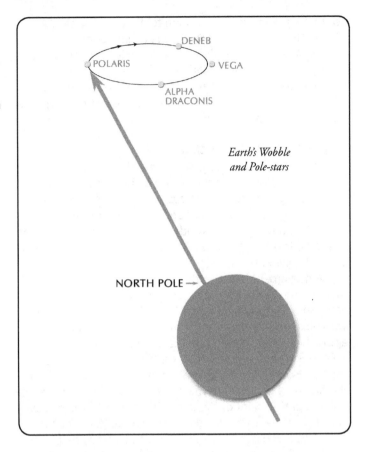

Earth's Wobble and Pole-stars

tions; energy flows don't affect centers, however — that's why middle ground serves as open courtyards.[5]

The Science of Ayadi

The professional practice of Vastu Vidya, the Vedic doctrine of space planning, employs zodiac-referenced mathematical calculations to harmonize a person's living (or work) area with his or her birth star — this is the science of Ayadi. An individual's Moon sign is used during important phases of the planning and building of a home or office. An edifice is considered a living being, influenced by the force of astrology.

Vedic Astrology uses a lunar-based system founded on twenty-seven signs, also known as nakshatras or lunar mansions. Each nakshatra has three specific orientations (North,

---

3. Jeffrey Armstrong, *God/Goddess the Astrologer: Soul Karma and Reincarnation: How We Continually Create Our Own Destiny* (Badger, CA: Torchlight Publishing), 38-39.
4. Ibid.

---

5. Pegrum, *Vastu Vidya*, 49.

South, East, and West) in relation to its ruling planet.[6] According to Hindu lore, Chandra, the Moon deity, married twenty-seven wives, each residing in their own constellate homes. Thus, Chandra visits one wife a day, completing the zodiac in twenty-seven days. Ancient astrologers perceive Chandra, though male, as feminine because of his perpetual female influence.

Vastu's Child — Feng Shui

Vastu is the parent: Feng Shui is the child. The science of Feng Shui is old; the practice of Vastu, however, predates its Chinese counterpart by thousands of years. And as the old saying goes, "The apple doesn't fall far from the tree." Feng Shui, the pattern of wind and water, relies on many of the same tools as Vastu to maximize the flow of energy in a particular living space.

The movement of chi — the vapor of life — is well documented in the history and culture of China. Practitioners of Feng Shui (pronounced fung-shway) depend on intricate, Vastu-like energy maps and a modified Paramashayika to apply these principles in practical applications.

Feng Shui evolved from two shaman Emperors, Fu Hsi of the San Huang Dynasty (twenty-ninth century BC) and Yü, the first ruler of the Xia Dynasty. Scholars credit Emperor Fu Hsi, the patron saint of the divination arts, with the discovery of Ho-t'u — the Earlier Heaven Pa-k'ua. (A pa-k'ua is similar to a Vedic yantra, another type of energy map). The revelation came to him after he witnessed a horse materialize from the Yellow River. On its side, he noted geometrical markings, which he later understood as the ideal structure of the universe and humanity.

Yü, the first emperor of the Xia Dynasty, ascended the throne approximately 700 years later. As a gift for saving the kingdom from a torrential flood, Shun, the reigning leader, named Yü his heir — a Prophecy fulfilled after Yü received the book Power Over Water from an immortal. As the floodwaters subsided, the future king observed a tortoise — its shell emblazoned with a pattern — emerge from the receding deluge. Yü recognized the ornamentation and identified it as the Later Heaven Pa-k'ua energy map.

☉	SU	Krittika North	Uttara Phalguni East	Uttara Ashada South
☽	MO	Rohini East	Hasta South	Shravana North
♂	MA	Mrigashira South	Chitra West	Dhanistha East
☿	ME	Aslesha South	Jyestha West	Revati East
♃	JU	Punarvasu North	Visahka East	Purva Bhadrapada West
♀	VE	Bharani West	Purva Phalguni North	Purva Ashada East
♄	SA	Pushya East	Anuradha South	Uttara Bhadrapada North
☊	RA	Ardra West	Swati North	Shatabisha South
☋	KE	Ashwini South	Magha West	Mula North

The 27 Nakshatras (Moon Signs) are the basis of the Vedic Science of Ayadi.

The interpretation of it can predict phenomena of flux and change. Today it's known as the Lo-shu.[7]

Feng Shui and the I Ching

The I Ching, also called the Book of Changes, is perhaps one of the oldest examples of Chinese texts in the vast timeline of the culture's history. It's an attempt to create order out of chaos based on the enduring principles of philosophy, cosmology, and mathematics.

Over millennia, scholars studied and recalculated the trigrammatic divination formulas of the Ho-t'u and the Lo-shu. Scholars credit Zhou Dynasty ruler King Wen with devising the sixty-four sequence hexagram. His grandson, Emperor Shing of the Chou Dynasty, combined these doctrines of divination; his knowledge of the compass; and the tenets of the I Ching to form the territory of terrestrial and celestial prediction.

6. Dennis Harness, *The Nakshatras: The Lunar Mansions of Vedic Astrology, First Edition* (Twin Lakes, WI: Lotus Press).

7. Eva Wong, *Feng Shui: The Ancient Wisdom of Harmonious Living for Modern Times* (Boston: Shambhala Publications, Inc.), page 15-16.

Niels Bohr, the 1922 Nobel Prize winner in physics, understood and appreciated the parallels of the I Ching's probabilistic concepts in relation to its prophetic application of popular phenomena. He even incorporated the Tai Chi symbol in his coat of arms when he was knighted in 1947. Other scientists, too, have attempted to apply I Ching principles in contemporary applications. For instance, the sixty-four hexagrams of the I Ching correspond to the sixty-four DNA condons of the genetic code.

The energy maps on these pages depict the legendary Lo-Ching. The first is the Earlier Heaven Pa-k'ua used with a compass for city planning. Practitioners apply the Later Heaven Pa-k'ua alongside landforms and the movement of the stars to design countermeasures for adverse conditions.[8]

The Science of Feng Shui Evolves

During the Tang Dynasty (618-960 AD) the geomancer's compass (lo-p'an) — used to identify the flow of Earth's energy — grew to seventeen rings and twenty-four directions. Feng Shui practitioners depend on a similar compass in contemporary applications. Since its early inception thousands of years ago, Classical Chinese Feng Shui describes the research and the observations of the Ancients:

1. The science of landform — the dragon's vein.
2. The interaction with the heavenly bodies.
3. Cycle of changes in the universe.
4. The science of burial sites.
5. Integration of numerology and symbology.
6. Classification of mountains.
7. The cycle of eras and small changes.
8. Analysis of an individual's karma in evaluating the Feng Shui of a location.
9. Auspicious timing.

The Path of Energy Movement through the Nine Palaces depicts the flow of energy through the Nine Palaces of Classical Feng Shui. The Nine Palaces comprise the eight directions of the compass plus the center. The five elements — water, earth, metal, wood, fire — and their cycles of creation and destruction form the underpinnings of this movement.[9]

---

8. Wong, *Feng Shui*, 18.
9. Ibid., 59.

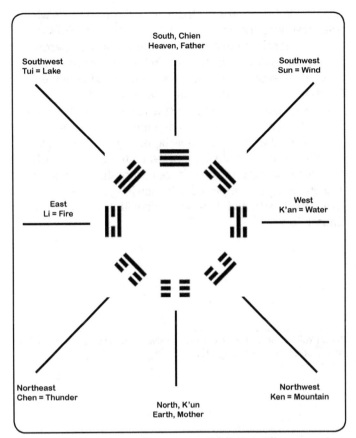

Chinese Pak'ua or Ba Gua Energy Map
Early Heaven devised by Fu Hsi.

The Three Gifts for Kali Yuga

Kali Yuga is one of the four stages of development the Earth experiences as its consciousness evolves (or deteriorates) as the case may be. According to ancient texts, the world entered Kali Yuga, or the Age of Quarrel, thousands of years ago when Maharaja Yüdhisthira noticed the Vedic antagonist darkening his kingdom. The king ceded his throne to his grandson Raja Parikshit, and the court, including its wise men, retreated to the Himalayas.

Wise and benevolent souls knew the consequences of these dire times, so the Seers, the Vedic rishis, and the Master Teachers gave humanity the following three gifts: the written word, Vastu Shastra, and Jyotish.

The sages prophesied that humans would suffer from diminished recall and an inability to sustain oral tradition, thus losing historical knowledge to oblivion — that's why they bestowed the alphabet on humanity. Vastu Shastra, the ancient science of geomancy, was the world's second gift. Maharaja Yūdhisthira's exile in the mountains created a dearth of Vastu knowledge among the Hindu people.[10] So, the ancient practice, in effect, reincarnated in another culture. Legend says Vastu Shastra leaped across the Himalayas where it conceived a child — the practice of Feng Shui. Most of all, the wise men knew humanity would need spiritual liberation from the cycle of death: the gift of Jyotish, the personal and intricate science of moksha (liberation). The ancient gurus imparted this knowledge of the soul's journey on Earth and its relationship with the Astral and Causal Bodies.

---

10. Sri Yukteswar, *The Holy Science*, Kaivalya Darsanam (Los Angeles: Self-Realization Fellowship), page 15.

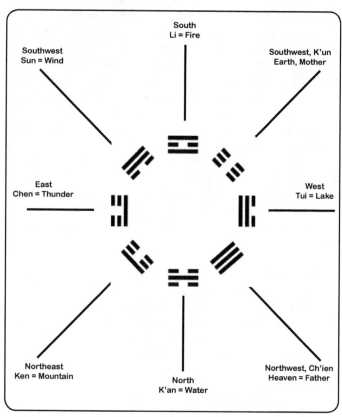

Chinese Pak'ua or Ba Gua Energy Map
Later Heaven devised by Yü.

Energy Movement Through the Nine Palaces of Classical Chinese Feng Shui

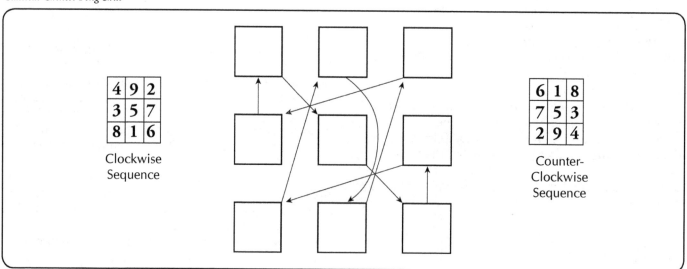

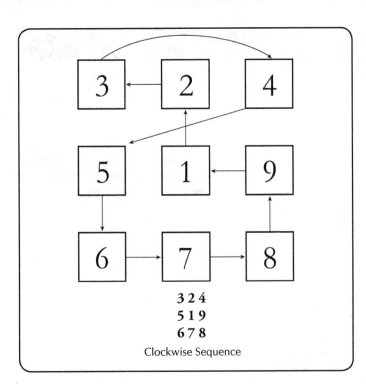

The Nine Movements of Consciousness
Through the Eight-sided Cell of Perfection the nine movements resemble the infinity sign, or the Yin-Yang formation through the figure eight.

3 2 4
5 1 9
6 7 8
Clockwise Sequence

World Map of the Nine Perfected Movements of Consciousness
Depicted below is the movement of energy and consciousness through the Eight-sided Cell of Perfection overlaid on a world map. It shows the possibilities for the movement of the Collective Consciousness. Please note that any place on the Earth could be referenced as the center, or the Temple of Being, and in doing so, would create entirely different Consciousness Zones on Earth. From this simplistic perspective, observe the different Zones of Consciousness by centering the first movement in Africa, the birthplace of the Aryan, and the second to a Southern orientation. Keep in mind, the number two, a feminine numeral, is present in the South, which also corresponds to the birth of femininity. The third movement is to the Southwest. This pattern continues to follow the sequence of energy movements described by Saint Germain in *The Ever Present Perfection*.
Map: *Robinson Projection*, not to scale.

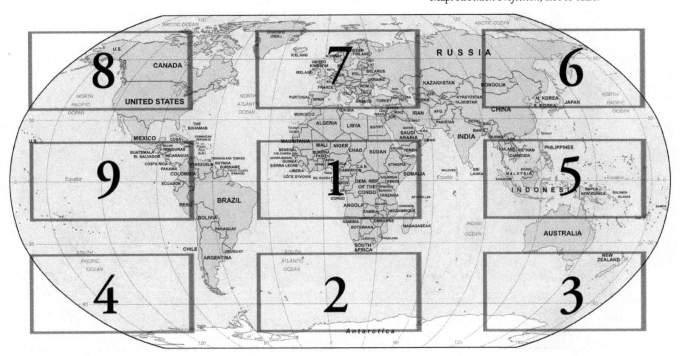

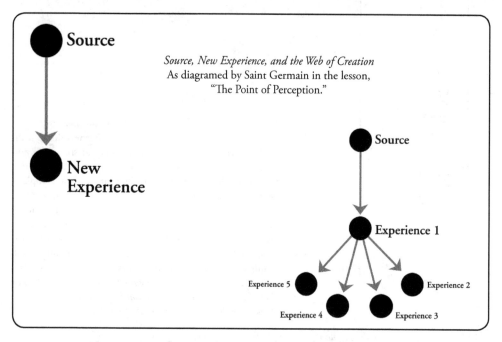

Source, New Experience, and the Web of Creation
As diagramed by Saint Germain in the lesson,
"The Point of Perception."

(Left) **Diagram for Simultaneous Points of Perception as taught by Saint Germain**

(Below) **Diagram for Not Less Than, Equal To as taught by Saint Germain**

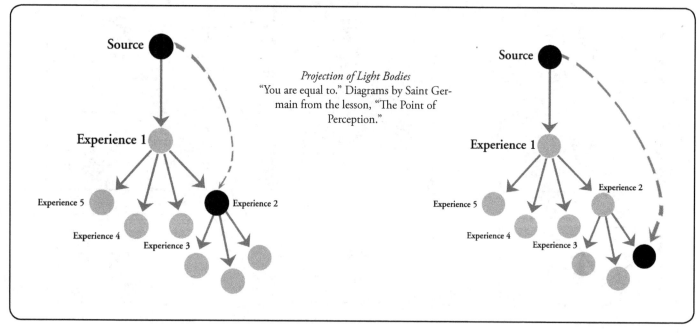

Projection of Light Bodies
"You are equal to." Diagrams by Saint Germain from the lesson, "The Point of Perception."

Star of the Hero
Nicolas Roerich, 1936.

Mahatma El Morya
Master Teacher and Hierarch of the Golden City of Gobean.

The Candle Meditation as Taught by El Morya

The Candle Meditation by El Morya is one of the first steps to experience the Divine Light within and calm the mind. Use a long tapered candle, not a jarred glass candle. For this exercise I prefer a white candle, but any color should work. Light the candle and establish a constant, stable flame.

First, sit comfortably; you may use a chair for back support if needed. Look and concentrate on the candle and give attention to the different layers of the light of the flame. You will notice these layers: the outer glow; the yellow-white layer of fire; the center of the wick; and the central inner glow, which sometimes contains a blue or violet hue at the base of the flame. Focus on the overall glow of the candle until you identify the layers of light. Breathe evenly and gently as you concentrate on the light.

As you observe the Flame of Light, continue your rhythmic breath as the light begins to expand and absorb the space between you and the flame. Continue this breathing until you have established a large ovoid of light, including the candle and yourself.

Remain focused in the circle of light and you will begin to notice you are in the flame; the light is even, and it flows with your breath. You may notice a pulse in the energy field you share with the flame. At this state you are ONE with the light.

Individuals who practice the Candle Meditation have reported feeling calm and peace, even in extremely stressful conditions. Sometimes this is accompanied by a high-pitch ring. El Morya asserts the application of the Candle Meditation imparts experience with the consciousness of the ONE and develops human consciousness into the HU-man. The Candle Meditation can be performed individually or in groups.

Angel with Censor and Candle
Mikhail Vrubel, 1887.

The Galactic Center

The above composite photograph by NASA, 2009, depicts the Galactic Center, the origin of the Seven Rays of Light and Sound. "In this spectacular image, observations using infrared light and X-ray light see through the obscuring dust and reveal the intense activity near the galactic core. Note that the center of the galaxy is located within the bright white region to the right of and just below the middle of the image. The entire image width covers about one-half a degree, about the same angular width as the full moon."

The Rays

A Ray, simply stated, divides its efforts into two measurable and discernable powers: light and sound. Alice Bailey, author of many spiritual and esoteric works, wrote in A Treatise on the Seven Rays, "A Ray is but a name for a particular force or type of energy, with the emphasis upon the quality which that force exhibits, and not upon the form aspect which it creates. This is a true definition of a Ray."[1] Bailey's work underscores the abstract elements of a Ray but omits its tangible importance. The presence of a Ray also creates many physical attributes, which are significant in Ascended Master teachings.

Light and sound are the building blocks of our universe; therefore, the Rays permeate everything in our world of thought, feeling, and action. A developed psychic may perceive the twin matrix powers of light and sound as specific colors and sound frequencies in the energy fields of an individual—the aura. Nature mimics a similar pattern: a plant blooms a variety of colorful flowers, a common mineral becomes a precious gem, a songbird's melody is distinct and characteristic to its species. Each color and sound contains an undeniable unique vibration.

Light and sound evoke attributes and properties that carry specific cultural meaning as well. In the Western world, black is often associated with darkness and evil; it is the hue of mourning and death. Yet in some Native American traditions, black represents the Great Mystery and is linked to the cardinal direction north on the medicine wheel. Though white is traditional attire for a Western wedding, white is often worn at funerals in Eastern cultures. Sound is no exception to cultural identity. Western music reflects the spectral experience of human emotion; Eastern music mimics the sounds of nature and its tranquil effect on human consciousness.

A person's culture will influence his or her experience of the Rays, creating a diverse spiritual interpretation. This cultural filter can cause misunderstandings, discrepancies, and confusion. That's why the esoteric translation of the Rays is often lost to the novice.

Ray Systems

Most teachings of the Ascended Masters offer various analyses of the Rays, their assigned qualities, and the accompanying Master Teachers and Archangels whose work resonates with various Rays. A variety of books also exist that explain Ascended Master Ray Systems. I recommend any book written by Alice Bailey. However, my favorite source book on the Rays is Law of Life, Volume Two by A.D.K. Luk. This series—known by many as the Yellow Books—was written by Luk, the former secretary to Guy Ballard, founder of the I AM Activity. This volume features a pullout Ray schematic on page 382, detailing various attributes and features.

Though some Ray Systems include up to forty singular Rays, it is best to stick with and memorize the basic seven Rays. Also, discard confusing numbering systems. Instead, focus on the color of the Ray to grasp its core meaning.

Below is a Ray System based on Ascended Master teachings and Vedic or Hindu astrology—Jyotish. In Sanskrit, Jyotish coincidentally means science of light. I have incorporated the Vedic system with the Ascended Master teachings for several reasons. First, it is perhaps the oldest astrology system on Earth (Jyotish traces back to 4,000 BC), and it articulates information on the Rays. Second, Jyotish and the Seven Ray System are uniquely compatible. It is likely the Vedic system is the same arrangement once studied by many of our contemporary Master Teachers.

Please note, the following two levels of attributes are given for each Ray: common qualities and cosmic qualities.

---

1. Alice Bailey, *Esoteric Psychology* (Lucis Publishing Co., 1962, New York, N.Y.), page 316.

The Astrological Planets
Ray Forces correspond to specific planets in our solar system.

The understanding of astrological planets is vital to grasping how Ray forces work in our solar system.

• Blue Ray
Common Attributes: steady, calm, persevering, transforming, harmonizing, diligent, determined, austere, protective, humble, truthful, self-negating, stern
Cosmic Attribute: Divine Will or Choice
Planet: Saturn

• Yellow Ray
Common Attributes: studious, learned, expansive, optimistic, joyful, fun-loving, generous, proper, formal
Cosmic Attribute: Spiritual Enlightenment
Planet: Jupiter

• Pink Ray
Common Attributes: loving, nurturing, hopeful, heartfelt, compassionate, considerate, communicative, intuitive, friendly, humane, tolerant, adoring
Cosmic Attribute: Divine Mother
Planet: Moon

• White Ray
Common Attributes: beautiful, pure, elegant, refined, sensitive, charming, graceful, creative, artistic, cooperative, uplifting, strong, piercing, blissful
Cosmic Attribute: Divine Feminine
Planet: Venus

• Green Ray
Common Attributes: educated, thoughtful, communicative, organized, intellectual, objective, scientific, discriminating, practical, discerning, adaptable, rational, healing, awakened
Cosmic Attribute: Active Intelligence
Planet: Mercury

• Ruby (Red) and Gold Ray
Common Attributes (Ruby): energetic, passionate, devoted, determination, dutiful, dependable, direct, insightful, inventive, technical, skilled, forceful
Cosmic Attribute (Ruby): Divine Masculine
Planet (Ruby): Mars
Common Attributes (Gold): warm, perceptive, honest, confident, positive, independent, courageous, enduring, vital, leadership, responsible, ministration, authority, justice
Cosmic Attribute (Gold): Divine Father
Planet (Gold): Sun

• Violet Ray
Common Attributes: forgiving, transmuting, alchemizing, electric, intervening, diplomatic, magical, merciful, graceful, freedom, ordered service
Cosmic Attribute: Divine Grace
Planet: Currently undetermined, but some systems place Uranus, the higher vibration of Saturn, or both under this Ray force.

The Seven Rays

BLUE	YELLOW	PINK	WHITE
Saturn	Jupiter	Moon	Venus
Divine Will Divine Power	Divine Teacher Divine Wisdom Guru	Divine Mother Divine Heart Divine Creatrix	Divine Feminine Divine Beauty Divine Love
Steady; calm; persevering; transforming; harmonizing; diligent; disciplined; determined; austere; protective; humble; truthful; self-negating; stern.	Studious; learned; expansive; optimistic; joyful; fun-loving; generous; proper; formal.	Loving; nurturing; hopeful; heartfelt; compassionate; considerate; communicative; intuitive; friendly; humane; tolerant; adoring.	Beautiful; pure; elegant; refined; sensitive; charming; graceful; creative; artistic; cooperative; uplifting; strong; piercing; blissful.
Blue Sapphire *Blue Topaz* *Lapis Lazuli*	*Yellow Sapphire* *Yellow Topaz* *Citrine*	*Pearl* *Moonstone* *Pink Tourmaline*	*Diamond* *White Sapphire* *Clear Quartz Crystal*
Myrrh, Frankincense, Cedar, Juniper	*Sandalwood, Lotus*	*Jasmine, Gardenia*	*Rose, Nag Champa*

Rays Blue through White
The first four Rays and their Planetary Force,
Archetype, qualities, gemstone, and scent.

The Seven Rays

GREEN	RUBY GOLD	VIOLET	AQUAMARINE GOLD
Mercury	Mars Sun	Saturn Uranus	Neptune Great Central Sun
Divine Child Divine Intelligence Divine Messenger	*Mars:* Divine Warrior Divine Masculine *Sun:* Divine Father Divine Creator	*Saturn:* Divine Grace *Uranus:* Divine Alchemy	*Neptune:* Divine Heaven *Great Central Sun:* Divine Man
Educated; thoughtful; communicative; organized; intellectual; objective; scientific; discriminating; practical; discerning; adaptable; rational; healing; awakened.	(Ruby): Energetic; passionate; devoted; determination; dutiful; dependable; direct; insightful; inventive; forceful. (Gold): Warm; honest; confident; positive; independent; courageous; leadership; responsible; ministration; authority; justice.	Forgiving; transmuting; alchemizing; electric; intervening; diplomatic; magical; merciful; graceful; original; freedom; ordered service.	Unifying; perceptive; intuitive; sensitive; cooperative; creative; integrative; spiritual; idealistic; self-realized.
Emerald *Green Tourmaline* *Peridot* *Jade*	*Mars (Ruby or Red Ray):* *Red Coral, Carnelian* *Sun (Gold Ray):* *Ruby, Red Garnet*	*Amethyst* *Purple Sugilite*	*Aquamarine* *Tourquoise*
Mint, Wintergreen	*Ruby Ray: Musk, Camphor* *Gold Ray: Ginger, Cinnamon*	*Lavendar, Lilac*	*Hydrangea, Bayberry, Sage*

Rays Green through Aquamarine-Gold
The second four Rays and their Planetary Force,
Archetype, qualities, gemstone, and scent.

Co-creation through the Rays: Mantras, Decrees, Gemstone, and Aromatherapy

As one begins to access the pure, restorative energy of each Ray force, changes will occur in all aspects of an individual's life. When a person calls upon the Rays, the soul becomes receptive to the process of Co-creation, thus spiritual growth and evolution are the outcomes. These changes are often subtle and require patience, diligence, and perseverance, but the results can also be immediate. The perfected support inherent in the power of a Ray encourages healing in many aspects of a person's life, including relationships, career, finances, and health. Spiritual healing through the Rays also improves and sharpens the super senses. Many people report enhanced psychic and telepathic links with Master Teachers after chanting mantras, decrees, or both. The healing energy of the Rays aren't just limited to individuals; groups and societies can benefit as well. Ray-oriented mantras and decrees when performed by a group of people often generate an exponential super-sensory experience and increase the collective consciousness, thereby creating a Group Mind. Fifth-dimensional energies are bridged to the physical plane by the collective consciousness of the Group Mind. The Ascended Masters refer to this anomaly as Oneship or Unana.

Sound is indeed the twin sibling of light. This esoteric aspect of the Rays cannot be overlooked or understated as El Morya, Master Teacher of the Blue Ray articulates: "Now understand, Dear Ones ... even sound itself works as a Ray. It is through this circular vibration, which we have explained as the spiral ... Light and Sound join to one another." Mantras invoke the energy of a Ray with scientific precision. Dr. David Frawley, an authority on Vedic and Hindu spiritual tradition, writes, "Mantras are seed sounds (the foremost of which is Om) that contain the laws and the archetypes behind all the workings of energy in the universe. Applying this mantric knowledge on different levels, any domain of existence can be comprehended in its inner truth. Through the mantra, the Rishis were able to be adept in all fields of knowledge, including Yoga, Philosophy, Astrology, Geomancy, Medicine, Poetry, Art and Music. This root knowledge of the mantra is thus an instrument on which all knowledge can be revealed by a shifting of scales."[1]

Try this experiment with the Bija-seed mantra, Om. Bija, by the way, means one—a one-syllable mantra. While slowly chanting Om, place your forefinger and thumb on your cheekbones. You will feel a vibration through your cheeks and a resonation in your skull, which will inevitably reach your spine. This same vibration affects your entire Chakra System. Some scholars claim that the sound vibration of a Bija-seed mantra simultaneously creates light frequencies in the human aura. I recommended a Ruby Ray Bija-seed mantra for a client, and she ardently chanted this mantra prior to a Kirlian photograph. [Editor's Note: Kirlian photography is alleged to capture the light energy surrounding a subject or object.] The photograph depicted her aura with shades and tones of red and ruby light. The Sanskrit Bija-seed mantras for each of the Rays are listed below.

Blue Ray: Om Sham or Om Shanti (Saturn)
Yellow Ray: Om Güm (Jupiter)
Pink Ray: Om Som (Moon)
White Ray: Om Shüm (Venus)
Green Ray: Om Büm (Mercury)
Ruby Ray: Om Ung (Mars)
Gold Ray: Om Süm (Sun)
Violet Ray: Om Hue (Higher aspect of Saturn; Uranus)

Decrees, similar to mantras, are yet another form of verbal prayer; however, decrees differ because of the added element of visualization, the spoken word, and the spiritual stillness of meditation. Some claim that decrees are one of the most powerful forms of prayer because they unite four chakras: prayer (Heart Chakra); spoken word (throat chakra); visualization (Third Eye chakra); meditation (crown chakra). [2]Violet Flame decrees are used worldwide by thousands of Ascended Master students. They can be spoken individually or used in groups to generate the benefic qualities of the Violet Ray: mercy, compassion, and forgiveness. One of my favorites is the simple Violet Fire decree by Mark Prophet, "I AM a being of Violet Fire! I AM the purity God desires!"

Decrees or mantras are often said rhythmically, in groups of seven, or in rounds of 108—the traditional Mala. [Editor's Note: A Mala is a prayer or rosary bead typically used in Hinduism and Buddhism, and a full Mala contains 108 beads with one final large bead often referred to as the guru bead.] Decrees and mantras are also repeated silently in the mind, similar to prayer, in preparation for meditation. El Morya lends further insight: " ... it is when this (decree) is consciously applied by the chela, through the work of the Violet Flame, or other mantra work they may engage ... light

---

1. David Frawley, *The Astrology of the Seers: A Guide to Vedic (Hindu) Astrology,* (Passage Press, 1990, Salt Lake City, Utah), page 38.

2. Craig Donaldson, *How to Get Great Results When You Pray,* http://www.ascension-research.org/prayer.html, (2010).

is then bonded to sound. Ultimately, this is the intertwining of consciousness with action." Simply stated, sound activates light, and light and sound together command the Ray into a force of conscious activity.

Gemstones are perhaps one of the most simple and powerful ways to correct Ray deficiencies or enhance and intensify the attributes of a Ray. Our aura, inner spiritual light, and overall vibration reflect the numerous lifetimes, experiences, and evolutionary journeys of our soul with the Seven Rays. Ray deficiencies appear as the under-developed aspects of the Rays and signify areas in our life that may need more individual effort, attention, and personal refinement. Chronic disease, relationship problems, financial setbacks, and personal suffering are often the result of Ray deficiencies. The qualified concentration of the Ray through specific, remedial gemstones can treat the undersupplied Ray by infusing the aura with its light. This supportive healing light can alter the trajectory of life's events and transform spiritual consciousness; corrective gemstones can ameliorate certain Karmic difficulties. Wear the gemstone so its facets touch the skin (this is classic in Jyotish), or hold a cluster of crystals to intensify a Ray force during meditation. Gem elixir—a liquid infused with the energies and essence of certain gemstones according to Vedic traditions—is also effective. Remember, never use a gemstone that is chemically dyed, heat-treated, or irradiated; unfortunately, today, many are. Vedic-quality gemstones are best for spiritual purposes. The list below identifies certain Ray forces contained in precious and semi-precious gemstones.

Blue Ray: Blue sapphire and blue topaz; lapis lazuli and turquoise.

Yellow Ray: Yellow sapphire, yellow topaz, and citrine.

Pink Ray: Pearl and moonstone. Pink tourmaline can give good results. The best metal to enhance energies of the Moon—the Divine Mother—is silver.

White Ray: Diamond and white sapphire. Very clear, high-quality quartz crystal works well. I have seen good results from large, high-quality, clear pieces of cubic zirconia.

Green Ray: Emerald and green tourmaline; green peridot and green jade work well too.

Ruby and Gold Ray: Ruby Ray: red coral. Gold Ray: Red ruby and red garnet are good gemstones for the energies of the Sun—the Divine Father. Red and raspberry rhodolite (a type of garnet) also work well. Good metals are yellow and white gold.

Lavender is associated with the Violet Ray.

Violet Ray: Amethyst is best; however, I have seen good results with purple sugilite.

The Scent of a Ray

Certain scents contain the essence of a Ray. Often, before the appearance of an ascended being or angel, a fragrance will imbue the area about to be occupied. Since these spiritual beings have focused their energies upon a specific Ray, their scent carries the same vibration of the Ray. This aroma often contains a healing power, or it intentionally heightens the energies of the space for the materialization of a Master Teacher and their ensuing teachings. Manifestations of Mother Mary are often accompanied by the faint perfume of rose, while Kuan Yin's scent is Neroli—orange blossom. Lavender or lilac most often heralds the presence of Saint Germain.

The practice of burning certain incenses and smudging a room with sage for purification has become increasingly popular. These religious and shamanic traditions enhance and reinforce certain Rays. The scents listed below are commonly associated with the following Rays:

Blue Ray: Myrrh, frankincense, cedar, and juniper.

Yellow Ray: Sandalwood and lotus.

Pink Ray: Jasmine and gardenia.

White Ray: Rose and nag champa.

Green Ray: Mint and wintergreen. Sage is good for the Green Ray ; it also vibrates to the Gold (Sun) Ray.

Ruby Ray: Musk and camphor.

Gold Ray: Ginger and cinnamon.

Violet Ray: Lavender and lilac.

The Great Central Sun and Movement of the Rays

In Ascended Master teachings, the energies of the Rays originate from the Great Central Sun. This mythic Sun is said to exist a great distance from our own solar system; it is perceived as a master intelligence. From its benevolent presence, the Rays of Light and Sound are sent to Earth, and humanity is educated and perfected through their influence. This same principle is present in Vedic astrology; however, this great Sun is known as the Galactic Center. The Galactic Center is renowned as Brahma, which means creative force or the navel of Vishnu. Dr. Frawley writes, "From the Galactic Sun emanates the light which determines life and intelligence on Earth and which direct the play of the Seven Rays of creation and the distribution of Karma."[1]

In the Vedic tradition, the planet Jupiter transmits the energies of the Galactic Center to our solar system. Mars initiates the Ray-force energy while the Sun stabilizes the Rays. This planetary trinity comprising the Sun, Jupiter, and Mars is commonly known as the Fire Triplicity.

Ray forces move by two scientific principles: emanation and radiation. Emanation means to flow out, as from a source or origin; radiation is defined as the emission and diffusion of Rays of heat, light, electricity, or sounds. According to Ascended Master teachings, Rays enter our solar system from the emanations of our Sun—hence, the use of Om before each Bija-seed mantra. From our Sun, a Ray completes its celestial journey at the core of the Earth; Ray forces then emanate from the center of the Earth to its surface. When we personally apply the energies of the Rays through gemstones, mantras, and scents, we are utilizing the second principle of Ray movement: radiation.

Ascended Masters, Archangels, and Ray Forces

Ascended beings and archetypes of evolution apply the Rays to receive and achieve higher states of perfection and knowledge. Through this profound diligence and submission to the grand interplay of the Rays, they have overcome Karmic reaction and retribution; they have opened the doors to liberation, higher states of consciousness, and enlightenment. Each Ascended Master individualizes his or her conscious energy upon a Ray force, especially while serving students and chelas as Master Teacher. The qualities and attributes of a Master's teaching clearly reflect the distinct energy of a Ray. You will note that before Saint Germain presents a lesson, he consistently qualifies each session through a Ray force by announcing, "I AM Saint Germain, and I stream forth on the Mighty Violet Ray of Mercy, Compassion, and Forgiveness."

Similarly, Archangels work on a specific Ray. Master Teachers and angels occasionally employ the energies of all of the Seven Rays to achieve a specific goal or mission. Certain Master Teachers, however, are best known for their work with specific Rays, which are listed below.

Blue Ray: Archangel Michael and Master Teacher El Morya.

Yellow Ray: Archangel Jophiel, Master Teachers Confucius and Lanto, and Peter the Everlasting.

Pink Ray: Archangel Chamuel, Beloved Mother Mary, and Paul the Venetian. [Editor's Note: Mother Mary is often identified with the Green Ray as well.]

Green Ray: Archangel Raphael and Master Teachers Hilarion and Soltec.

White Ray: Archangel Gabriel and Master Teachers Serapis Bey and Paul the Devoted. [Editor's Note: Paul the Devoted also serves the Pink Ray.]

Ruby and Gold Ray: Archangel Uriel, Lord Sananda, and Master Teacher Kuthumi .[Editor's Note: Lord Sananda is often identified with the Green Ray as well.]

Violet Ray: Archangel Zadkiel, Master Teacher Saint Germain, and Kuan Yin. [Editor's Note: Kuan Yin is often identified with the Pink Ray as well.]

History of the Rays in World Religions

H. P. Blavatsky, the founder of theosophy, introduced the Seven Rays in her first book The Secret Doctrine as the "primeval Seven Rays . . . found and recognized in every religion," as a type of "light substance conveying Divine Qualities." She later wrote that the symbolism of the Seven Rays was adopted by Christianity as the "Seven Angels of the Presence." The concept of the Seven Rays dates back to ancient religions and occult philosophies, as early as the sixth century BCE of Western culture, Egypt, and India. Esoteric historians note the presence of the Rays as both the Seven Rays of the ancient Chaldaean Mithra and the Seven Days of Genesis. In 1894 Harvard scholar S.F. Dunlap wrote, "The other planets which circling around the Sun lead the dance as round the King of heaven receive from him with the light also their powers; while as the light comes to them

---

1. Frawley, *The Astrology of the Seers,* page 48.

from the Sun, so from him they receive their powers that he pours out into the Seven Spheres of the Seven Planets, of which the Sun is the centre." Dunlap maintained the Seven Rays were the religious base for the ancient Chaldeans, Jews, Persians, Syrian, Phoenicians, and Egyptians. Nineteenth-century Egyptologist Gerald Massey theorized the unity of the Seven Rays as "the seven souls of the Pharaoh; the seven arms of the Hindu God Agni; the seven-rayed Sun-God of the Gnostic-stones; and, the seven stars in the hand of the Christ in Revelation."

Symbolic art of early Christianity depicts the emanation of the Seven Rays in union with the image of Mother Mary. The dove, symbolizing the Holy Spirit, is frequently accompanied by the golden ethereal Seven Rays of heaven. Of all the Seven Rays, perhaps the seventh—the Violet Ray—is distinct. Art historian and philosopher, Ananda Coomaraswamy, noted the complex iconology of the Seventh Ray that appears in Indian, Islamic, Chinese, Hellenic, and Christian symbolism. "(It) corresponds to the distinction of transcendent from immanent and infinite from finite . . . the Seventh Ray alone passes through the Sun to the suprasolar Brahma worlds, where no Sun shines . . . all that is under the Sun being in the power of death, and all beyond immortal."

When it comes to studying the Ascended Masters, a Ray chart is an invaluable and fundamental learning tool. It initiates the mind to archetypal thinking—the ability to perceive and recognize the ancient Gods and myths as part of our everyday experiences. This clarity helps the student connect and synthesize the theosophic concepts, characters, and characteristics so vital to understanding the Ascended Masters. But, thanks to cultural ambiguities and pedagogic differences, Ray charts do have imperfections.

For one, until recently little was known about the Mithraic mysteries. According to Franz Cumont, an authority on the subject, the genesis of Mithraism can be traced to a time when India and Persia shared a common language, as far back as 2,000 BCE. Time, cultural movement, and the shifting of political boundaries helped spread the practice of Mithraism throughout the Roman Empire later on. Its central character—a deity of light—shows up in Avestan and Vedic texts as Mithra and Mitra, respectively. Mitra represents the Divine Friend, a savior, and Lord of Mercy and Compassion. The story of Mitra, a benevolent Vedic Sun god, is one of creation. The deity is born from a sacred rock and sacrifices a bull (a likely symbol from the Age of Taurus),

Mithra and King Antiochus
King Antiochus (left) and Mithra (right) note the Rays streaming from Mithra's crown chakra. The depiction of Mithra is a relief from a Temple built by Antiochus I of Commagne, 69-31 BCE. Commagne was an ancient kingdom of the Hellenistic Age, located in south-central Turkey.

from which flows life-sustaining flora and fauna. Mitra also creates the archetypal energies of the Christ; while Maitreya, the prophesied future Buddha, derives his name from this ancient immortal. Mitra, the god of friendship and partnership, wears the Sun's crown of Divine Rays, comprising compassion, devotion, love, and cooperation. Many Mithraic doctrines were rooted in celestial and astrological references, which serve as a link to the ambiguous light of the Seven Rays. These teachings were reportedly well known in culturally cloistered India and the Middle East but virtually unheard of in the Western world.

Second, and probably even more importantly, the didactic underpinnings of Ray charts are riddled with confusing discrepancies, which are due, in part, to the wide-ranging interpretations of innumerable messengers, channels, and mediums who follow various spiritual leaders and divergent philosophies.

The source of these disparities comes from the venerated esoteric giants of theosophical thought themselves—H. P.

Mithra, the Sun God
Mithra as Sol, the Sun God. (Roman) Mithra holds the globe of power and Seven Rays stream from his crown chakra. According to Franz Cumot this is a representation of "Graeco-Roman Paganism" amd "Solar Pantheism."

*Taq-e Bostan: Investiture of Sassanid
Emperor Shapur II*
Investiture of Sassanid Emperor Shapur II (center) with Mithra (left)
and Ahura Mazda (right) at Taq-e Bostan, Iran, 309 AD (approx.), from
the Sassanid Dynasty.

Blavatsky, Annie Besant, Alice Bailey, Dion Fortune, and Nicolas and Helena Roerich. Naturally, their backgrounds and cultural experiences colored their perceptions and subsequent presentation of the subject matter. The Roeriches and Blavatsky were born in nineteenth-century imperial Russia amid social upheaval and political reformation, while Besant, Bailey and Fortune grew up in disparate regions of the United Kingdom during different times. Their seminal work has morphed into a vast and diverse body of spiritual education, which includes the I AM Activity (Guy and Edna Ballard); the Bridge to Freedom (Geraldine Innocente); White Eagle Lodge (Ivan and Grace Cooke); and the Summit Lighthouse (Mark and Elizabeth Prophet). The Seven Rays are, of course, a component of these teachings, but the resulting information is inconsistent for the reasons mentioned above.

The key to these irregularities lies in ideological differences. Consider the various Christian denominations—Catholicism, Baptism, Lutheranism, Methodism, and so on. The common denominator is Christianity: a monotheistic religion rooted in the teachings and life of Jesus Christ. The differences, however, are doctrinal. For instance, Catholics have seven sacraments; Protestants recognize only two. Often the greatest truths hold dichotomy and paradox.

The Ray Chart's Correlation to the Seven Traditional Planets

In 1996 I began to study the traditional astrology of India—Jyotish—the Science of Light. It is a complex, multifaceted, and comprehensive system of astrology. Not only does it incorporate the traditional zodiac of Western astrology, it embraces the twenty-seven goddesses, which serve as the foundation of Vedic and Chinese esoteric arts. The lunar mansions, or houses of the Moon, encompass the feminine-based astrology long forgotten by the West.

The twelve houses of astrology were likely derived from the twenty-seven signs of the goddesses, who in Vedic and Celtic lore are the wives of the Moon. Chandra, the Vedic God of the Moon, visits each Sister-wife every day of the month. This rotation ends in twenty-eight days, the length of the female menstrual cycle.

As my understanding and practice of Jyotish deepened, the obscure and vague teachings of the Seven Rays were clearly revealed as the seven traditional astrological planets: Jupiter, Saturn, Venus, Mercury, Mars, and the Sun and the Moon—the Earth's luminaries. This information filled in blanks, answered long-asked questions, and of course, satisfied an occultist's greatest desire—the discovery of layer upon layer of correlated information regarding the Seven Rays. Vedic astrology tracks an individual's relationship with the Seven Rays through thoughts, feelings, and actions, which are distilled from the following Hindu philosophical principles:

Vedic aims of life—kama (desire), artha (wealth), dharma (purpose), and moksha (liberation).

Gunas or qualities one may experience—sattvic (spiritual), rajasic (agitated), and tamasic (dark).

Elements of physical life—earth, water, fire, air, ether.

The Titan's Goblet
Thomas Cole, 1833.

The Seven Rays become conspicuous in the body by our level of health or disease; our foods and diet reflect the type of energy we receive and emit. Herbs, colors, flowers, scents, gemstones, and sounds resonate with specific Ray forces. In fact, prayers, mantras, and ceremonies dedicated to the planets—disguised as the Rays—are the cornerstones of Hinduism.

Unfortunately, the ancient Vedic principles that constitute Jyotish are rarely included in the construction of Ray charts. When the original data were assembled—in the late nineteenth and early twentieth centuries—it just wasn't available. In particular, esoteric scholars did not have access to the astrological knowledge of India, which according to some authorities dates back more than 5,000 years, and in my opinion, is an integral element of esoteric teaching. Vedic astrology is a vast, complex, and arcane area of study. The ability of one human being to grasp and distill this information is simply impossible, especially without the modern conveniences of technology and air travel. To give you an idea of the expansiveness of Vedic astrology, Jyotish comprises a mere one-sixth of the knowledge contained in the Vedanga—the six disciplines developed by Indian culture to understand the Vedas. The Vedas form the Sanskrit basis of Hinduism and were written by Rishis, the spiritual Masters from a time of greater light on Earth—likely Dvapara Yuga. Inaccessibility and inundation led to misinformation, especially in the theosophical interpretation of occult history. These mistakes were passed on to the lineages of Ascended Master teaching.

Archetypes of Evolution

Ideally the language of the Seven Rays is the language of the Gods. The Greeks and Romans recognized the polarity between their deities: the folly and the grandeur, the corruption and the honesty, the immorality and the morality—akin to the human and HU-man of the Ascended Masters. The Seven Rays live a mortal life within us, manifested in ignorance, fear, and ego. Simultaneously, they inspire immortality expressed as love, wisdom, and truth. This Ray chart incorporates Ascended Masters, Archangels, and Elohim. In Ascended Master teaching the Elohim are often depicted as the gods and goddesses of nature, typified by the Seven Rays and the deities that likely inspired their evolutionary journeys thousands of years ago.

The Mighty Elohim

Some esoteric historians perceive the Elohim—also referred to as the Els—as the ancient gods or Master Teachers of Lemuria and Atlantis. This area of the Ray chart seems logical but, again, filled with discrepancy, depending on the school of Ascended Master teaching you are studying. For my purposes, I have included the Elohim as described in the I AM America material—evolved nature gods. Some of the ancient deities actually make more sense to me than their contemporary counterparts, and I wanted to share these interesting tidbits.

The Titans are fierce elder gods overthrown by a race of younger deities. They represent the mature yet fierce experience of Saturn and the Blue Ray.

The White Ray through its affiliation with Divine Beauty represents literature and the arts, similar to the nine Muses of Greek mythology.

Kukulkan—the plumed serpent of the Mayan—is also known as Quetzalcoatl to the Aztecs. The astrology of ancient America was based on Venus.

According to some scholars, the compassionate centaur Chiron was the Master Teacher of young Apollo and Artemis. His renown as an astrologer and healer secures his placement on the Green Ray, which is associated with the ability to teach.

The Romans portrayed Jesus Christ as a Sun deity; his ardent devotion—the spiritual warrior—places him on the Ruby and Gold Ray.

The Greek cup-bearer of the Gods Ganymede represents the human ascent to spiritual liberation and perfection, qualities of the Aquamarine and Gold Ray.

BLUE	YELLOW	PINK	WHITE
EVOLUTIONARY ARCHETYPES			
Archangel Michael	Archangel Jophiel	Archangel Chamuel	Archangel Gabriel
Archeia Faith	Archeia Christine	Archeia Charity	Archeia Hope
El Morya	Lady Nada	Kuan Yin	Serapis Bey
Lady Miriam	Confucius	Mother Mary	Lady Master Se Ray
Lord Himalaya	Lanto	Goddess Meru	Paul the Devoted
Lady Master Desiree	Peter the Everlasting	Great Divine Mother	Lady Master Venus
Goddess of Light	Minerva	Paul the Ventian*	Reya
ELOHIM			
Elohim of Power	Elohim of Illumination	Elohim of Divine Love	Elohim of Purity
Hercules	Cassiopea	Orion	Claire
Amazonia	Lumina	Angelica	Astrea
DEITIES			
Shiva (Kala)	Brihaspati	Isis	Laksmi
Kali	Ganesh	Parvati	Venus
Yama	Saraswati	Chandra	Aphrodite
Durga	Lord Siddhartha-	Demeter	Hathor
Titans	Guatama Buddha	Ceres	Dionysus
Cronus		Luna	Kulkulcan
		Artemis	Tlahuizcalpantecuhtli
		Ix Chel (Mayan)	(Aztec)
		Sin (Sumerian)	
CHINESE ELEMENT / GUA			
Earth	Wood	Water	Metal
2,8	3, 4	1	6, 7
VEDIC ELEMENT			
Air	Ether	Water	Water
DAY OF WEEK			
Saturday	Thursday	Monday	Friday
MAHAPURUSHA YOGA			
Shasha Yoga	Hamsa Yoga	None	Malavya Yoga

*Serve on more than one Ray

The Seven Rays

The Deities of the Rays, Blue through White
Deities and Associated Qualities of the Rays.

BLUE	YELLOW	PINK	WHITE
EVOLUTIONARY ARCHETYPES			
Archangel Michael	Archangel Jophiel	Archangel Chamuel	Archangel Gabriel
Archeia Faith	Archeia Christine	Archeia Charity	Archeia Hope
El Morya	Lady Nada	Kuan Yin	Serapis Bey
Lady Miriam	Confucius	Mother Mary	Lady Master Se Ray
Lord Himalaya	Lanto	Goddess Meru	Paul the Devoted
Lady Master Desiree	Peter the Everlasting	Great Divine Mother	Lady Master Venus
Goddess of Light	Minerva	Paul the Ventian*	Reya
ELOHIM			
Elohim of Power	Elohim of Illumination	Elohim of Divine Love	Elohim of Purity
Hercules	Cassiopea	Orion	Claire
Amazonia	Lumina	Angelica	Astrea
DEITIES			
Shiva (Kala)	Brihaspati	Isis	Laksmi
Kali	Ganesh	Parvati	Venus
Yama	Saraswati	Chandra	Aphrodite
Durga	Lord Siddhartha-	Demeter	Hathor
Titans	Guatama Buddha	Ceres	Dionysus
Cronus		Luna	Kulkulcan
		Artemis	Tlahuizcalpantecuhtli
		Ix Chel (Mayan)	(Aztec)
		Sin (Sumerian)	
CHINESE ELEMENT / GUA			
Earth	Wood	Water	Metal
2,8	3, 4	1	6, 7
VEDIC ELEMENT			
Air	Ether	Water	Water
DAY OF WEEK			
Saturday	Thursday	Monday	Friday
MAHAPURUSHA YOGA			
Shasha Yoga	Hamsa Yoga	None	Malavya Yoga

*Serve on more than one Ray

The Seven Rays

The Deities of the Rays, Green through Aquamarine-Gold
Deities and Associated Qualities of the Rays.

This Ray chart also has its own inconsistencies, and I would like to point out that the Blue Ray is traditionally associated with Saturn. However, in Vedic teaching Saturn is the son of the Sun; and Surya—the Sanskrit name for the Sun—by ancestral lineage is related to the Blue Ray. While studying other Ray charts to corroborate this compilation, I noticed confusion and lack of clarity regarding the Pink and White Rays. Some esoteric scholars identify the Pink Ray as the Divine Feminine and the White Ray as the Divine Mother. Again, the baseline for this chart relies on the Vedic knowledge of the Moon and Venus. The Moon is the Divine Mother, the Divine Creatrix, and the heart of our emotions—the Pink Ray. Venus is the White Ray of the Divine Feminine, Divine Love, and the balance we achieve in our thoughts, feelings, and actions—beauty.

Please note that Ascended Masters can simultaneously serve on several Rays, and while archetypically identified with a particular Ray, he or she may temporarily give aid and service to humanity by serving on another Ray. Geraldine Innocente's work, Bridge to Freedom, often comments on this unusual but not uncommon occurrence. Sananda said he was "not limited by form of any kind" and would "take on any form or appearance for the task at hand."

The Elements: Chinese and Vedic

Chinese and Vedic astrology are both based on the planet Jupiter, however, Vedic astrology operates on sidereal or star-based calculations. It is interesting to compare the Chinese planetary interpretation of the elements—one of the foundations of Feng Shui—with the elements of Vastu Shastra, the Hindu science of architecture and construction. Remember that the Violet Ray is ruled by the two planets Saturn and Uranus, so this Ray 's elements are both earth and metal. Uranus does not specifically rule the element of metal; however, metal rules the hsiu constellations that include Uranus.[1]

Planetary Yogas (Unions)

According to the study of Jyotish, yogas are planetary unions that create and define certain astral conditions. Raja Yoga is the metaphysical union of Heaven and Earth, and it assures positive, evolutionary movement in our lives. A Sanskrit term meaning kingmaker, Raja Yogas give rise to

positions of political or social status. Theosophic scholar, Alice Bailey, took this concept a step further and linked Raja Yogas with specific Ray forces to further refine and clarify the connection between theosophy and Vedic thinking. This type of yoga, or union, merges two astrological houses—a trine and a quadrant—and almost every chart contains one or two of each. A trinal house (Astrological Houses One, Five, and Nine) are houses of dharma, purpose, and blessing; a quadrant house—also referred to as a kendra (Astrological Houses One, Four, and Ten) manifests earthly results. Vedic astrologers study the houses involved in Raja Yoga unions to determine how this energy will shape a person's life.

Mahapurusha Yogas comprise a powerful subset of Raja Yogas. Known in Sanskrit as combinations of a great being, these five unions increase the energy of a specific planet and its accompanying Ray. Mahapurusha Yoga planets are Saturn, Jupiter, Venus, Mercury, and Mars. The luminaries—the Sun and Moon—are not included. When the energy of a particular planet is imprinted and magnified by one of these benefic yogas, the recipient of its energy tends to express planet-specific qualities and characteristics, which is incorporated in the Ray chart and explained below.

Mahapurusha Yoga for Jupiter is Hamsa Yoga. Supports the strong qualities of Jupiter and the Yellow Ray ; expressed as an ethical, honest, and moral nature. Philosophical, religious, good teacher, fair disposition, optimistic, joyful, and spiritual. The Dark Side of this yoga produces self-promotion and self-righteousness.

Mahapurusha Yoga for Saturn is Shasha Yoga. This yoga endows power over people; it manifests in positions of authority and administration, control over material resources, and the creation of model workers. Vedic texts claim this person will become the leader of the village. This yoga may sustain detachment, happiness, and spiritual perception. The Dark Side of this yoga may foster cruelty, selfishness, ruthless, and the usurpation of another's wealth.

Mahapurusha Yoga for Venus is Malavya Yoga: Provides comfort and prosperity in life, including children, marriage and good fortune; is a common yoga for artists, beautiful women, and the wealthy and the affluent. This yoga also bestows charm, grace, culture, beauty, artistic talents, fame, and social influence. The higher side of Malavya Yoga inspires devotion, kindness, and compassion; the darker side

---

1. Christopher McIntosh, *A Short History of Astrology*, (Barnes and Noble Books by arrangement with Random House, UK, Ltd., 1994), page 49.

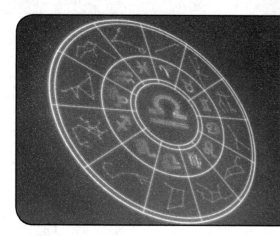

Hamsa Yoga: Jupiter
Malavya Yoga: Venus
Bhadra Yoga: Mercury
Ruchaka Yoga: Mars
Shasha Yoga: Saturn

Mahapurusha Yogas of the Planets

emphasizes hedonistic tendencies, including the excessive pursuit of sex, glamour, and sensuality

Mahapurusha Yoga for Mercury is Bhadra Yoga: Also known as the auspicious combination, this yoga blesses an individual with positive mercurial qualities, including good speech and communication, commerce, keen intellect, wit, humor, humanism, and a balanced psychology. This yoga is often seen in the charts of business people, writers, and intellectuals. The Dark Side of Bhadra Yoga creates an overly commercial orientation and a one-dimensional, intellectual experience of life.

Mahapurusha Yoga for Mars is Ruchaka Yoga: This yoga is also known as the radiant combination; it creates strong martial tendencies, including courage, force of will, decisiveness, independence, leadership, achievement, and the ability to take actions and achieve victory at any cost. Ruchaka Yoga overcomes enemies and emerges victorious. Many athletes, military leaders, generals, lawyers, and executives have this yoga. The Dark Side of this yoga creates aggression and violence; this person can be accident prone and fond of confrontation.

[Editor's Note: The above information was compiled from two Western classics written on the subject of Jyotish: Dr. David Frawley's The Astrology of the Seers, a Guide to Vedic (Hindu) Astrology, and Hart DeFouw's Light on Life, an Introduction to the Astrology of India.]

Aquamarine and Gold Ray

The Aquamarine and Gold Ray is a new addition to this chart. According to the Ascended Masters it began to influence humanity in the twentieth century. The influence of this Ray is destined to develop the higher spiritual qualities of humanity and guide Earth's entrance into the New Times—the Golden Age. This Ray is also associated with Unity Consciousness and is said to originate from the Galactic Center: the Great Central Sun.

The Rays of Golden Cities

Each of the fifty-one prophesied Golden Cities is said to represent and qualify certain Ray forces, which are broken down into the following categories:

Ray	Number of Golden Cities
Blue	Six
Yellow	Eight
Pink	Nine
White	Six
Green	Seven
Ruby and Gold	Six
Violet	Eight
Gold (only)	Three
Aquamarine and Gold	Three

Heart, Wisdom, Grace

As we enter the Golden Age, three Rays dominate the evolution of humanity and Earth: The Yellow Ray of Divine Wisdom; the Pink Ray of the Divine Mother and the Divine Heart; and the Violet Ray of Divine Grace. This suggests a transformation from the Unfed Flame's symbology of Love, Wisdom, and Power to: Heart, Wisdom, and Grace.

Location and Movement of the Rays through the Eight-sided Cell of Perfection

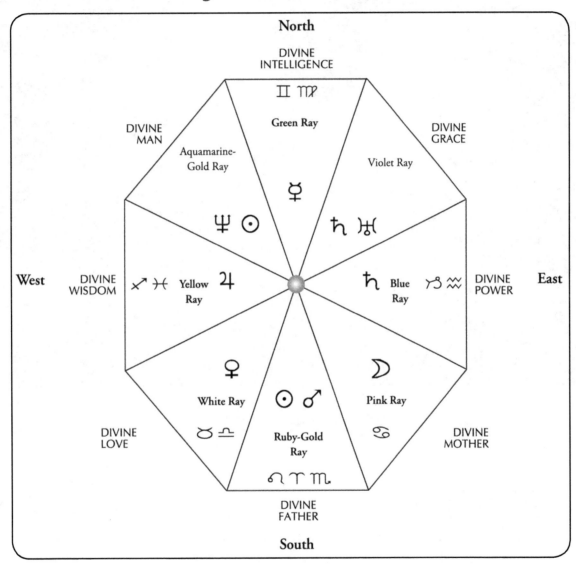

Eight-sided Cell of Perfection
Energy Map Depicting the Rays within the Sacred Cell.

The Sun
Edvard Munch, 1911-1916.

The Human Energy System and the Rays

Perhaps the most distinctive and personal system of the Seven Rays is the Human Energy System. The Seven Rays play a role in the formation of:

The Human Aura and its unique layers

The Auric Blueprint that maps the major and minor Energy Meridians and the gross and subtle Nadis (energy currents) of the Human Body

The Lunar Energy Current (Ida), the Solar Energy Current (Pingala), and the Golden Thread Axis (Medullar Shushumna); these three major Nadis of the physical body are related to the Kundalini. This is the familiar Caduceus, the ancient symbol of Hermes.

The Major Chakras—energy centers—located to the front of the Golden Thread Axis; the Crown and Base Chakra, located at the top and bottom of the Golden Thread Axis; and the Four Will Chakras, located at the back of the Golden Thread Axis.

Each of the Rays nourishes and encourages the growth of humanity through their specific qualities and characteristics. Accordingly, as humanity evolves so does the Human Energy System and many changes are noted in the Energy Fields and Chakras as the septenate forces unfold. A certain color may be associated with a functioning, ordinary chakra as normal, when in fact the chakra is still in its infant phase of development. The soul matures through stages of self-realization and the energy system reflects this transformation in the auric light. The Seven Rays expand, develop, advance, and establish the human into the HU-man, the Divine God Man, and prepares consciousness to enter the experience beyond earthly Karma—spiritual liberation.

The Seven Rays are carried by three major currents in the human body located in the spine which are the nexus of the Kundalini. The first is the Golden Thread Axis, also known in the Hindu tradition as the Medullar Sushumna. According to Ascended Master teaching, the Golden Thread Axis originates with our solar Sun, and the vibrant life-giving current spiritually connects each individual to their I AM Presence throughout each individual lifetime. Light energy penetrates at the top of the head, moves through the spinal system, and then onward through the perineum—the Base

Rod of Power
The *Rod of Power* symbolizes the human energy system's connection to the Sun and Earth.

Chakra. This ethereal cord travels onward through the Earth where it roots to the core of the Earth, also considered a latent Sun. According to esoteric teachers the Golden Thread Axis connects Heaven and Earth. Its visual symbol is known as the Rod of Power, which depicts the two Suns connected by a central beam. Ascended Master students and chelas frequently draw upon the energy of the Sun and Earth through the Golden Thread Axis for healing and renewal with meditation, visualization, and breath.

The vital energy of life—chi, or prana—pulsates through the Golden Thread, and its earthly presence is dissolved when the soul exits through death, or its energies are withdrawn by the individual to the spiritual planes through the Ascension Process.

Two vital currents intertwine around the Golden Thread Axis, and this foundation is distinguished in Yoga as the right and left eyes, representing the two petals of the Third Eye Chakra. Feminine energy travels up the spine by the inhalation (cooling) of breath through these six zodiacal signs: Aquarius, Pisces, Aries, Taurus, Gemini, and Cancer. Masculine energy descends into the spine by the exhalation (warming) of breath through the astrological signs of: Leo, Virgo, Libra, Scorpio, Sagittarius, and Capricorn. Yogic Astrology embraces the evolutionary fluidity of the Rays through the lunar energy (Moon), known as the Ida Current, and the solar energy (Sun), the Pingala Current. These currents intersect four times in their sacred journey around the axis, and each intersection creates a chakra ruled by specific planets and Ray Forces. The Seven Rays journey through these three important Nadis and chakras, and dispense Galactic energies according to the Karma and Dharma of the individual. This metaphysical human energy system is renown in ancient history and myth as the Caduceus.

Caduceus

The ancient symbol for the Greek Messenger Hermes became the emblem of the U.S. Army Medical Corps. In the Human Energy System the *Caduceus'* center staff represents the Golden Thread Axis; its wings, the Crown Chakra; the two eyes of the serpents represent the Third Eye Chakra; and their entertwining bodies represent the kundalini. Chakras form at the four intersections.

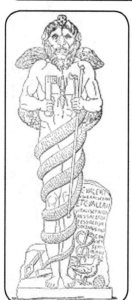

Mithra as Boundless Time

This is a reproduction of a statue found in the Mithraeum of Ostia (Italy), dedicated in the year 190 CE. The body is entwined six times by a singular serpent. The four wings are decorated with symbols of the Four Seasons. Symbols of the planets and ultimate authority, (sceptor, thunderbolt, wand of Mercury, the hammer and tongs of Vulcan), present Mithra as the embodiment of all of the powers of the Gods.

The Caduceus is often confused with the Rod of Asclepius, the traditional symbol of medical practice; however, the two symbols share common ancestry in the Greek myths of Apollo. Today the Caduceus is a universal medical symbol and its two serpents and wings were popularized by the US Army medical corps in 1902.

The serpentine energy of the symbolic Caduceus winds down the rod and meets in four distinct areas; the Crown Chakra is represented as a set of heavenly wings. Ancient depictions of Mithra in the Roman Mithraeum of Ostia (190 A.D.) depict the Caduceus entwined six times by only one serpent, and four wings are said to represent the four seasons.

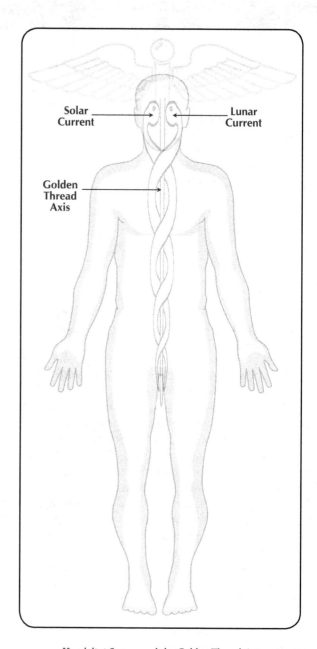

Kundalini System and the Golden Thread Axis
The Kundalini System depicting the Golden Thread Axis and the Lunar and Solar Currents

Kali Yuga and the Rays

Vedic Rishis claim the evolutionary status of humanity is contingent upon the quality of Ray Forces streaming to Earth as a non-visible quasar light from the Galactic Center—the Great Central Sun. While the Rays are invisible to the naked eye, their presence contains subtle electromagnetic energy and psychics may detect their luminous astral light. Ancient astrologers visually observed and experienced the Seven Rays of Light and Sound. Their astronomy, advanced beyond today's science, maintained that our solar Sun was in reality a double star. Our Sun rotates with a companion—a dwarf star which contains no luminosity of its own. This theory suggests that as our Solar System orbits the Great Central Sun, Earth experiences long periods of time when the dwarf star impedes the flow of the Rays from the Galactic Center; likewise, there are times when this important stream of light is unhampered. Since the light energy from the Central Sun nourishes spiritual and intellectual knowledge on the Earth, the Vedic Rishis expertly tracked Earth's movement in and out of the flow and reception of this cosmic light. This cycle is known as the Cycle of the Yugas, or the World Ages whose constant change instigates the advances and deterioration of cultures and civilizations. There are four Yugas: the Golden Age (Satya or Krita Yuga); the Silver Age, (Treta Yuga); the Bronze Age, (Dvapara Yuga); the Iron Age, (Kali Yuga). The dharmic Bull of Truth—a Vedic symbol of morality—represents this cyclic calendar. According to Vedic tradition the bull loses a leg as a symbol of Earth's loss of twenty-five percent of cosmic light with each cycle of time. During a Golden Age, the Earth receives one-hundred percent cosmic light from the Great Central Sun. In a Silver Age, Earth receives seventy-five percent light and in a Bronze Age, fifty percent light. We are now living in Kali Yuga: the age of materialism when Earth receives only twenty-five percent light.

Since the science of Vedic Astrology—Jyotish—was given to humanity in a time of greater light on Earth, it is possible that many of the recognized planets ruling chakras are functioning at abnormal levels. This is accounted for in the chakra tables that follow. [Editor's Note: Vedic and esoteric scholars speculate that the calculation for the timing of the Yugas may be faulty, and we are living in the infant stages of Dvapara Yuga. This opinion is based on the calculations of Sri Yuteswar, guru of Paramahansa Yogananda. Some Vedic adherents of the Puranas—ancient, reli-

The Dharmic Bull of Truth
The Bull of Truth loses one leg as Earth progresses through each declining stage of the Cycle of the Yugas.

gious texts—allege we are currently experiencing a minor upswing of Galactic Light, the Golden Age of Kali Yuga. It is important to understand the Golden Age of Kali Yuga is not a full force one-hundred percent Krita Yuga; however, the Master Teachers claim it is possible Earth may receive up to fifty percent Galactic Light, equal to a Bronze Age Dvapara Yuga at the height of this ten-thousand year period.

Chakras and the Endocrine System

Some esoteric scholars suggest certain chakras frequently represent the energies of the endocrine glands and their energies are responsible for the rising of the kundalini—a term for spiritual development. Specifically, two endocrine glands are linked to our psychic ability and regulate consciousness: the pineal gland and the pituitary gland. In recent studies at the Psi Research Centre in Glastonbury, England, researchers believe the pineal gland's production of pinoline is responsible for various psychic states of consciousness. "Pinoline is thought to act on serotonin to trigger dreaming. It also has hallucinogenic properties, and its chemical structure is similar to chemicals found in psychotropic plants in the Amazon. Studies suggest that the dream state is one in which we are most likely to have psychic experiences. Pinoline is believed to be the neurochemical that triggers this state of consciousness."[1] Animals and homing pigeons rely on the presence of magnetite—a magnetically sensitive compound of iron and oxygen—to sense the right direction during travel and seasonal migrations. Human

---

1. Cyndi Dale, *The Subtle Body, An Encyclopedia of Your Energetic Anatomy*, (Sounds True, Inc., Boulder, CO, 2009) Sounds True e-book.

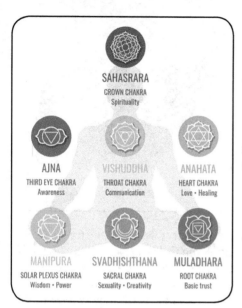

The Seven Chakras with their Sanskrit symbols and names.

Chakra	Endocrine Gland
Heart	Thymus
Throat	Thyroid/Parathyroid
Third Eye	Pituitary
Crown	Pineal

The following table is based on the research of Dr. Valerie Hunt, a professor of kinesiology at the University of California. Dr. Hunt has specialized in measuring human electromagnetic output to validate the existence of chakras. According to her research, the physical body emanates radiation in areas typically associated with the Seven Chakras. Her research data was mathematically measured by scientists in hertz frequency (Hz), the periodic speed of which something vibrates (movement) also known as cycles per second. Since the human eye can perceive only a small range of color, Dr. Hunt's research relied on information from auric readers and their use of clairvoyance. The results were remarkably consistent and these auric colors correlated with these frequency-wave patterns:

Color	Frequency
Blue	250-275 Hz plus 1200 Hz
Green	250-475 Hz
Yellow	500-700 Hz
Orange	950-1050 Hz
Red	1000-1200 Hz
Violet	1000-2000, plus 300-400; 600-800 Hz
White	1100-2000 Hz

[Editor's Note: The above table is derived from the book Hands of Light, by NASA research scientist and healer Barbara Brennan.]

Hunt's research expanded to include the frequencies of different types of individuals. She discovered the normal range for most people is around 250 Hz, which is the identical frequency range of the heart. However, when psychics were measured their frequency range was 400 to 800 Hz; mediums and channelers have a range of 800 to 900 Hz; and mystics—those continually connected to the I AM, or higher-self—were measured above 900 Hz. Cyndi Dale writes, "...the chakras can be stepping-stones to enlightenment, each inviting a different spiritual awareness and increasing the frequency of the subtle body."

sensitivity to magnetic fields may be explained by the presence of magnetite crystals located near the pituitary gland.

Color and Vibration

Human Energy Field researcher Dr. Shafica Karagulla (1914-1986) concluded chakras are affected and altered in color, luminosity, size, form, and texture during the disease process. An outgrowth of the detailed research discovered that medically diagnosed problems in the endocrine glands are also detected in the chakras. This research expanded knowledge regarding the traditional Seven Chakras, and added an additional chakra—the Spleen Chakra—located between the Creative and Solar Plexus Chakras. Her research also discovered the minor chakras that exist in the palms of hands, and soles of feet. Dr. Karagulla co-authored the book, Through the Curtain, with friend and theosophist Viola Petitt Neal. The book was published in 1983 after Neal's death. A version of this table is published in the introduction of the book:

Chakra	Endocrine Gland
Base	Spine/Glandular System
Creative	Ovaries/Testes
Spleen*	Spleen/Liver
Solar Plexus	Adrenals/Pancreas

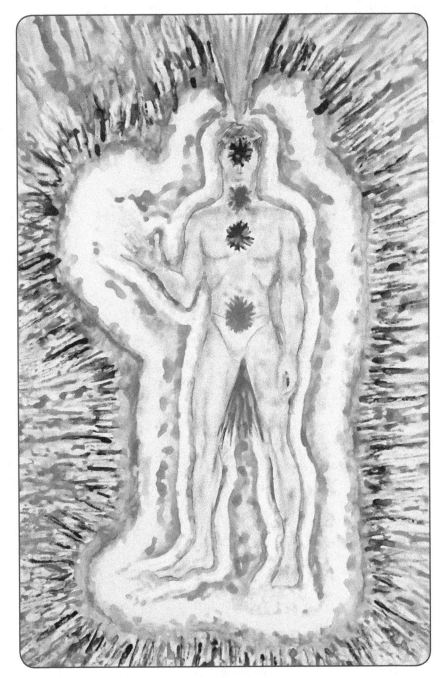

Layers of the Human Aura
The Hunan Energy System depicting the
Seven Major Chakras and Layers of the Energy Field

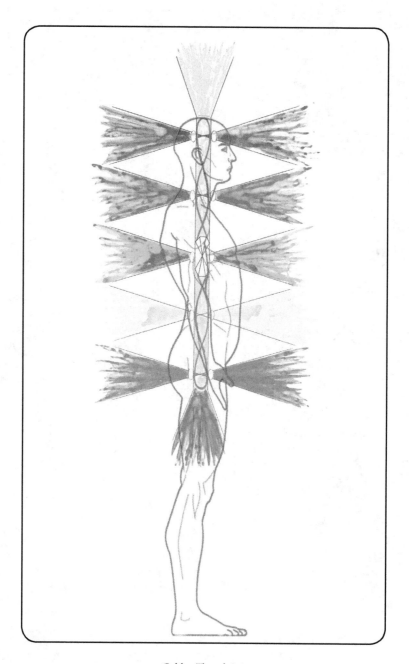

Golden Thread Axis
A depiction of the *Golden Thread Axis* and
the Major Chakra System

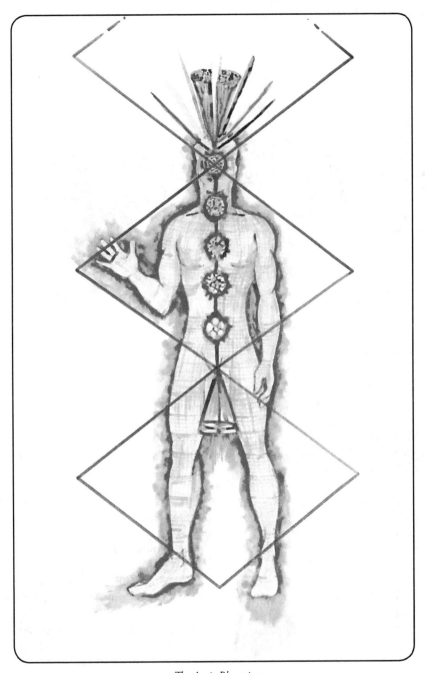

The Auric Blueprint
The *Auric Blueprint* depicting the Seven Major Chakras and the Energy Grids,
Meridians, and Nadis.

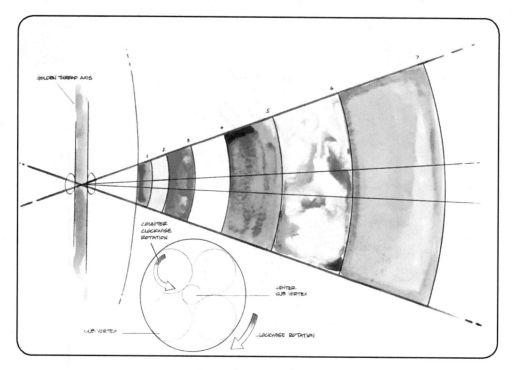

Layers of a Human Chakra
Illustration of the Golden Thread Axis, and cross section of Seven Layers of Light within the chakra.
Note sub-Vortices of chakra with clockwise and counter-clockwise motions.

First Chakra
Names: Root Chakra, Base Chakra, Muladhara.

Ruling Planet:

Average:	Earth
Evolved:	Saturn
HU-man:	Mars

Colors:

Average:	Dark Red
Evolved:	Blue
HU-man:	Ruby

Rays:

Average:	Red
Evolved:	Blue
HU-man:	Ruby-Gold

Location: Base of spine—the perineum; the energy of this chakra flows between the legs downward and connects to Mother Earth.

Main Aspect: Security and the will to live; is grounded to our Earth Mother and lives in the present moment.

Astrological Signs:

Lunar Current:	Aquarius
Solar Current:	Capricorn
Exaltation:	Mars in Capricorn

Attributes: Due to the influence of Kali Yuga on the human energy field, the average base or root chakras of most individuals are not in alignment with their environments. This may explain the lack of sustainability in many facets of current day affairs: economic, energy, climate, and government. This undeveloped chakra leads one to rashness and intensity without weighing the risks involved. However, this energy has good stamina and courage, which inevitably leads to development through the lunar current of Aquarius. Saturn rules elimination and support—the skeletal system, including the spine. Although it is a contracting planet and crude in nature, Saturn focuses and stabilizes the energies of the chakra towards structure, analysis, and science. Aquarius' sign of humanity civilizes the brash energies of the red Root Chakra, and Mars inevitably exalts in the solar current of Capricorn. This is the highest manifestation of Mars' qualities and the executive, hard-working efficiency of the Divine Warrior is present. The evolved base chakra resists disease and aging while focused on achieving goals through generous, protective acts.

Dark Side: Quick to anger and thinks it is okay to take from others; deceptive, reckless, and arrogant.

Second Chakra
Names: Creative Chakra, Sexual Chakra, Sacral Chakra, Svadhisthana.

Ruling Planet:

Average:	Rahu (Moon's North Node)
Evolved:	Jupiter
HU-man:	Venus

Colors:

Average:	Orange
Evolved:	Yellow
HU-man:	White, in developmental states, pastel colors may be detected.

Rays:

Average:	Will vary with each individual
Evolved:	Yellow
HU-man:	White

Location: Lower abdomen, between navel and genitals.

Main Aspect: Procreation and creativity.

Astrological Signs:

Lunar Current:	Pisces
Solar Current:	Sagittarius
Exaltation:	Venus in Pisces

Attributes: Rahu rules obsession and unpredictable behaviors, with a tendency towards materialism and worldliness. These lower energies influence the Creative Chakra in its developmental stages. Jupiter governs the reproductive system and the creative energy and the lunar current of this chakra in Pisces quickly evolves this chakra with wisdom, philosophy, spirituality, alongside a strong intuition and visionary ability. The lunar current of this chakra develops in Pisces and endows the individual with a nurturing and healing disposition, and a good family life with prosperous children. Jupiter's solar current in Sagittarius develops humanitarian social skills, and the capacity to inspire and lead others with progressive compassion. In the lunar half of Pisces, Venus exalts and is connected with the need to unite sex with love and harmony. The higher qualities of Venus and the White Ray are expressed through balanced artistic sensuality as the Divine Feminine is realized.

Dark Side: Overindulgent and too sacrificing; the individual may experience loss through misplaced sympathies, and is taken advantage of by marriage or partnership.

Third Chakra
Names: Solar Plexus Chakra, Navel Chakra, Manipura.

Ruling Planet:

Average:	Jupiter
Evolved:	Mars
HU-man:	Sun

Colors:

Average:	Yellow
Evolved:	Dark Red, during development stages some orange may appear.
HU-man:	Ruby-Gold

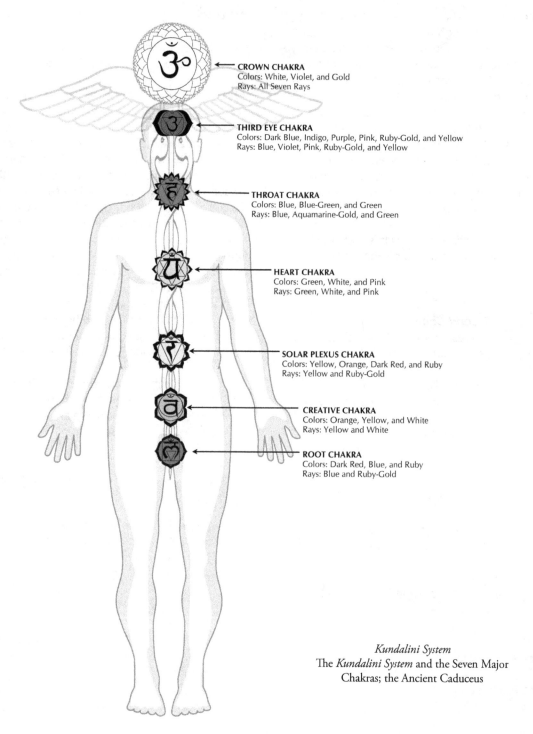

CROWN CHAKRA
Colors: White, Violet, and Gold
Rays: All Seven Rays

THIRD EYE CHAKRA
Colors: Dark Blue, Indigo, Purple, Pink, Ruby-Gold, and Yellow
Rays: Blue, Violet, Pink, Ruby-Gold, and Yellow

THROAT CHAKRA
Colors: Blue, Blue-Green, and Green
Rays: Blue, Aquamarine-Gold, and Green

HEART CHAKRA
Colors: Green, White, and Pink
Rays: Green, White, and Pink

SOLAR PLEXUS CHAKRA
Colors: Yellow, Orange, Dark Red, and Ruby
Rays: Yellow and Ruby-Gold

CREATIVE CHAKRA
Colors: Orange, Yellow, and White
Rays: Yellow and White

ROOT CHAKRA
Colors: Dark Red, Blue, and Ruby
Rays: Blue and Ruby-Gold

Kundalini System
The *Kundalini System* and the Seven Major
Chakras; the Ancient Caduceus

Rays:

Average:	Yellow	
Evolved:	Will vary throughout the development process, but will develop into the Ruby Ray.	
HU-man:	Ruby-Gold	

Location: Between the navel and base of the sternum.

Main Aspect: An intense feeling (intuitive) chakra which is known as the Center of Power and Balance in relationship to everything in life.

Astrological Signs:

Lunar Current:	Scorpio
Solar Current:	Aries
Exaltation:	Sun in Aries

Attributes: The Solar Plexus Chakra is our center of power, and distributes our ability to realize our goals and aspirations that inevitably lead to the fulfillment of our Dharma (purpose). Since this chakra manages digestion processes and digestive organs, it is also associated with our digestion of life's experiences as thoughts, feelings, and actions. Experience is the ultimate Guru, hence this chakra's affiliation with Jupiter in its seminal stages. Eastern systems relate digestion to the fire element, and as this chakra develops, it is associated with the planet Mars—considered by Vedic astrologers to be a good friend to Jupiter. The solar current of Mars in Scorpio manifests a strong warrior spirit with the ability to quickly resolve opposition with a sharp mind and intellect. However, as the Rays and chakra evolves, the lunar half of the energy current exalts the Sun in Aries, and the quick, impatient temperament must integrate with the vital will. The authority of the Divine Father is developed and realized through courage, leadership, innovation, and strength of character.

Dark Side: Too authoritative, dogmatic, impatient, active but incompetent, stubborn, and aggressive; these individuals are inept at sustaining or maintaining.

Fourth Chakra
Names: Heart Chakra, Anahata.

Ruling Planet:

Average:	Mercury
Evolved:	Venus
HU-man:	Moon

Colors:

Average:	Green
Evolved:	Green to White, pastel colors may be present during development.
HU-man:	White to Pink, pastel colors of green and blue may be present during developmental stages.

Rays:

Average:	Green
Evolved:	White
HU-man:	Pink

Location: The center of the chest; the heart.

Main Aspect: Love and Relationships; our ability to feel compassion, forgiveness, and our own feeling of Divine Purpose—the Heart's Desire.

Astrological Signs:

Lunar Current:	Taurus
Solar Current:	Libra
Exaltation:	Moon in Taurus; Saturn in Libra

Attributes: At the physical level the heart is the center of our body and emanates a thousand times more electricity and magnetism than our brain; and this is perhaps this chakra's foundational affiliation with the Green Ray. As an individual evolves the spiritual heart must open beyond physical needs, and our attachments to new ideas, fads, fame, and money inevitably change. A mystical approach to life opens the heart and creates balance in thoughts, feelings, and actions. This is the movement of intelligence into Wisdom. This energetic movement is related to the Divine Feminine as art and beauty, with an overall humanitarian approach. As the heart evolves the lower solar energies, the frequencies of the solar current create the Divine Will through the "higher principles of justice, order, and detachment, which are necessary in using our heart energy in the right way without bias or attachment."[1]

The lunar half of Venus evolves into the exalted Moon in Taurus. This is the birth of the Divine Mother within our heart and is the energy of openness, receptivity, generosity, and the fullness of life and love.

Dark Side: One may encounter over-indulgence, laziness, overly self-controlled, possessiveness, and jealousy; this makes one controlling in love, non-romantic, overworking, and fearful of change.

Fifth Chakra
Names: Throat Chakra, Vishuddha.

Ruling Planet:
Average:	Saturn
Evolved:	Neptune, Mercury
HU-man:	Mercury

Colors:
Average:	Blue
Evolved:	Blue-Green (Aquamarine)
HU-man:	Green

Rays:
Average:	Blue
Evolved:	Aquamarine-Gold
HU-man:	Green

Location: Throat

Main Aspect: Expression of truth, emotion, creativity, knowledge, and the sciences; the Oral Tradition.

Astrological Signs:
Lunar Current:	Gemini
Solar Current:	Virgo
Exaltation:	Mercury in Virgo

Attributes: Due to the influences of Kali Yuga, Saturn's pressure on the Throat Chakra has decreased our command of languages, memory, and our ability to learn and absorb new information. Naturally, this limits human development and ambitions; but is good for focusing on details at a slower pace, especially in communication and self-expression. As the lunar current evolves this chakra in the sign of Gemini, an individual's thinking becomes developed, tactical, inventive, and quick-witted. The mind readily absorbs music, literature, and technology. As the solar current evolves the Throat Chakra in the sign of Virgo, it reaches the point of exaltation and the sublime energies of the Divine Messenger. It is here that the intellect receives its highest levels of precision and advanced insight to readily absorb and express philosophically; initiate a quantum approach to the sciences; and receive advanced insight and intuition alongside a refined discrimination. This is the enlightened intellect of the Buddha.

Dark Side: Critical; lives in fantasy; demanding and argumentative; superficial, talks more than accomplishes; intellect interferes with common sense—analysis paralysis.

Sixth Chakra
Names: Third Eye Chakra, Ajna.

Ruling Planet:
Average:	Saturn
Evolved:	Moon and Sun
HU-man:	Jupiter

Colors:
Average:	Dark Blue, Indigo, Purple
Evolved:	Pink, Ruby, Gold
HU-man:	Yellow

Rays:
Average:	Blue, Violet
Evolved:	Pink, Ruby-Gold
HU-man:	Yellow

Location: Above and between the eyebrows.

1. David Frawley, *The Astrology of the Seers: A Guide to Vedic (Hindu) Astrology*, (Passage Press, 1990, Salt Lake City, Utah), page 231.

Main Aspect: The blending of thought and feeling as perception and projection for Co-creative activity.

Astrological Signs:
Lunar Current: Cancer
Solar Current: Leo
Exaltation: Jupiter in Cancer

Attributes: Solar and lunar currents meet and merge in the Third Eye Chakra, and due again to the lower energies of Kali Yuga, humanity is yet to achieve the fulfillment of the Ajna Chakra. However, in the infant stages of the development of this chakra, the Third Eye is often subjugated by the other chakras, and is readily influenced by external factors; especially by social and cultural pressures via politics and religion. Disciplined use of visualization will open and develop the Third Eye and promotes the expansion of engineering, science, and technology—areas humanity is currently developing as we enter the Golden Age of Kali Yuga. This promotes the evolution of the Third Eye Chakra through qualities of perception, sensitiveness, kindness, and wisdom through the lunar current of Cancer. The solar current of Leo further develops sensitivity through the royal sign of spiritual leadership. The developed chakra produces a blend of independent and intelligent insight that repels negativity with courage and stamina. At this stage, the chakra gains independence and initiates and directs the flow of consciousness. This gives rise to the exaltation status of the chakra, or the development of the Godman—the Divine HU-man, where the qualities of feeling and leadership expand into knowledge, devotion, merit, and a soft-yet-strong humane and spiritual ministration to humanity. This is the Divine Guru.

Dark Side: Over optimistic; indulgent; lazy; too sensitive and generous; susceptible to others troubles and becomes bossy, impatient, dominating and hot-tempered.

Seventh Chakra
Names: Crown Chakra, Sahasrara.

Ruling Planet: All planets, including the Great Central Sun—the Galactic Center.

Colors: White, Violet, Gold

Rays: All Seven Rays

Location: Top of or just atop of the head.

Main Aspect: Connection to the spiritual planes.

Attributes: The Seventh Chakra is perhaps the most unique of the seven chakras as this is where the Seven Rays enter the Chakra System. In the Hindu system the Crown Chakra is also known as the Chakra of One-Thousand Petals and "the petals represent the Sanskrit alphabet along with their twenty permutations."[2]
The Seven Rays, along with these subtle vibrations, govern and coordinate the other chakras according to the Divine Plan for the individual's spiritual growth and development for each lifetime. This chakra is easily located as it is the soft-spot at the top of the head in newborn babies. Some yogis claim as they liberate their Karmas from the earthly plane, Divine Rain falls from the petals of the lotus and dampens the head with the "dew of divinity."[3]
This chakra creates a sheath between the physical, astral, and causal bodies. As the HU-man fully develops and self-realizes through the Chakra System, the Ascension Process disintegrates the sheath and the soul is freed from the Wheel of Karma. According to certain Hindu traditions the freed soul enters into the three higher planes above the earthly body—Satyaloka, the Abode of Truth. Evolved yogis express this disintegration of the Anandamaya Sheath through the entrance into Samadhi, a state of bliss and transcendence of the Earth Plane.
Satyaloka is the highest of the seven lokas in the Vedic Cosmology of created worlds, and is the alleged home of Brahma and the Gods.

Dark Side: Over optimistic; indulgent; lazy; too sensitive and generous; susceptible to others troubles and becomes bossy, impatient, dominating and hot-tempered.

[The information on the Seven Chakras was compiled from information contained in the I AM America Teachings from the School of the Four Pillars, Dr. David Frawley's, *The*

2. Dale, *The Subtle Body*.
3. Ibid.

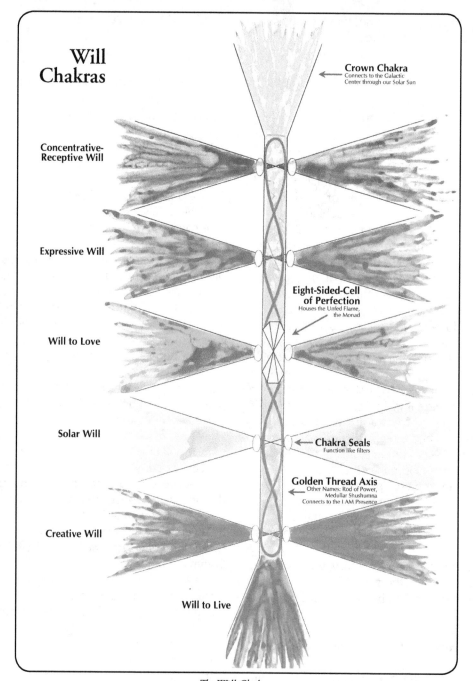

Will Chakras

Crown Chakra
Connects to the Galactic
Center through our Solar Sun

Concentrative-
Receptive Will

Expressive Will

Eight-Sided-Cell
of Perfection
Houses the Unfed Flame,
the Monad

Will to Love

Solar Will

Chakra Seals
Function like filters

Golden Thread Axis
Other Names: Rod of Power,
Medullar Shushumna
Connects to the I AM Presence

Creative Will

Will to Live

The Will Chakras
The Golden Thread Axis; Eight-sided Cell of Perfection; and the *Will Chakras*.
(Side View: Left represents the back of the body; Right represents the front of the body.)

Astrology of the Seers, A Guide to Vedic (Hindu) Astrology, William R. Levacy's, *Beneath a Vedic Sky, A Beginner's Guide to the Astrology of Ancient India*, and Cyndi Dale's, *The Subtle Body, An Encyclopedia of Your Energetic Anatomy.*]

Will Chakras

The Will Chakras are a specific series of six chakras located on the back of the human spine and the Root Chakra (kundalini system), and enable the personal actions and choices of the individual. Like the Frontal Chakras, Will Chakras absorb and process light and sound energy from Ray Forces. The entire Human Chakra System affects the Human Aura. A chakra spins, in fact, in Sanskrit *chakra* literally means, "spinning wheel." The anatomy of a chakra contains both an outer portion and an inner portion. The inner portion of the chakra is comprised of sub-Vortices; the number of sub-Vortices varies according to the type of chakra. Chakra movement absorbs and releases the energy of the Rays. A healthy chakra absorbs Ray Forces through the clockwise movement of the outer chakra and releases the energies through the counter-clockwise movement of the sub-Vortices. Will and Frontal Chakras both absorb and release energies; however, when energies enter a Frontal Chakra, the energy exits the Will Chakra; and vice-versa, when energies enter a Will Chakra, the energy exits through the Frontal Chakra. This flow maintains the health of the physical body through the balance of light and sound frequencies present in the Human Aura. Descriptions of the six Will Chakras follow:

Concentrative-Receptive Will: The ability to focus, while remaining open and receptive; centered and sensitive; Masculine and Feminine

Expressive Will: The will to express emotions and thoughts; the ability to communicate with clarity and personal truth; expansive and determined; Masculine

Will to Love: The Heart's Desire; Fulfills goals, aspirations, and desires conceived through the Creative Will. Nurturing and sustaining; Feminine

Solar Will: The ability to interact with others with personal power; receptive and protective; Masculine

Creative Will: The will to create through ideas, intentions, and goals; sensing; Feminine

Will to Live: Root Chakra connects to Mother Earth

Flow of the Rays through the Human Hands

Certain Ray forces are said to flow through human hands. The preceding diagram illustrates each digit of the left and right hands, including their associated Ray Forces, assigned planets, and defining energies. Please note the difference between the feminine side (left) and the masculine side. Of the four terminal digits, the ring finger radiates perhaps the most powerful energy of the Rays—the left ring finger emits the feminine energies of the Pink Ray (Moon) and the softer energies of the Ruby (Red) Ray (the healing, focused characteristics of Mars); while the masculine energies of the Gold Ray (Sun) and the forceful, masculine energies of the Ruby (Red) Ray emanate from the right ring finger. The Ruby Ray of Mars evolves into developed physical energy and insight from violence and aggression. This Ray is also affiliated with the index finger of both hands alongside Jupiter (Yellow Ray). The planets Saturn (Blue Ray) and Venus (White Ray) jointly govern the middle finger of the left and right hands. This energy represents converging sexual energy from the creative power of the developed will. Compassion, mercy, and forgiveness are characteristics of the Violet Ray. The thumb emits these qualities and represents an individual's developed grasp of power. As humanity evolves into the HU-man, according to the prophecies of the Ascended Masters, the Aquamarine Ray will emanate from the individual palms of both hands; it represents the power of unity and the consciousness of Unana.

A mudra is a symbolic ceremonial or spiritual gesture, mostly expressed by the hands and fingers. It is often used by evolved spiritual beings and Ascended Master to signify or emit spiritual energies. Mudras connect and link specific energy currents in the body, uniting Ray Forces symbolically and spiritually. Here are some classic Ascended Master mudras:

Index, middle, and ring fingers extended, thumb covers little finger: this is the mudra of love, wisdom, and power—a symbol of the Great White Brotherhood. In greetings the three fingers touch the heart (love), the Third Eye (wisdom), and the mudra is raised as a gesture to heaven (power).

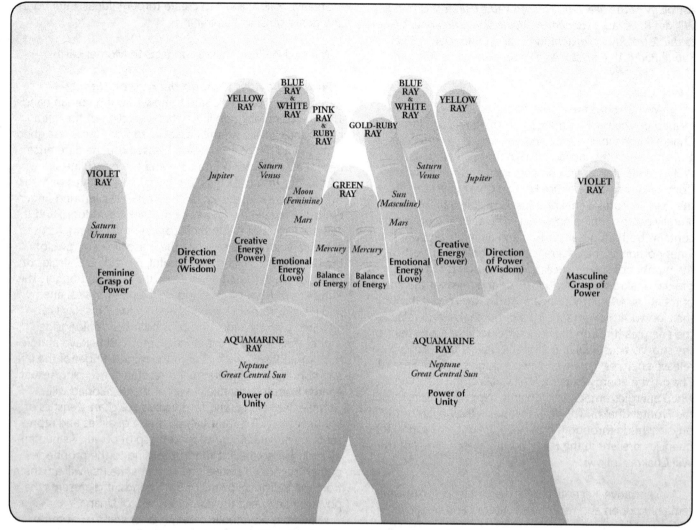

Flow of the Rays through the Human Hands
The Seven Rays and their corresponding locations and energy emission from the human hands.

Little and ring fingers touching palm; thumb and index and middle fingers extended. This is a common mudra often used by Sananda to transmit the energies of compassion, love, and mercy with force and direction.

Right hand held up, palm flat, all fingers extended pointing upward: greeting of unity and another symbol of the Great White Brotherhood.

Right hand held up, palm flat, all fingers extended pointing upward, left hand over heart. This mudra intentionally emits energies from the Heart Chakra of the individual and can be transmitted for Co-creative processes.

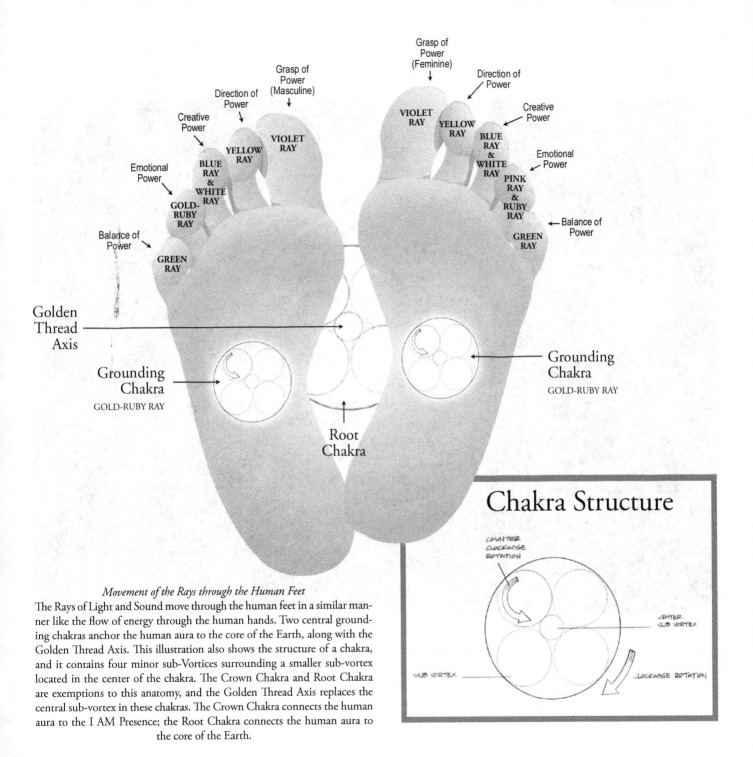

Chakra Structure

COUNTER CLOCKWISE ROTATION

CENTER SUB VORTEX

SUB VORTEX

CLOCKWISE ROTATION

Movement of the Rays through the Human Feet

The Rays of Light and Sound move through the human feet in a similar manner like the flow of energy through the human hands. Two central grounding chakras anchor the human aura to the core of the Earth, along with the Golden Thread Axis. This illustration also shows the structure of a chakra, and it contains four minor sub-Vortices surrounding a smaller sub-vortex located in the center of the chakra. The Crown Chakra and Root Chakra are exemptions to this anatomy, and the Golden Thread Axis replaces the central sub-vortex in these chakras. The Crown Chakra connects the human aura to the I AM Presence; the Root Chakra connects the human aura to the core of the Earth.

Seed of Life
Sacred geometry design based on the Flower of Life.

Sacred Geometry

Esoteric scholars suggest that many universal patterns, geometrical shapes, and geometric proportions symbolize spiritual balance and perfection. In other words, a fundamental mathematical order exists in the universe, one that is divinely inspired, because it cannot be explained by conventional means. Nature is rife with examples of Sacred Geometry, including the hexagonal cell of the honeybee, the chambered shell of the nautilus, and the spiral arms of a galaxy. Instances in the arts and sciences are also prevalent: the musical harmonic ratios of Pythagoras, the Spiritual Lokas of Vedic Cosmology, the mathematical beauty of the Golden Ratio, and Leonardo da Vinci's renowned Vitruvian Man. Meanwhile, the Sine Wave, the Sphere, Vesica Piscis, the Torus Tube, the Five Platonic Solids—Tetrahedron, Cube, Octahedron, Dodecahedron, Icosahedron; the Golden Spiral; the Tesseract four-dimensional hypercube; Fractals, the Star Tetrahedron (a Golden City shape); and the spiritually metaphoric Merkabah are just a few mathematical concepts that illustrate the ancient origins of this divine theory.

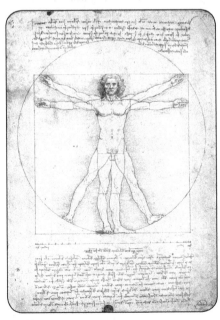

Vitruvian Man by Leonardo da Vinci, Galleria dell'Accademia, Venice, (1485-90), original drawing 1487.

Leonardo da Vinci's work serves as a compelling framework in which to study esoteric principles. Two of his pieces specifically—*Vitruvian Man* and his interpretation of the Flower of Life—investigate and illustrate the underlying elements of sacred geometry, which is a key concept in understanding Golden City Vortices. *Vitruvian Man* is ubiquitous in modern culture. He's on everything from t-shirts to NASA mission patches to international currency. There's a reason *Virtuvian Man* shows up all over the place—he's iconic, he simple yet complex, and he symbolizes the convergence of art, science, and metaphysics. In fact, Italy's prime minister, Carlo Azeglio Ciampi, said *Vitruvian Man* represents "man as a measure of all things." Da Vinci uses *Vitruvian Man* to express his ideals about human balance, proportion, and symmetry.

The rendering itself is of a male body in a square, arms out, feet together, superimposed on the same human form in a circle, legs spread-eagle, arms out but raised to meet the top of the head. *Vitruvian Man* is based on the work of the Roman architect Vitruvius, who postulated that the proportions of the human body were divinely inspired and thus perfect. Several centuries later Da Vinci expanded this notion—he felt the human body served as a microcosmic reflection of the universe. *Vitruvian Man* is a series of mathematical and geometric calculations that correlate measurements of the body using the distance between body parts, such as palms, hands, elbows, legs, and feet. For instance, the length of a man's outstretched arms is equal to his height. Da Vinci also relied on facial elements and dimensions to create his rendering— the distance from the bottom of the chin to the nose, for example, is a third of the face. At first glance, *Vitruvian Man* has two stances, but by combining various arm and leg positions, scholars have actually discovered sixteen poses. *Vitruvian Man* is considered a masterpiece and represents the inherent sacred geometry depicted in nature. Today *Vitruvian Man* represents the essential symmetry of the human body as an extension of the universe as a whole. He is often employed as a contemporary symbol of holistic and alternative medicine.

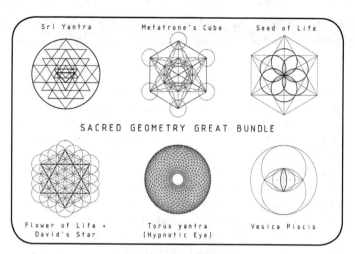

Sacred Geometry Collection

spiritual symbol. The *Flower of Life* is considered by many occultists as the foundation of sacred geometry and is associated with multiple spiritual beliefs, including Kabbalism, Judaism, and Wicca, while its geometric figures are noted throughout ancient Assyria, Egypt, India, Europe, the Middle East, Peru, and Mexico. Hermeticists, Kabbalists, and Pythagoreans have adopted it as a sacred symbol, one that represents the diagram of the Universal Seed of Life.

The pattern of the flower depicts the fundamental form of dimensional time and space. Its basis is the rotating or spinning octahedron, consisting of six vertices, eight faces, and twelve edges. Its spiritual influence is said to connect all patterns of life, especially to the Akashic Records, ethereal information that contains the breadth of knowledge of human experience. The *Flower of Life*, which blossoms in the following eight stages, forms the structural bedrock of the Tube Torus—the underlying geometric principle and structure of the Vortices.

1. Rotating Octahedron [Editor's Note: The symbol for the Fifth Dimension of the Golden City Vortices and an integral part of the Golden City's structure.]
2. Spherical Octahedron
3. Vesica Piscis
4. Tripod of Life—the Holy Trinity
5. Four intersecting rings
6. Five intersecting rings
7. Six intersecting rings
8. Seven interlocking rings

The *Flower of Life* is considered the initial structural foundation in the formation of Tube Torus—the underlying geometric principle and structure in Vortices.

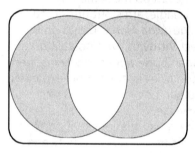

Vesica Piscis

Vesica Piscis appears in all kinds of religious, metaphysical, spiritual, and mathematical contexts throughout time. The shape itself is based on two interlocking circles of the same radius; the center of each circle lies upon the circumference of the other, forming an eye-shaped oval at its intersection, the Vesica Piscis. The mathematical ratio of the Vesica Piscis (width to height: 265/153) equals the square root of three—a metaphysical reference to the mystical triune, the Holy Trinity. Part of that ratio is also connected to the Gospel of John in the New Testament of the Bible and the number of fish caught in the Sea of Galilee in the teachings of Jesus Christ: 153. This phenomenon often referred to as the "miraculous draught of fish." The abundant iconography of the Vesica Piscis is prevalent throughout the art, architecture, and the symbology of Christianity. Vesica Piscis is also a dominant motif among the Freemason movement and Kabbalism.

Flower of Life

Though da Vinci did not create the *Flower of Life*, he was fascinated by its mathematical properties, which inspired him to produce his own rendition of this enigmatic

Planetary Life Forces of Our Solar System

Vedic astrologers claim that our Solar System occupies the nine o'clock position in Sagittarius, in relationship to the Galactic Center. The Rishis of the prior ages of greater light traveled in their astral bodies to explore the planets, observe their qualities, and subsequently record the effect of the planets on humanity and life on Earth. In fact, the bija-seed mantras attributed to the astrological planets are the alleged sounds of the planets heard by the Rishis as they journeyed to their faraway physical and supernal planes. Chanting each sound reproduces the life force and energy of the planet within our consciousness and spiritually activates the microcosmic Solar System within. Since the planetary force of the Rays structure and sustain life on Earth, this supra-intelligence guides our thoughts, feelings, and actions. Dr. David Frawley writes, "The stars and planets are not just outer entities; they are alive within us as well. They exist within our own minds as our guiding lights. Or rather, one could say that our own inner lights take shape outwardly as the stars and planets to guide the world evolution. The outer comes from the inner and not vice versa, though the outer can affect the inner. The same Rays of creation function outwardly in the heavens and inwardly in the heaven of our own higher mind."

Scientists theorize that our Solar System was formed 4.6 billion years ago after the collapse of a massive molecular cloud. The Sun will burn itself into a white dwarf—about the size of Earth—in about 5.4 billion years from now. The four smaller planets of Mercury, Venus, Earth, and Mars comprise the inner Solar System, and are dense and rocky, with minerals and metals with high melting points and no ring systems. The Earth has one natural satellite—the Moon—and Mars has two captured satellite asteroids: Deimos and Phobos. A system of yet again four more planets creates our outer Solar System, and they are known as the gas giants of Jupiter, Saturn, Uranus, and Neptune. These globes of hydrogen and helium with their gaseous rings and planet-sized Moons circle our Sun, along with the smaller planets, in the ecliptic plane interspersed with comets, centaurs (dwarf planets that act like asteroids and comets), asteroid belts, and the Kuiper belt.

The following table lists the spiritual life force of each planet in their highest potential as the representation of Cosmic Man:

From Planet Earth
Components of this image are from NASA.

Traditional Planets

Sun	Divine Self
Mercury	Divine Savior (Intelligence)
Venus	Divine Love
Earth	Divine Balance (Stability)
Moon	Divine Mind
Mars	Divine Energy
Jupiter	Divine Guru (Self-realization, Wisdom)
Saturn	Divine Will (Limitation and Impermanence)
Rahu, (North Node)	Divine Expansion
Ketu, (South Node)	Divine Liberation (Heaven)

Modern Planets

Uranus	Divine Awakening (Chaos, Change)
Neptune	Divine Inspiration (Imagination, Idealism)
Pluto	Divine Transformation (Renewal, Mastery)

Asteroids

Chiron	Divine Healer (Reconciliation)
Ceres	Divine Evolution (Cycles, Growth)
Juno	Divine Power (Relationship, Marriage)
Vesta	Divine Heart (Sacred Fire)

Oriot Messenger of the White Burkhant
Symbolic art by Nicolas Roerich, 1925, depicts the victory of the soul through
cultivating awareness and self-realization, inner harmony, and Mastery.

Golden City Dimensional Symbolism

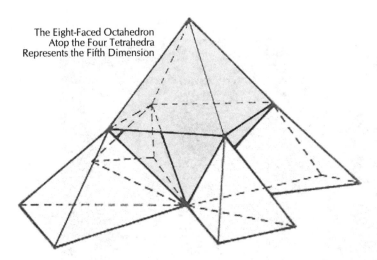

The Eight-Faced Octahedron
Atop the Four Tetrahedra
Represents the Fifth Dimension

Fifth Dimension: Golden City Vortex
The Fifth Dimension is represented by a Octahedron
in the Golden City Structure.

Fourth Dimension: Golden City Vortex
The Fourth Dimension is represented by
four Tetrahedra in the Golden City Structure.

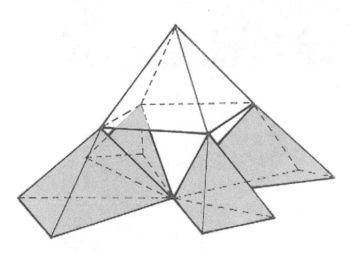

Third Dimension: Golden City Vortex
The three exposed faces of the Tetrahedra
represent Third Dimension in the
Golden City Structure.

Call of the Sky
Nicolas Roerich, 1936.

El Morya's Spiritual Teachings on Starting Anew, Restructuring Beliefs, Old Patterns, and Creating a New Mind

- First, identify your intention. The word intention derives its meaning from the Latin word intentio, or purpose. Further Latin derivations of proponere—purpose—means I declare or I propose. It is based on the Latin root word pono: to put or to place. The intentions, purposes, and thoughts we plant in our consciousness, according to El Morya, will define certain outcomes and subsequent actions.

- Our intention should properly reflect our purpose and plan: it should closely align or be in harmony with our will. Since our will is simply defined as the individual actions chosen, El Morya asks that we carefully consider our choices as a reflection of our will. The Ascended Masters often refer to the will as the Vertical Power Current.

- The inspiration to change is always found inside our hearts—this decision usually has no outer influence. Therefore, change often comes from internal thoughts and feelings. According to El Morya growth is "sparked from within" and travels energetically through its own current. Consider again the Vertical Power Current. Kundalini energy flows upward along its midline channel, influencing the Seven Chakras and an individual's Light Bodies.

- The creation of a new mindset often involves aligning the individual will to the Divine Will; however, El Morya's teachings state that this is not necessary. To restructure old patterns, beginners may choose instead to focus on an unattained desire or a simple wish. As time moves forward and the chela gains experience with this practice, intention becomes infused with conscience. This is the birth of the purposeful Divine Will.

- Equality is the underlying theme of any fresh start. Realizing the God-force within empowers "the body, the mind, and inevitably the consciousness to start fresh." Recognizing our equal divinity with the God-source induces new levels of harmony and cooperation—necessary components to achieving Ascension. El Morya suggests meditation to identify self-inhibiting beliefs, patterns, and fears. Discovery and identification of these limitations prepare our consciousness to release old ways and embrace new beginnings. "When one releases these fears, one becomes ready to begin anew! Make the choice from within."

- Take the time to evaluate your life; identify situations and circumstances that are not working. This may be difficult so have courage. Then write an outline of a personal plan you see for your life. Meditate upon this plan. "Have the courage to feel it, live it, and act it out," suggests El Morya. As a result of this process you'll gain experience and knowledge of what works for you and what doesn't.

Write and Burn Technique

The Write and Burn Technique helps students and chelas transmute any and all unwanted situations and circumstances, primarily undesirable dysfunctional life patterns. A venerated practice of the Ascended Masters, this type of journaling involves a handwritten letter—a petition—to the I AM Presence for Healing and Divine Intervention. The process encompasses two objectives: identifying and releasing unwanted and outdated energy or attracting and manifesting new and evolving energies. After the letter is written, it is then burned, either by fire or by light. Most students prefer to burn by fire. If, however, you choose to burn by light, place the document under a light source for twenty-four continuous hours. Insidious problems and complex-manifestation petitions may require up to one week of light exposure. The success of the light method and the subsequent acceptance of a petition depend on the reliability of the light source; the concentration of light must be continuous and without problems, e.g. blackouts, burnouts, and so on. If the issues are profound, you may need to probe deeper by identifying and addressing personal problem or life patterns. You may also want to consider rephrasing your approach to the problem, rewriting the letter, or both. Write and burn templates are provided below.

Transmute and Release Energy Patterns

Make one handwritten copy of this letter. In the name of I AM THAT I AM, I release this to the Universe to be transmuted. (List the energy or behavior patterns you have identified. Some students also insert various alchemic decrees to

the Violet Flame to dissolve, consume, and transform the energy.) Sign and date the letter. Burn the letter by fire or by light.

Attract and Manifest New Energy Patterns

Make two handwritten copies of this letter. In the name of I AM THAT I AM, I release this to the Universe to be fulfilled, maintained, and sustained in perfect alignment to the Divine Will. (List the new energy or behavior pattern you would like to Co-create.) Sign and date the letter. Burn one copy by fire or by light. Keep the other copy in a sacred place (e.g. personal altar, family Bible, favorite spiritual book) until you have achieved your goal or desired behavior change, and then burn that copy by fire.

Ascension Teachings of El Morya

Release the concept of drudgery! Seize life and all of its amazing experiences and gifts. "Live life for life!" Embrace the interconnectedness that exists in all circumstances and situations.

Use of the Violet Flame evokes the Blue Ray into action through Light Bodies. The Blue Ray clarifies intentions and assists the aligning of the will.

Time spent alone allows the unessential to fall away. Embrace spiritual simplicity when it comes to healing, solace, and important inner reflection. These principles engender introspection and inspired answers.

Don't expect to receive answers right away! El Morya encourages spiritual students to cast aside time. Some students may only need one day to identify their greater plan and connection to the ONE; for others, this may take many years. El Morya reminds us to remain patient with ourselves and not measure our results by earthly, illusive time. Personally integrating our experiences and feeling Unity from within are essential.

Saint Germain's Teachings on Starting Anew

The Violet Flame is known for its comprehensive healing properties, especially in matters of self-transformation and Karmic balancing. Saint Germain suggests the use of the Violet Flame to mitigate the following:

Harmful Cycles: release outdated, broken, and dysfunctional patterns. Lack of perfection: self-doubt, worry, and guilt. Saint Germain suggests the following decree to diminish fears of all kind:

> Violet Flame I AM, God I AM.
> Violet Flame, come forward in this instant.
> Manifest perfection in, through, and around me!
> Violet Flame I AM, God I AM Perfection, Violet Flame.

This decree is powerful enough to crack the voltage of the Blue Flame within the will. Its power is on a par with the electricity-producing force of lightning. Uttering this decree will create the Lightning Crack of Divine Intervention. The simple decree, "Violet Flame I AM, God I AM Violet Flame," from Saint Germain is meant for everyone. It instantly infuses the Violet Flame in our hearts. This decree lifts humanity out of suffering, limitation, death, and destruction, and into the hopeful vista of a New Day.

Forgiveness of Self: The Violet Flame assists the forgiveness of self. Use of its transforming fires transmutes any type of guilt. The Violet Flame is particularly helpful in transmuting the cause and effect surrounding memories that harness our consciousness with negativity and suppress our spiritual growth and evolution.

Sins of Self: Our own perceptions keep us trapped in a paradigm of death, decay, destruction, and catastrophe. Saint Germain sees this as a sin against self and encourages the dismantling of these destructive forces by applying the restorative energy of the Violet Flame and its Ray of transmuting light.

Know Thyself: Self-knowledge, along with the acknowledgement of our own doubts, limitations, strengths, and talents, is a key component of personal freedom.

The Co-creative Thought Process
As taught by Saint Germain

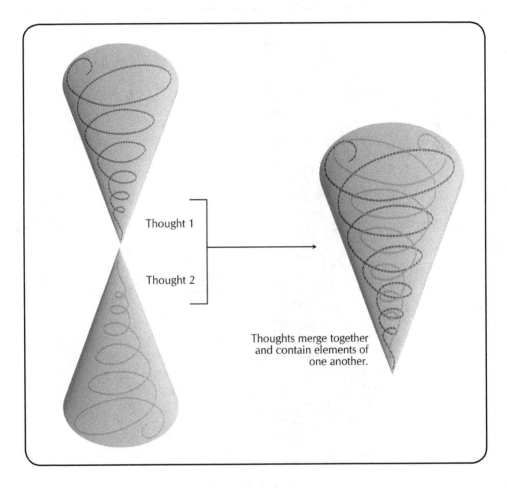

Thought 1

Thought 2

Thoughts merge together
and contain elements of
one another.

The Co-creative Thought Process
A diagram of the Co-creative thought process as
diagrammed by Saint Germain in *The Quickening*.

The Co-creative Thought Process
Under Time Compaction

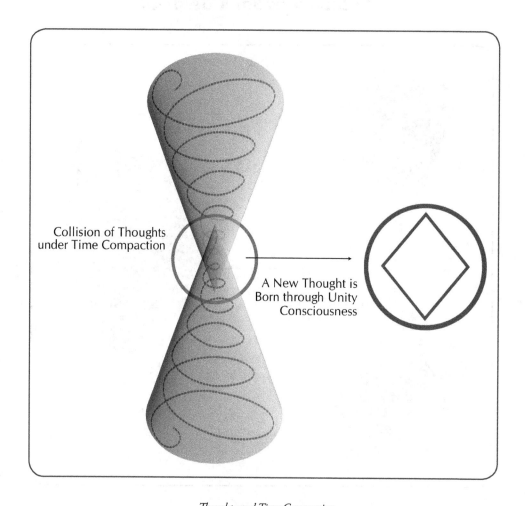

Collision of Thoughts
under Time Compaction

A New Thought is
Born through Unity
Consciousness

Thoughts and Time Compaction
Time Compaction changes our thought patterns
through the Co-creative process, and introduces a new
thought that functions beyond dualistic identity. This
ushers our entrance into Unity Consciousness, the
ONE, and the New Times.

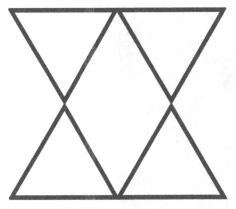

Native American Butterfly Symbol

Diamond Symbology

The diamond symbol is perhaps one of the most sacred geometrical designs, and its esoteric meaning is linked to immortality, harmony, time, and space, and the Ascension Process. It's enclosure in a circle represents the consciousness of One, Unana, and humanity's spiritual transformation process and entrance into the New Times.

Native Americans utilize the imagery of the diamond in the familiar design known as the butterfly. The butterfly lives a migratory existence, and in one lifetime may travel thousands of miles. Indigenous tribes welcome the annual return of the butterfly as the spiritual Homecoming. Most symbologists identify the butterfly as an icon of metamorphosis, transformation, and rebirth; however, the yearly return of the colorful Monarch also implies a profound metaphor of the soul's long journey to its true home. Avia Venefia writes about this insightful connection, "This encapsulates the divine journey in which man is born, moves through his world ever-gleaning more insight into his true identity and finally returns to the site of his first breath to realize he is immortal in his existence because of the path he chooses. In other words, man leaves a legacy, which is his key to immortality."

The Dagaz Symbol

Runic Alphabet

The Runic Alphabet, based on Germanic languages before the Latin alphabet was embraced, features a butterfly shaped symbol—Dagaz. It is possible the twenty-fourth symbol is derived from Lepontic inscriptions from ancient northern Italy; however, Dagaz is associated with this Anglo-Saxon poem, "Day, the glorious light of the Creator, is sent by the Lord; it is beloved of men, a source of hope and happiness to rich and poor, and of service to all."[1] Esoteric symbologists associate the Dagaz with the spiritual concepts of awakening, insight, clarification, epiphany, and new beginnings. Venefia writes, "It is also emblematic of time and space as complimentary elements. This rune speaks of the partnership between night and day with the center-point represented as the dawn."[2] The ancient Dagaz possesses similarity to Saint Germain's illustration of thoughts under Time Compaction; a metaphor to the dawn of the New Times and humanity's prophetic embrace of non-dualistic spiritual consciousness.

Ancient European groups often used the diamond as a symbol of life and depict the birth canal through the diamond motif. This association with the feminine and the birth of the New Energies through the cultivation of the intuition and the opening of Humanity's Heart is included in Saint Germain's new emblem for humanity's spiritual evolution.

The Magical Alphabet of the Viking Runes

1. Wikipedia, *Dagaz*, http://en.wikipedia.org/wiki/Dagaz, (2010).
2. Avia Venefia, http://www.whats-your-sign.com/diamond-symbol-meaning.html, (2009).

Night Startled by a Lark

The allegoric art of William Blake, 1820, illustrates Milton's poem *L'Allegro*. The angelic lark announces an Awakening, which includes essential communication and direction from the spiritual realm. In Blake's interpretation the individual must pass through a heavenly, crystalline gate — a metaphor for the developed HU-man entering the Ascension Process. Through this timely awakening we experience a quickening filled with humility, love, wonder, and awe.

Teachings on the Golden Cities by Saint Germain and El Morya in the Quickening

Inside Golden Cities, the Ascended Masters and Babajeran—Mother Earth—will interact to create peace, stillness, harmony, and an understanding of the ONE during the Time of Tribulation on Earth.

The Stars of Golden Cities consolidate the energy of that city's qualifying Ray, focusing its energy on a central location. The Master Teachers say that energy is concentrated in its most "direct force" in these specific areas.

The Star of the Golden City of Gobean is activated along with other Stars of Golden Cities during the Time of Change. Golden City activations create magnetism and psychic gravity inside the vortex. This type of radiation pulls students, chelas, aspirants, and initiates toward these geophysical locations for ceremony, prayer, and meditation. As humanity enters the New Times, many students will move to Golden City Stars to cultivate the spiritual attribute inherent in each Golden City Vortex. See following activation table. [Editor's Note: See Points of Perception, Activations and Subtle Energies.]

Each Golden City Star is a template of perfect thought, perfect feeling, and perfect action. These energies can be accessed and integrated for spiritual growth and evolution.

Certain Strategic Points inside Golden Cities are prophesied to physically manifest the energies necessary to move Earth and humanity toward the New Times.

Geophysical points inside the Gobean Golden City Vortex and the Star of the Gobean Vortex increase psychic awareness. Individuals who travel to, meditate in, and live near these geophysical points will develop spiritual insight and knowledge that will assist the manifestation of their choices and transformation and harmony processes while working within groups.

The infusion of Golden City energies present in the Stars and Adjutant Points of Gobean create an inner harmony with the Divine Will.

Stars and Adjutant Points of Golden Cities are interconnected. This connectivity first travels through the Stars of Golden Cities, then onward toward the Adjutant Points. Energies are subsequently disbursed throughout the Vortex.

This is known as the Golden City Network, which El Morya refers to as Template of Consciousness.

El Morya, Michael the Archangel, and Hercules the Elohim hold the Blue Ray in the Gobean Vortex. The Blue Ray blesses humanity with harmony in all of its creations for the New Times.

To sharpen your understanding of the Divine Intervention of Harmony, El Morya suggests traveling to the Adjutant Points of the Gobean Vortex and spending a day there to reflect "upon the intention" of your soul "to create Unity and Harmony within." The following cities and towns are near Adjutant Points in the Golden City Vortex of Gobean. [Editor's Note: According to estimates, a Golden City Adjutant Point can have up to a five, ten, and sometimes up to a forty mile radial electromagnetic energy flux. For more information see the *I AM America United States Golden City Map*.]

Socorro, New Mexico.
Magdalena, New Mexico.
Belen, New Mexico
Portal, Arizona (Chi.ricahua Mountains).
Safford, Arizona (Mount Graham, Pinaleno Mountains).
Benson, Arizona (Dragoon Mountains).
Globe, Arizona (Salt River Peak, near Lake Roosevelt).
Phoenix, Arizona (South Mountain Park, South Mountains).
Punkin Center, Arizona (Haystack Butte).
Sunflower, Arizona (Sycamore Creek and Diamond Mountain).
Cordes Junction, Arizona (Aqua Fria National Monument). [Editor's Note: This is near Arcosanti, an experimental town founded on the principle of arcology—ecological architecture—by the architect Paolo Soleri.]
Holbrook, Arizona (Painted Desert).
Payson-Heber, Arizona (Colcord Mountain).

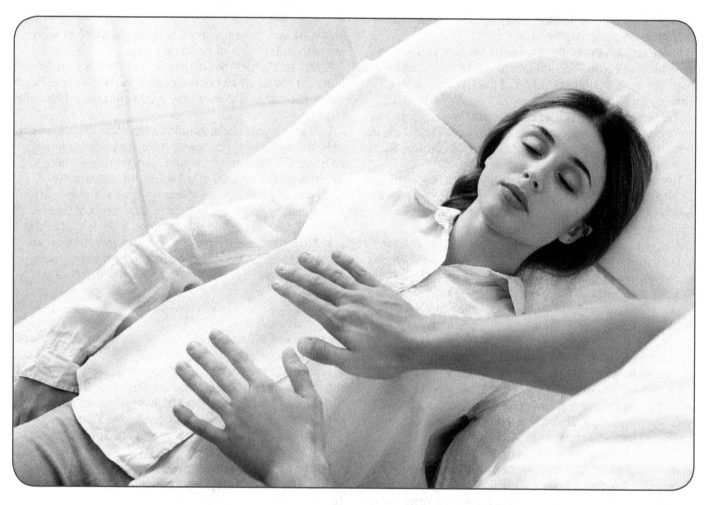

Energy Balancing
Energy work, or energy balancing, is a helpful technique to integrate Ray Forces
throughout the human aura. Choose a seasoned practitioner to assist you.

Saint Germain's Teachings on Golden City Rays

Ray Forces enter each Golden City through the apex under the direction of the Great Central Sun. These energies move in a circular motion and are disbursed by a process of emanation and radiation.

Individuals who seek to strengthen, integrate, or purify a Ray Force can achieve this goal by living near the apex or star of a Golden City Vortex. This produces the following results:

As one begins to work with Ray Forces, his or her energies function homeopathically, meaning a little of a Ray 's healing energy goes a long way. Therefore, Saint Germain suggests practicing patience with the integration process. Deliberately living in a Golden City to absorb a specific Ray Force will take time.

When new energy is first absorbed, the opposite results are often experienced. For instance, in Gobean, which focuses the energies of the Blue Ray, disharmony takes the place of harmony. According to Saint Germain, this is akin to personal spiritual purification—cleansing the astral field of unwanted thoughts, feelings, and past experiences.

Do not become alarmed—things may worsen before they improve. As the Ray Force integrates with Light Bodies, energies align light frequencies and vibrations with the Ray 's inherent power and force-field. Accordingly, seekers may also experience the need for more sleep as the body adjusts. Disharmonious relationships and other physical anomalies are also common.

The integration process is basically the same in all Golden Cities. The difference, however, is the Ray. Students may have different experiences, depending on the specific action and Divine Purpose of the Ray of a particular Golden City Vortex.

Ray activity affects the surrounding environment, including the Animal, Vegetable, Mineral, and Elemental Kingdoms contained in Golden City Vortices.

Breathwork is a great tool. Use it to integrate the Ray Force from the Light Bodies with the physical body. Chakra Breathing is a simple yet effective form of breathwork.

Energy work—or Energy Balancing—can also produce positive Ray Force integration. [Editor's Note: Types of Energy Balancing include the Four Pillars Technique, based on Ascended Master teachings; the Brennan Healing Science Technique, developed by NASA physicist, Barbara Brennan; Core Energetics, developed by John Pierrakos, M.D.; Reiki, developed by Buddhist, Mikao Usui; and Healing Touch, developed by holistic nurse Janet Mentgen.]

According to Saint Germain, various DNA, mixed genetics, and Karmas from past lifetimes may create challenges when identifying and assessing a student's dominant Ray Force. In these cases it may be necessary to utilize the energies of more than one Golden City Vortex to identify the Ascension process of an initiate. Most often, personal choices, preferences, and inclinations will reveal an individual's dominant Ray Force, disclosing its harmonizing yet balancing service.

Humanity has been subject to many embodiments on Earth. As a result, each individual has experienced different combinations of Ray Forces and a variety of genetic and racial types over time. This incarnated wisdom enhances the self-knowledge of the soul and the ability to work with light and sound.

In Saint Germain's Golden City of Wahanee, the Violet Ray creates a Divine Intervention, one that that releases cellular fear from the physical and Light Bodies via the following process:

The Violet Ray first works on the Solar Plexus Chakra, transmuting energies associated with death consciousness and cellular fear.

This process can drastically affect the physical body, causing flu-like symptoms and intestinal upset.

In its beginning stages, the Violet Ray galvanizes the Heart Chakra, moving energies along the Kundalini to the Crown Chakra—this is where the Ray 's higher purpose begins.

Saint Germain's decree to transmute death consciousness with the Violet Ray is "Down with death! Conscious immortality, arise!"

Saint Germain reminds students that healing is about repairing the body, the mind, the spirit, and the soul. Initiates can find this type of rejuvenation in Shalahah (Idaho and Montana, United States). This is where the Green Ray of Healing is located.

The Green Ray fosters revivification on many levels, including spiritual consciousness. It also repairs humanity's separation from God—or the Creator. As this level of healing progresses and is accepted from within, an individual will experience the Oneship. After this initiatory process, the chela is ready to move toward New Dimensions.

As the body, mind, and spirit are brought into balance and harmony, the result is natural abundance. Saint Germain encourages students who wish to manifest abundance and prosperity in their lives to travel to the Golden City of Shalahah. "Align yourself to the Green Ray," he says. Saint Germain also claims that this process deeply affects Heart and Solar Plexus energies. Growth and development culminate in true abundance and prosperity.

Safety. Overidentification with physical materialness makes one feel unsafe. "Safety is truly a matter of the heart."

Abundance streams forth into our lives by cultivating clarity and living in beauty (balance). "Abundance streams forth with clarity and beauty."

Ascension Energies of the Golden City of Klehma are similar to Shalahah; however, the White Ray assists the individual during the final release of the death urge. The White Ray completes the initiatory process that was instigated by the Violet Ray and Green Ray.

HU-man Power

Initiation and the Golden Cities

Spiritual migration is not a static process and virtuosity is never fully achieved. The journey can take a lifetime. Once a student or chela masters the spiritual migration of one Golden City, he or she may advance to other Golden Cities to experience the Ray Forces, Master Teachers, qualities, and characteristics within. Every Vortex embodies explicit spiritual teachings that are designed to reveal the presence of each Ray Force, its promise of personal integration, and the Mastery of its distinct spiritual process.

In all, fifty-one Golden Cities are located around the planet. Three individual sequences, or Ascension methods, consist of seventeen cities each, which are listed below.

Seventeen Initiations of the *I AM America Map*: Realization of and integration with the I AM Presence and establishment of the I AM Race.

	Golden City	Location	Presiding Ray	Master Teacher
1.	GOBEAN	United States	Blue Ray	El Morya
2.	MALTON	United States	Ruby-Gold Ray	Kuthumi
3.	WAHANEE	United States	Violet Ray	Saint Germain
4.	SHALAHAH	United States	Green Ray	Sananda
5.	KLEHMA	United States	White Ray	Serapis Bey
6.	PASHACINO	Canada	Green Ray	Soltec
7.	EABRA	Canada, US	Violet Ray	Portia
8.	JEAFRAY	Canada	Violet Ray	Archangel Zadkiel
9.	UVERNO	Canada	Pink Ray	Paul the Venetian
10.	YUTHOR	Greenland	Green Ray	Hilarion
11.	MARNERO	Mexico	Green Ray	Mary
12.	ASONEA	Cuba	Yellow Ray	Peter the Everlasting
13.	ANDEO	Peru, Brazil	Pink-Gold Rays	The First Sister, Goddess Meru, Beloved Constan
14.	BRAHAM	Brazil	Pink Ray	The Second Sister
15.	TEHEKOA	Argentina	Pink-Violet Rays	The Third Sister
16.	CROTESE	Costa Rica,	Pink Ray	Paul the Devoted
17.	JEHOA	New Atlantis Panama [The Eastern side of this Vortex is present-day Saint Lucia Island in the Caribbean.]	Violet Ray	Kuan Yin

Seventeen Initiations of the *Greening Map*: Personal and transpersonal healing of the feminine to balance Mother Earth and awaken her ecological alchemy.

	Golden City	Location	Presiding Ray	Master Teacher
1.	ADJATAL	Pakistan, Afghanistan, India	Blue and Gold Rays	Lord Himalya
2.	PURENSK	Russia, China	Blue, Yellow and Pink Rays	Faith, Hope, Charity
3.	PRANA	India	Pink Ray	Archangel Chamuel
4.	ZASKAR	China	White Ray	Reya
5.	GOBI	China	Ruby-Gold Ray	Lord Meru / Archangel Uriel
6.	ARCTURA	China	Violet Ray	Arcturus / Diana
7.	NOMAKING	China	Yellow Ray	Cassiopea and Minerva
8.	PRESCHING	China	Yellow Ray	Archangel Jophiel
9.	KANTAN	China, Russia	Green Ray	Great Divine Mother and Archangel Raphael
10.	HUE	Russia	Violet Ray	Lord Guatama
11.	SIRCALWE	Russia	White Ray	Group of Twelve
12.	ARKANA	Russia	White Ray	Archangel Gabriel
13.	GREIN	New Zealand	Green Ray	Viseria
14.	CLAYJE	Australia	Pink Ray	Orion
15.	ANGELICA	Tasmania	Pink Ray	Angelica
16.	SHHEAHAH	Australia	White Ray	Astrea
17.	FRON	Australia	Blue Ray	Desiree

Most numbers that show up in Ascended Master teachings have special metaphysical significance, and the number seventeen is no different. To humanity, it represents the Star of the Magi and the birth of Christ Consciousness. Ancient Chaldean numerology refers to the seventeen as the eight-pointed Star of Venus. Meanwhile, the seventeenth card of the Tarot—the Stars—signifies the Divine Powers of Nature.

Ascended Masters claim the nascent energies of the Christ Consciousness physically appear through three sets of seventeen Golden Cities; individuals who aptly apply esoteric principles begin this important development. The three sets of seventeen Golden Cities represent three separate spiritual techniques to rouse the internal sacred fire and actualize the Divine God Man—the HU-man.

While many Ascended Master students may choose to perfect the twenty-one movements of Spiritual Migration contained in a singular Golden City Vortex, the Master Teachers claim that any of the three sequential Ascension practices will quickly advance the chela. Perhaps the first initiatory sequence is considered the most straightforward; and most of the Golden Cities in this series are accessible.

Seventeen Initiations of I AM America

The Seventeen Initiations of I AM America is a spiritual process that helps students awaken and realize the power of the I AM Presence. As personal Mastery and command of the I AM Presence is achieved, individuals will join together to reestablish North America, Central America, and South

Seventeen Initiations of the *Map of Exchanges*: Self-realization of the HU-man through the exchange of heavenly energies on Earth that usher in the Golden Age.

	Golden City	Location	Presiding Ray	Master Teacher
1.	STIENTA	Iceland	Blue Ray	Nada
2.	DENASHA	Scotland	Yellow Ray	Nada
3.	AMERIGO	Spain	Gold Ray	Godfre
4.	GRUECHA	Norway, Sweden	Blue Ray	Hercules
5.	BRAUN	Germany, Poland, Czechoslovakia	Yellow Ray	Victory
6.	AFROM	Hungary, Romania	White Ray	SeRay and Claire
7.	GANAKRA	Turkey	Green Ray	Vista
8.	MESOTAMP	Turkey, Iran, Iraq	Yellow Ray	Mohammed
9.	SHEHEZ	Iran, Afghanistan	Ruby-Gold Ray	Tranquility
10.	GANDAWAN	Algeria	Ruby-Gold Ray	Kuthumi
11.	KRESHE	Botswana, Namibia	Ruby-Gold Ray	Lord of Nature and Amaryllis
12.	PEARLANU	Madagascar	Violet Ray	Lotus
13.	UNTE	Tanzania, Kenya	Ruby-Gold	Donna Grace
14.	LARAITO	Ethiopia	Yellow Ray	Lanto and Laura
15.	MOUSEE	New Lemuria [Present-day Pacific Ocean, Northwest of Hawaii]	Aquamarine-Gold Ray	Kona
16.	DONJAKEY	New Lemuria [Present-day Pacific Ocean, Northwestern Hawaiian Islands, Midway Islands]	Aquamarine-Gold Ray	Pacifica
17.	CRESTA	Antarctica [Antarctic Peninsula]	Aquamarine-Gold Ray	Archangel Crystiel

America as ONE expression of the I AM Race. An anagram derived from the word America, the I AM race is the prophesied new breed of man destined to serve as the nucleus of the New Times. The Violet Ray, the Pink Ray, and the Green Ray are the principal Rays of I AM America Golden Cities. The Archangel Zadkiel and various Master Teachers and Elohim serve as stewards of these Vortex cities.

Seventeen Initiations of the Greening Map

Mother Earth plays a central role in the Greening Map of Asia and Australia. The migratory path of these Golden Cities is intended to restore the Earth Mother physically, emotionally, and mentally by balancing prevailing oppressive male energies with the influence of the feminine. White and Pink Rays dominate this sequence, which means spiritual initia-

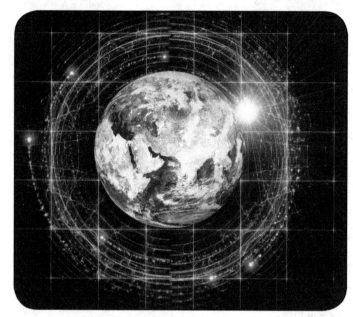

Many types of grids cover Mother Earth and include dynamic lei-lines, power points, inter-dimensional portals, and spiritual retreats.

Seventeen Initiations of the Map of Exchanges

The initiatory progression of the Map of Exchanges, which includes Europe, Africa, and the Middle East, is perhaps the most difficult spiritual sequence of all. It requires the guiding wisdom and focus of the Yellow Ray —the Divine Guru. The interplay of the Gold Ray in cosmic partnership with the Ruby-Gold and Aquamarine-Gold Rays helps the student realize the Yellow Ray 's hidden power, or Shatki and the Divine HUman. The progression of Golden Cities in this particular map is prophesied to anchor heaven on Earth and usher in God-actualized humanity. It is the birth of Unana. Throughout the seventeen Golden Cities of the Map of Exchanges, a student's Fourth- and Fifth-Dimensional Light Bodies are trained to step down heavenly energies that transmute and exchange with energies of the Third Dimension. It is an extensive Ascension process: doubt is exchanged for knowledge; fear is exchanged for courage; hate is exchanged for trust; and darkness is exchanged for light. Energies from the Galactic Center permeate the seventeen Golden Cities contained in the Map of Exchanges, lifting humanity and the planet toward the prophesied New Times and Golden Age. As Earth progresses toward the final exchange of enlightened energy, the heavenly filaments of the Galactic Web will illuminate the entire globe. This web of enlightened awareness is prophesied to link and expand individual consciousness beyond this planet and onward, toward a Galactic Consciousness that embraces the lokas—or the levels of spiritual development on all planets. Archangel Michael and Archangel Crystiel oversee the spiritual Ascension of humanity and Earth.

When encountering inaccessible Golden Cities, such as the submerged New Atlantis and New Lemuria, travel as close as possible to the Golden City's location to absorb spiritual energies. Students can also use the Star Meditation technique, which is as follows: Enter the Star of one Golden City Vortex and access the energies of any Golden City via the Fourth- and Fifth-Dimensional Golden City Network. This technique, however, is not for the novice. It requires patience and practice. [For more information see Points of Perception: Golden City Activations and Subtle Energies, Golden City Activation.]

tion focuses on the balance and integration of personal and collective feminine energies. The journey of healing through the seventeen Golden Cities of the Greening Map awakens Fourth- and Fifth-Dimensional attributes of Mother Earth to the magical and sensual expression of Ecological Alchemy. This spiritual practice opens initiates to the ONE and forges an indelible connection to the Earth Mother. This Ascension method is crucial in calibrating Earth's consciousness to the incarnating New Children. Meanwhile, many new and different species of flora and fauna are prophesied to inhabit Earth throughout the New Times. The Golden Cities of the Greening Map may instigate the healing of the tyrannical male energies—in governments, religions, cultures, and economies—that have dominated Earth's timely passage in Kali Yuga. As individuals integrate and apply the energies of these feminine Golden Cities, the global culture will heal the pain of harsh, exploitive power and open the Divine Heart of Humanity. Five Archangels serve in the seventeen Golden Cities of the Greening Map and assist the awakening of Earth's light grids and lei lines. Archangel Chamuel, Archangel Jophiel, Archangel Raphael, Archangel Gabriel, and Archangel Uriel comprise this cadre of spiritual stewards.

Determining the Dominant Ray Force

The presence of a Ray is usually obvious; an individual's dominant Ray can be expressed several ways. Physical appearance, personality traits, habits, and characteristics often provide many clues. A tall, thin, austere man shows the influence of the Saturnine Blue Ray; a beautiful, feminine woman embodies the White Ray of Venus, while a talkative, information-oriented personality reveals the Mercurial Green Ray. Sometimes, however, determining the dominance of a Ray Force is difficult. That's because several Rays may be vying for predominance in a person's life patterns. In this case Vedic Astrologers turn to Jyotish techniques to glean additional information, specifically *Shadbala* and *Atmakaraka*.

Shadbala measures the ascendency of a planet in an individual's horoscope. The power of a Ray is calculated by determining the strength of six planetary factors.

1. Positional strength (or the sign a planet resides in a chart);
2. Directional strength (or cardinal direction: North, East, South, West);
3. Temporal strength (based on time and date of birth);
4. The strength of motion (forward, direct, stationary, or retrograde);
5. The visual radiance of a planet (in this sequence: Sun, Moon, Venus, Jupiter, Mercury, Mars, and Saturn);
6. Aspectual strength (the strength a planet gains from being in proximity to other planets or Ray Forces).

By applying Shadbala, a particular planet and its Ray Force always gain prominence. The Ray that is discovered is considered the dominant Ray of that individual's current lifetime.

The Atmakaraka, or soul indicator, is the most important planet and Ray Force in a person's chart. The influence of the significator of self often reveals the disposition of an individual who embodies the natural aptitude, qualities, and characteristics of a particular Ray or planet. Some esoteric astrologers say the Atmakaraka indicates the soul group (or Star seed) or Ray Family of origin, which defines the soul's purpose. The planet positioned most powerfully in Shadbala is often seen as the Ray carrying the individual's obvious aspirations in a particular lifetime, whereas the Atmakaraka, also referred to as the Atma, indicates the essence of the soul and its core identity. For instance, an individual with the Sun

Soul's Purpose

(Ruby-Gold Ray) in the highest position in Shadbala may be driven toward leadership roles; however, the position of the Atmakaraka will indicate the area of leadership. For instance, an individual with a Mercury (Green Ray) Atma may prevail in commerce, business, science, or teaching; matriarchs or patriarchs may have a Moon (Pink Ray) Atma; and those who lead by their counsel or spiritual wisdom may possess a Jupiter (Yellow Ray) Atma. The power of a Ray relies on strengths and weaknesses to direct the course of lives and sculpt individual experiences. Low-strength Ray forces denote areas that may need improvement or refinement in this lifetime, known by Vedic Astrologers as Gnati Karaka—an astrological benchmark that defines a person's greatest obstacles and challenges in this lifetime.

The strongest Ray Force and Atma placement will also determine a person's preference for spiritual development and the most effective techniques for spiritual liberation. A strong Sun can provide great devotion; a powerful Moon, the ability for unconditional love; a well-placed Venus, a proclivity for forgiveness; Saturn fosters discipline, detachment, and self-negation; Jupiter provides the gifts of listening, direction, and advice (good teachers—gurus); and a solid Mercury offers the intelligence to grasp spiritual subtlety, nuance, and the ability to quickly integrate.

Angel I Will Follow You
Jacek Malczewski, 1901.

Golden City Names

The names of the Golden Cities are unusual, and each City's meaning is secret knowledge closely held by the Master Teachers. Through the years of our work with the Ascended Masters, several definitions of the names of Golden Cities have emerged, but never in great detail. Yet, each curious name is important, and reveals hidden qualities and spiritual characteristics of each Golden City. Some occultists refer to the veiled language of the mystics as Owaspee—the native tongue of Angels. The Divine Language, or the language of the Gods, is referred to in religious traditions including the Adamic language—the language spoken by Adam and Eve; Hebrew—the Jewish language of God; Greek, the mathematical language of harmony; and Sanskrit, the Divine Language of the Gods through Vedic spiritual traditions.

Divine Languages are often known as form languages. My Vedic teacher once explained the etymology of Sanskrit as "a Mother tongue," similar to the syntax and semantics of computer languages. According to Vedic legend our entire Earth was programmed, or created, through the spoken words of Sanskrit. Speaking a form language is powerful and commanding, and each spoken syllable has the ability to exactly create in form and substance its subject. Perhaps the creation story of Genesis says it best, "Then God said, 'Let there be light,' and there was light." (Genesis 1:3 New American Standard Bible)

The names and meanings of the Golden Cities, which originate in the causal plane of the Fifth Dimension, carry their emotive light and sound through the feeling worlds of the Fourth Dimension and integrate their activity to evolve the HU-man of Earth's Third Dimension. Golden City names are founded on the multiple languages of Earth. Their individual syllables are based on archetypal words from many cultures of the world, including ancient Sanskrit, Greek, Persian, Phoenician, and the lost tongue of Moriori. Their sounds also include Native American languages: Algonquian, Navajo, Shoshoni, and Cahto. Surprisingly, modern languages appear in the syllables of the names of Golden Cities: the universal language of peace, Esperanto; Tolkein's fictional language of Middle Earth, Elfish; and the contemporary, linguistic Minimalist Language.

The sounds and meanings of the Golden Cities's names are the evocations and myths for the New Times. Their resonance is the hope and the aspiration for progressive, positive change on behalf of humanity and the Earth. The theosophist George William Russell wrote, "The mind of man is made in the image of Deity, and the elements of speech are related to the powers in his mind and through it to the being of the Oversoul. These true roots of language are few, alphabet and roots being identical."

Meanings of the Fifty-One Golden City Vortices

ADJATAL: The Big Rainbow derives its meaning from the Suabo-Indonesian word *adja* ("big") and the Pashto-Pakistanian word *tal* ("rainbow"). The Golden City of Adjatal is located in Pakistan, Afghanistan, and India; the historical Khyber Pass (the ancient Silk Road) is located on the Western side of this Vortex city.

AFROM: This Golden City name means, "A Devotion." This meaning originates with the word from, which in German, Norwegian, and Swedish means "pious" or "devoted." The Ascended Masters claim this Golden City also means "to affirm."

AMERIGO: This European Golden City is Spanish for "I AM Race."

ANDEO: The Golden City of the South American Andes is likely named for this mountain range; however, the source of this Golden City of the Feminine is rooted in the Albanian word *anda*, which means "strong desire" and the Huli (New Guinea) word *andia*, which means "mother." Andeo's meaning translates into this phrase: "the Mother of Desire."

ANGELICA: The Native American Algonquian word *ca* means "at present" or "present"; therefore, Angelica's full meaning is "Angel Present," or "Angels at Present."

ARKANA: The nineteenth century created language of peace—Esperanto; and the Polish language both state that the word arkana means "Mystery."

ASONEA: The Golden City of Cuba and ancient Atlantis derives its meaning from the pristine Ason River of the Cantabria province in Spain and its mythological race of supernatural undines—the Xanas.

BRAHAM: Braham is also known as the Second of Three Sisters who preserves a maternal radiance over South America. Braham is the feminine version of Brahma, and this Golden City meaning is the "Mother of the New Manu."

BRAUN: The Golden City of Germany, Poland, and Czechoslovakia means "the Shining Strong One."

CLAYJE: Dialects from the Netherlands create this Golden City's name through the word *kla*—"clear." The word *je* in Bosnian, Croatian, Serbian, and Slovak languages means "is." The combination of these words constructs this Australian Golden City's meaning: "Is Clear."

CRESTA: In Spanish, Italian, and Brazilian Portuguese the word cresta means "the ridge or peak."

CROTESE: Located in the Cradleland of Central America, this Golden City means "the Attentive Cradle." Its meaning is derived from the French *cro*—"cradle," and the Etruscan *tes*—"to care for or pay attention."

DENASHA: This Golden City derives its meaning from the modern English name *Denesa*, which means the "Mountain of Zeus." This mythological Greek father of both Gods and men is also known in Roman myths as Jupiter, an ideal symbol for this European Golden City of the Yellow Ray.

DONJAKEY: Located on new lands prophesied to rise from the Pacific Ocean in the New Times, this Golden City's name comes from the Italian word *don*—"gift," and the Indonesian word key—"tree." Donjakey means "Gift of Trees," and is associated with new species of flora prophesied to appear on Earth.

EABRA: "The Feminine in Eternal Balance." This name is a derivative of several words, namely *bra* or *bodice*, which means "the pair" or the "wearing of pairs." *Ea* has several meanings: in Frisian (German) ea means "ever," in Romanian ea means "she." The word pair numerically indicates two, a number associated with femininity and balance.

FRON: The meaning of this Australian Golden City is "throne" in Albanian. In the Creole language, *fron* means "pious" and "devoted." The combination of these definitions creates Fron's meaning: "the Devoted Throne."

GANAKRA: The ancient Turkish City of Ankara means "anchor" in Greek; in Portuguese gana means "desire"; and *kra* is a Creole word for "mind." Ganakra's combined meaning is "Desires Anchored by the Mind," or "Desires of the Mind."

GANDAWAN: From the Sanskrit word *Gondwanaland* means "Forest of the Gonds." Located over the Sahara Desert, this Golden City represents this ancient culture that claimed to survive in present-day India. Contemporary Gond legends mirror the emergence stories of Southwest Native American tribes, and the Gond Gods surfaced from a cave and were adopted by the Hindu Goddess Parvati (Divine Mother) and were assisted by their tribal Goddess Jangu Bai. According to myth, the Gonds emerged from their cave in four distinct groups.

GOBEAN: The Ascended Masters claim the Earth's first Golden City for the New Times means to "go beyond." However, Gobean's etymology suggests the meaning: "Go Pray." This phrase is derived from the word *bea* or *be*, which in Frisian (German) and Norwegian means "prayer."

GOBI: Named for the Great Desert of China, Gobi in Mongolian means "the waterless place." Ascended Masters claim the Golden City of Gobi is a step-down transformer for the energies of the Earth's first Golden City—Shamballa. Gobi's esoteric definition comes from the Chinese translation of "go—across," and *bi* in Indonesian (Abun, A Nden, and Yimbun dialects) means "star." The Golden City of Gobi means "Across the Star," or "Across the Freedom Star." ("Freedom Star" is a reference to Earth in her enlightened state.) Gobi aligns energies to the first Golden City of the New Times: Gobean.

GREIN: Grein is an Icelandic, Norwegian, and Swedish word which means "branch." The Ascended Masters maintain that the New Zealand Golden City of Grein means "the Green Branch"—a symbol of the peaceful olive branch.

GRUECHA: The Golden City name of Norway and Sweden is a Norwegian word and means "Hearth."

HUE: According to the Ascended Masters, the word *hue* invokes the Sacred Fire, the Violet Flame. In Tibetan dialects, however, the word *hue* or *hu* means "breath."

JEAFRAY: The Golden City of the Ever present Violet Flame meaning translates to "Yesterday's Brother." This is based on the Gaelic word *jea*, which means "yesterday"; the word *fra* is English for "Brother" (friar). Since Archangel Zadkiel and the Archeia Amethyst serve in this Vortex retreat, "Yesterday's Brother" is a reference to the work of Saint Germain—as Sanctus Germanus (the Holy Brother)—and the many other archetypes of consciousness who tirelessly work for humanity's freedom and Ascension through the use of the transmuting fire.

JEHOA: It may be that this Golden City's name is based upon the Tetragrammaton YHWH; however, the etymology of this sacred haven of the Caribbean is based on the Russian word *YA*—meaning "I AM"—and hoa, which means "friend," from the Tahitian, Hawaiian, Maori, and Rapa Nui (Easter Island) languages. This translation elevates the various interpretations of Jehovah, the jealous God into the uplifting phrase, "I AM Friend."

KANTAN: This Golden City of China and Russia derives its name from the English (Cornish) word *kan*—which means "song," and the Korean word *tan*, meaning "sweet." The full meaning of this spiritual Vortex is the "Sweet Song."

KLEHMA: The meaning of the fifth Golden City of the United States is based on several Native American words. The first syllable *kle* (pronounced clay) comes from the Navajo word klê-kai—which means "white." The second syllable *ma*, is a derivative of the Shoshoni word *mahoi*—around, or encircling. Klehma's esoteric definition is the "Circle of White."

KRESHE: This African Golden City is known to the Ascended Masters as the "Silent Star," an esoteric reference to Venus. *Kres* is also a Celtic word for "peace."

LARAITO: This Ethiopian Golden City's meaning is "Our Home." Laraito's definition comes from the Brazilian, Portuguese, and Spanish word for home—*lar*. *Ito* is a Tanzanian word for "ours."

MALTON: The Ascended Master Kuthumi's Golden City meaning is derived from the Phoenician word *maleth*—which means "a haven."

MARNERO: Mexico's Golden City's steward is Mother Mary and the first syllable of Marnero—*mar*—is a Spanish, Italian, and Portuguese word which means "sea" or "ocean." The remainder of the name—*nero* translates into *ner*, a Hebrew word for "candle." The Golden City of Marnero's meaning is the "Ocean of Candles."

MESOTAMP: The Golden City of Turkey, Iran, and Iraq is likely linked to the ancient word Mesopotamia, which means the "land between rivers." The higher meaning of Mesotamp, however, is linked to the New Guinea word *meso*—"Moon," and the Turkmen word, *tam*—"house." Mesotamp's meaning translates into the "House of the Moon."

MOUSEE: This Golden City for the New Times means the "Ocean of Fish." This spiritual haven, prophesied to appear near Hawaii, combines the New Guinea word *mou*—"fish," and the Afrikaan word *see*—"sea" or "ocean." New flora and fauna is prophesied to appear as Earth enters the New Times.

NOMAKING: This Chinese Golden City means "Name of the King." Its meaning is based on the word *noma* (or *nama*) and in many languages ranging from Italian to Sanskrit simply means "name."

PASHACINO: "The Passionate Spirit." This Canadian Golden City's meaning is derived from the English word for "passion"—*pash*, and the Kurdish and Turkish word for "spirit"—*cin*.

PEARLANU: Madagascar's Golden City's meaning is based on the Malagasy (the national language of Madagascar) word *lanosina*, which means "to be swum in." Pearlanu's meaning translates to "Swimming in Pearls."

PRANA: Located in the heart of India, this Golden City of the Pink Ray meaning is "Life-giving Energy."

PRESCHING: This Chinese Golden City's meaning is linked to its topography. *Pres* is an English word which means "meadow," and ching is a Native American (Cahto) word for "timber and forest." Presching means the "City of Meadows, Grasslands, and Forests."

PURENSK: This Golden City means "Pure Intelligence" or the "Pure Message." This Russian and Chinese Golden City derives its esoteric meaning from the Danish, English, German, and French name *pur*—"pure," and the Turkish word, esk, for "intelligence" or "message."

SHALAHAH: Sananda is the steward of this United States Golden City which in Sanskrit means a "Sacred Place Indeed!" The syllables break down with these meanings: *shala*—"sacred place", "sanctuary"; *hah*—"indeed."

SHEHEZ: This Golden City located in Iran and Afghanistan is a Persian word that means "large," or "grand."

SHEAHAH: The Ascended Masters claim that the meaning of this Australian Golden City is, "I AM as ONE." The etymology of this Vortex meaning is undoubtedly related to the Feminine Energies prophesied to dominate and direct the New Times. The syllable *aha* in Tanzanian and Uganda means "here"; in Czechoslovakian aha stands for "I see." Therefore Sheahah's hidden meaning is actually prophetic: "She is here," or "She, I see."

SIRCALWE: The Russian Golden City of the White Ray derives its sacred name from the Turkish and Chinese languages—*sir*, which means "secret"; and the Elfish

language of Middle Earth—cal, meaning "light." The word *we* in the English, Korean, and Italian language is defined as "ours." These languages combine to give this Golden City Vortex name its meaning: "Our Secret Light."

STIENTA: This Golden City's name means "the path" in Norwegian.

TEHEKOA: Since this Golden City represents one of the Three Sister Golden Cities of South America, its meaning springs from the lost Moriori language and the Hebrew word Teku'a: "the City of Tents," "secures the tents." These meanings merge and Tehekoa means the "Wise Woman who Secures the City."

UNTE: This Golden City—located in Tanzania and Kenya—means in Brazilian, Spanish, and Portuguese "to anoint."

UVERNO: The Canadian Golden City of the Pink Ray translates in Slovak to "trust well."

WAHANEE: The third Golden City of the United States derives its name from Wahabu, the Nigerian name for the "God of Love." The etymological meaning of the final syllable *nee* in English, Italian, and French is "born." Wahanee's esoteric meaning is the "God of Love is born."

YUTHOR: In minimalist language, *Yu* means "union." Thor is the Scandinavian God of Thunder—"Power." The Golden City of Greenland's hidden meaning is the "Power of Union."

ZASKAR: This Golden City of the White Ray derives its meaning from the Czech and Slovak word *zas*—"again," "over again"; and the Basque word *kar*, which means "flame." This Chinese Golden City means the "Repeating Flame."

[Editor's Note: The Webster's Online Dictionary with Multilingual Thesaurus Translation was used extensively in creating this translation.]

El Morya's Historical Teachings on Shamballa and the Golden Cities

- The Golden City of Gobean aligns to, or is associated with the Golden City of Gobi—located in China. This Vortex covers the geophysical area which was once the earthly location of the fabled ancient Golden City of Shamballa.
- All of the Golden Cities of the Earth are interconnected.
- The Blue Ray Force is said to have brought Earth's first Golden City into physical manifestation. While many of Shamballa's first inhabitants came from the planet Venus, Mercury also played a significant role in populating the opulent city. Other planets from different solar systems were also involved in the population of Shamballa. The Ascended Masters refer to this galaxy-migrating populace as the Blue Race.
- Members of the Blue Race were immortal; death did not exist.
- The deterioration of Shamballa came about as the populace was invaded by other planets (Star seeds). Through this influence, the physical genetics and spiritual teachings of immortality were weakened and the Death Consciousness grew in strength. This brought the first disharmony, and thereafter strife and conflict spread through the once harmonious city. As the emanation of Shamballa deteriorated, the Masters of Wisdom decided to move the Golden City. However, this time the City of Perfection was physically built in such a manner that Shamballa was hidden; and entrance was given only to those who purposely sought its radiance and perfected vibration. Once again the city flourished as an abode for the immortals.
- According to El Morya, perfection is an emanation: "Seek your own perfection. (First) idealize it as a perfect crystalline thought in your mind."
- The second Golden City of Shamballa grew in energy and, through the principle of conductivity, once again influenced the Earth with perfection and harmony.

- Shamballa's second incarnation was again maligned by its citizens. This time the city's enlightened populace, who had risen in consciousness along with the venerated immortals, engaged in material excesses. The leaders of Shamballa made the decision to again destroy and rebuild the Golden City of Shamballa. However, the entrance to the new Golden City of Shamballa would not be built on the physical plane.
- The immortal leader Sanat Kumara set forth the edict for Shamballa's restructuring on the ethereal immortal plane, assuring that only those who had properly developed their Light Bodies (Astral Body) could enter the sacred city.
- Ashrams were established throughout Eastern Asia to train future members of the Shamballa community in the essential fundamentals of higher consciousness, which are the essential keys to open its Golden Gates.
- As the ethereal Crystal City of Shamballa flourished, directly underneath its radiating fifth-dimensional aura a new civilization of the Gobi Desert thrived. According to El Morya, this is the spiritual Law of "As above, so below," and this ancient culture advanced spiritual knowledge and healing techniques.
- The physical civilization that was once embraced by the golden ethers of the City of Shamballa disappeared upon Earth's entrance into the age of lesser galactic light: Kali Yuga.
- By the order of leader Sanat Kumara, the city limits of the Golden City of Shamballa were restricted to the ethereal Fifth Dimension; however, remnants of this once physically opulent metropolis can still be detected by archaeologists. The energies of Shamballa intertwined with the ancient light fields of the once physical civilization of Gobi. The process of ethereal consciousness, emanation, and conductivity produced the Golden City Vortex of Gobi.
- The Golden City of Gobi aligns to the First Golden City for the New Times: Gobean. Golden Cities represent a co-creation of Heaven and Earth. [Editor's Note: The Golden City of Gobi is located over the

Horses and Sand Dunes. Gobi Desert, Mongolia

Qilian Shan Mountains, with the Gobi Desert to the North. The word Qilian is pronounced Chee-layn, and closely resembles the word chela, a term commonly used by the Master Teachers which means disciple. Qilian is a Xiongnu word, and in this language means sky. Qilian Shan Peak is 5,547 meters, or approximately 18,199 feet high—the center, or apex of the Gobi Vortex and one of the highest mountain peaks in the Chinese Gansu Province.[5]

- The Golden City of Gobean and the Golden City of Gobi are connected, not only through the grid of worldwide Golden Cities, but through a spiritual, etheric connection. According to El Morya, meditation performed in the Golden City of Gobean can instantly transport your body. This is due to the level of perfection present in Shamballa. The process of bi-location is achieved through the Mastery of Perfection as perfect consciousness streams into body, mind, and heart.

- Through accessing the Blue Ray of Truth in the Golden City of Gobean, El Morya teaches that through meditation students and chelas can access Akashic Records of ancient times and civilizations. This allows information to be relayed seamlessly to fit each individual's educational spiritual developmental level. This technique circumvents recorded history slanted by another's perspective or beliefs that may dilute the effect of the information for the student. As each student or chela receives direct information, they also obtain ever-important experience.

- The Golden City of Gobean is permeated with the historical Akashic records of the Earth.

- According to El Morya, the lands that now comprise the physical proximity of the Gobean Vortex were once visited by the spiritual teacher and King of Egypt, Akhenaten (1351–1334 BC). Since he was able to project his consciousness to the higher planes, it is claimed that Akhenaten traveled in his Light Bodies to the ancient American Southwest and shared his teachings with the Native Peoples. This was one of the first initiatory preparations of Gobean, and from these earliest spiritual sparks, the Vortex grew in energy and power. Today, the Golden City of Gobean aligns in historical provenance to the Ancient Giza Plateau.

- According to El Morya, Shamballa is seen by the Master Teachers as the "Hall of Wisdom," and through its venerated teachings of the eons, it has guided humanity's spiritual growth and evolution.

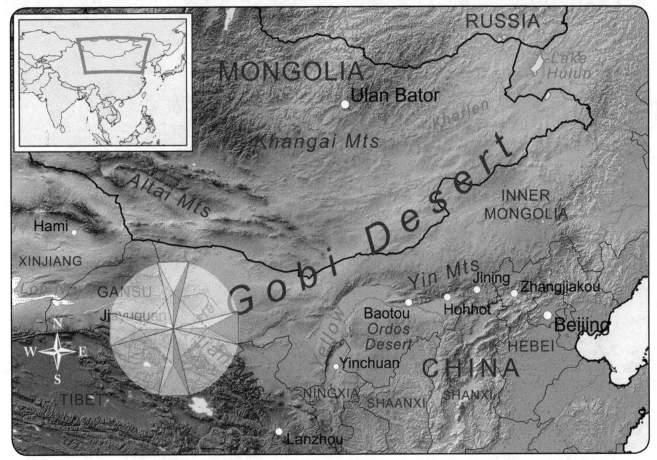

Golden City of Gobi

The *Golden City of Gobi* is located in China and Mongolia: Tibet is to the Southwest and the Gobi Desert to the North and Northeast. These areas are the People's Republic of China (PRC) Provinces and Administrative Divisions of: Gansu; Qinghai; Inner Mongolia. (Golden City Figure not to scale.)

Gobi Desert

Theosophists claim this desert region of China was once a fertile plain which bordered an inland sea and contained the "Sacred Island." This esoteric geology is said to date back to the times of Atlantis, Rama, and the Ancient Uiger civilization—an evolved culture that asserts the prehistoric use of aircraft (Vimanas).[1] The Sons of Will and Yoga took shelter on the mythological Sacred Island as humanity fell into states of lower consciousness. Theosophical texts define this time in humanity's history as one when, "Daityas prevailed over the Devas and humanity became black with sin." In Hinduism, Daityas were a race of evil giants, who resisted the Gods, or immortals; the Devas are the immortals who maintained the sanctity of Divine Creation. Cataclysm

---

1. Map Base Art: Wikimedia Commons, Kmusser, Map showing the Gobi Desert and surround area. Elevation data from SRTM, all other features from Vector Map (2011).

Edgar Cayce
The famous psychic predicted a Golden City would be discovered in the future Gobi Desert.

The Lineage of Shamballa to the Golden Cities

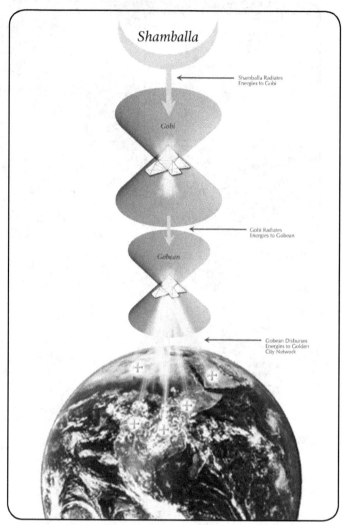

drained the inland sea, leaving the once bountiful land a wild and arid desert of mountains and sand.[2]

Prior to this catastrophe, the spiritual elders reestablished their school and library of teachings, known as the Thirteenth School in present-day Tibet. Occultists claim the Great White Brotherhood evolved from this early Mystery School and the famed philosopher Lao Tzu (born 604 BC) journeyed to its western headquarters—the mythological land of Hsi Wang Mu.[3]

Psychic Edgar Cayce referenced the Gobi Desert in many of his life readings and identified this area as the "Sun Land." Cayce also referred to a city buried under the desert sands as the City of Gold and prophesied its future discovery. His readings claimed that the Gobi civilization mirrored the prehistoric mound-builders of North America, and their architecture included terraced buildings and temples. Today the A.R.E.—the Association for Research and Enlightenment founded in 1931 by Cayce—alleges that a small ethnic group from the Gobi contains X Haplotype DNA, theorized to be related to the Atlantean Genetic Type, and a genetic link to the North American Iroquois tribe, ancient Iberia, and the Basques.[4, 5]

The Gobi Desert traverses Northern and Northwestern China and Southern Mongolia; it is the fifth largest desert in the world. The Himalaya mountain range creates the rain shadow that blocks rain from falling in the Gobi.

Lineage of Shamballa to the Golden Cities
This illustration depicts the flow of spiritual energies from Shamballa to the Golden City of Gobi (China); the energies step-down from the Golden City of Gobi to the Golden City of Gobean (Southwest, US); the Golden City of Gobean disburses the energies of Shamballa to all other Golden Cities through the Golden City Network. Fifth dimensional energies flow through a spiritual grid on the Earth and enter through the apex (center) of each Golden City Vortex.

2. Encyclopedic Theosophical Glossary, http://www.theosociety.org/pasadena/etglos/etg-hp.htm, (2011).
3. Top 10 Civilizations with Advanced Technology, http://ufo.whipnet.org/creation/ancient.advanced.civilizations/index.html, (2011).
4. Gobi Desert Mysteries, *China Pyramids and Mounds,*http://www.edgarcayce.org/AncientMysteriesTemp/gobidesert.html, (2011).
5. Modern Genetic Research Confirming Cayce's Story, http://www.edgarcayce.org/AncientMysteriesTemp/geneticevidence.html, (2011).

Akhenaten

Born in 1388 BC, the only surviving son of Amenhotep III, the King of Upper and Lower Egypt, Akhenaten strove to reform the Egyptian priesthood and unite the peoples of Egypt through a monotheist God, Aten. United in marriage at the age of twelve to the Egyptian Queen Nefertiti, Akhenaten was known to have fragile health, was a gentle and loving regent with an inclination to visions and dreams.

At the age of nineteen, Akhenaten broke with the corrupt priesthood of Amen. Historians record this fracture within the ancient Egyptian socio-political scene for several reasons. First, Amenhotep IV, known as Akhenaten, spiritually identified with the principles of Aten—symbolized by the Solar Disc—as a deity of one truth, and one light, who could unite the many secular deities of Egypt. Akhenaten—who had discovered the universal spiritual substance of light, good, and truth while meditating on the cosmic Sun—realized that, "the Sun did not shine upon Egypt alone, nor did its light and heat protect only the cities where it was honored. Its Rays shone beyond the mountains and beyond the deserts. Its light cheered the barbarians and sustained even the enemies of Egypt."[1]

Akhenaten's unfolding consciousness of the ONE and the unity of all life led him to issue orders that the name of Amen, and its implication of hierarchical adversity, be expunged from every inscription in Egypt. His break with the polytheistic religion of the kingdom created problems throughout the cultural state of Egypt, especially in ancient Thebes, the venerated City of his ancestors. To further implement his faith of Aten and his break from the traditional ancient faiths, Akhenaten relocated his capital City of Egypt on the East bank of the Nile River, approximately 160 miles South of present-day Cairo, where he constructed the intentional community of Khut-en-Aten (the Horizon of Aten) at the present-day site of Amarna. This is where Akhenaten oversaw the building of several of the most massive temples of ancient Egypt, including the Temple to the Formless One.[2]

A pioneer of monotheistic religion, Akhenaten embraced the Christ Consciousness, and some esoteric historians view him as a spiritual forerunner who led the way for the incarnation of Jesus, the Christ. Charles Potter in the History of Religion writes, "He was also the first pacifist, the first realist, the first monotheist, the first democrat, the first heretic, the first humanitarian, the first internationalist, and the first person known to attempt to found a religion. He was born out of due time, several thousand years too soon."[3]

According to the Master Teachers, Akhenaten is one of the prior lifetimes attributed to Ascended Master Serapis Bey, and in his lifetime as Akhenaten was able to split his consciousness to physically appear in the Southwest United States. Due to their discovery of an ancient rock-cut cave, esoteric archaeologists theorize that Ancient Egyptians may have left clues to their presence in the Grand Canyon. An April 5, 1909, Phoenix Gazette article alleged that the Smithsonian Institute was financing exploration of the Canyon during the cave discovery: "Discoveries which almost conclusively prove that the race which inhabited this mysterious cavern, hewn in solid rock by human hands, was of oriental origin, possibly from Egypt, tracing back to Rameses. If their theories are born out by the translation of the tablets engraved with hieroglyphics, the mystery of the prehistoric peoples of North America, their ancient arts, who they were and whence they came, will be solved. Egypt and the Nile, and Arizona and the Colorado will be linked by a historical chain running back to ages which stagger the wildest fancy of the fictionist."[4]

The Master Teachers further claim that during this phase of Akhenaten's spiritual development, he studied with the Lord of the Christ Consciousness, Quetzalcoatl. This may explain Akhenaten's spiritual presence among indigenous peoples of the ancient American Southwest.

1. Manly P. Hall, *Twelve World Teachers: A Summary of Their Lives and Teachings,* (Philosophical Research Society, Inc., 1965, Los Angeles, CA), page 21.

2. Wikipedia, *Akhenaten*, http://en.wikipedia.org/wiki/Akhenaten, (2011).
3. Hall, *Twelve World Teachers*, 16.
4. David Hatcher Childress, *Lost Cities of North and Central America*, (Adventures Unlimited Press, 1992, Stelle, IL), page 317.

Akhenaten and the Blue Crown
The Blue Crown evolved from the Crown of War and was worn by Egyptian Kings. It is associated with royal ceremonies. Cairo Museum. Jon Bosworth, *Akhenaten with Blue Crown*, Wikimedia Commons, 2007.

Hymn to the Aten in Hieroglyphics

Akhenaten wrote the celebrated poem, "Great Hymn to Aten," synthesizing many of the religious and spiritual teachings of Atenism:

How manifold it is, what thou hast made!
They are hidden from the face (of man).
O sole god, like whom there is no other!
Thou didst create the world according to thy desire,
Whilst thou wert alone: All men, cattle, and wild beasts,
Whatever is on Earth, going upon (its) feet,
And what is on high, flying with its wings.
The countries of Syria and Nubia, the land of Egypt,
Thou settest every man in his place,
Thou suppliest their necessities:
Everyone has his food, and his time of life is reckoned.
Their tongues are separate in speech,
And their natures as well;
Their skins are distinguished,
As thou distinguishest the foreign peoples.
Thou makest a Nile in the underworld,
Thou bringest forth as thou desirest
To maintain the people (of Egypt)
According as thou madest them for thyself,
The lord of all of them, wearying (himself) with them,
The lord of every land, rising for them,
The Aten of the day, great of majesty.[5]

---

5. Wikipedia, *Great Hymn to the Aten*, http://en.wikipedia.org/wiki// Great_Hymn_to_the_Aten, (2011).

The Golden City of Gobean Lineage of Gurus

The Golden City of Gobean Lineage of Gurus (Master Teachers)

Quetzalcoatl, known by many esoteric historians as a form of the Egyptian deity Thoth — an archetypal deity that dates as early as Atlantean times (52,000 BC) to ancient Egypt (1292 BC) — is known in Master Teachings as the Lord of the Christ Consciousness. The Master Teachers claim Akhenaten traveled in the ethereal planes to receive training from Quetzalcoatl Akhenaten was the reincarnation of the incarnated angel and architect of Shamballa, Serapis Bey. Serapis Bey, the Master of the White Ray of Purity and the Ascension Process, is guru to the Ascended Master El Morya, steward of the Golden City of Gobean. El Morya steps-down the ancient energies of Quetzalcoatl into Gobean through the spiritual energies of Transformation, Harmony, and Peace.

Golden Angel
Teodor Axentowicz, 1900.

Prophecies of Change by Master Kuthumi

- The Earth is beginning its process of purification. This is also foretold in Earth's astrology.
- Prayer can change many things, including humanity. Master Kuthumi suggests we pray to change from the inside first.
- There is great deceit and manipulation in world politics which places the United States economy in grave danger.
- The Elemental, Animal, Plant, and Mineral Kingdoms are all evolving, and their consciousness affects humanity's evolution. These Kingdoms serve us in various ways:
- Pets offer the consciousness of friendship and companionship.
- The Mineral Kingdom emits various qualities of Ray Forces.
- The Plant Kingdom offers its life force so we can live in and experience the physical plane.
- As each Kingdom experiences great change, so will humanity.
- As we all spiritually awaken telepathically, connections form between humans, animals, plants, and minerals. This helps to create awareness and knowledge of the power of consciousness. Master Kuthumi calls this the Bridge of Awakening.

Kuthumi's Teachings on the Ruby Ray

The Ruby Ray acts as a catalyst for the fulfillment of desires. Desires are not perceived as trappings of materiality or sinful craving, but as another aspect of God's promise of fulfillment. Hindu philosophies similarly teach that until man fulfills his desires, it is difficult to achieve liberation. Ultimately, Master Kuthumi views the human core of desires as, "an urge to know God."

Once all desires are obtained, often all that is left is the desire to know God. Master Kuthumi observes the quest to fulfill long-held desires as the greatest of all initiations, as it comes directly from the heart. Students and chelas who work intentionally to achieve desires through the Ruby Ray follow the Path of Desires as a liberation process.

As one becomes a practiced Master in the achievement of desires, the transparent cause of Unity and the ONE is realized. However, humanity is still in its infant stages of understanding this spiritual truth. In fact, Master Kuthumi claims that the simple desires of Peace and Happiness, which are constantly within the grasp of any individual, become almost impossible to obtain.

Since human nature craves demonstration of all things physical and is obsessed with materiality, one of the Golden City of Malton's purposes is to satiate desires.

Malton's higher purpose brings completion to the long-held desires of the human experience. Kuthumi asks students and chelas to assemble a list of the many unfulfilled desires held lifetime after lifetime. This step is critical before entering the upcoming initiatory steps of liberation—the Ascension process.

The Elemental and Nature Kingdoms assist the preparatory Path of Desire in the Golden City of Malton.

During the New Times, conscious phases of Instant-thought-manifestation demonstrate to humanity the supreme truth that this unseen world of heaven—the spiritual planes—exist.

Kuthumi's Teachings and Prophecies on the Gold Ray

- The Gold Ray will initiate human consciousness into a new vibration.
- The New Energies through air, water, earth, and fire are currently utilized by the Nature Kingdoms: Elementals, Plants, Animals, and Minerals. This is heightening of the overall vibration of the Earth.
- As humanity rises in consciousness and understands the new vibration, the consequent energy gives further assistance to these various Kingdoms creating a type of evolutionary spiritual eco-system (the Spirito-System).
- Around the year 2000 AD, the Earth was flooded with the Gold Ray. While the first infusions of this higher energy cause discomfort and disharmony, the overall outcome for the New Times will be determined by the qualification and utilization of this Ray Force for higher consciousness.

Gold Ray Meditation

- Master Kuthumi suggests a simple prayer for harmony and to adjust humanity's vibratory rate and frequencies to the Gold Ray: "The Prayer of a Thousand Suns "(Golden Ray) "Bring Harmony forth to my Brothers and Sisters, Let us be united as ONE, for we truly are."
- The Master claims that as the Gold Ray grows in strength and radiance on Earth, it will create the Light of a Thousand Suns to illumine minds with understanding; open hearts that are willing.
- The Gold Ray is a collective outpouring of illumined wisdom and love from the Lords of Venus.
- According to Kuthumi, vibration is keenly increased in Golden City Vortices, and this increase in vibration is a key to telepathy with Nature Kingdoms, Master Teachers, and Spirit Guides.
- In the New Times, personal suffering and worldwide misery will be lessened. This is due to shifts in energy and the rise in vibration of the Earth. This changes many of the perceptions individuals and humanity currently hold. Master Kuthumi prophesies that our perceptions of misery and suffering can be shifted into new realities.
- Two critical tools: Worldwide Peace and Unity are taught by Master Kuthumi to obtain this Co-creative Consciousness. However, consciousness must be honed without denying or judging desires in order to obtain peace. And desires need to be fueled by the Fire of Co-creation in order to obtain worldwide Unity.

Himalayas. Golden clouds on a purple sky.
Nicholas Roerich, 1940.

The Hiawatha Belt
The symbol of the Iroquois Nations, a dark-beaded belt of thirty-eight rows, with two white squares of both sides of a white heart. Photograph from Jamestown Exposition, New York State, 1907.

Greater Law or the Great Law

The Great Law is known as the Great Law of Peace, also recognized as Gayanashagowa: the oldest known constitution of our modern time, existing since 1000 BC. Lead by the Iroquois prophet Dekanawida, the Iroquois Nation's charter was formed by five Native American Lords who planted the metaphoric Tree of Great Peace, known as the Tree of the Great Long Leaves. The Tree of Great Peace was fundamental to the tenets of the Five Nations, comprising the Mohawk, the Oneida, the Onondaga, the Cayuga, and the Seneca. The roots of the Tree of the Great Long Leaves spread out to all four directions, and the Law of Gayanashagowa declared the name of each root as "the Great White Root and their nature are Peace and Strength."[1]

The doctrine of the Great Law entrusted the care of the nations to the Lords, known as fire-keepers of the Council Fire, each appointed through their mothers. Hereditary lines were matriarchal, and the status of Lord was considered a sacred and noble position signified by the wearing of deer antlers, an emblem of feminine distinction. The Lords were also considered spiritual mentors to their nations, and their constitution contains this declaration of Peace:

"Hearken, that peace may continue unto future days!

Always listen to the words of the Great Creator, for he has spoken. United people, let not evil find lodging in your minds. For the Great Creator has spoken and the cause of Peace shall not become old. The cause of Peace shall not die if you remember the Great Creator."[2]

The creed of Gayanashagowa urges the Lords to thicken their skins against anger, offensive actions, and criticism; to cultivate peace and goodwill within their minds and hearts; and to act with cool deliberation. The constitution states: "Look and listen for the welfare of the whole people and have always in view not only the present but also the coming generations, even those whose faces are yet beneath the surface of the ground — the unborn of the future Nation."

The physical symbols of the Great Peace are well documented and the five Lords of the nations physically contributed to the creation of five singular shell strings that were tied together to represent the completeness of their unity as ONE nation, formed by the union of the Great Law. The constitution also called for the binding of five arrows, enfolded as ONE head, ONE body, and ONE mind. Perhaps the best known symbol of the League of Iroquois Nations is the Hiawatha Belt: a dark beaded belt of thirty-eight rows, with two white squares on either side of a white heart — a symbol of the peaceful nation. "White shall here symbolize that no evil or jealous thoughts shall creep into the minds of the Lords while in council under the Great Peace. White, the emblem of peace, love, charity, and equity surrounds and guards the Five Nations."[3]

The prophet Dekanawida asked for the nations to lay down their weapons of war and abandon hostility in order to further establish the Great Peace among the tribal peoples:

"(I) now uproot the tallest pine tree and into the cavity thereby made we cast all weapons of war. Into the depths of the Earth, down into the deep under-Earth currents of water flowing to unknown regions we cast all the weapons of strife. We bury them from sight and we plant again the tree."[4]

Historians claim the creed of Gayanashagowa — the great work of Dekanawida — and the structure of the League of Iroquois Nations profoundly influenced the founding fathers and the formation of the Constitution of the United States. The opening words of Gayanashagowa suggest a moral pledge that spans the time of its origination; a living covenant with the Great Binding Law of Peace: "If any man or any nation outside the Five Nations shall obey the laws of the Great Peace and make known their disposition to the Lords of the Confederacy, they may trace the Roots to the Tree and if their minds are clean and they are obedient and promise to obey the wishes of the Confederate Council, they shall be welcomed to take shelter beneath the Tree of the Long Leaves."[5] [Editor's Note: The Golden City of Klehma, the fifth Golden City of the United States, associated with Native American culture, and the White Ray of Peace, is prophesied to lead the five Golden Cities of the United States during the New Times.]

---

1. "Constitution of the Iroquois Nations: The Great Binding Law, Gayanashagowa," http://www.constitution.org/cons/iroquois.htm, (2009).
2. Ibid.
3. *Constitution of the Iroquois Nations.*
4. Ibid.
5. Ibid.

Hiawatha

Thomas Eakins, 1874. It is claimed that the fierce Mohawk Chief, Hiawatha, worked with Dekanawida as his disciple to form the Iroquois Confederacy. After the five warring tribes buried their weapons Dekanawida symbolically planted the *Tree of Peace*, and the great prophet and adept disappeared from public life. Hiawatha was entrusted with the legacy of the newly formed confederacy, and became their leader. It is believed that the tenets of the Iroquois Confederacy, based upon a guiding constitution and democracy, would later direct the founding fathers of the thirteen American colonies to envision and create the United States Republic.

Spiritual Hierarchy

The term *Spiritual Hierarchy* often refers to the Great White Brotherhood and Sisterhood, however, this term also connotes the spiritual-social structure that exists within the organization, their members, and their various states of evolution. This includes the different offices and activities that serve the Cosmic, Solar, and Planetary Hierarchies. The following outline summarizes the Hierarchy's spiritual infrastructure:

1. **Cosmic Hierarchy, the Great Central Sun**
    a. The Silent Watcher: Galactic Architect
    b. Cosmic Beings
    c. The Galactic Suns
    d. Galactic Council
    e. Galactic Rays of Light and Sound
2. **Solar Hierarchy, our Solar Sun**
    a. Solar Rays of Light and Sound
        i. Elohim: Magnetize the Planetary Unfed Flame at the center of Earth
        ii. Archangels: Arch the Rays of Light and Sound to Earth
    b. Solar Manu: oversees the incarnation processes on various planets within this Solar System
    c. Planetary Silent Watcher: Architect of this Solar System
    d. The Cosmic I AM Presence: origination of the I AM Presence in the Creative Hierarchy
3. **Planetary Hierarchy**
    a. Karmic Board
    b. Manu: Protects the current race of humanity
    c. Axis of the Earth: Polaris (North) and Magnus (South)
    d. Earth's Elohim
        i. The Four Elements
        ii. Devas
        iii. Animal and Nature Kingdoms
    e. Earth's Archangels
        i. Seraphim
        ii. Cherubim
        iii. Angels
    f. Shamballa: Rules and balances the magnetism of Earth; keeper of the Rod of Power
        i. Lord of the World
            1. Great White Brotherhood
            2. Lords of Karma
            3. The Right-hand Path

    ii. World Teacher
        1. Spiritual Knowledge and World Religions
        2. Ascension Teachings
        3. The ONE
        4. Christ Consciousness
    iii. The Buddha
        1. World Buddha
        2. Kings of Shambahla: the Earth Protectors
    iv. The Temples of Shamballa
        1. Unity Temple
        2. Nine Temples of the Rays
        3. Temples of the Flame
        4. Temple of the Christ
        5. Temple of the Buddha
        6. Temple of the Violet Flame
    v. The Golden Cities: overseen by Saint Germain
        1. Adjutant Point Ashrams
        2. The Temples of Perfection
        3. Star Retreats
        4. The Star
  g. Lord of the Rays — Maha Chohan
    i. Seven Rays of Light and Sound
    ii. Seven Chohans of the Seven Rays
        1. Etheric Temples
        2. Spiritual Retreats
    iii. The New Ray Forces for the Golden Age
        1. Gold Ray
        2. Aquamarine Ray
  h. Heart of the Dove — Babaji

4. **Creative Hierarchy** (Human)
  a. The Ascended Master: the God-free being
  b. The I AM Presence: descends from the Cosmic I AM Presence as the Electronic Body
    i. Causal Body (Solar Angel)
        1. Abstract Mind
        2. Concrete Mind
    ii. Astral Body
        1. Christ-self
        2. Guardian Angel, Spirit Guides, and Spirit Teachers

c. The HU-man: the integrated and spiritually evolved human
   i. Master
   ii. Adept
   iii. Arhat
   iv. Initiate
       1. Bodhisattva
       2. Prophet
   v. Chela (disciple)
   vi. Aspirant (student)
d. The Human
   i. Unfed Flame: the spark of divinity
   ii. Eight-sided Cell of Perfection: the atom of God-perfection
   iii. Flame of Consciousness: the Intellectual Consciousness separates the Human from the Third Hierarchy
   iv. Higher Self: the Holy Spirit
   v. Lower Self: the animal nature

Esoteric historians claim the Spiritual Hierarchy embodies religious principles from Christianity, Hinduism, Buddhism, Neo-Theosophy, and Ascended Master Teachings. However, to correctly understand the provenance of the Spiritual Hierarchy, it is essential to embrace its unique and concurrent Creation Story. The Ascended Masters' chronicle of the mythological formation of our galaxy, our Solar System, and the Earth offers significant insight and knowledge regarding the Spiritual Hierarchy.

A Variety of Solar and Star Systems

According to the Ascended Master legend, the Silent Watcher embraces the Great Central Sun — the Galactic Center. This Cosmic Being is also known as the Galactic Architect who designed the galaxy along with its many Solar Systems. The Galactic Silent Watcher works in tandem with various Solar Silent Watchers who assist in the design of the individual Solar Systems within the galaxy. Scientists theorize that our Sun is one of 200 billion stars in the Milky Way, and so far, astronomers have discovered approximately seventy Solar Systems in our galaxy.[1] The Solar Systems of our galaxy are overseen by the Galactic Silent Watcher and the Galactic Council — comparable to a Galactic United Nations — which comprises many Ascended Cosmic Be-

ings from a variety of solar and star systems, including: the Sirius System, the Pleiades Cluster, the Arcturus System, the Constellation of Centaurus, the Constellation of Pegasus, the Constellation of Hercules, the Constellation of Volans, the Constellation of Aquila, the Orion System, and representatives from the neighboring DAL or DAHL Universe. At the time of this writing, scientific research discovered that the Earth may in fact originate from another galaxy: the Sagittarius Dwarf Universe.

Researchers surveying the sky with infrared light at the University of Massachusetts mapped a New Star Map, through the use of a supercomputer to sort out a half-billion stars. Through the study of star debris and by pinpointing the exact location of our Solar System — at the crossroads where two galaxies join — they discovered that the Milky Way Galaxy is absorbing smaller galaxies. The Sagittarius Dwarf Universe was discovered by a British team of astronomers in 1994, and in 2003 the Massachusetts team altered their angle of telescopic view to find the Earth in perfect alignment with the smaller galaxy, or what was left of it. Researcher Martin Weinberg believes this process is two-billion years in the making: "After slow, continuous gnawing by the Milky Way, Sagittarius has been whittled down to the point that it cannot hold itself together much longer...we are seeing Sagittarius at the very end of its life as an intact system."

---

1. "How Many Solar Systems are in Our Galaxy?," http://nasa.gov, (2011).

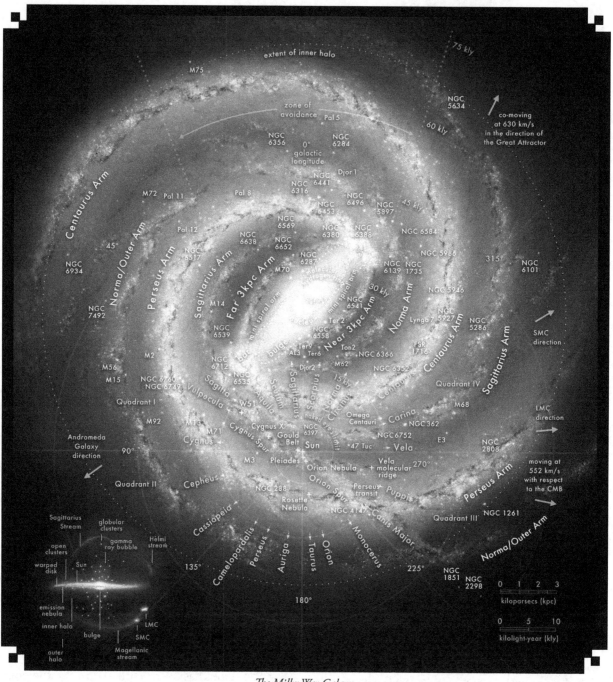

The Milky Way Galaxy

An artistic depiction of the Milky Way Galaxy. Our Sun is located in the Orion Arm, or the Orion Spur, approximately 26,000 light-years from the Galactic Center. Created by Pablo Carlos Budassi, 2021.

Metaphysicians theorize the discovery of the new galaxy may be the basis for the ending of the Mayan Calendar, because the Pleiades Star Cluster — which the calendar is based upon — is no longer a reliable point for celestial navigation as the Earth and its Solar System veer into a new direction.[2]

Elohim and Archangels

The Solar Hierarchy encompasses the Elohim and the Archangels. The Elohim (magnetism) are known as the Universal Builders and with the Archangels (radiation) — the Master conductors of the Rays — jointly formed a Creation Grid. At a central juncture of the grid the center of the Earth was created through the appearance of the Unfed Flame. To this day, the Unfed Flame is claimed to exist in the center of the Earth, and forms the cohesive power for the electrons and atoms of the Four Elements of the Earth.[3] Through the direction of the Rays, the Elohim managed the Four Elements (Virgo, Neptune, Aries, and Helios), the Gods of Mountains and Seas, and Amaryllis — the Goddess of Spring. The Devas created mountains, rivers, valleys, prairies, and lakes. It is claimed that the Ascended Beings Virgo and Pelleur oversaw the creation of the earth element to hold water, and from this substance the human form was ultimately created.[4] The Solar Manu — a Cosmic Being — holds the creative authority to sponsor a generation of incoming lifestreams (approximately 2,000 to 5,000 years). The office of Manu oversees humanity's spiritual evolutionary process throughout various epochs by protecting the current, incoming race. Two Manus protect incarnating souls; the Solar Manu protects the generations of souls incarnating throughout our Solar System, and the Planetary Manu protects souls incarnating on Earth. In the New Times it is prophesied that Mother Mary occupies the Earthly post as guardian of the Seventh Manu — highly-evolved souls currently incarnating on Earth.

The Four Elements

D. Stolcius von Stolcenberg, 1624. The Four Elements are governed by the Elohim in the Solar and Planetary Hierarchies. Ascended Master legend claims the Elohim, through the Four Elements (as the Elemental Kingdom, left to right, earth, water, air, and fire), magnetize the Seven Rays of Light and Sound.

Rod of Power

It is said that the gravity of the Earth is held through a mystical Rod of Power, a symbol of the office of Lord of the World that is kept securely in the Golden City of Shamballa. The mysterious wand is said to be constructed of orichalcum — the ancient metal of Atlantis — and encrusted with diamonds on either end.[5]

Hierarchal Offices

The history of Shamballa involves another important position in the Earth's Spiritual Hierarchy, the leader of the Great White Brotherhood: the World Teacher. I AM America Teachings assert Jesus the Christ is the resident of this appointment, and Lord Maitreya is the former World Teacher. The Golden Cities stream through the hierarchal radiance of

2. "Scientists Now Know: We're Not from Here!," http://viewzone2.com/milkywayx.html, (2011).
3. A.D.K. Luk, *Law of Life*, (A.D.K. Luk Publications, 1989, Pueblo, CO), Book II, page 206.
4. Ibid., page 207.

5. Wikipedia, *Orichalcum*, http://en.wikipedia.org/wiki/Orichalcum, (2011).

Seven Angels with Trumpets

From the Bamberg Apocalypse, Illustrator unknown. The Seven Archangels are depicted in this painting from the Bamberg Apocalypse. The eleventh-century manuscript containing the Book of Revelations was commissioned by Otto III of Germany. The Seven Archangels are said to radiate the energies of the Seven Rays of Light and Sound throughout the Solar and Planetary Hierarchies.

Shamballa, and their importance for the planet and evolving humanity during the New Times has equal significance to the Earthly hierarchal offices of the World Teacher and the Buddha.

On Earth, the office of the Lord of the Seven Rays is claimed to be held by the Maha Chohan, who oversees the Chohans (Lords) of the activity of the Seven Rays on Earth. The Lord of the Seven Rays is likely the archetypal Mithra. The Lords of the Seven Rays oversee vital Temples and Spiritual Retreats located in both etheric and physical locations on Earth. These spiritual sanctuaries provide a focus for the activity of the Rays of Light and Sound on Earth and shepherd humanity's continued spiritual education and evolution through the Rays. The Maha Chohan — which means the Major Lord — is said to be surrounded by the white light of all the Rays. The Maha Chohan instructs:

". . . the day of Our return into the consciousness of the mankind of Earth looms closer because the door has been opened by Faith and held back by the arms of Love, and the pathway of consciously dedicated energy passing out of your bodies and molded into form is witness before the great Cosmic Tribunal that the mankind of Earth do wish to walk and talk with a free Hierarchy, the Angels, the Devas, and the Gods once more. We come in answer to an invitation from your hearts — we have waited many centuries for such an invitation and Our gratitude to the lifestreams who are able to accept the logic within Our words and counsel cannot be mea-

La nouvelle Jérusalem

The City of the New Jerusalem. 14th Century Tapesty, Author Unkown. This 14th Century Tapestry depicts St. John's vision recorded in the Bible, the Book of Revelation. The Celestial City has diverse interpretations, and the prophecy indicates the heavenly construction of a New Heaven and Earth.

sured by any human concept, but it can be felt, I am sure, by those of you who are now sensitive enough to note the radiation of Our individual Presences."[6]

Creation of the Human Energy System

Ascended Master creation myths place the origination of the human soul from the heart of the Sun God-Goddess who constructs at the end of a Ray the Three-Fold (Unfed) Flame. This generates a Divine Presence, or a God-Flame; a Co-creator with the Source, the Cosmic I AM Presence. According to esoteric historians, some God-Flames choose to remain in the eternal embrace of the loving aura of the parental Sun; those who choose to progress further project their spiritual essence into two Rays — Twin Rays. The Twin Rays develop a new light substance: an electrical light field which separates the Rays into two distinct individuals. The I AM — the individualized presence of God — dwells within the newly formed soul, and the electrical field of light is known as the I AM Presence.[7]

The Presence of the I AM on Earth forms the nexus of evolution in the Creative, or Human Hierarchy. The Electronic Body of light is formed of both the Causal and Astral Bodies. The Causal Body is known primarily as a mental plane, and many Ascended Masters reside in the higher levels of the Causal Plane during their service to humanity and Earth.

6. Tellis Papastavro, *The Gnosis and the Law*, (Group Avatar, 1972, Tucson, AZ), page 119.

7. A.D.K. Luk, *Law of Life*, (A.D.K. Luk Publications, 1989, Pueblo, CO), Book II, page 208.

In Theosophical texts, the Causal body is known as the Karanopadhi, and its lower manifestation is associated with the causes bringing about re-embodiment on the Earth Plane; however, the Causal Plane is also associated with the Buddhi (Sanskrit for intellect) and the enlightenment of pure consciousness through discrimination between material and spiritual reality.[8] It is also the location of both the abstract and rational mind. The Astral Body or Astral Plane has various levels of evolution and is the heavenly abode where the soul resides after the disintegration of the physical body. Within the Astral Plane lie our individual desires and salvation from their incessant demands — the Christ. This plane of emotional energy becomes the proverbial heaven or hell.

The Ascended Master
The Ascended Master who is free from incarnating on Earth directs the Unfed Flame within the heart and builds a new etheric body focused through the immortal spiritual fire and light. Hence, the unascended are directed by the emotional desires of the Astral Body, symbolized by the earthly element of water. The Ascended Master has dissipated encumbering desires into a living flame; human desire is composed of etheric wandering. The human body is flesh; the Ascended Master is a body of spiritual fire — light. The luminous body of spiritual fire is developed through the use of the Unfed Flame in the physical plane.[9]

Collective Consciousness
Elohim focus their etheric Flame of Consciousness into the pineal gland of the human. This creates the Intellectual Consciousness. An outgrowth of the individual consciousness as thought, feeling, and action is the development of Mass Consciousness. Mass Consciousness is often measured by two methods: Collective Consciousness, the total consciousness of all forms of life currently present on Earth; and the Group Mind. Societal and cultural beliefs are the creators of the Group Mind's collection of thoughts, feelings, and actions.

---

8. *Encyclopedic Theosophical Glossary*, http://www.theosociety.org/pasadena/etglos/etg-hp.htm, (2011).
9. A.D.K. Luk, *Law of Life*, (A.D.K. Luk Publications, 1989, Pueblo, CO), Book II, page 214.

Lord Krishna in the Golden City
From the Harvivamsha, Mughal Dynasty (1556 — 1605). Krishna's legendary lost city of Dwarka was claimed to appear at his command from the ocean's waters. The city's golden radiance could be seen for miles. Myths claim that Krishna asked the Divine Architect Vishvekarma to design the magnificent city as an invincible fort; the haven was manifest on an island, and connected to the mainland by many bridges. The Golden City disappeared after Krishna left Dwarka's Earthly abode.

Spiritual Evolution
The Cosmic I AM Presence of the Solar Hierarchy projects into the Creative Hierarchy through the human heart, and radiates into the Unfed Flame; this is surrounded by the Eight-sided Cell of Perfection. Human growth evolves

through basic psychological and physical needs through ongoing spiritual interaction with the Guardian Angel, Spirit Guides, and Spirit Teachers. According to Theosophical thought, a spirit is incorporeal intelligence and can exist in almost limitless ranges of hierarchical classes: highest, intermediate, and lower.[10] Naturally, these interactions evolve the Lower Self, the animal nature within man, and awaken the Higher Self, as a direct and personal experience of our true nature.[11]Interaction with the Higher Self is also known as the Holy Spirit, a component of the I AM Presence. [Editor's Note: Some esoteric scholars claim that animals are evolved Elemental Beings of the Third Kingdom.]

The Awakened Human evolves to embrace the higher qualities of the Astral Body through the Christ-self (friendship, love, compassion), and the advanced characteristics of the Causal Body through the Solar Angel (leadership, confidence, respect, achievement). The I AM Presence instigates the human need for morality, ethics, Co-creation, and problem solving.

The Twelve Jurisdictions and Metaneeds

Psychologist Abraham Maslow identifies a similar pattern of human development through his theory of the hierarchy of needs, which identifies stages of human growth. As self-actualization is developed and evolved, the human needs change with the requirement for knowledge, beauty, and creativity. According to Maslow, these are the impulses of self-actualization, the birth of the HU-man. Maslow's metaneeds, the human ideals which drive consciousness toward self-realization, mirror the Ascended Master's Twelve Jurisdictions. The Twelve Jurisdictions are spiritual virtues, and when developed and applied, compel the growth of the HU-man and humanity's entrance into the Ascension process. The table below illustrates parallels between the two systems:

Jurisdiction	Metaneed: *Highest Need*
Harmony	Unity
Abundance	Richness, Complexity.
Clarity	Truth
Love	Goodness, Uniqueness, Individuality.
Service	Meaningfulness, Value.
Illumination	Truth and Goodness, Ease.
Cooperation	Perfection, Balance and Harmony.
Charity	Fairness
Desire	Aliveness and Spontaneity.
Faith	Autonomy, Self-Sufficiency.
Stillness	Simplicity, Essence, Beauty, Rightness of Form.
Creation	Completion
Creativity	Individuality (as individuus: the undivided), Unity.

Morning Prayer
According to the Master Teachers, the two most pivotal Jurisdictions to implement and integrate are Service and Faith.

10. *Encyclopedic Theosophical Glossary*, http://www.theosociety.org/pasadena/etglos/etg-hp.htm, (2011).
11. "Discovering Your Higher Self," http://www.thevoiceforlove.com/higher-self.html, (2011).

El Morya's History and Science of the Rays

- According to El Morya, the Lords of Venus, through an evolutionary process, re-directed the unrefined influence of the Rays on Earth. This process involved each individual Ray, and the spiral effect utilized light and sound at higher octaves, producing subtle, yet condensed, results.
- Again, a greater force of consciousness welds its hand at sculpting human destiny through the Rays of conscious evolution. As the Earth receives higher and refined energy from the Great Central Sun through the Golden Cities, history is created and our lives are re-shaped through changes in cultures, societies, politics, economies, and religious systems. El Morya compares this influence to a "ripple effect" and the pond is our Solar System; the pebble, the wave-inducing Rays.
- Light and sound spiral together, creating a circular vibration. Engaging any type of mantra or decree for a Ray Force is the "ultimate intertwining of consciousness with action."

El Morya's Teachings of At-ONE-ment

- First, to understand the spiritual transformation and evolution of At-ONE-ment, El Morya establishes the affirmation of the qualities of humanity:
- We are Divine.
- We carry within the same Source.
- All are equal to one another.
- When applying the above spiritual principles in thought and deed, light-bodies consciously align and unify, creating a unique sound, or tone.
- When applying the same spiritual process in a Golden City Vortex, the energies magnify, and the light-bodies grow exponentially.

- Initiates and adepts of this spiritual practice, upon reaching a level of intentional service, morph into Step-down Transformers of the Ray Force within the Golden City Vortex where they reside.
- Beginners of this practice are urged to start first with the Blue Ray, as it quickly brings the physical body and light-bodies into alignment.
- At-ONE-ment is an expression of beauty and creation. Through the Rays, light and sound frequencies work together as ONE. This is part of the Great Plan for humanity at this time.

Sunrise over Planet Earth
NASA captures this magnificent moment.

Himalayas - Blue Mountains
Nicholas Roerich, 1939.

Banner of Peace
Nicholas Roerich, 1931.

The Great Plan

The overall plan of the Spiritual Hierarchy's goal for humanity's spiritual growth and evolution is sometimes referred to by Theosophists and Ascended Masters alike as the Great Plan. The Hierarchy's strategy focuses on the development of the strength of the Inner Government of Earth to construct a higher and more enduring civilization based upon these ideals and metaphysical precepts:

- Humanity's recognition of the important parallels between scientific and spiritual laws.
- Love is the great teacher; love is the great educator; love is the great evolver.
- There is ONE Life, the limitless, incomprehensible from which all matter manifests.
- The human will is developed and evolved through conscious knowledge of individual thoughts, feelings, and actions.
- World conflict, combat, and division can be overcome through friendship, respect, support, service, cooperation, and equality.
- Eastern philosophy and religion's two greatest principles are the Doctrine of Karma (Cause and Effect; Universal Causation) and the Doctrine of Reincarnation. As a result, Eastern values are focused on family and community. The Christian West places great emphasis on the value of the individual (resilience; independence) and the Ideal of Service. As a result Western values are centered on the use of strength to help the weak overcome oppression.
- The Great Plan concentrates on the merging of both important philosophies and cultural values to realize the Ideal of Nations as one Family, and the Ideal of Universal Peace.
- The Law of Brotherhood is the basis of civilization; the Law of Sacrifice sustains civilization. The Temple of Humanity is built with Brotherhood, Love, Amity, and Freedom.

These eight precepts were outlined by Annie Besant, an early founder of the Theosophical Movement, in four lectures she delivered in London in June and July of 1921, "Britain's Place in the Great Plan."

Annie Besant
Annie Besant, one of the early founders of Theosophy, was a spiritual writer, teacher, and women's rights activist.

Emblem of the Theosophical Society
Contains numerous esoteric symbols including the Ouroboros, the Seal of Solomon, the Swastika (right-hand spiritual symbol), the Ankh, and the OM symbol.

The Angel of Peace
Walter Crane, 1900.

Breath Technique of the Blue Flame
(This technique is intended for students and chelas who are practitioners of the Violet Flame.)

1. First, visualize and focus the Violet Flame in the base of your spine.
2. Through visualization, raise the energies of the Violet Flame to the Heart Chakra.
3. Continue to focus on the Heart Chakra until you feel a burning sensation in this area. The Violet Flame energies as emanation will begin an expansion process.
4. As you focus on the Sacred Fire in your heart, see it transform into the Unfed Flame of Love, Wisdom, and Power
5. Separate the Unfed Flame into the three distinct Pink, Yellow, and Blue Flames.
6. Focus upon the Blue Flame, and move the Blue Flame to the Throat Chakra through rhythmic breath. You will feel the Blue Flame establish and expand in the throat area; the Blue Energy is cool, and you may have sensations similar to an electrical current: cool, calm; direct, but gentle.
7. Retain your focus on the Blue Flame in all of your communication; this is known by the Master Teachers as Divine Expression. As your work progresses with the Blue Flame, you will begin to recognize attributes of this flame in your will, choices, and a greater expression of service as Love. The energies will affect the physiology of the body, aligning its many systems to harmonize with light-bodies.

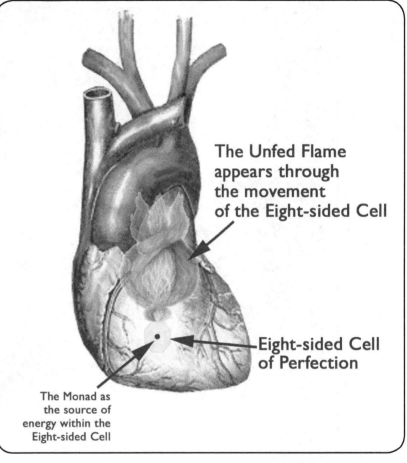

The Unfed Flame appears through the movement of the Eight-sided Cell

Eight-sided Cell of Perfection

The Monad as the source of energy within the Eight-sided Cell

The Unfed Flame
The Unfed Flame of Love (Pink), Wisdom (Yellow), and Power (Blue) overlaid the human heart. The Monad is the source of life and energy. Its God Radiation creates the Eight-sided Cell of Perfection — a perfect cell that initiates our Ascension Process into the Evolutionary Biome. Movement within the Eight-sided Cell through the Evolution Points creates and expands the growth of the Unfed Flame. As human spiritual evolution unfolds, the Unfed Flame grows in size and intertwines around the human heart. The three flames become recognizable in the human aura and radiate soft hues of Blue, Yellow, and Pink throughout the Heart Chakra. This illustration is not to scale, and expands the Perfect Cell for visualization purposes. The Eight-sided Cell of Perfection is atomic in size, and undergoes a duplication process.

Six Days of Creation
Hildegard of Bingen, 12th Century.

Saint Germain's Teachings on the Co-creation Process

1. Humanity's destiny lies in understanding our individual Co-creative nature. Saint Germain terms this the Heart's Desire:
   a. The Heart's Desire is a spiritual flame in the heart that seeks intention, understanding, and unfoldment.
   b. The "truth of life" is actualized through fulfilling desires and knowing and understanding your present Earthly work, or purpose.
   c. Freedom comes through Mastering each desire by identifying individual desires, fulfilled and unfulfilled.
   d. Saint Germain sees unfulfilled desires as illusive confinement, especially for those seeking spiritual liberation.
2. Unconscious creative desires ultimately foster spiritual growth and evolution, although sometimes we create and re-create the same circumstances and situations. This comes about through:
   a. Inability to identify the desire through unconscious knowing and understanding.
   b. Unconscious habits.
   c. Unconscious behaviors that are addictive or dysfunctional and the individual is unable to move forward to a constructive level.
3. The Aspirant seeks to discover and identify unconscious and conscious creations that assist growth of self-knowledge and personal unfoldment. This results in:
   a. A fuller, richer experience in the Co-creation process.
   b. Experience of the One in the flow and greater working of life. Saint Germain explains this as contacting the *River of Life*.
   c. The identification of intention(s).
   d. Observation of self: Saint Germain suggests keeping a journal to note everyday, small observations of self.

This journal is key to pinpointing and understanding repeated behaviors and patterns that block the fulfillment of desires.
   e. Knowledge of the Ray Forces and how they may qualify our experiences in lower and higher consciousness.
4. All desires manifest — this is a Universal Law. Saint Germain urges chelas to:
   a. Become aware of the desires you are manifesting.
   b. Note the manifestation process from unconsciousness to conscious awareness.
   c. Understand that desires exist as energy forces; they radiate from the Human Aura, and this process teaches and leads us forward in our evolutionary process as spiritual beings.
5. Dissolve unwanted patterns of creation that no longer serve your purpose (destiny) or conscious creations.
   a. If your creation no longer serves your best and highest good, Saint Germain recommends applying the Violet Flame to the situation or circumstance. Use of the Sacred Fire assures that Divine Intervention is present.
   b. Attune your skills of observation and perception to the situation in order to clearly identify dysfunctional patterns and repeating Karmas.
   c. One is unable to freely create trapped in the past while desirous of the future. This condition inhibits our experience of the present, the Ever Present Now. Saint Germain identifies this as the, "torture of ignorance."
   d. Use of the Violet Flame assists the healing process, and removes the emotional scars of the past. Saint Germain metaphorically reminds students that wholeness is not "walking with a limp."

River of Life

One overcomes unconscious creation through thoughtful, conscious experience. The Master Teachers often refer to this vital, profound life experience as the *River of Life*. The great philosopher Krishnamurti once commented, "But you can do that only when you leave the pool you have dug for yourself and go out into the River of Life. Then life has an astonishing way of taking care of you, because then there is no taking care on your part. Life carries you where it will because you are part of it; then there is no problem of security, of what people say or don't say, and that is the beauty of life."

The River of Life is present in both Christian and Buddhist doctrines.

Siddhartha sits at the edge of the allegoric river where he learns from the judicious ferryman Vasudeva. It is here that Siddhartha recognizes the endless, flowing, changeless rhythm of cycles:

"All the voices, all the goals, all the yearnings, all the sorrows, all the pleasures, all the good and evil, all of them together was the world. All of them together was the stream of events, the music of life...then the great song of a thousand voices consisted on one word: Om — perfection...From that hour Siddhartha ceased to fight against his destiny. There shone in his face the serenity of knowledge, of one who is no longer confronted with conflict of desires, who has found salvation, who is in harmony with the stream of events, with the stream of life, full of sympathy and compassion, surrendering himself to the stream, belonging to the unity of things."[1]

The metaphoric river is also portrayed in Pilgrim's Progress, the seventeenth century classic which is claimed as one of the most significant works of religious English literature. Pilgrim's Progress is translated into more than 200 languages and has never been out of print. The spiritual visionary and author John Bunyan conceived the allegorical tale while imprisoned for eleven years for his religious teachings and beliefs. Bunyan was discharged from prison after Charles II of England issued the Royal Declaration of Indulgence in 1672 which finally gave religious liberty to Protestant non-conformists. Like Siddhartha, the Pilgrim is carried on the metaphorical waters of the River of Life, and this creates deep spiritual introspection and transformation:

"I saw then that they went on their way to a pleasant river, which David the king called 'the river of God;' but John, 'the river of the water of life.' Now their way lay just upon the bank of this river: here, therefore, Christian and his companion walked with great delight; they drank also of the water of the river, which was pleasant and enlivening to their weary spirits. Besides, on the banks of this river, on either side, were green trees with all manner of fruit; and the leaves they ate to prevent surfeits, and other diseases that are incident to those that heat their blood by travel. On either side of the river was also a meadow, curiously beautified with lilies; and it was green all the year long. In this meadow they lay down and slept, for here they might lie down safely."[2]

The beauty of the River of Life exists internally through spiritual insight and growth, and it exists externally through the vital individual experience of life and the natural world. C. Adamson writes about the contrast of the two philosophies: "In some sense, Siddhartha is the eastern equivalent of John Bunyan's Pilgrim's Progress, which allegorizes the journey of Christian Life. One seeks enlightenment from within, the other from without. One seeks experience of self; one experience of Him via hope and faith."[3]

---

1. Chris Adamson, *The Right Answer; an Irreverent Journal of Thought and Opinion: Siddhartha,* http://chrisadamson.wordpress.com/2010/01/02/siddhartha, (2011).

2. John Bunyan, *Pilgrim's Progress: The Seventh Stage,* (Christian Classics Ethereal Library), http://www.ccel.org/ccel/bunyan/pilgrim.iv.vii.html#iv.vii-p0.2, (2011).

3. Adamson, *The Right Answer.*

Within Sight of the City to Which They Went the Pilgrim's Progress
Byam Shaw, 1907. A depiction of the sacred pilgrimage,
"The land of the shining ones upon the borders of heaven."

Pygmalion
Edward Burne-Jones, 1868-1869. A series of four paintings depict the Co-creative Process within the Heart's Desire. They are, top-left: "The Heart Desires." Next, top-right: "The Hand Refrains." Bottom-left: "The Godheard Fires." Next, bottom-right, "The Soul Attains."

The Heart's Desire

Sanat Kumara teaches the Heart's Desire is the Source of Creation, and this Ascended Master precept is the dominant crux of the Co-creation process. Since the Heart's Desire is one of the most influential principles underlying humanity's spiritual development and unfoldment, Ascended Master teachings give it utmost importance. It is considered a physical, emotional, mental, and spiritual presence that raises the un-awakened animal consciousness into the human, and onward to the awakened Aspirant and the devoted chela. Perhaps this spiritual principle lays the important developmental foundation that transitions the chela from passionate engagement with the River of Life to the detached Arhat — a necessary stage before entering the humanitarian duties associated with Mastery.

The Ascended Masters claim that the physical presence of the Flame of Desire lies within the heart nestled inside the Eight-sided Cell of Perfection. As students and chelas perfect the Co-creation process, some teachings suggest the Flame of Desire evolves alongside the Three-Fold or Unfed Flame of Love, Wisdom, and Power into the Four-fold Flame. In this physical, progressed state, it develops as the fourth White Flame of Creation.

Our innate ability to Co-create is alleged to be linked to humanity's unique DNA, and this is established through the service of the Archangels and their mythological ability to radiate the light of the Seven Rays from the galaxy to our human light-bodies. The advanced principle of desire, a psychology based on the creative spirit of humanity, is the Ninth Jurisdiction in the I AM America teachings. Its teachings recommend identifying activities that yield personal joy and happiness, and this delicate compass assists individuals to discover their Heart's Desire. The Master Teachers recognize the vibrant Source of Creation as the wellspring of abundance, love, and creativity. Eastern philosophy mirrors the same precepts as the soul's specific duty or purpose in life — Dharma. [Editor's Note: For more information on the Twelve Jurisdictions, see New World Wisdom, Book One.]

The dramatization of manifesting human ideals is illustrated by the Greek myths of Pygmalion: a Cypriot sculptor falls in love with his sculpture of the ideal woman, and she comes to life. This same story, which likely derives its narrative from the Roman poet Ovid's Metamorphoses, is also re-interpreted in the children's story *Pinocchio*, and in George Bernard Shaw's play *Pygmalion*, commonly known as the musical *My Fair Lady*. These themes explore the archetype of the Heart's Desire as the legend of the breath of life, and the transformation of dreams and beliefs into tangible human experience.

Edward Burne-Jones, a British artist and designer during the Arts and Crafts period, depicted the story of Pygmalion in a series of four paintings. The titles of the paintings create a poem that clearly synthesizes Ascended Master teachings pertaining to the Heart's Desire:

> The heart desires
> The hand refrains
> The godhead fires
> The soul attains.

Saint Germain on Identifying the Heart's Desire

1. Conscious awareness requires us to be spiritually awakened and aware of the world around us. Suggestions follow:
    a. Spend time in silence. Saint Germain explains silence as the quickener which awakens our sense of purpose.
    b. To know ourselves from within, silence as the Great Mystery assists the self-actualization process.
    c. Become aware of what fuels our desires, gives us positive energy, passion, or a positive outlook.

2. Saint Germain reminds us that in the pursuit of self-knowledge and the examination of our personal conscience there is no fool-proof method except returning within ourselves, to the Godhead — the I AM. It is here where we are all part of and connected to all of life.

3. While at times it seems our lives do not belong to us, and we have very little to do with our will, we belong to the Orchestration of the Great Central Sun. [Editor's Note: This is in reference to sidereal astrology.] Saint Germain assures us that through developing the will and the power of choice, while simultaneously identifying our desires, we are led to self-development.

Spiritual Prophecies

1. It is time to wake from the lethargic sleep of ego, illusion, and fear, and awaken to our true Divine Identity.

2. Worry, disease, and fear originate from our disconnected state to Mother Earth. The Law of Love demonstrates our interconnectedness to one another and the Earth mother.

3. This is a time when many will experience the death of the outer guru (teacher) to experience Truth and Divinity within. Saint Germain urges us to be cautious and to not give our power away to others' schemes and plans; create within, "your own dream."

4. From our shared vision and dream we will unite with our Brothers and create unity engendered with freedom.

5. We are often hindered by the patterns of past lifetimes that are the results of shame, doubt, and anxieties imposed by others. The Mercy, Forgiveness, and Compassion of the Violet Flame can awaken our consciousness from suffering, deception, and illusion.

6. An encounter with obstacles is often the old paradigm of consciousness rearing its ugly head. Remember that the paradigm is rooted in the past, and reaffirm the New Consciousness and the fact that a New Day has arrived. This gives positive energy to the new creation.

7. The I AM America Map concurrently shows the old and New Consciousness through devastated coastlines and wondrous Golden Cities. Saint Germain says, "Let the new creation come alive for the Age of One — Unana."

8. The old paradigm of consciousness is built on concepts of destruction: an eye for an eye; a tooth for a tooth. The New Consciousness redirects humanity to Grace, Divinity, Harmony — a New Age.

The Demon Mara and Buddha
Mara fails to tempt Buddha from attaining Enlightenment and her attempts to capture the Golden Throne are unsuccessful. (From a wall painting at a monastery in Penang.)

Saint Germain's Teachings on Prophecy

1. Prophecy is a philosophy to lift the human heart and to initiate understanding regarding human creation and the ramifications of those creations.
2. Prophecy is given in a timely manner to help humanity carefully consider their choices and their results.
3. Prophecy is not prediction. However, prophecy provides two vital processes.
   a. An evaluation of present collective circumstances, and from this a spiritual understanding, an awareness may be gleaned.
   b. An assessment of current needs further assists insight and knowledge for humanity and all life on Earth.
4. Prophecy is a spiritual teaching that addresses the interconnectedness of life. This spiritual understanding leads to:
   a. The development of compassion.
   b. The power of Divine Intervention.
5. Prophecy reveals our human experience through addressing individual and collective thoughts, feelings, and actions, and their link to personal Mastery. This evolves these processes:
   a. The lessening of suffering.
   b. The birth of wisdom and individual movement beyond Victim Mentality.
6. The spiritual teachings of Prophecy evoke a vision of hope and light for the future based upon the Law of Love.
7. Ideally, the teachings of Prophecy aid the individual to reveal and restore the true spark within: Divinity.

Saint Germain's Teachings on Consciousness and Co-creation

1. Aligned thoughts, feelings, and actions foster the creation process.
2. Collective Consciousness comprises the aligned thoughts, feelings, and actions of two or more individuals. This is the Co-creative premise of the Golden City Vortices.
3. The ONE is birthed from and based upon Collective Consciousness. Saint Germain refers to this manifestation process as the law.
4. The Law of ONE is defined as two individuals who gather (collect) their consciousness in unity through aligned thoughts, feelings, and actions. The ONE is prophesied to change humanity from within through evolving and transforming our spiritual values, cultures, and societies.
5. The creation process can be understood by visiting and understanding various scenarios as possible outcomes of one event. This helps us to understand the power of personal choice.
6. The Group Mind of Love: Saint Germain knows and understands how difficult it is to move beyond the ego and the needs of the individual versus the group. At this time, however, he sees mankind identifying with the Group Mind of destruction and cataclysm, versus the Group Mind of Love. Only though the Law of Love is the ONE realized.
7. Through the Law of the Great I AM our Divinity is affirmed and assured. The I AM is interconnected with Universal Life; this is known as the Law of Life. The I AM is contained in all creations, from the smallest sub-atomic particles to Solar Systems and galaxies of light. The focus and direction of our Co-creative energy through the I AM is key.

Triguna
Seema Kohli, 2008. The contemporary artist Seema Kohli depicts the feminine aspect of nature in the painting "Triguna." The three Sanskrit aspects of the mind (trigunas) — Sattva, Rajas, and Tamas — are represented as three goddesses. The Feminine Consciousness dominates and overwhelms the overgrown Patriarchal Consciousness.

Transforming Archetypal Prophecies of Doom and Gloom

The traditional Western viewpoint of Prophecy stems from a male, patriarchal archetype, which lends itself not only to limited, literal interpretation, but also to conflict and strife, which must first be overcome in order to realize goodness or light. The Christian Book of Revelations exemplifies this form of archetypal thinking which prophesies the Battle of Armageddon before the righteous are rewarded with the glory of heaven. Feminine archetypal thinking, which Saint Germain prophesies our culture is moving toward, embraces prophecy as metaphoric; and its story promises opportunity to move toward solutions that effectively address crisis, ultimately culminating in societal healing.

The old prophecies of doom and gloom likely are rooted in the philosophic fall of man, where nature is perceived as destructive and sinful. The feminine viewpoint, however, perceives the Earth as a Goddess and a Divine Manifestation. Joseph Campbell addresses these opposing positions as Sacrifice and Bliss, and these two distinct perspectives create societies and cultures with extreme variance. He writes:

> "Our story of the fall in the Garden sees nature as corrupt; and that myth corrupts the whole world for us. Because nature is thought of as corrupt, every spontaneous act is sinful and must not be yielded to. You get a totally different civilization and a totally different way of living according to whether your myth presents nature as fallen or whether nature is in itself a manifestation of divinity, and the spirit is the revelation of the divinity that is inherent in nature."[1]

These differences, while theoretically extreme, are often subtle — especially with Earth Changes Prophecies. The old patriarchal paradigm relates to change as inevitable and an opportunity to wipe the slate clean and begin anew. The feminine energies, while acknowledging change, embrace this time as an opportunity for evolution and healing and a maturation process for humanity. Earth Changes seen through the maternal lens transform death, doom, and gloom into a nurturing birth process. Saint Germain states, "The work of prophecy is to bring change within. This change begins at the individual level and extends onward — it grows exponentially. This is the Law of Love."

The Law of Love — which is the Alchemical root of the Christian faith — in Ascended Master teachings states "If you live fear, you will create fear. If you live love, you will create love."

Mother Earth
Components of this image are from NASA.

---

1. Joseph Campbell, *The Power of Myth*, (Bantam Doubleday Dell Publishing Group, Inc., 1988, New York, NY), page 91.

Group Mind

A Group Mind is formed by members of distinguished cultures, societal organizations, and more prominently by religious church members. The Group Mind is not a subjective energy body or thought-form, which often draws its energy from focus, concentration, and powerful emotion. Some subjective energy forms reside in the lower levels of the astral plane and induce addictive behaviors, and are capable of an independent existence outside the consciousness of their creator. [Editor's Note: For more information, see Subjective Energy Bodies, Points of Perception.]

The Group Mind is held together by the rituals and customs that are peculiar to its members; newcomers instantly sense the energies of the atmosphere, and will either accept or reject its influence. The physics of the Group Mind are important to comprehend, as the collective intelligence is formed to aid Aspirants to raise their consciousness beyond present limitations. This helps students to strengthen their will and power of visualization, and if formed of the appropriate emotion, "is capable of raising consciousness to the level of the angels or lowering it to the level of the beasts."[1]

Esoteric teachers claim the strength of the Group Mind rests on its ability to synthesize current energies that lead to spiritual evolution, based on the great cosmic laws. If these universal directives are not present, the Group Mind fades and dies, often a victim of dysfunctional psychologies and top-heavy irrationality. Dion Fortune describes the Group Mind:

"Anything which differentiates a number of individuals from the mass and sets them apart forms a Group Mind automatically. The more a group is segregated, the greater the difference between it and mankind, the stronger is the Group Mind thus engendered. Consider the strength of the Group Mind of the Jewish race, set apart by ritual, by manners, by temperament, and by persecution. There is nothing like persecution to give vitality to a Group Mind. Very truly is the blood of martyrs the seed of the Church, for it is the cement of the Group Mind."[2]

Perhaps this explains the use of ceremony and ritual in spiritual practice, and their inherent ability to enforce the Group Mind, which leads the Aspirant into the next initiatory phase into the guru/chela relationship. Fortune continues her instruction:

"It is for this reason that the secret of the Mysteries will never be entirely abrogated. However much is given out, something must always be kept in reserve and secret, because this something which, unshared with others and the focus of the attention of the group, is the nucleus of the Group Mind, the focus of its attention; it is to the Group Mind what the grain of sand is to the pearl forming within the oyster. If there were no grain of sand there would be no pearl. Remove that which differentiates the initiate from the rest of men and the Group Mind of which he forms a part will fall to pieces."[3]

The mysteries of the Group Mind rely heavily on the images of gods and saints, and visualizing their meditations and spiritual processes. The outpouring of this energy establishes a force in the Astral Plane, that is, if it is a representation of a natural force — as above, so below. These energies follow the natural channel of manifestation, and participants feel a result from their invocation. Fortune writes, "It is in this way that all anthropomorphic representations of the Godhead have been built up. If we think for a moment we shall see that the Holy Ghost is neither a flame nor a dove; neither is the maternal Earth-aspect of Nature either Isis or Ceres or the Virgin Mary. These are the forms under which the human mind contrives to apprehend these things; the lower and less evolved the mind, the grosser the form." Ideally, the Group Mind is a powerful tool to transform limitations of human consciousness and assists evolution to new levels of spiritual knowledge.

---

1. Dion Fortune, *Applied Magic*, (Weiser Books, 2000, Boston, MA), page 17.

2. D. Fortune, *Applied Magic*, 16.
3. Ibid, 17.

Illustration for Vyšehrad
Artur Scheiner, Czech Republic, 1863-1938.

Francis Bacon
Philosopher
1561-1626

Emanuel Swedonborg
Mystic and Scientist
1688-1772

Franz Mesmer
Scientist
1734-1815

Helena Blavatsky
Philosopher and Mystic
1831-1891

Georges Gurdijeff
Philosopher and Mystic
1866-1949

Helena & Nicolas Roerich
Mystics, Artists, and Spiritual Teachers
Helena: 1879-1955 Nicholas: 1874-1947

Edgar Cayce
Clairvoyant
1877-1945

Edna & Guy Ballard
Spiritual Teachers and Mystics
Edna: 1886-1971 Guy: 1878-1939

Paramahansa Yogananda
Yogi and Spiritual Teacher
1893-1952

Notable Founders of the New Age

(Top, left) Francis Bacon, philosopher who first coined the phrase, "New Age." (Top, middle) Emmanuel Swedonborg, known as the "Buddha of the North," communicated with the Angelic Kingdom and theorized the afterlife. (Top, right) Franz Mesmer pioneered the notion of energy transference and the practice of hypnotherapy. (Middle row, left) Helena Blavatsky, philosopher, author, and researcher co-founded theTheosophy Society. (Middle) Georges Gurdijeff, Russian mystic, philosopher, and spiritual teacher. (Middle, right) Helena and Nicolas Roerich, spiritual explorers of Asia and India and reknown Shambhala philosophers. The Roerichs founded the Agni Yoga Society. (Bottom, left) Edgar Cayce, healer and clairvoyant, founder of the Association for Research and Enlightenment — ARE. (Next) Edna and Guy Ballard, founders of the I AM Movement and the Saint Germain Foundation, introduced the spiritual tenets of Ascension. (Bottom, right) Paramahansa Yogananda, considered the Father of Yoga in the West, promoted spiritual teachings of meditation and Kriya Yoga.

New Age

The New Age movement is typically seen as a spiritual influence developed through the unique fusion of Eastern and Western spiritual and metaphysical traditions, and shaped in the last several decades through the self-help, motivational, and holistic health industries. Overall, the New Age movement is distinguished by its inclusive philosophies that incorporate Body, Mind, and Spirit, merging together science and religion, and producing criticism from some mainstream religious institutions. New Age theories of Unity and Oneness are not, however, religious maxims of the twentieth century and likely find their origins in the eighteenth and nineteenth century's esoteric works of Swedish philosopher Emanuel Swedenborg, the German holistic physician Franz Mesmer, Theosophy's founder Helena Blavatsky, and Russian mystic George Gurdjieff.[1]

The term New Age, however, was coined by the great English philosopher, scientist, and statesman of the seventeenth century Francis Bacon. A prophet of the Aquarian Age, Bacon envisioned his aspirations and idealistic hope for a New Age in his utopian essays in New Atlantis and Novum Organum. Francis Bacon called for a New Age to emerge through a United Brotherhood of the Earth — Solomon's Temple of the Future — built through the four pillars of history, science, philosophy, and religion. These important tenets could mature through the political development of Democracy, and their principles carried into commercial fellowship through Free Masonry, and guided by the religious light of the Rosicrucian Order. Bacon also appealed for a new nation of men, destined to become the nucleus for the future Utopia — America.[2]

The maturity of these organizations would likely take centuries, and even now the New Age is still considered in its infant stages. Bacon's vision, however, included all people of America as the combined "New Atlantis: North America, South America, Mexico, and Canada — affiliated in Brotherhood with the United Democracies of Europe and the Peoples of the World."[3] Marie Bauer Hall continues to write regarding Bacon's prophesied New Age, "The time of Man's coming into his great Inheritance, because his truly royal birth and spiritual Destiny, his claim to true Humanity has been recognized."[4]

Francis Bacon
An illustration from
A Natural History in Ten Centuries, by
William Rawley,
1588-1667.

---

1. Wikipedia, *New Age*, http://en.wikipedia.org/wiki/New_Age, (2011).
2. Marie Bauer Hall, *Foundations Unearthed*, (Veritas Press, 1974, Los Angeles, CA), pages 13–15.

3. M. Hall, *Foundations Unearthed*, page 62.
4. Ibid., page 64.

The Arhat and his Gurus, Ming Dynasty
This illustration depicts the Arhat meeting two contemporary teachers:
Confucius (the Adept) and Lao Tse (the Master). This illustrates the natural
progression of human evolution from Arhat, Adept, to Master — the spiritual
journey through Pyramids Eight, Nine, and Ten.

Great Triangle (Pyramid) of Solomon

The double interlaced Triangle of Solomon is also referred to by the Ascended Masters as the Pyramid of Solomon. Since it is the hidden basis for spiritual knowledge and understanding, it is also known as the two Ancients of the Kabalah: the God of Light and the God of Reflections. The figure contains the teachings of the Rays, Hermetic Law, and the Universal Microcosm and Macrocosm. The Pyramid of Solomon is also known as the Symbol or Seal of Solomon, and is a Western version of the Eastern Yin-Yang and the Chinese Pakua which is based on the I-Ching.

Eliphas Levi's modern translation of the Symbol of Solomon was first published in the nineteenth-century book Transcendental Magic. Levi explains the symbol as an energy map that illustrates the "creator of the greater world" and the "creator of the little world." Kabalistic teachings refer to this as the Macroprosopus and the Microprosopus — also known as the White Jehovah and the Black Jehovah. This is the proverbial law as above, so below, as all creation originates in the spiritual plane (light) and materializes in the illusive physical plane (darkness).[1]

Manly Hall revised the illustration to contain the Seven Rays of Light and Sound and explains this additional creative symbolism:

"From the point of the inverted triangle formed by the two eyes and the mouth of the Aged One stream the Seven Creative Hierarchies, which are concentrated in the single nature of the Demiurgus, or Lord of the World. From the apex of the upright triangle formed by the eyes and mouth of the inverted face, seven corresponding Rays ascend, blending themselves with reality on the horizon line between shadow and substance. The Seven Breaths are ONE in source and essential nature, but their divergence produces in the realm of nature the illusion of manyness. The divergent streams are again brought to a focal point in man — the Lesser Face — who is therefore an epitome of the agencies and elements of nature. In the secret doctrine of the Hindus the Seven Divine Breaths are symbolized by the seven-syllabled mantra, A-UM MA-NI PAD-ME HUM."[2] [Editor's Note: This same mantra is claimed to be the mantra of the Bodhisattva of Compassion, Kuan Yin.]

Great Triangle of Solomon
Interlocking triangles create the Great Triangle or Seal of Solomon.

Embedded within Hall's illustration is Saint Germain's mystical Maltese Cross, formed at the intersection of two lines: the Tree of Knowledge — the line of demarcation between spiritual and physical realities; and the Tree of Life, a central current present throughout the spiritual and physical planes of creation. In Ascended Master teachings, this is also known as the Golden Thread Axis, or Vertical Power Current.

The Symbol of Solomon is contained within the Eight-sided Cell of Perfection, and creates a pyramidal grid which reflects the individual state of spiritual evolution and conscious focus. Contemporary Native American Metis spiritual teacher Thunder Strikes refers to the Eight-Sided Cell as the Octagonal Mirror, and this template of energy resides near the heart and has "eight faces or camera filters called cognitive modes which determine how you will receive light."[3] When properly arranged through the Pyramid of Solomon, the perfect cell contains

---

1. Manly P. Hall, The Secret Teachings of All Ages: An Encyclopedic Outline of Masonic, Hermetic, Qabbalistic and Rosicrucian Symbolical Philosophy (The Philosophical Research Society, Inc., 1988, Los Angeles, CA), page 81.

2. M. Hall, The Secret Teachings of All Ages.
3. Thunder Strikes, Song of the Deer: The Great Sun Dance Journey of the Soul (Jaguar Books, 1999, Malibu, CA), Book II, pages 265–66.

Evolution Points of the Tree of Life within the Flower of Life

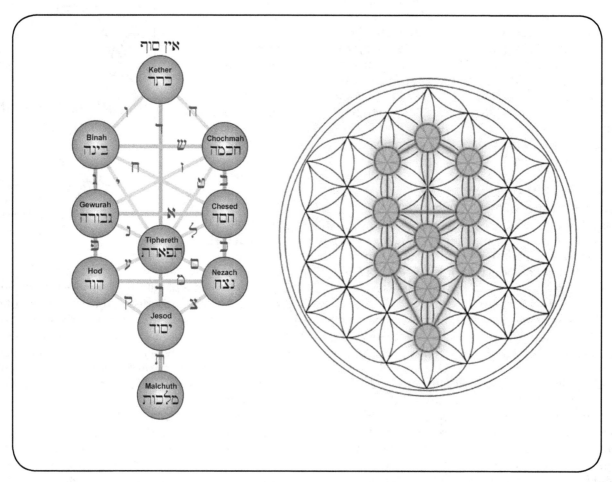

The Ten Sephirots of the Kabbalah Tree of Life
The Ten Sephirots and the Tree of Life within the Flower of Life
(Left) Tree of Life with the ten Sephirot and the 22 Hebrew characters as they
are presented in the "Sefer Yetsirah." (Right) This image depicts the Tree of
Life derived from the Flower of Life.

PYRAMID	DIMENSION OF EXPERIENCE	PURPOSE
1. Love	Third	Individualization
2. Wisdom	Third	Individualization
3. Power	Third	Individualization
4. Conscious Human	Third and Fourth	Conscience
5. Awakened Aspirant	Third and Fourth	Spiritual Awakening
6. Chela	Third, Fourth, and Fifth	Spiritual Discipline
7. Initiate	Third, Fourth, and Fifth	Spiritual Experience
8. Arhat	Third, Fourth, and Fifth	Spiritual Control, Buddha Consciousness
9. Adept	Fourth and Fifth	Spiritual Mastery
10. Master	Fourth and Fifth	Spiritual Liberation
11. Omega	Fourth and Fifth	Christ Consciousness
12. Alpha	Fourth and Fifth	Ascension
13. I AM	Fourth and Fifth	Ascended Master

thirteen initiatory Evolutionary Pyramids through which the individual spiritually progresses, develops, and inevitably attains spiritual liberation and Ascension. Each individual's spiritual growth and evolution determines which pyramidal lens tempers life's personal experiences and distinguishes the initiatory spiritual path for that specific lifetime. However, it is interesting to note that many Avatars and Christ-Consciousness archetypes often enter life as advanced Initiates, and move seamlessly through the next successive six Evolutionary Pyramids to demonstrate the attainment of the Ascension within one lifetime. The Thirteen Evolutionary Pyramids of the Eight-sided Cell of Perfection featured in the above table.

Twelve Points of Evolution are contained within the Eight-Sided Cell and represent twelve perfected spiritual virtues. Three Evolution Points assemble each Evolutionary Pyramid as a field of consciousness where congruent spiritual laws and Co-creative processes may be applied throughout the New Times. The Evolutionary Points are analogous to the ten Sephirots of the Kabbalah Tree of Life — ten illuminating spiritual processes: Keter (Crown); Chokhmah (Wisdom); Binah (Understanding); Chesed (Kindness); Gevurah (Severity); Tiferet (Beauty); Netzach (Eternity); Hod (Splendor); Yesod (Foundation); and Malkuth (Kingship).[4] Their emotional-psychological qualities bear resemblance to the consecutive Catholic Stations of the Cross (Via Dolorosa — the Way of Sorrows, or Way of the Cross); and Carlos Castaneda's shamanic Assemblage Points. However, it is important to remember the Ascended Masters consider the Evolution Points as attributes of godly perfection that lead to the development of the HU-man.

Symbol of Solomon by Eliphas Levi
Depicts the Macrocosm and Microcosm.

4. *Sephirot*, http://en.wikipedia.org/wiki/Sephirot, (2011).

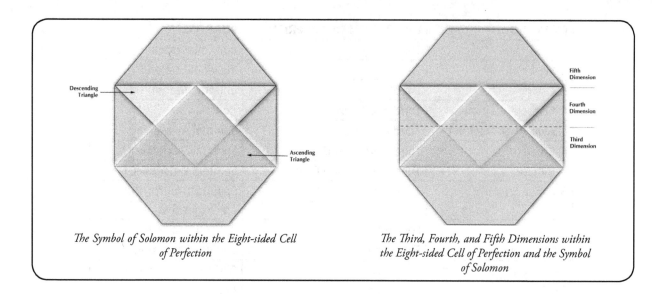

The Symbol of Solomon within the Eight-sided Cell of Perfection

The Third, Fourth, and Fifth Dimensions within the Eight-sided Cell of Perfection and the Symbol of Solomon

Point One: Harmony

The Law of Agreement is the Genesis of the HU-man. Through this vital Evolution Point, individual consciousness evolves through synergy, synthesis, and the recognition of Christ-consciousness.

Point Two: Abundance

The Law of Choice is a vital Evolution Point and develops the individual Will. Spiritual recognition of Universal Bounty and Manifestation leads to discernment and the acknowledgement of cause and effect through the Law of Attraction.

Point Three: Clarity

The Law of Non-judgment; the birth of Conscience, and recognition of the Divine Will. The Evolution Point of Clarity evokes the light of the Spiritual Awakening and opens the individual mind to the Co-creative possibilities of purpose and intention.

Point Four: Love

The Law of Allowing, Maintaining, and Sustainability; the manifestation of Light as intellect and knowledge. Cultivation of this point is crucial in order to attract appropriate spiritual teachers, an ancient tradition known as the Guru-chela relationship.

Point Five: Service

The Law of Love; the manifestation of the Cellular Awakening as Devotion, Brotherhood, and Compassion; the Universal Heart. In the Eight-sided Cell of Perfection this significant point creates the Eye of Horus, a spiritual representation of the individualization process completed through touch, taste, hearing, thought, sight, and smell. Evolution through this vital point births the HU-man, activates the spiritual Kundalini, and the consciousness of immortality through the development of the Clair Senses: Clairaudience, Clairvoyance, Clairsentience, Claircognizance, Clairgustance, Clairalience, Clairtangency, Clairempathy, and the Channel. Spiritual development through the Evolution Point of Service cultivates the apex of indivualization and is critical as the conscience develops and expands. For the Initiate, Service advances the vital contact with the guru — the spiritual teacher.

Point Six: Illumination

The ability to live without fear or judgment; the Light of Awakening as True Memory; Wisdom, Alchemy, and Co-creation. This essential Evolution Point advances the Initiate to the birth of the guru within: contact with the inner light. This prepares the Initiate to enter into the initiatory consciousness of the Arhat.

The Thirteen Evolutionary Points and Pyramids of the Eight-sided Cell of Perfection

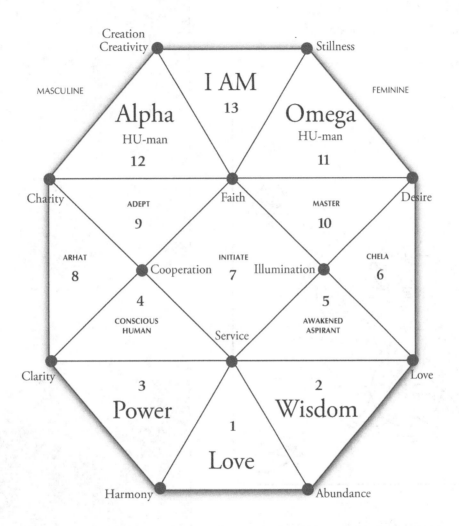

The Thirteen Pyramids and Twelve Evolution Points of the Eight-sided Cell of Perfection
The Thirteen Initiatory Pyramids (stages) of the growth of the HU-man and their states of consciousness depicted in the geometry of the Eight-sided Cell of Perfection. Also shown are the Twelve Evolution Points (Twelve Jurisdictions). Evolution Points are analogous to Adjutant Points; however, Evolution Points calibrate the HU-man Evolutionary Process. Adjutant Points regulate the Evolutionary Process inherent in a Golden City. Evolution Points and Adjutant Points play a vital role in creating the Evolutionary Biome—the responsive, Co-creative state of Unana. The Evolutionary Biome functions through the spiritual premise of the ONE.

Sacred Geometry of the Eight-sided Cell of Perfection and Evolution Points within the Flower of Life

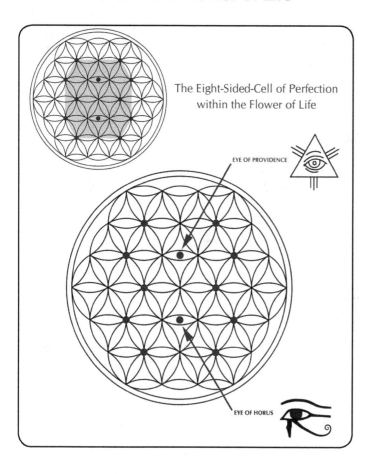

The Eight-Sided-Cell of Perfection within the Flower of Life

EYE OF PROVIDENCE

EYE OF HORUS

Eight-sided Cell of Perfection and the
Evolution Points within the Flower of Life
This illustration depicts the Eight-sided Cell of Perfection within the Flower of Life. The sacred geometry of the Eye of Horus (Service Point) and the Eye of Providence (Faith Point) are also shown.

Fu Hsi and Turtle
Fu Hsi is an archetype of the Eighth Evolutionary Point, also known as the Chartiy Point.

Close-up of Evolution Point

This illustration depicts the circular development of the Evolution Point. It is claimed that after twelve distinct radiations of each virtue is complete, the Evolution Point assembles, or integrates, and the individual's consciousness ascends to the next successive Evolution Point. The Evolution Point appears through conscious focus upon the spiritual virtue; each ring progresses through expanded spiritual perception and spiritual understanding.

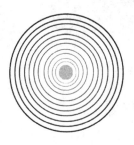

Point Seven: Cooperation

The ability to live with Beauty, Honor, and recognition of innate Divinity; the birth of the HU-man and entrance into the consciousness of the ONE — Unana. As this point is cultivated, conscience develops into devout principles and ethics which are critical for the Arhat. First, extremes may be experienced; and, as this Evolution Point progresses, the Middle Way is realized as balance, poise, and stability.

Point Eight: Charity

The ability to live with love and equity; this evolutionary point creates a humane detachment that results in spiritual transfiguration. The eighth Evolution Point is associated with the Arhat — the Buddha who has destroyed greed, hatred, and delusion; and the Adept who has the ability to control the Elemental Kingdom. The Ancient Chinese Sovereign Fu Xi, or Fu Hsi, is an archetype of this Evolution Point and, according to legend, is the inventor of calligraphy and taught the important arts of basic survival to humanity, including cooking, fishing, and hunting. Fu Xi is the acclaimed creator of the I Ching, the oriental spiritual system that governs the arrangement of Heaven and Earth, and is the foundation of Chinese Classical Feng Shui. Some esoteric scholars claim the myths of Fu Xi mirror the western Christian Biblical patriarch Enoch, who is similarly credited as the inventor of writing and a Master of astronomy and mathematics. Enoch means *initiated* and is also associated with the angel Metatron — the Divine Communicator of God's word. According to Judeo-Christian scholars, Enoch was taken directly to Heaven and received the title of Safra rabba — the great scribe.[5] This

---

5. *Enoch* (ancestor of Noah), http://en.wikipedia.org/wiki/Enoch_(ancestor_of_Noah), (2011).

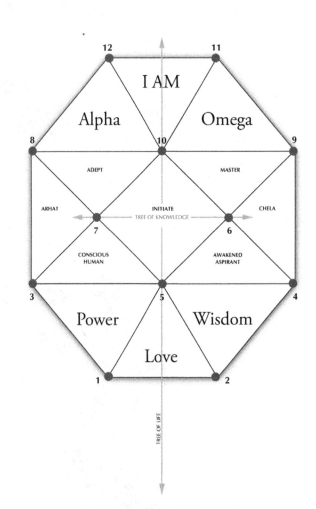

The Eight-sided Cell of Perfection with Tree of Knowledge and the Tree of Life

The Thirteen Initiatory Pyramids (stages) of the growth of the HU-man and their states of consciousness depicted in the geometry of the Eight-sided Cell of Perfection. Also shown are the Twelve Evolution Points (Spiritual Virtues), the Tree of Life, and the Tree of Knowledge.

Korean Shaman
The Ninth Evolutionary Point is affiliated with shamanism, shapeshifting,
White Magic, and miracles.

Bodhisattva Gautama with the Group of Five
Laotian Temple. The Buddha and Ascetic Practice.

suggests that spiritual cultivation of the eighth Evolution Point of Charity may directly lead to the achievement of the Ascension, circumventing the ninth and tenth Evolution Points. The Divine Tolerance, Divine Compassion, and Divine Benevolence inherent in Charity can quickly accelerate one from Arhat to Adept, and the attainment of the Buddha. This delicate balance of choice and the Divine Will interplays through theme and variation in the higher domain of the Fourth Dimension as its perimeters touch into the causal vibration of the Fifth Dimension.

Point Nine: Desire

The Heart's Desire is the source of creation and enlightenment. This point reassembles the individualization process, and consciousness identifies with individuus: one who cannot be divided. The ninth Evolution Point is affiliated with the esoteric Christian Magus or Mage from which the word Magi evolved. In Chinese culture, Magi is synonymous with the term Shaman or Sorcerer (Wu); albeit this level of attainment and Mastery over the Fourth Dimension has many degrees of realization, including Shapeshifting, White Magic, and the performance of miracles. A Shaman invokes their experience and knowledge through numerous of out-of-body experiences for transformation; a Sorcerer remains consciously aware and invokes spirits to take command of the elements. Both may employ the principle of devotion (bhakti) to invoke certain spiritual deities. While the Arhat and Adept often serve human culture and social order, the Shaman and Sorcerer often assist at a personal level,

Last Supper at Emmaus
Jacopo Pontormo, 1525. Jesus Christ with his disciples.
Note the *Eye of Providence* depicted above Jesus.

healing both physical and psychic trauma. As a mediator between the Fourth and Fifth Dimensions, the ninth Evolution Point of Desire opens the individual heart into the collective heart of humanity and retrieves the Divine Blueprint of the soul. This significant recovery of Divinity is analogous to the myth of the virgin birth, and represents the innate perfection of the Divine HU-man. Thus, the ninth Evolution Point is also affiliated with spiritual archetypes of Healing, Recovery, Spiritual Re-birth, and Transformation: Mithra, Quetzalcoatl, Zoroaster, Dekanawida, John the Baptist, and Jesus Christ.

The Triple Gem
In Ascended Master teachings the Triple Gem is the sacred iconography of the Unfed Flame.

Point Ten: Faith

This is the important point of Ascension, and its evolutionary location creates complete trust in the Divine Creative Birthright. This position is also referred to as the Lighted Stance and the attainment of the Seamless Garment. This important point in the Eight-sided Cell of Perfection creates the Eye of Providence, or the all-seeing eye of God. The Rays of Light and Sound stream into the Fourth and Third Dimension from this Evolution Point and epitomize the light and wonder of God. Faith represents Divine protection, Divine Intervention, and Divine guidance in the affairs of humanity by the Spiritual Hierarchy. In Buddhism this critical point is known as the Triple Gem, or the Three Refuges. The Triple Gem is reflected in the Third Dimension as the Unfed Flame held in the physical heart. In the Fifth Dimension, the Triple Gem embodies three important processes for humanity's spiritual unfoldment: 1) recognition of the innate Divinity that exists within all; 2) practice of the spiritual teachings that lead to liberation — Dharma; and 3) active membership among the community of those who have attained enlightenment and liberation: the Great White Brotherhood. Buddhists attribute the spiritual consciousness of the Triple Gem to the creation of the, "diamond mind which can cut through illusion."[6]

(Above)
Adoracao Dos Magos,
Vincent Gil,1498-1518. Depicts the three Magi visiting the Christ-child.

(Left)
Russian Shaman
Photograph of a Russian Shaman from the National Library of Russia, 1904.

6. *Three Jewels*, http://en.wikipedia.org/wiki/Three_Jewels, (2011).

The Annunciation
Paolo De Matteis, 1712. Archangel Gabriel announces the birth of Christ. Note the
rich symbology: the lily of the Evolution Point Stillness, twin-angels (Twin Flames)
descending in pairs, and the trinity of angels ascending above Mary.

The Assumption
Tiziano Vecelli, 1516–18. The Assumption by Titian depicts
Mother Mary's Ascension.

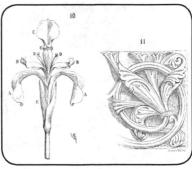

The Fleur-de-lis and the Lily
Eugene Viollet-le-Duc,
1856.

Point Eleven: Stillness

The Law of Alignment is the eleventh Evolution Point. It is considered the most advanced of the feminine points contained in the Thirteen Pyramids and is distinctively Yin. Theosophists concur that this point is affiliated with the Assumption, or the process of the physical body and the soul entering Ascension. Religious texts of the Koran similarly document Muhammad's physical Ascension in The Night Journey. Orthodox Christian Catholics however, view this process as the Dormition — falling asleep, or the sleep of human death before entering heaven. Ascended Master teachings maintain that the Point of Stillness or the Great Silence of Consciousness spiritually configures the soul for its evolutionary journey into Ascension and the Fifth Dimension. The esoteric symbol of the resurrection of the spirit through the stillness of Ascension is the Fleur-de-lis which is a symbol of royalty and literally means lily flower.[7] Like the Triple Gem of the Buddhists, some Ascended Master teachings compare the Fleur-de-lis to the Unfed Flame; however, it is more accurately portrayed as the sacred iconography of the Christian Annunciation, Mother Mary, and Archangel Gabriel. The Eleventh Evolution Point of Stillness comprises the final point in the Omega Pyramid of Consciousness and signifies the end of an initiatory series of lifetimes and the graduation of the soul's entrance into the immortal consciousness of the I AM and the Ascension.

---

7. *Fleur-de-lis*, http://en.wikipedia.org/wiki/Fleur-de-lis, (2011).

Yudishthira and His Dog, Ascending
Nandalal Bose, 1913. The eldest brother of the Pandava brothers of the Hindu epic, the
Mahabharata, was accompanied by his dog on an Ascension Spiritual Pilgrimage to the
Himalayas. It is claimed that Indra asked Yudishthira to abandon his dog, but he refused,
affirming the dog's impeccable loyalty and devotion. As Yudishthira enters the Ascension
Process his dog reveals his true identity as his godfather, a *Dharma Deva*.*

*From: The Story of Yudisthira, Mahabharata online.

Point Twelve: Creation-Creativity

The Law of Divine Order is the twelfth and final Evolution Point. This final point is considered masculine and therefore deemed Yang. Creation and Creativity are associated with the Christian ideology of the Annunciation — the declaration of the birth of Christ by the Archangel Gabriel to the Virgin Mary. In a universal context this Evolution Point is associated with the announcement of the Ascension of a Son of God. Since this is the final point in the entire series of Evolution Points, it may also be a beginning point for the soul's experience in the new realms as an Ascended Master; the point is also regarded as the commencement for a new soul's entrance into the Thirteen Pyramids. Creation and Creativity include the spiritual round of births and deaths; beginnings and endings. This Evolution Point is the cycle of life expressed as both the Creator and the Creation. It is the final point that completes the Alpha Pyramid of Consciousness and is contradictory since Alpha — a Greek word — means first. Alpha, however, derives its meaning from the first letter of the Ancient Phoenician alphabet Aleph. Aleph's historical mysticism is associated with truth, the Oneness of God, and assists the Hebrew formation of the name of God as I AM That I AM.[8] The sacred cycle of life through the Evolution Point of Creation-Creativity is best understood in the repeating text of the Bible's New Testament in the books of Matthew, Mark, and Luke that reiterates the message, "So the last shall be first, and the first last."

Anna Kingsford, esoteric scholar and Theosophist of the early twentieth century, extensively researched the Seal of Solomon in her 1916 essay The Credo of Christendom. The essay compares the seal's mystical symbolism to the esoteric teachings underlying Christianity and the creation of the Catholic Church as the "direct heir of the old Roman faith." She defines the philosophic underpinnings of the Catholic faith as a universal movement that intentionally captured all allegorical and archetypical Christ-Consciousness characters, legends, and their historical symbols present in both the East and West. Kingsford writes, "Thus the Catholic Church is Vedic, Buddhist, Zen, and Semitic. She is Egyptian, Hermetic, Pythagorean, and Platonic."[9]

The Kingsford treatise identifies the lower triangle of Solomon's Pyramid as the masculine Temple of Solomon, and the upper triangle as the feminine House of Wisdom. The upper regions of the interlaced triangles represent spirit in its purest state; the lower region embodies the manifest universe and the central region — whose sacred geometry forms a hexagon bisected by a cross. Spiritual and physical energies join at the central region, and a cross is formed by the horizontal Tree of Knowledge and the vertical Tree of Life. To Kingsford, the lower pyramid symbolizes the lesser mysteries, natural evolution, and man's subjection to Karma; the higher pyramid symbolizes the "abodes of the Gods," and the emanation of the Seven Rays. She points out numerous dual contrasts between the two planes: God — Nature; Un-manifest — Manifest; Abstract — Concrete; Un-create — Create; Absolute — Relative. These limitless comparisons also embrace religious thought: the upper triangle represents Heaven and the Holy Spirit; the lower triangle represents Earth as Jerusalem, and the creation of churches.[10]

Perhaps Kingsford's most provocative insight regarding the mystical Seal of Solomon is her theory of the middle ground: where spirit and matter meet. Her ideas invite a relationship to the Ascended Masters' prophetic New Times, the growth of the feminine in worldwide cultural experience, and the energetic grid of Golden City Vortices — a metaphorical New Jerusalem. She writes:

"It is the recognition of this dual character of Nature, and of the spiritual womanhood as the complement and crown of the spiritual manhood, that constitutes the best wisdom and supreme glory of the Catholic Church, and explains her uncompromising hostility to the Order of Freemasonry; for this system represents a perpetuation of the exoteric Judaism, in that it concerns itself exclusively with the lower triangle, and the building of the 'Temple of Solomon,' to the exclusion of the upper, the sphere of 'the

---

8. *Aleph,* http://en.wikipedia.org/wiki/Aleph, (2011).

9. Anna Bonus Kingsford and Edward Maitland, *The Credo of Christendom and other Addresses and Essays on Esoteric Christianity,* http://www.anna-kingsford.com, (2009).
10. Ibid.

The Five Pillars of the Eight-Sided-Cell of Perfection

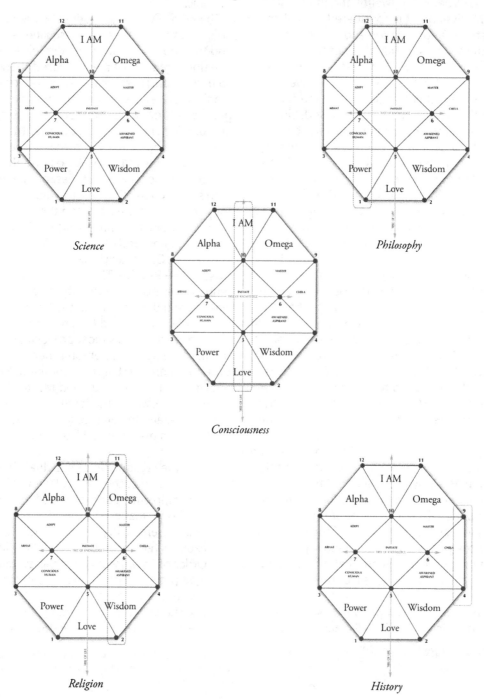

Science

Philosophy

Consciousness

Religion

History

woman,' and the 'city which cometh down from Heaven,' the New Jerusalem, or city of God. The whole, from top to bottom, is united by the vertical beam of the cross, called the Tree of Life. The horizontal beam is called the Tree of Knowledge, and the Measuring-rod of Adonai, wherewith the hold city of the Apocalypse is measured."[11]

The Eight-sided Cell of Perfection superimposed over the Pyramid of Solomon reveals humanity's potential stages of spiritual growth and development through the New Times and the Golden Age. As individuals progress from one field of conscious understanding, they advance to new spiritual ideals and paradigms in the next phase. Ascended Master teachings refer to this organic, innate, and yet inspirational spiritual process as a *Mantle of Consciousness* — humanity's Divine Destiny. Kingsford concurs:

"These kings of Edom, Adam, or Earth, are thus an occult figure of the seven progressive dominions, spheres, planets, or stages, through which the soul passes on her way to the heavenly royalty with and beyond the Earthly plane, where man perfected becomes 'Prince' or 'Israel with God.' At this stage only is the Life Eternal attained, since only as man does the soul finally secure immortality. All previous stages have, indeed, the potentiality of it, but they are only preparatory. The soul must pass through and rise out of them all in order to realize its Divine Destiny."[12]

The great philosopher Francis Bacon prophesied the evolved, democratic citizens of the future would build the Universal Brotherhood of Earth by cultivating the "four mighty pillars of history, science, philosophy, and religion."[13] The four lofty spiritual pillars of evolution exist within the Eight-sided Cell of Perfection and are joined with a fifth and critical pillar for humanity's progressive spiritual development throughout the New Times: consciousness. A contemporary viewpoint on the Five Progressive Pillars follows:

Science: Humanitarian effort based on systematic knowledge. The First Pillar of Science is built upon the Evolution Points of Clarity and Charity.

Philosophy: The science of truth, principles, or metaphysical knowledge underlying creation and the nature of reality. The Second Pillar of Philosophy is built upon the Evolution Points of Harmony, Cooperation, and Creation-Creativity.

Consciousness: Awakening to one's own existence, sensations, and cognitions. Collective Consciousness is the higher interactive structure of consciousness joining as two or more. The Third Pillar of Consciousness is built upon the Evolution Points of Service and Faith.

Religion: A code of ethics specific to shared belief and conduct. The Fourth Pillar of Religion is built upon the Evolution Points of Abundance, Illumination, and Stillness.

History: Ancestral knowledge of ancient and indigenous cultures of the past; our own personal account of events as written within ourselves; knowledge or systematic narratives, in order of time, recorded of past events. The Fifth Pillar of History is built upon the Evolution Points of Love and Desire.

The central horizontal division of the Seal of Solomon is known as the Tree of Knowledge, and classical interpretations of this line of energy are dualistic and state that if a "man lives uprightly, it is a Tree of Good, but if he lives unjustly, it is a Tree of Evil."[14] Kabalistic teachings of the Tree of Knowledge divide the sacred symbol into three divisions of the soul: the lower levels represent the animal instincts; the mid-region, the mind and reasoning powers; and the highest region represents the higher aspirations of the soul. Robert Wang writes in the Qabalistic Tarot regarding the progressive levels, or branches of the Tree of Knowledge, "All major religions teach that it is our heritage to return to some Primal Point from which we evolve. This is expressed as 'heaven' or 'nirvana,' or whatever is the ultimate happy state promised by faith. But of all the metaphysical systems in the West, only the Qabalah suggests the extent to which we progress through a natural course of development."[15]

Saint Germain explains the Tree of Knowledge and the various levels that grow horizontally beneath and above this divisional line as the Five Branches of the Tree of

11. A. Kingsford, *The Credo of Christendom*.
12. Ibid.
13. Marie Bauer Hall, *Foundations Unearthed* (Veritas Press, 1974, Los Angeles, CA), page 13.

14. Robert Wang, *Qabalistic Tarot: A Textbook of Mystical Philosophy* (Samuel Weiser, Inc., 1992, York Beach, ME), page 164.
15. R Wang, *Qabalistic Tarot*.

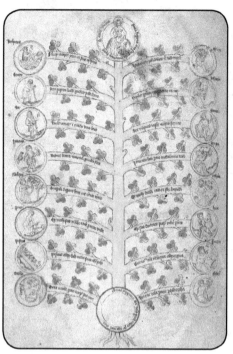

Tree of Wisdom
This medieval illustration depicts branches inscribed with verses that describe the Ages of Humanity.

Knowledge. Each distinct level of understanding incorporates various Evolution Points, and the individual moves forward in spiritual growth and development through the unique characteristics of the separate, yet connected, limbs of the sacred tree. The template of the Five Branches is based upon the Eight-sided Cell of Perfection and the HU-man — whose Divine, Innate Potential is innate within — and prophesied to emerge and self-actualize during the New Times and the Golden Age. Saint Germain claims the Five Branches are analogous to five levels of spiritual consciousness and awareness. The five are:

Physical: The lowest of the Five Branches comprises the Evolution Points Harmony and Abundance.

Emotional: The second lowest of the Five Branches comprises the Evolution Points Clarity, Love, and Service.

Mental: The middle branch of the Tree of Knowledge comprises the Evolution Points Illumination and Cooperation.

Astral: The second highest branch of the Tree of Knowledge comprises the Evolution Points Charity, Desire, and Faith.

Causal: The highest branch of the Tree of Knowledge comprises the Evolution Points Stillness and Creation-Creativity.

The Eight-sided Cell of Perfection contains three distinct levels of Energy Movement and three separate Energy Maps and should be treated as three diverse levels of information within the cell to assist personal knowledge regarding the development of the HU-man. Since each Energy Map of the Eight-Sided Cell addresses different spiritual functions and roles, each Energy Map has the ability to produce remarkably different spiritual perceptions and philosophies. In summary, the three Energy Maps of the Eight-sided Cell of Perfection are:

1. Movement of Consciousness through the Eight-sided Cell of Perfection: This map depicts the movement of conscious energy through the Eight-Sided Cell and the ability to lift difficult personal Karmas and Co-create new physical realities on Earth. This Energy Map integrates spiritual knowledge and philosophies from the East, primarily the Chinese Science of Feng Shui, the I-Ching, and the Hindu Science of Vastu Shastra. [For more information, Points of Perception.]

2. Movement of the Rays of Light and Sound through the Eight-sided Cell of Perfection: The Seven Rays interact with the perfection of the Eight-Sided Cell to assist individual healing processes while supporting and sustaining the perfect light of the Divine HU-man. This Energy Map assists the individual to identify psychological and Karmic themes through recognition of dominant and deficient Ray Forces. This Energy Map integrates Ascended Master teachings, Western and Vedic Astrology, and archetypal myth and allegory.

3. Evolution of Energy through the Eight-sided Cell of Perfection: As energy moves through the Thirteen Evolutionary Pyramids and the Twelve Evolution Points, this Energy Map charts the evolution of the soul, the potential of the HU-man, and the attainment of Ascension. This Energy Map integrates spiritual knowledge and philosophies from the West and esoteric Judeo-Christian viewpoints.

The Five Branches of the Eight-Sided-Cell of Perfection

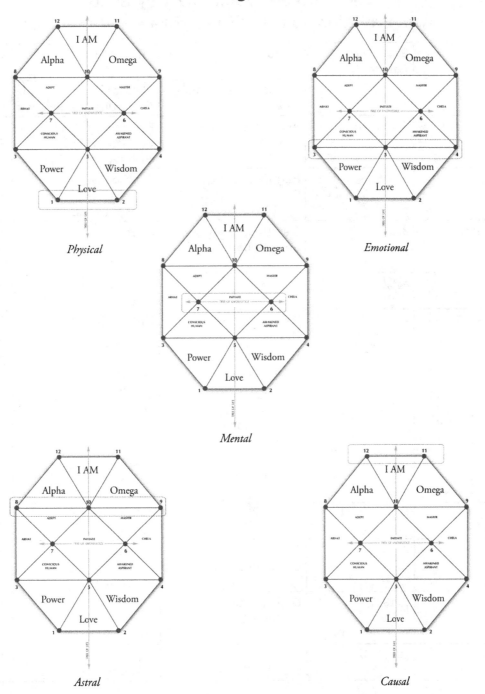

Physical

Emotional

Mental

Astral

Causal

The Thirteen Evolutionary Pyramids
with Evolution Points, Virtues, Pillars and Branches

Pyramid	Evolution Points	Virtues	Pillars	Branches
Love	1, 2, 5	Harmony, Abundance, Service	Philosophy, Consciousness, Religion	Physical, Emotional
Wisdom	2, 4, 5	Abundance, Love, Service	Religion, Consciousness, History	Physical, Emotional
Power	1, 3, 5	Harmony, Clarity, Service	Philosophy, Science, Consciousness	Physical, Emotional
Conscious Human	3, 5, 7	Clarity, Service, Cooperation	Science, Consciousness, Philosophy	Emotional, Mental
Aspirant	4, 5, 6	Love, Service, Illumination	Consciousness, History, Religion	Emotional, Mental
Chela	4, 6, 9	Love, Illumination, Desire	History, Religion	Emotional, Mental, Astral
Initiate	5, 6, 7, 10	Service, Illumination, Cooperation, Faith	Religion, Consciousness, Philosophy	Emotional, Mental, Astral
Arhat	3, 7, 8	Clarity, Cooperation, Charity	Science, Philosophy	Emotional, Mental, Astral
Adept	7, 8, 10	Cooperation, Charity, Faith	Science, Philosophy, Consciousness	Mental, Astral
Master	6, 9, 10	Illumination, Desire, Faith	Religion, History, Consciousness	Mental, Astral
Alpha	8, 10, 12	Charity, Faith, Creation-Creativity	Science, Consciousness, Philosophy	Astral, Causal
Omega	9, 10, 11	Desire, Faith, Creation-Creativity	Science, Consciousness, Philosophy	Astral, Causal
I AM	10, 11, 12	Faith, Stillness, Creation-Creativity	Consciousness, Religion, Philosophy	Astral, Causal

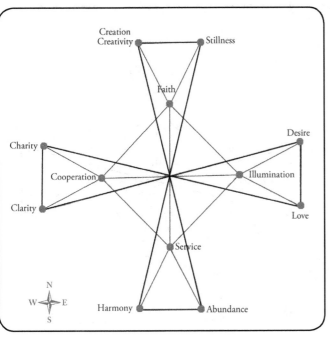

Evolution Points and Evolutionary Pyramids Overlaid the Golden City

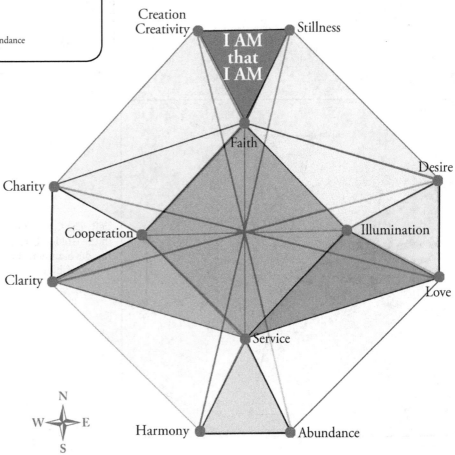

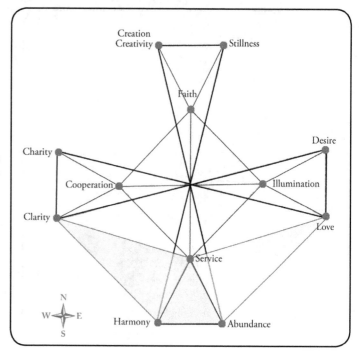

The Threefold Creation: Love, Wisdom, and Power
Right: *Unfed Flame within the Evolutionary Pyramids.*
The Unfed Flame as it exists in the three Evolutionary Pyramids within a Golden City Vortex. Pink represents *Love*, Yellow represents *Wisdom*, and Blue represents *Power*.

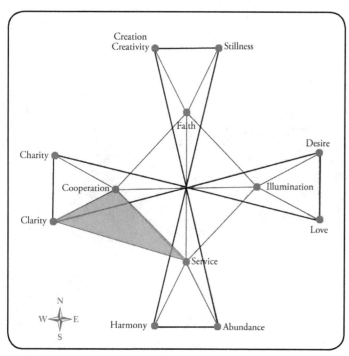

Conscience and Consciousness
Left: *The Evolutionary Pyramid of the Conscious Human.* Located in the Golden City Vortex. This field of spiritual experience drives the development of the conscience. This location helps to create states of higher consciousness alongside changes and shifts in vibrational frequency of consciousness.

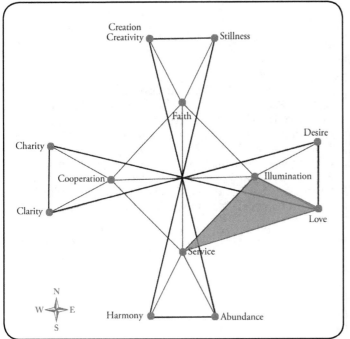

Spiritual Awakening

Left: *The Evolutionary Pyramid of the Aspirant.* This field of high frequency Galactic Energy creates and drives intense experiences of Spiritual Awakening.

Spiritual Discipline

Right: *The Evolutionary Pyramid of the Chela.* Located in the Eastern Door of the Golden City Vortex. This field of spiritual experience creates devotion and love for both the spiritual guru and their spiritual disciplines.

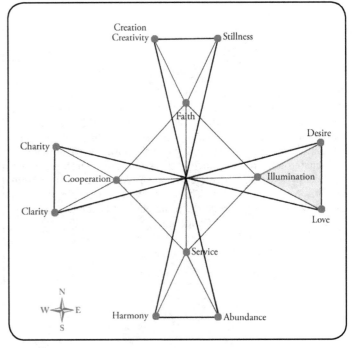

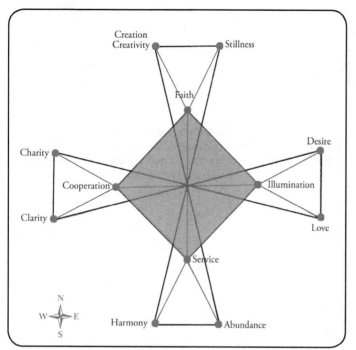

Vision and Compassion

Left: *The Evolutionary Pyramid of the Initiate.* This Evolutionary Pyramid drives visionary experiences. This field of energy is shaped as a square, but is actually two pyramids that represent both the *Prophet* and the *Bodhisattva*. This energy field helps to develop clairvoyance and clairaudience, "the eyes to see, ears to hear." This Evolutionary Pyramid also cultivates deep compassion, mercy, and forgiveness for self and others through applying the spiritual tenets of Service, Illumination, Cooperation, and Faith.

The Science of Spiritual Wisdom

Right: *The Evolutionary Pyramid of the Arhat.* This Evolutionary Pyramid assists individuals to cultivate and integrate the spiritual wisdom and intuition of the Evolutionary Biome. This is a field of experience that evolves spiritual intuition and insight into enlightenment. This creates profound spiritual knowledge. The Arhat is the trusted advisor, astrologer, feng shui practitioner, seasoned healer, or herbalist. In conventional thinking, the Arhat is one who has "overcome desire." This field of vibrational energy assists one to serve others through the principles of Clarity, Charity, and Cooperation.

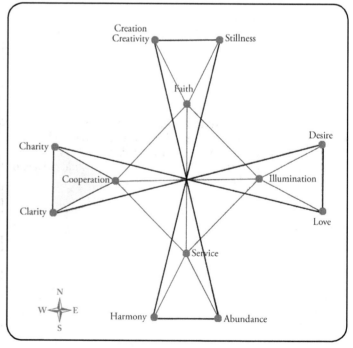

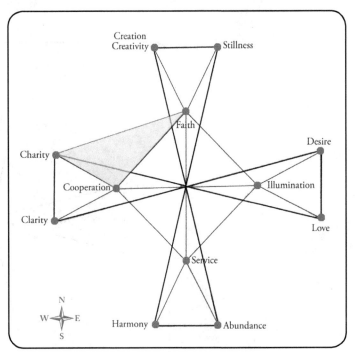

Strengthen the Soul

Right: *The Evolutionary Pyramid of the Adept.*
This Evolutionary Pyramid is located between the Golden City Western and Northern Doors. This field of remarkable energy produces the great soul—the *Mahatma*. Time spent in this Evolutionary Pyramid can help you to strengthen your resolve to overcome duality and reinforce the use of the Right-hand Path. The cultivation of conscious, deep meditation in this energetic field can lead to Astral Travel and train the soul for bi-location.

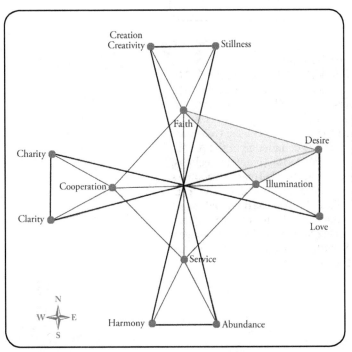

Mastery

Left: *The Evolutionary Pyramid of the Master.*
Mastery has many forms, and this field of energy helps you to realize your dharma, or great purpose. Since this Evolutionary Pyramid focuses upon your divinity, this energetic gives ideal support to progress your Ascension Process. These energies also help to recalibrate intention and objectives to achieve HU-man Development. Mastery possesses the consummate skill of command and self-realization over individual thoughts, feelings, and actions.

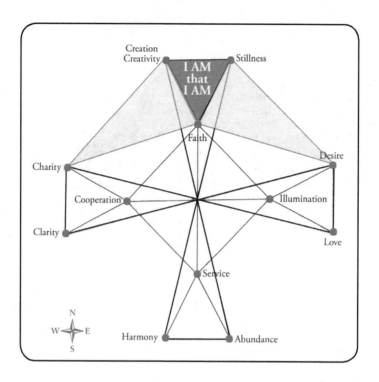

The Threefold Co-creator

Above: *The Evolutionary Pyramids of the HU-man and the I AM.*
The three final Evolutionary Pyramids of the North cultivate the
Evolutionary Points of Charity, Desire, Faith, Silence, and Creation-
Creativity. This is the domain of the HU-man, and time spent throughout these energetic fields will assist the realization of the God-man.
This is the final location to focus upon the completion of the Ascension. The Ascension is the process of Mastering thoughts, feelings,
and actions that balance positive and negative karmas. This allows
entrance into higher states of consciousness and frees a person from
the need to reincarnate on the lower Earth Planes. The threefold aspect
of the Creator mirrors and evolves the Unfed Flame of the Southern
Door. These principles are known as *beginning* (Stillness — Omega),
duration (Creation/Creativity — Alpha), and *transformation* (I AM
that I AM).

Lord Meru

Some accounts of Ascended Master teachings claim this Ascended Master is the blond and blue-eyed avatar who appeared in 15,000 BC to Atlanteans to warn of imminent Earth Changes. The myth alleges no one listened, and his radiant crystal sphere of light disappeared and five years later the continent—known as Meru, rolled to the East. The Atlantean culture led by Casimir Poseidon was forever submerged in cataclysmic ocean waters, and its once glorious history diluted to legend and myth.[1] In other esoteric teachings, the image of Lord Meru morphs into the great Native American teacher Lord Macaw; his symbol is the parrot, a representation of beauty, wisdom, and spiritual knowledge. The parrot is said to be the teacher of the birds of the Himalayans, and the White Parrot—also known as the Filial Parrot—hovers to the Bodhisattva Kuan Yin's right side as a symbol of ancestral respect. Lord Macaw's dark skin is contrasted by a colorful headdress filled with parrot, trogon, and quetzal bird feathers, a symbol of Quetzalcoatl—the Christ Consciousness.

Also known as the Great Sage of Ancient Mu—Ameru, Lord Meru was the Keeper of the Scrolls in Lemuria's final days. Esoteric historians claim the destruction of Mu began before 30,000 BC and continued for thousands of years. The final termination of the great civilization of the Pacific occurred between 9,000 and 12,000 BC, prior to the destruction of Poseidonis—the remaining lands of Atlantis.

1. "The Origin of the Brotherhood of the Seven Rays", http://www.seven-raystoday.com/secretoftheandes.htm, (2009).

The Spiritual Hierarchy entrusted Lord Meru and his partner and high priestess Amara-Mara, known as the Goddess Meru with scientific and spiritual records associated with the Right-hand Path and the Temple of Divine Light along with its venerated symbol and spiritual device: the Golden Disk of the Sun. Before the final cataclysms of Lemuria, it is claimed the pair traveled to Ancient South America in a "silver-needed airship" and safely re-established the sacred disk and the Brotherhood of the Seven Rays on the shores of the newly formed Lago Titicaca—Lake Titicaca.

Ascended Master myth claims Lord Meru spent many years as a spiritual ascetic wandering the new lands of South America, and he later joined forces with immigrants from the devastated lands. Through the use of the light forces concentrated within the Golden Disk, they cut blocks of stone to construct new buildings which became libraries and temples of Lemurian science, culture, spirituality, and esoteric knowledge. It is claimed these structures still exist to this day, and the ancient sanctuary of the Brotherhood of the Seven Rays is carefully guarded by the Great White Brotherhood.

Ancient Scrolls
It is claimed Lord Meru carried the Ancient Scrolls of Lemuria to South America.

Symbolism of the Great Sun Disk

(Right) *Aten and the Sun Disk: Relief of Akhenaten, Nefertiti and Two Daughters Adoring the Aten,* Ancient Egypt, 1372-1350 BCE. Painting of the Aten from Amarna.

(Next) *Sun Disk Sculpture* Sun disk on the roof of the Anahuacalli Musuem in Mexico City.

Aztec Calendar Stone
(Above) The Great Sun Disk depicted in Aztec culture. The Aztec Sun calendar is a circular stone with pictures representing how the Aztecs measured days, months, and cosmic cycles. 15th century Aztec "Sun Stone" sculpture, made into a diagram.

The Sun Disk in Egyptian Culture
Original artist unknown. Facsimile of a vignette from the *Book of the Dead of Ani*. The Sun disk of the god Ra is raised into the sky by an ankh-sign (signifying life) and a djed-pillar (signifying stability and the god Osiris) while adored by Isis, Nephthys, and baboons. Facsimile created 1890; original artwork created 1300 BCE. Scanned from *The Egyptian Book of the Dead: The Book of Going Forth by Day* by James Wasserman.

Mount Meru in Buddhist Cosmology
Bhutanese thanka of Mount Meru and the Buddhist Universe, 19th century.

Lord Meru's spiritual initiation began in the capital city of Lemuria, known as the Lands of Rama, now present-day Sri Lanka. The Lands of Rama are also known as the ancient empire of India which thrived until 10,000 to 15,000 BC.[2] The radiant energies of the once antediluvian temples of the city generate the etheric Mount Meru—acclaimed in both Hindu and Buddhist cosmology as the center of Earth's spiritual and metaphysical universes—home of the Devas. The spiritual mountain is said to be four to nine miles high, shaped like an hourglass, and guarded by the Four Great Kings of the Earth: the four directions. Before Lemuria's geological demise, Lord Meru's brother, Lord Himalaya, also immigrated from the Lemurian capital to the present-day Pamir Mountains, northeast of Kashmir, and established the Retreat of the Blue Lotus.[3]

The two spiritual refuges of Lemuria founded by two brothers deeply influenced the post-Atlantis' New World spirituality. Lord Himalaya's Retreat of the Blue Lotus radiated spiritual energy to the Eastern culture of Sumera—Ancient Mesopotamia, India, and China. Lord Meru's Brotherhood of the Seven Rays impacted spiritual growth in the West and the lands of Ameru—now known as America. In the New Times the Ascended Masters state the island of Sri Lanka, the once Lemurian sanctuary of Lord Meru and Lord Himalaya, will be known as the Holy Island. Today Lord Meru, Lord Himalaya, and the Goddess Meru each steward these Golden Cities—respectively, the Golden City of Gobi, which step-downs the energies of Shamballa into the entire Golden City Network; the Golden City of Adjatal located near the Retreat of the Blue Lotus, whose name means the Big Rainbow, (Adjatal is a tribute to the ancient Brotherhood of the Seven Rays); and the Golden City of Andeo, located in present-day Peru, which radiates much needed Feminine energies throughout the New Times to assist the incoming souls known as the Seventh Manu.

The Lineage of Manus

Lord Meru and Lord Himalaya both participate in the Earthly lineage of Manus. In Ascended Master terminology, Manus are the spiritual sponsors of each current or incoming race of souls on Earth. The Office of Manu in the Spiritual Hierarchy is considered of equal significance to the Karmic Board, the Seven Elohim and Seven Archangels, Shamballa, and the Lords of the Seven Rays. A Manu may sponsor a Root Race, (e.g., the Lemurian or Atlantean); or a Manu may serve one of seven sub-races of each major Root Race, (e.g., the Toltec, Mongolian, or Persian). H. P. Blavatsky introduced the idea of the Root Race in her book The Secret Doctrine, although the concept of tracking the stages of human evolution was explored earlier by the esoteric Frisian (Dutch) work the Oera Linda Book, written in the nineteenth century.[4] Ascended Master, Theosophical, and Hindu teachings concur on many points regarding the lineage of humanity's Manus; however, Theosophical and Hindu teachings conceptualize the Manu as a progenitor of the human race, while Ascended Master teachings perceive the Manu as a spiritual guardian and spiritual protector of the current or incoming race of humanity. A list of well-known Manus follows:

Manu	Epoch	Root Race/Sub-Race
Asuramaya	Lemuria	Third Root Race
Narada	Atlantis	Fourth Root Race
Lord Himalaya	Atlantis	Fourth Sub-race of the Fourth Root Race (Turanian)
Melchizedek	Atlantis	Fifth Sub-race of the Fourth Root Race (Semitic)
Lord Rama	Aryan	Fifth Root Race
Mother Mary	Aryan	Prophesied Seventh Sub-race of the Fifth Root Race
Lord Meru	New Times	Prophesied Manu of the Sixth Root Race

2. ABH Alexander, *Ancient Rama Empire of India, The Wonders of a Lost Civilization,* http://www.associatedcontent.com/article/110678/ancient_rama_empire_of_india.html, (2011).
3. A. D. K. Luk, *Law of Life and Teachings by Divine Beings* (ADK Luk Publishing, 1978, Pueblo, CO), Book III, page 558.

4. Wikipedia, *Root Race,* http://en.wikipedia.org/wiki/Root_race, (2011).

Island Del Sol, Lake Titicaca, Bolivia

Lord Meru's Influence in South America

Lord Meru's retreat near Lake Titicaca is also known as the Temple of Illumination and is affiliated with the vibratory action of the Feminine. "The feminine aspect of Meru is yet such a subtle activity that it is not apparent to the outer consciousness...it will increase in its irresistible force and be a tremendous assistance in the blanketing of the individual emotional nature and the peace-commanding Presence, which will enable (one) to much more easily Master (their) own feeling world."[15] The Ascended Masters state that the Golden City of Andeo is one of three Feminine aspects prophesied to envelop the spiritual consciousness of South America and influence the New Times. These three aspects are: Consistency (Golden City of Andeo); Nurturing (Golden City of Braham); and Devotion (Golden City of Tehekoa).

Regarding the great Manu of the Sixth Root-Race, A. D. K. Luk writes, "Lord Meru is the archetype of the entire Sixth Root Race, with all its seven sub-races. This means that He is the perfect God image for each one of these millions of spirit sparks called forth for evolution upon the planet Earth by His God Flame. All the individuals who belong to the Sixth Root Race are His special charge. He can never know full freedom of release from responsibilities of guardianship, until every one of these individual souls are developed and matured in the schoolroom of Earth's experience. When His particular children do evolve spiritually, He will establish a great civilization in South America, which will be a Golden Age of great perfection, enduring for over 10,000 years."[5]

_____

5. Luk, *Law of Life*, Book II, page 323.

The Map of the Ancients

In the I AM America Teachings, Lord Meru, or Lord Macaw, as he prefers to be called at this time, shares one of the eternal records he rescued ages ago from the Lands of Lemuria: the Map of the Ancients. This map of the world simultaneously portrays the lands of Rama, Mu, and Atlantis. No date or timeframe is given for this ancient map; however, its landforms insinuate an epoch before our current geologic period and postdate the theorized existence of the dual continents of Laurasia and Gondwana. These massive continents allegedly broke apart the super-continent of Pangaea and are scientifically estimated to have existed 200 to 180 million years ago. Perhaps Lord Meru purposely left the date off of the ancient map. According to many esoteric teachings, galactic light calibrates scientific development and understanding, and contemporary science may not yet be able to properly interpret this map's geologic and evolutionary implications. However, Lord Meru states that the purpose of the Map of the Ancients is to illustrate the migration and evolution of human consciousness as shaped through the Seven Rays, and it identifies nine civilizations the Rays have influenced and formed. Geologists who ascribe to the theory of Plate Tectonics and the hypothesis of Continental Drift believe that approximately 135 Mya (million years ago) the South American Plate and the African Plate separated and began to form the familiar map of the Earth we recognize today.

Ameru

Some esoteric historians refer to Ameru as Ameru—the Incan Christ, Quetzalcoatl. From Ameru comes the word America, and, according to Manly P. Hall, "Ameruca is literally translated 'Land of the Plumed Serpent.'" The ancient peoples of America were known as the Red Children of the Sun and worshipped Quetzalcoatl, a prophet of the Christ Consciousness, a messenger from our solar sun.[1]

Ameru and the Right-Hand Path

The provenance of Ameruca—the Land of the Plumed Serpent—is the lost history of Mu, Lemuria, and Atlantis.

Manly Hall
Well-known esoteric historian and philosopher Manly P. Hall wrote about Ameru and the secret destiny of America.

The Plumed Serpent metaphorically represents the developed Chakra System of the Divine God-man, the Ascended Masters' HU-man. The plume of light atop the head is the developed crown chakra, and the serpent's coils represent the mature Kundalini system, or human energy system comprised of seven chakras. It is claimed that many Lemurians and Atlanteans had the advanced capacity to function in both the Fourth and Fifth Dimension as Spiritual Masters and Shamans where an Alchemical and spiritual battle ensued: the Left-Hand Path versus the Right-Hand Path. Spiritual development at this level of consciousness endows power over the Elemental Kingdom, and the unascended Spiritual Master is often pitted between both malevolent Black Magic and constructive White Magic.

According to Theosophical history, the Lemurian and Atlantean epochs overlap and it is alleged that the lands of Lemuria, also known as Shalmali, existed in the Indian and Southern Pacific Oceans and included the continent of Australia. Lemuria is the remaining culture and civilization of Mu—an expansive continent that once spanned the entire present-day Pacific Ocean.[2] Some esoteric writers place the destruction of Mu around the year 30,000 BC; others place its demise millions of years ago. The apparent discrepancy of these timelines is likely due to two different interpretations of the Cycle of the Yugas—large recurring periods of time employed in the Hindu timekeeping system. The older classical method of calculation literally applies time spans of millions of years; the contemporary method, revealed in 1894, applies cycles that are much shorter.

---

1. Manly P. Hall, *The Secret Teachings of All Ages: An Encyclopedic Outline of Masonic, Hermetic, Qabbalistic and Rosicrucian Symbolical Philosophy* (The Philosophical Research Society, Inc., 1988, Los Angeles, CA), Diamond Jubilee Edition, page 194.

2. Wikipedia, *Root Race*, http://en.wikipedia.org/wiki/Root_race, (2011).

LANDS OF THE
NORTH
Red Ray - Mars

LANDS OF THE
NORTH
Red Ray - Mars

ANCIENT CITY OF
SHAMBALLA

LAND OF
BRIHASPATI
Yellow Ray - Jupiter

LAND OF
PLUMED
SERPENT
Ameru
White Ray - Venus

GALACTIC
HEART

FUTURE LANDS OF
EUROPE
Violet Ray - Urahus

LAND OF
BRIHASPATI
Yellow Ray - Jupiter

LAND OF
RAMA
Blue Ray - Saturn

ATLANTIS
White Ray - Moon

ANCIENT LANDS OF
QUETZALCOATL

CRADLE OF
KNOWLEDGE
Green Ray - Mercury

INFLUENCE OF THE
FEMININE
White Ray - Moon

LAND OF
MU
Gold & Ruby Rays
Sun

Map of the
ANCIENTS
A Migration and Evolution of Consciousness
The Seven Rays and the Nine Civilizations they have formed.

Map of the Ancients
This map is a depiction of Earth given by the Ascended Master Lord Meru to illustrate the spiritual evolution of
humanity through the Seven Rays of Light and Sound. This map of the world simultaneously portrays the lands of
Rama, Mu, and Atlantis. No date or timeframe is given for this ancient map; however, its landforms insinuate an
epoch before our current geologic period and postdate the theorized existence of the dual continents of Laurasia and
Gondwana. The Ancient Lands of Quetzalcoatl rise and fall under the waters of both the present-day Pacific and
Atlantic Oceans. These lands later evolve into sections of present-day North America, Mexico, and Central America.

Map of the Ancients and the influence of the Seven Rays on Nations.

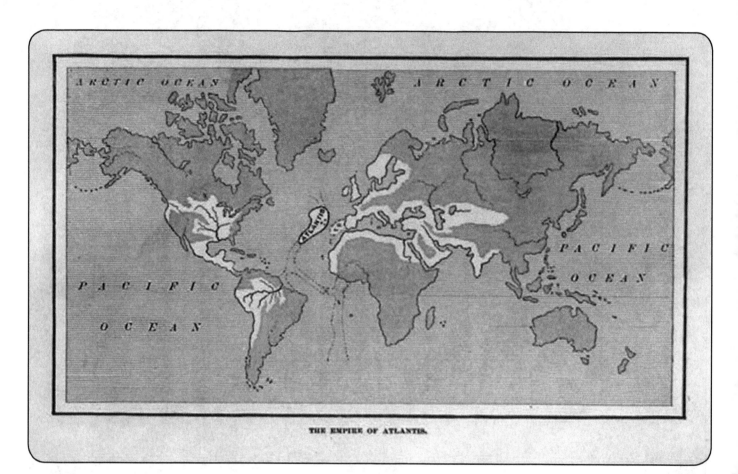

Atlantis Map
Ignatius Donelly, 1882

Lemuria

Short or long, the cycles of the world's ages contain similar archetypes of consciousness and the ever-important ebb and tide of cosmic lessons humanity is destined to learn. The traditional Lemurian was said to live "close to nature" yet was culturally and technologically sophisticated, placing a high value on spiritual and personal growth. Lemurian citizens lived in an esteemed agrarian utopia which attracted migrants from other countries in the ancient pre-Atlantis world. Prior to a polar shift, it is claimed Lemuria suffered civil strife and economic breakdown through illegal immigration. Spiritually and morally unable to expel the foreigners, Lemurians clung to their spiritual aspirations that someday the non-citizens, "who had all the advantages of citizens and cared little about personal growth or taking citizenship training," would later join fellow Lemurians in their spiritual quest.[16] Apparently there was little that could be done. The Lemurian economy could not sustain its empirical growth and needed the immigrant workforce; to further complicate matters, the discontented non-citizenry broke into two conflicting groups: the Pfrees and the Katholis. Inevitably open combat erupted between the two cultures.[17] "The non-citizens eventually divided into two opposing groups: those who prized practicality and those who prized spirituality. The citizenry were more balanced, and valued each equally. The Lemurian Fellowship calls the practical minded non-citizens Pfrees and the spiritually minded non-citizens Katholis," writes David Hatcher Childress in the book Lost Cities of Ancient Lemuria and the Pacific. Hatcher describes the Lemurian cataclysm:

"The continent had been subsiding for hundreds of years, when a Pole Shift caused the Pacific continent plate to sink amid much juggling of the tectonic plates. The once great cities were suddenly a thousand feet underwater. The Pfrees had already established their main colony on another continent (actually an island group at that time), Atlantis, while the Katholis established a colony of their own, later to be known as the Rama Empire, in India."[1]

Hatcher claims the venerated Elders of Lemuria also escaped the global tragedy by moving to an uninhabited plateau in central Asia. This similar account mirrors Ascended Master teachings and Lord Himalaya's founding of the Retreat of the Blue Lotus. By Hatcher's explanation, the Lemurian elders re-established their spiritual teachings and massive library as the Thirteenth School. It is claimed these teachings and spiritual records became foundational teachings in the Great White Brotherhood of the mystical lands of Hsi Wang Mu (the Abode of the Immortals), and the Kuan Yin Lineage of Gurus.

Ameru and the Rise and Fall of Atlantis

During the spiritually enlightened phase of the civilization of Atlantis, the rule of the Toltec Sub-race—the reputed ancestors of today's Native American—created a world society of architectural beauty, unrivaled Earth-friendly technology, with organized armies, governments, and elegant social amenities. The lands of Mu, Ameru, and Atlantis formed the vast empire of the spiritually evolved Atlantean. Spiritual teachings, grand ceremonies, spiritual meditation, and the magnificent Atlantean temples were all dedicated to the worship of the sun.[2] Some esoteric texts allege that the Lands of Mu and the Lands of Rama were home to the spiritual elite—the ancient priesthood of Lemuria; the homeland of Atlantis housed the central government and its wondrous buildings and temples; and the Lands of Ameru remained mostly uninhabited, with a few small cities colonized by Atlanteans. At the height of Atlantean culture, the lands of Ameru were intentionally held in environmental stewardship primarily

1. David Hatcher Childress, *Lost Cities of Ancient Lemuria and the Pacific* (Adventures Unlimited Press, 1988, Stelle, IL), page 128.
2. Ibid., page 152.

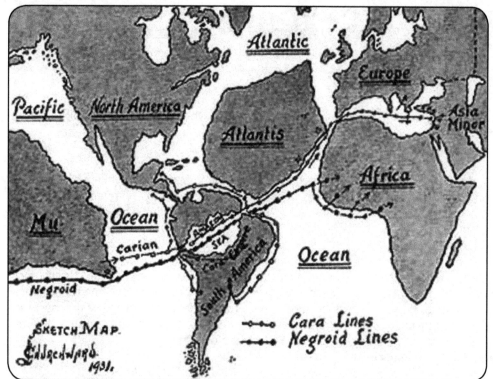

The Churchward Map
James Churchward. Churchward's map showing how he thought Mu refugees spread out after the cataclysm through South America, along the shores of Atlantis and into Africa. James Churchward (1851 — 1936). Book: *The Lost Continent of Mu.*

today. Not then arid or very sparsely inhabited, though vastly colder in winter, owing to the nearness of the vast glaciers of the north. The Nevada lakes were not then mere dried up beds of borax and soda, nor the 'Great Salt Lake' of Utah a bitter, brackish body of water of its present comparatively small size. All lakes were large bodies of fresh water and the Great Salt Lake was an inland sea of fresh floods, bearing icebergs from the glaciers on its northern shores. Arizona, that treasure-house of the geologist, had its now marvelous desert covered with the waters of Miti, as we called the great inland sea of that region…On the shores of Miti was a considerable population, and one city of no small size—colonists all, from Atl."[3]

It is claimed that secluded Atlantean Temples were established in the lands of Ameru. Oliver describes an Atlantean Temple in the Teton Mountains of Idaho discovered in an 1870s expedition of the Yellowstone region led by the U.S. geologist Ferdinand V. Hayden:

"On its top he found a roofless structure of granite slaps, within which, he said, that 'granite detritus was a depth indicating that for eleven

for agricultural use; fruit and grain crops grew bountifully alongside roaming herds of genetically bred wild game—elk and deer. Frederick Oliver writes about the abundant lands of Ameru colonized by Atlanteans in the esoteric classic *A Dweller on Two Planets*:

"Successively we came to the Isthmus of Panama, then over four hundred miles in breadth; to Mexico (South Incalia) and to the immense plains of the Mississippi. These latter formed the great cattle-lands where Poseid drew most of its supplies of flesh-foods, and where, when the modern world discovered it, enormous herds of wild progeny of ancient stock roamed at will. Buffalo, elk, bear, deer and mountain sheep—all off-spring of the remotest ages—to the west lay in what early American days were called the 'great plains.' But in the days of Poseid they had a far different appearance from that which they bear

3. Frederick Spencer Oliver, *A Dweller on Two Planets or The Dividing of the Way by Phylos the Thibetan* (Harper and Row Publishers, 1974, San Francisco, CA), page 170.

thousand years it had been undisturbed'...He was examining a structure made by Poseid hands one hundred and twenty-seven and a half centuries ago . . ."4

Religious teachings and colorful motifs of the Children of the Sun allegedly migrated into the preceding cultures of ancient Egypt, the Mayan, and are said to have influenced both the Aztec of Mexico and the Native American tribes of North America. Occultists link Atlantean culture to North Africa and the surrounding areas of the Mediterranean: Greece, Italy, Portugal, and Spain. Perhaps one of the best known accounts of ancient Atlantis was written by Ignatius Donnelly in 1882. His book Atlantis, the Antediluvian World was revised in 1949 by mythologist Egerton Sykes (1894–1983). Hugh Cayce, son of the renowned psychic Edgar Cayce writes:

"Donnelly's arguments are based largely on evidence of similarities between the culture of Egypt and the Indian cultures of Central and South America. On both sides of the Atlantic one finds the use of a 365-day calendar, the practice of embalming, the building of pyramids, legends of a flood, etc. Donnelly argues that both the ancient Egyptian and American Indian cultures originated in Atlantis, and spread east and west when Atlantis was destroyed. An Atlantean heritage, Donnelly suggests, would explain the fact that the Basques of the Spanish Pyrenees differ from all their neighbors in appearance and language...Donnelly says Spain, Portugal, and the Canary Islands would be likely landing spots for refugees from sinking Atlantis."5

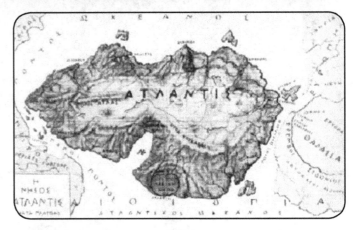

Atlantis

(Top) Depiction of the ancient entrance to Atlantis, alleged to have had entrance pillars and harbor walls. (Next) Patroclus Kampankis, 1891. Originally drawn in 1891, first published in his book "The procataclysm *Communication of the Two Worlds via Atlantis*," Constantinople 1893.

---

4. Oliver, *A Dweller on Two Planets*.
5. Hugh Lynn Cayce, *Edgar Cayce on Atlantis* (Warner Books, 1968, New York, NY), page 18.

Rama with a Squirrel

Artist unknown, 1940. It is claimed that Sri Rama appears on Earth during times of darkness and evil. According to Hindu legend, Sri Rama incarnated during Treta Yuga, the same timeline of Atlantis and the Land of Rama, as an incarnation of Vishnu.

Land of Rama

The Land of Rama grew and developed alongside the great Atlantean civilization, and was ruled by magnificent kings—spiritual priests, adepts, and Master Teachers known in Sanskrit as Rishis. It is claimed that seven great cities emerged in the Rama Empire, known as the Seven Rishi Cities. David Childress writes, "The Rama Empire spread out to include most of the Indian sub-continent. It probably extended as far west as Iran or so, and as far east as Burma."[1] The Rama Empire rivaled Atlantean culture with its technology and it is claimed both countries developed sophisticated air-flight; however the Rama Empire was known for its creation of the Vimana, a double-decked aircraft that flew "with the speed of the wind," and "weapons such as fireballs that could destroy a whole city."[2] Many ancient Indian texts including the Ramayana and the Mahabharata describe Rama's splendor and beauty alongside its endurance of horrific wars and battles. Perhaps one of the most eclectic accounts of this prehistoric civilization, from the Lemurian Fellowship, uniquely describes the clash between Lemurian rivals, now world-powers, the once practical Pfrees—Atlanteans; and the Katholis—the spiritually adept Rama Empire.[3]

> "The Atlanteans (sent) a well-equipped army to India in order to subjugate the Rama Empire and bring it under the sovereignty of Atlantis. Equipped with a formidable array of weapons the Atlanteans landed their valixi (aircraft) outside one of the Rishi Cities…sent a message to the ruling Priest-King of the city that they should surrender. The Priest-King sent word back to the Atlantean general, 'We of India have no quarrel with you of Atlantis. We ask that we be permitted to follow our own way of life.'"[4]

The Atlanteans, equipped with advanced weaponry and technology, perceived their enemy weak, sensed an easy victory, and replied, "We shall not destroy your land with the mighty weapons at our command provided you pay sufficient tribute and accept the rulership of Atlantis."[5] The Priest-King responded, "We of India do not believe in war and strife, peace being our ideal. Neither would we destroy you or your soldiers who but follow orders. However, if you persist in your determination to attack us without cause and merely for the purpose of conquest, you will leave us no recourse but to destroy you and all of your leaders. Depart, and leave us in peace."[6]

The Atlantean army began their invasion, while the great Rishi watched from his hilltop palace. The Priest-King of Rama raised his arms upwards and spiritually evoked the power of heaven through yogic technique. The Atlantean General and each of his descending officers dropped dead to the ground—their hearts burst. The Atlantean force, without leadership and organization, panicked and retreated.[7]

Inevitably after the humiliating defeat, the government of Atlantis, instead of subjugating the ancient Indians, decided to destroy the major cities of the Rama Empire with nuclear attacks. Hatcher claims the Mahabharata is a historical account of the use of nuclear weaponry, and the Atlantean destruction of the magnificent Rishi Cities.[8]

> "Gurkha, flying a swift and powerful Vimana,
> Hurled a single projectile
> Charged with all the power of the Universe.
> An incandescent column of smoke and flame,
> As bright as ten thousands Suns,
> Rose with all its splendor."
> –the Mahabharata

---

1. David Hatcher Childress, *Lost Cities of Ancient Lemuria and the Pacific* (Adventures Unlimited Press, 1988, Stelle, IL), page 70.
2. Ibid., page 71.
3. Ibid.
4. Ibid., page 72.
5. David Hatcher Childress, *Lost Cities of Ancient Lemuria and the Pacific*.
6. Ibid.
7. Ibid.
8. Ibid.

H. P. Blavatsky claims that prior to the invasion of the Rama Empire, a new sub-race of Atlanteans incarnated on Earth: the Turanians. According to Theosophical history, the Turanian sub-race was a young group of souls: selfish, materialistic, and inevitably they overcame the wise stewardship of the Atlantean Toltecs.[9] The advanced science and technology of Atlantis sadly morphed into egotistical self-indulgence with continued violence and cruelty against other nations. Extreme supernatural experience prevailed during the Atlantean cultural downturn and led Atlantean geneticists to create a bizarre sub-race of Animal-Humans—chimeras. The chimeras were abused as sex slaves and later bred into vicious armies of cruel, blood-thirsty warriors.[10] The psychic readings of Edgar Cayce reiterate the myths of the chimeras, and the moral conflict their presence created in Atlantis between the Sons of the Law of One and the Sons of Belial.

> "In Atlantis when there (was turmoil) between children of the Law of One and Sons of Belial, found Sons of Belial desirable for gratification of material emotions and desires."[11]

The account of this conflict describes the Sons of the Law of One seeking higher consciousness to spiritually affect the Group Mind of Atlantis and lift the spiritual consciousness of the nation to overcome the conflict,

> ". . . through the concentration of the Group Mind of the children of the Law of One, they entered into a fourth-dimensional consciousness—or were absent from the body."[12]

Clearly, the Sons of the Law of One saw the chimeras as developing souls; the Sons of Belial saw these creations

Christ in Desert
Nicholas Roerich, 1933.

merely as property—common chattel. The Cayce readings further explain:

> "This is not intended to indicate that there is transmigration or transmutation of the soul from animal to human; but the comparison is made as to trait, as to mind, as to how those so domesticated in the present are dependant upon their masters for that consideration of their material as well as mental welfare—yet in each there is still the instinct, the predominant nature of that class or group-soul impregnation into which it has pushed itself for self-expression."[13]

9. Wikipedia, *Root Race,* http://en.wikipedia.org/wiki/Root_race, (2011).
10. Ibid.
11. Hugh Lynn Cayce, *Edgar Cayce on Atlantis* (Warner Books, 1968, New York, NY), page 102.
12. Ibid., page 103.

13. H. Cayce, *Edgar Cayce on Atlantis.*

Atlantean spiritual life spiraled downward into the polarized misuse of occult energy and black wizardry, and sorcery denigrated the great Mystery Schools; in the later Atlantean period human sacrifice and gross idolatry disabled the once mighty civilization, facilitating its inevitable destruction through massive Earth Changes.

The demise of Atlantis was unavoidable; however modern-day geologists, archaeologists, and occultists disagree about its timing. Ascended Master teachings affirm that Atlantis—a continent whose geo-physical and political existence probably spanned well over 100,000 years—experienced several phases of traumatic Earth Change. This same belief is held by occult historians who claim that the Earth repeatedly cycles through periods of massive Earth Change and cataclysmic Pole Shifts that activate tectonic plates and subsequently submerge whole continents and create vital new lands for Earth's successors. Theosophists and the psychic readings of Edgar Cayce agree that a massive deluge occurred in Atlantean times somewhere between 75,000 and 50,000 BC; this was followed by another period of Earth's instability around 28,000 BC.[14], [15] However, both groups conclude that the Atlantis finale took place around 10,000 BC, and it was described by the Greek philosopher Plato in the historic dialogues Timaeus and Critias.

Prior to the Atlantean epoch, Mu and Lemuria had suffered a similar fate; yet the sinking of Atlantis remains to this day etched in humanity's archetypal consciousness. The Edgar Cayce readings claim that many of the souls who once walked, lived, and loved the lands and the mystical times of Atlantis are today reincarnated in America—Ameru, the beloved land of the Toltecs. Hugh Cayce writes, "Along with technological abilities, they bring tendencies for being extremists. Often they exhibit individual and group karma associated with selfishness and exploitation where others are concerned. Many of them lived during one of the periods of destruction, or geological change in Atlantean history. If Edgar Cayce's prophecies are correct, a similar period of Earth Changes is imminent."[16]

_____

14. Ibid., page 28.
15. Wikipedia, *Root Race*.
16. Cayce, *Edgar Cayce on Atlantis*.

The Right-hand Path

The Spiritual Masters who fled Atlantis and re-established their spiritual temples and sanctuaries in the New Lands held their chelas to the sacred vows of the Right-Hand Path which today is practiced in Buddhism and Christianity as Compassion, Tolerance, Unity, the Brotherhood of Man, Mercy, and Forgiveness. This holy vow is reiterated in the Ascended Masters' Awakening Prayer: "Great Light of Divine Wisdom, stream forth to my being; and through your right use let me serve mankind and the planet . . ."

Theologians of Ascended Master teachings claim Lord Meru's temple was founded in the New World to embrace the Western ideals of the Right-Hand Path, and teach spiritual liberation and Ascension attained by way of Sainthood through the rigor of humane service in the Ninth Pyramid of HU-man Consciousness. Today, many evolved Arhats choose to circumvent the spiritually arduous lure of the Tenth Pyramid and the horrifying conflict once experienced in the final days of Atlantis. Only the Adept is capable of venturing into the dualistic nomenclature of the Spiritual Master. Initiates of the Tenth Pyramid must properly prepare and strengthen their resolve with intimate knowledge and experience regarding the pitfalls of necromancy and reinforce the spiritual practice of the Right-Hand Path attained through the proper use of Alchemy, Transmutation, and God-Protection. The Master Jesus Christ fasts for forty days and nights and faces the temptations of Satan in the demanding spiritual tests inherent in the Tenth Pyramid of Consciousness. The soul-trying conflict is illustrated in this Christian story:

1. Jesus Christ is asked by Satan to turn stones into bread—an abomination of the Elemental Kingdom; he responds, "One does not live by bread alone..."
2. Satan challenges Jesus Christ to jump off a temple's rooftop; after all, since he was a Son of God, surely an Angel will catch him. Unable to misuse the Divine Power entrusted to him, Jesus Christ responds, "You shall not put the Lord, your God, to the test." Will L. Garver, metaphysical author of the Victorian Age, clarifies this spiritual precept in the classic occult novel Brother of the Third Degree, "Remember that

Painting of Native American
N. C. Wyeth, 1907. Esoteric historians claim that numerous Native American
tribes hold the ancient lands of Ameru in spiritual purity until they unite in
the future as the "Land of the Plumed Serpent."

the Great Brotherhood requires no tests except those which are mental and moral in nature."[17]

3. During this period, all of the Kingdoms of Creation are revealed to Jesus Christ: the Mineral Kingdom; the Vegetable Kingdom; the Elemental Kingdom; the Animal Kingdom; the Creative Hierarchy (the Human Kingdom); and the majestic Kingdoms of the Elohim and Archangels. Again, Jesus Christ is asked by Satan to assert his complete dominion, power, and authority over their realms; yet, Jesus Christ responds: "The Lord, your God, shall you worship and him alone shall you serve," affirming the spiritual principles of Unity, Cooperation, and the Sanctity of life through the Right-Hand Path.

America's Secret Destiny

The Ascended Masters claim America's destiny is linked to both the Lemurian and the Atlantean histories, and in the New Times its populace is prophesied to spiritually self-actualize as a nation, and realize the HU-man. Esoteric freemasonry reflects a similar spiritual knowledge and restates the hidden potential in the Seal of Solomon and the Thirteen Pyramids of Consciousness in the Eight-sided Cell of Perfection. "Theosophists and Rosicrucians believe that America was the thirteenth step in evolution," states Dr. Robert Hieronimus in America's Secret Destiny. Apparently these esoteric teachings perceive the contemporary American as the culmination of thirteen evolutionary phases, or in Theosophical terms, sub-races of spiritual human development. The thirteen phases includes one sub-race of Lemuria, the seven sub-races of Atlantis, and the five sub-races of the Aryan. Dr. Hieronimus writes, "The thirteenth race is expected to mother a sixth sub-race, which in turn will foster the sixth root race. By the year A.D. 2600, the seeds of the sixth root race will have germinated, and a great part of America's destiny will have been fulfilled."[18] H. P. Blavatsky prophesied the birth and evolution of the Aryan sixth sub-race in the United States in the early twenty-first century.[19] Ascended Masters prophesy this sub-race as the New Children, who will lead the mass consciousness to apprehend the individualized HU-man. The Seventh Manu—or the seventh and final sub-race of the Aryan—is prophesied to incarnate in South America, and it is claimed this race's evolved spiritual vision will unite Canada, the United States, Mexico, Central and South America as ONE nation—America—once again as the Land of the Plumed Serpent.

Throughout thousands, if not millions of years of human evolution and spiritual development, the destiny of the world's nations has been guided by a hierarchy of elder Brothers and Sisters who have assisted humanity's development at each critical stage. It is claimed that four great Ascended Masters—Kuthumi, El Morya, Saint Germain, and Djwal Kul—were vital in the founding of America, and continue this essential mentoring to this day. "Some of the founders of America may have been consciously or unconsciously students of these teachers, just as some contemporary Americans are pupils of these masters." Dr. Hieronimus adds, "In fact, the motto of the hierarchy of world teachers is identical with America's destiny—the brotherhood of man and the Fatherhood of God." In the I AM America teachings, El Morya, Kuthumi, Saint Germain, Sananda, and Serapis Bey are the Master Teachers of the United States Golden Cities. [For more information on the Master Teachers of the Golden Cities throughout the world, see Freedom Star Book.]

From the Scene at the Signing of the Constitution of the United States Howard Chandler Cristy, 1940. It is alleged that Saint Germain was physically present at the signing of the US Constitution, inciting the delegates at a critical juncture to, "Sign, not only for yourselves, but for all ages!"

17. Will L. Garver, *Brother of the Third Degree* (Garber Communications, 1989, Blauvelt, NY), page 183.
18. Robert Hieronimus, *America's Secret Destiny, Spiritual Vision and the Founding of A Nation* (Destiny Books, 1989, Rochester, VT), page 94.
19. Wikipedia, Root Race, http://en.wikipedia.org/wiki/Root_race, (2011).

Krishna and Balarama Ride Forth to Proclaim Yudisthira to be World Ruler
From the *Ancient Text of the Lord*, Bhagavata Purana, 1785.

The Cycle of the Yugas

Vedic Rishis claim the evolutionary status of humanity is contingent upon the quality of Ray Forces streaming to Earth as a non-visible quasar light from the Galactic Center—the Great Central Sun. While the Rays are invisible to the naked eye, their presence contains subtle electromagnetic energy and psychics may detect their luminous astral light. Ancient astrologers visually observed and experienced the Seven Rays of Light and Sound. Their astronomy, advanced beyond today's science, maintained that our solar Sun was in reality a double star. Our Sun rotates with a companion—a dwarf star which contains no luminosity of its own. This theory suggests that as our Solar System orbits the Great Central Sun, Earth experiences long periods of time when the dwarf star impedes the flow of the Rays from the Galactic Center; likewise, there are times when this important stream of light is unhampered. Since the light energy from the Central Sun nourishes spiritual and intellectual knowledge on the Earth, the Vedic Rishis expertly tracked Earth's movement in and out of the flow and reception of this cosmic light. This cycle is known as the Cycle of the Yugas, or the World Ages whose constant change instigates the advances and deterioration of cultures and civilizations. There are four Yugas: the Golden Age (Satya or Krita Yuga); the Silver Age, (Treta Yuga); the Bronze Age, (Dvapara Yuga); the Iron Age, (Kali Yuga). The dharmic Bull of Truth—a Vedic symbol of morality—represents this cyclic calendar. According to Vedic tradition the bull loses a leg as a symbol of Earth's loss of twenty-five percent of cosmic light with each cycle of time. During a Golden Age, the Earth receives one-hundred percent cosmic light from the Great Central Sun. In a Silver Age, Earth receives seventy-five percent light and in a Bronze Age, fifty percent light. We are now living in Kali Yuga: the age of materialism when Earth receives only twenty-five percent light.

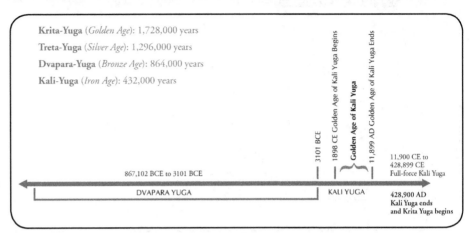

Classical Calculation of the Yugas

The classical calculation of the Yugas is depicted above, with Kali Yuga beginning in the year 3,101 BCE with the death of Krishna. According to Vedic Prophecies the Golden Age of Kali Yuga begins in the year 1898 CE and ends in the year 11,900 CE. The above illustration includes the prophesied 10,000-year period of the Golden Age of Kali Yuga.

The science of Vedic Astrology—Jyotish—was given to humanity in a time of greater light on Earth. Vedic and esoteric scholars speculate that the calculation for the timing of the Yugas may be faulty, and we are living in the infant stages of Dvapara Yuga. This opinion is based on the calculations of Sri Yuteswar, guru of Paramahansa Yogananda. Some Vedic adherents of the Puranas—ancient, religious texts—allege we are currently experiencing a minor upswing of Galactic Light, the Golden Age of Kali Yuga. It is important to understand the Golden Age of Kali Yuga is not a full force one-hundred percent Krita Yuga; however, the Master Teachers claim it is possible Earth may receive up to seventy-five percent Galactic Light, equal to a Silver Age Treta Yuga at the height of this ten-thousand year period.

The Four Gifts for Kali Yuga

According to ancient texts, the world entered Kali Yuga, or the Age of Quarrel, thousands of years ago when Maharaja Yūdhisthira noticed the Vedic antagonist darkening his kingdom. The king ceded his throne to his grandson Raja

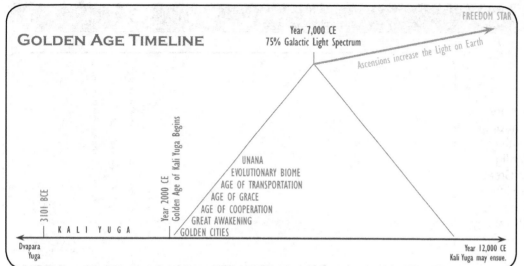

GOLDEN AGE TIMELINE

FREEDOM STAR

Year 7,000 CE
75% Galactic Light Spectrum

Ascensions increase the Light on Earth

3101 BCE

Year 2000 CE
Golden Age of Kali Yuga Begins

UNANA
EVOLUTIONARY BIOME
AGE OF TRANSPORTATION
AGE OF GRACE
AGE OF COOPERATION
GREAT AWAKENING
GOLDEN CITIES

K A L I   Y U G A

Dvapara
Yuga

Year 12,000 CE
Kali Yuga may ensue.

Golden Age Timeline
This chart represents the beginning of Kali Yuga, our entrace into the Golden Age of Kali Yuga, and the anticipated rise of energies. The principles of the Ascended Masters, i.e. the Golden Cities, the Age of Cooperation, and Unana are not presented as a timeline. They are listed to remind the reader of the important philosophical and scientific principles that help to create the New Times. It is prophesied in the year 7,000 CE, energies will either continue to rise, or begin a decline.

Parikshit, and the court, including its wise men, retreated to the Himalayas.

Wise and benevolent souls knew the dire consequences of the lessening of Galactic Light on Earth, so the Seers, the Vedic rishis, and the Master Teachers gave humanity the following three gifts: the written word, Vastu Shastra, Jyotish, and the science of the Golden Cities.

The sages prophesied that humans would suffer from diminished recall and an inability to sustain oral tradition, thus losing historical knowledge to oblivion—that's why they bestowed the alphabet on humanity. Vastu Shastra, the ancient science of geomancy, was the world's second gift. Maharaja Yūdhisthira's exile in the mountains created a dearth of Vastu knowledge among the Hindu people.[1] So, the ancient practice, in effect, reincarnated in another culture. Legend says Vastu Shastra leaped across the Himalayas where it conceived a child—the practice of Feng Shui. Most of all, the wise men knew humanity would need spiritual liberation from the cycle of death: the gift of Jyotish, the personal and intricate science of moksha (liberation). The ancient gurus imparted this knowledge of the soul's journey on Earth and its relationship with the Astral and Causal Bodies.

1. Sri Yukteswar, *The Holy Science*, (Los Angeles: Self-Realization Fellowship), page 15.

Evolutionary Biome and the Golden Cities

Finally, the Golden Cities possess the ability to enhance the Evolutionary Biome—the Consciousness of Unana—through their network of intricate Adjutant Points. This accelerates humanity's spiritual evolution and Ascension Process. Remember, the Golden Age of Kali Yuga is not a one-hundred percent Galactic Light spectrum Satya Yuga. Yet, the waves of increased light from the Galactic Sun and our solar system's entrance into a highly charged plasma field that potentiates Galactic Light rapidly evolves life on Earth. The Ascended Masters claim that the Golden Cities can further increase evolution during this relatively short evolutionary period of ten-thousand years to the heights of a full-fledged Treta Yuga. This is a Silver Age with seventy-five percent Galactic Light spectrum!

According to the prophecies of the Ascended Masters, we noticeably entered the Golden Age of Kali Yuga in the year 2,000 CE. This is when the Earth and humanity began to demonstrate effects from the energies from the Galactic Center, alongside our solar system's entrance into the light enriching plasma field that researchers often refer to as the *Photon Belt*. We will experience a growth of energies for 5,000 years until the year 7,000 CE. After the zenith of energies in 7,000 CE, the next 5,000 years cycle into a progressive decline of energies until the year 12,000 CE. Then our solar system exits the energy-calibrating plasma field and the Galactic Light spectrum decreases, resulting in Earth's return to a full force Kali Yuga. The Ascended

Masters concur that the ongoing evolution and Ascension of humanity may alter this scenario altogether, and evolution on Earth may continue to increase from the year 7,000 CE forward. This is due to the Evolutionary Biome of Ascension on Earth as self-sustaining light propels Earth onward into the Freedom Star. [For more information see: *New World Wisdom, Book Two*.]

The Vedic viewpoint concerning the Golden Age of Kali Yuga, however, is quite different with varying cycles of ascending and descending Galactic Light.

Yugas and the Yuteswar Theory

Galactic Light is said to regulate the intelligence of humanity during the Cycle of the Yugas, and some Vedic teachers claim the mathematical calculations made during the darkness of Kali Yuga are inaccurate. This is the theory of Sri Yukteswar, disciple of the Avatar Babaji and Paramahansa Yogananda's Master Teacher. He writes in *The Holy Science*:

> "The mistake crept into the almanac for the first time about 700 BCE, during the reign of Parikshit, just after completion of the last Descending Dvapara Yuga...together with all the wise men of his court, (he) retired to the Himalayan Mountains, the paradise of the world. Thus there were none in the court of Raja Parikshit who could understand the principle of correctly calculating the ages of the several Yugas."[2]

The Yukteswar Yuga Cycle theorized the use of a shorter cycle with 24,000 years completing a cycle of four yugas. The longer, traditional Yuga Cycle contains a total of 4,320,000 years with 432,000 years allotted to the fourth cycle—Kali Yuga. Here's a comparison, using the Yukteswar approach, Kali Yuga ends in the year 1700 CE and by the year 2010 CE, Earth has experienced 310 years of Dvapara Yuga in an ascending cycle of light. It is also important to note that the Yukteswar Yuga Cycle, also known as the Electric Cycle, is based on the movement of light through both declining and ascending cycles. This descending cycle ceases at the lowest point and then begins an upward motion in the ascending cycle to the highest point of light. From a practical point of view, this makes sense as the longer method of calculation prophesies a Golden Age to immediately arise after the completion of the darkest hours of Kali Yuga. From this perspective, the Yukteswar method reflects a more natural progression of light—i.e., the flow of the seasons from spring to summer; fall to winter; dusk to dawn; twilight to night-time.

According to both Vedic systems, the cycle of Kali Yuga began in the year 3102 BC; however, the longer method presently places humanity's development approximately 5,000 years descending into the mire of 432,000 years of spiritual darkness. The shorter cycle positions humanity at the onset of evolution in the cycle of Dvapara Yuga.

The Golden Age of Kali Yuga

Optimistically, the shorter cycle is a much more pleasant viewpoint, marking an obvious upward trend for humanity's growth and evolution. It is, however, entirely possible that we are currently experiencing both cycles simultaneously. This is the position of contemporary Ascended Master teachings that prophesy humanity's entrance into a cyclic Golden Age filled with opportunity for spiritual growth, enlightenment, and liberation—the Ascension Process. While some global devastation and tragedies may be endured, this destruction is almost necessary in order for humanity to recognize, re-assess, self-actualize, and then re-construct a sustainable paradigm and global infrastructure that aligns and harmonizes with the New Times. Present-day Vedic scholars concur that the timing of the traditional Yugas may be interrupted with a small, minor upward cycle of Galactic Light prophesied in the Brahmavaivarta Purana to occur 5,000 years after the beginning of Kali Yuga, known as the Golden Age of Kali Yuga.[3] Dr. David Frawley, Vedic authority and teacher of the ancient wisdom, addresses the issue:

> "I see humanity to be in a greater dark age phase, because even in the Golden and Silver Ages of the lesser cycle as evidenced in the Vedas, the great majority of human beings appear to remain on a materialistic or vital plane level, concerned mainly with the ordinary goals of family, wealth, and personal happiness. Only the higher portion of

2. Yukteswar, *Holy Science*, 16.

3. Stephen Knapp, *Vedic Prophecies*, http://www.stephen-knapp.com, (2003).

This table represents the contemporary method of calculating Yugas, advocated by Sri Yuteswar, taught to him by the Avatar Babaji.

11,501 BCE				12,499 CE	

DESCENDING CYCLE   6,701 BCE   7699 CE   ASCENDING CYCLE

3101 BCE   4099 CE

701 BCE   1699 CE

499 CE

DESCENDING LIGHT	AGES:	ASCENDING LIGHT
11,501 BC to 6701 BC	GOLDEN (Krita)	7699 AD to 12,499 AD
6701 BC to 3101 BC	SILVER (Treta)	4099 AD to 7699 AD
3101 BC to 701 BC	BRONZE (Dvapara)	1699 AD to 4099
701 BC to 499 AD	IRON (Kali)	499 AD to 1699 AD

humanity, the cultural elite of a few percent, appears to experience the full benefits of the ages of light. This is the same as today, when the majority of human beings live on the same emotional level as before, and only a few really understand the secrets of science and technology, though all benefit from them."[4]

The Hindu avatar Krishna prophesies a Golden Age of 10,000 years to begin in the descending cycle of light 5,000 years after the beginning of the Age of Kali Yuga. In essence, Vedic scholars describe the Golden Age of Kali Yuga as an age within an age. It is important to remember that this period of time is not a full force, or one-hundred percent, Galactic Light Krita Yuga Golden Age. Instead, this is a minor short cycle of ascending light within the larger descending influences of Kali Yuga. It is claimed that the 432,000-year cycle of Kali Yuga begins in 3102 BCE; this places the commencement of the Golden Age of Kali Yuga around the beginning of the twentieth century. Krishna's prophecy and the timing of the short-cycled Golden Age give confluence to the I AM America prophecies. According to this calculation, we may have experienced over one-hundred years of this short ascending cycle of light, a little over one percent of the total 10,000-year cycle. It also explains the overall downward and material influence of Kali Yuga on our governments, political leadership, technologies, cultures, and societies. The I

AM America interpretation of the Golden Age explains the sudden influx of positive energies that drive the Great Awakening. [Editor's Note: Vedic scholar Stephen Knapp places the beginning of the Golden Age of Kali Yuga around 1500 CE, with the birth of Lord Caitanya (Sri Caitanya Mahaprabhu) who placed a great emphasis on congregational devotional singing and chanting the names of God to elevate consciousness as a means for spiritual liberation. According to Knapp's timing, we have already experienced approximately 500 years of the Golden Age of Kali Yuga.[5]]

The crest of enlightened energy during the Golden Age of Kali Yuga is realized in the year 6899 CE. Subsequently, light energies incrementally decline when the 10,000-year cycle ends in 11,899 CE. At that time, Vedic authorities claim, the full effects of Kali Yuga will ensue. Many prophecies in Vedic texts describe the decline of life on Earth throughout the remaining 417,000 years of the Age of Kali Yuga.

4. David Frawley, *The Astrology of the Seers, A Guide to Vedic (Hindu) Astrology* (Passage Press, 1990, Salt Lake City, UT), page 59.

5. Knapp, *Vedic Prophecies*.

Lord Meru's Prophecies

1. The time of the shaking of the Earth is now.
2. It is also the time of the shaking of the inner self, and Lord Meru prophesies humanity at large will begin to spiritually develop. This will happen in several ways:
    a. Personal development of the inner dialogue with the I AM Presence.
    b. Realization of the deep, inner truths that circumvent the doubt and skepticism associated with outer truths.
    c. As the bonds of trust are strengthened through contact with the I AM, so are the bonds of love.
    d. Love awakens (the Aspirant) and initiates the spiritual student, who becomes the chela of a Master Teacher.
    e. This process rests on the acquisition of patience, love, and understanding (the trinity of love, wisdom, and power) which awakens the energies of the Kundalini, and the Tao (the understanding of Feminine-Yin energies balanced and interacting with Masculine energies—Yang).
    f. As energy shifts and changes around the awakened Aspirant, he or she magnetizes the tutelage of a Master Teacher.
    g. Each Master Teacher works upon the Ray Force that is currently most dominant in the chela's aura and energy system.
    h. Once the chela has identified his or her dominant Ray Force, adherence to spiritual principles is necessary in the initiatory steps. The first principle is recognition and understanding of the One Ray Force, and its interaction with Earthly law. The second principle is utmost reliance and adherence to the inner dialogue which will continue to foster and guide spiritual awareness and growth.
3. Since the Great Central Sun is connected to the center (fiery-core) Sun of our Earth, the Great Central Sun acts as a type of universal life force, much like an umbilical cord of life, which regulates the heartbeat of our Earth. As our Mother Force, the Great Central Sun controls all life on Earth, and the life on other planetary schemes that she is connected to. The Earth, along with other sibling planets, vibrates to the Great Central Heart of the Great Central Sun or Galactic Center.
4. This umbilicus connection between Earth and the Great Central Sun—not to be confused with Ray Forces—is currently located in the United States and is known as the Heart of the Dove.
5. The Heart of the Dove is prophesied by Lord Meru to become a center for learning and understanding the Quetzalcoatl (Christ) Energies and their link to America—the Land of the Plumed Serpent.
6. The Quetzalcoatl Energies, as explained and taught by Lord Meru, are akin to the Christ energies when applied in the esoteric Western Christian tradition. This ancient spiritual teacher, however, predates Christianity and likely has its roots in Alchemic Atlantean (Toltec) teaching. According to Lord Meru, the spiritual focus of the teaching is aimed toward the opening of the Third-Eye Chakra through the activation of the Kundalini system. Lord Meru claims the teaching was practiced throughout Central and South America, but over time and as the teaching spread to North America, its spiritual impact and practice was diluted. The teaching faded, leaving its Divine Purpose unfulfilled and incomplete. Lord Meru prophesies the Golden City Vortices play an important role in the resurrection of this spiritually vital teaching which allows students to Master their Kundalini energies through the balanced power of love and wisdom.
7. In the future we will gain the technical expertise to accurately forecast the waxing and waning cycles of

our Sun. This information sheds light on forecasting Earthly events and greatly contributes to our present astrological systems—both Vedic and Western.

8. North America's evolution has and will continue to be influenced by the Lords of Venus.

9. The continent of Australia is prophesied to continue to be a free-floating continent, like the lands of the ancient Golden Disk of Pangaea. In the Golden Age, Meru prophesies, Australia will become a center for enlightened thinking and living, "Throughout the Golden Age it shall become a capstone for (spiritual) understanding." [Editor's Note: In the Freedom Star World Earth Changes Prophecies, Australia splits in two; however, it does not conjoin other continents.]

10. Meru prophesies the first six Rays—the Blue Ray, the Yellow Ray, the White Ray, the Green Ray, and the Ruby (Red) and Gold Ray—will conjoin as One force; and raise the Earth to one of the highest energies and spiritual frequencies of Harmony ever experienced.

11. The energies of the Six-Ray Force create a perfection of the Quetzalcoatl-Christ energies; Meru terms this the Dual Christ. The Quetzalcoatl-Christ energies harmonize the cultures, nations, and all countries of the world. Lord Meru states, "Each in their purity…their Tao—their balance."

Lord Meru's Teachings on the Rays

1. The Rays are part of the flow of energy that has inundated the Earth since time immemorial. The energy of the Rays originates with the Great Central Sun, moves onward to Earth, flows upon the Earth, and engulfs the human Chakra System (aura).

2. Each Ray Force is the individualized presence of the source—the ONE.

3. The Rays never separate themselves from the ONE; however, they are individualized expressions of the ONE.

4. Rays individualize in expression so the work and service of the ONE can flow in balance.

5. Each Ray Force identifies with both sound and light—the dual processes of life on the Earth Plane and Planet.

6. Sound and light unify through the Rays. The Rays are the building blocks of the higher dimensions of Earth.

7. The knowledge of the Rays is natural law that liberates man and his consciousness to the higher planes. According to Lord Meru, technology cannot achieve this; in fact, technology is a hindrance to this evolutionary, spiritual process.

8. Lord Meru's teachings rely on breath-work as key in the integration of light and sound. When properly applied, breath increases the absorption of the life forces (i.e. prana, orgone, chi), and the higher spiritual energies are absorbed through the Light Bodies. These energies raise the Kundalini and open the Third-Eye Chakra.

9. An opened Third Eye is essential for the education and training of a chela. This vital inner instruction includes:
   a. The inner dialogue: Connection to the I AM Presence; instruction on and maintenance of the evolved HU-man energy systems, (light-bodies); experience and instruction from the I AM Presence.
   b. The Godhead: Instruction concerning innate Divinity; use and instruction of the God-force; preparation and instruction of the light-bodies for Ascension.
   a. Initiation into the teachings of the Earthly and Galactic Brotherhoods. These teachings often include personal instruction from these types of Ascended Beings:
      i. Ancient Sages and Seers
      ii. Ancient Gods, Messiahs, and Saviors
      iii. Master Teachers
      iv. Archangels and Elohim

10. Ray Forces contain dual forces, and their energy flow waxes and wanes from Masculine (Yang) expression to Feminine (Yin) expression. Meru teaches that both our Sun and Moon contain and emit these dual, cyclic natural forces.

11. Rays Forces follow a cyclic flow, similar to the respiration process of the human body. The Rays pulsate through cycles that contain both inflow and outflow. During the cyclic inflow, the Ray infuses its energies; during the cyclic outflow, the Ray releases energy.

12. Through understanding and comprehending the cyclic flow of the Rays, students recognize opportune times to absorb Ray energies (inflow), and to purify Ray energies (outflow). According to Lord Meru, this

The Sun and Moon
Lord Meru claims that the cyclic influence of the Sun and Moon calibrates the Rays' effects upon the Earth.

esoteric knowledge of the Rays is an immutable law.

13. The cyclic solar influences of Ray Forces have varied effects on historic events, weather patterns, world economies, and the births and deaths of great and lowly souls.

14. Ray Forces utilize beneficent astrological placements of the Sun to build Masculine Energy on planets. When building Feminine Energies on Earth, Ray Forces use waning cycles of the Sun, alongside beneficent energies from the Moon.

15. The eco-system of the Rays exists through a constant recycling of energy from the Great Central Sun to Earth. Lord Meru claims Ray Forces—once absorbed at the Earth's core-sun—emanate to the Earth's heart center. Energy from the Earthly heart center radiate and ultimately emanate energies to the Galactic Center, where they are re-absorbed into the Cycle of the Rays.

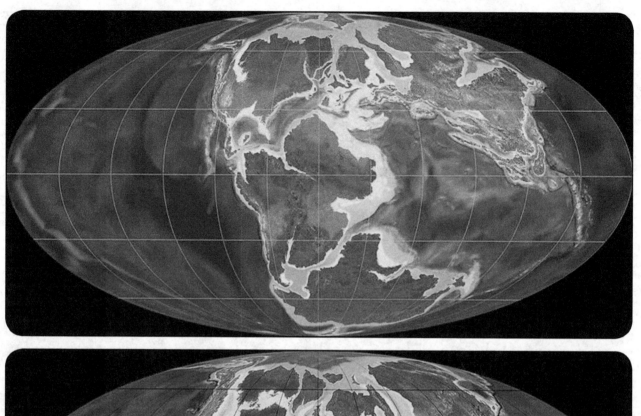

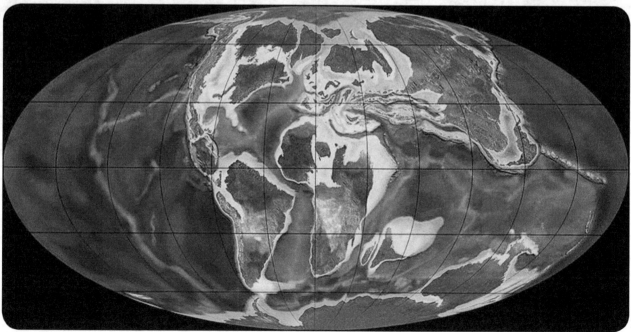

Prehistoric Earth
Ron Blakely's depiction of prehistoric Earth, before and after South America and Africa split.

The Colonization of the Earth as Taught by Lord Meru

The first souls to inhabit schoolhouse Earth originally came from other planets. This colonization process was energetically orchestrated by the Great Central Sun in a threefold process. First, the energies established themselves upon the Earth through the Emanation-Radiation Process of the Rays. Once a single Ray Force established a stronghold in the collective planetary consciousness, the attraction of various lifestreams from other planets toward Earth ensued, and various Ray(ces) populated on Earth through the incarnation process—sometimes esoterically referred to as the Transmigration of Souls. Others arrived physically as space-travelers from our Solar System. Altogether, Meru claims souls and life forms from eight planets originally colonized Earth. While other Master Teachers have mentioned the presence of souls and lifestreams from other solar systems and galaxies, Lord Meru focuses on the esoteric history of the extraterrestrial immigration from these planets: Saturn, Jupiter, our Sun, the Earth's Moon, Mercury, Venus, Uranus, and Mars.

The spiritual and physical leaders of each immigrant group of Ray(ce) Souls in Ascended Master teachings is referred to as a Lord. Meru claims Lord Rama led the first wave of immigrants from the planet Saturn to Earth. Today portions of the geological area where the Saturnians (also known as the Blue Ray) once colonized are present-day India. In the Lineage of Manus, Lord Rama is known as the Manu of the Aryan Race. Ray Forces from Saturn, the Sun, and the Great Central Sun assisted the rise of this great civilization.

According to Lord Meru, the second Ray(ce) to populate Earth originated from Jupiter—the Yellow Ray. Meru refers to this civilization as the Land of Brihaspati—Brihaspati is a Sanskrit term and astronomically refers to Jupiter—a term likely coined by the colonial Ramans. This group of souls is alleged to have originally settled on lands which today geologically comprise the Japanese Archipelago. It is claimed that the mountain range of the Lands of Brihaspati eventually morphed into the Himalayas, and the genetic seed of this Ray(ce) are the ancient Kirata and Tibetan cultures. The Mahabharata recounts this mythological race

of people as "gold-like…unlike the Dasas (Ramans) who were dark (dark blue)."[1] It is claimed that the I-Ching (the sixty-four hexagrams) is the foundation of the lost language of Mu, which likely originated with the Brihaspatites.[2] The Raman and Brihaspati cultures produced the post-diluvian Elders of Lemuria who later migrated to the Himalayans during cyclic Earth Changes. [Editor's Note: See Lord Meru.] Hsi Wang Mu—a name assigned to the mystical lands West of the Lands of ancient Brihaspati—became synonymous for the goddess Kuan Yin as the Goddess Hsi Wang Mu: the Merciful Guardian, Queen Mother of the West. Lao Tzu was said to travel to Hsi Wang Mu (the Thirteenth School), and before he embarked on the spiritual journey from which he would never return, he wrote in the famous book Tao Te Ching, "The Ancient Masters were subtle, mysterious, profound, responsive. The depth of their knowledge is unfathomable. All we can do is describe their appearance; watchful, like men crossing a winter stream. Alert, like men aware of danger; courteous, like visiting guests; yielding, like ice about to melt; simple, like uncarved blocks of wood."[3]

Lord Meru claims that the lands of Earth were once one large super-continent, similar to the scientific theories of Pangaea. Geologists estimate Pangaea to exist about 250 million years ago. During this time of greater spiritual light on Earth, esoteric myths maintain the continent floated over one continuous ocean. The land drifted on a blissful, calm sea and followed the ever present light of the Sun. The land, its nature kingdoms, and its peoples never experienced the duality of day and night until the super-continent broke apart and permanently affixed to the Earth. [Editor's Note: For more information, see Lord Meru's Map of the Ancients. Lord Meru does not place a date on this map, yet it is possible that this map depicts the Earth after the birth or destruction of continental land masses known as Mu. Also, lands located Southwest of Atlantis are described by Meru to have once been above the ocean. It is

1. *Kirata,* http://en.wikipedia.org/wiki/Kirata, (2011).
2. David Hatcher Childress, *Lost Cities of Ancient Lemuria and the Pacific* (Adventures Unlimited Press, 1988, Stelle, IL), page 95.
3. Ibid, page 48.

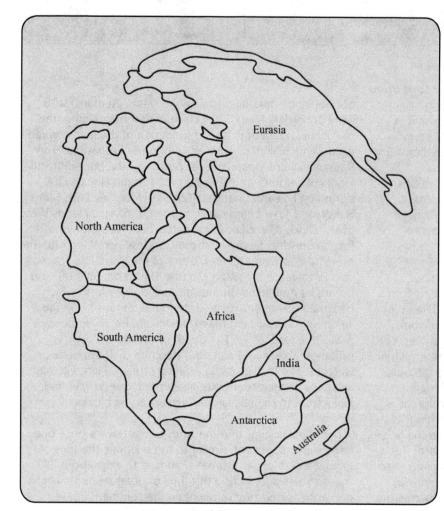

Pangaea
A depiction of Pangaea.

4.6 Billion Years BC: This is the estimated time of creation of the Earth theorized by geologists and scientists.[4]

250 MYA (Million Years Ago**):** Pangaea exists.

200–180 MYA: Earth experiences the breakup of Pangaea and two super-continents emerge: Laurasia and Gondwana.

145–65 MYA: Laurentia exists as an independent continent which is known today as North America.[5]

135 MYA: South America and Africa split. [Editor's Note: Ancient Earth entered Dvapara Yuga at approximately 135.5 MYA—the estimated date of Lord Meru's Map of the Ancients. Kali Yuga follows Dvapara Yuga around 136.3 MYA and this event likely marked Kali's entrance with global Earth Change.]

65.95 MYA: A mass extinction occurs on Earth of all life; scientists refer to this as the Cretaceous-Tertiary Extinction. Eighty-five per cent of all species on Earth died including the dinosaurs; and scientists believe this catastrophe was likely caused by asteroid impacts alongside massive volcanic activity.[6] [Editor's Note: Scientists have recently improved their process for dating rocks and fossils, and according to Paul Renne, director of the UC Berkeley Geochronology Center, the "best date for the Cretaceous-Tertiary boundary is now 65.95 million years ago, give or take 40,000 years."[7]

wrong to presume Lord Meru's representation of the world would remain unchanged. It is likely new lands emerged in short periods of time as this geologic epoch developed and ended; whole continents changed or disappeared as yet another geological epoch ensued. The idea of Earth Change embraces the concept that Earth experiences and is susceptible to constant cycles of descending and ascending galactic light through the Cycle of the Yugas; therefore, humanity is simultaneously changing and adapting to these phases.]

The following timeline may help us understand potential timeframes and geographical possibilities:

4. *Geological History of Earth*, http://en.wikipedia.org/wiki/Geological_history_of_Earth, (2011).
5. *Laurentia*, http://en.wikipedia.org/wiki/Laurentia, (2011).
6. *Cretaceous-Tertiary Extinction Event*, http://en.wikipedia.org/wiki/Tertiary_extinction_event, (2011).
7. Science Daily, "When Did Dinosaurs Go Extinct? Cretaceous-Tertiary Boundary Dating Refined," http://en.wikipedia.org/wiki/Kirata, (2011).

North American Craton
By the United States Geological Survey, Geology of Ameru, also known by geologists as Laurentia. The brown area shows the part of the North American continent that has been stable for over 600 million years. This region is made up of a basement older Precambrian metamorphic and igneous rock.

This gives plausible evidence as to the accuracy of the Cycle of the Yugas, which places the beginning of a Kali Yuga at 66.2 MYA. According to the Vedic succession of the Classical Yugas, Kali Yuga is identified as a period of Earthly decline and strife, which is immediately overcome once the Krita Yuga (Golden Age) begins. According to the Puranic method of Yuga calculation, Earth entered this vulnerable period at approximately 66.2 MYA. Since a Kali Yuga lasts for a period of 432,000 years, the episode of destruction was likely endured until 67.6 MYA. Applying the slop-factor of 40,000 years, the Cretaceous-Tertiary Extinction could be placed as early as 66.35 MYA, during a Kali Yuga period on Earth.]

55–39 MYA: Europe, Greenland, and North America drift apart.

34–23 MYA: The continents continue to drift to their present locations.

23–.5 MYA: The land-bridge between South America and North America disappears and reappears. North America (Laurentia) crashes into South America and forms the super-continent America.[8]

3,891,102 BC: The last Krita Yuga (full-force Golden Age) on Earth ensues, using the Puranic, or classical timing of Yugas.

2.58 MYA to Present: The Earth enters its fourth Ice Age: the Quaternary Ice Age. Scientists believe Earth entered its worst Ice Age from 850 to 635 MYA, when ice covered the entire globe. The Ascended Masters prophesy that as we enter the New Times, Earth will enter a phase of Global Warming and the polar ice-caps may melt.[9]

2,163,102 BC: Treta Yuga begins. According to the revered Sanskrit poet Valmiki, Ramayana (the Lands of Rama) flourish in this time period.

2 to 1.5 Million Years BC: The civilization of Mu develops at the end of Treta Yuga (a Silver Age on Earth).

---

9. Wikipedia, *Geological History of Earth.*

---

8. Wikipedia, *Laurentia.*

1.8 MYA: The Pleistocene Ice Age—a subdivision of the Quaternary Ice Age—begins and glaciers form on all continents of Earth. This glacial period ends almost 12,500 years ago as ice sheets and continental glaciers retreat.[10]

867,102 BC: Dvapara Yuga begins and the races of men that will eventually civilize the societies of Lemuria and Atlantis are born.

780,000 BC: Earth's magnetic field reverses.

778,000 to 400,000 BC: Ancestral human remains exist. Present-day archaeologists have found and dated them within this time span; locations of remains include: Ancient Israel, Ancient Britain, Northern Europe, Ethiopia, Indonesia, and Germany.[11]

638,000 BC: The massive Yellowstone Caldera erupts in North America. Scientists believe the Supervolcano also erupted in 2.1 MYA and 1.3 MYA.[12]

300,000 BC: According to author and researcher Zecharia Sitchen, the Annunaki—a race of extraterrestrials on Earth—genetically engineer through in-vitro fertilization a race of genetic workers to labor in their gold mines.[13]

278,000 to 250,000 BC: Ancestral human remains exist. Present-day archaeologists have found and dated them within this time span; locations include: China, Northern Siberia, Central Mexico.

200,000 BC: According to James Churchward, Lemuria is inhabited by over sixty million people, consisting of ten diverse tribes, united by one government.[14]

128,000 BC: Humans are voyaging across the Ancient Mediterranean Sea, according to evidence discovered by present-day archaeologists.[15]

100,000 BC to 50,000 BC: Lord Meru claims that by 100,000 BC civilizations of Atlantis co-exist with the civilizations of Lemuria.

73,000 BC: The super volcano Toba erupts in Indonesia. Scientists theorize that the global temperature drops five degrees for many years on Earth, substantially reducing its population.[16]

70,000 BC: According to James Churchward, the Uighur Empire of Lemuria flourishes as a world power, just north of present-day Burma.[17]

40,000 to 24,000 BC: The Great Barrier Reef is above water—according to Aboriginal myths.[18]

24,000 BC: Lemuria, also known as Mukulia, Rutas, Hiva (Polynesian), and Pacifica, undergoes massive Earth Changes.[19]

20,000 BC: Geologists estimate sea levels begin to rise on the Great Barrier Reef and coral skeletons initiate the construction of the present-day natural wonder on an older platform estimated to be over 600,000 years old.[20]

10,000 to 15,000 BC: An Ice Age ensues, and remaining coastlines of Lemuria disappear under the ocean waters. Today, present-day Australia also known by ancient Egyptian gold-miners as the ancient Land of Punt, is the remainder of the once great continent of Mu and Lemuria.[21]

10,000 BC: Earth enters the Holocene geological epoch regarded as a warmer period, also known as an interglacial period, within the Quaternary Ice Age. Scientists credit the stable climate of the Holocene period to the development of humanity and its current urbanization. Many believe this era marks a permanent end to the current Ice Age.[22]

10. *Last Glacial Period*, http://en.wikipedia.org/wiki/Last_glacial_period, (2011).
11. Etznab Mathers, *Historical Timeline 4 Million B.C.*, http://mirrorh.com/timline4mbc.html, (2011).
12. *Yellowstone Caldera*, http://en.wikipedia.org/wiki/Yellowstone_Caldera, (2011).
13. E. Mathers, *Historical Timeline 4 Million B.C.*
14. Ibid.
15. E. Mathers, *Historical Timeline 4 Million B.C.*

16. Ibid.
17. Ibid.
18. David Hatcher Childress, *Lost Cities of Ancient Lemuria and the Pacific*, page 128.
19. Ibid., page 152.
20. *Great Barrier Reef*, http://en.wikipedia.org/wiki/Great_Barrier_Reef, (2011).
21. Childress, *Lost Cities of Ancient Lemuria*, 95.
22. Holcene, http://en.wikipedia.org/wiki/Holcene, (2011).

9,628 BC: Atlantis sinks; although many esoteric texts claim Atlantis' geologic Earth Changes occurred in three partial cataclysms. 9,628 BC is the estimated year of Atlantis' final demise.

3,102 BC: Kali Yuga begins.

360 BC: Plato writes about the lost continent of Atlantis.[23]

Lord Meru claims the teachings of the Map of the Ancients is for esoteric students to grasp the interaction of Ray Forces, and how their natural power and energy sculpts societies, cultures, and the civilizations of Earth. Ray Forces work together in a harmonic, instead of a defined, focus. For example, Lord Meru teaches that civilizations from the Moon, Venus, and Mercury appeared simultaneously. The civilizations from these Ray Forces developed in ancient America, Atlantis, and the prehistoric lands of South America and Africa.

Venus is perhaps one of the most unique planets in our Solar System. Meru claims Venus is not originally from our solar scheme, and initially functioned like a large, planetary satellite that was intentionally placed in our Solar System by members of the Galactic Brotherhood to resurrect and restore impoverished Ray Forces throughout our Solar System. No date is given for this event; however, Meru claims this action alone saved the Earth from imminent annihilation through spiritual depravity. Lord Meru states a similar spiritual intervention by Venus; in the twentieth century, it gave humanity yet another reprieve from obliteration; and the construction of the spiritual infrastructure of the Golden City Vortices by the Spiritual Hierarchy ensued.

The Ray Forces of the Moon and Mercury aided the birth and growth of an ancient civilization claimed to once exist in the present-day Sahara Desert of Africa. Meru states this empire was intellectually adept and communication was primarily telepathic; although an alphabet and written language were also developed. The same energies and their influence gave rise to the Osirian Culture of Egypt and initiated ancient settlements of present-day Central and South America. The pre-American civilizations were conceived millions of years ago on the super-continent of conjoined South America and Africa. [Editor's Note: These

Plato
It is claimed that the dialogues of Plato describe the Ancient Kingdom of Atlantis, a parable of a failed utopian empire.

Native American cultures likely flourished in the early centuries of Dvapara Yuga.]

The Greater and Lesser Antilles chain of islands, along with the island of Cuba was once a land mass where Lord Meru claims the pre-American civilizations of Quetzalcoatl developed. This society was sponsored by the Ray Force of the Moon and the White Ray; its culture was inordinately feminine.

The esoteric Christian tradition finds its roots under the sway of the Ruby-Gold Ray and to this day many Christians are deeply impacted by the healing benevolence of this religious faith. However, the esoteric, historical influence of this Ray split its effect over two continents: the Lands of Mu, which later evolved into Lemuria and present-day Australia; and lands located near the North Pole—present day Russia. Meru claims this Ray developed the healing arts which profoundly influenced the spiritual cultures of Mu and Lemuria. The Ray Force draws its energy from Mars and our Sun, with overtones from the White and Green Rays—the planets Venus and Mercury. Altogether the Rays formed an aggregate energy which became the nexus for two new Ray(ces)—the Lemurian and Atlantean—both birthed on the Motherland of Mu.

Prehistoric Tectonic Plate

Lord Meru refers to this geological plate, which is in reference to the Pacific Plate, as an oceanic tectonic plate beneath the Pacific Ocean. Esoteric historians theorize that the Pacific Plate, through periodic geologic upheaval and Earth Changes formed the submerged lost continent of Lemuria. Some Earth Changes theories claim Pole Shifts caused entire continents to rise or fall due to Tectonic Plate Theory.[24]

---

23. *Atlantis*, http://en.wikipedia.org/wiki/Atlantis, (2011).

24. Childress, *Lost Cities of Ancient Lemuria*, 36.

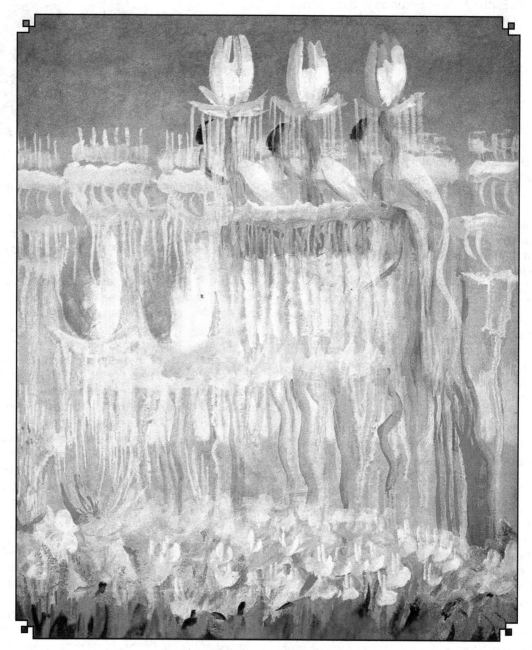

Creation of the World XIII
Mikalojus Konstantinas Ciurlionis, 1906.

Flora and Fauna of the Ancient Lands of the Plumed Serpent

Plants: According to Lord Meru, plants grow in harmony and cooperation with the Mineral Kingdom. Since humanity subsists primarily on a vegetarian diet at this time—likely due to the increased light and the spirituality of Dvapara Yuga—ancient species of nuts, grains, and fruits are harvested after their maturation process. According to scientific theory, this time frame marks the evolution of flowering plants—angiosperms. Honey is collected through domestic beekeeping, and many occult teachings claim bees were brought to Earth from their homeland planet of Venus. The evolved cultures of Earth ate certain foods to enhance or strengthen specific Ray Forces, according to health needs.

Animals: Meru claims few wild animals (mammals) existed in the ancient land of Earth during the Dvapara Yuga millions of years ago, however certain animal species were cultivated domestically as pets and were likely wiped out in the Cretaceous-Tertiary Extinction. The group-souls of these animal companions still exist today as the domesticated horse, dog, and cat. Meru describes a domestic ox that once existed millions of years ago on Earth. It is claimed that colonies of ancient dolphins and whales habituated the ancient oceans, and their presence increased the spiritual vibration of the Earth.

Diet: A vegetarian diet prevailed throughout the ancient Dvapara Yuga, due to the highly sensitized human Kundalini system which could not bear the vibration of flesh-eating. Since foods were chosen to complement specific Ray Forces, this resulted in the deepening of spiritual knowledge and development alongside the "demonstration of the physical laws of cooperation." Lord Meru states that the land resonated with Beauty and Harmony.

Insects: It is claimed the Lords of Venus introduced butterflies and bees to our Earth. The golden nectar of honey is claimed to support the human intellect in obtaining enlightenment and spiritual illumination.

(Top) *Pando, Ancient Quaking Aspens.* Scientists theorize that this ancient colony of Aspens, located in Utah, is over a million years old. It was discovered they are one single tree that share one common root system. The tree covers an area of 106 acres. (Above) Ascended Master Teaching claims that eating honey increases spiritual growth and development.

Lord Meru's History of the Violet Ray

The Violet Ray was introduced to Earth during the end times of the Land of the Plumed Serpent with explosive and catalyzing results. Its energies brought tremendous change to the once harmonious lands, and its lower, immature energies quickly associated with the dark, undeveloped side of Saturn; this seeded civilizations which were the basis for much of Europe. The young Ray(ce) germinated adolescent energies of the Violet Ray with an explosive, conflicted, and revolutionary consciousness in stark juxtaposition to the past epoch of the Quetzalcoatl-Christ harmonic. The Galactic Suns—the great Lords of Galactic Consciousness—held their constant, conscious out-picturing for the positive qualities of the Violet Ray, as a tremendous force to eventually purify and transform the new wave of souls comprising Earth's new humanity. The puerile energies of the Violet Ray were almost intolerable, and the Lords of the presiding Six Rays requested that the power of the Seventh Ray be held back until humanity gained spiritual maturity. However, the Galactic Suns unleashed the Violet Ray's fury with the promise and hope its power would inevitably lead humanity to ONE Mind and steward Earth's imminent destiny—Unana.

The lower qualification of the Violet Ray brought rebellion and shadows to the Feminine Knowledge. Masculine energies moved away from the guidance of paternal wisdom, and the Earth, along with her cultures and civilizations were led into psychopathic exploitation. The Feminine Path of Beauty became subject to Male Tyranny. Lord Meru explains this dark time of Earth's pubertal relationship with the Violet Ray:

1. Humanity's spiritual ancestry and knowledge of the Great Central Sun, the Galactic Center, and the Galactic Suns were severed. This wisdom would not be recovered for ages.
2. Millions of souls from other galaxies entered the transmigration process on Earth, causing a mass co-mingling of Ray Forces, inevitably resulting in race wars.
3. The purity of Lemuria—a harmonic of the Blue, Yellow, and Red and Gold Rays was irretrievably broken. This resulted in the development of a caste system for humanity and human slavery.
4. The once sacred pact of humanity's companionship with animals was abandoned; and the few types of animals that existed on Earth were technologically bred for religious sacrificial use and human consumption.
5. Dietary standards were abandoned, and with flesh-eating and the lack of knowledge of the Ray Forces in association with their influence through diet, humanity experienced a lowering of the Kundalini, with drastic effects on the light-bodies. The Third-Eye closed, and the spiritual knowledge of its existence vanished among the masses.
6. Shamballa's energies suffered denigration, and its Golden Gates were closed. Only those who had preserved the ancient wisdom of Open Eyes, Open Ears (the Third-Eye) could obtain entry into its schools of higher knowledge.
7. As technology developed, the abilities of the HU-man arrested; yet, eventually the wisdom of the Galactic Suns prevailed, and the genetic inbreeding and mutations finally resulted in small soul groups who realized the Godself through the higher qualities of the Violet Ray. One of these great souls is Saint Germain.
8. Through the evolutionary work of the Violet Ray, its flame began to integrate and penetrate the mutated and hybrid light-fields. The Violet Flame is revered for its ability to spiritually awaken the chela to obtain the valuable instruction contained in the inner dialogue, preparing a path to Ascension.
9. With the birth of Jesus Christ, the Lords of the Rays deemed humanity fit and ready to tame the explosive force of the Violet Ray. A span of over 2,000 years was needed to calm this Ray Force, and initiate its purposeful constructive use.

Aged Angel
Odilon Redon, 1903.

Kuan Yin
The Bodhisattva Kuan Yin, also known as Kun Iam, was one of Saint Germain's gurus of the the Violet Flame. The Violet Flame produces the Divine Intervention of Mercy, Compassion, and Forgiveness.

10. Lord Meru claims the introduction of the Violet Ray set humanity back in evolution over 10,000 years. Humanity's destiny, however, lies in our ability to apply the Ray's Alchemical power, transmute the consciousness of duality, and usher our collective entry into the ONE.

11. In its infant-stage, the piercing energies of the Violet Ray tore Man away from God, and into the "structures and organizations," of Man. Lord Meru prophesies the important role the Alchemical Ray asserts in humanity's Divine Destiny:

 a. The Violet Ray produces the consciousness of Unity—Unana.

 b. The Violet Ray cultivates Divine Compassion—empathy. This is the result of people accepting humanity's dark side and the development of the ego. The Violet Flame transmutes the ego to the light of true spiritual identity.

 c. Even though the identity of self superseded the development of

Unity—the evolutionary process has served the ONE.

Saint Germain's Closing Thoughts on Lord Meru's Teachings

1. The Violet Flame produces the Divine Intervention of Mercy, Compassion, and Forgiveness.

2. These qualities are the greatest tenets and attributes to develop as the foundation of Christ Consciousness.

3. The Christ Consciousness develops the higher chakra centers and opens the Third-Eye.

4. Saint Germain recommends the following decree to abet the individual and collective dark-side of humanity's fascination with violence, wars, and destructive technology. The Master of the Violet Ray claims this decree unites the true-self as ONE, "with the universe . . ."

 "Mighty Violet Ray Come Forth!
 And transmute all discord, all dis-harmony,
 So I may move forward in ONE Beauty and Cooperation."

Saint Germain's Teachings on the Violet Flame

1. The Violet Flame is similar to the Rays. It finds its source at the Galactic Center, and travels with the Rays from the Great Central Sun to Earth. [Editor's Note: The activity of the Violet Ray is known as the Violet Flame.]

2. The Violet Flame is considered by Saint Germain to be a natural law; he refers to the transmuting fire as a "Mighty Law in Action."

3. The Violet Flame calms and focuses the mind. This assists the student to accept the perfection of conscious thoughts, feelings, and actions which activate the will and inhibit self-doubt. Overall, this practice counteracts negative thoughts that may harm or impede the Co-creative process.

4. Self-acceptance of innate perfection awakens the Eight-sided Cell of Perfection within the Chamber of the Heart. The awakened, perfect cell affects other cells, and they simultaneously awaken as a complete, spiritual whole. This process evolves the light-bodies to a new state of conscious physical presence known as the Lighted Stance.

5. The Lighted Stance is a state of conscious perfection—a precursor to Ascension. In this state of consciousness, the individual contacts innate Divinity, the Godhead. This initiates a transformational process that spiritually and genetically reconnects the physical body to eternal life. The Mask of Forgetfulness, purposely imposed over human consciousness before birth, fades and reveals memories of previous lifetimes. This process is described by Saint Germain as contact with the soul's eternal memory, the Oneship, and the true self.

Spiritual Prophecies

1. Humanity encounters the prophesied Time of Testing, a period of time within the New Times when personal trials and world changes converge. In order to navigate these turbulent times, it becomes necessary to develop spiritually and consciously cultivate the Lighted Stance.

2. Our ability to consciously experience and understand events and circumstances beyond the Mask of Forgetfulness is contingent on our ability to apply forgiveness. This opens the heart to unconditional love and the higher attributes of Compassion, Brotherly Love, and Gratitude.

3. According to Saint Germain, many other civilizations have risen to great heights of conscious awareness; however, these civilizations inevitably fell and were unable to sustain a peak consciousness due to several factors:

    a. Members of these civilizations were unable to develop the necessary, yet evolutionary, steps that involved self-awareness, Divinity, and contact with the true self.

    b. Due to the inability to contact the Divine Self, these societies were unable to develop a Group Mind to embrace compassion for the human condition.

    c. Compassion opens human consciousness to the Fourth Dimension through developing necessary states of empathetic awareness toward life. This produces experiences of interconnectedness and the perception of the ONE.

    d. Thoughts and perceptions of division produce separation. Miscommunication and lack of cooperation create disjointed realities; and, as we move into the New Times, division between all people will intensify.

4. Through the presence of simultaneous realities, individuals may jointly perceive the Time of Change with great sorrow and great joy. Many will perceive the Time of Testing as a period of loss. This loss may encompass both the loss of financial and personal security; yet, simultaneously cause

Kamiak Butte
Photograph taken atop Kamiak Butte, near Palouse, Washington, the westerly point of Ascension Valley.

tremendous change within and the arrival of self-actualization, self-knowledge, and acknowledgment of the existence of the true self, and the consciousness of the ONE—Unana.

5. Ultimately, the Master Teachers remind us that the Time of Testing is a phase for self-development through Co-creation and the activation of the will—choice. This assists individual empowerment of humanity's Divine Nature and destiny, which the Ascended Masters have pledged to foster, encourage, leading every individual to the freedom from re-birth into the Ascension.

6. Ascension Valley, located in the Golden City of Shalahah and the Transportation Vortex, located near Coeur d'Alene, Idaho, are geo-physical energy models, which in the New Times are prophesied to greatly assist the light and Ascension bodies to experience and master interdimensional movement. According to the Master Teachers, this can be achieved without the aid of technology and

is the natural result of the individual awakening to perfection within the heart and the cultivation of the Seventh Chakra.

Prophecies of Change

1. During the Time of Testing, many of the Golden City Vortices mature, and their energies assist humanity in one of history's most definable transformations through cooperative group efforts and worldwide spiritual awakening.

2. Living in Golden City Vortices helps to enhance physical and spiritual contact with the Fourth and Fifth Dimensions. This is necessary to adjust our bodies, minds, and spirits in preparation to birth the New Times—the Golden Age.

3. As we enter the Times of Change and experience the Fourth and Fifth Dimensions, many will experience simultaneous realities. This experience can temper the fury of the Great Purification and assist the creation of the Golden Age.

Teachings on Spiritual Migration

1. Spiritual Migration includes the intentional re-location to a Golden City Vortex to absorb and integrate its spiritual energies and teachings. Serious students are advised, before entering this spiritual process, to understand the initiatory steps. According to the Ascended Masters, these are:

   a. Identify the dominant Ray guiding and directing your life's current experiences and spiritual growth.

   b. Establish a rapport and inner dialogue with the I AM Presence.

   c. Establish a rapport and inner dialogue with the Master Teacher of the Golden City Vortex you are guided to.

   d. Each Golden City Vortex represents a step in spiritual growth and embodies a series of initiatory steps with possible challenges to hone your spiritual evolution.

   e. The Golden City Vortex and the tutelage of its Master Teacher utilize inherent, subtle energies which instigate the growth of the Ascension light-bodies. This method transpires individually for each chela's Ascension process, and collectively for the Earth's global transformation.

2. When moving to a Golden City Vortex, first, it is recommended to live on the outer periphery of the Vortex—just outside the Golden City's circular boundary to acclimate to the spiritual energies. This process may take as little as two weeks or as long as two years, depending on the spiritual

development of the student initiate. Of course, each student's experience will differ; however, here are a few indicators that may signify the readiness of the chela to migrate forward:

   a. Hear a constant high-pitch ring.

   b. Experience vivid dreams.

   c. Instruction by the Master Teacher in meditation.

   d. Calm emotions alongside an intuitive urge.

3. Once the Golden City Vortex energy of each Doorway has properly adapted your light-bodies, you are ready to integrate more intense energy. Move onward, closer to the Golden City Star. The spiritual energy of the Golden City Vortex is at its peak in this location. [Editor's Note: Ascended Master teachings recommend to first travel through the Four Golden City Doorways before entering the Golden City Star.]

4. By slowly absorbing the Golden City energies, the chela is able to integrate the subtle Vortex energies. As this spiritual process proceeds, the light-bodies begin to align, harmonize, and balance.

5. As the chela embraces the science of Spiritual Migration, it is recommended to spend a minimum

Pilgrimage at Sunset
Ascended Master teachings recommend to first travel through the Four Golden City Doorways before entering the Golden City Star.

Love Leading the Pilgrim
Edward Burne-Jones, 1877-1896.

of sixteen months to two years in each successive location. Again, this assists the light-bodies and their assimilation and integration of Golden City energies.

6. Students and chelas engaged in the first phases of Spiritual Migration may live on the perimeter of Golden Cities. Ascended Masters claim the Golden Cities contain a flux of twenty to thirty miles.

7. Each progressive move within the Golden City may take a student initiate up to twenty-four months, depending how quickly energies are assimilated.

8. Once chelas have advanced in their integration process of Golden City energies of the Four Doorways, migration to the Star is recommended.

    a. According to the Master Teachers, the Star rapidly advances self-knowledge and rapid assimilation of energies. Due to this intensity, it is recommended to carefully approach the Star, and to begin by living within forty to thirty miles from its radius.

    b. Since the center of each Golden City Star carries the strongest concentration of the Ray forces, it is best to have developed the indelible connection with the I AM Presence, and rely on this communication to monitor results before moving closer.

    c. Living in Golden City Stars intensifies the connection between the Golden City and its Master Teacher. This accelerates the chela's inner instruction. As this spiritual process deepens, the Ascension bodies develop and strengthen.

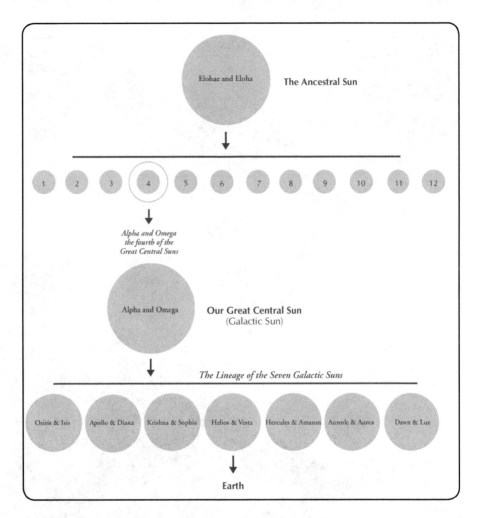

The Lineage of the Seven Galactic Suns

According to Ascended Master teachings, our solar Sun is one of seven evolved Suns from the lineage of Twelve Ancestral Suns. Alpha and Omega—our current Great Central Sun—is overseen by a larger ancestral Sun, known in Ascended Master myth as the Mighty Elohae-Eloha. It is claimed that of the twelve Great Central Suns, Alpha and Omega is the fourth, and from their lineage, seven smaller solar Suns evolve: the Seven Galactic Suns. Currently, Helios and Vesta serve as Earth's solar Sun. It is claimed that each of the Seven Galactic Suns emit spiritual light which guards, protects, and evolves incarnating souls in these solar systems.[1]

---

1. Tellis Papastavro, *The Gnosis and the Law*, (Group Avatar, 1972, Tucson, AZ), page 31.

Diana
Correggio, 1519. Diana is also known as Lumina, the Moon Goddess. Diana is the Divine Complement to the Galactic Sun and Spiritual Teacher Apollo.

Apollo
Briton Rivière, (1840—1920). Apollo often accompanies Sanat Kumara and is considered one of the Ancestral Teachers of Ascended Master Teaching. It is claimed that Apollo is the Master of Music, and is depicted with his lyre, whose stringed vibrations calm the Animal Kingdom. Briton Rivière was a British illustrator, famous for his realistic paintings of animals.

Apollo and Diana
Giovanni Battista Tiepolo, 1757.

Apollo

Apollo is Saint Germain's teacher, and joins the Master of the Violet Flame's lineage of venerated gurus. Lord Apollo is the spiritual sponsor of the Twelve Jurisdictions in the I AM America teachings, and he is revered in myth as the God of Prophecy and Music. Some spiritual teachings suggest Apollo was a primordial god from the second-root race of Earth, the culture of the Hyperborean described in H. P. Blavatsky's Secret Doctrine.[1]

Archetypically renowned as a Sun God, Apollo is claimed to have evolved beyond the Avatars of Earth, serving as one of seven Galactic Suns—ancient planets which have ascended into Suns of our galaxy, alongside Helios and Vesta, the deities of our solar Sun.[2] The Galactic Sun Apollo is assisted by his feminine companion Diana, an ancient Elohim and Goddess maiden; both are deities of the second solar Sun in the Ascended Master cosmology of the Milky Way.

Esoteric teaching claims Apollo is the ultimate protector of the Christ Consciousness for humanity and is somewhat considered another form of Mithra. Alongside Lumina—Diana, Goddess of the Moon—Apollo's ever present light of the Yellow Ray of Wisdom radiates in an ethereal retreat above Germany. In the Golden Age it is prophesied that millions of angels will be released from this luminous sanctuary and assist the Ascended Masters Lord Meru, Gautama Buddha, Lord Himalaya, Lord Maitreya, Lord Sananda, and Kuthumi. The Angels of Illumination and the Master Teachers will advance humanity's spiritual enlightenment and entrance into the Golden Age.[3]

1. *The Secret Doctrine*, http://en.wikipedia.org/wiki/The_Secret_Doctrine, (2011).
2. Tellis Papastavro, *The Gnosis and the Law*, (Group Avatar, 1972, Tucson, AZ), pages 24–32.

3. *Nature and Elohim: Apollo and Lumina, Elohim of the Second Ray*, http://www.tsl.org/Elohim/ApolloAndLumina.asp, (2009).

Love
Martiros Sarian, 1906.

Saint Germain's Teachings on the Law of Love

Lord Sananda is one of Saint Germain's gurus, and he taught the Master of the Violet Flame these significant insights regarding the Law of Love.

1. It is natural to question ourselves while learning to live with love on a daily basis. Yet, since the Law of Love serves humanity, love makes our lives rich and full.
2. We all thirst for the Law of Love to quench our needs; however, few find their innate need for love satiated.
3. True love creates peace. According to Saint Germain, this understanding is a great truth; a treasure that is timeless and transforming.
4. When applied, True Love has the ability to heal any wound, cause bitter enemies to join together in mutual purpose, and end the conflict of warring nations.
5. The Law of Love is so powerful it can transmute Akashic Records and the Karmic requirement to return to the Earthly, physical plane.
6. Inevitably, the embrace of the Law of Love is freeing. The vibration of love can remove the death consciousness. This is achieved through detachment, which loosens the ropes of expectation, especially when applied with the Violet Flame. Saint Germain refers to this nuance of consciousness as *Love Eternal*. The following Violet Flame decree transmutes traumatic memories through detachment:

   "May freedom ring supreme in the hearts of all mankind! Mighty Violet Flame, blaze in, through and around all situations of memory that hold me from my eternal freedom and my true self. Mighty Violet Flame, come forth now! And remove such memories that may keep me bound into the rounds of birth and death. Mighty Violet Flame, come through and set me free. Mighty Violet Flame, let me truly be."

7. The Law of Love and the Violet Flame unite in their intention and objective, which inevitably frees individual desires, wants, expectations, and consciousness to explore new psychological arenas of detachment and freedom

Spiritual Prophecies

1. Humanity is currently experiencing the Time of Tribulation, as prophesied by Jesus Christ, in Matthew 24:21: "for then there will be a great tribulation, which has not occurred since the beginning of the world until now, nor ever shall."[2] The prophesied tribulation of the Bible is reference to signs that mark the return of Christ—the Christ Consciousness—and the end of the current age. Saint Germain prefers to call this prophesied time of tribulation the Time of Testing.
2. During the Time of Testing it may seem humanity, both individually and collectively, is tested spiritually. These inner tests of love, forgiveness, and transformation may first seem like a type of punishment; however, Saint Germain reminds us that these experiences are given so we may individually examine and measure our own spiritual growth as we enter the Global Ascension or liberation process.
3. As humanity spiritually awakens its True Memory, past histories and civilizations are better understood and comprehended. This reveals a great deal about humanity's past: genealogy, culture, social mores, and religions. This assists humanity's unification at a critical juncture and gives guidance and direction for the New Times.
4. As True Memory is restored among humanity, the consciousness of humanity expands.
5. During the Time of Testing, some individuals may experience difficulty absorbing information via the Oral Tradition and totally rely on written information.

is likely a reference to Krita Yuga—an epoch experienced millions of years ago, often referred to as a Golden Age. Due to this esoteric history, the presence of this state of awareness and consciousness of humanity created a Group Mind, or information field, that exists eternally on Earth. This unique energy survives during times of lesser vibration and during the time we are now experiencing—Kali Yuga. The memory of higher states of perfection is permanently embedded into the Earth Plane, and while mankind may not be able to outwardly express the qualities of these blissful states of higher consciousness, many souls instantly recognize and identify with this inherent truth.

2. Those who instantly recognize and relate to this heavenly truth of Embedded Group Memory likely experienced a Krita Yuga in another lifetime. Saint Germain explains the memory of this state of consciousness as One with Source.

3. The Unfed Flame symbolizes metaphorically and literally our HU-man connection and HU-man memory with purity and perfection. This Divine Spark drives our desires to unveil the truth within, which assures our evolutionary path to express higher states of love, wisdom, and power. Saint Germain refers to this great truth as the Causeless Cause, which leads the spiritual journey onward to the God Light, and the consciousness of Desireless Desire.

6. Reliance on the Oral Tradition and developing our memory through this ancient technique breaks the illusive hold many are currently experiencing, and it opens our hearts to inherent Divinity and the Law of Love.

7. Opening our spiritual heart through cultivating compassion and love allows the development of perception and readies our experience to recall past lives. Saint Germain refers to this as the "thousand eyes of many."

Teachings on True Memory

1. According to the Master Teachers, humanity once existed at a higher vibratory rate of consciousness and held a purer state of memory function. This

The Cycles of Human Perception and Consciousness

The epochs of time—the Vedic Yugas—play a role in predicting the scope of humanity's perception and comprehension of past cultures. This relates to the metaphysical concept that a culture cannot thoroughly comprehend or understand another culture that is higher in spiritual evolution and vibration than itself.[1]

This pattern is also due to the constant flux of descending and ascending world ages, based on the precessional cycles of galactic light received by our solar Sun from the Galactic Sun, also known as the Great Central Sun in Ascended Master teachings. According to this precept, galactic light controls man's evolutionary journey on Earth and therefore controls our present level of intelligence, our memory function, our ability to grasp and respect spiritual knowledge, and the length of our lifespans. This subtle light is further regulated by a dwarf Sun orbiting our solar Sun, and astrologers speculate its juxtaposition between the Earth and our Sun obstructs, and therefore controls, the flow of this important galactic energy to Earth. Recent discoveries by astronomers theorize the premise of the dual Sun as Binary Companion Theory.[2] [Editor's Note: For more information, see the Four Great Yugas and Yugas and the Yuteswar Theory.]

Scientific research led by archaeoastronomer Walter Cruttenden at the Binary Research Institute in California suggests the motion of the Sun is best explained through a binary orbital path. Essentially this theory supports the knowledge of Ancient India and astrologer Sri Yukteswar regarding the twin stars comprising our Sun. According to studies, the twin stars rotate around a common center of mass, which drives scientific thinking beyond Newtonian forces. This idea introduces a new approach to the precession of the equinoxes, or the slight wobble of the Earth, which, according to the Binary Research Institute, is speeding up due to the elliptical orbit of our dual-starred

Sri Yuteswar
Revered guru of Paramahansa Yogananda and the author of *The Holy Science*, a comprehensive outline of the four yugas and their relationship to human evolution.

Sun. Binary theory maintains that the energy of the two stars rotating around one another causes the Sun to curve in its elliptical path in space—contrary to the long-held scientific model of lunisolar theory, based primarily on Sir Isaac Newton's theories of gravity and the effect of the Sun and Moon on Earth's wobble.[3] Mark Heley writes about the two opposing ideas, "The binary star theory asks us to take an imaginative leap that is equal to the one Copernicus asked the medieval world to take."[4] The contrast is obvious. One idea is centered on the Earth and its position to our Moon and Sun. The second theory grasps the notion of our Sun as part of an infinite and

1. David Frawley, *The Astrology of the Seers: A Guide to Vedic (Hindu) Astrology*, (Passage Press, 1990, Salt Lake City, UT), page 59.
2. Walter Cruttenden, *Binary Research Institute*, http://www.binaryresearchinstitute.org, (2011).

3. Walter Cruttenden, *Comparison of Precession Theories: An Argument for the Binary Model*, http://www.binaryresearchinstitute.org/bri/research/papers/ComparisonPaper.pdf, (2011).
4. Mark Heley, *The Change from a Heliocentric to a Galactocentric World-view*, http://www.netplaces.com/guide-to-2012/the-binary-star-theory/the-change-from-a-heliocentric-to-a-galactocentric-worldview.htm, (2011).

Ancient Astrology Clock

extensive galaxy. "Instead of being important members of a small and exclusive club of less than ten planets, we now have to learn to live with the mind-boggling vastness of the galaxy, where we are just one solar system out of countless billions. These may be the first steps from a heliocentric perspective to a galactocentric or galaxy-centered cosmos."[5]

According to the Master Teachers, the ideal position for the dwarf Sun is tucked behind its luminous twin so the Earth basks in the beneficial light received from the Galactic Center via the bright twin. When the Sun's dark companion begins to hinder galactic light, a descending cycle ensues, and Earth's humanity slowly moves toward a phase of materialism and overall lack of spirituality. Likewise, as the shadow of the dwarf Sun's cycle fades, an ascending cycle begins and the Sun again receives the benefit of pure galactic light and emits the energy to Earth. Infused with these energies, the Golden Age (Krita Yuga) and the Silver Age (Treta Yuga) of Earth are the past epochs of Earth's history credited with cosmic awareness and spiritual wisdom likely due to humanity's self-realization and cooperation with Angels, Nature Beings, and the emissaries of the Gods.[6] The Puranic method depicts the timing of the Yugas in the illustration of the Ancient Bull of Dharma. Allegedly the Bull of Dharma loses one leg of truth as we descend into each period marked by less galactic light.

According to the Master Teachers, each culture of humanity can only recognize and understand a culture of equal or less galactic light from the preceding cycle. For example: a culture receiving fifty-two percent galactic light in an ascending cycle will only comprehend the spectrum of past cultures from the previous descending cycle up to the threshold of fifty-two percent light. Human consciousness and perception is driven by the Yugas, and this knowledge may help us to understand why we presently cannot unlock the mysteries of the Pyramids or the Naza Plains, yet thoroughly comprehend and annotate the histories of Ancient Rome or Greece.

Traditional Puranic timing of the Yugas predicts only a lengthy descending cycle of galactic light, interrupted at the moment of almost complete darkness and spiritual corruption on Earth—Kali Yuga—by the sudden effulgence of one hundred percent galactic light, a Krita Yuga. Other Vedic authorities claim as we descend out of darkness, we slowly ascend into light. This suggests a natural incremental flow of light and allows for both cycles of descending and ascending light. Overall, this viewpoint makes sense, and places Earth in a time period of ascending infancy, with hope for humanity's spiritual growth and inevitable development.

5. M. Heley, *The Change from a Heliocentric to a Galactocentric Worldview.*
6. David Frawley, *The Astrology of the Seers*, page 56.

Saint Germain's Prophecies of Change

1. During the Time of Transition, an Aggregate Body of Light was built by the Divine Beings to assist humanity to experience a global Spiritual Awakening. This energy force—much like a Group Mind—enabled humanity to enter a new period of evolutionary growth and development through obtaining knowledge and experience with the Fourth Dimension, the Fifth Dimension, and the New Dimensions.

2. The great Aggregate Body of Light prepared humanity to enter and experience the Time of Testing. The souls who developed a keener awareness during the Time of Transition will experience new opportunities for spiritual development, growth, and further spiritual awakening during the Time of Testing.

3. Alongside our personal and collective growth and Spiritual Awakening, we will also experience periods of testing as we expand our consciousness. This testing is not a trial or punishment; rather, an opportunity to realize and experience our expanded growth. Saint Germain says, "This is the time and the time is now."

4. While humanity's entrance into the Golden Age will broaden humanity's current overall educational knowledge (e.g., science, technology, mathematics, physics), the greatest attribute marking our entrance into the new times is the development of the Will and the realization of personal choice.

5. As our ability to see and understand our personal choices and our roles in situations and circumstances increases, there is a new-found level of human sensitivity. This new role of personal accountability and responsibility for our life and its direction moves the soul forward into the first levels of spiritual initiation, and this seems like a type of purification.

6. The collective energy of humanity moving into the rites of self-knowledge and the simultaneous surges of purification are mirrored throughout the Earth by numerous Earth Changes events. As we individually and collectively purify, the Earth enters its own purification.

7. More importantly, as the Earth and humanity jointly enter the purification process, an alignment process simultaneously takes hold. The alignment is both physical and spiritual: the Earth begins to absorb more benefic energy from the Great Central Sun—the Galactic Center. This causes an even greater spiritual evolution of humanity and personal clarity regarding each individual's purpose on Earth at this time.

8. The Master Teacher El Morya serves the Golden City of Gobean through his universal application of the Blue Ray and the ray's inherent qualities of purity, which help humanity to align, harmonize, and ultimately transform as we enter the New Times.

HU-man in Yoga Pose
The HU-man aura responds to the Ascended Masters'
Aggregrate Body of Light.

Earth Pater Noster
Nicholas Roerich, 1907.

The Great Purification

Primarily considered a Native American term, the Great Purification signals the end of one period of time for humanity and the beginning of a New Time. The Hopi Prophecies state the Great Purification will occur in several stages with prophesied Earth Changes, global wars, Climate Change, and nuclear devastation by the dropping of a "gourd full of ashes."[1] The final stage, known as the Great Day of Purification, is a culmination of world and social events; the crisis will force rich and poor, "to struggle as equals in order to survive." The Hopi further prophesy that "man still may lessen the violence by correcting his treatment of nature and fellow man."[2]

The Native American Sioux tradition defines the Great Purification as an escalation of prophetic events to a point of no return. Brave Buffalo, Brule Sioux Nation states, "It is time for the Great Purification. We are at a point of no return. The two-legged are about to bring destruction to life on Earth. It's happened before, and it's about to happen again. The Sacred Hoop shows how all things go in a circle. The old becomes new; the new becomes old. Everything repeats."[3]

Contemporary prophets view the Great Purification as a time for humanity to heal and transform individually and collectively. These actions create an opportunity for the Brotherhood of Man and a new society built on the ideals of cooperation rather than competition. This viewpoint asks humanity to throw away progressive Darwinian ideals regarding modern culture and cultivate spiritual growth for humanity's survival and to heal our compromised and fragile environments. The common linear theory of time that implies that the constant drive of evolutionary progress is always bigger and better is only illusion, and perilously leads humanity to the edge of destruction. According to Prashant Trivedi, we must remember the cycles of time taught by ancient civilizations and that "Humanity was faced with the same situation about 12,000 years ago, when great floods destroyed flourishing civilizations which had become overly materialistic as they too approached the end of their age."[4]

The Great Purification signals everyone that there is the opportunity to spiritually grow and develop relationships beyond greed, consumption, and exploitation. At this critical time, our inherent Divinity can move us toward balance, away from the precipice of cataclysm. "It is up to each of us to discover the true meaning of life by inquiring within our own minds. If someone tells you how you should live, what you should do, what your path might be, and if you follow that road, it will lead you nowhere," and Trivedi reminds us that spiritual wakefulness is perhaps our greatest ally at this tumultuous time. "Learning along our path is a continuous and effortless process, but one must stay awake, mentally, and not allow oneself to be influenced by the conditioning of this world. One can only stay awake mentally with a mind that is not already conditioned by society, rules, orthodoxy, nationality, religion, and so on."[5] It is time to move away from "dying systems," and move toward self-reliance and sustainable methods that harmonize with nature and Earth.[6]

Hopi Symbol of Gourd of Ashes
According to the late Hopi Elder, Grandfather Dan Evehma, Maasaw (a Hopi immortal deity) carries a gourd of ashes. "He is carrying with him his own gourd of ashes, and one day he will drop it. When he does, all fighting will cease all over the world. Enemies will just go to sleep. Maasaw will drop ashes on everyone, so they won't have to fight."

1. Thomas Mails, *The Hopi Survival Kit*, (Penguin Group, 1997, New York, NY), page 209.
2. Ibid., page 210.
3. Brave Buffalo, *Brule Sioux Nation*, http://www.dreamscape.com/morgana/hyperio2.htm, (2009).

4. Prashant Trivedi, *The Great Purification: Creation and Destruction*, http://www.osfa.org.uk/essay-32.htm, (2009).
5. Ibid.
6. Ibid.

Violet Flame Meditation

Various Applications of the Violet Flame

"It is important to understand there are many applications of the Violet Flame." ~ Saint Germain

The Violet Flame, which is a spiritual prayer, decree, philosophy, action, and meditation of forgiveness, detachment, compassion, and ultimately transformation, has many applications and devotional practices. These are a few techniques the Master Teachers have specifically taught or mentioned throughout the years; however, in reality, the use of the transmuting alchemical fire is in fact as varied and unique as snowflakes—no two are alike!

1. Decrees: Written and spoken
2. Mantras: Chant the HU and Bija-seed mantras
3. Take purifying salt baths with lilac or lavender essential oils
4. Meditation upon the Violet Flame; visualize the color violet while meditating.
5. Hold purple beads or an amethyst Mala while meditating. You can use amethyst crystals to invoke the presence of the Flame.
6. Invoke the presence of the Violet Flame Angels for protection, assistance, and healing.
7. Prayers and worship to Shiva (detachment) and Kuan Yin (compassion).
8. Develop bhakti—the Hindu principle of compassionate love.
9. Use of Dahana Shatki, which comes from the Vedic Nakshatra Krittika, one of the twenty-eight lunar mansions of Vedic Astrology—Jyotish. The sign of Krittika is represented by the six brightest stars of the Pleiades constellation and are mythologically represented as the six wives of the Great Seers: Alcyone, Celaeno, Electra, Taygete, Maia, and Asterope. The symbolic Shatki, or energy, has the ability to transformationally burn or cut away negativity to get to the deepest truth.[11]
10. Kriya Yoga

The Violet Flame Breath

This technique is recommended by Saint Germain to assist the Re-membering Process for mental, emotional, and physical blocks that play a role in pain, suffering, and disease. This technique is unique, as it is a physical breathing exercise that exposes suppressed and past-life memories, initiating release. Steps in this process are:

1. Close your eyes, and focus your attention upon the pineal gland—the Third-Eye.
2. Visualize the Violet Flame spinning and opening the Third-Eye Chakra.
3. Visualize a thread of energy that expands into a globe, and then develops into a Vortex shape. The Vortex is filled with the energy of the Violet Flame and moves to the Heart Chakra, connected by the pulsating thread.
4. Now, both the Third-Eye Chakra and Heart Chakra are connected by the luminous thread and function together as ONE.
5. From the Heart Chakra, visualize yet again a second thread of energy that moves to the sacral area, and another globe of fiery Violet Flame energy develops and radiates. All three centers—the pineal, the heart, and the sacral area—are connected through vibrant, transmuting Violet Flame energy. According to Saint Germain, the front, or anterior, positions of the Seven Chakras connect through this visualization process.
6. As you begin your first intentional breath, start at the base of the spine and, with the power of your breath merged with your visualization, move a golden, invigorating energy of light through each of the three Violet Flame centers. Breathe from the sacral to the heart; from the heart to the pineal. Then breathe moving the light downward through the Violet Flame centers. Your inhale moves the light up; your exhale moves the light down. Each breath completes a loop, upward toward the front; downward toward the back, or posterior position

Amethyst Crystals
Place amethyst crystals nearby or hold a crystal while meditating upon the Violet Flame
to increase and stengthen the process of transmutation.

of the chakras. Repeat each breathing cycle seven times.

7. Carefully still your mind and note any area of your body where energy is not moving or is stagnating as you continue the breathing technique. The Violet Flame is a continuous looping circle through the three centers.

8. Carefully breathe and work through blockages. In your mind, break the blockage apart and move any residue in the continuous, steady river of energy through the Violet Flame Breath.

9. Continue this process until you feel a mass of energy accumulate in the pineal area.

10. Visualize the pineal mass as a large white television screen. Carefully view any experiences that are associated with the energetic obstacle.

11. You may need to repeat this technique several times, depending on the severity of the blockage.

12. According to Saint Germain, the Violet Flame Breath Technique assists the body and soul to restore balance and to continue the journey of spiritual growth and evolution. "Once you become aware of the experience you have suppressed and held [this technique] allows a full experience [Remembering]. The pain will cease and you will begin to understand the Alignment Process."

Seventh Manu

In past teachings, the Master Teachers describe the Seventh Manu as a large group of souls that incarnate for over 1,500 years on Earth (1981 AD to 3650 AD). The purpose of the Seventh Manu soul-group is to raise the overall vibration of Earth through their spiritually evolved understanding of Freedom and Peace. Saint Germain expands this definition in the teaching The New Children to include:

1. Many of the souls incarnating as the wave of souls known as the Seventh Manu have not incarnated on Earth for thousands of years; and some were last present on Earth during the time of Atlantis.
2. Some souls of the Seventh Manu have a natural talent and propensity toward the technological sciences, which inevitably assists the Earth and its evolutionary process.
3. Previous incarnations on diverse planets and different solar systems are common among Seventh Manu souls. According to Saint Germain, the system of evolving souls does not consider physical proximities restricted only to Earth. The soul is "timeless" and is not bound by the Third Dimensional aspects of time and space. When viewed through this understanding, the veil separating physical and spiritual realities is a thin line of demarcation, and the soul's consciousness often evolves between galaxies and star-systems literally thousands of light-years away.

[Editor's Note: The idea of the timeless, deathless soul was explored by Paramahansa Yogananda in the book Autobiography of a Yogi, The Resurrection of Sri Yuteswar. Yogananda accounts the astral visit of his spiritual mentor who had passed away on March 9, 1936, and appears to him at a Bombay Hotel:

"Yes, my child, I am the same. This is a flesh and blood body. Though I see it as ethereal to your sight it is physical. From Cosmic Atoms I created an entirely new body, exactly like that cosmic-dream physical body which you laid beneath the dream-sands of Puri in your dream-world. I am in truth resurrected—not on Earth but on an Astral Plane."[1]

The resurrected Yuteswar continues with his detailed explanation of the Astral Plane as a frequent location for the soul's journey after Earthly death and describes the Astral Cosmos: "There are many astral planets, teeming with astral beings. The inhabitants use astral planes, or masses of light, to travel from one planet to another, faster than electricity and radioactive energies."[2]]

4. The New Children are prophesied as spiritual Masters who will incarnate on Earth at a critical juncture of humanity's evolutionary process to help the masses transmute difficult Karmas and lead many into the liberation, or Ascension Process.
5. Children of the Seventh Manu are also known as the Indigo Children. Seventh Manu refers to the Seventh Alchemic Ray—the Violet Ray. The scientific wavelength of the color Indigo is between Blue and Violet; however, many consider Indigo analogous to Purple.
6. Since Seventh Manu souls carry a higher vibration and less Karmic burden than the average Earth soul, they are prophesied to lead humanity into the Age of Transportation. During this Earth epoch, spiritual technology

1. Paramahansa Yogananda, Autobiography of a Yogi, (Self-Realization Fellowship, 1994, Los Angeles, CA), page 400.
2. Ibid., page 402.

Yoga in the Forest
The New Children, also known as the *Seventh Manu*, are spiritually evolved and wise beyond their years.

    will embrace the ancient practice of bi-location and the spiritual ideals of timelessness.

7. The Spiritual Technology of the children of the Seventh Manu is prophesied to develop and is derived from varied experiences gleaned from their incarnations in different galaxies. This exposes the Earth to new ideas, processes, and perceptions that evolve our current sciences and reshape much of our current technology.

8. The influence of the New Manu children will shape human consciousness for several thousand years. As these souls are wise beyond their years, they will be seen as the new elders of Earth. The New Children will lead a renaissance in reformation of our societies, cultures, religions, and scientific knowledge.

9. While this group of souls is highly evolved, Saint Germain explains that they, too, have their own unique Karmas and "Time of Testing," to be played out upon the Earth Plane and Planet.

Mother Mary, the Western Goddess and Archetype of the Feminine

The Ascended Master and Western Goddess of the Feminine Archetype was an initiate of the ethereal Temples of Nature before her incarnation as Mary, Mother of Jesus Christ. It is claimed that as a child Mary was raised in the mystical traditions of the Essenes, and throughout her lifetime as Mother Mary, she was constantly overshadowed by the Angelic Kingdom. Some Ascended Master texts claim Mary was once a member of the heavenly realm.

Mary's lifetime as the mother of Jesus Christ was planned in-between lifetimes on Earth, "Her embodiment as Mother of Jesus was in the Divine Plan long before she entered the physical realm. She went through a severe initiation at inner levels to test her strength some time before taking embodiment."[1] Throughout her life as the Master's mother, Mary was attuned to the spiritual planes which gave her strength and insight to fulfill her role as the Mother of Jesus. And, no doubt, Mary or Maryam, as

1. A. D. K. Luk, *Law of Life, Book II,* (ADK Luk Publications, 1989, Pueblo, CO), page 344.

The Mythological Trinity: Osiris, Horus, and Isis, Karl Baedeker.

she is known in Aramaic, lived in perilous times. The Biblical story in the Book of Matthew accounts the Holy Family's flight to Egypt to avoid King Herod's Massacre of the Innocents. It is claimed that Mother Mary made a vow to assist anyone who had lost their life as a Christian martyr to obtain the Ascension in a future life.[6] Mary the Mother of Jesus became an archetype of the Cosmic Mother for all of humanity.

As an archetype of the Feminine, Mary is also a form of Isis, the Virgin of the World of Hermetic Teaching. The name Isis draws its meaning from Hebrew and Greek sources, which means wisdom or to serve.[2] However, the myth of the Virgin Goddess is contained in the ancient language of Scandinavia as Isa; and is similarly portrayed as the Eleusian Goddess Ceres and Queen Moo of the Mayans. Manly Hall writes, "She was known as the Goddess with ten-thousand appellations and was meta-morphosed by Christianity

Isis
Roman statue of Isis-Persephone, 180-190 CE.

2. Manly P. Hall, *The Secret Teachings of All Ages: An Encyclopedic Outline of Masonic, Hermetic, Qabbalistic and Rosicrucian Symbolical Philosophy,* (Philosophical Research Society, Inc., 1988, Los Angeles, CA), page 45.

بخال تو عیسی و مریم برآمد بگویم حقیقت بگویم خوش آمد

در خستهٔ و روزی برویت کشاده شوه تا قیامت تو کردی سپاه آمد

Maryam and Issa
Virgin Mary and Jesus, old Persian miniature. In Islam, they are called Maryam and Isa.

an alphabet for written language, astronomy, and the science of seamanship. Isis helped humanity to overcome paternal tyranny through instructing men to love women and children to love and respect their elders through the philosophic teachings of beauty as truth, and the intrinsic value of justice. The teachings of Isis are not for the irreverent. The discipline of emotion and the acquisition of wisdom are required in order to access and understand the evolutionary energies of the Feminine.

Ancient initiates were advised to keep silent their venerated knowledge of the spiritual truths underlying the vulgar and profane.[3]

In Christianity Mary is known as the Virgin Mother of Jesus; however, Catholics and Protestants differ regarding their worship of the Mother of the Son of God. In Islam, the Virgin Mary is esteemed as the mother to the Prophet Issa.[4] Jesus' birth was prophesied by the Archangel Gabriel in a visit to Mary during her betrothal to Joseph, and the Archangel declared, "She was to be the mother of the promised Messiah by conceiving him through the Holy Spirit."[5] The New Testament places Mary at Nazareth in Galilee, the daughter of Joachim and Anne. Apocryphal legend claims Mary's birth was also a miracle—her mother was barren. To many Roman Catholics, Mary was the perfect vessel to carry the Christ, and was "filled with grace from the very moment of her conception in her mother's womb and the stain of original sin."[6] This spiritual precept is known as the Immaculate Conception of Mary.

into the Virgin Mary, for Isis, although she gave birth to all living things—chief among them the Sun—still remained a virgin, according to legendary accounts." As the eldest daughter of Kronus the Ancient Titan, and the wife and sister to Osiris, Isis was the student of the great Master Hermes Trismegistus. Through this affiliation it is claimed the laws for humanity were developed, including

3. M. Hall, *The Secret Teachings of All Ages*.
4. *Mary (Mother of Jesus)*, http://en.wikipedia.org/wiki/Mary_(mother_of_jesus), (2009).
5. Ibid.
6. Ibid.

The Immaculate Conception
A depiction of Mother Mary by Bartolome Esteban Murillo, 1660-1665.

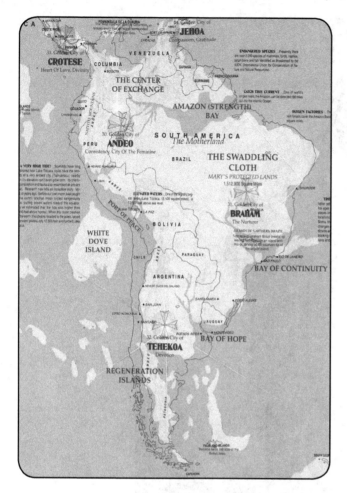

The Swaddling Cloth from Freedom Star Map

An area of over a million square miles located in Brazil, South America. According to the Ascended Masters, this area is the primary prophesied physical location for the incarnation of the children of the Seventh Manu. The Swaddling Cloth is protected by the Ascended Master Mother Mary.

Contemporary interpretations of the Immaculate Concept state this spiritual practice is the Alchemy of holding the image of perfection through the use of prayer, meditation, and visualization. Thought-forms of "Beauty, poise, and grace on behalf of others," is claimed to create Divine Energies of purity and protection.[7] David C. Lewis

writes regarding the spiritual exercise of holding the Immaculate Concept for ourselves:

> "Ultimately we must first hold the immaculate concept for ourselves by attuning to our own Higher Self and maintaining a vigil of Oneness through presence and awareness of our own Divine Nature. Once we have learned to live in this unified field of stillness and beingness and maintain our spiritual poise, especially during challenging times and situations, we can more easily practice the science of the immaculate concept on behalf of others."[8]

The Swaddling Cloth

According to the Ascended Masters Mother Mary holds the Immaculate Concept for the incoming generations of the Seventh Manu through the energies of the Swaddling Cloth, located in Brazil, South America. In the I AM America teachings, Mother Mary often merges her energies with Kuan Yin, the Feminine Bodhisattva of Mercy and Compassion, and together they channel the energies of the Divine Mother to Earth. Divine Mother is an archetype of Feminine Unity and the ONE. Beloved Mary is known to appear at times of physical or emotional crisis, often to convey the healing power of wholeness and unconditional love. Mother Mary's Temple of the Sacred Heart, located in the Fifth Dimension, prepares souls for re-embodiment.[9] She is the Ascended Master sponsor of the Golden City of Marnero, located in Mexico. Marnero means the ocean of candles; its quality is Virtue; and this Golden City is affiliated with the Green Ray.

---

7. David C. Lewis, *The Immaculate Concept: Creating Alchemical Change,* http://www.theheartscenter.org, (2009).

8. Lewis, *The Immaculate Concept.*

9. A.D.K Luk, *Law of Life,* Book II, (ADK Luk Publications, 1989, Pueblo, CO), page 347.

Fantasy in Twilight
Robert Edward Hughes, 1911.

The Encounter
Paul Gauguin, 1892.

Glossary

Absolute Harmony: Order and peace permeate throughout.

Absolute Perfection: State of completion and purity without lack, blemish, or fault.

Abundance: The second of the Twelve Jurisdictions is the principle of overflowing fullness in all situations, based upon the Law of Choice. In Divine Destiny, Abundance, as a Meta-need, is defined as richness and complexity. Abundance, perceived as an Evolution Point, is synonymous with the Law of Choice, and develops the individual will; hence, the spiritual recognition of Universal Bounty and Manifestation leads the spiritual student to the discernment and the acknowledgement of the Hermetic principles of Cause and Effect through the Law of Attraction.

Acceleration: A rapid rate of change of velocity, especially with respect to Spiritual Development and the perception of time.

Adept: An unascended Master of thought, feeling, and action (physical plane), and an initiate of the Great White Brotherhood.

Adjutant Point: Power points that form where the lei-lines of the geometric Maltese cross formation of a Golden City traverse or intersect. Adjutant points support the infrastructure of a Golden City, both geometrically and spiritually, and assist and disburse the unique energies held by Babajeran, the Ascended Masters, and the Golden City's Ray Force.

Age of Cooperation: The age humanity is currently being prepared to enter; it occurs simultaneously with the Time of Change.

Age of Transportation: A prophesied epoch on Earth humanity will experience once we leave the current Information Age (late eighties through the twenty-first century). The Transportation Age will see humanity's consciousness evolve into Mastery beyond the human maxims of time and space. During this period, which is prophesied to run concurrently with several periods of the Golden Age—the Age of Cooperation and the Age of Peace—humanity will begin interstellar travel, alongside leaps in evolutionary growth resulting in telepathic communication, spiritual technologies, and bi-location.

Age of Peace: The time period prophesied to exist after the Earth Changes.

Aggregate Body of Light: The sum or mass of our individual energy bodies.

Agreement Formation: Agreement Formation is an early tenet of the I AM America Teachings, the Law of Agreement is also known as the First Jurisdiction, Harmony. Agreement is the sacred meeting of two minds which on one formative side reflects our intent and commitment. The results of our agreements with others reflect our choices and our responsible actions that ultimately define the quality of our life force.

Akashic Records: The recorded history of all created things from time immemorial, and constructed with the fifth cosmic element: ether.

Akhenaten: The ancient king of Egypt (1388 BC) embraced the unfolding consciousness of the ONE, which culturally replaced the polytheistic religion of his Kingdom. A pioneer of monotheistic religion, Akhenaten embraced the Christ Consciousness and some esoteric historians view him as a spiritual forerunner who led the way for the incarnation of Jesus Christ. According to the Master Teachers, Akhenaten is one of the prior lifetimes attributed to Ascended Master Serapis Bey.

Alchemy: The process of Transmutation.

Alignment: Convergence or adjustment. Balance.

Ameru: The ancient lands of America from which the word Ameruca is derived, and means, "Land of the Plumed Serpent." Esoteric historians allege Ameru is the beloved land of the Toltecs, the ancestral forefathers of today's Native American; geologists suppose the lands of Ameru are the North America Craton, the ancient continent of Laurentia.

Ancestral Planet: A hidden planet, whose view is obscured by the dark, twin Sun. Its inhabitants are highly evolved Spiritual Beings who assist humanity during times of evolutionary darkness.

Anchor: One of three models of soul groups prophesied to inhabit Earth during the New Times. The anchor securely affixes spiritual energy from the Fourth Dimension to the Third Dimension. Compassionate in disposition, the Anchor resonates with the Elemental, Deva, and Nature Kingdoms, and can readily hold the transformative energies of the Violet Flame for the collective consciousness.

Apex: The center, especially the top of a Golden City Vortex.

Archangels (the Seven): The seven principal angels of creation are: Michael, the Blue Ray; Jophiel, the Yellow Ray; Chamuel, the Pink Ray; Gabriel, the White Ray; Raphael, the Green Ray; Uriel, the Ruby Ray; and Zadkiel, the Violet Ray.

Archetype(s): A pattern or form, from which a thing is modeled, especially a forward-moving, transcendent state of human consciousness, often known as an Archetype of Evolution.

Armies of Light: Members of the Angelic, Deva, and Elemental Kingdoms, who work with and are under the direction of our Earth Mother, Babajeran. Their service is primarily given to the Heavenly Ashrams of the sublime Adjutant Points within the Golden Cities.

Aryan: The fifth Root Race of humanity is identified primarily with Active Intelligence, and the development of the prefrontal lobes of the brain (prefrontal cortex). This is the dominant Root Race currently incarnated on Earth.

Ascended Master Consciousness: A higher frequency of thought, feeling, and action which embraces the unity of humanity through the principle of the Oneship.

Ascended Masters: Once an ordinary human, an Ascended Master has undergone a spiritual transformation over many lifetimes. He or she has Mastered the lower planes—mental, emotional, and physical—to unite with his or her Godself or I AM Presence. An Ascended Master is freed from the Wheel of Karma. He or she moves forward in spiritual evolution beyond this planet; however, an Ascended Master remains attentive to the spiritual well-being of humanity, inspiring and serving the Earth's spiritual growth and evolution.

Ascending Culture: A culture that emerges from the upswing of galactic light from the Great Central Sun. Ascending cultures are constantly moving towards the light of truth that is yet to be defined or fully realized.

Ascension: A process of Mastering thoughts, feelings, and actions that balance positive and negative Karmas in the physical planes. Once engaged, the soul's Ascension Process often involves successive lifetimes, and engages the transmutation of Karma (actions), and the conscious achievement of spiritual immortality. Ascension allows entry to a higher state of consciousness and frees a person from the need to reincarnate on the lower earthly planes, or lokas of experience. Ascension is also known as the process of spiritual liberation, moksha, or spiritual transcendence. The attainment of physical immortality is also associated with Ascension; however, an Ascended Being is not limited by form of any kind, and may take any shape or outward appearance necessary for the task at hand.

Ascension Process: The Ascension Process, according to Saint Germain, gathers the energies of the individual chakras and expands their energy through the heart. The Law of Love calibrates the energy fields (aura) to Zero Point—a physical and philosophical viewpoint of neutrality. From there, the subtle and fine tuning of the light bodies is effectuated through the higher chakras, sequentially including the Throat Chakra, the Third Eye Chakra, and finally the Crown Chakra. Zero Point is crucial in this process and it is here that the energies of all past lives are brought to psychological and physical (karmic) balance. Then the initiate is able to withdraw their light bodies from the physical plane into the Astral Light of the Fourth Dimension. The Ascension Process may take several lifetimes to complete and the beginning stages are defined through the arduous process of obtaining self-knowledge, the acceptance of the conscious immortality of the soul, and the use of Alchemy through the Violet Flame. Intermediate stages may manifest the anomalies of Dimensional Acceleration, Vibrational Shifting, Cellular

Awakening and Acceleration, and contact with the Fourth Dimension. Use of the Gold Ray at this level accelerates the liberation process and unites the individual with soul mates and their beloved Twin Ray. Later stages of Ascension include the transfiguration of light bodies and Fifth Dimensional contact through the super-senses as the magnificent Seamless Garment manifests its light. It is claimed that the Golden Cities assist the Ascension Process at every stage of development. According to the Master Teachers diet and fasting will also aid the Ascension Process at various phases.

Ascension Valley: According to the I AM America Prophecies, Ascended Masters appear in physical form in the Golden City Vortices during and after a prophesied twenty-year period. At that time, Mass Ascensions occur in the Golden Cities, at the Golden City Star locations, and in select geophysical locations around the world, which are hosted by the complimentary energies of Mother Earth. A model of this geophysical location is Ascension Valley, located in the Shalahah Vortex. The energy of Ascension Valley prepares students to integrate their light bodies and spiritual consciousness into the Oneship, the divinity within, and further prepares the body, mind, and spirit to experience and travel into the New Dimensions.

Ashram: A secluded community or retreat, especially of spiritual students and seekers.

Astral Body or Plane: The subtle light body that contains our feelings, desires, and emotions. It exists as an intermediate light body between the physical body and the Causal Body (Mental Body). According to the Master Teachers, we enter the Astral Plane through our Astral Body when we sleep, and many dreams and visions are experiences in this Plane of vibrant color and sensation. Through spiritual development, the Astral Body strengthens, and the luminosity of its light is often detected in the physical plane. Spiritual adepts may have the ability to consciously leave their physical bodies while traveling in their Astral Bodies. The Astral Body or Astral Plane has various levels of evolution and is the heavenly abode where the soul resides after the disintegration of the physical body. The Astral Body is also known as the Body Double, the Desire Body, and the Emotional Body.

Aspirant: A newly awakened spiritual student, whose ambitions create aspiration; the student has yet to find or acquire a guru—a teacher who can assist their evolutionary journey on the spiritual path. The aspirant is the first level of HU-man development, and occupies the fifth of the Thirteen Evolutionary Pyramids of the Eight-sided Cell of Perfection: Spiritual Awakening.

Atlantis: An ancient civilization of Earth, whose mythological genesis was the last Puranic Dvapara Yuga—the Bronze Age of the Yugas, and its demise occurred around the year 9,628 BC. The legends of Atlantis claim the great empire co-existed with Ameru, Lemuria, and the Lands of Rama. According to Theosophical thought, Atlantis' evolving humanity brought about an evolutionary epoch of the Pink Ray on the Earth, and the development of the Astral-Emotional bodies and the Heart Chakra. Ascended Master provenance claims the Els—now the Mighty Elohim of the Seven Rays—were the original Master Teachers to the spiritual seekers of Atlantis. Esoteric historians suggest three phases of political and geophysical boundaries best describe its ancient record: the Toltec Nation of Atlantis (Ameru); the Turian Nation of Atlantis (the invaders of the Land of Rama); and Poseid, the Island Nation of the present-day Atlantic Ocean. The early civilizations of Atlantis were ruled by the spiritually evolved Toltec and their spiritual teachings, ceremonies, and temples were dedicated to the worship of the Sun. Atlantean culture later deteriorated into the use of nuclear weapons and cruelty towards other nations, including the use of genetic engineering. The demise of Atlantis was inevitable; however, modern-day geologists, archaeologists, and occultists all disagree to its factual timing. Ascended Master teachings affirm that Atlantis—a continent whose geo-physical and political existence probably spanned well over 100,000 years—experienced several phases of traumatic Earth Change. This same belief is held by occult historians who allege the Earth repeatedly cycles through periods of massive Earth Change and cataclysmic pole-shifts that activate tectonic plates which subsequently submerge whole continents and create vital new lands for Earth's successors.

At-ONE-ment: The spiritual practice and state of Unity. This spiritual ideal is philosophically affirmed through the recognition of humanity's innate divinity, equality, and human connection to ONE source of creation. This results in the At-ONE-ment, and the advanced practitioner morphs into a Step-down Transformer of the Seven Rays of Light and Sound as an expression of beauty and creation. The At-ONE-ment facilitates the consciousness of Unana.

Aura: The subtle energy field of luminous light that surrounds the human body.

Avatar: The Divine Manifestation of a perfected spiritual consciousness in human form has several meanings. The Siddha is a perfected being; the Jivanmukta is freed while living; and the Paramukta, similar to an Ascended Master, is supremely free, with full power over death. A Paramukta or Ascended Being purposely creates a physical body and descends to Earth to either assist humanity or to spiritually bless or balance a disordered world. The perfected, death-free body of a Paramukta does not cast a shadow or leave footprints. Such Masters never appear in the gross public, and have the ability to become invisible. There are, however, Living Avatars who incarnate in a human body to help the masses to spiritually awake and transform at critical times in Earth's history. According to Ascended Master teachings there are twelve Living Avatars present on Earth at any time. This insures specific levels of vibration, radiance, and spiritual energy to foster humanity's growth and evolutionary requirements.

Awaken: To rouse from the sleep of illusion and become spiritually aware and attentive to one's internal truth. This first level of spiritual evolution is often identified as the Spiritual Aspirant. It can also indicate a new level of spiritual wakefulness or growth, sometimes known as the restorative and vibrant Quickening.

Axiotonal Bodies: Light bodies of the Human Aura defined by magnetic energy lines, similar to acupuncture lines on the human body and lei-lines on Mother Earth. It is claimed Axiotonal Lines connect our human biology to resonating star systems within our galaxy, affecting human chemistry and genetic change.

Babajeran: A name for the Earth Mother that means, "grandmother rejoicing." Feminine form of Babaji.

Balance: "Put into proper order."

Belief: An opinion, conviction, or doctrine based upon insufficient grounds, or proof.

Belt of Golden Light: This etheric Golden Belt of high-frequency energy has been in place since the early 1950s. It holds back catastrophic Earth Changes until humanity has a better chance to evolve. The belt also plays a significant role in mankind's spiritual growth.

Bija-Seed Mantra: A one-syllable word spoken aloud to produce spiritual healing and intervention, alongside spiritual growth and insight. Bija-Seed Mantras are said to contain the spiritual laws and patterns of the underlying energy of creation, and their sound vibration recalibrates the energy bodies and light-fields of the Human Aura which affects the physical world of the individual.

Bi-locate: The ability to consciously move the physical body through the spiritual development of the light-bodies. Some spiritual Masters use bi-location to be physically present in two or more locations simultaneously.

Bi-location: The ability to be in more than one place at one time in the physical dimension.

Binary Intellect: Dual, human intelligence, based upon the difference of the left brain and the right brain.

Bliss of the Eternal Ocean: The state of consciousness that immerses the individual into constant bliss.

Blue Flame: The activity of the Blue Ray, based upon the activation of the individual will, manifests the qualities of truth, power, determination, and diligence in human endeavors. The Blue Flame is associated with the transformation of our individual choices, and its inherent processes align the individual will to the Divine Will through the HU-man qualities of detachment, steadiness, calm, harmony, and God-protection.

Blue Flame Angels: A group of angels associated with Archangel Michael who assists humanity with the manifestation and Co-creation Process.

Blue Ray: A Ray is a perceptible light and sound frequency, and the Blue Ray not only resonates with the color blue, but is identified with the qualities of steadiness, calm, perseverance, transformation, harmony, diligence, determination, austerity, protection, humility, truthfulness, and self-negation. It forms one-third of the Unfed Flame within the heart—the Blue Ray of God Power, which nourishes the spiritual unfoldment of the human into the HU-man. Use of the Violet Flame evokes the Blue Ray into action throughout the light bodies, where the Blue Ray clarifies intentions and assists the alignment of the Will. In Ascended Master teachings the Blue Ray is alleged to have played a major role in the physical manifestation of the Earth's first Golden City—Shamballa and six of fifty-one Golden Cities emanate the Blue Ray 's peaceful, yet piercing frequencies. The Blue Ray is esoterically linked to the planet Saturn, the development of the Will, the ancient Lemurian Civilization, the Archangel Michael, the Elohim Hercules, the Master Teacher El Morya, and the Eastern Doors of all Golden Cities.

Breathwork: The conscious, spiritual application of breath, often accompanied by visualization and meditation forms the nexus of Breathwork. Ascended Master teachings often incorporate various breathing techniques to activate and integrate Ray Forces in the Human Aura and light bodies.

Cause and effect: Every action causes an event, which is the consequence or result of the first. This law is often referred to as karma—or the sixth Hermetic Law.

Causeless Cause: In Ascended Master teachings, the spiritual and philosophic notion of chaos. This gives rise to the creation of the Seven Rays of Light and Sound.

Cellular Awakening: A spiritual initiation activated by the Master Teachers Saint Germain and Kuthumi. Through this process the physical body is accelerated at the cellular level, preparing consciousness to recognize and receive instruction from the Fourth Dimension. Supplemental teachings on the Cellular Awakening claim this process assists the spiritual student to assimilate the higher frequencies and energies now available on Earth. Realizing the Cellular Awakening can ameliorate catastrophic Earth Change and initiate consciousness into the ONE through the realization of devotion, compassion, Brotherhood and the Universal Heart.

Cellular Fear: The cumulative emotion of fear held in the light bodies which simultaneously affects human DNA. This energetic build up is carried by the individual to the astral plane after physical death and passed to the next lifetime until it is released by the soul.

Ceremony: Intentionally using the language of symbols to initiate or activate consciousness and subtle energies.

Chakra(s): Sanskrit for wheel. Seven spinning wheels of human-bioenergy centers stacked from the base of the spine to the top of the head.

Chalice: A Cup which represents the field of neutrality, zero point, and balance. The metaphoric Cup or chalice is best known as the goblet used by Christ in the Last Supper. During spiritual wars of good and evil, the Divine Chalice is carried by Angels of Neutrality to represent the spiritual attribute of Divine Grace during human battles of fear and desire. In its purest state, the Angels of Neutrality pour the cup upon humanity to restore harmony, abundance, and peace.

Chela: Disciple.

Chi: Energy.

Chohan: Another word for Lord.

Choice: Will.

Christ, the: The highest energy or frequency attainable on Earth. The Christ is a step-down transformer of the I AM energies which enlighten, heal, and transform all human conditions of degradation and death.

Christ Consciousness: A level of consciousness that unites both feminine and masculine energies and produces the innocence and purity of the I AM. Its energies heal, enlighten, and transform every negative human condition and pave the way for the realization of the divine HU-man.

Circle of Known: A measurement of all known knowledge is contained in the circle; the unknown falls outside the circle.

Closure of Understanding: The completion and release of a Karmic lesson.

Co-creation: Creating with the God-Source.

Collective Consciousness: The higher interactive structure of consciousness as two or more.

Compassion: An attribute of the Violet Flame is the sympathetic understanding of the suffering of another.

Conductivity: The transmission of vital energy.

Conscience: The internal recognition of right and wrong in regard to one's actions and motives

Consciousness: Awakening to one's own existence, sensations and cognitions.

Cooperation: The seventh of the Twelve Jurisdictions advises joint actions, work, and assistance to faithfully adhere with fairness, honesty, and the acknowledgement of the Divine Presence.

Cosmic Teacher: A teacher of the Ascended Masters.

Cosmic Wave Motion: Belts of energy that weave a pattern throughout the universe; they originate from the Sun.

Cup: A symbol of neutrality and grace.

Cup Within a Cup: A remedial measure constructed in the center of a Golden City Community that opens a heavenly gateway.

Cycle of the Elements: The interactive cycle of the elements on Mother Earth is dualistic—both masculine and feminine, and constructive or destructive. The cycle contains a creative, nourishing cycle: metal creates and nourishes water; water nourishes wood; wood feeds and nourishes fire; fire creates earth; earth creates and nourishes metal. The counterpart of this cycle is destructive: metal destroys and weakens wood; wood weakens earth; earth contains and weakens water; water destroys or weakens fire; fire melts and weakens metal.

Dark Government: The dysfunctional aspect of leadership that knowingly or unknowingly creates tyrannies of fear, control, destruction of life, and the suppression of human rights.

Dark Side: The energy and force of the common man that draws power from raw human emotions like: pain, hatred, passion, and attachment.

Dead Zone: A consciousness of slumber and unawareness.

Decree: Statements of intent and power, similar to prayers and mantras, which are often integrated with the use of the I AM and requests to the I AM Presence.

Denasha: The Golden City of Denasha is primarily located over Scotland, and the Ascended Masters assert this Vortex holds the energies of Divine Justice for all of humanity. Denasha is also the Sister Golden City to Malton (Illinois and Indiana, USA) and both Vortices mutually distribute energies to the Nature and Elemental Kingdoms during the New Times. The Master Teacher is Lady Nada; the Ray Force is Yellow; and Denasha's translation means, "Mountain of Zeus."

Descending Culture: A culture that emerges during the downswing of galactic light from the Great Central Sun. Cultures birthed in descending cycles strive to protect their traditions and spiritual heritage whose origin is from a period of greater light and enlightenment.

Desire: Of the source.

Deva: Shining one or being of light.

Dharma: Purpose.

Dimensional Rifting: An anomaly caused by the individual absorbing evolutionary Ray Forces from the Great Central Sun. It is associated with the healing of trauma and painful experiences associated with past lives and unfulfilled desires. This allows one to complete and liberate from karmas, initiating the liberation process of the soul, known as Ascension.

Dis-ease: Lack of harmony.

Disembodied Spirit: A person or thought-form that survives the death of the body but maintains consciousness.

Divine Cloak: A heavenly, protective Veil of Energy.

Divine Mother: The Mother Goddess or feminine aspect of God.

Divineship: The essence and presence of the Divine is present within the individual.

Divine Feminine: The Mother Creative principle as the highest expression of being. Femininity is akin to the Goddess. She comprises one half of the gender-neutral God force. Feminine energy represents love, beauty, seduction, sensitivity, and refinement—characteristics of the Goddess Venus. On the dark side, it reflects vanity, superficiality, fickleness, and exhaustion. Femininity is also the intuition—a nurturing force that, above all, produces the first creative spark in our Sun of Truth. The female essence serves as the inspiration and aspiration for life's goodness and purity—a devotion to truth.

Divine Inheritor: The enlightened understanding that affirms our divine status through an innate connection to spiritual knowledge and spiritual heritage.

Divine Mind: The principle or idea that a universal mind or soul creates a rational order in the cosmos.

Divine Plan: The outcome of creative and Co-creative processes that provoke spiritual growth and evolution. From a traditional viewpoint, the will of God.

Divine Spark: A Gnostic principle that God is contained in the human body. The Divine Spark is encouraged to grow and reunite with the I AM Presence.

Divine Will: The idea of God's plan for humanity; however, from the perspective of the HU-man, the Divine Will is choice.

Divinity: Derived from the Sanskrit word Deva, this notion is the transcendent power of light or God. The creative energy of the Source is in all things created, and this philosophy includes ideas, thoughts, emotions, and feelings. As our comprehension of innate divinity evolves, our beliefs often shift and we experience equanimity, harmony, and cooperation.

Dove: A symbol of peace and renewal.

Duality: An understanding that the world is divided into two perceptible categories.

Eabra: The seventh Canadian Golden City located in the Yukon and Northwest Territories. Its qualities are joy, balance, and equality; its Ray force is violet; and its Master Teacher is Portia.

Dvapara Yuga: The Age of Bronze, both equal in sin and virtue, when Earth receives twenty-five to fifty percent of light from the Galactic Center.

Earth Changes: A prophesied Time of Change on the Earth, including geophysical, political, and social changes alongside the opportunity for spiritual and personal transformation.

Earth Plane: The dual aspect of life on Earth.

Earth's Grids: Geometrical patterns that cover the Earth and follow symmetrical links to sacred geometry and crystalline shapes.

Eastern Door: The East side of a Golden City gateway, also known as the Blue Door.

Eighth Light Body: Known as the Buddha Body or the Field of Awakening, this energy body is initially three to four feet from the human body. It begins by developing two visible grid-like spheres of light that form in the front and in the back of the Human Aura. The front sphere is located three to four feet in front of and between the Heart and Solar Plexus Chakras. The back sphere is located in front of and between the Will-to-Love and Solar Will Chakras. These spheres activate an ovoid of light that surrounds the entire human body; an energy field associated with harmonizing and perfecting the Ascension Process. This is the first step toward Mastery. Once developed and sustained, this energy body grants physical longevity and is associated with immortality. It is known as the first level of Co-creation, and is developed through control of the diet and disciplined breath techniques. Once this light body reaches full development, the spheres dissipate and dissolve into a refined energy field, resembling a metallic armor. The mature Eighth Light Body then contracts and condenses, to reside within several inches of the physical body where it emits a silver-blue sheen.

Eight: The eight is considered a sacred number to ancient mystics, as it reaffirms the existence of the monad. This is a holy number to the Ascended Masters, and is associated with divinity and perfection.

Eight-Sided Cell of Perfection: An atomic cell located in the human heart. It is associated with all aspects of perfection, and contains and maintains a visceral connection with the Godhead.

El Morya: Ascended Master of the Blue Ray, associated with the development of the will.

Elemental: A nature-being.

Elemental Kingdom: A kingdom comprising an invisible, subhuman group of creatures who act as counterparts to visible nature on Earth.

Elemental Life Force: The life energy of the Nature Kingdoms that are associated with an invisible, subhuman group of creatures who act as counterparts to visible nature on Earth.

Elohim: Creative beings of love and light that helped manifest the Divine idea of our solar system. Seven Elohim (the Seven Rays) exist on Earth. They organize and draw forward Archangels, the Four Elements, Devas, Seraphim, Cherubim, Angels, Nature Guardians, and the Elementals. In Ascended Master teaching, the Silent Watcher—the Great Mystery—gives them direction. It is also claimed the Elohim magnetize the Unfed Flame at the center of the Earth. Some esoteric historians perceive the Elohim—also referred to as the Els—as the Ancient Gods, or the Master Teachers of Lemuria and Atlantis.

Emanation: To flow out, issue, or proceed as from a source or origin.

E-motion: The harmonizing Vibration of Sound, sometimes defined as feeling plays a critical role in the Co-creation process by melding and harmonizing thought and feeling. The E-motion is a charge which ignites and inflames the kernel of thought-feeling into action.

Emotional Body: A subtle body of light that exists alongside the physical body. It comprises desires, emotions, and feelings.

Energy Field Balancing: Healing modality which energizes, heals, and stabilizes the light bodies comprising the Human Aura. Also known as Energy Work, Energy Balancing is a healing technique applied by a trained practitioner who balances the Chakra System of an individual through hands-on-healing and energetic adjustment of the energy fields and light bodies.

Energy Field(s): Distinct and definable layers of energy that exist around all forms of physical life: mineral, plant, animal, and human.

Energy-for-energy: To understand this spiritual principle, one must remember Isaac Newton's Third Law of Motion: for every action there is an equal and opposite reaction. However, while energies may be equal, their forms often vary. The Ascended Masters often use this phrase to remind chelas to properly compensate others to avoid karmic retribution; and repayment may take many different forms.

Ever Present Now: Time as a continuous, unencumbered flow without past or future.

Expanders: One of three types of soul groups now present on Earth who work with consciousness and light. They primarily develop and increase spiritual knowledge and work best with Infusers.

Fear Substance: Energy associated with threat, pain, and terror. According to Ascended Master Teachings, the fear substance is created through intense emotion, then physically absorbed and retained in the physical body after death. Plants, animals, and humans create the fear substance; however, plants do not retain this substance after harvest. This physical essence permeates all animal food products, especially meats after slaughter. The fear substance is considered to be addictive to evolving HU-mans, and is associated with spiritual devolution, decay, and destruction. The Violet Flame and dietary discipline is key to removing the fear substance from the human and evolving HU-man body.

Feminine: Esoteric philosophy considers the Mother Creative principle as the highest expression of being. Femininity is akin to the Goddess; it comprises one half of God whose gender is neutral. Feminine energy represents love, beauty, seduction, sensitivity, and refinement—the characteristics of the Goddess Venus. On the dark side, it reflects vanity, superficiality, fickleness, and exhaustion. Femininity is the intuition, a nurturing force which, above all, produces the first creative spark in our Sun of Truth; the female essence serves as the inspiration and aspiration for life's goodness and purity—a devotion to truth.

Feng-shui twenty-year cycles: According to Taoist understanding, the Earth undergoes a cyclic series of nine twenty-year segments. This is known as the Nine Cycles, a total of one hundred and eighty years. A further division of the one-hundred and eighty years is the Three Eras—sixty years each, comprised of upper, middle, and lower. Universal energy is said to change during each of the Three Eras, and Earth is currently in the Lower Era which started in 1984. Each era contains three cycles of twenty years each, hence the Nine Cycles. According to Taoist philosophy small changes occur between cycles; considerable changes occur between eras. Currently Earth is in the eighth cycle that began in 2004. The ninth cycle begins in 2024. The flow of universal energy significantly changes between each of the Nine Cycles, or every twenty years. The Ascended Masters often refer to the twenty-year cycles of the Earth, and their influence on culture, societies, and individuals. They prophesy a twenty-year period that is likely the Ninth Cycle, in the year 2024, or the Beginning of the Upper Era (first cycle) in 2044, when the spiritual Masters appear on Earth, in physical bodies to teach and heal the masses.

Fifth Dimension: A spiritual dimension of cause, associated with thoughts, visions, and aspirations. This is the dimension of the Ascended Masters and the Archetypes of Evolution, the city of Shamballa, and the templates of all Golden Cities.

Fire Triplicity: Energies from the Great Central Sun, or Galactic Center triangulate to our Solar System through these three planets: the Sun, Mars, and Jupiter. These three planets are known as the Fire Triplicity and represent three forms of spiritual fire: the Sun is the spiritual leader; Mars is the spiritual pioneer; and Jupiter is the spiritual teacher.

First Spiritual Body: A highly developed spiritual body of energy comprised of both the Astral and Causal light bodies. It is a timeless, non-corporeal body and can demonstrate the higher manifestation of Universal Law.

Five: According to the ancients, the five represents nature. In Ascended Master teaching, the five represents the divine HU-man.

Focus: The point where the Seven Rays of Light and Sound radiate and meet.

Fourth Dimension: A dimension of vibration associated with telepathy, psychic ability, and the dream world. This is the dimension of the Elemental Kingdom and the development of the super senses.

Free Energy: A continuous, abundant state of energy that heals and restores the spirit, mind, and physical body. Many of the spiritual teachings of Saint Germain are based on the use of this universal substance. Free energy creates health and joy in the path of Mastery, adeptship, and immortality.

Freedom Flame: An energy field that covers the entire American continent; it holds within it the principles of sovereignty, free will, and choice.

Freedom Star: The Earth's future prophesied name.

Freedom Star Map: The I AM America Map of prophesied worldwide Earth Changes.

Galactic Light: Energy streams from the Great Central Sun, or Galactic Center, as the Seven Rays of Light and Sound to Earth. Galactic Light calibrates the level of intelligence on Earth through memory function; the ability to absorb, recognize, and respect spiritual knowledge; the length of lifespans; and our ability to access the Akashic Records. The amount of Galactic Light streaming to Earth at any given time is classically measured through the Hindu Puranic timing of the Yugas, and through a contemporary method—the Electric Cycle—advocated by the Eastern Indian guru Sri Yuteswar.

Galactic Suns, the: Planets which have ascended into Suns. The Galactic Suns oversee evolving races throughout several solar systems in our Galaxy, and are also known as the Lords of Galactic Consciousness. Helios and Vesta are the Galactic Suns for Earth, and assist the evolutionary process of the human to the HU-man.

Galactic Web: A large, planet-encircling grid created by the consciousness of all things on Earth—humans, animals, plants, and minerals. Magnetic Vortices, namely the Golden Cities, appear at certain intersections.

Gateway: A doorway of a Golden City.

Gateway Adjutant Points: Two Golden City power points that are located on either side of each directional gateway of a Golden City Vortex and are situated to the outer perimeter of the Vortex.

Geometric Language: The symbols of sacred geometry.

Geo-Sensitive: A person who is sensitive to and can read the Earth's energies.

Gobean: The first United States Golden City located in the states of Arizona and New Mexico. Its qualities are cooperation, harmony, and peace; its Ray force is blue; and its Master Teacher is El Morya.

Gobi, Golden City of: Steps-down the energies of Shamballa into the entire Golden City Network. This Golden City is located in the Gobi Desert. It is known as the City of Balance, and means Across the Star; its Master Teachers are Lord Meru and Archangel Uriel.

Godhead: The I AM

God-state: The attainment of Unity Consciousness.

Golden Age: A peaceful time on Earth prophesied to occur after the Time of Change. It is also prophesied that during this age human life spans are increased and sacred knowledge is revered. During this time the societies, cultures, and the governments of Earth reflect spiritual enlightenment through worldwide cooperation, compassion, charity, and love. Ascended Master teachings often refer to the Golden Age as the Golden-Crystal Age and the Age of Grace.

Golden Age of Kali Yuga: According to the classic Puranic timing of the Yugas, Earth is in a Kali Yuga period that started around the year 3102 BCE the year that Krishna allegedly left the Earth. During this time period, which according to this Puranic timing lasts a total of 432,000 years—the ten-thousand year Golden Age period, also known as the Golden Age of Kali Yuga, is not in full force. Instead, it is a sub-cycle of higher light frequencies within an overall larger phase of less light energy. This Golden Age is prophesied to raise the energy of Earth as additional light from the Galactic Center streams to our planet. This type of light is a non-visible, quasar-type light that is said to expand life spans and memory function, and nourish human consciousness, especially spiritual development. There are many theories as to when this prescient light energy began to flow to our planet. Some say it started about a thousand years ago, and others claim it began at the end of the nineteenth century. No doubt its influence has changed life on Earth for the better, and according to the I AM America Teachings, its effect began to encourage and guide human spiritual evolution around the year 2000 CE. The Spiritual Teachers say that living in Golden Cities can magnify Galactic Energies and at their height, the energies will light the Earth between 45 to 48 percent—nearly reaching the light energies of a full-spectrum Treta Yuga or Silver Age on Earth. The Spiritual Teachers state, "The Golden Age is the period of time where harmony and peace shall be sustained."

Golden City Activation: A full comprehension of the word "activate" is key to understanding this spiritual phenomena. The following dictionary definitions describe its usage: "to make active;" "to make more active;" "to hasten reactions by various means"; and "to place in active status." So, the term Golden City Activation includes several meanings and applications to illustrate the four types of Golden City activations. (1) Ascended Master Activation: Made Active. The Spiritual Hierarchy first conceptualized the idea of the Golden Cities by the perfect out-picturing of these spiritual centers. Certain Master Teachers, Archangels, and Elohim—in cooperation with Mother Earth Babajeran—sponsor specific Golden Cities. Their task: to gather the energies of each divine municipality. The grid structure of Earth—in tandem with the focus of the appropriate Ray—is held in immaculate concept by each steward and coalesces the energies of each Golden City. And as consciousness increases, members of mankind seek its Fifth Dimension power as spiritual retreats. (2) Geophysical Activation: More Active. The interaction of Mother Earth and the Golden Cities—Fifth Dimensional structures—produces Third and Fourth Dimensional characteristics. This phenomenon creates a more active activation. The significance of Third Dimensional activation lies in its ability to generate a Vortex at the intersection of lei-lines. When eight of these invisible coordinates crisscross, a Vortex emerges, including the formation of Golden City Vortices. Vortices move in a clockwise/counterclockwise motion. Geophysically activated Golden Cities have a profound effect on humans: they experience longevity, greater healing abilities, and physical regeneration. In the Fourth Dimension, Nature Kingdoms begin to interact with Vortex energies; human visitors experience telepathic and psychic abilities, and lucid dreaming. (3) Ceremonial Activation: To Hasten Reactions by Various Means. Ceremonial activations, inspired by humans who seek an intense result from a Golden City, occur on an emotional-astral level in areas throughout these sacred Vortices. Similar to pujas or yagyas—known in Hindu as sacrifices—fire or water-driven ceremonies neutralize difficult karmas and enhance beneficial human qualities. (4) Great Central Sun Activation: To Place in Active Status. Produced by a greater timing or origin, this type of activation relies on the energies that emanate from the Great Central Sun or Galactic Center. Some theosophical scholars say power from the Galactic Center sends subtle energies to our solar system via the planetary Fire Triplicity: Jupiter, Mars, and the Sun.

Golden City Doorway: The four gateways of the Golden City Vortex based on the cardinal directions of North, East, South, and West. They comprise the North Door (or the Black Door); the East Door (or the Blue Door); the South Door (or the Red Door); the West Door (or the Yellow Door). The center of a Golden City is known as the "Star" and is affiliated with the color white.

Golden City Gateway Lei-line: An electromagnetic, arterial lei-line that exists across the outer span of the directional gateway of a Golden City Vortex. The length of this Golden City arterial lei-line is 64 miles.

Golden City Grid: The matrix comprised of all Golden Cities covering the Earth.

Golden City Vortex: A Golden City Vortex—based on the Ascended Masters' I AM America material—are prophesied areas of safety and spiritual energies during the Times of Changes. Covering an expanse of land and air space, these sacred energy sites span more than 400 kilometers (270 miles) in diameter, with a vertical height of 400 kilometers (250 miles). Golden City Vortices, more importantly, reach beyond terrestrial significance and into the ethereal realm. This system of safe harbors acts as a group or universal mind within our galaxy, connecting information seamlessly and instantly with other beings. Fifty-one Golden City Vortices are stationed throughout the world, and each carries a different meaning, a combination of Ray Forces, and a Divine Purpose. A Golden City Vortex works on the principles of electromagnetism and geology. Vortices tend to appear near fault lines, possibly serving as conduits of inner-earth movement to terra firma. Golden Cities are symbolized by a Maltese Cross, whose sacred geometry determine their doorways, lei-lines, adjutant points, and coalescing Star energies. Since their energies intensify experiences with both the Fourth and Fifth Dimensions, Golden City Vortices play a vital role with the Ascension Process. The clockwise motion of the Vortex absorbs energy from its Ray Force, Ascended Master Hierarch, the Great Central Sun, and Mother Earth – Babajeran. Its counterclockwise motion releases energy. The spin of the Vortex creates a torsion field.

Golden Flame: An energy field of spiritual enlightenment. The teachings of the Golden Flame are said to originate from the Pleiades.

Golden Harmonies: The sciences of sacred geometry and sacred numerology.

Golden Perfection: A spiritual acceleration in the physical body, mind, and light-bodies which enables an individual to bi-locate and achieve physical immortality.

Golden Thread Axis: Also known as the Vertical Power Current, the Golden Thread Axis is physically comprised of the Medullar Shushumna, a life-giving nadi physically comprising one-third of the human Kundalini system. Two vital currents intertwine around the Golden Thread Axis: the lunar Ida Current, and the solar Pingala Current. According to the Master Teachers the flow of the Golden Thread Axis begins with the I AM Presence, enters the Crown Chakra, and descends through the spinal system. It descends beyond the Base Chakra and travels to the core of the Earth. Esoteric scholars often refer to the axis as the Rod of Power, and it is symbolized by two spheres connected by an elongated rod. Ascended Master students and chelas frequently draw upon the energy of the Earth through the Golden Thread Axis for healing and renewal with meditation, visualization, and breath.

Gold(en) Ray: The Ray of Brotherhood, Cooperation, and Peace. The Gold Ray produces the qualities of perception, honesty, confidence, courage, and responsibility. It is also associated with leadership, independence, authority, ministration, and justice. The Gold Ray vibrates the energies of Divine Father on Earth. Its attributes are: warm; perceptive; honest; confident; positive; independent; courageous; enduring; vital; leadership; responsible; ministration; authority; justice. The Gold Ray is also associated with the Great Central Sun, the Solar Logos, of which our Solar Sun is a Step-down Transformer of its energies. According to the Master Teachers, the Gold Ray is the epitome of change for the New Times. The Gold Ray is the ultimate authority of Cosmic Law, and carries both our personal and worldwide Karma and Dharma (purpose). Its presence is designed to instigate responsible spiritual growth and planetary evolution as a shimmering light for humanity's aspirations and the development of the HU-man. The Gold Ray, however, is also associated with Karmic justice, and will instigate change: constructive and destructive. The extent of catastrophe or transformation is contingent on humanity's personal and collective spiritual growth and evolutionary process as we progress into the New Times.

Grace: Neutrality, calmness, peacefulness.

Great Central Sun: The great Sun of our galaxy, of which all of its solar systems rotate. The Great Central Sun is also known as the Galactic Center, which is the origin of the Seven Rays of Light and Sound on Earth.

Greater Mind: An outgrowth of the Ascension Process, this mind differs from the deductive and inductive reason of the Rational Mind, and the sporadic, yet instant insights gleaned from the Intuitive Mind. The Greater Mind is activated by self-revealed wisdom versus acquired knowledge.

Great Law, the: The Law of Peace.

Great Mystery: The source of creation; all elements of life contain the sacred and are aspects of the Divine.

Great Pyramid of Solomon: Also known as the Great Triangle of Solomon, the double interlaced triangles are the hidden basis for spiritual knowledge which represents the macrocosm and microcosm in all created things: the God of Light, and the God of Reflections.

Great Purification: Primarily considered a Native American term, the Great Purification signals the end of one period of time for humanity and the beginning of a New Time. The Hopi Prophecies state the Great Purification will occur in several stages with prophesied Earth Changes, global wars, Climate Change, and nuclear devastation. Contemporary prophets view the Great Purification as a time for humanity to heal and transform individually and collectively. These actions create an opportunity for the Brotherhood of Man and a new society built on the ideals of cooperation rather than competition.

Great Silence: The Master Teachings encourage a contemplative period of quiet and stillness to intensely apply spiritual energies in certain circumstances and situations. This period of tranquil power is often referred to as the Great Silence.

Great White Brotherhood and Sisterhood (Lodge): This fraternity of ascended and unascended men and women is dedicated to the universal uplifting of humanity. Its main objective includes the preservation of the lost spirit, and the teachings of the ancient religions and philosophies of the world. Its Mission: to reawaken the dormant ethical and spiritual spark among the masses. In addition to fulfilling spiritual aims, the Great White Lodge has pledged to protect mankind against the systematic assaults—which inhibit self-knowledge and personal growth—on individual and group freedoms.

Green Ray: The Ray of Active Intelligence is associated with education, thoughtfulness, communication, organization, the intellect, science, objectivity, and discrimination. It is also adaptable, rational, healing, and awakened. The Green Ray is affiliated with the planet Mercury. In the I AM America teachings the Green Ray is served by the Archangel Raphael and Archeia Mother Mary; the Elohim of Truth, Vista—also known as Cyclopea, and Virginia; the Ascended Masters Hilarion, Lord Sananda, Lady Viseria, Soltec, and Lady Master Meta.

Grey Man: An archetype of an ordinary man, who easily fades into the background and blends into the crowd. He is often used to carry out the secret Missions of the dark government.

Group Mind: A conscious intelligent force, formed by members of distinguished cultures, societal organizations, and more prominently by religious church members; the Group Mind is held together by the rituals and customs that are peculiar to its members; newcomers instantly sense the energies of the atmosphere, and will either accept or reject its influence. The physics of the Group Mind are important to comprehend, as this collective intelligence is purposely formed to aid the Aspirant to raise human consciousness beyond present limitations.

Guru: Another name for teacher.

Harmony: The first virtue of the Twelve Jurisdictions based on the principle of agreement.

Harmony of the Spheres: A superior form of music, founded on beauty and harmonious combination, heard by those who have developed the ears to hear—clairaudience.

Heart Chakra: Known in Sanskrit as the Anahata. The location is in the center of the chest. Its main aspect is Love and Relationships, and includes our ability to feel compassion, forgiveness, and hold our own Divine Purpose.

Heart of the Dove: Also known as the Center of Fire, this energy anomaly is prophesied to exist Northwest of Kansas City, Missouri. It is here that Master Teachings claim an umbilicus connection between Earth and the Galactic Center exists, creating time anomalies and the potential for time travel in the New Times. The Heart of the Dove is also prophesied to become a spiritual center for learning and self-actualizing the consciousness of Quetzalcoatl—the Christ.

Heart's Desire: This Ascended Master teaching recommends by identifying activities that yield personal joy and happiness, one may discover their Heart's Desire. The Heart's Desire is the wellspring of abundance, love, and creativity. Eastern philosophy often refers to this principle as the soul's specific duty or purpose in a lifetime—Dharma. The Heart's Desire is analogous to the principle of desire—the Ninth Jurisdiction. This evolved perception of desire is based on the true etymology of the word. De, is a French word that means of, and the English word sire, means forefather, ancestry, or source. From this context, Sanat Kumara teaches, "The Heart's Desire is the source of creation." Since the Heart's Desire is one of the most influential principles underlying humanity's spiritual development and unfoldment, Ascended Master teachings give it utmost importance. It is considered a physical, emotional, mental, and spiritual presence that raises the un-awakened animal consciousness into the human, and onward to the awakened aspirant and the devoted chela. The Ascended Masters claim that the physical presence of the Flame of Desire lies within the heart nestled inside the Eight-sided Cell of Perfection. As students and chelas perfect the Co-creation process, some teachings suggest the Flame of Desire evolves alongside the Three-Fold or Unfed Flame of Love, Wisdom, and Power into the Four-Fold Flame. In this physical, progressed state it develops as the fourth White Flame of Creation.

Helios and Vesta: The God and Goddess of our physical Sun.

Hermetic Law: Philosophical beliefs and principles based on the writings of Hermes Trismegistus, the Greek sage who is analogous to the Egyptian God Thoth.

Higher Self: The Atma or Atman. This is the true identity of the soul which resides in the spiritual planes of consciousness, and although it is energetically connected to each individual in the physical plane, the Higher Self is free from the Karmas of the Earth Plane and identification with the material world.

Hilarion: Ascended Master of the Green Ray and associated with the attainment of personal truth and the development of faith.

His-story: The re-telling of the story of circumstances directly related to one's level of spiritual understanding, perceptions and personal experience.

Hitaka: "So be it."

Holy Christ Self: Another name that identifies the presence of the I AM, or the great ambassador to the Oversoul. Esoteric teachings refer to the Christ Self as the higher, refined Astral Body.

Holy Spirit: An individual manifestation of the light and spiritual energy of the I AM Presence. Collectively, this same energy is known as the "Holy Comforter." The Holy Spirit is also known as the Higher Self.

HU or HUE, the: In Tibetan dialects, the word hue or hu means breath; however, the HU is a sacred sound and when chanted or meditated upon is said to represent the entire spectrum of the Seven Rays. Because of this, the HU powerfully invokes the presence of the Violet Flame, which is the activity of the Violet Ray and its inherent ability to transform and transmit energies to the next octave. HU is also considered an ancient name for God, and it is sung for spiritual enlightenment.

HU-man: The God-Man.

I AM: The presence of God.

I AM Presence: The individualized presence of God.

I AM THAT I AM: A term from Hebrew that translates to, "I Will Be What I Will Be." "I AM" is also derived from the Sanskrit Om (pronounced: A-U-M), whose three letters signify the three aspects of God as beginning, duration, and dissolution – Brahma, Vishnu, and Shiva. The AUM syllable is known as the omkara and translates to "I AM Existence," the name for God. "Soham," is yet another mystical Sanskrit name for God, which means "It is I," or "He is I." In Vedic philosophy, it is claimed that when a child cries, "Who am I?" the universe replies, "Soham – you are the same as I AM." The I AM teachings also use the name "Soham" in place of "I AM."

I AM America: A sacred name that affirms the power of the I AM and contains the hidden lexigram: I AM Race. This new race of man is destined to serve as the nucleus of the planet's future Utopian society through fostering the Ascension Process and the development of the divine HU-man.

I AM America Map: The Ascended Masters' Map of prophesied Earth Changes for the United States**.**

I AM Race: A new race of man destined to serve as the nucleus of the planet's future Utopian society. It will inherit the work and the development of fellowship among the nations of the world.

Immortality: Everlasting and deathless. Spiritual immortality embraces the idea of the eternal, unending existence of the soul. Physical immortality includes the notion of the timeless, deathless, and birthless body.

Individualized: A state of wholeness and cannot be divided.

Infusers: One of three types of soul groups now present on Earth who serve naturally as Step-down Transformers of transcendent energy. They work best with the Violet Flame and are pioneers of the New Consciousness.

Initiation: Admission, especially into secret, advanced spiritual knowledge.

Inner Dialogue: Clear and effective communication with the I AM Presence, which fosters spiritual growth and awareness.

Inner Marriage: A process achieved through the spiritual integration of the masculine and feminine aspects of self, uniting dualistic qualities into greater balance and harmony for expression of self-Mastery.

Inner Earth: Below the Earth's Crust lie many magnificent cities and cultures of various break-away races of humans, evolved HU-mans, and extraterrestrials. The Inner Earth is filled with reservoirs, streams, rivers, lakes, and oceans. According to metaphysical researchers the Earth is honey-combed with pervasive caves and subterranean caverns measuring hundreds of miles in diameter. This viewpoint is held by the Ascended Masters and shared throughout their Earth Changes Prophecies and historical narratives.

Instant-Thought-Manifestation: The clear and concise use of thought to Co-create desires. The Master Teachers often refer to this process as Manifest Destiny. Experiences with Instant-Thought-Manifestation are said to prepare our consciousness to enter into the ONE.

Intention: Acts, thoughts, or conceptions earnestly fixed on something, or steadfastly directed. Intentions often reflect the state of an individual's mind which directs their specific actions towards an object or goal.

Interplay: Reciprocal action and reaction.

Jiva: The immortal essence of a living thing that survives death.

Judgment: The act of forming negative assumptions and critical opinions, primarily of fellow human beings.

Kali Yuga: The Age of Iron, or Age of Quarrel, when Earth receives twenty-five percent or less galactic light from the Great Central Sun.

Kama: Desire

Karma: Laws of Cause and Effect.

Klehma: The fifth United States Golden City located primarily in the states of Colorado and Kansas. Its qualities are continuity, balance, and harmony; its Ray force is white; and its Master Teacher is Serapis Bey.

Kuan Yin: The Bodhisattva of Compassion and teacher of Saint Germain. She is associated with all the Rays and the principle of femininity.

Kundalini: In Sanskrit, Kundalini literally means coiled, and represents the coiled energy located at the base of the spine, often established in the lower Base and Sacral Chakras. Kundalini Shatki (shatki means energy) is claimed to initiate spiritual development, wisdom, knowledge, and enlightenment.

Kuthumi: An Ascended Master of the Pink, Ruby, and Gold Rays. He is a gentle and patient teacher who works closely with the Nature Kingdoms.

Land of Brihaspati: A mythical land and civilization that according to Lord Meru originated and thrived on the ancient Japanese Archipelago whose civilizations later migrated to the present-day Himalayans. It is claimed the ancient Kirata and Tibetan cultures came from the Land of Brihaspati, and the Mahabharata recounts the ancient people as, "Gold-like."

Land of the Plumed Serpent: The ancient lands of Ameru, from which the word America is derived. The ancient peoples of America were known as the Red Children of the Sun and worshipped Quetzalcoatl, a Prophet of the Christ Consciousness, a messenger from our solar Sun. The Plumed Serpent metaphorically represents the developed Chakra System of the Divine God-man, the Ascended Masters' HU-man. The plume of light atop the head is the developed crown chakra, and the serpent's coils represent the mature Kundalini system, or human energy system comprised of seven chakras.

Land of Rama: The ancient civilization of India once co-existed with Ancient Atlantis and is claimed to have extended as far West as present-day Iran, and as far East as present-day Burma. The Land of Rama is claimed to have been a nation of spiritual adepts, priests, and Masters—Rishis.

Laws of Attraction and Repulsion: Like charges repel; unlike charges attract.

Laws of Cause and Effect: For every action there is another event, which is the consequence or result of the first.

Law of Correspondence: "As above, so below."

Law of Death and Rebirth: Reincarnation.

Law of Life: The great Universal Law states life is for the joy of living and the joy of creation. Life is ever present, immortal, and deathless.

Law of Love: Perhaps every religion on Earth is founded upon the Law of Love, as the notion to "treat others as you would like to be treated." The Law of Love, however, from the Ascended Master tradition is simply understood as consciously living without fear, or inflicting fear on others. The Fourth of the Twelve Jurisdictions instructs Love is the Law of Allowing, Maintaining, and Sustainability. All of these precepts distinguishes love from an emotion or feeling, and observes Love as action, will, or choice. The Ascended Masters affirm, "If you live love, you will create love." This premise is fundamental to understand the esoteric underpinnings of the Law of Love. The Master Teachers declare that through practicing the Law of Love one experiences acceptance and understanding; tolerance, alongside detachment. Metaphysically, the Law of Love allows different and varied perceptions of ONE experience, situation, or circumstance to exist simultaneously. From this viewpoint the Law of Love is the practice of tolerance.

Law of Opposites: Every action has an equal and opposite action.

Law of Polarities: Everything in the universe can pursue two opposite paths, each with its own essence. Following this logic, all pairs exist in a spectrum comprising an infinite number of points among ends. Diametric termini are identical in nature but different in degree; they contain the possibility of the other in its essence. Everything encompasses its opposite; therefore, the macrocosm embraces the microcosm.

Law of Reciprocity: In Biblical texts this is known as, "Give, and it will be given to you." The Master Teachers rephrase this to mean, "Energy flows within, energy flows without."

Law of Rhythm: Everything ebbs and flows; rises and falls. The swing of the pendulum is universal. The measure of the momentum to the right is equal to the swing of the left.

Law of Synchronicity: Nothing is happenstance: "There is no mistake ever, ever, ever!"

Laws of Octaves: The relationship of planets, colors, and musical notes are based on the Law of Octaves, also known as the Law of Seven.

Law of ONE: All of created life interacts with and is indelibly connected to the ONE.

Lei-lines: Lines of energy that exist among geographical places, ancient monuments, megaliths, and strategic points. These energy lines contain electrical or magnetic points.

Lemuria: According to Ascended Master Teachings, Lemuria primarily existed in the present Pacific Ocean and esoteric historians theorize the oceanic tectonic Pacific Plate, through periodic geologic upheaval and Earth Changes forms the submerged lost continent of Lemuria. Spiritual teachings claim the evolutionary purpose of the ancient civilization developed humanity's Will (the Blue Ray of Power), and Lemurian culture venerated the Golden Disk of the Sun and the Right-hand Path. Lemuria, while claimed to be one the earliest cultures of humanity, ultimately integrated with the Lands of Rama, and Sri Lanka is alleged to have been one of the empire's capital cities. Asuramaya is one of the great Manus of Lemuria's Root Race. According to Theosophical history the Lemurian and Atlantean epochs overlap and it is alleged the lands of Lemuria, also known as Shalmali, existed in the Indian and Southern Pacific Oceans, and included the continent of Australia. Lemuria is the remaining culture and civilization of Mu—an expansive continent that once spanned the entire present-day Pacific Ocean. Some esoteric writers place the destruction of Mu around the year 30,000 BCE; others place its demise millions of years ago. The apparent discrepancy of these timelines is likely due to two different interpretations of the Cycle of the Yugas. It is claimed the venerated Elders of Lemuria escaped the global tragedy by moving to an uninhabited plateau in central Asia. This account mirrors Ascended Master teachings and Lord Himalaya's founding of the Retreat of the Blue Lotus. The Lemurian elders re-established their spiritual teachings and massive library as the Thirteenth School. It is claimed these teachings and spiritual records became foundational teachings in the Great White Brotherhood of the mystical lands of Hsi Wang Mu (the Abode of the Immortals), and the Kuan Yin Lineage of Gurus. Today, present-day Australia once known by Egyptian gold-miners as the ancient Land of Punt is the remainder of the once great continent of Mu and Lemuria which likely existed in the time period of Dvapara-Yuga, over 800,000 years ago.

Light: "Love in action."

Light Body: A body of subtle energy surrounding the human body. It survives death, and develops and evolves over lifetimes. Also known as the aura, the light body divides into layers of light energy. These strata are referred to as light bodies or layers of the field of the aura.

Lighted Stance: A state of light the body acquires during Ascension.

Light of Awakening: A prophesied wave of cosmic light, originating from the Galactic Center, is destined to evolve humanity into the Golden Age by altering our human genetics and transforming our sensation of fear.

Light Side: Evolves the human to the HU-man, and the HU-man to the ONE, and is aligned with honesty, compassion, mercy, love, and self-sacrifice.

Lineage of Gurus: The venerated ancestral root of certain spiritual teachings. Kuan Yin and Lord Apollo are two of Saint Germain's spiritual teachers; therefore, they compose his Lineage of Gurus.

Lord Meru or Lord Machah: An Ascended Master of the Ruby and Gold Ray is also known as the great Sage of Ancient Mu. Lord Meru is a teacher of the ancient civilizations of the Earth and considered a spiritual historian of their mythological records. Lord Meru is also known as Lord Machah—the parrot—a symbol of beauty, wisdom, and spiritual knowledge. Lord Machah's

dark skin is contrasted by a colorful headdress filled with parrot, trogon, and quetzal bird feathers, a symbol of Quetzalcoatl—the Christ Consciousness. In the New Times, Lord Meru is prophesied to steward the Golden City of Gobi.

Lords of Venus: A group of Ascended Masters who came to serve humanity. They once resided on the planet Venus.

Lotus: An Eastern symbol of the maternal creative mystery—the feminine. The lotus signifies the unfolding of spiritual understanding, and the opening and development of the chakras. It also represents the growth of man through three periods of human consciousness—ignorance, endeavor, and understanding. This idea is mirrored in nature, too. In Oriental philosophy the lotus manifests in three elements, earth, water, and air. Thus, man exists on the material, intellectual, and spiritual planes. In Western culture, the symbology of the rose is similar to the lotus.

Love: "Light in action." The fourth of the Twelve Jurisdictions evolves our understanding of love as the Law of Allowing, Maintaining, and Sustainability.

Maltese Cross: The Maltese Cross, a symbol often used by Saint Germain, represents the Eight-Sided Cell of Perfection, and the human virtues of honesty, faith, contrition, humility, justice, mercy, sincerity, and the endurance of persecution.

Malton: The second United States Golden City located in the states of Illinois and Indiana. Its qualities are fruition and attainment; its Ray force is ruby and Gold; and its Master Teacher is Kuthumi.

Mantle of Consciousness: Ascending to or attaining a new level of conscious awareness that produces tremendous change and spiritual development.

Mantra: Certain sounds, syllables, and sets of words are deemed sacred and often carry the ability to transmute Karma, spiritually purify, and transform an individual and are known as mantras.

Map of the Ancients: Lord Meru rescued this ancient map ages ago from the Lands of Lemuria: the Map of the Ancients. This map of the world simultaneously portrays the lands of Rama, Mu, and Atlantis. According to Lord Meru the Map of the Ancients illustrates the migration and evolution of human consciousness as shaped through the Seven Rays, and identifies the nine civilizations the Rays have influenced and formed.

Map of Rings: This Map depicts Earth covered with a worldwide grid of interlocking circles. The circles portray the elements of Earth: air, water, fire, and earth. Their interaction with one another results in the physical manifestation of Earth and her many alchemical and spiritual processes.

Masculine Energy: The Father creative principle. In esoteric literature, this is referred to as the Monad.

Mask of Forgetfulness: The soul purposely imposes the Mask of Forgetfulness over their human consciousness before birth, and this diminishes the memories of previous lifetimes.

Master Teacher: A spiritual teacher from a specific lineage of teachers—gurus. The teacher transmits and emits the energy from that collective lineage.

Master Within: The Mighty I AM Presence that can respond immediately to individual concerns and problems.

Mastery: Possessing the consummate skill of command and self-realization over thought, feeling, and action.

Meissner Field: A magnetic energy field that does not contain polarity. It is produced during a transitory state of superconductivity. Ascended Master teaching associates this type of energy field with HU-man development, Unana, and Christ Consciousness.

Mental Body: A subtle light body of the Human Aura comprising thoughts.

Michael: The archangel of the Blue Ray. Archangel Michael is the protector of chelas and initiates of the Ascended Master tradition through the activity of the Blue Flame.

Migratory Pattern or Sequence: A Golden City spiritual pilgrimage that travels through a certain progression of Adjutant Points. The progression of each sacred site may vary, dependent on the desired spiritual result for the chela or initiate. Some sequences focus on healing processes; others focus on integration of Golden City Energies, especially certain Golden City Doorways.

Mind: The aspects of consciousness manifested as thought, perceptions, true memory, will, and imagination.

Mirroring: "As (when looking in) water, face reflects face, so does one's heart find reflection in another's." *Proverbs 27:19*

Monad: From an Ascended Master viewpoint, the Monad is the spark or flame of life of spiritual consciousness and it is also the Awakened Flame that is growing, evolving, and ultimately on the path to Ascension. Because of its presence of self-awareness and purpose, the Monad represents our dynamic will and the individualized presence of the Divine Father. Ultimately, the Monad is the spark of consciousness that is self-determining, spiritually awake, and drives the growth of human consciousness. The Monad is the indivisible, whole, divine life center of an evolving soul that is immortal and contains the momentum within itself to drive consciousness to learn, grow, and perfect itself in its evolutionary journey.

Mother Mary: Ascended Goddess of the Feminine who was originally of the angelic evolution. She is associated with the Green Ray of healing, truth, and science, and the Pink Ray of love.

Mudra: A symbolic ceremonial or spiritual gesture, mostly expressed by the hands and fingers. It is often used by evolved spiritual beings and Ascended Masters to signify or emit spiritual energies.

New Children: The evolution of the Aryan sixth sub-race, who will lead the mass consciousness to apprehend the individualized HU-man. The New Children are prophesied as spiritual Masters who will incarnate on Earth at critical junctures of humanity's evolution. They will help the masses to transmute difficult karmas and lead many into spiritual liberation or the Ascension Process. The New

Children are the predecessors to the Seventh Manu, the seventh and final sub-race of the Aryan.

New Day: The spiritual ideal of positive energy and a fresh start.

New Dimensions: As humanity enters the New Times, subtle elements and aspects physically appear and spiritually and simultaneously enable HU-man consciousness to embrace allowing, alignment, transformation, and self-knowledge. The Ascended Masters claim this spiritual growth is the result of New Dimensions.

New Times, or New Age: Prophesied by Utopian Francis Bacon, the New Age would herald a United Brotherhood of the Earth. This Brotherhood and Sisterhood would be built as Solomon's Temple, and supported by the Four Pillars of history, science, philosophy, and religion. These four teachings would synergize the consciousness of humanity to Universal Fellowship and Peace.

Northern Door: The North side of a Golden City gateway, also known as the Black Door.

Om Manaya Pitaya or **Om Manaaya Patiya:** This Ascended Master statement has several meanings. Two spiritual translations are: "I AM the Light of God," and "I AM the Seer of the Lord." The Sanskrit translation means: "Amen, honored Lord."

Omni-presence: Present everywhere.

Omniscience: Infinite knowledge.

ONE: Indivisible, whole, harmonious Unity.

Oneness: A combination of two or more, which creates the whole.

Oneship: A combination of many, which comprises the whole, and when divided contains both feminine and masculine characteristics.

Open Ears, Open Eyes: The ability to see and hear spiritual truths.

Open Heart: Evolved love of openness, sharing, and Brotherhood.

Oral Tradition: According to the Master Teachers and many indigenous teachers, the Oral Tradition, or learning through oral instruction, is the preferred medium to receive spiritual knowledge. This method requires the use of memory and memorization and also instigates the recognition of vital, yet subtle nuances that engender spiritual comprehension and may include the Master Teacher's use of telepathy, clairaudience, and clairvoyance.

Out-picturing: To envision in the mind and project to the outer world.

Oversoul: This refers to the soul in its relationship to the ONE, which is infinite and from which finite souls draw sustenance and light.

Peak Adjutant Lei-line: This arterial lei-line of a Golden City is formed through energies surging from two points within the Golden City Gateway.

Peak Adjutant Point: This power point is energetically defined by the merging of both masculine and feminine Gateway Adjutant Points. The Peak Adjutant Point is also referred to as a Golden City Child Point, as it contains and expresses a pure and concentrated energy of both points of the Golden City Doorway.

Perceive: To observe, feel, sense, and have awareness of.

Perception: Awareness and intuitive recognition.

Pillar of Light: A tube of protective light, impenetrable to anything not of light that surrounds the subtle light bodies and the physical body.

Pink Ray: The Pink Ray is the energy of the Divine Mother and associated with the Moon. It is affiliated with these qualities: loving; nurturing; hopeful; heartfelt; compassionate; considerate; communicative; intuitive; friendly; humane; tolerant; adoring. In the I AM America teachings the Pink Ray is served by the Archangel Chamuel and Archeia Charity; the Elohim of Divine Love Orion and Angelica; and the Ascended Masters Kuan Yin, Mother Mary, Goddess Meru, and Paul the Venetian.

Pitris: Derived from the Sanskrit word pitr, Pitris is a generic word in Theosophical terminology and Ascended Master teaching for any progenitor of the human race.

Pleiades: A seven-star cluster that exists in the same Orion Arm of the Milky Way Galaxy near Earth. Also known as the Seven Sisters, the Pleiades is located in the Taurus Constellation. Its seven stars are: Sterope, Merope, Electra, Maia, Taygeta, Celaeno, and Alcyone.

Point of Perception: A certain position of understanding that allows for immediate or intuitive recognition. A Co-creation teaching of the Ascended Masters and its processes pivot on the fulcrum of choice. By carefully choosing certain actions, a Master of Choice opens the world of possibility through honing carefully cultivated perceptions, attitudes, beliefs, thoughts, and feelings. This allows the development of outcome through various scenarios and opens the multi-dimensional door to multiple realities and simultaneous experiences that dissolve linear timeframes into the Ever present Now.

Portals of Entry: These geological locations on Earth are prophesied locations where energy anomalies occur. Portals of Entry are also prophesied sites where new energies will enter the Earth and affect her evolution physically, emotionally, mentally, and spiritually.

Portia: The Goddess of Justice and Opportunity. She represents Divine Justice on Earth. Her action is balance, expressed as the scales. Harmony holds balance. Some say her electronic pattern, a mandala, is the Maltese Cross.

Prana or Prahna: Vital, life-sustaining energy. The Masters Teachers often refer to Earth as Prahna.

Prediction: A forecast or conjecture of an upcoming circumstance or event.

Projection of Consciousness: The ability acquired through a Mastery of meditation and enables the individual to split their consciousness (existence, sensations, and cognitions) to another physical location or plane, while retaining the physical body in the physical dimension.

Prophecy: A spiritual teaching given simultaneously with a warning. It's designed to change, alter, lessen, or mitigate the prophesied warning. This caveat may be literal or metaphoric; the outcome of these events are contingent on the choices and the consciousness of those willing to apply the teachings.

Prosperity: Comfort and ease, the result of spiritual growth and development.

Protective Grid: The world-wide network of Golden Cities that exist on the Earth's surface, and within the inner Earth. As the Protective Grid expands into space it is known as the Galactic Web.

Purification: A clearing process, especially in spiritual practice, which frees consciousness from encumbering or objectionable elements.

Quetzalcoatl: The Quetzalcoatl Energies, as explained and taught by Lord Meru, are akin to the Christ energies when applied in the esoteric Western Christian tradition. This ancient spiritual teacher, however, predates Christianity and likely has its roots in alchemic Atlantean (Toltec) teaching. Quetzalcoatl, in contemporary terms, is the Incan Christ.

Radiation: The emission and diffusion of Rays of heat, light, electricity, or sounds.

Rainbow Bridge: The esoteric term that describes the human aura, which contains a spectrum of light bodies, similar to a rainbow. A perfect rainbow of color, with definition and brilliance, is often seen in the aura or light field of an Ascended Being.

Ray or Ray Force: A force containing a purpose, which divides its efforts into two measurable and perceptible powers, light and sound.

Rayce: A civilization influenced by a singular Ray Force.

Re-embodiment: Reincarnation.

Refreshing Drink: A metaphor for the Universal Supply of Life.

Re-membering: The process of recalling past events may be painful or wounding or the recalled presence creates obstacles to spiritual growth. Often, these events occur in this lifetime, but sometimes are past-life memories. The Re-membering Process uses mind, thought, and perception to recalibrate memory into conscious activity.

Ring of Fire: A geographical area, which encircles the basin of the Pacific Ocean, prone to volcanic eruptions and earthquakes.

River of Life: The thoughtful, conscious experience of life. It is also recognized as a silver-white current of high-frequency energy that separates the Third Dimension and the Fourth Dimension. It is alleged as the soul passes from this life that it travels upon this sublime river of effervescent, flowing energy of light to the heavenly levels of the Astral Plane.

Rose: The Western symbol of the maternal creative mystery — the feminine. It represents the chakra as a spiritual Vortex; a garland of roses typifies the seven chakras and their unfolding and attainment. In Eastern culture the symbology of the lotus is similar to the rose.

Rosicrucian: An ancient mystery school with its teachings rooted in the study of Western esoteric teachings. Also known as the Rose Cross, its foundation is the study of Alchemy through Hermetic-Christian traditions.

Ruby Ray: The Ruby Ray is the energy of the Divine Masculine and Spiritual Warrior. It is associated with these qualities: energetic; passionate; devoted; determination; dutiful; dependable; direct; insightful; inventive; technical; skilled; forceful. This Ray Force is astrologically affiliated with the planet Mars and the Archangel Uriel, Lord Sananda, and Master Kuthumi. The Ruby Ray is often paired with the Gold Ray, which symbolizes Divine Father. The Ruby Ray is the evolutionary Ray Force of both the base and solar chakras of the HU-man; and the Gold and Ruby Rays step-down and radiate sublime energies into six Golden Cities.

Sacred Fire: The Unfed Flame of Divine Consciousness within the human heart. Also, the term Sacred Fire is synonymous to the Violet Flame.

Sacred Geometry: Esoteric scholars suggest diverse universal patterns, geometrical shapes, and geometric proportions symbolize spiritual balance and perfection.

Sacred Numerology: A specific assignment of numbers to alphabetic letters. This creates esoteric knowledge and insight regarding names and specific dates. Numbers are also assigned secret meaning that provides further insight.

Sacrifice: The spiritual ideal that through giving selflessly, or taking a short-term loss, that a greater long-term return for others is created.

Saint Germain: Ascended Master of the Seventh Ray, Saint Germain is known for his work with the Violet Flame of Mercy, Transmutation, Alchemy, and Forgiveness. He is the sponsor of the Americas and the I AM America material. Many other teachers and Masters affiliated with the Great White Brotherhood help his endeavors.

Salt Bath: A spiritual healing technique that cleanses the human aura. Its formula is two cups of any type of salt, used in the bath water with essential oils such as lavender or other floral scents.

Sananda: The name used by Master Jesus in his ascended state of consciousness. Sananda means joy and bliss, and his teachings focus on revealing the savior and heavenly kingdom within.

Sanat Kumara: One of the original Lords of Venus who founded the Great White Brotherhood at Shamballa. The Bible refers to him as Ancient of Days. Sanat Kumara is a Venusian Ascended Master and the venerated leader of the Ascended Masters, best known as the founder of Shamballa, the first Golden City on Earth. He is also known in the teachings of the Great White Brotherhood as the Lord of the World, and is regarded as a savior and eminent spiritual teacher. Sanat Kumara is the guru of four of the Twelve Jurisdictions: Cooperation, Charity,

Desire, and Stillness. These spiritual precepts are based on the principles of Co-creation, and are prophesied to guide human consciousness into the New Times. These four Jurisdictions reiterate the symbolic revelation of Sanat Kumara's four-fold identity as the Cosmic Christ, which assist humanity's evolutionary process into the New Times. As Kartikkeya, the commander of God's Army, Sanat Kumara teaches Cooperation to overcome the lower mind; as Kumar the holy youth, Sanat Kumara imparts Charity to conquer the darkness of disease and poverty; as Skanda, the son of Shiva and the spiritual warrior, Sanat Kumara offers Desire as the hopeful seed of God's transformation; and as Guha, the Jurisdiction Stillness restores the cave of all hearts.

Sattva: Harmonious response to vibration; pure and spiritual in effect.

Seamless Garment: The Ascended Masters wear garments without seams. This clothing is not tailored by hand but perfected through the thought and manifestation process.

Sea of Consciousness: A refined state of higher consciousness, developed through the individual practice and application of the Twelve Jurisdictions, which allows one to enter into a state of Unity Consciousness, or the ONE.

Serapis Bey: An Ascended Master from Venus who works on the White Ray. He is the great disciplinarian—essential for Ascension; and works closely with all unascended humanity who remain focused for its attainment.

Service: The fifth of Twelve Jurisdictions is a helpful act based upon the Law of Love.

Sense of Reason: The use of this term is a reference to the human mind and its primary existence as a blank slate—tabula rasa.

Seven Rays: The traditional Seven Rays of Light and Sound are: the Blue Ray of Truth; the Yellow Ray of Wisdom; the Pink Ray of Love; the White Ray of Purity; the Green Ray of Healing; the Gold and Ruby Ray of Ministration; and the Violet Ray of Transmutation.

Seventh Manu: Highly evolved lifestreams that embody on Earth between 1981 to 3650. Their goal is to anchor freedom and the qualities of the Seventh Ray to the conscious activity on this planet. They are prophesied as the generation of peace and grace for the Golden Age. South America is their forecasted home, though small groups will incarnate other areas of the globe.

Seventh Moon: A storied Earth Changes legend that recounts a large-asteroid impact on Earth. It occurred near the present-day Yucatan Peninsula, forming the Gulf of Mexico.

Shalahah: The fourth United States Golden City located primarily in the states of Montana and Idaho. Its qualities are abundance, prosperity, and healing; its Ray force is green; and its Master Teacher is Sananda.

Shaman: An intermediary between the natural world and the spirit world. Indigenous Shaman place a strong emphasis on their environments; nature spirits and animals play important roles and act as omens, messengers, and spirit guides.

Shamballa: Venusian volunteers, who arrived 900 years before their leader Sanat Kumara, built the Earth's first Golden City. Known as the City of White, located in the present-day Gobi Desert, its purpose was to hold conscious light for the Earth and to sustain her evolutionary place in the solar system.

Silicon-based Consciousness: A level or state of consciousness that humanity is moving toward. Silicon-based consciousness is a form of crystalline consciousness that quickly interconnects with others through compassion, empathy, and telepathy. It is associated with clarity, purity, and is uniquely humanitarian. This level of consciousness evolves from our current state of carbon-based consciousness.

Simultaneous Realities or Experiences: A transmigratory experience based on a non-linear perspective of time. It holds all the possibilities of past, present, and future events. Simultaneous realities maintain the capacity for multiple experiences and outcomes. Each reality exists side by side. A person could consciously open himself or herself to these scenarios to gain insight and self-knowledge.

Six-fold Path: A spiritual discipline based on six principles: tolerance, study of the Twelve Jurisdictions, forgiveness, respect of life, respect for Mother Earth, and harmony.

Six-Map Scenario: A series of six maps of the United States. The Ascended Masters prophesied this schematic to illustrate choice, consciousness, and their relationship to Earth Changes.

Soletata: The feminine.

Soul: The self-aware immortal essence unique to every living being.

Soul Mate: Two people who have known each other in the journey of lifetimes through many different types of relationships, e.g. lovers, friends, parents, children, Brothers, Sisters, and so on. Attracted by this affinity, the souls—before entering physical bodies—plan the specific and important roles they will play to each other in their lifetime together.

Source and destination: The teaching of a fundamental process that moves conscious energy from one point to another.

Southern Door: The South side of a Golden City gateway, also known as the Red Door.

Spirit Guide: A spiritual ancestor or teacher who gives individual guidance and teaching at critical junctures for spiritual growth and evolution.

Spiritual Awakening: Conscious awareness of personal experiences and existence beyond the physical, material world. Consequently, an internalization of one's true nature and relationship to life is revealed, freeing one of the lesser self (ego) and engendering contact with the higher (Christ) self and the I AM.

Spiritual Family: Soul groups that are connected through past lives and share spiritual goals and values. They frequently encounter one another from one lifetime to the next.

Spiritual Hierarchy: A fellowship of Ascended Masters and their disciples. This group helps humanity function through the mental plane with meditation, decrees, and prayer. The term Spiritual Hierarchy often refers to the Great White Brotherhood and Sisterhood. However, the term also connotes the spiritual-social structure for the organization, its members, and the various states of member evolution. The hierarchy includes the different offices and activities that serve the Cosmic, Solar, Planetary, and Creative Hierarchies.

Spiritual Liberation: The Ascension Process is also known as moksha in Hindu tradition.

Spiritual Migration: The process of moving to and living in certain geophysical areas to purposely integrate and assimilate Earth's sacred energies for spiritual growth and evolution. The intentional use of the Golden City Vortices to transmute personal Karmas and initiate the Ascension Process through physically accessing Golden City energies is also known as Spiritual Migration. This spiritual process involves the metaphysical knowledge of the four doorways—the four directions—of a Golden City and pilgrimage to their locations.

Spiritual Technology: Spiritual Technology is the practical application, process, methods, and techniques associated with spiritual and sacred knowledge.

Sponsorship: To support and engender spiritual growth and evolution,

Star: The apex, or center of each Golden City.

Star seed: Souls and groups whose genetic origins are not from Earth. Many remain linked to one another from one lifetime to the next, as signified by the Atma Karaka, a Sanskrit term meaning "soul indicator." Star seed consciousness is often referred to by the Spiritual Teachers as a family or soul group whose members have evolved to and share Fifth-Dimensional awareness. Star seeds can also contain members who have not yet evolved to this level, who are still incarnating on Earth.

Star seed Consciousness: The Star seed is a family or soul group whose members have evolved to Fifth-Dimensional awareness. Star seeds can also contain members who have not yet evolved to this level and are still incarnating on Earth. Ascended Master teachings also refer to a Star seed as an indication of a soul group or Ray Family of origin of which the individual possesses a natural aptitude of its qualities and characteristics.

Step-down Transformer: The processes instigated through the Cellular Awakening rapidly advance human light bodies. Synchronized with an Ascended Master's will, the awakened cells of light and love evolve the skills of a Step-Down Transformer to efficiently transmit and distribute currents of Ascended Master energy—referred to as an Ascended Master Current (A.M. Current). This metaphysical form of intentional inductive coupling creates an ethereal power grid that can be used for all types of healing.

Strategic Points: Strategic Points exist throughout the Golden Cities and are prophesied to physically manifest the energies necessary to move Earth and humanity into the New Times. Adjutant Points are perhaps the most powerful Strategic Points one may access for interaction with Golden City energies.

Subjective Analysis: Identifying the presence of subjective energy bodies in homes, land, and other Earthly landscapes or locations. This psychic residue can be cleared through various means.

Subjective Energy Body: This type of energy is similar to a thought-form, which causes behavioral changes when triggered. They are created through intense emotions, addictive behaviors, and the use of addictive substances, and often contain elements of lower consciousness.

Super senses: Primarily the supernormal powers of telepathy, clairvoyance, and clairaudience, as they naturally unfold through the Law of Love and Unity Consciousness. These are the senses of the developed HU-man.

Sympathetic Resonance: A physical phenomenon where a passive material (stringed instrument, glass, and tuning forks) responds to an external vibration from an altogether different source, as the two share similar and harmonic likeness.

Telepathy: According to the Master Teachings, telepathy is the result of human consciousness rising in vibration and is considered one of the Super-senses. The incidence of telepathy, or the ability to non-verbally communicate from one mind to another, develops Oneness—also known as Unity Consciousness.

Terra: Earth.

Third Dimension: Thought, feeling, and action.

Third Eye: The inner eye, referring to the ajna (brow) chakra.

Thought, Feeling, and Action: In Ascended Master teachings and tradition, thought, feeling, and action are the cornerstones of the creation process. Thought represents the Mental (Causal) Body and the Yellow Ray. Feeling represents the emotional (astral) body and the Pink Ray. Action represents the physical body and the Blue Ray.

Thought Transference: Telepathy—the process of a person randomly or intentionally, feeling or knowing the thoughts and emotions of another person.

Thousand Eyes: This term refers to the endless rounds of death and rebirth the soul encounters before entering the Ascension Process of spiritual liberation.

Threefold Flame: The Unfed Flame of Love, Wisdom, and Power.

Time Compaction: An anomaly produced as we enter into the prophesied Time of Change. Our perception of time compresses; time seems to speed by. The unfolding of events accelerates, and situations are jammed into a short period of time. This experience of time will become more prevalent as we get closer to the period of cataclysmic Earth Changes.

Time of Change: The period of time currently underway. Tremendous changes in our society, cultures, and politics in tandem with individual and collective Spiritual Awakenings and transformations will abound. These events occur simultaneously with the possibilities of massive global warming, climactic changes, and seismic and volcanic activity—Earth Changes. The Time of Change guides the Earth to a new time, the Golden Age.

Time of Testing: In the year 2000 a new era, called the Time of Testing, got underway. While prophesied to last a span of seven years, the Time of Testing may occur for a longer time period alongside the Time of Change. This period is identified with unstable world economies and political insecurity alongside the convergence of personal trials and world change. Many may perceive the Time of Testing as a period of loss. This loss may encompass both the loss of financial and personal security; yet, simultaneously cause tremendous change within and the arrival of self-actualization, self-knowledge, and acknowledgment of the existence of the true self, and the consciousness of the ONE—Unana. These years are also defined by the spiritual growth of humanity; Brotherly love and compassion play a key role in the development of the Earth's civilizations as mankind moves towards the Age of Cooperation.

Time of Transition: This favorable twelve-year period began in the mid to late eighties of the twentieth century and ushered in tremendous spiritual exposure and growth through a proliferation of alternative self-help and healing groups, spawning a renewed zeal for other forms of faith. Beginning in 1988 and ending in the year 2,000 AD, (some I AM America prophecies suggest a longer duration), the beloved Ascended Masters, Archangels, and Elohim flood the Earth with light (the Rays) to restore mankind's spiritual growth and acuity. Spiritual development achieved in this period proves essential as the events which mark the end of its benevolence introduce the Time of Testing.

Time of Tribulation: Humanity is currently experiencing the Time of Tribulation, as prophesied by Jesus Christ, in Matthew 24:21. The prophesied tribulation of the Bible is reference to signs that mark the return of Christ—as the Christ Consciousness—and the end of the current age.

The Ascended Masters refer to this prophesied Time of Tribulation as the Time of Testing.

Transfiguration: Changes encountered during the Ascension Process.

Transformers: A fourth soul group prophesied to incarnate on Earth as the New Children. As a new wave of souls, this group is highly evolved and can alchemize energy in all three previous manners: anchoring, infusing, and expanding.

Transmutation: Alchemy and the transformation of a lower energy into a higher energy, nature, or form.

Transportation Vortex: Prophesied to develop as we enter the New Times, a model of this energy anomaly will exist in the Golden City of Shalahah hear Coeur d'Alene, Idaho (USA). This inter-dimensional portal functions through the developed projection of the mind. As our understanding of Ray Forces evolves, our bodies take on a finer quality in light and substance and we are able to bi-locate through these energy Vortices. In the New Times this becomes an accepted form of travel.

True Memory: Memory, as defined by Ascended Master teachings is not seen as a function of the brain, or the soul's recall of past events. Instead, True Memory is achieved through cultivating our perceptions and adjusting our individual perspective of a situation to the multiple juxtapositions of opinion and experience. This depth of understanding gives clarity and illumination to every experience. Our skill and Mastery through True Memory moves our consciousness beyond common experiences to individualized experiences whose perceptive power hones honesty and accountability. The innate truth obtained from many experiences through the interplay of multiple roles creates True Memory, and opens the detached and unconditional Law of Love to the chela.

True State Economy: An economy based solely on the trading of metals, natural resources, and goods.

Tube of Light: Light surges from the tributaries of the Human Energy System: Chakras, meridians, and nadis—to create a large pillar of light. Decrees, prayers, and meditation with the Tube of Light increase its force and ability to protect the individual's spiritual growth and evolution.

Twelve Jurisdictions: Twelve laws (virtues) for the New Times that guide consciousness to Co-create the Golden Age. They are Harmony, Abundance, Clarity, Love, Service, Illumination, Cooperation, Charity, Desire, Faith, Stillness, Creation/Creativity.

Unana: Unity Consciousness,

Unfed Flame: The three-fold flame of divinity that exists in the heart and becomes larger as it evolves. The three flames represent Love (pink); Wisdom (yellow); and Power (blue).

Universal Laws: Laws that apply to the entire universe; considered a fundamental basis of nature and reality.

Vertical Power Current: The Ascended Masters often refer to the Vertical Power Current as the Golden Thread Axis or the Vibral-Core. A portion of this major energy current links the soul to the higher mind and is known as the Hindu Antahkarana. According to the I AM America teachings, the Vertical Power Current connects to our solar Sun and its resident deities Helios and Vesta. Its energies travel to the I AM Presence and stream from the Presence through the Crown Chakra, and flow through the physical spine of the individual (Kundalini), and the current grounds into the center of Earth's core—itself considered a latent, fiery Sun. In Hinduism, the portion of the Antahkarana that enters the physical planes and the Earth's core is known as the Sutratma, or Silver Cord. [See Golden Thread Axis]

Vibration: The moving, swinging, or oscillation of energy. In Ascended Master teachings, vibration is associated with light's movement during physical and spiritual activities, as well as in the presence of the Masters.

Vibrational Toning: A process of spiritual Transmutation that affects the physical body

Violet Flame: The Violet Flame is the practice of balancing karmas of the past through Transmutation, Forgiveness, and Mercy. The result is an opening of the Spiritual Heart and the development of bhakti—unconditional love and compassion. It came into existence when the Lords of Venus first transmitted the Violet Flame, also knows as Violet Fire, at the end of Lemuria to clear the Earth's etheric and psychic realms, and the lower physical atmosphere of negative forces and energies. This paved the way for the Atlanteans, who used it during religious ceremonies and as a visible marker of temples. The Violet Flame also induces Alchemy. Violet light emits the shortest wavelength and the highest frequency in the spectrum, so it induces a point of transition to the next octave of light.

Violet Flame Angels: Legions of Violet Flame Angels are claimed to carry the energies of the transmuting Violet Flame whenever they are called upon. The Angels of the Violet Flame protect the flame in its purity and dispense its transforming vibration.

Violet Ray: The Seventh Ray is primarily associated with Freedom and Ordered Service alongside Transmutation, Alchemy, Mercy, Compassion, and Forgiveness. It is served by the Archangel Zadkiel, the Elohim Arcturus, the Ascended Master Saint Germain and Goddess Portia.

Vortex: A Vortex is a polarized motion body that creates its own magnetic field, aligning molecular structures with phenomenal accuracy. Vortices are often formed where lei-lines (energy meridians of the Earth) cross. They are often called power spots as the natural electromagnetic field of the Earth is immensely strong in this type of location.

Wahanee: The third United States Golden City located primarily in the states of South Carolina and Georgia. Its qualities are justice, liberty, and freedom; its Ray force is violet; and its Master Teacher is Saint Germain.

Water of Knowledge: According to the Master Teachers, consciousness requires nourishment—much like the physical body—in order to grow and develop. When the Ascended Masters choose a chela or student to work with, they emit this vital energy to the individual, which transmits an essential substance known as the Water of Knowledge. The Water of Knowledge functions like an oceanic tidal system, and transfers waves of conscious energy of differing degrees of power, force, and intention designed to stimulate and impact the student's consciousness through various effects.

Wenima: A Hopi and Zuni name that means "Coming Home." Wenima Valley is the proposed site of a Golden City Community, located in Arizona and the Golden City of Gobean.

Western Door: The West side of a Golden City gateway, also known as the Yellow Door.

White Ray: The Ray of the Divine Feminine is primarily associated with the planet Venus. It is affiliated with beauty, balance, purity, and cooperation. In the I AM America teachings the White Ray is served by the Archangel Gabriel and Archeia Hope; the Elohim Astrea and Claire; and the Ascended Masters Serapis Bey, Paul the Devoted, Reya, the Lady Masters Venus and Se Ray, and the Group of Twelve.

White Star: Nibiru, or Planet X. Its appearance ushers in a period of spiritual awareness and spiritual consciousness for humanity.

Will: Choice.

Witness: An aspect of the soul, which has seen, heard, and experienced firsthand all of the events, incidents, and encounters involved throughout numerous lifetimes, and this includes the timeframe that is said to exist in-between lifetimes.

Write and Burn Technique: An esoteric technique venerated by Ascended Master students and chelas to transmute any unwanted situation or circumstance, primarily dysfunctional life patterns. This technique involves hand-writing and then burning a letter—a petition—to the I AM Presence for Healing and Divine Intervention.

Yellow Ray: The Ray of the Divine Wisdom is primarily associated with the planet Jupiter and is also known as the Divine Guru. It is affiliated with expansion, optimism, joy, and spiritual enlightenment. In the I AM America teachings the Yellow Ray is served by the Archangel Jophiel and Archeia Christine; the Elohim of Illumination Cassiopeia and Lumina; and the Ascended Masters Lady Nada, Peter the Everlasting, Confucius, Lanto, Laura, Minerva, and Mighty Victory.

Yin and Yang: Feminine and masculine.

Yuga: Large recurring periods of time employed in the Hindu timekeeping system.

Index

Vierge Aux Colombes
Carlos Schwabe.

I AM America Teachings
Four Pillars viii
Iamblichus 93, 297
I AM Presence 325, 419, 420, 425, 426, 427
engendered by Sanat Kumara 325
I AM Race 397
I AM THAT I AM 236
definition 552
I-Ching 336, 449, 455, 503
Ida Energy Current
lunar current 361
illusion 73, 179, 235
and death 127
immaculate concept 99
Immaculate Conception of Mary 534
immortal consciousness 175
immortality 389
definition 552
physical 205
immortals
of Shamballa 203
incarnation process 73, 503
India 107
ancient geology 244
Indian Ocean earthquake 250
indigenous people
North and South America 106
Indigo Children 277, 531
individuality 116
sovereign 127
individualization 451
individualized 81, 104
Indus River 106
infinity 136
Ninth Direction 136
Infusers
definition 552
initiate 326, 451, 533
initiation 73, 269
injustice 127
inner dialogue 241, 499, 500, 510
and Shamballa 247
and Spiritual Migration 515
definition 553

Inner Earth
definition 553
Inner Marriage 250
definition 553
inner-self
cleansing 104
shaking of 241
Inner Spark 58
innocence 212
insanity 69, 114
symptom of vibrational shifting 112
insects
ancient 509
instant-thought-manifestation 163, 185
and the Golden City of Malton 197
definition 553
integration 179
of Ray Forces 196
integrity 89
intellectual consciousness
creation of 426
intention 72, 168, 170, 177, 181, 200, 229, 261, 385
definition 553
interconnectedness of life
and Prophecy 441
interdimensional movement 514
interdimensional travel 278
intermediate colors 331
internal creation 232
interplay
definition 553
of the Rays 171, 351
Invocation of the Violet Flame for Sunrise and Sunset 609
involution of consciousness 58
Iraq War 250
Isis
Roman statue 533
"Virgin of the World" 533

Janmot, Louis
The Poem of the Soul: 16, Flight of the Soul 604
Japan
ancient geology 244
Japanese Archipelago 503
Japanese earthquake 250
jasmine 62, 84
Jeafray
Golden City of
meaning 403
Jehoa
Golden City of
meaning 403
Jesus Christ 510, 533
Akhenaten, spiritual forerunner 409
and the temptations of Satan 491
Prophet Issa 534
revelation of the Spiritual Hierarchy 493
Jiva 58, 59, 100
definition 553
joy
"is lived each day as chosen" 106
judgment 63, 128, 192, 209
definition 553
"...exists within yourself." 171
Juno 381
Jupiter 310, 323, 369, 371, 375, 381, 503
Lords of Brihaspati 244
Jyotish xlix, 337, 345, 363, 495

Kabbalah
the two Ancients 449
Tree of Life
the Ten Sephirots (illuminating spiritual processes) 451
Kali Yuga 204, 262, 280, 337, 363, 398, 405, 495, 496, 497, 498
and the Violet Plume 188
begins 507

One-hundredth monkey 122
Oneness
    and the Violet Flame 224
    definition 557
    of Kuthumi, El Morya, and Saint Germain
        210
    through telepathy 175
Oneship 56, 59, 63, 69, 83, 87, 195, 250,
    513
    and Ascension Valley 199
    and prophecy 233
    and the Violet Flame 271
One World Government 87
open ears, open eyes 262
    definition 557
    the Third Eye 510
open heart
    definition 557
opening the heart 77, 80
Open Society 89
opposites
    attracting 118
Oral Tradition 261, 372, 521
    definition 262, 557
    illustration 522
orange blossom 84
orichalcum 423
Osiris 533
out-picturing 103, 138, 145, 148, 213
    definition 557
overshadowing 324
oversoul 133
    definition 557
Owaspee 401

P

Pacific Ocean
    and ancient MU 240, 481
Paine, Thomas 240
pakua 336
Pando, Ancient Quaking Aspens 509
Pangaea 481, 503
paper money 69

Paramukta
    Ascended Being 256
parenting 88
parrot
    symbol of Lord Macaw 475
Pashacino
    Golden City of
        meaning 404
past
    and future 75
past life 76, 263, 522
Path of Adeptship 74
Path of Unities 120
peace 61, 70, 90, 187, 212, 259, 521
    and the Violet Ray 276
"peace out of turmoil" 75
Peak Adjutant Lei-line
    definition 557
Pearlanu
    Golden City of
        meaning 404
perceive
    definition 557
perceive-receive 147
perception 110, 142, 158, 269
    and Karma 265
    and memory 260
    and Ray Forces 163
    creates reality 143
    definition 557
    Point of 147
        bi-location 150
        creating bodies 149
    shifting 143
    tool of consciousness 214
perfection
    "...is an emanation." 204
    "perfection mirrors more perfection" 133
perfection within the heart 514
perfect thought 57
perfect world 87, 195
Perkins, John 143
perseverance 145, 181
pesticides and chemicals
    in food 70

petrochemicals 88
pets 211
Pfrees 485, 489
philosophy
    and the Five Progressive Pillars 464
Photon Belt 1, 496
physical body
    and the Violet Ray 275
    purification 267
physical immortality 69, 205
physical life 73
Physical Plane and the Five Progressive
        Pillars 466
physiology
    changes 62
Pierrakos, John 393
"Pilgrim's Progress"
    and the River of Life 436
Pillar of Forgiveness 64
pillar of light
    definition 124
Pillar of Light
    definition 557
pineal gland 70, 125, 256, 363
Pingala Energy Current
    solar energy current 361
Pink Flame 172
Pink Ray 179, 346, 375, 399
    definition 557
pinoline 363
Pisces 369
Pitris 243
    definition 558
pituitary gland 364
Plane of Cause 76
Plane of Neutrality 78
Planetary Logos 321
planetary systems
    and Ray Forces 170
planets
    are life forces 170
Plasma Field 496
Plate Tectonics 481

The Voices
Gustave Moreau, 1867.

Discography

This list provides the recording session date and name of the original selected recordings cited in this work that provide the basis for its original transcriptions.

Toye, Lori

Points of Perception:

Earth Healing, Earth Healing - Forgiveness, I AM America Seventh Ray Publishing International Audiocassette. © ℗ No. 062294, June 22, 1994.

Love's Service, I AM America Seventh Ray Publishing International, Audiocassette. © July 11,1994.

Changing the Guard, I AM America Seventh Ray Publishing International, Audiocassette. © October 27, 1994.

The Fourth Dimension, Fourth Dimension - Teachings on the Golden Cities, I AM America Seventh Ray Publishing International, Audiocassette. © ℗ No. 071495, 1994.

The Work of a Master, I AM America Seventh Ray Publishing International, Audiocassette. © November 22, 1994.

No Need for Change?, I AM America Seventh Ray Publishing International, Audiocassette. © December 30, 1994.

Weaving the New Web, I AM America Seventh Ray Publishing International, Audiocassette. © May 29, 1995.

Golden City Classes, I AM America Seventh Ray Publishing International, Audiocassette. © July 14, 1995.

Vibrational Shifting, I AM America Seventh Ray Publishing International, Audiocassette. © August 7, 1995.

Closing the Circle, I AM America Seventh Ray Publishing International, Audiocassette. © August 17, 1995.

The Fountain of Life, I AM America Seventh Ray Publishing International, Audiocassette. © September 27, 1996.

The First Golden City, Three Shamballa Messages, I AM America Seventh Ray Publishing International, Audiocassette. © ℗ No. 500, 1996.

The Ever Present Perfection, I AM America Seventh Ray Publishing International, Audiocassette. © December 11, 1996.

The Point of Perception, The Point of Perception, I AM America Seventh Ray Publishing International, Audiocassette. © ℗ No. 102497, 1997.

Light of Awakening:

Light a Candle, I AM America Seventh Ray Publishing International Audiocassette. © February 19, 1998.

Emanation, Instruction on the Rays, I AM America Seventh Ray Publishing International, Audiocassette. © April 10,1998.

Behind the Interplay, The Service of the Rays, I AM America Seventh Ray Publishing International, Audiocassette. © April 14, 1998.

A New Day, I AM America Seventh Ray Publishing International, Audiocassette. © June 26, 1998.

A Quickening, Gobean Ready, I AM America Seventh Ray Publishing International, Audiocassette. © June 3, 1998. ℗ No. 070398, 1998.

Golden City Rays, Rays of the Golden Cities, I AM America Seventh Ray Publishing International, Audiocassette. © July 23, 1998. ℗ No. 072398, 1998.

Blue Illumination, Gobean and El Morya, I AM America Seventh Ray Publishing International, Audiocassette. © July 31, 1998.

The Light of a Thousand Suns, Golden Harmony, I AM America Seventh Ray Publishing International, Audiocassette. © September, 9, 1998.

Divine Destiny:

Template of Light, The Blue Flame, I AM America Seventh Ray Publishing International Audiocassette. © September 19, 1998.

Conscious Creation, Desires and Elixirs, I AM America Seventh Ray Publishing International, Audiocassette. © November 18, 1998.

Divine Destiny, A Blessing, I AM America Seventh Ray Publishing International, Audiocassette. © February 2, 1999.

Map of the Ancients, I AM America Seventh Ray Publishing International, Audiocassette. © April 7, 1999.

The Time of Testing, I AM America Seventh Ray Publishing International, Audiocassette. © September 28, 1999. ℗ No. 092899, 1999.

Memory is Freedom, True Memory, I AM America Seventh Ray Publishing International, Audiocassette. © February 24, 2000. ℗ No. 022402, 2000.

Growth of the Soul, I AM America Seventh Ray Publishing International, Audiocassette. ©
March 2, 2000. ℗ No. 030202, 2000.

The New Children, I AM America Seventh Ray Publishing International, Audiocassette. ©
March 2, 2000. ℗ No. 031002, 2000.

A Birch Grove Spots of Sunlight
Arkhip Kuindzhi, 1895.

Illustrations / Photos Endnotes

Blakely, Ron. *Prehistoric Earth*. Wikipedia, March 17, 2010. http://en.wikipedia.org/wiki/File:TectonicReconstructionGlobal2.gif.

Chavez, Phillipe. *Taq-e Bostan: Investiture of Sassanid Emperor Shapur II*. WikiMedia Commons, 2010.

"El Morya," Hall, Manly P., The Phoenix: An Illustrated Overview of Occultism and Philosophy. Los Angeles, CA: Philosophical Research Society, 1983.

El Morya. Summit Lighthouse. Accessed July 17, 2021. Summitlighthouse.org/el-morya.

Four Elements in Viridarium Chymicum. Wikimedia Commons, August 16, 2009. https://commons.wikimedia.org/wiki/File:Four_elements_in_Viridarium_chymicum.jpg. Excerpt from the book D. Stolcius von Stolcenberg, 1624, Viridarium chymicum, Frankfurt am Main. It shows the four elements: from left to right, earth, water, air and fire.

Ginolerhino. *Naqsh i Rustam. Investiture D'Ardashir*. March 28, 2006. *Wikimedia*. https://commons.wikimedia.org/wiki/File:Naqsh_i_Rustam._Investiture_d%27Ardashir_1.jpg.

Hiawatha Wampum Belt. Hiawatha Wampum Belt (1909). Wikimedia Commons, July 30, 2014. https://commons.wikimedia.org/wiki/File:Hiawatha_Wampum_Belt_(1909)_(14779431751).jpg. New York at the Jamestown Exposition, Norfolk, Virginia, April 26 to December 1, 1907.

Kuthumi. Summit Lighthouse. Accessed July 17, 2021. , Summitlighthouse.org/kuthumi. .

Lord Meru. Metaphysical School of Maitreya. Accessed July 2018. http://metafisicacdelu.blogspot.com/2012/08/lunes-dia-de-iluminacion-dioses-meru.html.

Mithra and King Antiochus. The Origins of Mithraism. Sacred Texts. Accessed July 30, 2021. https://www.sacred-texts.com/cla/mom/mom04.htm.

Mithra as Boundless Time. The Doctrine of the Mithraic Mysteries. Sacred Texts. Accessed July 30, 2021. https://www.sacred-texts.com/cla/mom/mom07.htm.

Mithra, the Sun God. The Origins of Mithraism. Sacred Texts. Accessed July 30, 2021. https://www.sacred-texts.com/cla/mom/mom04.htm.

Morris, William. *Aztec Calendar Stone*. Wikimedia Commons, February 10, 2014. https://commons.wikimedia.org/wiki/File:117-AZTEC_CALENDAR_STONE.jpg.

Prithu and Four Kumaras. December 10, 2012. *Mythnosis*. https://mythnosis.wordpress.com/2012/12/10/lord-brahmas-step-1-the-four-kumaras-or-the-catursana/back-to-godhead-prthu-maharaja-with-four-kumaras/.

Saint Germain. March 1, 2017. The Summit Lighthouse. https://tsl.org.au/saint-germain-help-me-now/.

Sanat Kumara. 2019. *Era of Light*. , shekinah-el-daoud.com/2019/01/09/sanat-kumara-shielding-and-setting-boundaries-is-more-important-than-ever-genoveva-cole/.

Serapis Bey. Ascension Now. Accessed July 17, 2021. https://anow.org/.

Suvorov, Valdimir. Archangel Zadkiel. December 4, 2013. Valdimir Suvorov Art. http://annacatharina.centerblog.net/rub-vladimir-suvorov-art-.html.

Violet Flame Chalice in the Moutains. Summit Lighthouse. Accessed July 17, 2021. https://www.violetflame.com/the-secret-of-the-violet-flame/.

The Poem of the Soul: 16, Flight of the Soul
Louis Janmot, 1831-1881.

Bibliography

Bhaktivedanta, A. C. *Bhagavad Gita As It Is*. Watford: Bhaktivedanta Book Trust, 2014.

Blavatsky, H. P. *Secret Doctrine*, 1979.

Brennan, Barbara Ann. *Hands of Light: A Guide to Healing through the Human Energy Field: A New Paradigm for the Human Being in Health, Relationship, and Disease.* Toronto: Bantam Books, 1993.

Childress, David Hatcher. *Lost Cities of North & Central America*. Stelle, IL: Adventures Unlimited Press, 1993.

"Lost Cities of Ancient Lemuria & the Pacific." Adventures Unlimited Press, 2002.

Dale, Cyndi, and Richard Wehrman. *The Subtle Body: An Encyclopedia of Your Energetic Anatomy.* Boulder, CO: Sounds True, 2009.

Frawley, David. *Astrology of the Seers: A Guide to Vedic/Hindu Astrology.* Twin Lakes, WI: Lotus Press, 2000.

Hall, Manly P. *The Secret Teachings of All Ages: Being an Interpretation of the Secret Teachings Concealed within the Rituals, Allegories and Mysteries of the Ages; an Encyclopedic Outline of Masonic, Hermetic, Qabbalistic And Rosicrucian Symbolical Philosophy.* London: Duckworth, 2006.

Hall, Marie Bauer. *Foundations Unearthed*. Los Angeles, CA: Veritas Press, 1974.

Harness, Dennis M. *The Nakshatras: The Lunar Mansions of Vedic Astrology.* Twin Lakes, WI: Lotus Light, 2000.

Luk, A. D. K., *Law of Life and Teachings by Divine Beings.* Oklahoma City, OK: Luk, 1978.

King, Godfré Ray. *Unveiled Mysteries (Original)*. Schaumburg, IL: Saint Germain Press, 1982.

Ouspensky, Peter. *In Search of the Miraculous: Fragments of an Unknown Teaching*. New York: Harcourt, Brace & World, Inc., 1949.

Papastavro, Tellis S. *The Gnosis and the Law*. Tucson, AZ: Papastavro, 1972.

Stone, Joshua David. *The Complete Ascension Manual: How to Achieve Ascension in This Lifetime.* Sedona, AZ: Light Technology Pub., 1994.

Wong, Eva. *Feng-Shui: The Ancient Wisdom of Harmonious Living for Modern Times*. Boston: Shambhala, 1996.

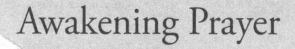

Awakening Prayer

Great Light of Divine Wisdom,
Stream forth to my being,
And through your right use
Let me serve mankind and the planet.
Love, from the Heart of God.
Radiate my being with the presence of the Christ
That I walk the path of truth.
Great Source of Creation.
Empower my being,
My Brother,
My Sister,
And my planet with perfection
As we collectively awaken as one cell.
I call forth the Cellular Awakening.
Let wisdom, love, and power stream forth to this cell,
This cell that we all share.
Great Spark of Creation awaken the Divine Plan of
Perfection.
So we may share the ONE perfected cell,
I AM.

Wings of the Morning
Edward Robert Hughes, 1905.

And We Are Not Afraid
Nicholas Roerich, 1922.

Invocation of the Violet Flame
for Sunrise and Sunset

I invoke the Violet Flame to come forth in the name of I AM that I AM,

To the Creative Force of all the realms of all the Universes, the Alpha, the Omega, the Beginning, and the End,

To the Great Cosmic Beings and Torch Bearers of all the realms of all the Universes, And the Brotherhoods and Sisterhoods of Breath, Sound, and Light, who honor this Violet Flame that comes forth from the Ray of Divine Love — the Pink Ray, and the Ray of Divine Will — the Blue Ray of all Eternal Truths.

I invoke the Violet Flame to come forth in the name of I AM that I AM!
Mighty Violet Flame, stream forth from the Heart of the Central Logos, the Mighty Great Central Sun! Stream in, through, and around me.

Sir Galahad - the Quest of the Holy Grail
Arthur Hughes, 1870.

Illustrations Resources

Earth Changes Maps, Golden City Maps:
I AM America Maps
iamamerica.com

Saint Germain and Visionary Art:
Susan Seddon Boulet
susanseddonboulet.com

El Morya, Kuthumi, and Spiritual Art:
Summit Lighthouse
summitlighthouse.org

Archangel Gabriel, Astrea, and Visionary Art:
Marius Michael-George
mariusfineart.com

Prince Ragoczy (Saint Germain)**, Symbolic Prints and Posters:**
Philosophical Research School
prs.org

Angelic Art:
Howard David Johnson
howarddavidjohnson.com

Visionary Art:
Celeste Korsolm
artsedona.net

Visionary Art:
Pamela Matthews Art of the Soul
grail.co.nz

Ascended Master Art:
Suvorov Vladimir
artnow.ru

Ascended Masters and Sacred Images:
Saint Germain Press
saintgermainpress.com/pictures

About Lori & Lenard Toye

LORI TOYE is not a Prophet of doom and gloom. The fact that she became a Prophet at all was highly unlikely. Reared in a small Idaho farming community, as a member of the conservative Missouri Synod Lutheran church, Lori had never heard of meditation, spiritual development, reincarnation, channeling, or clairvoyant sight.

Her unusual spiritual journey began in Washington State when, as advertising manager of a weekly newspaper, she answered a request to pick up an ad for a local health food store. As she entered, a woman at the counter pointed a finger at her and said, "You have work to do for Master Saint Germain!" The next several years were filled with spiritual enlightenment that introduced Lori, then only twenty-two years old, to the most exceptional and inspirational information she had ever encountered. Lori became a student of Ascended Master teachings.

Awakened one night by the luminous figure of Saint Germain at the foot of her bed, her work had begun. Later in the same year, an image of a map appeared in her dream. Four teachers clad in white robes were present, pointing out Earth Changes that would shape the future United States.

Five years later, faced with the stress of a painful divorce and rebuilding her life as a single mother, Lori attended spiritual meditation classes. While there, she shared her experience; encouraged by friends, she began to explore the dream through daily meditation. The four Beings appeared again, and expressed a willingness to share the information. Over a six-month period, they gave over eighty sessions of material, including detailed information that would later become the I AM America Map. Clearly she had to produce the map. The only means to finance it was to sell her house. She put her home up for sale, and in a depressed market, it sold the first day at full asking price.

She produced the map in 1989, rolled copies of them on her kitchen table, and sold them through word-of-mouth. She then launched a lecture tour of the Northwest and California. Hers was the first Earth Changes Map published, and many others followed including 21 books on Ascended Master teachings, with three more in the works. The maps, as well as the *New World Wisdom Series* (recently updated) became bestsellers.

From the tabloids to the New York Times, The Washington Post, television interviews in the U.S., London, and Europe, Lori's Mission was to honor the material she had received. The material is not hers she stresses. It belongs to the Masters, and their loving, healing approach is disseminated through the I AM America Publishing Company operated by her husband and spiritual partner, Lenard Toye.

Lenard Toye, originally from Philadelphia, PA, pursued his personal interests in alternative healing after a successful career in Europe as an opera singer. He attended Barbara Brennan's School of Healing to further develop the gift of auric vision. Working together with his

wife Lori, they formed the *School of the Four Pillars* which included holistic and energy healing and Ascended Master Teachings. More recently, they have fostered a national and international mentoring program that embraces the teachings Lori has published, the *I AM America Spiritual Teachings.* This transformative information is based on over thirty years of published sessions with the Ascended Masters. Len continues to monitor Lori's channeling sessions and also mentor students.

During the course of the channeling sessions, Lori and Len were directed to build the first Golden City community at Wenima Valley, in Arizona. The *I AM America Atlas* includes those areas called the "Golden Cities." These places hold a high spiritual energy, and are where the Masters encourage the building of a new heaven on Earth; sustainable communities that use solar energy and renewables.

The first community, Wenima Village, has been surveyed over the last twenty years by professionals and Spiritual Masters for the purpose of identifying lots and grids, as well as locating energy points to harness this energy for future spiritual and community development. The surveys have also considered classical feng shui engineering/infrastructure, indigenous precepts, and astronomical alignments. This achievement has included identification, by numerous master practitioners and shamans, of the dormant indigenous energies on the land. Lei-lines, Earth protectors, and subtle energies have been reactivated and have raised the vibration of the site to herald a future for healing, learning, and spiritual development.

While the Golden Cities are key spiritual locations on the Maps, the other maps show possible Earth Changes. Concerned that some might misinterpret these maps' messages as doom and gloom and miss the metaphor for personal change, or not consider the spiritual teachings attached to the Maps, Lori emphasizes that the Masters stressed that the Maps are a prophecy of "choice." Prophecy allows for choice in making informed decisions and promotes the opportunity for cooperation and harmony. Lenard and Lori's vision is to share the Ascended Masters' prophecies as spiritual guidance to heal, rebuild, and renew our lives.

As such, those who have risen above the noise and polarity of their environment and the current social and political upheaval are already Ascending. We encourage you to work on building one of the Golden Cities, to offer a respite to those souls who have a higher vision and long for a new heaven on Earth. Nothing is static, everything is always changing. The way we embrace the changes is of vital importance. To live in peace and harmony and experience personal growth and self-development is the aim of Ascension.

Lori's latest book, *Evolutionary Biome*, features twenty lessons that focus on the interactive and multidimensional Spiritual Pilgrimage to Golden Cities that activate and enhance the Ascension Process. This spiritual education includes detailed knowledge of the Western Shamballa lineage, its numerous ethereal temples of light, and how to apply the rich traditions and legacy of the Ascended Masters that interface the Evolutionary Biome onto our Earth. Three more books are in the process of being written. These Ascended Master Teachings are available on *Amazon, Barnes & Noble* and other platforms worldwide.

Evening Bells
Carlos Schwabe, 1895.

The Lady of the Isenfluh
Ferdinand Hodler, 1902.

About I AM America

I AM America is an educational and publishing foundation dedicated to disseminating the Ascended Masters' message of Earth Changes Prophecy and Spiritual Teachings for self-development. Our office is run by the husband and wife team of Lenard and Lori Toye who hand-roll maps, package, and mail information and products with a small staff. Our first publication was the I AM America Map, which was published in September 1989. Since then we have published three more Prophecy maps, thirteen books, and numerous recordings based on the channeled sessions with the Spiritual Teachers.

We are not a church, a religion, a sect, or cult and are not interested in amassing followers or members. Nor do we have any affiliation with a church, religion, political group, or government of any kind. We are not a college or university, research facility, or a mystery school. El Morya told us that the best way to see ourselves is as, "Cosmic Beings, having a human experience."

In 1994, we asked Saint Germain, "How do you see our work at I AM America?" and he answered, "I AM America is to be a clearinghouse for the new humanity." Grabbing a dictionary, we quickly learned that the term "clearinghouse" refers to "an organization or unit within an organization that functions as a central agency for collecting, organizing, storing, and disseminating documents, usually within a specific academic discipline or field." So inarguably, we are this too. But in uncomplicated terms, we publish and share spiritually transformational information because at I AM America there is no doubt that, "A Change of Heart can Change the World."

With Violet Flame Blessings,
Lori & Lenard Toye

For more information or to visit our online bookstore, go to:
www.iamamerica.com
www.loritoye.com

To receive a catalog by mail, please write to:
I AM America
P.O. Box 2511
Payson, AZ 85547

I AM America Books:

The I AM America Trilogy

ISBN 978-1-880050-44-6
(Paperback) 235 pages
eBook through Amazon
Audiobook through Audible

BOOK ONE: I AM America Trilogy

A Teacher Appears
An Introduction to the Ascended Masters of the I AM America Teachings

Are you a student who is ready for a teacher? If so, then welcome to *A Teacher Appears*.

As a twenty-two-year-old sales rep in a small town in the Pacific Northwest, Lori Toye had never even thought about meditation, let alone asking spirit teachers for help. But all that changed in 1983 when she got a middle-of-the-night bedside "visit" from Master Saint Germain, an eighteenth-century Frenchman and "Ascended Master" . . . who later returned with four of his friends — teachers in white robes who presented a map of America with a new geography, along with a message: it is time for worldwide healing. Despite her questions and doubts, Lori surrendered to their requests and began disseminating their wisdom and messages — the earliest of which are published for the first time in *A Teacher Appears*.

Why is it helpful to get information from spirit entities? How and why should we change? We've noticed the drama going on in our weather, on the planet, in our culture. What is that about? What about manifesting money; what about fear, social disharmony, and my excruciating headaches? What am I doing here, how can I prepare for my future, and why on earth would spirit entities need *my* help? Lori asked these questions and many more.

A Teacher Appears offers fifty-one small but simple channeled lessons about Earth Change and humanity's opportunity to open to and accept the I AM Presence — your individualized presence of God. All it requires is inspiration, appreciation, love, and a good teacher.

BOOK TWO: I AM America Trilogy

Sisters of the Flame
An Introduction to the Ascended Masters of the I AM America Teachings

ISBN 978-1-880050-26-2
(Paperback) 196 pages
eBook through Amazon
Audiobook through Audible

Imagine sitting around a kitchen table with a small group of women friends asking compassionate Master Teachers — Saint Germain, Kuthumi, Sananda, Kuan Yin, Mary, and others absolutely anything you wanted . . . and getting detailed answers.

Join such a group of women, affectionately named by Master Saint Germain the "Sisters of the Flame." Read transcripts of their question and answer sessions — sessions that took place over the course of many long, hot summer evenings while the crickets sang and air conditioners hummed in the small town of Asotin, Washington. These spiritual teachings focus on the important lessons of Love, Emotion, and the Awakening. Learn about the Angels who serve each of us. Enjoy clear explanations about the roles of minds, bodies, chakras, and sounds. Do you have questions about freewill, collective thought, and cooperation? Here are answers. What about personality and the ONE; fear and safety; science, technology, and healing; Christ and Anti-Christ? Or are you more concerned about jobs, relationships, smoking, or Bigfoot? From the transcendent to the mundane, to the personal and quirky, the lessons in *Sisters of the Flame* provide everyone with a questioning mind and concerns about our future information to help us welcome what many of us perceive to be cataclysmic times. No, say the Masters, it is not a time for despair. Instead, consider it to be a monumental opportunity in this school room we call Earth — an opportunity to become our highest selves. Through *Sisters of the Flame*, you will learn how.

ISBN 978-1-880050-50-7
(Paperback) 196 pages
eBook through Amazon

Fields of Light

An Introduction to the Ascended Masters of the I AM America Teachings

Who are you? Can you really know in an objective way? And how can you grow and change in a healthy way—a way that becomes healing to those around you and our beautiful ailing planet?

In this third book of the I AM America trilogy, mystic Lori Toye blends her entertaining personal love story (with mystic Lenard Toye) and the teachings of Ascended Masters, spirit beings dedicated to helping humanity. Saint Germain, her first Master, visited Lori unbidden and proceeded to school her—giving her visions of a new Earth with altered land and water formations as well as the possibilities of changing, averting the very prophecies of devastation he was sharing.

If you want to know who you are, learn from Saint Germain and his colleagues how the universe mirrors back to us our own thoughts so we can learn discernment, the power of choice, and rewarding responsibility. In twenty lessons you will take a journey to freedom and an experience of perfection and the higher love of a developed soul. Learn acceptance, detachment, sacrifice, and forgiveness. Each lesson from the Spiritual Masters develops and reinforces the inner quest for spiritual expansion—the liberation process better known in these teachings as Ascension. Learn to benefit from challenging partnerships, deal with the inevitable results of our choices, resolve seemingly unsolvable problems, and connect with spirit and the higher realms to find solace, love, resolution, and finally your inner fields of light.

"The world is in need of your light and your love," says Saint Germain. "Come forth in your light and expand to all around you."

ISBN 978-1-880050-04-0
(Paperback) 84 pages

Freedom Star
Prophecies that Heal Earth

This book contains detailed and stunning Earth Changes Prophecies for the Americas, Europe, Africa, Japan, Asia, and Australia, as well as a pull-out Earth Changes Map of the World (8 ½ x 11). These prophecies offer spiritual teachings and they map practical and simple solutions to the coming challenges—solutions that, if heeded, can alter the course of the most catastrophic events.

The power of prophecy has always been dependent on the nuance, intelligence, and power of their interpretation. The Oracles of Delphi were surrounded by five interpreters who gave their insights on each prophecy. Native American prophets traditionally utilized one or several steadfast translators to share their messages, and Ancient Hebrew Prophets never allowed prophecy to be heard unless if it had been scrutinized three times. In all cases of ancient prophecies, it was extremely rare for the prophet to interpret or to publicly share the gift of prophecy. In this rare and unique booklet, Lori Adaile Toye acts as prophet, translator, and interpreter, using the Ancient Threefold Technique for the Ascended Masters' World Earth Changes Map—*Freedom* Star.

For more information or to purchase, go to:
iamamerica.com

ISBN 978-1-880050-50-7
(Paperback) 174 pages
eBook through Amazon
Audiobook through
Audible

Ever Present Now
A New Understanding of Consciousness and Prophecy

With her bestselling *I AM America Maps*, Lori Toye has led and inspired thousands to understand the ongoing "Time of Change"—a period in Earth's history of tumultuous change in society, culture, and politics in tandem with individual and collective spiritual awakenings and transformations. These events occur simultaneously with the possibilities of massive global warming, climatic changes, and worldwide seismic and volcanic activity - Earth Changes. The "Ever Present Now," is a compilation of insights notes, and articles that contain simple reasoning, current anecdotes, in-depth research, and esoteric spiritual teachings. Predictions are for doomsayers, but the nuanced perspective of Prophecy, is carefully explained by well-known mystic and founder of *I AM America*—Lori Toye—through Prophecy's inherent gift of hidden metaphor and its power to guide and change people in unpredictable times. *The Ever Present Now* is a new way of enlightened thinking and understanding—a valuable skill-set for the current times. Learn how collective consciousness can morph and reshape drastic Earth Changes through the Seven Rays of Light and Sound and the Ascended Masters' network of Golden City Vortices. Familiarize yourself with the Fourth Dimension and the evolution of Unity Consciousness and personal transcendence—the Ascension Process. The "Time of Change" is now!

New World Wisdom Series

ISBN 978-1-880050-53-8
(Paperback) 386 pages
eBook through Amazon

New World Wisdom, Book One
Teachings from the Ascended Masters

Can we transform our tumultuous society? Is it even possible to save our ailing planet? Yes, say the teachings in this book—channeled wisdom from a team of Ascended Masters, one of whom made his presence known to the young mother and mystic Lori Toye when she least expected it and could do little about it. It took decades to channel, transcribe, and publish the prophecies and counsel in this book, and even more time—and a second revised printing—for Toye to understand the meaning of the material: Prophecies are not predictions! Such messages are both metaphorical and literal. They are warnings with solutions to avoid what is prophesied. The chapters in this book contain information that explains how human consciousness has the ability to change and transform, and how this microcosmic effect literally extends—guiding social and cultural values, physically reshaping the planet's weather, sensitive ecosystems, and geography.

Yes, we can change—by accepting our spiritual virtue and innate goodness; by learning to consciously cultivate the *Twelve Jurisdictions*, shared by the spiritual teachers; by engaging in our own personal Ascension process. The Spiritual Teachers who contributed their Wisdom call this process the "BE-Coming." Be. Come. Add your effort to engender the growth of a new global, cultural consciousness—the Golden Age. (Formerly *New World Atlas, Volume One*.)

For more information or to purchase, go to:
iamamerica.com

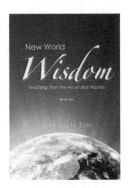

ISBN 978-1-880050-66-8
(Paperback) 344 pages

New World Wisdom, Book Two
Teachings from the Ascended Masters

To keep your light hidden at this time is indeed almost a criminal activity," says the Spiritual Teacher Saint Germain in this channeled book of wisdom, warnings, and prophecies. What are the consequences of choosing ego attractions and aversion over those that come from your heart? Why should we choose heart over ego? How can we tell the difference? Through intimate lectures, Saint Germain, Sananda (Christ), Mother Mary, and Kuan Yin delineate not only the steps to "transfiguration" (when we transform ourselves into beings who function from a place of enlightenment), but they lay out the consequences to Earth and our sensitive environments if we do nothing. In vivid detail, we see a world where land masses have turned into oceans and continents divide. Through Mystic Lori Toye, we hear about a future that has already begun—due to global warming and climatic change. But what beyond use of fossil fuels causes this future? What thought patterns and consequent actions are directing us to behave as we do? This and more is clarified in this second book of a series of three in the *New World Wisdom Series*. Book Two of the New World Wisdom Series contains the prophecies for Japan, China, Australia, and India. This new revision also contains updated prophecies for the United States through the *6-Map Scenario*—six possible Earth Changes scenarios, based upon the insight of the Spiritual Teachers and Earth's potential and possibility for catastrophic change predicated through human collective consciousness.

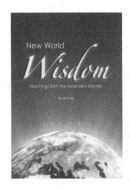

ISBN 978-1-880050-69-9
(Paperback) 480 pages

New World Wisdom, Book Three
Teachings from the Ascended Masters

New World Wisdom offers a hopeful message: Human consciousness plays a pivotal role in creation, both individually and globally. In other words, "Group consciousness creates climate." The Ascended Masters' teachings in this book, channeled by Lori and Lenard Toye, clarify this, emphasizing that our individual consciousness is not a cause of what is going on, but rather will result in stagnation and destruction of the whole if we choose to do nothing to change our individual movements to affect the dance of group consciousness.

According to the teachings of Ascended Masters, we are in a "Time of Change"—a period of tumult in world societies, environments, climates, cultures, and politics. The good news is that all this upset comes in tandem with individual and collective spiritual awakenings and transformations. These will occur simultaneously with a literally shifting terrain; there will be new lands and oceans. We can experience these changes with fear and loathing, or we can choose to become part of them—literally changing the way we think and behave toward ourselves, each other, and the planet. To do this, we must choose self-knowledge and acknowledgment of the existence of the true self and the consciousness of the ONE—Unana. By sharing the New World Wisdom, we can begin to consciously change, and by doing so, change the group consciousness. Throughout this complex, convoluted time of tipping past almost every point of no return, we most definitely can choose to make a difference. The Spiritual Teachers in this book offer their best advice: it is time for *our* spiritual growth and evolution.

For more information or to purchase, go to:
iamamerica.com

Golden City Series

ISBN 978-1-880050-57-6
(Paperback) 328 pages

BOOK ONE: Golden City Series

Points of Perception
Prophecies and Teachings of Saint Germain

In this time of massive upheaval and transition—through weather and Earth Changes, with governments crashing and new ones being born—is it possible that the words from Genesis, "And it was very good" still apply? Yes, says Saint Germain, an Ascended Master channeled by a gentle and amazing prophet named Lori Toye. Yes!

Learn why what appears to be chaos is actually the beginning of a new harmony and why disasters are necessary. Learn how devastation is an invitation to humanity's new life of love and service. It augurs a time to release guilt and enter into an evolution of consciousness and new creation and new levels of life itself. Learn about Golden Cities—real places with a pivotal role in the prophesied Time of Change.

For people who are new to New Consciousness thinking as well as people who have been studying metaphysics for years, the teachings in *Points of Perception* offer personal instruction. Included in the book are a detailed glossary and appendices featuring contemporary terms, language, and definitions for those who are interested in non-biblical prophecy, the upcoming changes, the New Times, and self-Mastery alongside the Ascension Process.

ISBN 978-1-880050-58-3
(Paperback) 264 pages

BOOK TWO: Golden City Series

Light of Awakening
Prophecies and Teachings of the Ascended Masters

In the year 2000, our planet was flooded by light—albeit extrasensory light that you may or may not believe was sensed by extra-sensed people, one of whom is prophet, channel, and author Lori Toye. What cannot be disputed is that there have since been massive disruptions of the social, political, and economic systems that continue today. According to leading scientists, our earth is experiencing climatic and extreme weather events, geologic change, severe damaging earthquakes, comet and asteroid sightings, and continuous magnetic pole shift—Earth Changes. The same scientists, analysts, economists, and spiritual leaders agree that more drastic change is approaching. In *Light of Awakening*, Lori Toye, channeling wisdom from Ascended Masters, chronicles the critical passage of humanity's evolution into the New Times—a time that is aligned with the hope of Unana (Unity Consciousness) alongside polarizing wars and worldwide economic calamity. Spiritual teachers claim this prophesied period of large-scale difficulty is reference to the return of Christ as the Christ Consciousness. This second volume of the Golden City Series reveals the spiritual lineage that predates Christianity through the Egyptian King Akhenaten (1388 BC) and his association to the Mayan Christ figure, Quetzalcoatl.

Through Toye, the Master Teachers describe prehistoric cataclysms which shaped contemporary occult schools and their spiritual traditions. They connected prophesied Golden Cities to Shamballa, the fabled city of Buddhist lore, which lights the New Grid of Earth. Learn how these sanctuaries expand our psychic energy and increase spiritual awareness to enable us to transcend the destructive End Times.

The steady radiance of Love, Wisdom, and Power that twinkles, glows, flames, and blazes throughout Ascended Master Teaching is known as the classic Seven Rays of Light and Sound. The teachings in this book begin with the metaphoric flicker of the light of a single candle, and end in the brilliant luminosity of a thousand suns: the *Light of Awakening*.

Golden City Series (cont'd)

ISBN 978-1-880050-60-6
(Paperback) 334 pages

BOOK THREE: Golden City Series

Divine Destiny
Prophecies and Teachings of the Ascended Masters

Have you ever wondered about Atlantis, or the lost continent of Mu, or the lands of Lemuria? What united the ancient people of earth, and what led them into terrible, divisive wars that depleted their economies and inevitably led to their demise? *Divine Destiny* presents the lands of our myths and legends, with the geologic science that corroborates the prophecies and spiritual teachings of the Ascended Masters.

Lori Toye is best known for the *I AM America Maps of Earth Changes*, however, in 1999 she was contacted by Lord Macaw—an ancient tribal leader within the Toltec nation of Ameru—and given a compelling map of Ancient Earth: *The Map of the Ancients*. The map depicts another time on earth, when men were spiritually realized as divine beings (the HU-man) through the Quetzalcoatl (Christ) energies, and the great kingdoms of Rama, Mu, and Lemuria flourished. *Divine Destiny* shares spiritual teachings from Lemuria that are grounded in the foundational teachings of the lost Thirteenth School and the Right-Hand Path (the right use of energies), and their traditions and spiritual wisdom which were re-established in the New World after world-wide cataclysmic Earth Change.

Divine Destiny assists humanity's passage through 2012 and the critical years ahead, with important insight regarding humanity's upcoming shift in consciousness. This book—the third volume of the *Golden Cities Series*—continues the vital instruction regarding the use of the Golden Cities (the prophesied New Jerusalem) and their role in achieving spiritual initiation through the Ascension Process.

ISBN 978-1-880050-22-4
(Paperback) 290 pages

BOOK FOUR: Golden City Series

Sacred Energies of the Golden Cities
Ascended Master Prophecies and Teachings for Integrating the New Energies

A Guidebook to Right Now—our incredibly turbulent times, our "Time of Testing"

The channeled lectures and study lessons in Sacred Energies tell us exactly what is going on—the big picture—and how to benefit from it: How to perceive it in a way that helps us grow and become our best, loving selves, and how, by appreciating the transcendent nature of what may feel scary and horrible, perhaps we may even experience gratitude.

Take heart:

"As the polarity of politics subsides and humanity begins to cultivate and achieve the Christ Consciousness, we enter the neutral point. This neutral point is described as unity and Oneship and ushers in a new period for humanity; poverty is removed as true abundance reigns on Earth."

And, according to channeled Ascended Master Saint Germain, "When darkness seems to produce an all-time low, it is also the greatest opportunity for light."

Sacred Energies features an in-depth study regarding the metaphysics of the Golden Cities—real locations where our spiritual growth can be expedited during the ongoing Time of Change.

Golden City Series *(cont'd)*

ISBN 978-1-880050-27-9
(Hardcover) 256 pages

BOOK FIVE: Golden City Series

Temples of Consciousness
Ascended Master Teachings of the Golden Cities

A Spiritual Guide for the Great Awakening - the Ascension Teachings for Right Now.

   We are now living in the tumultuous Time of Change, a period of worldwide uncertainty and chaos, both physically and spiritually. In this unpredictable time of both global revolution and personal transformation, can we skillfully adjust and thrive while safely acclimating to the ongoing changes?

   The Ascended Masters offer a path of spiritual protection and evolution in this fifth book of the Golden City Series, Temples of Consciousness. The journey from our first whiff of self-conscious awareness to life in a state of spiritual liberation is the "Ascension Process"—a process that contains numerous noteworthy spiritual passages that awaken, shock, confirm, align, and inevitably empower the human to HU-man evolution.

   This time of personal spiritual growth and global change alongside activating Golden Cities is known as the "Great Awakening." The lessons in these pages help us to nurture and expand our newfound awareness. Learn how to release genetically held fear and how every negative situation we encounter is an opportunity to learn through polarity—making sense out of the senseless and finding balance within turmoil. Also included are suggestions to attune our diet and break negative addictions while cultivating compassion, especially for self. Discover and develop your super senses and to identify and feel subtle, heavenly energy. Then travel to a Golden City and enter one of its magnificent doorways to a new age of forgiveness, cooperation, healing, and harmony.

ISBN 978-1-880050-28-6
(Hardcover) 284 pages

BOOK SIX: Golden City Series

Awaken the Master Within
Golden Age Teachings of Saint Germain

   Do you yearn for your next precious step of spiritual growth that wholly engages your Ascension Process? Are you ready to transform your Earthly, carbon-centered perceptions into the oneness of telepathic silicon-based consciousness? If so, your time is now.

   This is the appointed time that your divine self awakens and spiritually evolves alongside our beloved Mother Earth—Babajeran. And according to the Ascended Master Saint Germain, this global awakening rouses humanity alongside a tenuous backdrop of planetary change and upheaval with the prophetic arrival of the White Star—also known as the planet Nibiru. These invaluable teachings address our current time of chaotic culture, politics, and ecology that were surprisingly received nearly two decades ago by mystic Lori Toye. This published instruction was purposefully held back until this moment, when worldwide events evolved as if to prime our receptivity to listen—waited for our spiritual 'eyes and ears' to be developed enough that we could thoughtfully see and perceptively hear its message. Yes, the time is now!

   Whether you have just picked up this book and are new to the I AM America Teachings, or you've been studying for years, you won't find information like this anywhere else. Awaken the Master Within is a manual for students and teachers alike. These teachings are designed to help you to reaffirm your innate divinity via contact with your true self—the Master Within.

Golden City Series *(cont'd)*

Digital Format Only
Available at the I AM
America Bookstore

BOOK SEVEN: Golden City Series

Soul Alchemy
Ascended Master Teaching on Golden City Community

This is the seventh book in the Golden City Series, and recommended for advanced students of the I AM America Spiritual Teachings. Saint Germain, El Morya, and Lord Kuthumi conclude and evolve many of their introductory, yet complex, Golden City Teachings.

How do you build a Golden City Community? Is it based on the loving camaraderie of chelas and initiates of the Ascended Masters, or is it constructed of physical buildings with a carefully planned infrastructure? According to the Spiritual Master El Morya a community is not found within walls, "It is found in hearts!"

The teachings of Soul Alchemy, however, focus on both the spiritual and physical ideal of a Golden City Community. In these channeled spiritual lessons through mystic Lori Toye, the Master Teachers of the I AM America Spiritual Teachings describe and share their knowledge of the Golden Cities and how their transcendent energies can shepherd HU-man Consciousness to new dimensions beyond conventional sensing, a necessary development as we evolve through the Ascension Process. Soul Alchemy features metaphysical knowledge about our environment, describing and delineating the living, breathing energy of mountains and the singing flow of water. Mother Earth — Babajeran — is flourishing, blooming, and buzzing with physical, spiritual, and multi-dimensional energies that channel and define the heavenly energies of Shamballa upon our Earth.

This collection of spiritual teachings features the diverse teachings of Quetzalcoatl — prophet of Christ Consciousness, use of the Vedic Sudharshanna (Victory) and Bhumi (Earth Blessing) puja, and the auspicious Buddhist Windhorse supplication. Teachings on physical remedial measures feature the alchemical Golden City Rock technique, use of energy regulating calibration points, and Lord Kuthumi's mystical "Cup within a Cup," and culminate to the identification of a self-born Shiva Lingam. Undoubtedly, Soul Alchemy is filled with the unveiled mysteries of traditional spiritual knowledge entwined with the promise of Ascended Master wisdom, our HU-man evolution, and Ascension.

For more information or to purchase, go to:
iamamerica.com

I AM America Books and Collections

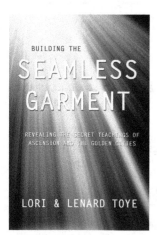

ISBN 978-1-880050-10-1
(Paperback) 288 pages

I AM AMERICA COLLECTION

Building the Seamless Garment
Revealing the Secret Teachings of Ascension and the Golden Cities

Is there a way to master our individual thoughts, feelings, and actions, thereby balancing our inevitable negative and positive karmas? Can we get out of the loop of incarnation-death-reincarnation? Can we conceive of something beyond both the incarnate and the spirit body? According to the channeled teachings of Masters Saint Germain and El Morya, the answer to all these questions is "Yes." The lessons in this book focus on the hidden teachings of Ascension—the spiritual and mental processes and the spiritual techniques that can free us from the confines of the need to reincarnate.

After a conventional Christian upbringing, Lori Toye had her life rocked when she was visited by a spiritual Master, who went on to become her teacher. Over the course of more than thirty years, she has been given information that she shares with others who similarly long to know esoteric truth. In Building the Seamless Garment (the literal growth to final liberation from the reincarnation cycle), Lori and her husband, Len, share detailed soul-freeing techniques and spiritual disciplines for ordinary people who are driven by a longing for Ascension and the dedication to try.

This material is a living text—as alive as you are. Read and reread these words in order to fully comprehend their enlightening message as you begin the soul-transcending journey of building your light bodies of eternal freedom and Ascension.

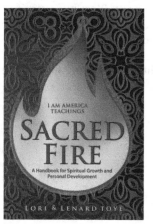

ISBN 978-1-880050-41-5
(Paperback) 288 pages

I AM AMERICA COLLECTION

Sacred Fire
A Handbook for Spiritual Growth and Personal Development

The soul-freeing process of Ascension is considered the utmost peak of human spiritual development and its precious states of consciousness have been sought by spiritual avatars and adepts of all ages. This book is a practical workbook that explains how to apply numerous Ascension techniques that access this miraculous energy of rejuvenation, strength, and spiritual fortification.

Each lesson in this selection of I AM America Ascension Teachings focuses on methods that set-up dynamic energies that create new HU-man brain connections. Each progressive spiritual technique converges to help you to develop a personal, experiential spiritual practice that evolves both your inner and outer light. As the frequencies of the Earth continue to progress into the Golden Age, you will advance into a seasoned Step-down Transformer of the Gold Ray.

Throughout this unique compilation of channeled lessons received by mystic Lori Toye, Ascended Master Saint Germain focuses many of his teachings on the Violet Flame, the vibrant sacred fire of forgiveness and transfiguration and shares numerous insights on how to apply its energies through decree, visualization, meditation, and breath technique. You will also learn about valuable spiritual methods of meditation, specific use of decree and mantra, and how to identify and release karmic patterns.

Sacred Fire contains a unique collection of important prayers and numerous decrees from the Ascended Masters of the I AM America Teachings that fortify and increase your spiritual light during this critical time of collective Spiritual Awakening and worldwide Ascension.

I AM America Books and Collections *(cont'd)*

ISBN 978-1-880050-33-0
(Hardcover) 412 pages

ISBN 978-1-880050-14-9
(Paperback) 412 pages

Golden Cities and the Masters of Shamballa
The I AM America Teachings

This book holds the long-kept secrets of the Masters of Shamballa and is your next step on the spiritual path to Ascension. However it's not just a step, but a literal Spiritual Pilgrimage through the words and instruction of the Ascended Masters, to Golden Cities—locations throughout the world where you can accelerate your spiritual development in this Time of Change and Great Awakening.

Through the Adjutant Points, lei-lines, and magical portals described in these pages, you will learn about the growth of HU-man Consciousness and gain entrance into the once guarded knowledge of Master Teachers who aspire for humanity's freedom. You will discover treasured spiritual techniques that rapidly expand and cultivate your Ascension Process while experiencing Spiritual Migration, a real Spiritual Pilgrimage to each Master's Golden City. Migratory patterns help to improve self-awareness, a relationship, or integrate spiritual virtues, like harmony, love, illumination, or charity. But as the teachings of this book progress, you will be trained to enter an umbilicus portal for the world—the Heart of the Dove. Here, through simple straight-forward instruction, you experience the Group Mind with other students to focus energies for specific spiritual intentions and causes. These methods accelerate your Ascension Process, and offer a potent spiritual upgrade to all who enter the ONE of Group Mind.

Golden Cities and the Masters of Shamballa contains the detailed, authentic transcripts from the most recent channeled sessions through mystic Lori Toye, and this book was rushed to print because of recent world events and planetary changes. Filled with easy-to-understand full color illustrations, you will read exact instructions on building the New Shamballa, that is, the Golden Grid of Light that holds and contains the wondrous Golden Cities. You will learn more about the newly revealed Ascended Masters and Teachers who will guide and lead us into the New Times as you are introduced into their Shamballa Lineage of Golden City Teaching. This includes the physical locations of their ashrams, retreats, and temples within a Golden City, the Shamballa provenance, and organizational aspects (Spiritual Hierarchy), as you are guided to apply the spiritual techniques and practices for Ascension.

As the Gold Ray bathes our planet and initiates the Golden Age of Kali Yuga, you are fortunate and privileged to learn this timely, soul-freeing wisdom.

For more information or to purchase, go to:
iamamerica.com

I AM America Books and Collections *(cont'd)*

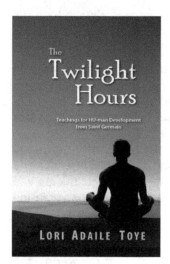

ISBN 978-1-880050-40-8
(Paperback) 230 pages

The Twilight Hours
Teachings for HU-man Development from Saint Germain

In the brief period of Earth's soft transition through dusk or dawn, our planet gains access to the energies of the Fourth Dimension. Spiritual Masters refer to this momentary shift in frequency and light as the heavenly, "Meeting of the Archangels," and leverage this auspicious time with focused spiritual practice and technique.

The Twilight Hours contains specific details regarding the soul-evolutionary methods that rapidly advance your spiritual development into the HU-man—a consciously integrated and telepathic state of Ascension. These teachings progress your Ascension Process through the cultivation of the Twilight Breath of Luminous Light, a rhythmic breath technique designed to drive the sacred, alchemic fire of the Violet Flame to every cell in your body. For those interested in dynamic, experiential Ascended Master Teaching and especially for practitioners of the Violet Flame, this is your next step.

Throughout five insightful channeled lessons received through mystic Lori Toye, Saint Germain describes how to attain the Evolutionary Body, an essential Ascended Master support system that initiates our soul's journey to spiritual freedom. This comprehensive teaching includes the addition of fire ceremony to cleanse chakras and dissolve the death urge, instructive details on the Twilight Breath that transmute fear and open multi-dimensional experience, and a rigorous Spiritual Migration through the four physical doorways of a Golden City Vortex. As you learn each treasured spiritual secret and apply their methods for Ascension, you will evolve into the expansive HU-man. This is our perfect Oneness, and the foundation of Unana—Unity Consciousness.

In this time of entering the unknown, as global economies implode and our worlds wobble and shift through polarized culture in the prophesied Time of Change, take heart, and know that Earth is ascending. The Ascended Masters' wisdom and teaching in The Twilight Hours sheds thoughtful light on darkness, as our inner luminosity initiates a HU-man Revolution of Ascension on Earth.

For more information or to purchase, go to:
iamamerica.com

I AM America Books and Collections (cont'd)

ISBN 978-1-880050-30-9
(Paperback) 492 pages

Evolutionary Biome
The Pilgrimage to Ascension

As the conventional world hurtles uncontrollably through economic uncertainty, pandemic, and constant social and cultural polarity, a new world of abundance, health, harmony, and Oneness offers light to humanity's continuous struggle with shadow. This luminous, creative world is the Evolutionary Biome.

The Evolutionary Biome is the wondrous world around us, from atomic particles to the green grass under our feet. It is contained in all biologic organisms to seemingly inert objects on Earth, from the running water in our kitchen taps to a flowing river during a spring thaw. Its energies are present in all of life. The Master Teachers, as channeled by mystic Lori Toye in the many I AM America books, describe it simply as "Oneness."

Through this book, you will take a journey—literal or meditative—to the worldwide Golden Cities—an evolutionary path enabling us to receive unique and vital energies for the Golden Age. This journey comprises spiritual, mental, and physical forces influenced by the dynamism of Group Mind. On this path you will learn how the Evolutionary Biome seamlessly connects our inner life to the outer life, perfect and imperfect, with sequential chaos and rhythm, beauty and order. With practice and guidance from the many exercises, become a Co-creator of the Golden Age we all long for.

In twenty lessons the Ascended Masters share inspiring and fascinating details that include one of the best collections of contemporary teachings regarding the Western Shamballa Lineage and its invaluable knowledge of the Golden Cities. This spiritual education features Pilgrimages to engage your evolutionary Ascension Process, information regarding Shamballa and its numerous ethereal temples of light, specific instruction on the use of Cup Ceremony, and the rich traditions and legacy of the Ascended Masters that interface the Evolutionary Biome onto our Earth.

Commit to your spiritual evolution and, through the pages of Evolutionary Biome, take an inner and an outer Pilgrimage, intentionally choosing Light that restores and expands our heritage as Light Beings.

For more information or to purchase, go to:
iamamerica.com

I AM America Books and Collections *(cont'd)*

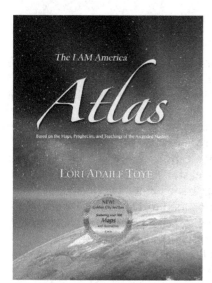

ISBN 978-1-880050-32-3
(Paperback) 254 pages

I AM America Atlas
Based on the Maps, Prophecies, and Teachings of the Ascended Masters

How can we navigate the prophesied troubled times ahead? Perhaps by seeing them—literally and metaphorically. A lot has changed since the first presentation of the *I AM America Earth Changes Maps* over thirty years ago, and perhaps we have required that time to fully appreciate what they offer: a look into our possible future, and through contemplation of the literal pictures—land masses, cities, and roads—the opportunity to understand how beliefs create thoughts, that create actions, that create reality. So how can we best create a healthy, humane alternative to the prophesied disaster pictured in this book—changes that the scientific community now acknowledges (global warming) and we are witnessing firsthand as hurricanes and earthquakes besiege us? The *I Am America Atlas* offers perhaps one of the best anthologies of Earth Changes Maps ever produced. In the decades since each Map was received by mystic Lori Toye, our insight has matured. We encourage you to contemplate these Maps. What do they mean to you? How do these pictures arise? What insights arise when you entertain the notion that changing ourselves will change our environment? What are the changes you long to embody? What can you do right now to begin your transformation—and the subsequent transformation of our future maps?

For more information or to purchase, go to:
iamamerica.com

CPSIA information can be obtained
at www.ICGtesting.com
Printed in the USA
JSHW052143021221
20942JS00006B/102

9 781880 050484